HISTORY

OF THE

CHURCH OF THE BRETHREN

OF THE

EASTERN DISTRICT OF PENNSYLVANIA

BY

THE COMMITTEE
APPOINTED BY
DISTRICT CONFERENCE

PRESS OF
THE NEW ERA PRINTING COMPANY
LANCASTER, PA.

1915

Copyright, 1915
By THE COMMITTEE
Elder S. R. Zug, Chairman

DEDICATED

TO THE

MEMORY OF THE FATHERS

WHO, BY THE GRACE OF GOD, ESTABLISHED
THIS WORK TO HIS GLORY

BY THE COMMITTEE

INTRODUCTION.

History, whether ancient or modern, is always interesting, and instructive to the average reader. It is, however, of special interest to him when he studies the history of his own native land, his own people, his own kindred.

So while our people read with deep interest the history of other religious denominations, once they turn to the narrative that chronicles the history of our own fraternity, her organization in the Fatherland, her early trials and persecutions, the flight across the ocean, the settlement in the new world, the bitter trials and sufferings, as well as the remarkable deliverances, triumphs and blessings, the spread of the Gospel, the new organizations through her consecrated efforts, the story becomes intensely interesting and fascinating.

At District Meeting of 1911 a committee composed of the following Brethren was appointed, viz.: S. R. Zug, John Herr, G. N. Falkenstein, J. G. Francis and D. C. Reber to gather statistics and facts concerning the activities and work of the Church of the Brethren in the territory then constituting the Eastern District of Pennsylvania from the beginning of the Brethren in America to the present time and compile the same in book form. This beautiful volume placed into the hands of the reader is the result of the untiring, persistent faithful effort of these men of God.

We do not stop to quote Eccl. 12: 12, or to apologize for introducing this new history of the Church of the Brethren of Eastern Pennsylvania for reasons that follow. The volume fills a unique place and a long-felt want with our people, and will be hailed with joy by thousands in our own State District and throughout the Brotherhood.

In reading and examining the manuscript, the writer was impressed with the amount of new data and material that is here given in book form for the first time. No one will ever know the amount of hard labor and sacrifice it has cost the Committee during these four years to compile, and get this work ready for the press. They read volume after volume; they corresponded, traveled, visited, gathered data from tombstones, and monuments; they examined Bible, Church, and Court records; and left no stone unturned that would add interest to their solemn trust. The Committee met often and consulted patiently together for long hours in order to raise this monument that will stand as a memorial in honor to the devout and pious fathers and mothers in Israel, whose unselfish labors, and unswerving faithfulness through severe trials have made possible the blessings we now enjoy, and placing into our hands privileges and opportunities for Christian activity and worldwide evangelization such as was never accorded to any other people.

It is especially gratifying to the Brotherhood that the work was compiled before the departure of the senior member of the Committee. His vast amount of knowledge, and his remarkable memory has added much information that could not have been obtained through any other source. The Committee found itself much handicapped because of the indifference of some who could have rendered valuable aid, and because so few records were kept of church work in earlier years.

M. G. Brumbaugh in his preface of the History of the Brethren has well said, "History at best is a beggarly gleaner in a field where death has gathered a bountiful harvest." *So* much that would be valuable and precious has vanished and was forgotten when the fathers fell asleep, and will remain unknown history until the archives of Heaven shall make known all the deeds of the children of men.

May the spirit of the heroic lives which are here recorded live in a larger, fuller measure in the hearts and lives of the many thousands who shall read; and the work will have reached the aim and design for which it is published!

"Thus saith the Lord, Stand ye in the ways, and see, and ask for the old paths, where is the good way, and walk therein, and ye shall find rest for your souls." Jer. 6: 16.

JACOB H. LONGENECKER.

PREFACE.

The activities of the Church of the Brethren during the two centuries of her existence have been recorded and published in several excellent general works such as Brumbaugh's "A History of the German Baptist Brethren in Europe and America," in 1899, and Falkenstein's "History of the German Baptist Brethren Church," in 1901.

In 1908, Elder D. H. Zigler, of Virginia, published his book, entitled "History of the Brethren in Virginia," which differs from the general histories just mentioned in that it attempts to narrate the work of the church in a single state.

At a fourth of July Sunday-school and Missionary Meeting held in Mohler's Church House near Ephrata in 1908, the topic, "A Brief History of the Lancaster County Churches," was assigned to and discussed by Elder G. N. Falkenstein. The interest taken in the general discussion of this subject showed the existence of a strong sentiment for the publication of a more comprehensive history of the congregations comprising the Eastern District of Pennsylvania than was in existence at this time, since some of the leading Brethren were still living whose memory retained many personal reminiscences and much important information not recorded nor heretofore published in print, and who possessed memoranda of valuable historical data relating to church growth and extension.

In 1911, the Elizabethtown Church of the Brethren placed a query before the District Meeting of that year held at Manheim, Pa., as follows: "We, the Elizabethtown Church, petition the District Meeting of 1911 to appoint a committee of five Brethren who shall take steps to gather statistics and facts concerning the activities and work of the Church of the Brethren in the territory that now constitutes the Eastern

District of Pennsylvania from the beginning of the Brethren in America to the present time and compile the same in book form." This petition was passed by the District Meeting and the following committee was appointed: S. R. Zug, John Herr, G. N. Falkenstein, J. G. Francis, D. C. Reber. This committee met at Elizabethtown on May 15, 1911, and organized as follows: Elder S. R. Zug, Chairman; Elder G. N. Falkenstein, Secretary; Elder John Herr, Treasurer.

The Committee discussed plans of procedure and assigned the work of gathering material as follows: Elder Zug was to write up the churches constituting the White Oak Group, also Big Swatara, Spring Creek and its subdivisions, and Harrisburg. To Elder Falkenstein was assigned the church from its beginning at Schwarzenau, Germany, to the close of the American Revolution, also the following congregations: Germantown, the Indian Creek Group of Churches, and the Maryland Congregations in Garoline and Talbot counties.

Excepting those congregations assigned to Elder Zug, Elder John Herr was given the task of preparing a history of the Swatara Group. In addition to this, he was also to write the history of the Home Mission Board of Eastern Pennsylvania. J. G. Francis, A.B., B.D., was to prepare a history of the Philadelphia Churches, the New Jersey Churches, and the churches composing the Coventry Group. Brethren Falkenstein and Francis were given certain biographies to write. D. C. Reber, A.M., Pd.D., was asked to prepare a sketch of the Conestoga Group of Churches. To him and Elder Zug was given to prepare historical accounts of the benevolent, and educational activity of the District.

Elder Zug contributed the valuable articles on District Meetings, Annual Meetings and about seventeen biographical sketches. At the solicitation of Elder Herr the biographical accounts of Elder George Klein and Elder George Miller were secured for the book. Bro. Francis secured Kurtz's " The Very Ancient Church of the Brethren in Lancaster Co., Pa.," from the *Gospel Visitor* of 1855, and contributed the "First District Meeting of Eastern Pennsylvania."

The matter of securing photographs for the illustrations of the book and having cuts prepared from the same was assigned to Brethren Herr and Francis. The Committee decided that only photographs of church houses, tombstones or farms, but no pictures of persons, should appear in the book. A number of churches in the District decided not to have any photographs of their houses of worship in the book; hence, they do not appear. All, however, were given the privilege of putting in as many as they were willing to pay for.

Brethren Falkenstein and Reber were constituted as the committee on editing and printing.

After nearly four years of diligent labor, in the face of numerous obstacles, such as lack of records or minutes of many congregations, disinterestedness and failure to coöperate with the Committee on the part of Elders and others, after considerable correspondence and travel and many meetings of the Committee, success has attended its labors due in a large measure to the assistance and coöperation of many faithful Elders, deacons and lay Brethren who have rendered valuable service cheerfully and gratuitously. To these, as well as to the general histories of the Brethren Church already mentioned, due credit is hereby gratefully acknowledged.

D. C. REBER.

TABLE OF CONTENTS.

PART I.

FROM THE MOTHER CHURCH AT SCHWARZENAU TO THE CLOSE OF THE AMERICAN REVOLUTION—1708-1783.

		PAGE.
CHAPTER I.	The Mother Church at Schwarzenau	1
CHAPTER II.	Other Churches Organized. Spread of the New Denomination	5
CHAPTER III.	Persecutions	7
CHAPTER IV.	First Emigration	13
CHAPTER V.	A New Denomination in Colonial America	17
CHAPTER VI.	Organized Missionary Endeavor	23
CHAPTER VII.	Conrad Beissel	32
CHAPTER VIII.	Growth and Development. Trials. Second Emigration	44
CHAPTER IX.	Alexander Mack, Sr.	56
CHAPTER X.	Germantown	63
CHAPTER XI.	Closing Decades of the Pre-Revolutionary Period	71
CHAPTER XII.	Early Conestoga, by Elder Henry Kurtz	81

PART II.

GERMANTOWN GROUP.

CHAPTER I.	Germantown—1723	88
CHAPTER II.	Philadelphia.	
	A. First Brethren—1813	107
	B. Geiger Memorial—1906	136
	C. Bethany—1910	142
CHAPTER III.	Upper Dublin—1840	153

PART III.

THE JERSEY GROUP.

CHAPTER I.	Amwell—1733	168
CHAPTER II.	Sandbrook—1849	175
CHAPTER III.	Bethel—1876	189
CHAPTER IV.	Union—1896	193
CHAPTER V.	Biographical	196

CONTENTS.

PART IV.

COVENTRY GROUP.

			PAGE.
CHAPTER	I.	Coventry—1724	205
CHAPTER	II.	Green Tree—1845	230
CHAPTER	III.	Parkerford—1898	250
CHAPTER	IV.	Royersford—1901	257
CHAPTER	V.	Harmonyville—1913	264
CHAPTER	VI.	Biographical.	
		A. Autobiography of Geo. Adam Martin	269
		B. John H. Umstad	273

PART V.

INDIAN CREEK GROUP.

CHAPTER	I.	Great Swamp—1735	280
CHAPTER	II.	Indian Creek—1785	289
CHAPTER	III.	Mingo—1869	307
CHAPTER	IV.	Hatfield—1868	313
CHAPTER	V.	Springfield—1868	319
CHAPTER	VI.	Norristown—1901	323

PART VI.

CONESTOGA GROUP.

CHAPTER	I.	Conestoga—1724	325
CHAPTER	II.	West Conestoga—1864	334
CHAPTER	III.	Ephrata—1864	337
CHAPTER	IV.	Lancaster City—1891	341
CHAPTER	V.	Mechanic Grove—1897	346
CHAPTER	VI.	Spring Grove—1897	350
CHAPTER	VII.	Springville—1899	352
CHAPTER	VIII.	Akron—1913	354
CHAPTER	IX.	Lititz—1914	359
CHAPTER	X.	Biographical.	
		A. Jacob Stoll	362
		B. Abraham Zug	365
		C. Christian Bomberger	366
		D. Samuel Harley	367
		E. John B. Gibbel	368

CONTENTS.   xiii

PART VII.

WHITE OAK GROUP.

			PAGE.
CHAPTER	I.	White Oak—1772	369
CHAPTER	II.	Chiques—1868	396
CHAPTER	III.	Mountville—1882	399
CHAPTER	IV.	Fairview—1902	405
CHAPTER	V.	West Green Tree—1902	406
CHAPTER	VI.	Elizabethtown—1902	407
CHAPTER	VII.	Biographical.	
		A. Peter Hummer	422
		B. Christian Longenecker	422
		C. Johannes Zug	422
		D. Andreas Eby	422
		E. Henry Gibbel	423
		F. Daniel Fretz	423
		G. Jacob Haller	425
		H. Christian Longenecker, the Second	427
		I. David Gerlach	428
		J. John S. Newcomer	429
		K. Samuel R. Zug	429

PART VIII.

SWATARA GROUP.

CHAPTER	I.	Big Swatara—1798 or 1800	436
CHAPTER	II.	Little Swatara—1798 or 1800	445
CHAPTER	III.	Tulpehocken—1841	457
CHAPTER	IV.	Spring Creek—1868	472
CHAPTER	V.	Maiden Creek—1866	475
CHAPTER	VI.	Schuylkill—1877	485
CHAPTER	VII.	Harrisburg—1896	488
CHAPTER	VIII.	Shamokin—1897	490
CHAPTER	IX.	Reading, 1898	492
CHAPTER	X.	Midway—1901	496
CHAPTER	XI.	Annville—1912	504
CHAPTER	XII.	Conewago—1912	506
CHAPTER	XIII.	Biographical.	
		A. George Klein	509
		B. George Miller	511
		C. Who My Ancestors Were	512
		D. Valentine Balsbaugh	515
		E. Lorenz Etter	517
		F. George Beshor	517

CONTENTS.

	PAGE.
G. Jacob Hollinger	518
H. John Zug	520
I. Philip Ziegler	523
J. William Hertzler	523
K. John Hertzler	525
L. Jacob W. Meyer, Sr.	526
M. Abraham Pfautz	527
N. Christian Bucher	528

PART IX.

Missionary Group.

Chapter	I.	Peach Blossom—1882	530
Chapter	II.	Ridgely—1884	533
Chapter	III.	Brooklyn—1899	536

PART X.

Miscellaneous.

Chapter I. Annual Meetings.
    A. Those Held in Eastern Pennsylvania 541
    B. Those Held Elsewhere 546
    C. Changes in Holding Annual Meetings 563
    D. Annual Meeting of 1846 by Abrm. H. Cassel 568
    E. Annual Meeting of 1871 571

Chapter II. History of District Meetings.
    A. First District Meeting of Eastern Pennsylvania 579
    B. District Meetings 585

Chapter III. Ministerial Meetings 592
Chapter IV. Missionary History 593
Chapter V. Benevolent Activities.
    A. Brethren Home 608
    B. Children's Aid Society 617

Chapter VI. Elizabethtown College 622
Chapter VII. Statistical Tables.
    A. Table of Churches 642
    B. Table of Elders 644
    C. Sunday School History 651
    D. Local Missionary and Sunday School Meetings 652

Index 653

LIST OF ILLUSTRATIONS.

Germantown Brethren Church ....(*Frontispiece.*)
                                                                        FACING PAGE.

The Baptismal Pool on the Wissahickon	5
Seal of Alexander Mack, Sr.	62
Old and New Tombstone of Alexander Mack, Sr.	62
Old Stone Church and Old Stone Parsonage	62
Old and New Germantown Brethren Church	63
Graves of Alexander Mack, Sr., and Jr.	56
Grave of Elder Peter Becker	88
Grave of Elder Christopher Sower	88
Grave of Elder Peter Keyser	88
Grave of Elder John Fox	88
Brethren Church, Dauphin above Broad	107
Geiger Memorial Church	136
Home of Bethany Mission	142
Upper Dublin Church	153
Amwell Church	168
Old Amwell Cemetery	169
Sand Brook Church	175
Grave of Elder Israel Poulson, Sr.	175
Grave of Elder John P. Moore	175
Coventry Church of To-day	205
Farm House where Annual Meeting was Held	222
Second Coventry Church	222
Coventry Graveyard	223
Green Tree Church	230
Graves of Elder John H. Umstad and Wife	240
Graves of Elder Isaac Price and Wife	240
Graves of Elder Jacob Z. Gottwals and Wife	240
Graves of John U. Francis and Wife	240
Union Church, Port Providence	250
Parkerford Church	250
Royersford Church	257
Mennonite Cemetery	284
Brecht and Rothrock Cemetery	284
Old Cemetery, Hellertown	285
Indian Creek Meeting House	289
Price Cemetery, Indian Creek	302
Grave of Elder Samuel Harley	303
Grave of Elder Henry A. Price	303
Hatfield Meeting House	313
Springfield Meeting House	320

xvi LIST OF ILLUSTRATIONS.

FACING PAGE.

Brethren Church, Quakertown	321
Barn of Division	326
Graves of Conrad Beissel and Peter Miller	326
Monastery Buildings, Ephrata	327
Diagram of Conestoga Churches	328
Bird-in-Hand Meeting House	332
Eby Meeting House	333
Middle Creek Meeting House	334
Grave of Elder Jacob Stoll	335
Grave of Elder Michael Pfautz	335
Grave of Elder Jacob Pfautz	335
Grave of Elder Christian Bomberger	335
Title Page Stoll's Book	336
Ephrata Brethren Church	337
Brethren Church, Lancaster	341
Mechanic Grove Meeting House	348
Kemper's Meeting House	349
Mohler Meeting House	352
Akron Meeting House	354
Steinmetz's Meeting House	355
Grave of Ludwig Mohler	355
Grave of Elder Samuel Harley	355
Ulrich Zug Monument	374
Grave of Elder Abraham Zug	374
Grave of Elder John Zug	374
Grave of Michael Zug	374
Longenecker's Meeting House	395
White Oak Meeting List	396
Grave of Elder Daniel Fretz	396
Mount Hope Meeting House	396
Mountville Meeting House	398
Petersburg Meeting House	399
Neffsville Meeting House	402
Manor Meeting House	402
Salunga Meeting House	403
Elizabethtown Brethren Church	406
Stevens Hill Church	407
Hanoverdale Meeting House	436
Big Swatara Meeting List	437
Moyer Meeting House	444
Heidelberg Meeting House	458
Tulpehocken Meeting House	462
Richland Brethren Church	463
Spring Creek Meeting House	472
Old Spring Creek Meeting House	473
Pricetown Meeting House	476

LIST OF ILLUSTRATIONS.

	FACING PAGE.
Mohrsville Meeting House	477
Mohrsville Cemetery	477
Samuel Haldeman Letter	486
Harrisburg Brethren Church	487
Reading Brethren Church	492
Midway Meeting House	496
Lebanon Brethren Church	497
Annville Brethren Church	504
Conewago Meeting House	506
Bachmanville Meeting House	507
Klein Cemetery	510
Grave of Elder George Miller	511
Graves of Elders Valentine Balsbaugh and Lorenz Etter	516
Grave of C. H. Balsbaugh	517
Grave of Elder Jacob Hollinger	517
Grave of Elder William Hertzler	517
Union Church, Talbot County, Maryland	530
Ridgely Brethren Church	534
Brooklyn Brethren Church	536
Place of Annual Meeting, 1815	542
Place of Annual Meeting, 1820	543
Place of Annual Meeting, 1827	544
Place of Annual Meeting, 1846	545
Place of Annual Meeting, 1871	572
Place of Annual Meeting, 1902	573
Home of Lake Ridge Mission	601
Brethren Home	616
Detention Home, Aid Society	617
Elizabethtown College	622

PART I.

FROM THE MOTHER CHURCH AT SCHWARZENAU TO THE CLOSE OF THE REVOLUTIONARY WAR.

CHAPTER I.

THE MOTHER CHURCH AT SCHWARZENAU.

Introduction.—It would be interesting to trace the events that led up to the organization of the Brethren at Schwarzenau, and the general religious conditions that prevailed throughout Germany preceding this time, but these do not fall within the scope of our present history. Our story is to begin with the Mother Church at Schwarzenau, not where she came from, but her condition, why she left there and where she went.

Geography.—It is necessary to locate, geographically, the heretofore unimportant little town of Schwarzenau, since these religious movements, chiefly the organizing of the Church of the Brethren, have made this insignificant little village famous for two hundred years. Schwarzenau is in the province of Wittgenstein, in Westphalia (German "Westfalen"), in the western part of Prussia, toward the valley of the Rhine, and Holland still a little farther to the west. And now let us speak a little more definitely in regard to the small province of Wittgenstein. "Still more came to the lonely hills and vales in Wittgenstein, which was then controlled by Hedwig Sophia (1693–1712) of Berleburg, who ruled the northern two-fifths of Wittgenstein, and Count Heinrich Albrecht, of Laasphe, who governed the remaining three-fifths of the country, which includes Schwarzenau. Hedwig Sophia was herself a Pietist and her son, Count Casimir, was very devout. There was the freest intercourse between the Pietists that lived at Berleburg and those at Schwarzenau, even though the latter place was governed by Prince Henry. He, too, was a devout man and spent much of his time in the castle (Schloss) at Schwarzenau. His two daughters were Pietists, and lived with the Pietists at Schwarzenau."[1]

It is interesting to notice a description of the town itself, and its immediate surroundings. "We have found a secluded little German village far away from the rush and bustle of the busy world of travel. It is one of those quaint old-fashioned towns that are quite out of place in the present. It belongs to the past and has not yet awakened to the impulse of the age, which has taken hold of Germany. Its peace and quiet have never been disturbed by steam whistle or rumbling of trains of cars. For centuries it has rested in the beautiful valley through which, like a thread of silver in a ribbon of green, flows the historic river Eder. The village is built on both sides of the Eder and contains, as we were informed by one of the inhabitants, about 600 souls. . . . On both sides of the river stand the quaint-looking old houses with high gables and steep roofs, covered with straw or red tile, which make up the ancient village of Schwarzenau. . . . A well kept lawn is not more evenly mowed than are the grassy slopes of the Eder. . . . Here is a quiet, enchanting beauty which exceeds anything I can now recall ever having seen, even in picturesque America. Perhaps the associations connected with the place have their influence upon our estimate of its surpassing beauty; but after making due allowance for all this, I am not willing to say less than has been said."[2]

So much of the geography of Schwarzenau, and its ideal and beautiful local setting, shall serve as a background for our further consideration.

[1] "Origin, Church of the Brethren," D. W. Kurtz, 1910.
[2] "Girdling the Globe," pp. 70, etc., Elder D. L. Miller, 1898.

Religious Conditions at Schwarzenau.—As noted above, in the division of the province, the rulers were devout persons and members of their households were Pietists themselves. These were ideal conditions for protection and encouragement from the civil authorities, for a time. It is interesting to note how these favorable external conditions contributed to the highest ideals of Christian life and character for the Brethren. With these surroundings of everything that was noblest and purest in Pietism, in its best sense, it is not surprising that many remained Pietists, and their lives of devotion, and earnest endeavors for personal piety, were in sharp contrast to the cold and formalistic ritualism of their times. For a time the Brethren were all that this soil could produce, but the genus and spirit of their loyalty to Gospel ideals, and service to the Christ they confessed, developed higher and better things. Therefore, in the memorable words of Alexander Mack,[3] "The crisis for the camp to move forward was now arrived; they were now made willing in the day of the Lord's power." Here, then, came the line of great divide, and he has not failed to make a definite record when he says:[4] "here, also, some turned back again to the religion from whence they came out, being offended at the discipline of the cross; others fostered a spirit of libertinism, more to be dreaded in its consequences than their former depravity."

While we have noted carefully these external religious conditions of a friendly government, and pious rulers, and religious and spiritually minded neighbors and friends, we must look deeper for religious conditions of mind, and for grace in their hearts, that set them as beacon lights of history, and sent them forth into the forefront of the world's religious conflicts, in which they were spiritual heroes. I quote again from Bro. D. W. Kurtz, who was granted the unusual privilege of making research in the archives of the present ruling family at Schwarzenau, and read letters of

[3] "German Baptist Brethren Church," by the author, p. 22.
[4] *Ibid.*, pp. 19 and 20.

one of the daughters of Prince Henry, writing to her father while she was sojourning among the Brethren. He says, "I have read several letters written by one of them to her father, in which she describes minutely the daily life of these people, especially about the "Täufer," whose lives were full of 'good works,' of 'prayers and Bible study,' and 'much kindness and charity to the poor.'" This is a beautiful picture and it is remarkable that we should be permitted to see it after two hundred years. It is another illustration that the integrity of historic records is often preserved in a providential manner, that demands our grateful appreciation, and should inspire us to be worthy of our spiritual inheritance.

We are not informed how long some of these who became members of the Church of the Brethren sojourned at Schwarzenau before the formation of a definite series of doctrines, and a formal organization at the baptism. Without doubt they were there for some years, as we know many remained there for some years after the organizing, and thus Schwarzenau became an important center of definite religious activity. Under these favorable external religious conditions noted, and of saving grace, and living lives of prayer and Bible study, and living practical Christianity in charity to the poor, we may well hope the Brethren are well equipped for the awful experiences that were awaiting them. We leave for a time, therefore, the mother church, and notice the spread of the new denomination in other parts, and the dark clouds rapidly forming, that indicated all too clearly the terrific storm of persecution soon to break upon God's faithful ones.

By *Julius F. Sachse.*

THE BAPTISMAL POOL ON THE WISSAHICKON.

CHAPTER II.

OTHER CHURCHES ORGANIZED.

Spread of the New Denomination.

While the mother church at Schwarzenau continued to be the most important center throughout, it will be remembered that the Brethren soon carried the gospel doctrines far and wide, and the new denomination spread with remarkable rapidity. Of this period of growth Alexander Mack says: "After this evidence of their love to God, by obeying his command they were powerfully strengthened and encouraged to bear testimony for the truth in their public meetings, to which the Lord added his blessing, and believers were more and more obedient, so that in the short space of seven years their society became numerous, not only at Schwarzenau, but also in various places in the Palatinate. A society was likewise formed at Marienborn, to which the awakened from the Palatinate attached themselves, for in endeavoring to form a society for themselves, they were persecuted and banished. And even at Marienborn their external privileges were soon blasted, for as the light diffused itself the truth spread, and their numbers increased; it excited alarm and envy; persecution arose; they were driven out as exiles, and under the direction of Providence found an asylum at Crefeldt, under the jurisdiction of the King of Prussia." There were also members at Epstein, and perhaps an organized church, and there seems to be good authority for saying, there were many members living in Switzerland, and persecution drove some to Holland. The secret, of course, of the spread of the new doctrines, and the rapid increase of membership in the new denomination was that there were many workers, and aggressive missionary work. Like the

Apostolic Church, the Church of the Brethren has, in all her history, been a missionary church, and must continue to be so, as long as she is apostolic in faith and doctrine. Of this period when the "society became numerous," in the short space of seven years, Alexander Mack says: "Within this short space of time, it pleased God to awaken many laborers among them, and send them into His vineyard, whose names and places of abode are as follows: John H. Kalklöser from Frankenthal; Christian Libe and Abraham Dubois from Epstein; John Naas and others from the North; Peter Becker from Dilsheim; John H. Traut and his brothers; Henry Holtzappel and Stephen Koch; George B. Gantz from Umstadt; and Michael Eckerlin from Strassburg; the greater number of whom resorted to Crefeldt; some few, however, atttached themselves to the society at Schwarzenau." There was evidently a definite policy of providing workers, and we do well to maintain always a fixed and definite policy of having, as far as possible, a body of faithful and efficient ministers. It is probable that we shall never fully know of the spread of the Brethren and their doctrines to the fullest extent, but it is still to be hoped that later researches among the archives, and translations of hitherto untranslated works, will throw new light upon this unexplored field, and we shall perhaps find that they covered a much larger field than we generally suppose. The further growth and development of the great work already established, and the changes in location of congregations, and the moving to other parts, can more properly and logically be treated in the next chapter, for long before now, as indicated by the above development, powerful influences had been set to work to stop its spread and destroy the workers and their work. We shall see how far these opposers of the truth succeeded.

CHAPTER III.

PERSECUTION.

Retrospect.—Such childlike faith, and unfaltering trust and pious devotion was the seed of a church. What self-forgetfulness, and what self-abnegation! It was early in the morning, in 1708; this is all we know. The month and the day are studiously avoided. They covenanted not to reveal the name of the one who baptized the leader, and they kept their vow; we shall never know on whom the lot fell. They had traveled over Germany to collect the opinion of the awakened upon the subject of baptism; they had diligently searched history for apostolic and primitive Christian practice; they prayerfully studied the New Testament; there was but one conclusion. The crisis came and the camp moved forward. They knew the consequences but they faltered not. Blessing and prosperity followed the new congregation, and converts were added in such numbers as to arouse the spirit of envy in the established churches; opposition and persecution were at once instituted. The twenty-one years of the church's existence in Germany were eventful years. We know the struggle, but history is silent on many things we should like to know. We may know more, sometime we shall. The Schwarzenau congregation flourished and in seven years the society was numerous. There was a congregation established at Marienborn, to which the awakened from the Palatinate attached themselves. These members were all driven out as exiles in 1715, but found a refuge, or asylum at Crefeldt, under the jurisdiction of the King of Prussia, whence also came the congregation from Epstein.

Persecution.—Persecution did we say, in the preceding retrospect? Yes, persecution; religious persecution! In the most enlightened country in Europe, in the eighteenth century, within two hundred years from the present, religious persecution! Surely the saddest, and most heart-touching subject in all history is the history of persecution. The most inhuman treatment of barbaric savagery, because they are savages, is tame as compared with the indescribable torture and most horrible cruelty inflicted, by the so-called Christian church, in putting its helpless victims to a lingering death. It is impossible to understand the history of the Brethren at this period, or the true inward spirit of their lives, unless we can get at least a partial view of this persecution. Perhaps it is all we can get; we shall never know its full meaning, and the bitterness of their struggle.

First of all, let us get the historic setting of this period, and we shall, perhaps, be able to measure, at least in part, its real import. The agitation, conflict, and persecution that followed the overthrow of Catholic domination, at the time of the Reformation, finally broke out in the Thirty Years' War (1618–1648), which involved all continental Europe. The valley of the Rhine became the theater of war, and the pious Germans suffered the horrors of continual persecution, rapine and murder. "The state church in various parts of Germany was now Catholic, now Protestant. When the Catholics were in power they persecuted the Protestants. When the Protestants were in power they persecuted the Catholics. As the Protestants divided up into sects they persecuted each other. Cruel persecution for religious belief and practice was a daily occurrence. The government was changing, unstable, and often insincere. It was neither able nor inclined to give protection. It may be said in brief, that for one hundred years, from the beginning of the Thirty Years' War, the Rhine countries were scenes of almost constant carnage."[1] The bloody struggle of the Thirty Year's War was ended by the Treaty of Westphalia (1648), sometimes called the Treaty of Münster, and by

[1] T. T. Myers in "Two Centuries of Brethren."

this treaty, the Catholic, Lutheran, and Reformed Churches were leagued into a new persecuting power.

"The three state churches denied to all others the right to exist in the German Empire. Whoever found his religious convictions running counter to these; whose faith was of a different sort; who interpreted his Bible in another sense; who worshiped God in his own way; found life a burden and a cross. Church and state vied with each other in their zeal to persecute dissenters. The harmless Mennonites, the God-fearing Schwenkfelders, the Pietists, and the Mystics were all reviled, persecuted, and regarded as fit subjects for insane asylums or prisons. What happened to these in the closing years of the seventeenth century became also the fate of the Täufers in the opening third of the eighteenth century."[2]

We cannot further follow out in this connection and give full particulars of the sufferings of the Brethren as their persecutors drove them from place to place, and inflicted punishments of severe labor, deprivations, fines, and imprisonments. As already intimated the Marienborn and Epstein congregations, and refugees from the Palatinate, were driven out as exiles, and banished from their homes, with their goods confiscated, and finally found refuge in Crefeldt. Here the new organization flourished, for several years, and many were added to their number, but bitter experiences awaited them. Members were received by baptism from all shades of belief, as a result from previous teaching and training, and often it was a slow process of assimilation and indoctrinating. In the Crefeldt congregation there was a diversity of opinion that occasioned general discussion and finally broke out into an open rupture and division, that was fraught with momentous results. The main facts in the case were somewhat as follows: There was a young minister

[2] M. G. Brumbaugh, "Eighteenth Century Influences in Germany"; Seidensticker's "German Emigration to America"; D. K. Cassel's "History of the Mennonites"; Sachse's "Pietists of Colonial Pennsylvania"; Pennypacker's "Historical and Biographical Sketches."

by the name of William Häcker who had been baptized, but was preaching for the Mennonites, who paid him 800 guilders. He became acquainted with a young woman who was not a member of the church, the daughter of a merchant, and finally married her. This unfortunate incident caused a great excitement, and an open rupture. Christian Libe with four Brethren rose up and expelled Häcker, though John Naas and the congregation disapproved, and wished only to suspend him from bread-breaking. Other expulsions followed, and the congregation suffered much from this confusion. Häcker took sick and died. Peter Becker, who had been his special friend, continued to be so, and ministered to his comfort to the time of his death.

It is remarkable that these things happened, but the most remarkable part of this sad struggle and experience, is that the results were so serious, when the large majority of the congregation opposed the expulsion of Häcker, and disapproved of Libe's course. It is important to us, at this time, to note causes that made such a condition possible, and the final resultant effects produced.

Refugees from all over Germany had come to Crefeldt, with widely different teaching and training. It was impossible to assimilate rapidly the diversified views of these converts to the Brethren's doctrines. While this was the internal condition, among the members, there were powerful external conditions of many refugees not in fellowship with the Brethren, who brought to bear every possible influence against the work of the Brethren. In the next place, while Christian Libe was only assistant Elder in the Crefeldt Congregation, he was a powerful preacher, and a man of large influence. In this unfortunate controversy, he was either insincere, or afterwards drifted entirely from his moorings. He himself, afterwards, did as Häcker had done, married outside of the congregation, and proved unfaithful to the Brethren's doctrine by finally becoming a wine-merchant. He never came to America. As a result, or effect, of all this, it may be said, it was a step in the direction of more fixed principles of doctrine, and a more definite policy of church government among the Brethren.

This Crefeldt territory seemed to be especially under the persecuting influence of the Reformed Church, as will be seen by the following accounts:

"The Crefeldt congregation had many remarkable experiences. In 1714 six members of the reformed congregation at Solingen became concerned on the question of infant-baptism, its lawfulness and its necessity. This resulted in their joining the Crefeldt congregation through holy baptism. These six were Wilhelm Grahe, Jacob Grahe, Luther Stetius, Johann Lobach, Wilhelm Kueppus and Johann Henkels. The youngest, Wilhelm Grahe, was twenty-one years old. They were immersed in running water in the river Wupper.

"This raised a great storm. The synods of the Berg Province and the Reformed general synod heard of this with deep regret. The secular government called these six Brethren as well as the landlord of Wilhelm Grahe, Johann Carl, before the judge, who was a Catholic. On February 26, 1717, they were taken to Dusseldorf and thrown into prison.[3]

"Here they had to endure great hardships, digging trenches, wheeling dirt, performing all sorts of menial services.[4] This imprisonment lasted four years. In their misery they were visited by Stephen Koch, who gave them spiritual consolation. They became quite sick in prison and in their suffering they were also visited by Gosen Gojen and Jacob Wilhelm Naas.

"This Gosen Gojen was a Mennonite preacher of the Crefeldt congregation. He afterwards became convinced that immersion was the only Christian baptism, and in Septem-

[3] The prison of Gulch.
[4] For a full account of their sufferings see Goebel's "Christliches Leben," Vol. III, p. 238 et seq.

ber, 1724, he was immersed in the Rhine after the apostolic manner.

"The Jacob Wilhelm Naas named above was a son of John Naas, Elder at Crefeldt, and a member of the congregation of Täufers or Brethren."

The official action of the Synod, that brought about this imprisonment, will be seen in the following ecclesiastic censure: *ad acta* Montensis, 144, held at Solingen, "The Synod General must learn with regret that several heretofore Reformed church members have been by Dompelaers, living at Crefeldt, rebaptized in rivers and other running waters."

When, later, the General Synod learned that the Brethren had left Crefeldt, the assembled preachers expressed their joy in the following official record: Acta Synod General, 1719, 21 ad 44, "The preachers of the Meuro Classe have received the confession of faith of the so-called Dompelaers staying at Crefeldt, and they have sent their 'remonstration' to his gracious Majesty the King of Prussia. However, this *Fratres Meursanae Synodi* report with pleasure that these Dompelaers, who have been so injurious to our church, have betaken themselves away by water and are said to have sailed to Pennsylvania."[5]

[5] Brumbaugh's "History of the German Baptist Brethren," p. 50.

CHAPTER IV.

FIRST EMIGRATION.

The Brethren had been at Crefeldt about four years, and there were at least two operating causes why there was soon to be brought about a change fraught with tremendous and far-reaching results, in the centuries to come. On the one hand, persecution was pressing harder and harder, on every side; for, as baptisms multiplied, the churches were aroused afresh into bitter persecution. On the other hand, the Brethren had every opportunity to become well informed on the subject of Pennsylvania, and especially the settlement at Germantown, the first permanent German settlement in America, which had been made in 1683, by 13 families, or 33 persons, from this same Crefeldt community. The Brethren knew Germantown for years, knew Penn's province of religious liberty, and a few of the older ones, no doubt, heard Penn preach in the valley of the Rhine and in Holland. They had every opportunity to learn full particulars of the now prosperous settlement of the Germans in the Quaker province, the foundation of which had been laid by the Crefeldt settlers thirty-six years before.

Crefeldt, therefore, was destined to furnish the first company of Brethren for emigration and settlement in the new world, just as it had furnished the first emigrants for the first settlement of Germantown. Here there had been many trials and scenes of persecution, and many were now ready to do anything or go anywhere, so there was but the assurance of religious freedom and liberty of conscience. To these people the endearments of home remained only as a sad memory. They were all exiles and pilgrims among strangers and enemies. Their persecutors pressed them hard everywhere. Finally their hearts almost sank within them.

Regretfully, they turned their eyes away from the beloved "Vaterland" and looked wistfully, hopefully, to the land of promise in the New World. Brave souls those, who, in those days, could face the horrors of an ocean voyage, in unseaworthy, comfortless, death-breeding old hulks. But there was hope beyond, as an anchor to their souls. Did they not count the cost, nor measure the sacrifice? They could not realize all, but they trusted Him whom they followed and for His sake they were willing to endure all things. The uncivilized Indian was to be preferred to the enemies at home, inhospitable shores to a land of persecution; they would find some new friends for those they left behind, and at great sacrifice, they would have other homes for those of their childhood. The enjoyment of religious liberty, in the "province of peace," would pay for all they leave behind, and all they should endure, and the darkness of the hour of the sacrifice of all things, proved to be just preceding the dawn of the day of their salvation. The company consisted of about twenty[1] families, it is said, perhaps one hundred and twenty persons, and organized with Peter Becker as their leader. He was a minister at Crefeldt and is known as a man gifted in prayer with earnestness and fervency, and as a sweet singer, but not noted as a preacher. The story of this journey and voyage to America, so momentous in its results, is briefly told. They came in the year 1719; that is almost all we know.

The voyage is said to have been a stormy one, which is likely true. Landing at Philadelphia, the procession moved to Germantown, the place that was to be so inseparably connected with their future history. It would be exceedingly interesting to know the names of all those that composed this company, but we must be satisfied with the names of those that sat at the first love-feast and communion service, four years later.

The principal settlement was made in Germantown, while

---

[1] Goebel says, 40 families, 200 persons.

small settlements were made at distant points—some scattering to Skippack, Falckner's Swamp and Oley. There were new experiences awaiting these hardy pioneers, as they marched forth into the primeval forests. The reliance upon God, which they had learned in the school of bitter persecution, no doubt served as their support and comfort in many a new trial and dark hour. They were face to face with a series of struggles. They were struggling to conquer the forest wilds, to make them fruitful fields. They were struggling to establish homes. They were struggling to adapt themselves to new and strange conditions and circumstances in life. And, above all, they were struggling to adjust religious differences and prejudices that marred their fellowship and prevented their united effort in Christian work.

It is sometimes sad to record the facts of history, and it may seem sad to some to record this fact of religious differences among the first Brethren in America, and the consequent first few years of spiritual drought. Historians have seized the opportunity of speaking of "jealousies and bickerings" among themselves, without stopping to consider reasons or results In considering the religious conditions at this time, it is necessary to make a careful inquiry into the cause or causes, in order that we may understand future results. To the careful student and the impartial investigator, it is gratifying to know that differences in views produced discord among them, or at least lack of full fellowship. It only proves that the real spirit of the Brethren Church was at variance with the mystic influences and all kindred forms of error which some had absorbed in Germany. Some of the Brethren did not wholly escape the influence of the disciples of Boehme. There had been prolonged trouble in the Crefeldt congregation. The members discussed their differences while crossing the ocean, and the agitation was kept up after they came here, and in fact, continued until some left the communion of the church, a few years later. But in addition to all this, there were the hardships of a frontier life to overcome. The settlements were widely separated, forest and stream intervening, poor roads, or none at all, and no transportation. Some had become indifferent, like most of the German settlers who had preceded them, and among whom they had settled. All of these things tended to hinder the work for three years, and saddened many hearts, but there were earnest souls praying for relief from this spiritual famine, and the Lord soon answered in refreshing showers of spiritual awakening, and we are about to record a most important event in the religious history of Pennsylvania.

CHAPTER V.

A NEW DENOMINATION IN COLONIAL AMERICA.

It must be remembered that these members who were so earnestly praying and working, were not raw recruits, but seasoned veterans. They were battle-scarred spiritual heroes, disciplined in the hardest battles that Christian men are ever called upon to fight. The very highest type of Christian character alone survived the severest test of persecution through which they passed. The weak and faint-hearted had fallen by the wayside. This is why, in later years, the little German church on the slope of wooded hills on the old Indian trail was ready to do such splendid things, without parallel in the province, and thus contributed so large a part of the glorious history of two hundred years.

While there were some services held in the vicinity of Germantown, from the beginning, there was no special organized religious effort made until the fall of 1722. At that time Becker, Gommere, Gantz and the Traut Bros. visited the scattered Brethren. The result of this visit was the unification of sentiment and the awakening of new interest in their religious activity. It was the beginning of a new era. In the fall of the following year important events occurred that constituted an immediate step toward organizing themselves into a church. The climax of this series of events was the application of six "persons on the Schuylkill" for baptism. These "persons on the Schuylkill" lived thirty-five miles up the river, and comprised Martin Urner and his wife and four neighbors. "This organization of the Germantown church and baptism of these first six converts took place on the 25th day of December, 1723."[1]

Of these important events, the "Chronicon" gives the

---
[1] See "Urner Family," p. 9, Isaac N. Urner, LL.D., Philadelphia, 1893.

following account: "In August of the year 1723, a rumor was spread through the country that Christ. Libe, a famous Baptist teacher who had long been in the galleys had arrived in Philadelphia. This moved some newly awakened persons on the Schuylkill to go forth to meet him. The whole thing, however, was a fiction. These persons were persuaded by the Baptists (Brethren) to go with them to their meeting, during and after which they heard so much of the Germans' awakening that they went home very much edified. Soon after a second visit was made to Germantown, by which both parties were so much edified that the German Baptists (Brethren) promised them a visit in return which they made four weeks afterwards with great blessing. The newly awakened ones were thereby stirred up still more, so that they begged to be received into their communion by holy baptism. This was the occasion of important proceedings among the Brethren in Germantown, for they still had in mind the misunderstandings which had arisen between them and their Brethren at Crefeldt. Besides, they were indeed a branch of a congregation, but yet not a congregation that dared to presume to administer the sacraments. The worst was that they were divided among themselves and had only lately commenced to draw nigh to one another again. After they had seriously pondered over these things in the spirit, they finally agreed to consent to the request. Accordingly, after the candidates for baptism had chosen Peter Becker as their baptizer, they were baptized in the stream Wiskohikung, (Wissahickon,) near Germantown, on December 25th, of the year 1723. And as these were the firstlings of all baptized among the high German in America, their names shall be here recorded and given to posterity, namely: Martin Urner and his female housemate, Henry Landis and his housemate, Frederick Lang and Jane Mayle. The evening following they held the first lovefeast ever celebrated in America at John Gommere's, which created a great stir among the people of that neighborhood, Peter Becker, mentioned before, ministering at the same.

"Through such a Divine happening the Baptists (Brethren) in Pennsylvania became a congregation."

The importance of this event justifies these quotations and extended considerations. To Julius F. Sachse belongs the credit of working out many an interesting fact of the early history of the Brethren, and it is only fitting to quote in this connection his interesting descriptive sketch of the events of this memorable day of Organized Beginnings in America. (See "German Sectarians in Pennsylvania," Philadelphia, 1899.)

"Returning once more to our story, it was on the morning of Wednesday, December 25, 1723 (Christmas Day), that a number of German settlers who had located within the bounds of the German township, wended their way towards the humble weaver's shop where Conrad Beissel had served his apprenticeship, at the extreme end of the borough limits in what was known as Van Bebberstown. History has unfortunately failed to preserve for posterity the exact location of Becker's humble abode. This, however, is but of secondary importance. We know that it was in Van Bebber's township, on the North Wales road. Tradition strongly points to the vicinity of the present church, where the earliest meetings were held. However, be this as it may, upon the day in question the solemn scenes which took place on the Eder, in Germany, fifteen years before were to be repeated here in the western world and the foundation laid for a new Christian denomination. The seed sown in Germany was to be transplanted into our virgin land, where it was destined to take root and flourish far beyond any expectation of the devout band on either the Eder or the Wissahickon.

"It was a typical winter's day, and the air crisp and cold, the sky clear, the ground hard and frozen, with a thin covering of snow. Many were the sad memories of the Fatherland that came into the minds of these pilgrims in a far-off land, as they plodded over the frozen ground; separated, as it were, from both kin and church, they thought of the joyous Christmas at home.

"The day was a well chosen one for their object—the fervent desire to organize a church home for themselves, to found a new Christian sect in the New World. The series of devotional meetings held by Peter Becker and his helpers was about to become the grain of seed which was to bring forth a mighty tree with wide-spreading root and branches. Their aim was to form a Gemeinde or commune of their own—to give them the benefit of religious instruction, and at the same time emancipate them from what Falkner calls 'the melancholy, saturnine Quaker spirit' which then prevailed in the province.

"It was well-nigh noon when the party assembled and devotional exercises were commenced. After these were over it was found that there were present seventeen persons who had been baptized in Europe, viz.:—Peter Becker, Johann Heinrich Traut, Jeremias Traut, Balser Traut, Heinrich Holzappel, Johannes Gumre, Stephan Koch, Jacob Koch, Johannes Hildebrand, Daniel Ritter, George Balser Gansz, Johannes Preisz, Johannes Kampfer, Magdalena Traut, Anna Gumre, Maria Hildebrand, and Johanna Gansz. These persons proceeded formally to organize themselves into a congregation, and constituted Peter Becker their Elder.

"Six postulants now presented themselves and asked to be baptized as by Scripture ordained, and then received into fellowship, viz.: Martin Urner, his wife, Catherina Urner; Heinrich Landes and his wife; Friederick Lang and Jan (Johannes) Mayle. Thus they became the first Anabaptists among the high Germans in America. In the church records this band of converts is always referred to as the 'First Fruits.' The immersion took place the same day. After a noon day meal had been served the party went in solemn procession down the old Indian trail, which led from the North Wales road to a ford on the Wissahickon, and thence beyond the ridge towards the Schuylkill. This trail, which long since has become a public highway, was known north of the township line successively as Morgan's and Trullinger's lane, now Carpenter Street. South of the dividing line the trail was successively known as Gorgas, Milner's, Garseed's and Kitchen's lane. The course of the creek at this point makes a sharp turn and here comes nearest to Germantown. The distance from Bebberstown, or the upper part of Germantown, to the Wissahickon is but a short one. The distance traversed by the party was about one and one-half miles; it was a short journey for the sturdy Germans of that day. The objective point of the party was a level bank, or strip of land on the estate of Johannes Gumre, adjacent to the creek, where easy access could be had to the flowing water. The ravine of the

Wissahicken is a rugged one, with towering rocks upon either bank, making the shore inaccessible, except in a few places.

"The strip of land in question is about two hundred yards north of Kitchen's lane. There, recession of the rocky ravine forms a space large enough to accommodate quite a respectable number of people. While the rocks are covered with evergreens, the alluvial soil on the bank has fostered the growth of the catalpa and other deciduous trees. In former days, at the time of the scene we are now describing, when the country was yet covered with a fine forest growth, a rivulet broke over the rocky wall in the background and formed a picturesque waterfall as it leaped from rock to crag in its wild flight down to the bottom of the ravine.

"When the party reached the banks of the Wissahickon, the afternoon was already well advanced, so little time was lost. After a fervent invocation to the Throne of Grace and the reading of a passage from Luke XIV, the newly constituted Elder entered the water through the thin ice, leading by the hand the first candidate. This was Martin Urner, a native of Alsace, who had been brought up in the Reformed faith, and who, together with his two brothers, for a short time had been members of the Hermits on the Ridge.

"The scene was a solemn one. The small procession on their way to the creek was reinforced by some of the Hermits from the heights on the other side of the stream, and some others who were attracted out of curiosity, so that by the time the party arrived at the banks of the frozen stream the company was quite a goodly one—witnesses who were to assist by their presence at what was to be the founding of a new Christian denomination in America.

"Clear above the sound of the rushing waters and the rustle of the leafless branches rose the solemn German invocation and the singing of the baptismal hymn composed by Alexander Mack, 'Ueberschlag die Kost, Spricht Jesu Christ, wann du den Grund wilt legen.'[2] Numerous as had been the mystic rites and occult incantations held on the rugged ravine and valley of this stream since the gentle Kelpius and his band settled there thirty years before, none were more fervent or brought so great and lasting results as this solemn rite upon the narrow strip of rockbound land on the shore of the Wissahickon. There stood the administrator deep in the cold water: before him knelt the

[2] "Count the cost, says Jesus Christ, when the foundations thou wouldst lay."

rugged Alsatian; thrice was he immersed under the icy flood. As he arose the last time the Segenspruch was pronounced and Martin Urner once more entered the material world to become a factor in the religious development of his adopted country. His wife, Catherina Reist, was the next candidate, followed by the other four persons, the same scenes being repeated in each case.

"Long before the solemn rite was ended the winter sun was well down over the Schuylkill hills and the sky covered with leaden clouds. The party now proceeded to the house of Johannes Gumre where dry clothing was provided. In the evening a lovefeast was held, the rite of foot-washing was observed, at which the newly constituted Elder officiated as a token of his humility. This was followed by the breaking of the bread and the administration of the Holy Communion, and was partaken of by the seventeen constituents and the six newly baptized converts, making twenty-three members in all.

"Thus was perfected the organization of the first 'Congregation of the Brethren in America.'"

CHAPTER VI.

ORGANIZED MISSIONARY ENDEAVOR.

What a scene for a master's hand this reproduction of "The Last Supper," and we may well wish that it might have been placed upon canvas. But what we have is enough, and we are devoutly grateful. The spiritual blessings which we enjoy as the fruits of their labors would indeed in itself be enough. Let us be thankful for each fact of additional interest. It was Christmas Day. What an appropriate day for the memorial observance of the Ordinances, which He commanded! To that memorable day which should be dear to the heart of every Christian, is now added a three-fold interest for every member of the Church of the Brethren in America, viz: The First Organization, The First Baptism, The First Love-feast and Communion Service. There were twenty-three persons for the twenty-three years of the new century, surrounding the Lord's table. What a gathering from two continents, and various tongues and nations; and the aggregate number of miles this entire company travelled in fleeing persecution and coming to the truth and this blessed fellowship, was more than sixty thousand miles. Not only the number of persons that were there, but their names, are recorded, and what history they have made. Of the original eight at Schwarzenau, not one of them sat at this table. The Lord in His Providence has dealt kindly and leads us gently on. Not only have we the day and date, and the facts of the day, and the number of persons, and the names of the persons, but Mr. Julius F. Sachse gives us the reasonable assurance of the identification of the spot where these important events transpired. If so, there is added interest, as the present writer not only walked in their footsteps over the historic route from Germantown and stood on the banks of the baptismal pool in the beautiful Wissahickon, but also stood within the walls where they were seated around the table of the Lord. These ruined walls are all that is left of the once comfortable home of John Gumre. Before me rolls the Wissahickon, famous in story and song, while on the hills above are towering forest trees, standing like sentinels, the guardians of these hallowed scenes. As I stand in the midst of these reflections, and as I look upon the rugged grandeur around me, and into the historic past, there comes such a flood of inexpressible thought that I stand in silence and look up in mute adoration.

Immediate Results.—It is not difficult to understand that there were immediate results from these wonderful events which we have just cited, as well as remote and far-reaching. The immediate results were of a two-fold character,—internal and external. The effect upon the membership was very marked. It was a visible demonstration of the Lord answering the earnest prayers of the faithful ones. Such great blessings brought new life and hope to the congregation—indeed they had not been a congregation before. The desire that all might enjoy such blessings of fellowship as they enjoyed, was intensified. The truth must now be spread. Missionary enterprise was commenced. It has already been noted above that these memorable Christmas-day scenes "created a great stir among the people of the neighborhood." Here then were inside and outside results, incentives, opportunities. Steps were at once taken to improve these favorable opportunities, but the " winter proved to be an exceedingly hard and stormy one and the meetings were discontinued until spring. They were resumed early in May, and continued with great success. Efforts were also made to reach and influence the youth and to educate them in matters spiritually. Many were attracted to the services and 'taught to walk in the fear of the Lord and to love the Brethren.' As the fame of this awakening spread abroad there was such an increase of attendance that no room could be found large enough to accommodate the worshippers; so, whenever the weather permitted, the assembly was held in the open air." (German Sectarians.)

There was, however, another immediate result. Such present blessings and such bright prospects for the future were not to be shared alone by those here in America. What glad news this will be to send across the ocean and what joy it will bring to the dear brethren and sisters in the faraway German Fatherland. They shall know of it soon that they may share in the joy of this good news and, perhaps, be induced to come to America and share in this promising work.

A Message to the Home Land.—The "Chronicon Ephratense" gives the following interesting account of this message: "Under these circumstances they deemed it well to make a detailed report of this new awakening to their Brethren in Germany. Therefore they prepared in common a writing addressed to them, in which they informed them that they had become reunited in Pennsylvania, and that hereupon a great awakening had resulted in the land, which was still daily increasing; that of the awakened several had joined their communion, to which they had to consent, as they dared not withstand the counsels of God." It would be interesting to know that message in full, to have the exact words and know the real heart throbs that pulsated through them, but we shall probably never know more than we know now. The above quotation, no doubt, gives us a fair conception of the scope of the letter, and we furthermore know the effect this and other reports had upon the Brethren in Germany. Two Continents are now interested in the struggles in this new and, to them, unknown world. Other messages go from time to time to the Home Land. The earnest prayers from both sides of the great ocean strengthen the hearts of the brave leaders, as they go forth, over the hills and down the valleys, through the forests and across the rivers, bearing the message of the "Man of Galilee"— for he said, "Go ye therefore, and teach all nations, baptizing them in the name of the Father, and of the Son, and of the Holy Ghost: Teaching them to observe all things whatsoever I have commanded you: and, lo, I am with you alway, even unto the end of the world. Amen."[1]

Organizing for Work.—One of the strongest elements in a successful leadership is a proper organizing of the forces to be led, or directed. United and concerted action and effort is as necessary in church work, as it is in military or industrial matters, or in business enterprises. Elder Peter Becker and his coworkers saw an open door to a great field of opportunity, and they were wide awake to organize on a scale large enough to meet the needs. The subject was discussed by the congregation which gave encouragement and hearty support. And so the year 1724 was destined to be scarcely less eventful and important than the previous year. No one who is a careful student can dwell upon the events of this year without feeling that they were of the utmost importance to the German pioneer settlers, and far-reaching in their influence and permanent results. It was deemed advisable that all the scattered settlements of Brethren should be visited at once and brought under organized spiritual influences. For this purpose a missionary party was organized, with Peter Becker as the leader. Its great importance justifies its careful consideration, for this is the most remarkable missionary tour to the frontier in all Pennsylvania colonial history, and is absolutely without parallel in colonial times. Leaving industry and loved ones behind, these pioneer preachers of the gospel, and their assistants, with true German devotion to the cause they loved, marched forth, seven horsemen and seven footmen. On the fields of martial conquest there never marched a more gallant band than these in commission of the Prince of

[1] Matt. 28: 19–20.

Peace. It was a worthy representation of the importance of the cause they sought to establish, as well as a worthy representation of the work accomplished in their continued devotion. What a mission was theirs, pushing out to the frontier lines to battle with callous indifference and skepticism, or mysticism and materialism among their fellow countrymen! And so October 23, 1724, was a memorable day for the Germantown Settlement, and what an impressive scene it must have been to behold the gathering of the company of cavalry and infantry, and then behold the company as it slowly moved out of the settlement, northward, over the old Indian trail. The scattered settlers have gathered in little groups here and there to discuss the journey and mission of their neighbors and friends, and with deep interest watched them until they vanished over the slopes of the distant hills.

There is some confusion as to the route taken, and the stops made, especially as to the first stages of the journey. The Chronicon states, "They first went to Schippack." Sachse, in German Sectarians, says,—"The first stop was made in the beautiful Skippack Valley, where a number of Germans had settled. Here several meetings were held with much success." Brumbaugh, In The German Baptist Brethren, says "Their first visit was to Brother John Jacob Price on the Indian Creek." The facts likely are, members both on the Indian Creek and in the Skippack valley, or different places of Skippack township, were visited, for we are informed that some of the members of the emigration of 1719 settled in the Skippack, and we further learn that in the visitation of 1722, "they traveled through the regions of Skippack." The John Jacob Price referred to, settled, we are informed by the old records, "on a large tract of land on the Indian Creek, in Lower Salford Township," in 1721, and is the Johannus Preisz who was at the first lovefeast, and a minister of note, in the early church, in Europe and America, and likely the father of all the Prices in the Brotherhood. This, therefore, marks the establishment of an important field, or region, of activity, that later became the early Indian Creek Congregation, and, in later years, subdivided into a number of congregations.

From the above named place, or places, more properly, they went northward, crossed the Perkiomen and continued on through Providence to Falckner's Swamp, when a halt was made at the house "of a Brother named Albertus." Here revival meetings were held, closing with a Lovefeast and Communion Service, which was attended, we are informed, by the Chronicon, "with great blessing." From here they went to Oley, in Berks County, near Douglassville, "where a similar work was done with similar blessing." From Oley the party went southward and crossed the Schuylkill, to visit their newly-baptized Brethren, going direct to the house of Martin Urner, one of the "First Fruits," "who, since his baptism, had permanently settled in Coventry, Chester County, immediately opposite the present town of Pottstown."

"Martin Urner, from the time he came to Coventry, exhorted his neighbors whenever opportunity offered, besides holding meetings at his own house on Sundays with more or less regularity. One of the results of his labors was that when Peter Becker and his party reached there they found two persons prepared for baptism in addition to the settlers who were ready to form a congregation.

"On the next day, November 7, 1724, a meeting was held in Urner's house, at which Elder Becker presided. The two candidates were baptized in the Schuylkill, and the ceremony was followed by the usual Lovefeast and breadbreaking in the evening.

"Upon this occasion was organized the Coventry Brethren Church, of which Martin Urner was made preacher. The following nine persons were the constituent members: Martin Urner, his wife, Catharine Reist Urner; Daniel

Eicher and wife, Henrich Landes and wife, Peter Heffly, Owen Longacre and Andrew Sell."[2]

This seems to have been the end of the contemplated missionary tour, two weeks had been spent, the usual time for a "series of meetings" at this time. It would have been about time for some busy preachers to go home, to look after the family and business. But these preachers were after their "Father's business." They heard of some awakened souls in the Conestoga country, and they decided to go there, which was then known as the western part of Chester county.

Upon leaving Urner's the party divided, the horsemen following the road and staying all night, Monday, November 9, at the house of Jacob Weber, in the Conestoga Valley, near Weberstown, in Leacock township. The footmen took a shorter route, over the Welsh mountain, and spent the same night at the house of Johannus Graff "This was in Earl township, at what is now known as Graffsdale, at the lower end of Earl township. The original tract of 1,419 acres was situated on Graff's run, a branch of the Mühlbach (Mill Creek). Johannus Graff was the earliest and wealthiest settler in the vicinity. The foundation stones of the cabin which he built in 1718 are yet to be seen upon the property of a lineal descendant."[3] The next day, Tuesday, November 10, they journeyed to the house of Hans Rudolph Nagele, a Mennonite preacher, when both horsemen and footmen once more united, and passed the night of Tuesday, with Stephen Galliond.

Early the next morning two Brethren were sent to Henry Hohns, to announce their coming. On Wednesday, November 11, therefore, the party retraced their steps and journeyed towards the valley of the Pequea. The special purpose seems to have been to bring about an awakening among the Mennonites, who had been brought into great confusion by Bauman, in teaching his pernicious "Newborn" doc-

[2] "German Sectarians."
[3] *Ibid.*, p. 100.

trines. A largely attended meeting was held at Heinrich Hohns.

As its authors were directly interested, I quote from the Chronicon, an account of this meeting, and its immediate results: "A meeting was held at Hohn's on the following day, November 12 (Thursday), at which the Superintendent (Beissel) was present. At this meeting extraordinary revival-powers were manifested. The Baptists spoke with such power concerning baptism and the divine purpose concerning fallen man involved therein, that after the close of the meeting five persons applied for baptism, namely the aforementioned Hohn, his housemate, John Mayer and his house-mate, and Joseph Shafer, who were at once baptized in Apostolic-wise, by Peter Becker, in the Pequea stream. Soon a sixth one followed these, namely, Veronica, the wife of Isaac Frederick. Now the Superintendent (Beissel) fell into great perplexity. For, to withstand this ordinance of God seemed to him great presumption; at the same time, the calling of these people was not deemed important enough by him, for he had been the recipient of a weighty testimony from God, and feared that, if he associated with them, he might lose all the good he had reached through so much pain. Suddenly, however, his heart was enlightened by a bright ray from the Gospel, in whose light the whole purpose of God was revealed to him, namely, that Christ also had permitted himself to be baptized by one who was less than himself, and had said thereof: 'Thus it becometh us to fulfill all righteousness'; and that, in order to make this work easier for us, God himself had thus gone before, and first sought out the field in which he would sow his grain of wheat.

"Consequently, after the Sister referred to before came out of the water, he came down from his spiritual pride, humbled himself before his friend Peter Becker, and was baptized by him on the same day in Apostolic-wise, under the water.

"After the baptism they spent the rest of the day in edifying conversation unto the praise of God, until evening, when a 'Lovefeast' was held at Hohn's, the first ever held in Conestoga since the country began to be cleansed from its heathenish inhabitants; it was held on November 12, 1724."

There was one more meeting held at the house of Sigmund Landert, at which time he and his wife were baptized. The leaders of the missionary party now informed the Brethren in the Conestoga, that on account of the distance from Germantown, they must arrange their matters as best they could, as a separate congregation. The little body of six Brethren and six Sisters now chose Conrad Beissel as their minister, and he remains in fellowship with the Brethren for about four years. The chapter following will treat of the history of Beissel, and his relation to the work of the Brethren in the Conestoga. After the kiss of peace was given, the Germantown Brethren started on their homeward journey on the fourteenth of November.

To bring out important lessons and results and fundamental principles of action, may be regarded as sufficient reason for devoting much space to a description of these events, which had a significance far beyond their local setting. Here are characteristics of the church that have made history; elements of strength, and principles of action, adopted in Germany, and here reëstablished, that have directed the progress of the church ever since. Alexander Mack was an evangelist of note before he organized the Brethren Church, and there are many evidences of the missionary activities of the church while yet in Germany. This tour, after the organization in America, was the first step in that missionary enterprise which has been such an important factor in the life of the Brethren Church. The immediate result was, two churches were organized, and the foundation laid for several more and both of these became prosperous and important in a few years. It is remarkable how large a part of the District was covered by this tour, and how many present day congregations are the result of this early missionary endeavor.

CHAPTER VII.

CONRAD BEISSEL.

Introduction.—In order that we may understand the association, and historic relation, and later antagonism, to the Brethren, it is manifestly necessary to give some biographical account of Conrad Beissel; and sketch, briefly, some of the moulding influences of his erratic life. As the "Chronicon Ephratense" is the official record of the Superintendent, and his communal life, its facts and dates, as relating to him, are made the basis of this sketch.

Birth.—He was born in April, 1690, at Eberbach, a small town on the Neckar, in the Palatinate, and received the family name of John Conrad Beissel. His father, a baker by trade, died two months before the child was born. Having spent all his means by his dissolute habits, the widow was left destitute, and with a numerous family. Under this burden of care and great responsibility the mother, a devout person, only lived seven years.

Environment.—It would seem that now almost his last blessing was gone, and "from that time on he led a sorry life, after the manner of the country, until he was old enough to learn a trade," when the local authorities apprenticed him to a master baker to learn the trade. It seems from the account that these years were spent in the most wretched poverty, without cheer or comfort to lighten the darkness in his miserable life.

Education.—He seems to have had no school advantages whatever, but there were evidences of natural gifts, for we are told, " He showed a wonderful facility in learning many things without any instruction, merely by his own reflection;

so much so that his oldest brother often said to him, 'Your studying will make a fool of you yet.'"[1]

Apprenticeship.—The choice of a master for the young apprentice was most unfortunate, and now to the life of former misery and wretchedness was added unrestrained frivolity. His master was a musician, and he soon learned to play the violin, and assisted his master at weddings, "at which, when exhausted with fiddling, he would betake himself to dancing, and from this again return to the former."[2] This life of pleasure and excess seems to have brought convictions of sinfulness; and "the awakening Spirit knocked so loudly at his conscience that his whole being was thrown into the utmost perplexity, and so the foundation was laid for his conversion."[2]

Wanderings.—Having finished his apprenticeship, he started out on his wanderings as a journeyman, according to the custom of the country, first going to Strasburg. After remaining here some time, he finally entered the service of a man in Mannheim. Here he fell into a quarrel with his employer's wife, and for her violence he called her Jezebel, on account of which he was obliged to leave the house. From Mannheim he returned to Heidelberg, and for a time matters spiritual and temporal were very favorable and prosperous. He gained the confidence of the master bakers, and they made him treasurer of their guild. But when Beissel criticised them for their idle practices at their banquets, they had the city council put him under arrest and in jail,—and so closes this epoch, as the curtain falls upon the journeyman baker when the jail door closes behind him.

Religious Struggles.—There is an entire change of scene. The conflicts now are of a religious character. In order to have a full understanding of his religious convictions and theories, it is necessary to trace the teaching and experiences

[1] The "Chronicon."
[2] *Ibid.*

of these years, that made such a lasting impression, and moulded his future life. As noted before, from the excessive frivolity, he fell under strong conviction of sin; and, though temporarily brought low in the spirit, he earnestly sought for a higher spiritual development. "It was at Strasburg that Beissel was first introduced into Inspirationist and Pietistical circles. The chief spirit of the latter was one Michael Eckerling, a cap-maker by trade, whose four sturdy sons were destined to play so prominent a role in the Ephrata Community."[3]

When he arrived at Heidelberg, he found many *Pietists;* but he attended, for some time at least, the regular services of the Lutheran church, and heard several prominent preachers of the times.

"He also made the acquaintance of a learned mystic and theosophist, named Haller, who was a friend and correspondent of Gichtel. Through him Beissel obtained an introduction to, or was initiated in, the local Rosicrucian chapter held under the name or guise of a Pietist conventicle, which organization counted many of the most learned and distinguished men in the community among its membership. But, being under the ban of the secular as well as religious authorities, they were forced to hold their meetings in secrecy, in an almost inaccessible fastness of the forest. Here, within the tiled precincts of the weird, rocky chasm (Felsenschleugt), by the fitful light of resinous torches, Conrad Beissel followed his guide, was brought to the true Light, taught the first steps of the Brotherhood, and received instruction in the rudiments of the secret rites and mysteries of the Fraternity of the Rosy Cross."[4]

The "Chronicon" states: "He was astonished beyond measure when these dear people the first time called him Brother. He often said that he had passed through three awakenings, in which he always had to deal with newly

[3] "German Sectarians," Vol. I, p. 37.
[4] *Ibid.,* pp. 39-40.

awakened ones; but he must confess that the greater part of his heart remained at the first awakening at Heidelberg. Therefore, his references to these precious souls never passed off without tears, particularly as in after times so much bitterness and gall were served him by his followers." As noted before, he was lodged in jail by the instigation of his own bakers' guild. Once more in conflict and trouble. "Meanwhile his trial took place, and there it appeared that the charge was not sufficient to have him kept under arrest. His accusers, however, knew how to help themselves, and declared that he was a Pietist. This brought the matter before the ecclesiastical court. The clergy of the three dominant religions took him in charge, and gave him the choice, either to join one of the three dominant religions, or to leave the country," says the "Chronicon." He refused to join either of the churches, and so he was banished. His friends interceded for him, but all efforts were in vain.

He was now an outcast, not merely a wanderer. He bade farewell to his Brethren in Heidelberg, whom he never saw again; and, then departing, went to his home town of Eberbach, to say farewell to his relatives. He hurried away, but had barely gone when soldiers arrived to arrest him.

The experiences of this banishment brought him to such severe trials and suffering and deprivations that he came near retracting, and was nigh unto death. He fell into excessive penitence-labors, suffering such violence thereby that he contracted consumption. His declining strength, from his severe penance, excited public attention, and made of him an object of pity, for it seemed that the thread of his frail life was about to be severed. He wandered about from place to place, ekeing out a miserable existence by wool-spinning, and similar employments. He sojourned for a short time with the Brethren at Schwarzenau, and then joined the Inspirationists. He soon invoked their displeasure, and the "Chronicon" states that they wished to transfer him from the Adults' to the Children's meeting, on account of which he withdrew himself from them.

A Retrospect.—Born of a godly mother, but a worthless drunken father—at the age of seven the mother also dead—he grew up an object of public charity or neglect, living in wretched poverty and misery; apprenticed to a master baker from whom he learned unrestrained frivolity in dancing and fiddling; under conviction of sin, he sought spiritual comfort and light in all sorts of ways, and through all kinds of experiences, from the regular services in the Lutheran churches, individuals, the Pietists, Separatists, and down to the Rosicrucian mystics; as a journeyman baker, he wandered about, quarreled with his employer's wife, and driven from the home; criticized the bakers' guild, whose treasurer he was, who had him arrested and put in jail; brought to trial, he was charged with being a Pietist, and was banished from the country; wandering about almost starving, and under violence of severe penance, contracting consumption, he visits the Brethren at Schwarzenau, joins the Inspirationists, and after violent disagreements withdraws from them; thus were the thirty years of Conrad Beissel's life in Germany spent.

His two intimate friends, Stiefel and Stuntz, now induced him to journey to America. He resolved to go to Pennsylvania, and join the chapter of Perfection under Kelpius, called the "Woman in the Wilderness," on the Wissahickon, and there spend his life in solitude. When the Pietists heard of this, they tried their best to persuade him not to go. Stuntz offered to pay his way, and so in the year 1720 he left the fatherland, the scene of so much history, accompanied by his aforesaid friends, Stiefel and Stuntz, and others, as traveling companions.

The Arrival.—They arrived at Boston the same autumn. What the name of the ship was, or where she sailed from, or who commanded her, in which Beissel and his friends came to Boston, we are not told, neither do we know in what manner they transported themselves from Boston to Philadelphia. We are simply informed "that the party arrived well and in good spirits at Germantown toward the close of the autumn of the year 1720." It is impossible to realize their sore disappointment upon their arrival, nor appreciate the vast difference between their expectations and the real conditions of things as they found them. They had endured the hardships of a long and tedious ocean voyage, only to find that the community they sought to join had ceased to exist some years prior to their departure from the Fatherland, but for some reason this news had not reached that part of Germany. So it was necessary to change the whole plan and purpose of their coming, because of the changed conditions. According to "German Sectarians": "Beissel and his companions expected to find here an ideal spiritual community, whose chief interest centered around the Tabernacle in the primitive forest, where the time was spent in prayer and a nightly watch was kept to obtain the first glimpse of the harbinger in the skies, who should appear to announce the coming of the celestial bridegroom: a community where the world with its allurements was secondary to the state of spiritual regeneration."

"In place of this expected elysium they found the tabernacle deserted, the nocturnal watch upon the tower long since abandoned, Magister Kelpius dead, while of the other leaders, Köster, had returned to Europe, and the Falkner brothers were itinerating in the adjoining provinces."

Commenting upon this condition, the "Chronicon" states, "After their leader died, the Tempter found occasion to scatter them, as those who had been most zealous against marrying now betook themselves to women again, which brought such shame on the solitary state that the few who still held to it dared not open their mouths for shame."

"In such times the Superintendent (Beissel) arrived in Germantown; but kept very quiet as to his projects for a solitary life, for many, who had maintained a very proper walk in Germany, had here hung up their holy calling on a nail; and, what was worse, would give no one credit for zeal or diligence. Among these were several who in the Palatinate had let themselves be driven from house and home, but had left great wealth behind them after their death. All this caused him much concern; for he everywhere saw the pious sitting at the helm and exercising magisterial offices."

Beissel in the New World.

Religious Aspect.—In tracing the religious experiences, and struggles, and conflicts in the life of Beissel, in his foregoing biography, we see the religious conditions and excesses of his times that constituted such a powerful influence over him, and prepared him for such tremendous acts, that made him the central figure of so much dramatic history.

Beissel indeed found himself now in a new world. He had hoped for speedy realization of mountain-tops of spiritual ecstasy on the Wissahickon Heights, but instead he was down in the valley of disappointment and humiliation. Instead of things wholly spiritual, he found his feet on hard terra firma, and so face to face with the stern necessity of physical subsistence. He perhaps remembered the condition of starvation in Germany, and he once more turned to the Brethren for material comfort.

A New Start.—The Brethren had preceded Beissel by more than a year, as already noted in their coming in 1719. Peter Becker had already established himself as a master weaver of Germantown. Beissel, seeing that his baker's trade would be of no use to him, in this new country indentured himself to Peter Becker, as an apprentice, to learn the weaver's trade, and so his whole purpose had to undergo a complete change.

New Environments.—With his plans and purposes changed, he indeed found himself in new environments. Beissel now became a member of a busy industrial community, self-supporting, and a producing factor in the interests and welfare of his fellows. He became a part of the social life of his immediate surroundings, and, it is to be hoped, he added his share to the religious tone and atmosphere, that tended to the uplift of the settlement. As an apprentice, he entered the home of Peter Becker, and became a member of his household; and, as such, we are assured, by the "Chronicon," they were on most friendly and intimate terms in their religious discussions. Under these conditions, he was in constant association with the Brethren, and entered fully into all their social and religious life. He knew much of the Brethren at Schwarzenau, had sojourned among them for a time, knew their history and their persecution, and, in part, had been a fellow sufferer. The Brethren at Germantown, with whom he now associated, had come from Crefeldt, on the Rhine, which had been for some time a general asylum for persons of all shades of religious belief, who had fled from their persecutors. Mysticism in all shades was to be found among some of these refugees at Crefeldt. Such diversity of religious belief influenced some of the early Brethren, and they brought some of it to Germantown. Beissel had every opportunity to know every phase of religious tendency at Germantown, and his familiarity with all conditions enabled him to see where he could find some sympathy, as a foundation for antagonizing the Brethren's doctrines. It is not surprising, therefore, that, in years after, his inroads were to a considerable extent successful in disrupting the Germantown Church. For a time, it seems, Beissel was able to adapt himself quite well to his new environments, but the change must have been so great that he could not long endure the strain. In less than a year he broke his contract of apprenticeship, and left Germantown.

In the Wilderness.—The unexpected surely once more has happened. History is silent as to the developments that bring about so great a change from the home of Peter Becker, in the busy industrial village of Germantown, to the wilderness Solitude. But no doubt the year at Germantown was one of thoughtful preparation and planning for his future work. He had carefully examined the soil where were growing some prospective adherents.

We are indebted to the official "Chronicon" for an introduction into the very midst of the new scenes, and that without ceremony, or knocking at the cabin door, and waiting for an invitation. The "Chronicon" says: "In order to carry out his purpose, he went, in the autumn of the year 1721, into the upper country known as Conestoga, now Lancaster County, which at that time was inhabited by but few Europeans; and there, with the aid of his traveling companion, Stuntz, erected a solitary residence at a place called Muehlbach, where they lived happily for a while. A young Hollander by the name of Isaac Von Bebern soon after joined them, with whom he also made a journey to Maryland, probably to visit the remnant of Labadists, who lived there." The rapidity of change of scenes and the development is now truly remarkable. Perhaps there is no better way to show the diversity of teaching in the midst of which the Brethren had to labor, and the religious excesses against which they had to contend, than to note, briefly, how these conditions influenced Beissel, and how he finally became a conglomeration of social and political conditions of society, and religious doctrine with which he came in contact.

These Labadists had located on the Bohemian Manor, in Maryland, about forty years before, living a communal life, and had become prosperous and wealthy. The young Hollander desired to visit his near of kin, perhaps his father and his uncle, who had left the Mennonites and joined the Labadists. Beissel was interested in this mystical community, and we shall see that what he saw and learned on this visit was a moulding power on his whole future career.

"There can be but little doubt that, although the community at the time of Beissel's visit was already in a state of dissolution, it was due to his visit to Bohemian Manor and the conferences with Sluyter, together with a number of books and papers, both printed and in manuscript, of Labadie and Yoon Von, which Beissel obtained, that we owe many of the peculiar features of the Ephrata community. Not the least important one was the separation of the sexes.

"This visit was made none too soon, for soon after the two pilgrims had departed, Peter Sluyter died, and, there being none to replace him or wield the necessary authority, the few remaining members separated, and the community passed into history."[5]

It is plainly apparent, from the time of this visit, that Beissel was now a convert to the fundamental teaching of the Bohemian Labadists. Soon after the return of Beissel and Van Bebber from their pilgrimage to the Bohemia Manor, to their hut on the Mühlbach, they were joined by George Stiefel, a traveling companion, as noted before, on the voyage to America. These four enthusiasts now resolved to dwell together in a brotherly and communal manner. About this time, or soon after, Beissel commenced to express views in regard to the observance of the Sabbath. He paid visits to the Sabbatarians in Chester County, at Providence and Newtown. He soon after made a public announcement that he would observe the Sabbath. This caused a disagreement with his companions, but they finally acquiesced.

The "Chronicon" relates the effect of this new order of things as follows: "He declared himself to his brethren that now he would observe the Sabbath, and work on Sunday, which did not suit them very well. This strange mode of life aroused much attention among the few settlers, of

[5] "German Sectarians," p. 59.

whom some were continually coming and inquiring what it meant." Thus matters continued for some time, until the severity of the discipline and the short rations commenced to tell on his companions. Finally Stiefel and Van Bebber declared that they could not live that way, and took their departure. Stuntz finally sold the cabin, and thus in part re-imbursed himself for the money he had advanced to Beissel as passage money.

Trials Without and Within.—Homeless and alone, Beissel, smarting under his recent treatment, penetrated deeper into the forests, and determined to make a new start. By the end of the summer of 1723, he had built with his own hands a small log cabin, about one mile distant from the former one. Here he was soon joined by a new companion, and, because of the importance of this new fellowship, we quote from the "Chronicon," as follows: "There it came to pass that Michael Wohlfahrt, on his journey to Carolina, visited him for the first time. He was a Pietist, born at Memel on the Baltic Sea, but had grown cool in his faith, and had lost much of it on his many travels. He had come to the Superintendent while Stiefel and Stuntz were still with him, and had so fallen in love with his life that he promised to settle there with him when he should return from Carolina. Meanwhile, when in the year 1724 he came back to him, they had left him. As he laid before him his whole condition, the Superintendent received him in faith. In this man the latter found abundant exercise for his patience, and gained much profit through him in spiritual things. Indeed he fared better with him than he had with his former companions; for, though at times they disagreed, yet Michael Wohlfahrt had such high respect for him that he always confessed himself in the wrong." This companionship continued until broken by death.

While outward conditions were once more adjusted so far as home and companions were concerned, there was a growing inward conflict. There was a remarkable struggle between his self-exaltation and conceit, on the one hand, and his growing conviction, on the other, that he should bow in humble submission to the divine command. The "Chronicon" expresses the whole matter and condition in very candid language, as follows: "Now also we arrive at the reason why God obliged him to again renounce this seraphic life, and to enter into a communion with others. According to this, the life of a hermit is only something granted for a time, but not at all the end itself; since no solitary person can be fruitful. Accordingly, however innocent his walk before God and man at that time was, it was not yet right in itself; for with all his renunciations he still had not renounced himself. What was needed was a soil into which he might sow his grain of wheat to die, so that it should spring forth and bear fruit to the glory of God. It has before been mentioned how baptism, as a transplanting into the death of Christ, was again brought to light; now he had become abundantly convinced on that subject, but at that time he knew neither of a congregation according to his own mind, nor of a man who would have been worthy to baptize him. Once he made an attempt to baptize himself in the waters of Mill Creek; but his conscience was not satisfied; nor was the transaction valid, since there were no witnesses present. He was to obtain it through men, and that was difficult for him. How, at last, he humbled himself under the ordinance of God, and became a child of the new covenant, this shall be shown forth in the following chapter, although another excursion from the subject will be necessary, in order to trace the matter to its origin." So we leave, for the time, Beissel and the religious conditions of these times as a separate and distinct subject, and turn now to the consideration of how all these were related to the Brethren and their work.

CHAPTER VIII.

GROWTH AND DEVELOPMENT. TRIALS. SECOND EMIGRATION.

We are in the midst of years that are full of history. Events of importance are crowding each other in rapid succession. Amazing changes come like a flood. For the most part, the labors of the Brethren at Germantown, Coventry, and other places, were blessed, "and the Lord added to the church such as should be saved." Acts 2:47. Meetings multiplied, and the influence spread into new fields. In a few years a great change had been effected in America by the infant church, for the Lord strengthened the hearts of his people. By the close of 1724, there were three congregations organized, all in less than one year: Germantown, Coventry, and Conestoga.

Darkening Days.—In the midst of all of this glorious spiritual prosperity and blessing, when the Brethren were so much encouraged and strengthened by the spiritual showers of refreshing from the presence of the Lord, there was a gloom hanging over Conestoga. Dark clouds were gathering that looked threatening and indicated all too clearly the approaching storm. Dark days were coming that were full of new and strange and sad experiences. We cannot study all of these things in detail, but we must be satisfied with a rapid sketch, a kind of panoramic view of the principal facts and results. As has already been stated, in treating of the religious condition at the time of settlement in this country, some members had not entirely escaped the influence of mysticism at Crefeldt and other places, and they brought some of it to this country. For a time it prevented their fellowship, but was finally swallowed up for a time at least, in the general interest of the revival services.

But the spirit of mysticism was only waiting for a favorable opportunity for its development, through the leadership of some one. Conrad Beissel knew all this; he had learned it at Germantown a few years ago. We have seen him as a poor uneducated man, a strange character, with a strange history in Europe, and now, lately, living a life of dreamy solitude in the Conestoga, but an extreme egotist, in shrewd selfishness, coveting leadership. His most marked characteristic seems to have been his wonderful capacity to absorb all new and strange beliefs wherever found—whether the extreme and sweeping grounds of Pietism, or the ethereal conceptions of the Rosicrucian Mystics, or the solitary meditations of the Hermits on the Wissahickon, or the new doctrine of the Keithian Quakers on French Creek. He seemed to have had the unique experience, too, of coming in contact with more strange doctrines than anyone else, and so his own beliefs passed through many evolutions from time to time. When the Brethren established the work in Conestoga and largely gave it into his hands, he received what he had so much desired. He saw the opportunity, and seized it with earnestness. He desired leadership, and planned for it at any cost. Let us note the view of the "Chronicon," on this point, as follows: "Whoever considers this journey, together with the great blessing accompanying it, must confess that God was with them, at least up to the time when that man was found whom he had destined for a more important work. It is also certain that the Superintendent (Beissel) dealt with them in sincerity, and entered into communion with them with his whole heart. Had they not in the beginning permitted their suspicion against him to over master them, but had they condescended to him as he had done to them, he would have been the man through whom they would have recovered again their first vocation received at Schwarzenau; for he had a higher witness than they; such an unpleasant division would not have taken place."

The "Chronicon" is clean cut: "God was with them, at least up to the time when that man was found whom he had destined for a more important work."

And, again, "had they condescended to him as he had done to them, he would have been the man, etc;" "for he had a higher witness than they." The authors of the "Chronicon" understood the position and purpose of Beissel on this matter well, and they were in full sympathy with him, and they put it on record as a standing rebuke to the Brethren for not submitting themselves to this self-appointed and self-exalted leader. Again, as indicating how the Lord had cast off the Brethren, and chose Beissel, the "Chronicon" says: "Accordingly, as they failed in God's trial of them, his choice passed from them, and with the election all blessing also, unto the person of the Superintendent." In speaking of his ministry, the "Chronicon" says: "His ordination to this office he received from the same one who had bestowed it upon Elijah, John the Baptist and other reformers, who were awakened specially and directly to come to the help of a church fallen asunder." Testimony might be multiplied, if it were necessary. The time has come when at least the church should know the reason for his bitter antagonism.

With well defined plans and purposes, Beissel entered upon his ministry with enthusiasm. As to the manner of his preaching, the "Chronicon" says: "He conducted all Meetings, however, with astonishing strength of spirit, and used so little reflection over it, that even in the beginning he was not suffered to use a Bible, so that the testimony in its delivery might not be weakened by written knowledge." (It will be noticed by this, that the revelation came direct, without the medium of the Bible.)

"He began his discourse with closed eyes, before a large crowd of hearers; and when he opened his eyes again the most of them were gone, not being able to endure the Spirit's keenness." These revelations are then discussed at some length, by the "Chronicon."

But scarcely was he fairly started in his preaching when he began to present his doctrines regarding the Sabbath and to defend likewise certain Jewish laws in regard to meats, etc. This preaching was, of course, resented. Agitation and discussion upon these topics soon produced lack of harmony and restlessness which laid the foundations for dissension and confusion. The confusion seemed about complete, when, soon after, he presented his mystic speculations which produced so marked an effect that, while some thought him inspired, the others thought him crazy. There were some converts, however, and Beissel baptized them. Communications between the Sabbatarians on French Creek and Beissel and his adherents, became more and more frequent, and he presented his Sabbatarian views more positively and most bitterly antagonized those who differed on doctrine. This bitterness against the Brethren was carried by those who went to proselyte to all the settlements and finally reached Germantown; and when Elder Peter Becker and some others came on a visit to the Conestoga, Beissel attacked him most bitterly in public in his sermon. It was very evident that he was now openly committed to the policy that if he could not control the Brethren in leadership, he would destroy their work, and build his own upon the ruins. Thus was the breach constantly widened, and the Conestoga congregation itself was divided into two parts: those who adhered with Beissel to the Sabbath and those who adhered to the Lord's Day or Sunday. The leader of the latter was Johannus Hildebrand, who had moved to the Conestoga from the mother congregation at Germantown. It was very evident that matters could not go on at this rate and it seemed almost out of the question to restore harmony and reach a peaceful settlement. Beissel made a special effort to reach and influence the various Brethren settlements and that he succeeded will be noted further on in the history. These circumstances bring us to the latter part of the year 1728 and a paragraph from German Sectarians, page 138, will show conditions at that time: "The Germantown Baptists now reproached Beissel for his ingratitude toward them, as it was at their hands that he had received baptism. This, instead of rallying him, only tended to increase his vehemence against his former friends. At the same time he was forced to acknowledge the truth of their argument. How to overcome this dilemma was a serious question. At last, however, a way was found out of the difficulty, which was worked to their own satisfaction. This was the novel proposition to renounce the Becker baptism and return it to the old congregation, and then to have such of the Beisselianer as had been immersed by Becker rebaptized. This strange scene was enacted toward the close of December, evidently in the Mühlbach or the Conestoga. Upon the appointed day a general meeting of the Sabbatarians was held, during which three brothers and four sisters were selected for the chief ceremony. It had been decided that it was proper for the Sabbatical number to be the foundation of the rebaptized congregation. The number seven and the two sexes were therefore chosen. According to the teachings of the Rosicrucians the number seven represents the union of the square and the triad, and is considered the divine number, in the same sense in which forty is the perfect numeral. Jan Meyle and Beissel were the first to enter the icy water; special hymns were sung, and after an invocation, in which both men renounced their former baptism, Meyle immersed Beissel thrice backwards, and immediately afterwards repeated the operation thrice forwards, thus baptizing the candidate. Beissel then repeated the same ceremony upon Meyle and the others in turn. This act completed the separation between the Germantown and Conestoga Baptists." The babyish act of Beissel in his desire to "return" his former baptism, has received no end of ridicule, but if we can overlook his self-righteousness and self-exaltation and his ambition to lead, the poor man is to be pitied rather than laughed at. This was the condition of things when Alexander Mack with the larger part of the Schwarzenau congregation arrived in the following year, 1729. Several attempts were made at reconciliation, but without success. The Rosicrucian was now more than a mystic; he was partly a Jew, and a strict Sabbatarian, on which latter doctrine the separation largely came about. But not this alone, nor was this all of his system. He was a Labadist, and had already advocated celibacy and a communal life. One of his special missions now was to invade the sanctity of the home, separate husband from wife and wife from husband and parents from children. To many a home, for peace and happiness, he gave sorrow and separation and many of his victims were filled with remorse and regret.

Thus was the separation complete. By the very nature of the case, the system of doctrine, and the character of the leader and defender of that doctrine, complete separation was an absolute necessity. Owing to the peculiar conditions and circumstances of those early times, the system flourished for a number of years under a kind of hero worship. But the world is not looking for a religion behind cloister walls, or locked inside of convent gates. The world is longing for a religion of hope, of cheer, of charity,—a religion that can comfort, that can feed the hungry, that can soothe the broken hearted, with a salvation that proves *the joy of living is the joy of service.*

Some historians and others have regarded and classed these people as a branch of the Brethren Church. This seems strange to anyone who has studied the system of doctrine of these people. That the German Sabbatarians or Seventh Day Baptists under Beissel were a schism or split in the first place from the Brethren Church is unquestioned; but his monastic Community is no more a branch of the Brethren Church from which he separated than the Lutheran Church is a branch of the Catholic Church. There could be nothing more foreign in doctrine or more opposite in practical working. While the Master said: "Go ye into all the world, and preach my gospel to every creature," Mark 16:15, Beissel sought to confine his gospel behind cloister walls. The system was inherently selfish and was destined to die with the brain that conceived it. It was a system whose very foundations were so fallacious in character as to bring about its own destruction and annihilation. The historian, writing for popularity, has regaled himself on its unique character, but Beissel and his work linger only as a memory of the past generations. Long since has the stern hand of destiny laid low the actors, and while time has silenced the turmoil and the turbulence, and has gently stilled the sobs of broken homes and soothed the heartaches, let us cover these scenes of the past with the mantle of charity.

It will be remembered that we left the Mother Church at Schwarzenau, under favorable civil conditions, enjoying religious prosperity from 1708, for many years, being protected and even defended by Prince Henry. When he could no longer protect them, he spoke in most kindly terms in their defense after they had gone away. I wish to quote once more, from "The Origin of the Church of the Brethren":[1]

"These good people were, however, not left in peace. Objections came from all sides that godless people were living there who did not attend the state church nor did they submit to its ordinances. On Easter morning of 1719 the soldiers came and took the babes out of the mother's arms by force, and took them to the state church, where they were sprinkled. A cousin of Prince Henry, from Wetzlar, brought suit against Henry for permitting the 'Täufer' in his territory. Evidently Henry saw that he could no longer defend these people. Most likely he told them this and they, thankful for past favors and not wishing to cause him any trouble, went to West Friesland. I read the letter

[1] By D. Webster Kurtz in "Brethren Almanac," 1911.

where Henry defends himself, saying that he had no such persons in his territory. He did have, but two hundred persons,—forty families,—had just left, and now no one was there except Lutherans, Calvinists and Catholics. In a previous defense Henry says he does not harbor godless and wicked people, but the people whom he had were the 'best people he ever saw' and 'they had more religion than any of the members of the state church.' 'Their religion is genuine, but the religion of many others is sham.'"

Little is known of the church during the stay of nine years in this place of refuge. It is well known, however, that "some Hollanders were won to the church," which is evidence that the activity and growth of the church was maintained. "It was at this place that they received the news of the promising mission fields among the Germans in Pennsylvania. They decided to cast their lot with their friends and Brethren in the New World, the land of religious liberty. They sailed from Rotterdam, in July, on the good ship *Allen,* James Craigie, master, and qualified at Philadelphia, September 15, 1729."[2]

Upon his arrival, Alexander Mack again became the leading spirit of the church, as he had been in the beginning, in the capacity of the "leader and first minister" at the time of organization in 1708. As some so-called historians speak of him as the "founder" of the church of the Brethren, there should be a clear and definite understanding that the Brethren do not regard Mack as either the "founder," or the "foundation." He was only one of eight to organize the work, but because of his previous experience and activity as a minister and evangelist, he naturally became the leader and the leading spirit.

As to foundation, we accept the words of the Apostle Paul, I Corinthians 3: 11—"For other foundation can no man lay than that is laid, which is Jesus Christ." It may be well to recall Alexander Mack's recital of the covenant of

[2] "German Baptist Brethren," by the author, p. 52, and footnote.

the eight: "Under these circumstances some felt themselves drawn powerfully to seek the footsteps of the primitive Christians, and desired earnestly to receive in faith the ordained testimonies of Jesus Christ according to their true value. At the same time they were internally and strongly impressed with the necessity of the obedience of faith to a soul that desires to be saved.

"Finally, in the year 1708, eight persons consented together, to enter into a covenant of a good conscience with God, to take up all the commandments of Jesus Christ as an easy yoke, and thus to follow the Lord Jesus, their good and faithful shepherd, in joy and sorrow, as his true sheep, even unto a blessed end."—German Baptist Brethren, page 62 and 63.

This is a clear statement of those who, having come from different beliefs, accepted Christ and His Gospel as fundamental principles. True to the leadership of Alexander Mack and his associates, there is no other creed or confession to-day, but the Church of the Brethren still accepts only the New Testament as the rule of faith and practice.

We have already set forth the difference in doctrine on which the line of separation was made by Beissel. It is necessary to have some understanding now as to the policy of antagonism and destruction that was inaugurated by Beissel, and his faithful dupes, in order to show what Alexander Mack and Peter Becker had to grapple with at this time. In the Conestoga, the confusion and dissension had become a veritable Babel. Many resented the teaching and acts of Beissel, and withdrew, and so was formed later the Conestoga Church of Brethren. The general condition of the congregation, and the conduct of the leaders is thus set forth in the "Chronicon," p. 42: "About this time, namely, in the year 1728, the power of God manifested itself palpably in the meetings, witnessing against the old Adam and his many false sanctuaries; whereat many were offended and separated themselves from the congregation.

These Separatists, like men sick with a plague, finally banded together, and set up a meeting of their own; so that in those times there were more apostates than there were righteous ones; which, however, by no means confounded the Superintendent; for he had reckoned on all these, and yet worse, quarrelings, when he left his beloved solitary state and waded into the sea of humanity. Since it was known that these apostates were supported by the Baptists of Germantown, M. W., (Michael Wohlfahrt), felt himself moved to go into the meeting of these Baptists and thus spoke to them: 'Men and Brethren, thus saith the Lord, ye have gone mad; this is a city that is destroyed, and unto you, Peter Becker, the Lord saith, why dost thou declare my rights and hast my covenant on thy lips, while yet thou hatest order and throwest my words behind thee!' After he had thus done, he went his way again. This occurred in December, 1728."

After recording some other matters, on other subjects, the "Chronicon" again proceeds: "Now we will take the new congregation in hand again. The witness of God concerning the judgment against the old Adam, as it was applied by the Superintendent with much severity, was the cause of one revolt after another among his followers. This continued until his death; yes, some followed him with slander even after his death. No meeting was held at which some did not fall to quarreling, and mostly it was on the subject of the matrimonial estate; for he was accused of seeking to prescribe laws and rules for the same, and this was regarded as a teaching of the devil. It was mentioned above concerning the apostates that they organized an own congregation, in which J. H. (John Hildebrand) and D. E. (Daniel Eicher) were teachers. To these a Brother, Joel by name, went in their meeting, and spoke thus: 'To you, J. H., I have a word from the Lord to say, Thus saith the Lord: Thou shalt no longer go forth and preach to others, but first thou and thy house must be converted, then thou canst go forth and convert others. If thou heed not this warning voice, the judgment of the Lord shall come upon thee because thou hast not done according to his Words. Moreover this day it shall be made manifest whether we or you are the congregation of God; for God will to-day perform a wonder and sign in me, in that if I shall fall down before your eyes as one that is dead, and you will pray for me that I may rise again, then God hath not sent me unto you, and you are the Lord's congregation. But if I do not fall dead before your eyes, but shall go out of the door again well and hearty, then ye shall know that the Lord hath sent me to you this day, and that you are not the Lord's congregation. Eight days ago as I was in your meeting, I said that there were wolves among you'; and after seizing one of them, Henry Hohn by name, by the arm, he said, 'Here is a wolf,' and then went away with his companion."

The "Chronicon" states that Joel "went away" showing that he did "not fall dead," and thereby proving that the Brethren were "not the Lord's congregation."

These denunciations were called prophesying, by delivering a message from the Lord, announcing certain destruction of the good Brethren who had incurred the displeasure of Beissel by refusing his self-imposed leadership. Beissel himself also delivered such testimony, or prophesy. Some of these testimonies were written,—some printed, in both English and German.

It is interesting to know just how the congregation of Beissel regarded this method of antagonistic attack upon the Brethren, and Peter Miller does not fail to state in his usual frank way ("Chronicon") and the results:

"Some of the congregation thought as much of this testimony, (Joel by name,) and also of that of M. W., recorded above, as if the Holy Spirit had dictated it; therefore they had them carefully written out. But another Brother, Amos by name, who looked upon this as idolatry, with the sanction of the Superintendent gained possession of these testimonies by craft and burned them, saying he would try whether they could endure the fire-test. The sensible reader will know how to take the best out of this." The best is not plainly apparent even to the "sensible reader."

The company of Alexander Mack consisted of about thirty families and so large an addition to their numbers greatly stimulated the work, and cheered the Brethren in Pennsylvania. But the heart of this devoted man was saddened when he found the deplorable condition of things among his Brethren, as a result of the Beissel confusion. His life was full of heroism, however, and his true and moral bravery failed him not now. He went resolutely to work, once more, to win the last great battle of his life. Perhaps he little realized that it was to be the last great struggle. After several vain attempts to reconcile Beissel, all efforts were concentrated to bring harmony out of the the confusion and chaos, and once more organize his forces for united Christian work. The result of these united efforts is perhaps best indicated by pointing to the fact that a number of churches were organized in the course of a few years. The following is at least a partial list of the churches and the dates of their organization: The Oley Church, in 1732; the Great Swamp Church, in 1733; Amwell Church, New Jersey, in 1733; the Cocalico, or Conestoga Church, in 1735 (reorganized from the Beissel wreck); the White Oakland, in 1736 (only partly organized); and others soon after. But he saw only a part of the fruits of his latter labors. His life was too intense, too full of sacrifice and service, to last long; and at the early age of fifty-six, he passed away. A brief biography will be found in the following chapter.

CHAPTER IX.

ALEXANDER MACK, SR.[1]

Birth.—In the foregoing chapters we have much account of the activities and labors of this man of God, yet because of the importance of his ministry and leadership for twenty-seven years, it will be of interest to relate briefly such biographical facts as have come down to us. It may be said, however, that we know but little, comparatively, of this great and good man, outside of the organized activities of the Church of the Brethren with which he is so inseparably connected. He was born in 1679, at Schriesheim, about midway between Manheim and Heidelberg, in the Electorate of Palatia, or the Palatinate, now forming a part of the grand duchy of Baden, in southern Germany. Of his parents we have little positive information. From what his biographers say of him, we know that his parents were respectable, wealthy and religious.

His Education.—Inasmuch as "After the Reformation Heidelberg was long the headquarters of German Calvinism and gave its name to a famous Calvinistic catechism," it is altogether likely that Alexander Mack received careful instruction in the Heidelberg catechism, since he was born and raised only a few miles from that city. Elder James Quinter writes, in 1867: "Although we know but little of his ancestors, it appears he descended from a very respectable and wealthy family. He was a Presbyterian (Reformed), and educated in the Calvinistic faith. Of his literary acquirements we know nothing but what we can gather from his writings, and from these it does not appear that he had a classical education."[2]

Occupation.—It seems that in early life he was a miller, and operated his milling interests. Morgan Edwards, writ-

---

[1] This biographical sketch is placed as Chapter IX, of Part I, because his life belonged to the whole Brotherhood.

[2] Memoir of Alexander Mack, Sen., Brethren's Encyclopedia.

GRAVES OF ELDERS ALEXANDER MACK, SENIOR AND JUNIOR.

ing in 1770, says: "He had a handsome patrimony at Schriesheim, with a profitable mill and vineyard thereon, but spent all in raising and maintaining his church at Schwarzenau."[3]

Marriage.—In the year 1700, at the age of twenty one, he was married to Anna Margaretha Klingin, a native of the same place and about his own age. To this union were born five children, three sons and two daughters: Johannes, John Valentine, Alexander, Christina, and Anna Maria.

His Life-Work.—His life-work began at an early age. He was only twenty-nine years of age when the Church was organized and he was chosen the first minister. He however had been active already for a number of years before this time. Being dissatisfied with the religious system in which he had been brought up, he directed his prayerful attention to the Scriptures in searching for "the old paths," for he was anxious to ascertain the mind of the Lord as therein revealed. This soon brought persecution and in a few years he was an exile from his splendid estate at Schriesheim. He took his wife and little ones, and with many others found a refuge at Schwarzenau under the mild rule of Count Henry. Here he found many active Pietists and among them Ernest Christoph Hochmann von Hochenau who was an active evangelist and with whom Mack traveled much, for they had much in common. There is no doubt but that Hochmann's Confession of Faith encouraged and confirmed Mack considerably in his own convictions; but Hochmann seemed to lack the courage of his convictions and his work ultimately came to naught and he died in sorrowful poverty. The work of the Church of the Brethren was organized here in 1708, as has already been noticed, and was continued for twelve years, or until 1720; when upon the death of the mild and friendly Count, they were driven to Holland. But the year 1720 is emphasized for sadness, in the life of this good man, in addition to persecution and exile. From Quinter's Memoir, I quote as follows:

[3] "Materials toward a History of the American Baptists," Vol. I, Part IV.

"But he had domestic afflictions to endure, as well as those arising from persecution. In 1720, twenty years after they were united in the bonds of matrimony, and twelve years after they were united to Christ by a living faith and gospel obedience, his companion was taken from him by death. She is said to have been a meek Christian and virtuous wife. She found in death what she and her husband had sought in vain for on earth, a calm retreat from the storm of persecution. Within one week of the death of his wife, his oldest daughter, then about six years old, also died. It is said that the child was uncommonly fond of its mother, and out of regard, perhaps, to the fondness which existed between the mother and child, as well as out of regard to the circumstances of persecution under which the father and child were placed, the Lord in His wisdom and goodness may have taken the little daughter to the quiet home of the mother where it could enjoy her fond caresses, rather than leave it where it must endure the hardships and troubles of persecution in common with its father. Thus in about one week, in addition to the troubles consequent upon the great persecution which was then raging, he had to bear the loss of a kind and Christian wife and a dear little daughter. After seeking unsuccessfully for a retreat from persecution in his native country, he with his three sons, and a number of his Brethren, emigrated to America in 1729, and settled as a poor man, poor in this world's goods but rich in faith, on a small lot of ground near Germantown, in the vicinity of Philadelphia."

Thus it will be seen that the wife of Alexander Mack did not accompany him to America in 1729, as some historians assert, and such assertion has, therefore, been the cause of much confusion.

The Character of this "Man of God."—Though he probably was not classically educated, his writings have lived for two hundred years. He was, perhaps, not an eloquent preacher, but his consistent life and consecrated devotion wonderfully impressed the truth he professed and defended. He was truly loved and deeply mourned by those who followed his leadership. His death at this time was a very serious loss, coming as it did so soon after the confusion of the Beissel Secession; and it would certainly have proven fatal if his followers had builded on the personality of their leader. But he was so anxious about the permanent establishment of the truth of God, that he had carefully eliminated his own personality. Perhaps the truth of this statement is best illustrated by the following incident.

Some time before his death, he said to his family, "Now when I am gone, don't mark my grave, or they might sometime want to erect a monument over my grave." The sons were grieved to think that his grave should be lost sight of, and so they protested against an unmarked grave. It is said he then yielded to the wishes of his loved ones and gave them privilege to place his initials on a small stone slab. This incident seems well established as a fact; it is at any rate entirely consistent with the man's life and character, and the unpretentious bluestone, scarce two feet in height, has been a silent witness for more than a century and a half, to multitudes of his followers.

No monument has yet been erected, and none will be. He needs none. His name is written in the Book of Life; his spiritual devotion and living sacrifice to principle are inscribed in the hearts of his spiritual descendants. What a simple story of such a heroic life. "Hier Ruhen | die Gebeine | A.M. | geboren 1679. | gestorben | 1735. | Alt 56 Jahr." Succeeding generations of his own family, not connected with the Brethren, had lost the grave entirely. To the Brethren, all these years the simple epitaph was eloquent with meaning.

"His Christian character appears to have been that of a primitive follower of Christ. Humility, zeal, self-denial, and charity were conspicuous among the graces that adorned his character. The high estimation in which he was held by his Brethren is seen in the circumstances that he was chosen by them to be their minister. He was the first minister in the little Christian community organized at Schwarzenau in 1708, and labored zealously and successfully to enlarge the borders of their Zion. Of his private character as a Christian father we may infer favorably from the circumstances that all his sons became pious and were united to the church before they had completed their seventeenth year. And what seems somewhat remarkable, they all made a public confession of religion in the seventeenth year of their age."[4]

"To Alexander Mack the church must ever turn with gratitude and reverence. In the midst of persecutions and in an age of religious fanaticism, surrounded by men of all shades of belief, he heroically stood for the truth as he saw it. Around him, no doubt impressed by his piety and honesty, gathered faithful followers—men and women who abandoned former religious organizations and stood with him for the truth of God as revealed in Christ. To him we are indebted for our church organization and for the principles that bind into a Christian unity, the members of God's visible Church."[5]

We need a larger vision of the times and condition in which he lived, and of the scope of the work he helped to establish, so that we may place a higher estimate upon the life and character of Alexander Mack, and assign his proper place as a factor in the religious history of the world. Such high type of Christian leadership leads men and women back to God.

His Seal.—To study his seal is of real significance. Some years ago some of his descendants from the west commenced a research for the purpose of recovering his seal. They seemed certain enough that there was or had been a seal, but the search proved fruitless, and it now seems likely that the seal of Alexander Mack will never be found. Such a seal indicates the prominence of his family. What was the character of this seal, and what was its symbolic representation? Did he not leave its impress somewhere, just as he left his impress of his character upon the hearts and lives of his followers? Yes, after being lost perhaps more than a century, and even its character unknown. Beside his official signature on an old parchment deed, at Germantown, is his official impress of his personal or family seal. It is in red sealing wax and is in perfect condition. See illustration, which shows that the seal consisted of several symbols, each of which had a religious significance. The entire combination constitutes a remarkable index to the character of its owner.

[4] Quinter's Memoir.
[5] "German Baptist Brethren," M. G. Brumbaugh, page 71.

It is circular in shape. In the center is the cross, which means sacrifice; the heart means devotion, and placed on the cross, further means sacrificed in devotion; the branches of the vine mean fruit-bearing. Thus the seal may be interpreted to read: a devoted, fruit-bearing, sacrificed life. How significantly true is this of the life of Alexander Mack?

The Removal.—When Alexander Mack died in 1735, there was but one graveyard in the neighborhood, called the Upper Burying Ground of Germantown or sometimes called Axe's Burying Ground, after the man who owned the ground. The cemetery connected with the Brethren church, located now near the spot where he died, was not opened until the close of the century, or about sixty-five years after Mack's death. So with loving hand his body was laid away to sleep in the midst of strangers. This ancient cemetery has long since been but little used, and many removals have taken place within recent years. Because of the growing neglect of the place for years, it was a matter of much regret and real sorrow of heart, when I first discovered that he reposes in so forlorn and neglected a place. The Brethren cemetery was a beautiful, and an ideal spot in which to lay away loved ones. Why should not his remains repose in the midst of his own people, and especially in the midst of five generations of his own descendants? But he was buried one hundred and fifty-nine years, and why should his dust be disturbed. A proposition of removal was presented to some of the descendants, for they alone had the right to authorize. They quickly consented but scarcely one of them knew of the place of his burial. Necessary official arrangements were made, and on November 13, 1894, the removal took place. The inscription on the small stone slab said: " Here rest the bones A. M." This was literally the truth, strange as it seems to one who knows not the condition of the ground that preserved the bones for so long a time. All the bones were there, even to the smallest, perfect in form and shape, but without hardness, or toughness, only the mineral constituents. These bones, with the brown layer of dust surrounding them, we carefully and gently gathered together, and placed in an oak box. For a short time these remains reposed in the historic meeting house, while we conducted brief funeral services, Eld. T. T. Myers, then of Philadelphia, assisting. The oak box, with the mortality of Alexander Mack, was then carried to the cemetery in the rear of the church, and placed in a grave in the midst of his own family. The former small slab was retained for a footstone, and for a head-stone there was erected a plain white marble slab about five feet in height, with the following inscription:

Alexander Mack, Sr., | the first minister | and organizer of the | Church of "The Brethren" | in the year 1708. | Born at Schriesheim, | Germany, 1679. | Came to Germantown | 1729, died 1735. | Removed from | Axe's Burying Ground, | 1894.

SEAL OF ALEXANDER MACK, SR.

OLD AND NEW TOMBSTONE OF ALEXANDER MACK, SR.

OLD STONE CHURCH AND OLD STONE PARSONAGE, GERMANTOWN.
By Julius F. Sachse.

OLD AND NEW GERMANTOWN BRETHREN CHURCH.
OLD CHURCH BUILT 1770.   NEW CHURCH DEDICATED MAY, 1897.

By Julius F. Sachse.

CHAPTER X.

GERMANTOWN.

It will be remembered that from the beginning, Germantown has always occupied a conspicuous place in the activities of the Brethren. It was the center of authority and organized effort; and so, in the preceding chapters, Germantown has often been referred to and much of its history traced directly, and much more indirectly and in a general way. Nothing more, therefore, need be said of these earlier years, but we have now arrived at a period when it is necessary to consider Germantown very carefully, for here are concentrated all the vital interests of a great religious crisis.

A Retrospect.—Beissel had invaded Falckner's Swamp,[1] and during the years, from 1727 to 1729, had made many converts. It was here that an effort was made at reconciliation, but like all others proved fruitless. After seven years from the beginning of this awakening, these converts of Beissel broke up their homes and moved to the Settlement, in 1734. Encouraged by his success in Falckner's Swamp, during these first years, Beissel decided to make a visit into the Tulpehocken country, where he met with astonishing success, because of the high standing of the converts in the Reformed and Lutheran churches. The recital of this awakening had no bearing on the subject under consideration, except by mere reference to it to show Beissel's proselyting methods at this time.

Michael Wohlfahrt the over-zealous servant, was ever ready to do the bidding of Beissel, at all hazards. As noted in a previous chapter, he, with one Joel by name, interrupted the Brethren, in their meetings in Conestoga. He had been of service in Falckner's Swamp, until, "he fell from his office with shame and disgrace." He was now ready to serve his master in a new field, and other places.

[1] For account of the work in Falckner's Swamp, see "History of Coventry Church."

The *Chronicon* makes a final comment on this method of work, and gives another example of this style of harangue, viz.:

"It was mentioned above that M. W. (Michael Wohlfahrt) had borne prophetic witness against the Baptists (Brethren) in Germantown. He did more such work in those days. For on October 19, 1729, he and another Brother went into a meeting of the Quakers in Philadelphia, and, after he had listened a long while to a female preacher, he finally began to speak,—'My friends, I beseech you to hearken unto me, for I have a few words from the Lord to you; therefore, I demand that you hear me. For I will not leave this place until I have delivered my message which I am sent to bring, that I may be guiltless before the Lord, and may go my way hence again in peace.' The speeches and replies are in print, but are too lengthy to reproduce here."

The civil law has long ago made provision for such conditions, and if any one were to tramp around the country now disturbing religious meetings, he would likely be arrested and fined, or imprisoned. But the very audacity of these dupes, and the very positive boldness with which they announced their preposterous claims of a direct revelation from the Lord to pronounce judgment upon the people, made a profound impression upon some of the hearers. All of these things had an influence upon some people, and they could not fail to affect those at Germantown who had already such tendencies, and contributed to their further developmen. However, with the coming of Alexander Mack, in 1729, the whole situation assumed a changed aspect. The powerful influence of his personal leadership was at once felt and recognized,—in checking Beissel's influence and work, and in giving inspiration and enthusiasm to the cause of the Brethren. During the next six years the work was much extended, and new churches were organized.

Other Influences at Work.—It will be necessary to a clear understanding now, to trace some of the *internal* conditions which contributed so largely to the final results. Reference was made in the beginning to the mystical influences that hindered the Brethren in the earlier years, in their work at

Germantown. After a time these influences seem to have been overcome; but they were only lying dormant for a time, and in years after rebounded with consuming force. One person was largely responsible for this element in the religious crisis, as will be seen by an account of his doings.

"Among the Creyfelt members who came with Peter Becker to Germantown in 1719, no one affords a better illustration of the mystical influences that saddened and retarded the growth of the Church than Stephen Koch.

"Before 1715, he was a minister at Creyfelt, but not an ordained Elder. With the more consecrated element of the congregation he engaged in active evangelistic work, traveled much, preached fearlessly, lived nobly. When he came to America, he allowed the spirit to decline. In 1723, he was at the first love feast, a humble member; but the collected membership chose Becker to conduct the services. Whether this in any way affected the zeal of Bro. Koch is not known. Perhaps he already had developed such traits of mysticism as to render his leadership unwise. At all events, the Ephrata community had a charm for him.

"In August, 1726, the Brethren at Germantown paid a fraternal visit to the Conestoga congregation, then in full fellowship, and presided over by Conrad Beissel. On this visitation Henry Traut and Stephen Koch left the party and visited Jacob Stuntz.

"Stuntz came to America in 1720 with Beissel and Steifel. Stuntz paid Beissel's passage to Boston. He also, in 1721, accompanied Beissel into the wilderness and lived a solitary life. About 1724, Stuntz sold the house in which he and Beissel lived in order to recover the money advanced to Beissel on coming to America. This caused Stuntz to suffer the displeasure of Beissel. When Beissel founded the church, Stuntz also became a member. Stuntz married, and under censure of having married a near relative, Beissel placed him under the ban.

"To restore Stuntz to fellowship was the purpose of Traut and Koch's visit. In this they were successful. But in doing so they incurred the censure of Beissel who claimed that he alone had the power to restore Stuntz to the communion of his Brethren. Beissel, therefore, not only renewed his opposition to Stuntz, but censured these Brethren as well."[2]

Some of Koch's Doings.—I have made this somewhat extended quotation, in order to give some facts of Koch's earlier life, some phases of religious tendencies, and Koch's relation to Germantown as well as to Beissel. We are, therefore, the better prepared to consider the conditions at Germantown, in which Koch became so important a figure. Koch was a man of large experience as a minister, of some ability as a writer, and among other things, he wrote a long account of himself, and his doings at Germantown, which is recorded in the *Chronicon*. This account is very largely the index to his life and character. From 1726 to 1739, he passed through many and very varied experiences. He more and more yielded to his mystical tendencies. He lived for a time, at least, a solitary life, but the *Chronicon* says, "he forsook his celibacy, and betrothed himself to a widow." From this course he repented with many tears of penitence, and returned to his solitary life. In an introductory way, the *Chronicon* says, "at that time there was among the Baptists at Germantown, an old experienced Solitary Brother, Stephen Kock by name, who stood in good repute because of his piety." But he grew more and more out of harmony with the Brethren. He says, in his own account,—

"for they recognize no one as a Brother who has not been baptized, even though he should surpass them in knowledge and experience; such an one has to be satisfied with the title of friend. They went still further in this literal and narrow manner and committed the teaching office mostly into the hands of married men. Thereby they brought matrimony into high favor."

This seems to be the real ground for his course, that he did not receive the consideration he felt was due him, the reason for such lack, of course, being that his teaching was wholly at variance with the Brethren. Koch began to have ecstatic visions, as early as 1732; some of these he wrote out in full for publication,—first published in Europe, and

[2] "German Baptist Brethren," Brumbaugh, pages 133–134.

afterwards reprinted, by Saur, in 1744 and 1748, with other "*apparitions*," etc. These are too lengthy to appear in this work.[3]

But new experiences came to him besides his betrothal, and remarkable visions and apparitions. He says:

"About this same time, however, an important Brother, Henry Traut by name, passed out of time into eternity, on Jan. 4, 1733. When with sorrowful heart and deeply grieved I saw him pass into eternity, it made so deep an impression on me that I continually sighed unto God whether it were not possible that in this life yet I might attain unto health of conscience."

Traut and Koch had been very intimate, for they had much in common, and had some similar experiences. To this penitence, and to visions, and to this grief, however, one thing more must be added. He says:

"In this way I spent several years, and had, besides, great pain from stones in the bladder, so that I often lay two or three days in the greatest extremity, and had death ever before me, until I was again relieved from it for a time. But God finally regarded my misery, and came to my help in a wonderful manner, on the 3rd of May, 1735."

The Reaction.—As stated above the six years, from 1729 to 1735, during Mack's leadership, were years of religious prosperity for the Brethren, notwithstanding Beissel's aggressive opposition from without, and Koch's mystical influences from within. But the year 1735, the year of Mack's death, was especially a sad one for Germantown. The time seemed most unfortunate.

"A great crisis was approaching among the Germans in Pennsylvania. Beissel was especially active and aggressive, and while he had confined himself to the Brethren settlements in various places, he now branched out and began to proselyte among the Lutherans and Reformed in the Tulpehocken and other places. It was in 1735 that Rev. Peter Miller and Conrad Weiser and other prominent Germans

---

[3] See the *Chronicon,* "German Sectarians," and Brumbaugh's "German Baptist Brethren."

accepted Beissel's doctrine, and removed to Ephrata. Beissel now seemed to put forth every effort possible to destroy the Brethren congregations. He organized large parties, sometimes as many as twelve in a party, to visit the settlements of Pennsylvania and New Jersey. He laid claim to following the Brethren's doctrine in the observance of all the commandments of the New Testament and everywhere threatened the church. He found in after years that his work was too aggressive, for he had many converts he could not hold, and many he did not want, for he could not assimilate and use them to his own ends. This at least partly explains the reason why so many prominent persons, who became converts of Beissel, remained at Ephrata only long enough to find out the man and the character of his work."[4]

Under these conditions, it is not strange, therefore, that there was a serious reaction when Mack died. Some of the newly organized churches were not yet well established, but the full force of the blow fell on Germantown. Here were those who had come with him in 1729, and who had never known any other ministry and leadership. They who knew him best, loved him most, and most deeply mourned their loss of his personal presence. Among these was Alexander Mack, Jr., then a young man of 23 years, very active in the church, but disheartened when his father died, whom he dearly loved. He was despondent, and believed that he too would soon die. It was at this time that Koch first related to him his wonderful visions and experience. It made a deep impression upon him, in his despondent condition. Koch also greatly influenced Henry Kalckglässer, who was at this time the oldest minister in the congregation at Germantown. By this condition, Koch was much encouraged in his work, and began to hold public meetings of his own. He came to live with Alexander Mack and he refers to their further association, and the result as follows:

"We often had similar conversations with each other, and it was not long before he also came to an awakened condition. As he was a ready speaker, he began to speak

[4] "German Baptist Brethren," by the author, page 74.

in the meeting so powerfully that it was a marvel to hear him, and aroused much notice in the congregation. . . . At that time we had a meeting for the unmarried every Sunday afternoon, where we also spoke together as narrated above. At last the spirit of revival came upon all who were assembled together, so that one often heard with astonishment how they praised God; however, with many it did not last long."

These meetings have sometimes been called a Sunday School because held on Sunday afternoon. But let it be remembered, first, it was "a meeting for the unmarried"; second, the teaching theme was Koch's visions and Beissel's doctrine of celibacy; third, the teachers were Beissel's disciples. These meetings received every possible encouragement from Ephrata, and Peter Miller and others from Ephrata frequently were present to address the meetings. After these Germantown Brethren and Sisters had gone to Ephrata, they continued the Sunday meetings there, for many years.

A Divided Congregation.—Thus matters continued for several years, with increasing gloom hanging over Germantown. There could be but one result,—a divided congregation, a disrupted church. The *Chronicon* gives the following, as to conditions at this time:

"The fame of it (the awakening) soon resounded through the whole land; for they held their meetings in the woods, and then walked through Germantown hand in hand, which attracted much attention. Besides, they had frequent meetings at night. The teachers of the Baptists themselves went astray in this movement. Some of them, like Henry Kalckglässer, Valentine Mack, John Hildebrand, supported it; while others, like P. Becker, Naass, etc., [Peter Becker, John Naas,] who had had a similar experience in Germany, opposed it. Yes, Peter Becker often said to them: 'Dear children, it is the seventh-day spirit of Conestoga!'"

And so, the crisis was at hand. Beissel had won, but at tremendous cost, and the victory was worse than the defeat. Koch and his companions and adherents marched out of Germantown, most of them never to return. They journeyed to Ephrata, there to bury themselves in seclusion behind monastic walls. Germantown had lost a host, Beissel added a few names to his monastery lists. It was the saddest day in the history of Germantown, for many valuable members had been lost, and some of the best families were represented. A few, when they realized their disappointment, repented and returned; others there were who died in the sadness and solitude of their disappointment. There was only one thing that saved Germantown in this trying ordeal, and that was the faithful devotion of Elder Peter Becker and those who stood with him.

The following names are given as composing the exodus of 1739, mostly on March 27: Heinrich Kalckglässer, and wife; Valentine Mack, and wife Maria (Hildebrand); Louis Höcker, his wife Margretta, and daughter Maria; Johannes Hildebrand and wife; Johannes Péttikoffer, and wife Anna Elizabeth; the widow Gorgas and her children. Among the single persons who joined the celibates, or Solitary, were: Stephen Koch, Alexander Mack, Johannes Reismann, Christian Eckstein, Heinrich Höcker, Martha Kinsing, Miriam Gorgas and Elizabeth Eckstein. And so the curtain forever falls upon the unwritten tragedy.

CHAPTER XI.

CLOSING DECADES OF THE PRE-REVOLUTIONARY PERIOD.

General Survey.—It is necessary, at this time, to take a view of the whole field of the Brethren activities. During the closing decades of this period, the work is much extended, far beyond the borders of the field covered by this volume. These can only be referred to, in order to show to what extent the work has spread at so early a date. There was much colonization at an early day, and with this colonizing went the doctrine and influence of the Brethren. This migration and colonization was first to the southern counties of Pennsylvania, and then into various counties in Maryland and Virginia, and even south as far as North Carolina.[1]

Virginia.—There were probably no organized churches of the Brethren in Virginia before the Revolution, but settlements by the Brethren had commenced; and, also, several by followers of Beissel, some of whom here, as in other places, soon came into full fellowship with the Brethren, upon the disintegration of Beissel's work.

Maryland.—Several well-established churches must have existed in Maryland, by the close of this period. The first Brethren Church was probably that of Middletown Valley, in Frederick County, organized in 1760. "Many members went to the Conococheague and to Monocacy, from the various congregations in Pennsylvania; and among them were prominent and efficient ministers, but we know little of their work in the early days. The scores of congregations of the present day, however, attest the faithful devotion of these pioneers, and the success of the migration to the Southland."[2] Among the prominent Elders and minis-

---

[1] See "History of the Brethren in Virginia," by D. H. Zigler; also, "The Church Before the Revolution," in "Two Centuries of the Church of the Brethren," by J. W. Wayland.

[2] "German Baptist Brethren," by the author, page 98.

ters who went to Maryland early, before 1770, were:—
Elder Jacob Donner, from the Codorus Church, York
County; Elder Daniel Leatherman and Elder Nicolas
Martin, both from Little Conewago Church, in York
County, Pennsylvania. These were prominent and active
elders, and frequently returned to the Pennsylvania churches
on preaching tours, and important church councils. This
much must suffice for a notice of the work to the southward,
from Pennsylvania. We hope that soon the Brethren in
Maryland will make a thorough research of their ante-
cedents, and after having gathered all available data possible,
make a careful study of their history, and publish the fruits
of their labors, for the instruction and inspiration of the
coming generations.

A Momentous Period in American History.—It is well
to note some of the external conditions with which our
Brethren were surrounded during the latter years of this
period under consideration. It was indeed a momentous
period in American history, as to political and military conditions. In this period fall two wars in which the Americans and the English fought against the French; and it also
marks the beginning of a far greater one, in which the
Americans and the French fought against the English. In
the former wars, the French lost their empire in America;
and in the latter, in the succeeding period, England forever
lost a vast empire, and the beginnings of a mighty nation.
It was scarcely less momentous from educational and religious considerations. The following panoramic sketch is
full of interest, as well as thoughtfully suggestive:—

"It was in this period under review that Thomas Jeffer-
son was born; that Washington rose from a forest ranger to
a general's rank; that Franklin became famous as a printer,
and an inventor, and won some notoriety for his antipathy
to the Pennsylvania Dutch; that Jonathan Edwards published his work on the freedom of the human will; that Zinzendorf the Moravian, Mühlenberg the Lutheran, Schlatter
the German Reformed, and Whitefield the Methodist, all
came to Pennsylvania or neighboring colonies; that the
northern Indian tribes rose in that mighty conspiracy under

CLOSING DECADES OF PRE-REVOLUTIONARY PERIOD. 73

the crafty Pontiac; that the Stamp Act was passed by the British Parliament one year and repealed the next; that Patrick Henry and James Otis set the land aflame with words and ideas; and that there was fired one April morning in the dim light at Lexington, near Boston, 'the shot heard round the world.'

"It was a stirring time; a period of aggressive strivings, momentous beginnings and of rapid developments; and, unfortunately for us, a period of too scanty records. Our fathers of that time were too busy subduing wild nature, and overcoming want and long distances, to pay much attention to writing history. They were making it, not writing it. We have entered into their labors with joy and thanksgiving, but we long to know more of their story."[3]

In Southern Pennsylvania.—This field is exceedingly interesting, from the fact of its early beginnings and rapid developments. The Brethren at an early day crossed the Susquehanna, entered what is now York County, and occupied many hundreds of its fertile acres. The strong congregations within the county to-day attest their prosperity for one hundred and seventy-five years. The Little Conewago Church was the first to be organized, in 1738, with Elder Daniel Leatherman as their minister; and upon his moving to Maryland, Elder Nicholas Martin was their minister. He also went to Maryland, as noted before, and when the Church was thirty-two years old, in 1770, Brethren Jacob Moyer and James Henrich, not ordained, were the ministers. The Conewago Church was organized, three years later, in 1741; Elder George Adam Martin was the minister. Later Leatherman and Martin, from the Little Conewago, also ministered to them, until they left the state. In 1770, George Brown, not ordained, was the minister; the Church, with a membership of 77, was the next to the largest church in the Brotherhood, Conestoga alone being larger. The Codorus Church was organized in 1758 with Elder Jacob Tanner, or Donner, as their minister. When he went to Maryland Henry Neff was their minister in 1770. The Bermudian Church was organized by Beissel, in 1758,

[3] " Two Centuries, Church of the Brethren," J. W. Wayland.

but he was too feeble, in a few years, to serve them; when Peter Miller and George Adam Martin preached there for a time. When Miller ceased his visits, and Martin went to Stony Creek, in Bedford County, the Bermudian Church passed entirely under the influence and control of the Brethren. Henry Lowman, not ordained, was the minister in 1770. The Antietam Church in Franklin County was organized in 1752, when George Adam Martin was also an active minister. The Stony Creek Church was organized in 1770.

"This church also is the offspring of Ephrata (for the most part); the seventh-day sabbath is kept.

"The minister is Rev. George Adam Martin, of whom mention has been made before. He was born near Landstuhl in Germany in the year 1715; was bred a Presbyterian; embraced the principles of the Baptists in 1737, and was ordained by Peter Baker (Becker) in 1739. Afterwards he resided at Little Conewago, where some misunderstanding arose between him and the people and occasioned him to remove to Antitum (Antietam). In the year 1762 he adopted the sentiments of the seventh-day Baptists, and preached at Bermudian. From thence he went to Stony Creek this year."[4]

After the death of Martin, the Stony Creek Church passed into the hands of the Brethren, as Bermudian had done before. For full accounts of the colonial Brethren Churches at this period, 1770, see German Baptist Brethren, by the author, pages 80–102, quoting Rev. Morgan Edwards; see, also, Brumbaugh, quoting from same. These accounts are very interesting, but too lengthy to be inserted here. See tabulated list at the close of this chapter.

"At some time between 1750 and 1760 certain Tunkers (Brethren) became the first permanent settlers in what is now Blair County, locating in the southern end of Morrison's Cove. They are said to have held religious services before the year 1756."[5]

[4] Morgan Edwards, in 1770.
[5] J. W. Wayland, Bicentennial address, 1908.

CLOSING DECADES OF PRE-REVOLUTIONARY PERIOD. 75

These brief accounts must suffice for a general survey of the work and activities of the Brethren in other parts.

Our Own District.—In this district, the colonial churches for the most part are elsewhere fully considered. The Conestoga Church will be found in the following chapter, discussed by Elder Henry Kurtz.

The Coventry Church is found in Chapter I, Part IV, *Coventry Group,* and nothing more need be said, by way of addition to general references in early colonial conditions, and the special chapter devoted to the history in detail.

The colonial church in New Jersey, Amwell, will be found in Part III, *The Church in New Jersey, Introduction.*

White Oak Church, for a long time a part of Conestoga, is fully discussed in its separate existence, in Chapter I, Part VII, *The White Oak Group.*

The Big Swatara, The Little Swatara, The Northkill, and The Oley Churches, are covered by the discussions in Chapters I, II, and V, of Part VIII, *Swatara Group,* which chapters cover the territorial divisions of the former colonial churches above-named.

The "Greatswamp" (Big Swamp) Church, organized in 1735, receives due consideration in Chapter I, Part V, *Indian Creek Group.*

As our definite and specific information of these times largely closes with the year 1770, the time when Morgan Edwards published his researches, this pre-revolutionary period must largely close with that date. The foregoing general survey, though necessarily brief, gives a fair view of the condition of the Brethren Churches in 1770, and shows really a remarkable development during thirty years, since the time when that dark cloud hung over the Germantown Church. Before closing this period it will be necessary to name a few things that happened there in thirty years.

Germantown.—As everywhere else, so at Germantown, a great change has taken place. The entire leadership, of the earlier years, has passed away, by the close of this period. Not one remains. At no other place was there so great a change in conditions, and so remarkable a change in leadership, as at Germantown. With the death of Mack in 1735,

Peter Becker was once more the leader; and with the exodus to Ephrata in 1739, when at least three ministers left Germantown, and another one having died, it may be that Becker was the only minister left at the time. Perhaps at no other time was his character and personality brought to a greater test, and perhaps at no other time did he show greater fervor and devotion, and higher elements of leadership. He reorganized his shattered forces, and prepared Germantown for a period of greatest strength, and highest development.

Elder Peter Becker.[6]—Much has been said of him, in the preceding chapters, in the discussion of the religious activities of the Brethren, but it is necessary to give a few biographical facts, in closing his life. He was born at Dilsheim in Germany, in 1687. He was educated a Presbyterian, but embraced the principles of the Brethren at Crefeldt, Germany, in 1714. He was the leader of the first emigration, and arrived in America in 1719. At the organization of the Church at Germantown, he became the first Elder, the administrator at the first baptism, and officiated at the first love-feast. He was a weaver by trade, and owned twenty-three acres of land, which he cultivated in cereals and flax.

Marriage and Family.—He was married to Anna Dorothy Partman, by whom he had two daughters, Mary and Elizabeth. The first was married to Rudolph Harley, and the other to Jahob Stump; both of which settled in the neighborhood and had large families, and most of them became members of the Brethren at an early period. In 1746, his wife died, and he removed to Indian Creek, and lived with his *daughter,* the wife of Rudolp Harley. Here he lived twelve more years, and labored faithfully in his ministry in the Indian Creek Church, but his life's record belongs to Germantown, rather than Indian Creek.

His Character.—It is said of him, that he was not an eloquent and forceful preacher, but a sweet singer, and a

[6] For fuller biography, see "Some Who Led," Brethren Publishing House; also "History, German Baptist Brethren," Brumbaugh, pp. 191-210.

man remarkably gifted in prayer. He is noted for his piety and true devotion to the cause he loved. He seems to have been a wise counselor, a safe leader in trying times, when some others lost their balance, and were *swept* away by the influence of visionary theories, and mystical doctrines of the spirit of the times. He was a rock of safety, in the stress of a great crisis. He was not the most gifted man, but, next to Mack, one of the most used of the Lord in the early church.

A Center of Influence.—Not alone the leadership of Peter Becker saved and re-established Germantown, but gradually and powerfully, other influences contributed to a great change in conditions, and the development of a new leadership. Prominent in the new order of things is the beginning of a printing establishment that in due time reached to the remotest parts of Colonial America. This printing business was commenced by Christopher Saur (Sower) the First, and afterwards, continued by his son, Christopher Second, one of the Bishops, or Elders, of the Germantown Church for many years. This same Sower family has continued the publishing business in various places ever since, and the Christopher Sower Publishing Co., of Philadelphia, was established by the late Chas. G. Sower, and incorporated by him to perpetuate the name of his ancestors. This Sower press soon became famous, and the Brethren early came into full control of large publishing interests, and issued many books, and pamphlets, and especially Bibles and hymn books. The Leiberts and Schreibers were also printers, and book-binders. These literary and publishing activities made the Germantown Church a center of widespread influence, throughout all the German settlements in all the colonies.

The New Leadership.—It will be remembered that with the exodus from Germantown to Ephrata, went Alexander Mack, Jr., then a young man. Just how long he remained is not known, and what he did while there is not an essential part of our story. He did remain, however, long enough to convince himself that Ephrata is not the place for him to spend his life, and to do his life's work. He returned to

Germantown, before 1748, for in that year, he was not only in full fellowship with his Brethren, but also in their full confidence. Christopher Sower records in his diary, "On June 7, 1748, there were placed upon me and Brother Sander (Alexander) Mack the oversight (Aufsicht) of the Brotherhood (Gemeinschaft) on trial.[7] Brother Brumbaugh adds:—

"Prior to this Alexander Mack must have returned and made fitting apology for his absence, and lived long enough among the members to win their confidence and love. Otherwise they would not have given him the joint oversight of the congregation. This closes his career as a wanderer and marks the beginning of fifty-five years of continuous service in the ministry of the Church of the Brethren."

According to the further record in the diary of Elder Sower, they served as Elders *on trial* for five years, and were then ordained with the laying on of hands by Elder Peter Becker, on June 10, 1753. These two Elders, the successors of Alexander Mack, Sr., and Peter Becker, became the most prominent Elders in their generation, during the closing years of this period, and during and after the Revolutionary War. Under their joint Eldership the Germantown Church prospered, and their influence extended throughout the entire Brotherhood.

Prominent Elders.—Some of the Elders who constituted a tower of strength during a part of, or all, of this period of 30 years, from 1740 to 1770, are the following: Peter Becker, Germantown; Alexander Mack, Germantown; Christopher Sower, Germantown; John Naas, New Jersey; First Martin Urner, Coventry; Second Martin Urner, Coventry; Michael Frantz, Conestoga; Michael Pfautz, Conestoga; George Klein, Northkill; John Jacob Beshor, Swatara; George Adam Martin, Conewago; Abraham Duboy, Big Swamp; Jacob Donner, Codorus; Daniel Leatherman, Little Conewago; Nicholas Martin, Little Conewago.

[7] "German Baptist Brethren," Brumbaugh, p. 219.

Pennsylvania Churches in 1770.[8]

Name of Church.	Name of Place.	When Organized.	No. of Members.
Germantown	Germantown	1723	57
Greatswamp	Bucks County	1735	28
Coventry	Chester County	1724	40
Conestoga	Lancaster County	1724 1735	86
Oley	Berks County	1732	20
White Oak	Lancaster County	1736	65
Big Swatara	Lancaster (now Dauphin) County	1756	39
Little Swatara	Berks County	1757	45
Northkill	Berks County	1748	11
Codorus	York County	1758	35
Little Conewago	York County	1738	52
Conewago	York County	1741	77
Bermudian	York County	1758	58
Stony Creek	Bedford County	1762	17

"Thus we see that there are in this province fifteen churches of Tunker Baptists, to which appertain eight ordained ministers, elders, or bishops, and thirteen exhorters, or probationers, and four meeting houses; the reason of their having no more places of worship is, that they choose rather to meet from house to house in imitation of the primitive Christians. We see also that their families are about four hundred and nineteen, which contain about two thousand and ninety-five souls allowing five to the family, whereof seven hundred and sixty-three persons are baptized and in communion."[9]

It must be noted that in the above paragraph, from Morgan Edwards, in giving his statistics, he includes the Ephrata congregation with one hundred and thirty-five members. I may say, in passing, that, at this time, 1770, Beissel is in his grave, and his Monastic community has commenced to decline, but it is not necessary to describe in this connection Ephrata, because it forms no part of the Brethren history at this period. For almost all matters of statistics at this time, and many important facts, we are indebted to Rev. Morgan Edwards, and we need to give full recognition to the value of his writings, and descriptions of

[8] These facts and figures are taken from the accounts of Morgan Edwards.
[9] Morgan Edwards, "Materials for History of the Baptists."

the early congregations of the Brethren. It is to be regretted exceedingly, that the facts which he put on record in reference to the Brethren Churches in Maryland, were not published; but remained in manuscript form, until the big fire in the Baptist Publication Society building, in Philadelphia, some years ago, when these with other very valuable manuscripts and historical records were all destroyed. Many of these valuable historic records can never be replaced. This is another warning that everything possible should be done to preserve our own invaluable historic data, by proper publication from time to time, and in such form as to insure permanency. It is to be hoped that every local church, and every state district will fully wake up on this important subject.

CHAPTER XII.

THE VERY ANCIENT CHURCH OF THE BRETHREN IN LANCASTER CO., PA.

According to manuscript records, kept in said church, and entrusted to the writer for investigation, it consisted on the 29th of September, 1734, as on the day when MICHAEL FRANTZ was baptized, who was afterwards their first teacher, of the following members:

BRETHREN.	SISTERS.
Legan,	Rollin,
John Keppinger,	Koch,
John G. Koch,	Kalkglaser,
Rudolph Bollinger,	Latshaw,
Earnest Stoll,	Luy,
Joseph Latshaw,	Keppinger,
Lewis Kalkglaser,	Hildebrand,
——— Luy,	Krapf.
Samuel Gut,	
John Hildebrand,	
Gottfried Geiger,	
Michael Frantz.	

Altogether of 20 members.

Counting from the above date, September 29, 1734, this church in Lancaster is now (1855) over 120 years old. Truly a venerable mother-church, whose daughters are to be found in the most distant parts of our great country, as we have reason to conclude from the names of the members in that church.

"Afterwards," continues the record, "hands were laid on MICHAEL FRANTZ by Elders, and he was ordained as Elder and overseer of the church in Conestoga and White Oak; and thus by the grace and blessing of God the church has been multiplied and increased continually." And how great the blessing was that rested upon this church the continued lists of those who were baptized by them, and were added unto them from the Seventhday Baptists and from elsewhere, show.

In the list from 1735 to 1739 are 32 names of newly-received members, and among them we find the following: Segrist, Etter, Frantz, Royer, Martin, Landis, Roland, Bollinger, Miller, Longenecker, &c. In the year 1739 were further baptized 21 persons, among whom were MICHAEL PFAUTZ, the successor of the first overseer, and three Brethren by the name of Mohler.

In the year 1740 were received *seven;* in the year 1741, *ten;* in the year 1742, *twenty-eight,* among whom were the names of Stucky, Gehr, Alterffer, Schwartz, Flory, Hag, Funderburg, Weis, Schneider, Lichty; and others occur.

In the year 1743 was the number of newly received members *twenty-four,* among whom was Jacob Sontag of whom particular mention is made afterwards. Anno 1744 only *four* persons were baptized, and brother *Michael Pfautz* chosen for the ministry. In 1745 *four* were baptized, and six brothers and six sisters from Amwell (probably in New Jersey) received. In 1746 thirteen persons, and in 1747 nineteen persons were added unto the church.

In the following year we find the following note. "In the year 1748 is our elder and overseer (MICHAEL FRANTZ) departed this life, and has exchanged time with eternity, after being well tried by affliction." To this are added a few lines of poetry, of which we have endeavored to make a translation.

> Farewell on the chariot of God!
> We do not envy thee thy rest.
> By angels thou'rt carried the road
> Toward the abode of the blest;
> To join in that heavenly abode
> The host of the angelic choir,
> To sing and rejoice in thy God,
> To praise him forever and e'er.

When we stand still here at the death of the first elder and overseer, MICHAEL FRANTZ, and look back on the first fourteen years of this church, we are compelled to say to the glory of God, that the time of the ministry of this old Brother, who has died more than a hundred years ago, was richly blessed, inasmuch as the church increased "by the grace and blessing of God," and its numbers were multiplied from year to year in such a manner, that and until it grew in fourteen years from a little flock of 20 members to a company of nearly *Two hundred.* "This is the Lord's doing, and is marvelous in our eyes."

The year when the first teacher and overseer died, was a memorable and singularly blessed year for the church. As we read of *Samson,* Judges 16: 30, "The dead which he slew at his death were more than they which he slew in his life," so we might say of MICHAEL FRANTZ, as blessed as his former years of ministry were, the year of his death was still more blessed. Of this we find the following recorded in the manuscript already mentioned:

"In the year 1748, the 25th of September, Brother MICHAEL FRANTZ, overseer of the church in Conestoga and White Oak has laid his hand upon Bro. MICHAEL PFAUTZ (who, as we have seen already, had been chosen to the ministry in the year 1744), and has ordained and confirmed him in his place, with the united assistance of the Brethren. Thus the church has been blessed and enlarged by the grace of God through Brother *Michael Pfautz,* who has been ordained by the Elders to be an Elder." Again it says, "In this year brother *Jacob Sontag* was chosen as a minister (or deacon) in the church."

How much the share of each of these *three* ministers was in the great blessed awakening, which came this year upon the church, cannot be made out, and is also of no consequence, whether we know it; but this much we may safely believe, that they must have labored together in unity of spirit, without which unity no blessing can be expected. And whether the one sows, and the other reaps; whether the one planteth, and the other watereth; whether one stands with MOSES on the mountain, and raiseth up his hands in prayer, and the other with JOSHUA is fighting against Amalek, and the third stands by the side of him that prays, or him that fights (the battle of the Lord); still "neither is he that planteth anything, neither he that watereth; but God that giveth the increase."

And how great the increase was of this year 1748 we may gather from the following simple statements as they were recorded at the time:

In the year 1748 were baptized Brothers Ulrich, Shively, Henry Gibbel, &c.

March 6 in all	7 persons.
April 24	11 persons.
May 1	2 persons.
June 12 and July 24	15 persons.
August 7	6 persons.
August 14	4 persons.
September 4	2 persons.
October 16	4 persons.
October 23	6 persons.

Altogether in this one year, or rather within less than six months, 57 persons; truly a harvest-blessing not often repeated, and reminding us of Pentecostal times.

To the encouragement of those who might think such blessed times happened of old, but are now-a-days rare among the Brethren, and to the honor of God and his word we cannot refrain from noticing, what we lately have learned, namely that during the past summer and fall (1854) the Lord has revealed himself as of old in different churches, and that for instance in one church not one hundred miles west from here there were baptized more than thirty, and in two other adjoining churches in the southeast over sixty souls. Blessed be the Lord for his grace which is yet to-day proving its efficacy for the salvation of the children of men!

But even in our dear Lancaster church it was not every year alike, for we find, that there were baptized in the year

1749 only	8 persons.
1750	14 persons.
1751	6 persons.
1752	18 persons.
1753	12 persons.
1754	10 persons.
1755	11 persons.

and then we find the following note: "Here I must say, that much trouble and temptation has fallen upon the overseer, so that he has recorded nothing in seven years." These then were undoubtedly dark, gloomy times; not only for the overseer, but without fail also for the church. What a pity it is, when after the blessing of God having visibly rested upon a church, the enemy and destroyer of all good finds means again to make an entrance, and to cause confusion! And, oh, how should ministers and members be on their guard, that the temptation may not come upon them unawares while asleep!

Over those first fourteen years of the ministry of the second overseer *Michael Pfautz* hovered then quite a different providence. The first half from 1748 until 1755—seven years—were most eminently blessed, and the latter half from 1755 until 1762—again seven years—remind us almost of the seven years of famine, which *Joseph* predicted unto *Pharoah,* where all the plenty should be forgotten, that was before. Let us then, dearest members, make good use of the advice of *Joseph,* in plenteous years to gather and take care of all "spiritual blessings in heavenly places," when they are given us richly, that we may not want in times of distress and famine.

Without much research and thought this much is plain from the information at hand, beyond which we do not wish to go at the present time, that the seven years of trial of the overseer, Michael Pfautz, had now at last come to an end, that he came forth out of this trial of fire like fine gold, cleansed and purified, and that from now on he worked mightily and with rich blessings toward the upbuilding of the congregation, for in this same year, 1763, in which the aforesaid circumstance with Jacob Sonntag took place, we find that no less than eighteen or nineteen persons were added to the church through baptism..

Here many of our dear readers might ask: "Were there then none at all baptized in the former seven years, and did then the work of God stand entirely still so long?" Thereupon we can answer, that our records do not say so, but only state that much trouble and temptation had been encountered by the Elder, and that, therefore, he had not written up anything. We may, therefore, conclude with some confidence that, notwithstanding nothing had been written up,[1] the congregation of God in this community had continued its course, that meetings were held, and that the word of God, the Gospel of Jesus Christ, which is the power of God unto salvation to all who believe in it, was preached, also that it showed its power toward souls at this time and made them willing to establish the bond of a good conscience toward God, and that consequently probably souls were baptized at this time, and their names were written up in Heaven.

Since we must soon again send back the little books (manuscripts) which have been entrusted to us, we still want to copy out the most important parts and postpone all further observations to the future. As is evident from the book written in Michael Pfautz's own hand, he worked on in the vineyard of the Lord from 1763 to his end; and from year to year, and from time to time, they who were saved were added to the church. Acts 2: 47.

In the year 1764, we read in another little book, that "Christian Longenecker was chosen to the service of the church in peace and harmony on Dec. 1, as a helper to the Elder. And in the year 1769, on May 4, he was ordained to the place of Michael Pfautz our Elder. I have come thus far through good and ill report."

Then it stands written: "On May 14, 1769 (ten days after the ordination of Christian Longenecker) our dear brother Michael Pfautz, the Elder of the congregation in Conestoga, fell asleep in the Lord, after much trial and suffering, in the sixtieth year of his age. God cared for him well, and made him an elect one in the furnace of affliction. He served and led as the Elder and overseer of the church in Conestoga and White Oakland, very nearly twenty-one years." They also sang for him the same lines which they sang for the first overseer (which are this time reproduced in the original German).

[1] For names of persons baptized from 1755-1763 see "History of Conestoga," by D. C. Reber, p. —.

CHURCH OF THE BRETHREN IN LANCASTER CO.

"Fahre wohl auf Gottes Wagen,
　Wir gönnen dir die Ruh',
Dasz du von den Engeln wirst getragen
　Dem schönen Himmel zu,
Dasz du bei der Engel Chor und Reih'n
　Dich ewig, ewig konntest freu'n."—

Now follows a list of those baptized, which is carried forward to the year 1799.

There are also written the disclosures of a drunkard and degraded person, on the 29th of autumn month, 1773. It is also worthy of note that after the names of all those baptized stands the word, "Gestorben," "died." Dear reader, this will also some time come to our name. Therefore, let us in time learn to die to sin and seek life in Christ's word and death.[2]

[2] Published in the *Gospel Visitor* of 1855 by Eld. Henry Kurtz.

PART II.

GERMANTOWN GROUP.

CHAPTER I.

GERMANTOWN.

Introduction.—To write a complete history of the Mother Church, and the labors of her principal men, would fill a large volume. There are, of course, many facts buried in oblivion, that never can be recovered; and things so long forgotten, they can never be recalled. In the preceding chapters, necessarily, much of the early history of Germantown has been interwoven with the history of the Brotherhood in general, during the time of organization, struggles, trials, and development in the first fifty years in America. Chapter X treats, especially, of Germantown at the time of a great crisis. Chapter XI treats of great changes of leadership, far-reaching influences of publishing interests and literary activity, and a period of rapid development of the work in general. In the present treatment of Germantown, therefore, nothing further can be said in a special and detailed way of the earliest times, except on such points that especially need to be connected consecutively with later development. It must be remembered, too, that in so brief a space as can be allotted to the subject here, only a few of the more important matters can be treated, and some of them far too brief for the importance of the subject. This volume occupies so large a field, that it is manifestly impossible to say all on this important subject that should be said, and all that the reader would like to know. It is especially gratifying to know that much interest has been manifested in what has been written from time to time on German-

GRAVE OF ELDER PETER BECKER,
INDIAN CREEK.

GRAVE OF ELDER CHRISTOPHER SOWER,
METHACHTON.

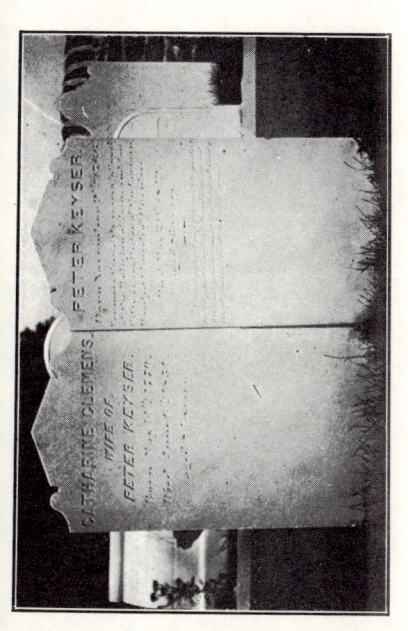

GRAVES OF ELDER PETER KEYSER AND WIFE,
GERMANTOWN.

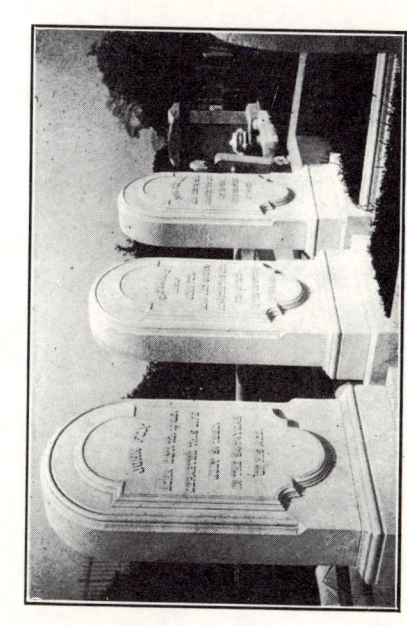

GRAVE OF ELDER JOHN FOX, GERMANTOWN.

town, and it is to be hoped more will be written in the future.

A Permanent Place of Worship.—In the beginning religious services were held in the homes of the members, and, in the summer time, out of doors under some large trees, or in a grove; especially was this the case, when the assemblies became too large to be accommodated in the homes. These services were held in the vicinity of Germantown, but considerable distances apart. It is interesting to trace the history of the present location of worship and it is all that can be said at this time. As the history of this old town is interesting, so also is the history of the mother congregation near it that has been in existence here for almost two hundred years. There is a large amount of historical matter bearing on the Germantown Church directly or indirectly; but it became much scattered years ago by careless or unfaithful custodians; and much of it being now in the hands of private individuals, it is difficult to collect and confirm the necessary facts for a much-needed reliable account of many points. There is considerable material lying on the surface, as is always the case, that passes current as history, and yet is entirely worthless to the reliable historian until confirmed by thorough research, and a careful study of original data. It would seem that in this respect Germantown has been singularly unfortunate in its experience of being at the mercy of the unscrupulous historian.

The usual reference is made that Johannes Pettikoffer received the ground as a gift, from one Peter Schilbert; and then some add that Schilbert had much difficulty in gaining possession of the land again, when Pettikoffer went to Ephrata, as he did in 1739. Now all this is sheer nonsense, the absolute creation of somebody's fancy, without a grain of truth, and yet these statements are copied again and again, apparently without any attempt being made to know the facts, when the records of the office of the Recorder of Deeds are at all times accessible to all who care to investigate. It seems necessary, therefore, that a truthful account of this matter should be given, and doubly so, for the reason that the facts and the truth are intensely interesting. In tracing the history of the ground, I can only give the bare statement of the transfers[1] that were made from time to time. The evidence of ownership will be presented in each case in regular order, and it will be sufficient for the present study to begin with the ownership of Peter Shoemaker.

Peter Shoemaker to Johannes Pettikoffer.—On August 4, 1731, Peter Shoemaker, Turner, and Margret, his wife, sold to Johannes Pettikoffer for the sum of five pounds and five shillings ("to them in hand paid by the said Johannes Pettikoffer, the receipt whereof they do hereby acknowledge, and thereof do fully acquit and forever discharge"). This is perhaps enough to show that he did not get the lot from Peter Schilbert as a gift. This land carefully described in the deed is declared to be a half an acre and twenty perches, and constitutes what is now the northern half of the present Church property, or the part on which the church buildings are located. It will be seen by this deed, that Pettikoffer paid a fair price for his half acre, considering that it was nearly half a mile out of the settlement of Germantown as it then was, and that the settlement altogether had not more than twenty houses. He paid at the rate of fifty dollars per acre, entirely unimproved. These original papers should be sufficient testimony to prove that Johannes Pettikoffer did, on August 4, 1731, acquire title to his half acre from Peter Shoemaker, and at a good price. But to some historians, it does not make much difference whether they say Peter Schilbert or Peter Shoemaker,—one Peter is as good as the other Peter. To them the facts of history are not so essential, they have plenty of fancy to fill the gaps.

Johannes Pettikoffer to Johannes Mack and Andreas Bonney.—On the twenty-second of August, 1739, Johannes Pettikoffer and Ann Elizabeth, his wife, sold the aforesaid half acre, together with the house he had built upon it, to Johannes Mack and Andreas Bonney, for the sum of sixty-

---

[1] See "History of German Baptist Brethren," by the author, for brief quotations from the original parchment deeds, pp. 117–128.

five pounds, each of the two holding a half interest. It will be noticed, that whereas he had paid for the ground five pounds and five shillings, Pettikoffer now receives on his sale sixty-five pounds, thus valuing his improvements fifty-nine pounds and fifteen shillings. It thus appears that there is no documentary evidence to sustain the old fable that Pettikoffer received the lot as a gift and then begged the money to build the house. This house was built in 1732, and because of its importance in later years, we shall give some description of its interesting history and notice it hereafter as the "Pettikoffer House."

Andreas Bonney to Johannes Mack.—The future deeds indicate that after Johannes Pettikoffer had vacated his house, Andreas Bonney, who owned the one-half interest of the property, lived in the house, or did so, on October 6, 1741, on which date he did devise by "his last will and testament," his half interest unto the said Johannes Mack for the consideration of twenty-nine pounds and ten shillings. Why Bonney sold his interest for less than he had paid does not appear but it may be that Mack had advanced some money, or that Bonney had lived in the house without paying rent, and so Mack would be entitled to a lower price for Bonney's half. This Bonney (Bony) was one of the original eight, at Schwarzenau, and had come to America with the second emigration, in 1729.

Johannes Mack to Peter Schilbert.—On July 20, 1742, Johannes Mack, stockingweaver, and Margrett, his wife, sold to Peter Schilbert the aforesaid property, house and lot, for the consideration of seventy-three pounds. Thus, it will be seen, that instead of Peter Schilbert being the original owner and giving this lot to Pettikoffer, as "historians" say, the ownership, as I have clearly shown, runs as follows:

Peter Shoemaker, Johannes Pettikoffer, Johannes Mack and Andreas Bonney, Johannes Mack, Peter Schilbert; and all these changes in the eleven years from 1731 to 1742. These old historic writings are exceedingly interesting,—quaint in their expressions, unique in conditions, and often intensely specific, and at other times very wordy indeed, and altogether too lengthy to be quoted here.

Bastian and Johanna Hoech to Theobold Endt and Henry Slingloff.—It was evidently the intention of Peter Schilbert to present this half acre and the "Pettikoffer House" to the Brethren congregation, but he died with the property legally in his possession. The deed of a later date says,—"The said Peter Schilbert dying (in effect) intestate." After some years of delay, this was finally accomplished, as will be seen by the quotation that follows. The deed further recites,—("He having made only a noncupative will) the right of the inheritance of his said possessions depending legally unto Johanna Hoech the wife of Bastian Hoech which Johanna being the only issue and heir of Abraham Schilbert who was the brother and heir at law of the said Peter Schilbert." On the twenty-sixth day of August, 1746, the said Bastian Hoech, and Johanna, his wife, deeded *in fee* to Theobold Endt and Henry Slingloff, two well-known Brethren. Just under what conditions, or why, is not apparent, but the property was held by them for fourteen years.

Theobold Endt and Henry Slingloff to Alexander Mack, Christopher Sower, Peter Leibert and George Schreiber.— The consideration at this transfer was ten pounds, and bears date August 11, 1760. It is not difficult now to see the purpose of this new transfer, when it is noted that these four men to whom the property was deeded, were four of the principal men of the Brethren congregation. On the following day, these four men, the first two Bishops, and the other two perhaps ministers, issued, and published, the famous Declaration of Trust. They first make definite acknowledgment of the grant unto them, "by the direction and at the appointment of the persons who are members of the Religious Society or Community of the people called Dutch (German) Baptists and belonging to the Meeting of that People in or near Germantown aforsd."[2]

After having stated the grant, and the body under which they act, the Trustees declare the use, etc., under their trust, viz.: "To the use and interests hereinafter mentioned and declared and under the Conditions and Restrictions

[2] The Declaration of Trust.

hereinafter limited and Restricted and to no other use or purpose whatsoever, That is to say, One Room in the said Messuage (Pettikoffer House), to be made use of for a Meeting place of the said People living at or near Germantown aforesaid and for such other as the said Community may think proper to admit thereto. The which Room may be improved or enlarged for the better convenience of the said Meeting at the discretion of the said Community in such Manner as they may think Meet And on Room and kitchen of the sade Messuage to be made use of for a dwelling place for some Widow woman of the said Society or Community to live in Rent free and that the said Society or Community Shall and do keep the said Messuage or Tenement of pieces or parcels of Land or ground in repair from time to time Towards the Charge of which they are to have the use, Rents Issues & Profits which may accrue or arise yearly from the remaining part of the premises."[3]

It is further expressly provided that in case this Society or Community shall cease to exist, the property shall be sold and the proceeds given to the poor. The entire Declaration is very interesting indeed, and it was the means of setting in operation influences that have ever marked the high ideals of the Brethren Church. Thus is established the first permanent place of worship, or a place especially provided for that purpose, but it is very probable that this same place had been used for some time for worship.

"*The Old Folks' Home.*—While the said Declaration of Trust tells us of the regular and permanent meeting-place, it also tells in a very interesting manner how one room and the kitchen were set apart for some widow to dwell 'rent free'; thus showing how early the Brethren thought of making special provision and providing a home for the 'widows.' I know of no instance where any other denomination made a similar public provision for its widowed poor, at so early a date. The history of this Home is interesting. While it is probably true that in a few years the congregation so increased that perhaps the entire home was needed for purposes of worship, we do know that when the new stone meeting-house was dedicated in 1770,

[3] The Declaration of Trust.

the 'Pettikoffer House' was set apart anew for the comfort of the widows, and it remained such a home until 1861, or a period of 101 years from the time it was first set apart. There are many people living to-day (1900) who remember the place well as the 'Widows' Home. I am indebted to Charles M. Benson, of Germantown, and also Rachel Douglass Wise, of Philadelphia, for facts that enable me to describe the 'Pettikoffer House' as it appeared fifty years ago. The main part of the house was about twenty feet long by sixteen feet wide, built of logs, with frame gables, and shingle roof. The house fronted south, with gables east and west. The spaces between the logs were chinked and plastered, and the entire house whitewashed. It had a good cellar, with an outside trapdoor, which was located between the pavement and the outside door leading into the east room. There were four windows and one outside door. There were two windows in the west gable towards the street, one upstairs and one downstairs. Then there were two additional windows in the west room, one on the north side and one on the south side There were two rooms upstairs and two rooms downstairs. At the east end of the east room, there was a large fireplace which was in constant use from 1852 until the time the house was taken down in December, 1861, so my informer tells me. The meeting-room was the west one, well lighted with three windows. The ceilings were of good height. The house was still in good condition in 1861, when it was torn down, after such an interesting history of one hundred and thirty years.

"Immediately to the rear of the above described house there stood many years ago a good-sized frame building, whose history I have not been able to unravel. Many suggestions have been made of its probable history, but I have been unable to confirm anything so that I can safely regard it as history. I hope the future may yet reveal the purpose of this ancient structure."[4]

The Old Church.—On this same half acre which we have been considering, or the northern half of the present Church grounds, are located the Church buildings, consisting of the old stone meeting-house which was built in 1770, and the more imposing, modern stone one, built in 1896–1897. A brief description of this old church building will be of

[4] "German Baptist Brethren," by the author, 1901, pp. 129–130.

interest, for it has long since become a landmark in the midst of the passing centuries. Considering the time in which it was built it is singularly complete in its appointments. Its substantial character may well be judged from the fact that it has stood so long, and is in excellent state of preservation, barring accident, might do service for another century. It is thirty feet square, built of native Germantown stone, with walls eighteen inches thick. There is a large well-appointed basement, under the entire building, of good height, where there was a large fireplace for cooking and making the necessary preparations for love-feast occasions. In the corner, near the fireplace, is a large flat stone, hollowed out trough-like, built into the wall, on which the waste water was poured to drain out of the building. The floor in the audience-room is yellow pine, full of pitch and very hard. The boards were carefully selected, very wide, almost every board has a heart in it, no sap boards, and there has been no decay in all these years. But there is another reason why these boards are neither decayed nor worm-eaten. The floor rests on a bed of mortar, which is supported beneath by a layer of split oak lath. Hand-made nails are used throughout. About thirty-five years ago the audience-room was remodeled, but formerly the ceiling was about eight feet high, plastered and whitewashed; and a heavy wooden girder, supported by two posts, was visible. There was a large loft, very roomy and well-lighted, supplied by four windows, two in each gable. It seems to have been built and arranged for some special purpose, perhaps largely unknown at this time. There was an outside entrance to this loft, making access easy, and without disturbing in any way, or entering, the audience-room. Many years ago these gable ends were rough-cast, covering up all traces of this loft-door and windows, and all knowledge of them seems to have been lost, until some years ago, when we restored this front. Upon removing the rough-cast, there were the outlines of the door and windows distinctly visible. At this time I made the following measurements: the door was four feet, three inches wide and six feet, six inches high, a very large door, if it was a single one. The windows were three feet, two inches wide and four feet, six inches high. To what different uses this story was put, is not known. It was large enough to make a roomy dwelling for a small family. The place seems to have been extensively used for storing the unbound sheets of publications that required months to run through the press. It is said that Elder Christopher Sower so occupied the place, with his third edition of the Bible, in 1777, and that the unbound sheets were confiscated by the British soldiers, and used for gun-wads and for bedding their cavalry horses.

The Old Parsonage.—The south half of the Church grounds need a brief account. The Brethren came into possession of this portion many years after acquiring title to the north half. This part was bought by Johannes Mack from Peter Shoemaker in 1730. On August 29, 1751, Johannes Mack and Margaretta, his wife, sold the same to Christopher Sower. It consisted of seventy-eight perches and had two houses thereon. On September 24, 1753, Christopher Sower and Catharina, his wife, sold the same to Philip Weaver, for sixty pounds, and he, in the year 1756, erected his large stone dwelling, that in the next century became known as *The Old Parsonage.* On March 18, 1796, John Weaver, Philip Weaver and Susanna Keyser, three children and heirs of the above Philip Weaver, deeded the property to Abraham Keyser, for the sum of four hundred pounds; and on the following day, the said Abraham Keyser deeded the same, for the same amount, to Philip Weaver, one of the sons and heirs of the first mentioned Philip Weaver. On April 4, 1804, Philip Weaver and his wife, Ann, sold the same to the Trustees of the Brethren congregation, for the consideration of four hundred and thirty pounds. This stone residence has an exceedingly interesting history, like unto the *Pettikoffer House,* or (Meeting House and Widow's Home), and the *Old Stone Church.* The Weaver house was rented by the Brethren as a private residence, and then in the early decades of the nineteenth century, before the time of the public school system, Sister Susan Douglass occupied the house with her large Select School.[5] After the closing of this school the Parsonage was again rented, for many years, as a private residence. While this Weaver house, that stood in three centuries, was known for many years as *"The Old Parsonage,"* it was in reality the residence of the pastor, only eight years, from 1893 to 1901, when it was occupied by the author and his family, during his pastorate in the Mother Church. Some ten years ago, this famous old landmark of Germantown was torn down, to make room for the new parsonage.

The Old Cemetery.—This cemetery is a very interesting place, it is furthermore a beautiful spot, and often did I hear people say, they wished they could be buried there. So far as grave-stones indicate, the first burial took place in 1797. Many of the old families of Germantown are represented, in some cases several generations, and in a few cases five and six generations. Many of the members, and especially of the officials, for several generations are buried here. From all the walks of life, the humblest, as well as those noted, and of religious and social prominence, rest here side by side. Among other noted persons, Miss Harriet Livermore lies buried here, in an unmarked grave, the woman who opened our National Congress with prayer in 1832; the "Evangelist," "The Guest" of Whittier's *Snow Bound;* the "Pilgrim Wanderer" in the Holy Land, and in Egypt; the "Watcher" on Mt. Sinai in the immediate expectation of the coming of Christ. After she had wandered all over the world her tired body was laid to rest in this beautiful God's acre, in the lot of Sister Worrell, in the midst of these historic surroundings. This cemetery is still much used as a place of burial; it is kept in excellent condition, and receives constant care and attention.

Two Prominent Bishops.—Germantown has been blessed with a remarkable line of active ministers and prominent Bishops. Of the latter, she had five, from 1723 to 1850, or 127 years, any one of whom would have been sufficient

---

[5] For account of Weaver Log-House, and The Select School, see "German Baptist Brethren," by the author, pp. 134 and 135; also Pennsylvania-German Magazine.

to give luster to the history of any church. From 1723 to 1747, she had Peter Becker and Alexander Mack, Sr., whose lives and labors have been so fully recounted in the history of the Church of the Brethren with which they were so inseparably connected. These two Bishops were contemporary at Germantown for only six years, from 1729 to 1735; but succeeding them were two who were contemporary from 1748 to 1784, or a period of 36 years. These were Alexander Mack, Jr., and Christopher Sower. It is impossible to give here a biography of these two prominent Bishops, such as their lives and labors would so justly deserve. We must be satisfied, at this time, with very brief biographical data and some records of their activities; especially so, because there is so much of their lives already recorded.[6]

Alexander Mack, Jr.—He was born January 25, 1712, at Schwarzenau; and baptized in 1728, in his seventeenth year, likely in Holland. He emigrated to America with his father the next year, in the Second Emigration, 1729. He resided at Germantown from 1729 to 1739, when, in the Koch excitement, as before noted,[7] he removed to Ephrata. For his marriage and family, see *Mack Family,* at the close of this sketch. Disappointed and utterly discouraged with the conditions and work at Ephrata, he returned to Germantown, and was destined to become his father's eminent successor. His election, ordination as Elder, or Bishop, and his leadership have been noted. He was a man of great energy and far-reaching influence. He was the most eminent man, without doubt, that the Church of the Brethren ever had in America, considering the times and circumstances of his eventful life, and his times. He was an able man as a preacher and counselor in church work. He was well known and greatly beloved all over the church. He was a gifted hymn-writer, and wrote much in defense of the doctrine of the Brethren. For more than half a century, he served the Church ably and faithfully. His life was full of good deeds and was a great blessing to many. He died

---

[6] "German Baptist Brethren," by the author, pp. 136-140; also by Brumbaugh; also "Some Who Led," Brethren Publishing House, 1912, Alexander Mack, Jr., pp. 23-26.

[7] See Part I, Chapter X, a Great Religious Crisis; also Chapter XI.

at the ripe age of 91 years, 1 month, and 20 days. The following is his epitaph, composed by himself a short time before his death:

> "Gott
> der uns hat
> aus Staub gemacht
> und wiederum
> zum Staub gebracht
> wird zeigen
> Seiner Weisheit macht
> wann wir nach Seinem
> Bild erwacht."

A rather literal translation would be as follows: "God who created us out of dust, and brings us again to dust, will certify His wisdom's power, when we awake with His likeness."

It should be stated that much of its beauty is lost in any translation. In its original setting, it is as fine a conception of thought as I have found in any language. He lies buried at Germantown.

List of Baptisms.

Some of the baptisms performed by Alexander Mack, Jr., at Germantown, after the year 1766:

1766.—May 15, Margretta Hartzbach.
" October 3, Nathaniel Schrieber.
" October 17, Henry Schlingluft, Jr., Catharine Schlingluft, Dorothea Fox.
1767.—July 12, Charles Lang.
" August 7, Anna B. Van Lashett and Elizabeth Schlingluff.
" August 16, Jacob Bauman and Maria Barbara, his wife.
" October 2, Conrad Good, William Spira and Maria Spira.
1768.—March 27, Christina Schlungluff, Jr.
" September 25, Hannah Stamm.
1769.—May 14, Sarah Baker.
" July 27, Christopher Saur, Jr.

1769.—September 3, Michael Keyser, Sarah Mack and Susana Baker.
" October 5, Peter Keyser and Hannah, his wife, Henry Sharpnack and Sarah, his wife, John Schlingluff, Conrad Stamm, Maria Fendt, Elizabeth Raab.
1770.—September 2, John Weber, William Leibert, Dirock Keyser and Rachel, his wife.
" September 30, Julius Roberly and Appolonia, his wife.
1771.—May 19, Thomas Langstoth and Catherine, his wife, Hannah Mack, Hannah Stier.
" September 8, John Kaempfer.
" November 10, Rudolph Harley and Barbara, his wife, John Harley and Margaretta, his wife, Ulrich Stouffer and Hannah, his wife.
1772.—April 19, Michael Corbit, Garehart Clemens and Gertrude, his wife, Jacob Landis and Maria, his wife.
1773.—January 4, John Prisz.
" January 20, Phillipina Vernon.
1774.—March 27, Edmund Langstroth.
" May 12, Edward Bright and Elizabeth, his wife, Elizabeth Painter, Ruth Silence.
" July 3, Cornelius Neisz, William Heisler, David Meredith, Jacob Raab, George Duke John Leibert, Anna Leibert, Susanna Hinckle, Hannah Knorr, Lydia Keyser, Catherine Bauman.
" October 16, William Prisz and Susanna Knorr.

Here occurs a break in the records for the period of nine years.

1783.—October 20, Susanna Weaver, John Weaver's wife, and Catherine Keyser, Michael Keyser's wife.
1785.—March 6, Emanuel Fox and his wife, Margarett, Jacob Zigler and Lydia Kulp. I regret very much that I cannot present a complete list of his baptisms, but it has been impossible to confirm a part of the list. There is no complete record extant.

The following is a partial list of baptisms by Christopher Sower:

1748.—November 3, Elizabeth Weiss, Catherine Buchmarin, Susanna Miller.

1749.—April 2, Jacob Ganz.
1755.—May 18, Andrew Menichinger.
1758.—March 26, Uly Rinder and wife.
1781.—July 15, George Becker and his wife, Catherine Nancy Becker, their daughter, Catherine, daughter of Frederick Stamm.
1783.—November 6, Adam Weber.
1784.—June 10.—Martin Urner and wife, Barbara Baugh.

When Christopher was dead and Alexander Mack was past seventy-two years of age, the second Martin Urner baptized some at Germantown, and the following is perhaps a complete list:

1784.—August 15, Derick Keyser and his wife, Elizabeth, and Susanna Weaver, Philip Weaver's daughter.
1785.—September 25, Nicholas Oliver, Benjamin Lehman, and Peter Keyser, Jr.
1786.—September 14, Henry Rinker, William Keyser and his wife, Barbara, Elizabeth Lehman and Mary Heisler.
1788.—September 4, Charles Hubbs and his wife, Mary, Catherine Clemens and Hannah, the daughter of Derick Keyser.

Christopher Sower.—Bishop Christopher Sower was the only son of Christopher Sower, the first.[9] According to his own record in his diary, "I was born on the twenty-sixth of September, 1721, in the town of Laasphe in Witgenstein, about six hours from Marburg." At the age of three years, his parents brought him to America, and for two years resided in Germantown. At the end of this time, 1726, they removed to Lancaster county where they resided until 1730, when his mother joined the Solitary of Beissel, and was made subprioress of the Sisterhood. The following year, 1731, the father with his now motherless boy of ten years, returned to Germantown, where they permanently resided. It was not until 1744, that the young man was able to induce his mother to leave Beissel, and return to her husband in Germantown, and he had the joy of seeing his

---

[9] See "German Baptist Brethren," Brumbaugh, "The Two Christopher Sowers," p. 338.

parents live happily together for seven years, when she died in 1752. At the age of 16 years, he was baptized February 24, 1737. He was elected a deacon of the Germantown congregation in 1747. On June 7, 1748, he, with Alexan-

MACK FAMILY.[8]

1st. Gen.	Date of Birth.	Place.	Date of Marriage.	Place.	Date of Death.	Remarks.
Alexander	1679 "	Germany "	1700 "	Germany	1735 1720	Anna Margaretha Kli gen.
2d Gen. John Valentine		" "	(?) 1731 (?) 1731	America "	1755 8-11-1758	Maria Hildebran Mack.
John		"		"		Sneider.
Alexander	1-28-1712 9-25-1725	"	1- 1-1749 1- 1-1749	"	3-20-1803 5- 6-1811	Ordained, 1748. Elizabeth Nice Mack.
3d Gen. William	10-31-1741	America	10-13-1772 10-13-1772	"		Blacksmith. Agnes Gantz Mack.
Anna Maria	10-29-1752	"	6- 6-1769 6- 6-1769	"	4- 5-1770	Death in childbirth. Husband.
Sarah Marg.	12-23-1753 2-17-1753	"	2- 2-1776 2- 2-1776	"	9- 8-1799 1-23-1822	Baptized, 9-3-1769. Husband, Jacob Zigle
Hannah	9-10-1755 1-20-1756	"	8-27-1775 8-27-1775	"	4- 6-1816 8-30-1815	Baptized, 5-19-1771. Husband, Adam Weaver.
Alexander	1-18-1758	"		"	3-26-1760	
Lydia	1- 4-1761	"	1779 1779	"	12-14-1785	Baptized, 3-6-1785. Husband, Dielman Kulp.
			7-15-1788			Husband, John Lentz Baker.
Elizabeth	5- 2-1763	"		"	5-29-1770	Died of smallpox.
Anna Marg.	7-31-1765 1764	"	8-22-1784 8-22-1784	"	5-29-1838 3- 2-1833	Baptized, 3-6-1785. Baptized, 3-6-1785. Husband, Emanuel Fox.

[8] Three generations of Alexander Mack's family, the third being Alexander Mack, Jr.'s, children. For a full account of Life and Writings of Alexander Mack, Jr., see "German Baptist Brethren," M. G. Brumbaugh, pp. 211-273.

der Mack, Jr., was elected Bishop, *on trial.* Five years later, June 10, 1753, these two, having been fully proven, were duly ordained by Peter Becker, by the laying on of hands, and thus were they fully established in their long and useful service.

His Marriage and Family.[10]—He was married to Catherine Sharpnack, April 1, 1751, and to them were born nine children, and have left numerous descendants. In 1754 his father transferred to him the publication of English books. His father died in 1758, and he became sole proprietor of his father's large printing and publishing business, as well as other interests, and became possessed of large wealth, and one of the most extensive business interests of his times. During the Revolutionary War, he was arrested by the Colonial Government, and, without a trial or a hearing, was imprisoned and all his property confiscated. Released finally in 1778, penniless, he received assistance in money and provisions from some friends, and his daughter ministering to him, as his faithful housekeeper, he lived in obscurity and poverty until 1784, when he died. Alexander Mack wrote a hymn in his memory, which was sung at the funeral. His age was 63 years, while his contemporary, Alexander Mack, Jr., lived 91 years, and died in the beginning of the next century.

Peter Keyser.—The next notable Bishop of Germantown was Peter Keyser. He was born November 9, 1766,—and was baptized, September 28, 1784. He was elected to the ministry, 1785, and ordained a Bishop in 1802,—having been the intimate associate of Alexander Mack, Jr., during all those early years of his ministry. He was Bishop of Germantown for almost fifty years, also of Philadelphia, which for many years was regarded as a branch of Germantown. For full biographical facts, and his life, and service, see the following: Chapter II, "The Philadelphia Church"; "Some Who Led," pp. 27–30; and, also, "The Keyser Family," by Chas. S. Keyser, Esq., Philadelphia, 1889. A mere reference to these records must suffice, for the life of one who would well deserve a full discussion here.

Later History.—In more than one hundred years, very few elections for ministers were held in Germantown. In consequence, with the death of Peter Keyser, in 1849, the work gradually, but steadily, declined. For many years the preaching was supplied, in part, by the Philadelphia

---

[10] See "*Sower Family Chart,*" by Chas. G. Sower.

ministers, John W. Price, from Fitzwatertown, and others, from adjoining churches. For a period of almost twenty years there was no resident minister. At times deacons conducted the preaching services. Finally, there were no resident deacons, and when the present writer became pastor, in 1893, there was neither minister nor deacon in the congregation. For many years there are very few, or no records at all, they having passed into the hands of individuals, and, no doubt, some were lost and destroyed. A peculiar condition existed in Germantown, as in Philadelphia, that for many years the only records were the records of the Board of Trustees. The present records seem to date from 1863, when the Board consisted of John Price, Chairman, Stephen Benton, Secretary, Benjamin Lehman, Treasurer, Amos Cowell, J. G. Hammer, J. Sheetz, John Price, Jr., and Chas. M. Benson. Several committees were appointed to conduct the business of the Church. On October 27, 1867, W. W. C. Paul and Bro. James Kirk were elected trustees in place of Bros. Benton and Cowell, deceased. January 19, 1868, Bro. Britton was elected in place of Bro. Lehman, deceased.

On February 9, 1870, James Kirk and Chas. M. Benson were elected deacons.

There was a Sunday School in 1872.

In 1875, Willis, Ambers, and Unruh were elected trustees. Bro. Kolb was elected to fill the vacancy of Hammer, resigned. In 1877, the minutes imply that Bro. J. T. Meyers had been in the service of the Church three years. In 1877 William Price was elected trustee. By the year 1881, Brethren Kolb and Britton had died, and Paul resigned, Brethren John Thomas and Harry Shugard, and Thos. B. Hammer were elected. In 1885, John Thomas resigned as trustee. In 1888, the cemetery was enlarged. In 1889, Bro. Francis W. Price was elected trustee. In May, 1890, Joseph Sheetz resigned as sexton and trustee. In 1890, efforts were made to secure a resident preacher. Bro. W. B. Stover now in India, served the Church for about one year though residing in Philadelphia. The Church having called the writer, through the General Mission Board, he arrived at Germantown, from Mt. Morris, Ill., with his family, on June 9, 1893, and preached his first sermon in the "Old Stone Church," on June 11, following. This pastorate lasted eight years, the facts, and events of which can not be recorded in detail here. A few facts from the minutes of the Church (which are now regularly kept) and from the minutes of the Board of Trustees must be sufficient for lack of space. The New Stone Church was built in 1896 and 1897. The church minutes contain the following record: "New Church dedicated May 17, 1897. Preaching morning, afternoon and evening. Church filled at each service, especially in the afternoon. Speakers were G. N. Falkenstein, J. T. Myers, T. T. Myers, Jesse Ziegler, S. R. Zug, M. G. Brumbaugh and others. F. W. Price, Clerk." This new church building cost $8,000. The following is from the minutes: "F. W. Price and Alpheus Fahnestock elected deacons, September 2, 1897. General Mission Board in charge." Having resigned, to take charge of the new school to be organized as Elizabethtown College, the following appears on the minutes of the board of trustees, December 1, 1900: In view of the resignation of our pastor, Bro. G. N. Falkenstein, we herewith petition the District Mission Board to secure for us at the earliest possible opportunity, a regular pastor who shall take charge of the work of this church." The appointments continued to be filled by the writer, until in February, 1901, coming from Elizabethtown every week, when on account of sickness in the family, his preaching had to cease. For a time the appointments were filled by supplies. Then followed the pastorate of Bro. T. T. Myers, of Philadelphia, of about one year; and that of Walter Long, of about two years, from 1902 to 1904. On November 13, 1905, the Church decided to call Bro. M. C. Swigart to become pastor.

I regret very much indeed that limited space absolutely forbids me giving as full an account as I would like to give of the work of these five pastors, extending over a period of 22 years, from 1892 to 1914. I must close this History with but a brief account of the present pastor and his work. Bro. M. C. Swigart was born in Mifflin Co., Pa., December

28, 1868, and was baptized in June, 1888. He was elected to the ministry in 1894, and advanced to the second degree in 1900. Before coming to Germantown he taught in the public schools, and preached in his home church. He came to Germantown April 4, 1906, and has since had a very successful pastorate. He has organized a number of Church activities, and baptized 74. The membership has increased in these 8 years from 50 to about 126. There is a flourishing Sunday School, with an enrollment of over 200, with a well sustained Home Department, and Cradle Roll, and collections ranging from $5.00 to $7.00 a Sunday. The Sisters' Aid Society supports a native worker in India, and contributes $50 to $60 to Home Mission Work. The Missionary contributions, in 1913, were $2.61 per member. The preaching services are well attended, both by the members of the Church, and outside people, at times filling the house, so that extra seats have to be provided. Bro. Swigart was ordained to the eldership in 1912, which was probably only the second ordination, in the Mother Church, since 1802.

BRETHREN CHURCH, DAUPHIN ABOVE BROAD, PHILADELPHIA.

CHAPTER II.

THE PHILADELPHIA CHURCHES.

A. First Brethren Church.

Peter Keyser is the father of the church in Philadelphia. Here he lived, though being a member at Germantown. He was public spirited; he was a part of the growing city, and he longed that his city should have its highest possible blessing—the benediction and benefaction of the pure Christianity of the Church of the Brethren. The truest devotion of the Brethren to public education is manifested in the alliance of the Brethren Church with it in her first work in Philadelphia. The Brethren first held services in Philadelphia in a schoolhouse on the northwest corner of Fourth and Vine Sts.[1] The hearty service of the Brethren in the cause of education on their first entrance into the semblance of congregational existence in Philadelphia, her first preacher here being also a school director, is now duly repaid by a brother being at the head of the educational work of this most truly American of all our great cities.

It is not clear, however, as claimed by Bro. M. G. Brumbaugh that the Philadelphia church was organized in 1813, though this is not saying, however, that preaching services did not begin at this time. For many years after the meeting-house was erected in 1817, Philadelphia continued an integral part of the congregation at Germantown, all the love-feasts being held in Germantown till 1826. From this date until 1858, they alternated between Germantown and Philadelphia, the spring feast being held in Philadelphia. The process of separation was long and gradual, and almost imperceptible. In fact all the preachers of Philadelphia up to 1865, including Henry Geiger, David Harley, and Christian Custer are on the list of Germantown preachers.

[1] See Brumbaugh's "History," p. 509.

When in 1817 it came to the question of building a meeting-house in Philadelphia, the members in Philadelphia held council meetings, seemingly apart from the members at Germantown, kept minutes, and appointed a treasurer. But it does not appear that this meant more than permission from the general Germantown congregation to the members in Philadelphia to go ahead for themselves in the matter of erecting a convenient house of worship for themselves and for the purpose of extending the borders of Zion; in other words that Philadelphia was at this time anything more than a mission of the Germantown church. But congregational lines, both from the point of view of territory and of organization, were not so sharply drawn in those days. A general oneness with Germantown, however, seems to have been recognized till after 1860.

For a local history of the church in Philadelphia all the minutes recorded relative to building the Crown Street church would be in place, but for the history of the church in Eastern Pennsylvania, only an abridged form is in place.

"NEW CHURCH ON CROWN STREET.

"*Minutes of the First Meeting Held in regard to Building a Church in Philadelphia.*

"At a meeting of the subscribers and contributors for purchasing a lot of ground, and building a meeting-house for the use of the Church of Christ in Philadelphia (commonly called German Baptist) held March 19, 1817, for the purpose of considering the expediency of progressing in the undertaking. When after hearing the report of the Funding Committee, stating that nearly Five Thousand Dollars are already subscribed, and considerably more is calculated on, it was resolved unanimously that it is expedient to proceed in the undertaking. Whereupon James Lynd, George Gorgas, Jacob Ziegler, James Gorgas, and John Rink, were appointed a committee to procure a lot of ground suitable for the purpose, and report at our next meeting.

"Adjourned."

If the heading of these minutes is to be taken strictly, that this was the "first meeting" relative to this project held in Philadelphia, then the "Funding Committee" mentioned in the Minutes must have been appointed at a council held in Germantown, and the claim that the Philadelphia organization was effected in 1813, seems without foundation.

Five days later, March 24, the Philadelphia Brethren again met in council. The committee for procuring a lot of ground reported that they had purchased "from Jesse Stillwaggon a lot of ground situated between Crown and Fourth streets, a little south of Callowhill Street, 45 ft. front on Crown Street, and running that breadth to Fourth Street, say from between 75 and 86 feet deep, for Four Thousand, Two Hundred and Fifty Dollars."

It was unanimously agreed that it is expedient to proceed without delay to the collection of the subscriptions, or so much of them, as to enable the lot committee to meet their engagements with Jesse Stillwaggon. After considering the matter it was deemed expedient to appoint a treasurer to receive the amounts collected from time to time. James Lynd was the unanimous choice of the meeting.

It was deemed expedient also to appoint trustees, to whom the lot of ground might be conveyed in trust. The trustees appointed were: Peter Keyser, Jacob Ziegler, Sr., James Lynd, John Heisler, John Fox, Jacob Ziegler, Jr., Christian Lehman, George Gorgas, Joseph Gorgas, Christopher S. Langstroth, Michael Keyser, and John Leibert—twelve in all.

A Building Committee was also appointed at this second council meeting of March 24, which consisted of the following persons: Jacob Ziegler, Sr., James Lynd, George Gorgas, John Heisler, James Gorgas, Peter Keyser and John Rink—seven in all.

Cost of materials and what different contractors and business men contributed is mentioned in the minutes. There is however no mention of the cost of lumber. Inasmuch as Peter Keyser was a lumber merchant, we shall take the liberty to conjecture that he furnished the lumber free, and that he had learned how to keep the doings of his right hand from the knowledge of his left.

There was a gallery in the church, built after the pattern

of the one in the Friend's Meeting-house on 12th Street. The meeting-house was dedicated on October 12, 1817.[2]

How many members lived in Philadelphia at the time of the building of the Crown St. meeting-house we have not learned. Those whose names are given in the preceding pages were certainly at least the most prominent ones, and may have constituted a large percentage of the male members. Peter Keyser was the preacher living in Philadelphia. He was elected already in 1788

The first minister elected in Philadelphia after the erection of the church on Crown St., which election was held April 2, 1826, proves conclusively that at that date yet, Philadelphia and Germantown were one congregation. The church record of this election is as follows:

"At a church meeting held in Germantown, April 2, 1826, all the members present; our Brother Timothy Bangor was duly acknowledged and approved as a minister of the Gospel in the church of German Baptist. And on the following Sabbath evening, the church in Philadelphia, in convention ratified the proceedings of the Church at Germantown, and acknowledged and approved in like manner Timothy Bangor as a minister and helper in the Gospel of Christ.

" Signed on behalf of the church.
PETER KEYSER, *Sec'y*."

On October 12, of this same year in which Timothy Bangor was made a minister, the first love-feast was held in Philadelphia. From now on Philadelphia had the spring feast, with the exceptions of 1834 and 1843, when both were again held in Germantown.

Sometimes the Philadelphia feast was omitted altogether. In 1858 Philadelphia for the first time had both a spring and an autumn feast. This however was only an exception, and did not occur again until 1866. After 1867 we find the feast in Germantown neglected. The first communion service in the new church on Marshall Street was held October 9, 1873.

[2] Elder Peter Keyser preached three sermons on that day, from Hebrews 9: 1-5; Luke 19: 46; and Acts 26: 22, 23. The meetings were largely attended. On March 5, 1818, Elder Keyser presented to the congregation a beautiful pulpit Bible. Brumbaugh's "History," p. 509.

The first fruits of the new church were Christian Flower and Catherine Evans, baptized on Easter day, April 6, 1817, by Peter Keyser. Catherine Evans became one of the saintly characters of the Philadelphia church. "Her works follow her in the living members she brought into the fold by her religious ministrations, who are endeavoring to walk in the footsteps of her holy example."

Not very much is recorded of the Philadelphia church from 1817 to 1854, or to about the time that Dr. Henry Geiger was elected to the ministry. ·Some church officers were elected in this interval. John Righter and Thomas Major were elected to the ministry, November 18, 1841, in the Crown St. meeting-house, the former receiving twenty-nine votes and the latter twenty-seven. They were likely the first ministers elected in Philadelphia, for while Timothy Bangor was received here, he was elected in Germantown. James Lynd and John Heisler are on the list of Philadelphia preachers, following Peter Keyser and coming in before Timothy Bangor, but these two were likely also elected at Germantown. John Fox was "elected elder," September 28, 1844. But, as in New Jersey, the terms elder and preacher seem to have been synonymous. John Fox was ordained to the eldership in the regular order of the Brethren, November 16, 1867.

On May 4, 1854, two more ministers were elected: Dr. Henry Geiger, who received thirty-one votes, and David Harley, who received twenty-five. Christian Custer was elected December 24, 1861. Had the old custom of receiving the one with the next highest number of votes prevailed when these votes nearly equalled the first choice, there would have been another dual election, for Jonathan Eisenhower had thirty-three votes to Custer's thirty-six. The last election from the membership of the Philadelphia church was the one held on the removal of Elder J. P. Hetric in 1882, when Joel Reiner, son of Elder Jacob, of Pine Run, was the choice. These last two elections made a lot of trouble for the Philadelphia church.

A very interesting entry is found in the books of the Philadelphia church, which is herewith copied:

"Names of Elders of the German Baptist Church in Germantown and Philadelphia from the year 1793 down to this date, February 22, 1865.

    Alexander Mack   James Lynd
    Philip Weaver   John Heisler
    Peter Leibert   John W. Price
    Thomas Langstroth   John Righter
    Charles Hubbs   Thomas Major
    Justus Fox   Sara Righter
    John Weaver   John Fox
    Peter Keyser   Amos Crowell
    John Sellars   Henry Geiger
    Peter Bruster   David Harley
    John Van Lashett   Christian Custer
    Timothy Bangor

"I have heard all these Brethren preach,
                "Your Brother in the Lord,
                      "JOHN FOX, *Elder*."

There were also some deacons chosen during this period:

1. Peter K. Gorgas, elected January 13, 1842.
2. John Fox, elected January 13, 1842.
3. John Goodyear, elected February 23, 1858.
4. Christian Custer, elected February 23, 1858.
5. John Fry, elected January 31, 1863.
6. Isaiah G. Harley, elected January 31, 1863.

We now come to what might be called

The Constitutional Period

of the Philadelphia church—a period of reorganization, of readjustments to meet changing conditions, a period of transition from the old-time church preachers to the modern pastorate. During this time the Sunday School gained admission. The church began keeping regular, systematic records. Poor funds were developed. The Trustees were organized. The church was incorporated as a legal body with a corporate seal. The struggle was begun for the development of a church edifice that would properly house her manifold activities. And she formulated a constitution.

This period we may say in a general way extended from 1850 to 1870, from the death of the old founder, Peter Keyser, to the coming of J. P. Hetric, the first pastor. And yet this evolution was felt before and after these dates.

The Church Property.

In a meeting on January 15, 1850, the surviving trustees were empowered "to remove the discrepancy between the deed and the article of agreement" (whatever this was), and the following new Board was elected, to whom the surviving trustees of the original deed were authorized to convey the legal title now standing in their name. The second Board of Trustees, elected on the motion of John Fox, was as follows:

1. John Righter,
2. John Fox, only old trustee,
3. Joseph E. McIlhenny,
4. John Hagey,
5. John Harley,
6. John Dismant,
7. John Goodyear,
8. George H. Spencer,
9. Jacob Harley,
10. Benjamin Lehman,
11. Peter K. Gorgas,
12. James Lynd, Jr.

A meeting was called February 20, 1862, in the meetinghouse, for the purpose of taking into consideration the incorporation of the property belonging to the said German Baptist Church, located on Crown Street, below Callowhill, east side. Thirty members were present, the names of all of whom are given in the minutes. Bro. Geiger read the legal writings drawn up for the above named purpose, in which the following named persons were named as Trustees:

1. John Fox,
2. Stephen Benton,
3. James Lynd,
4. Henry Geiger,
5. John Goodyear,
6. Jonathan Eisenhower,
7. Isaiah G. Harley,
8. Jacob Harley,
9. Joseph A. Price,
10. Samuel Hershey,
11. John Fry,
12. John Hagey.

The act of incorporation as read was unanimously adopted.

At this same meeting, on Bro. Fox's own motion, a committee was appointed to examine the church books, city bonds or loans, etc., in his possession, for the purpose of having them transferred to Bro. Goodyear. This matter involves the poor fund, which we shall consider later.

"PETITION TO THE COURT FOR INCORPORATION.

"*To the Honorable, the Judges of the Court of Common Pleas for the County of Philadelphia.*

"The Subscribers, citizens of the State of Pennsylvania have agreed to associate themselves for the purpose set forth in the annexed Article, Constitution of the Society of the Church of Christ (worshipping in Crown Street, city of Philadelphia) commonly called German Baptists, and are desirous of acquiring and enjoying, in accordance with the articles, conditions and objects, and under the name, style and title in said annexed articles, set forth the powers and immunities of a corporation and body politic in law, and they pray that your Honors may examine the said articles, and if the objects and conditions therein shall appear lawful and not injurious to the Community, may direct the same to be filed in the office of the prothonotary of the Court aforesaid and also direct the necessary advertisement of this application.

"And as in honor bound your petitioners will ever pray, etc. (Signed)

"JOSEPH A. PRICE SAMUEL HERSHEY
JACOB HARLEY JOHN FOX
JAMES LYND HENRY GEIGER
ISAIAH G. HARLEY JONATHAN EISENHOWER
JOHN HAGEY JOHN GOODYEAR"
JOHN FRY

The trustees figured very prominently in this work, as much as to call forth protest. A meeting was held July 5, 1864, to reconsider the Constitution and By-Laws. Bro. Custer objected to Art. III, Sec. 2, on the ground that too much power was vested in the trustees, and thought that the word "Church" should be substituted in place of "Trustees." No motion was made to this effect, but the protest went on the minutes.

It seems that a Constitution is necessary to present to the Civil Court in order that the church may be recognized as a corporate body in law. It, therefore, has to do with the temporal side of church work, and rightly falls within the sphere of the Trustees. The entering of the protest on the Minutes seems to indicate that the church recognized the danger of the Trustees feeling their power, to being led to usurp authority in the church not belonging to them, but not recognizing any such usurpation as having taken place. The Church in her spiritual functions is above, not subject to Civil Courts, but where she has dealings in the affairs of this life, she recognizes the Civil Courts as of God to look after these matters, and submits to their regulations in matters temporal. The submission of such a Constitution is not to be interpreted as the Church subscribing to a confession or Creed. The creed of the Church of the Brethren is as always the New Testament.

On May 25, 1864, the Board of Trustees met and organized as follows: *President,* Jonathan Eisenhower; *Secretary,* I. G. Harley; *Treasurer,* John Goodyear. Two days later, on May 27, Samuel Hershey resigned his trusteeship and his membership in the church. Silas Thomas was elected in his place.

A motion is recorded, made likely about this time, the mover being Elder Jacob Spanogle, as follows: "*Resolved,* that the Society of the church of Christ commonly called German Baptist adopt a corporate seal for the use and purpose of said Society, and that we hereby adopt a said corporate seal, one of which the following is a true and correct impress."

The first annual meeting of the Trustees was held Jan. 30, 1865. At this meeting it was decided to repair the church, repairs consisted of "painting and fixing up," cost $347.35.

To the Trustees is the credit also due of getting the church to keep regular minutes. The following written report was submitted on the date of the above meeting. The report speaks for itself.

"PHILADELPHIA, Jan. 30, 1865.
"TO THE MEMBERS AND TRUSTEES OF THE GERMAN BAPTIST CHURCH.

"*Dear Brethren:*—Being instructed by the Board of Trustees, at a meeting held May 25, 1864, to purchase a Book for the use of the German Baptist Church, and to record therein the Act of Incorporation, By-Laws, and the Minutes of all meetings held from that date," etc.

The name of the person who secured the book is not given. It was likely I. G. Harley.

Jacob Harley is the first secretary of whom we have record. He served in 1854. Henry Geiger was secretary in 1856 and 1858; and Silas Thomas in 1864. But these seem to have been only appointments *pro tem.*

We find the treasurer's work also being gotten in shape. In 1865 the treasurer gave reports for several years back, for 1862, 1863 and 1864; also a report of poor funds since 1858. After 1864 he gave a regular annual report of all receipts and expenditures, and also separate annual reports of the poor funds. The total cost of running the church in 1862, including cost of light, heat, water, $150 interest on a mortgage, and $80 sexton's salary for eight months, amounted to $252.97. The next year it was $301.99. In the light of present day conditions, we may well call this the day of small things. But even this burden the members did not have to bear, the receipts being as follows:

Rents from lot and cellar ($150 and $60)	$210.00
Contributions from R. Harley Fund	5.00
Quarterly Collections	11.97
From ex-Treasurer John Fox	32.37
Total receipts	$259.34

Notwithstanding the low cost of running the church, the congregation had been borrowing heavily from the poor funds. Surely the members had not been taught to give. No wonder that the windows of heaven had not been opened in blessings. The shortage in funds continued to increase; and in order to stimulate the members in giving, shortages for three years were read, being as follows: in 1864, $92.55;

in 1865, $213.54; in 1866, $395.84. It being recognized as illegal to use the poor funds, the following action was taken in a special meeting of Trustees at Bro. John Fry's, on the evening of January 28, 1867:

"*Resolved,* That the proceeds of the legacies to the Crown Street German Baptist Church, be appropriated and used alone for the purpose for which they were bequeathed—to the assistance of the Poor members of said church."

John Goodyear, John Fry and I. G. Harley were appointed a committee to liquidate the debt. The board suggested, "that the present debt of the church be subscribed for and paid, that a permanent church fund be raised by quarterly or half yearly subscriptions, from each member of the church in such amounts as each member may feel able and willing to pay."

A meeting of the church was called to present the matter to the members, when it was decided to do away with the quarterly collection of Sunday morning, "and that each member subscribe in a book furnished by the deacons, what they may feel willing and able to give, and that it be payable half yearly, on the first of November and on the first of May in each and every year." It will thus be seen that the burden of financing the church devolved largely upon the trustees.

The personnel of the Board has been kept pretty well before us.

The following letter was received by the Board:

"PHILADELPHIA, May 18, 1865.

"MR. JONATHAN EISENHOWER, President of Board of Trustees of the German Baptist Church, Phila.

"*Dear Sir,*—I hereby tender my resignation as a member of the board over which you preside. Please have my resignation accepted and entered on the minutes of your transactions.

"H. GEIGER."

This resignation was accepted with no little reluctance. Dr. Geiger's influence for good as a trustee, as well as in other lines of church work, was considerable. George Spencer was elected in his place.

John Fox resigned as a trustee, February 11, 1867, and Jacob Spanogle was elected in his place. Bro Spanogle was a preacher and had moved to Philadelphia a few years before.

Joseph Price having moved to Norristown, resigned as a trustee, July 26, 1869. Isaac Hunsberger was elected in his place.

February 13, 1871, John S. Thomas was elected a trustee in place of George H. Spencer, deceased.

Jacob Harley resigned as trustee, January 29, 1872. Christian Custer was elected to fill the vacancy. At the same time John Eisenhower resigned as chairman of the Board, and was succeeded by John S. Thomas.

The Poor Fund.

In the matter of funds for the poor the Philadelphia church holds an enviable position. Up to the end of the period of this congregation's history now under consideration, she had three—The Hannah Keyser Fund, the Rudolph K. Harley Fund, and the Christian Lapp Fund.

Hannah Keyser by her will left $1,000 as a poor fund, to the Germantown and Philadelphia churches. The interest was to be divided equally between the two churches and to be given to their poor and needy. The money was invested in City Loan at 6 per cent. By January 1, 1865, the income had amounted to $379.23. Of this amount $260.16 had been paid out, leaving a balance on hand of $119.07. The funds seem to be in care of the Philadelphia church, which pays Germantown her share.

Rudolph K. Harley bequeathed to the Philadelphia Church forty-two shares of Northern Liberty Gas Stock, $25 per share, making $1,050. John Fox originally had the care of it, but resigned in 1869. He was succeeded by I. G. Harley. The income from this fund up to October 5, 1864, was $994.12. $522.14 had been paid out, leaving a balance, January 1, 1865, of $471.98. $5 were given annually to defray expenses of the church. The Gas Stock paid very large dividends, but in 1865 was likely soon to be paid over to the church.

Christian Lapp Fund was originally $470.11. But with 6 per cent. interest by 1864 amounted to $656.23. Of this amount $512.50 were invested. The balance on hand, January 1, 1865, was $143.73.

The total balance from the poor funds, January 1, 1865, was $642.33. As already stated the church had been in the habit of borrowing from this fund. Nearly $100 were due the poor fund on the preceding date. When the question of repairing the church came up before the Board of Trustees, May 22, 1865, the President stated that the poor fund could not be used and that the amount owed should be paid back. In 1858 the sole duty of the treasurer seemed to be disposing of the income from these funds.

The Philadelphia Sunday School.

The following account of the Philadelphia Sunday School is the one read at the meeting of the Brethren's Historical Society at Harrisonburg, Va., in 1909. The information concerning its origin was received direct from Sister Mary Geiger of Philadelphia, the widow of its founder.

"Dr. Henry Geiger moved to Philadelphia in 1852. About two years later, in 1854, he was elected to the ministry. At this time no services were held on Sunday except preaching, morning and evening. This was in the old Crown Street Church."

The Doctor refused to serve unless a Sunday School was organized. This stand brought the Sunday School, and brought it permanently. Dr. Geiger was elected superintendent.

During a trip east James Quinter was with the Philadelphia church on Sunday, December 28, 1856. He says::

"The Brethren here have a Sunday School; and on Sunday afternoon our talking was more particularly directed to the teachers and scholars. We were pleased with the interest manifested, and hope God will bless all concerned, and make them a blessing. Our meetings here were characterized by solemnity and attention. We felt, I think, that it was good to be together. There are zealous brethren and sisters in this church. And we hope God has blessings in store for them. We enjoyed ourselves very well with our Christian friends here."—*Gospel Visitor* of 1857, pp. 57 and 58.

The Philadelphia school was purely Brethren at the start; the one at Coventry was union in origin, yet it was securely intrenched in the church with a brother as superintendent before the Philadelphia school was started, so it may rightly claim to be the older school. Many of our church enterprises were started as individual concerns. If, however, the position be taken that that is not a Brethren school which was not purely one at the beginning, then to Dr. Geiger must be conceded the distinction of standing at the head of our Sunday School work. It would give us great pleasure to grant him the distinction, because of the indirect blessing he has been to the church. Dr. Geiger did the work of a surgeon in the Civil War. This not only brought an end to his preaching and Sunday School work, but cost him his membership. May the good he has done the church return to him in blessing!

The Philadelphia school was the first to receive notice in our church paper, so that its influence was doubtless more widespread and called into being more schools than did the Coventry school. James Quinter's visit was in mid-winter. He visited Coventry as well as Philadelphia. Coventry is in the country and her school had likely closed for the winter.

So much for the account to the Historical Society.

The Sunday School has ever been a potent factor in shaping church architecture. We shall here insert a statement from the old minute book which may seem out of place.

"Our holy and beautiful house where our Fathers worshipped was injured by fire, October 5, 1854. We congregated in the old school room, corner of Vine and Fourth Streets, until January 28, 1855, when we turned our feet once more to the little Sanctuary." Bro. M. G. Brumbaugh evidently places this construction on the above: "We congregated in the old school room, corner of Vine and Fourth Streets, where we had congregated before the Crown Street house was built."

The question of leasing again the lot back of the church was considered at a special meeting of the Board of Trustees, May 26, 1869. It was then stated that the teachers and scholars of the Sunday School were dissatisfied with the gallery of the church, the place which was then used by the school. They complained that they could not build up the school unless they had better accommodations for the scholars, and asked that something might be done to relieve them, whereby they might retain all the scholars and increase the school. It was proposed to erect a school room on the lot, but on this point there was lack of agreement. The next proposition was to sell the church and lot and to build a new church elsewhere with basement for Sunday School, it being thought the church was not in the right place to do good. It was decided to call a meeting of the members to consider the matter.

This meeting was held June 24, 1869, in the church building. The object of the meeting was laid before the members by the President of the board, and all were requested to express their views. Bro. John S. Thomas thought the church wasn't in a place to do good, being surrounded by "Lager beer saloons," and other "annoyances," and that he could not see how any member could object to selling the church, and building or buying one in some more suitable place. Brother Spanogle tried to dispel any fears of additional cost by stating that the property could be sold for $18,000 or more, and that for this amount a lot could be purchased and a plain meeting-house erected. Bro. John Fox had no objection to selling if sufficient could be realized on the old property. He said that when the house was built in 1817, it was in the center of the membership, but now the members were more up town. His remarks seemed to set forth the general view of the church. Those present were unanimously in favor of selling and a committee was appointed to take the vote of those present. A written vote of the whole membership was taken and resulted as follows: "Yes," 84; "No," 8; refused to vote, 8; not seen, 5. It will thus be seen that the membership of the church in 1869 was 105. In 1862 it was 96.

It was decided in council, September 6, 1869, to sell the Crown Street property. Isaac Hunsberger, John L. Fry, Silas Thomas, and I. G. Harley were appointed to attend to the matter, and also to see about buying a new lot. An offer of $12,000 for the property was refused. The matter dragged on till September 3, 1872, when it was decided to accept an offer of $13,000. A new committee had been appointed in June of this year—Brethren Hunsberger, Custer and Fry—to look up a building lot, to draw up a plan for the new church and to secure estimates of cost. Two sites were found—one on the corner of 8th and Thompson Streets and the other on Marshall Street below Girard Avenue. The latter was taken for $7,600. A two-story brick church was erected on this lot, and dedicated the second Sunday in September, 1873. Elder Isaac Price, of Green Tree, preached the dedication sermon.

The Philadelphia church began keeping council records apart from the minutes of the trustees in 1865. Troubles among the ministers seem to have brought this desirable result. Lack of harmony, running too fast, unkindness, assuming authority, jealousy, lack of care in truthfulness, and attending services elsewhere when there were meetings in the home church, were faults found in the ministry; and the chuch was rebuked for schism. The committee of elders present were Christian Long, John L. Glick and Samuel Harley. Elder Andrew M. Dierdorff was also present.

But this committee was not able to put an end to the trouble. The ministers involved were Brethren Custer, Heyser and Fox. The committee met the church in January, 1866; but the next year it was necessary to have another. The committee consisted of John Zug, Graybill Myers, John Wise, Jacob Reiner and Daniel M. Holsinger. This was November 14, 1867. After the members had subscribed themselves as "willing to abide by the decision of this committee and never oppose it unless it can be shown that it is contrary to the Scriptures," the committee gave its report as follows:

"After patiently hearing all the testimony offered, the following are our

Unanimous Conclusions.

"WHEREAS, We, having examined the writing and verbal declarations made before us, after mature deliberation found that many members have done wrong;

"*Therefore, Resolved:* That after hearing the acknowledgements made by brethren in public council, we do not require any further acknowledgements from any, but that all the members shall humble themselves before God, confess their sins to him and turn from them.

" Also, *Resolved,* That we set the ministers in order according to the general order of the Brethren by promoting Brother John Fox to the office of Bishop, or Ordained Elder; and Bro. Custer be continued in the ministry in the first degree.

" And the members *shall submit* unto this decision and whoever shall stir up anything that has occurred before this time shall fall into the judgment of the church.

" Philada., Nov. 16, 1867.

" Signed
JOHN WISE, *Moderator*
DANIEL M. HOLSINGER, *Clerk*
GRAYBILL MYERS
JACOB K. REINER
JOHN ZUG"

Bro. John Fox was very old when he was ordained. When it came to receive him as bishop, as is the custom, the brethren received him with the right hand of fellowship and the salutation of the kiss, then the sisters gave the right hand of fellowship. The first three gave the hand only but the fourth seized his hand and kissed him. All the sisters that followed kissed him also.

The next year another committee waited on the church to set them in order in regard to feetwashing, the supper, the salutation, and use of the Lord's Supper. In the council of October 5, 1869, it was decided to carry out the decision of the committee, to have "Beef, Bread, Rusk and Coffee" for the Supper.

Action of the church November 10, 1869, Bro. Graybill Myers being present, showed further progress in the matter of getting fully into the order of the Brotherhood. After some consultation the following proposition and resolution were unanimously accepted.

"WHEREAS, a few of our members have sometimes communed with other denominations, and others have fellowshipped Wm. C. Thurman, an excluded member of the Brotherhood; and, Whereas these things are contrary to the order of the Brethren, and thereby have brought trouble and contentions into our congregation,

"*Therefore, Resolved,* that, forgiving one another all that is past, we will henceforth by the help of the Lord, avoid giving offence, in the particulars named above, and furthermore, that we will enforce discipline upon all those members who hereafter thus offend."

Meeting was held for the last time in the old Crown St. Church, on Sunday, September 22, 1872. Services were held morning and evening.

"The Brethren and Sisters having tried to worship the Lord our God, in accordance with the teachings of the New Testament in that house for fifty-five years, feel sorry to leave the dear, sad spot. But believing it to be for the best, to promote the cause of Christ, and the salvation of precious never-dying souls, have consented and are willing to make sacrifices, and thereby assist in the building of a new house, wherein to continue by the blessing and assistance of our God our worship in a more convenient place."

Meetings were held in a hall on the corner of 6th St. and Girard Ave., from September 29, 1872, to the second Sunday in Sept., 1873, when as previously stated, the new house was dedicated.

The first quarterly council meeting held in the Marshall St. house was on Thursday evening, July 2, 1874. Bro. J. T. Myers was appointed chairman, and I. G. Harley was secretary.

October 1, 1874, it was decided to have a minister read the opening chapter instead of a deacon as heretofore. It being stated that reading in order was not the general custom of the Brethren, Bro. John Fox stated that the reading of the chapter in order, by one of the deacons, has been done here and at Germantown, as long as he can remember; but he did not object to a change. A psalm was also read at the opening of the morning service, by the minister, but he was not in favor of too much reading and thought the long chapters should be divided.

While the Philadelphia Church was getting in line with some of the old regulations of the Brotherhood, new measures were constantly being introduced.

The question of a pool came up at this time. Bro. Fox thought the time had come for a pool. The readiness of change in a man so old is remarkable. There was great difficulty in baptizing in the River. They must always wait for the tide or baptize in the mud, and they did not know how soon they would be deprived of that privilege. The vote was seventeen to one for a pool.

Elder J. P. Hetric first comes to the front in the third council in the new church, and it was in the interest of church government. He stated that the order among the Brethren is, when business is to come before the church of which the church is not fully informed of its nature, to submit it to a special council of the official members, who approve or disapprove as they think proper, and thus occupy the relation to the council meeting, that the Standing Committee does to the general Annual Council, after which our church meetings are modelled; and if the church wishes to transact its business after the order of the Brethren, this is the way they should proceed.

Brother Hetric came from Armstrong Co., Pa. John Wise, of that county, informs the Brotherhood in the *Gospel Visitor* of August, 1866, that "The congregation on Red Bank held an election for a minister—and called Bro. Jesse P. Hetric to the ministry." Bro. Hetric came to Philadelphia in April, 1874, and remained as pastor of the Philadelphia church to June, 1882. In this interval, April, 1877, he met with the great loss and sorrow of his life, in the death of his estimable wife. He had had the pleasure of baptizing her into the church for which he was laboring, September 6, 1874. "Broken down in physical health and discouraged in heart, he took up the duties of life alone in the city church." And for five years more he rendered very acceptable service. During his pastorate forty-three were added to the church. He held some very successful revival services in the churches in the country roundabout. Bro. Hetric wished to go to the country, but not because of any dissatisfaction in the church, which desired him to stay. He advocated the election of a minister from the membership. Bro. Joel Reiner, son of Elder Jacob, was elected. There was a rival, and dissensions and withdrawals followed. After some years of service Bro. Reiner fell away from the church.

Then Brethren from a distance were called in to look after the flock. These were E. A. Orr, I. M. Gibson and Howard Miller. Though there are members still living who have " pleasant memories of Christian fellowship in the Marshall Street Church," yet the work did not prosper. The membership became weak and scattered. The church was sold in March, 1890; and a lot was bought at the N. E. corner of Dauphin and Carlisle Streets in June of the same year.

For about a year the members worshipped in a hall at 22d St. and Columbia Ave. During this time the Sunday School was suppressed. Bro. W. J. Swigart of Huntingdon preached every other Sunday. The pulpit was filled on the other Sunday as best they could. Prayer-meetings were held in the homes. The last sermon in the hall was preached Sunday, April 26, 1891, by Bro. T. T. Myers, of Illinois, it being his first to the Philadelphia members. The new church was dedicated May 3, 1891. Eld. W. J. Swigart preached the sermon. At the same time Bro. Myers assumed the pastorate of the little flock, now numbering about forty. The total membership in Philadelphia was seventy-four. This was the beginning of prosperity for the Philadelphia church. Up to February 8, 1891, four hundred and nine persons had held membership in the Philadelphia church.

There were about twenty of the Marshall St. members who were worshipping at Dover Hall. These too might have been built up into a strong congregation had they been supplied with a good resident pastor. They were organized into a congregation and became known as the

North Philadelphia Church.

They first represented at District Meeting in the year 1888. This was while E. A. Orr was preaching at Marshall St. J. K. Reiner was the preacher in North Philadelphia. He and J. H. Hartman represented the church this year. These with J. W. Steiner were the only representatives of this church till 1893, when it was taken under the care of the District Mission Board. We have the following minutes in the District records of this year:

"The Northern Philadelphia Church at a council in the fall of 1892 decided to ask the District Mission Board to take charge of them, which we agreed to do. J. K. Reiner, their only minister, was charged with improper conduct and improper expressions in preaching, to which he plead guilty. Whereupon, in the presence of the writer (name not given) and Elders Wm. Hertzler and F. P. Cassel, he was deposed from the ministry; and at the next council, he and wife disowned, by their request. Four councils attended there during the year. This church was assigned to Elder Wm. Hertzler to care for them in the name of the Mission Board, and they are supplied with ministerial service by ministers from other churches."

J. H. Hartman continued to represent this church at District Meeting; and the District Mission Board spent considerable money in ministerial supplies here. Jesse Ziegler and J. Z. Gottwals preached most frequently.

In 1894 the report at District Meeting was that one was baptized, that meetings were held every Lord's day, and that the members are much in need of a better place of worship.

In 1895 the work was in charge of Elder H. E. Light, and he was unable to give a very encouraging report. "They still continue to hold their meetings in Dover Hall. Every Sunday the appointments are filled by supplies from H. E. Light, Cassel, Gottwals, Price and Ziegler, or their substitutes. A few had to be disowned, and no addition during this year. Four councils and one love feast were held during the year. The committee appointed to see for a better place of worship did not succeed as yet in getting a new place."

The report to the District Meeting of 1896 was: "Philadelphia Northern Church was disorganized by the mutual consent of the members and the committee from A. M." The members went to the

Carlisle and Dauphin St. Church.

Here Bro. T. T. Myers was doing a quiet, steady work that was bringing results. During his first year twenty-two were baptized; during the second, thirty-five; the third, thirty-seven; the fourth, twenty-eight; the fifth, nine (this year he visited the Holy Land); the sixth, forty. During these years he received sixty-two by letter; and dismissed by letter perhaps twenty.

In the spring of 1892 it was necessary to build a Sunday School addition. It consisted of two rooms, an infant room and a general Sunday School room. The building and furnishing, costing about $7,000, were the gifts of Sister Mary Geiger. This building was dedicated October 2, 1892. The first Sunday School at the new Carlisle and Dauphin St. house was held May 10, 1891, with W. S. Price, now of Royersford, as superintendent.

Bro. T. T. Myers continued to serve this congregation till he was called to the chair of New Testament Theology in the Juniata Bible School, with the exception of one year, from May, 1901, to May, 1902, when W. S. Long was pastor. Bro. Long and C. C. Ellis were each assistant pastor for a short time.

In 1896 a mission Sunday School was started at 26th Street and Lehigh Avenue. Bro. J. W. Cline was placed in charge of the work. Through the generosity of Sister Geiger a lot was purchased and a church and parsonage built, which were dedicated in the fall of 1898. This church is fittingly called Geiger Memorial.

The Carlisle and Dauphin St. church was enlarged and a tower built on it in 1905. Bro. M. G. Brumbaugh preached the dedication sermon on Sunday morning, January 1, 1905. A sermon was preached in the evening by Eld. I. N. H. Beahm. The membership of the church at this time, including the mission at 26th and Lehigh, was about four hundred and fifty. Besides the different departments of the Sunday School and Bible Classes, there were a Mother's, a Young People's and a Junior Christian Endeavor, a Young Woman's Christian Temperance Union, a Society of King's Daughters, Sewing Circles, a Beneficial Association, a Young Men's Association, a Junior, and A Young People's Choral Society. The feeling of the church was: "Surely the Lord has been and is with us, and He will continue to be with us if we show to Him a spirit of real devotion."

A brief acquaintance with some of the old preachers of the Philadelphia Church will be of interest to all. First and foremost among them will ever be

Peter Keyser.

An interesting account of him is given in the book, "Some Who Led," which is no doubt accessible to nearly all. He came of good old Mennonite stock, and little wonder that he became a tower of strength.

Peter Dirck Keyser, great-grandfather of Elder Peter, came to America in 1668, and settled at Germantown. The subject of this sketch was born November 9, 1766. When he was three years old his father joined the Church of the Brethren. He himself joined the church, September 28, 1784, in his eighteenth year. In 1785 he was called to the ministry; and in 1802 was ordained to the eldership. For sixty-four years he was preacher and for forty-seven years was bishop of the Germantown and Philadelphia churches. He died May 21, 1849.

Bro. Abraham H. Cassel has a few words more for us about him: "I was well acquainted with the Rev. Peter Keyser. He told me some of his early life; that his father had been a tanner, and that he was early put at the bark mill for grinding. Above it he made a shelf, on which he kept an open Bible, and as the grinding went on he would read a passage in it, memorize it; and so he would take up verse after verse and chapter after chapter, until he had completely memorized the whole of the New Testament. Of the Old Testament he memorized the whole of the Psalms and the Prophets, and the five books of Moses—the whole of the New and the greater part of the Old Testament."

James Lynd.

James Lynd succeeded Peter Keyser as elder of the Philadelphia Church, and survived him only a little over two years. He died December 28, 1851. We give the following lines written on him after his death by J. E. M. I. They indicate that the spirit of poetry was cultivated in this city church.

"He has finished his course,
  He has fought the good fight;
He has reached the bright realms
  Of peace and delight.
* * * * * * * *
"No storm of affliction
  Shall bear on him now
The crown of rejoicing
  Is placed on his brow.

"Then joyfully thronging
  With melody sweet,
And harps all attuned,
  Their brother to greet.

"The saints of all ages
  Appear on the plain,
And join in one sweet
  And enrapturing strain.
* * * * * * * *
"What bliss to behold
  Midst the bright ones above,
The brethren and friends,
  Whom on earth he did love;

"And join in the praises
  That never shall end,
To Jesus their Savior,
  Redeemer and Friend."

John Righter and Thomas Major.

November 18, 1841, a notable event occurred in the Philadelphia church. On this day were elected to the ministry, one with twenty-nine, the other with twenty-seven votes, John Righter and Thomas Major, the father and husband of Sarah Righter Major, the noted woman preacher of the Church of the Brethren.

The year following this election, in 1842, Sarah exchanged her father's home for the home of a husband. Both guarded and encouraged her in her work of prophesying. We feel that she was the central figure, and that the other two existed for her.

For a very interesting account of Sarah Righter Major, see "Some Who Led," pp. 70-72.

The *Gospel Visitor* tells us of the home going of John Righter.

"Died in Philadelphia, August 10 (1860) our beloved brother in the Lord, Elder John Righter, in the seventy-seventh year of his age. He was fifty-one years a member of the church, and nineteen years a preacher of the Gospel. He was in delicate health for several years, and suffered much, which he endured with more than usual Christian fortitude. His end was like the going down of a balmy, summer evening's sun. He was sensible to the last, and with patience waited for his end, when his disembodied spirit should go home to dwell with the saints, who have made their robes white in the blood of the Lamb. Funeral services by brethren John H. Umstad and John Fox. Subject— 'It is better to go to the house of mourning, than to the house of feasting.'

"We who are left to mourn his departure can say with truth, —Another of God's servants hath put on the garment of salvation, has laid aside Earth's heavy raiment, and arrayed in light, has gone to enjoy the house of many mansions. We weep that he has left us alone. In grief we tread life's desert pathway, but when life hath passed, we may go to him and claim his hand, to lead us where the living waters flow."

Thomas Major moved from Philadelphia in 1843 to Highland County, Ohio. He died in 1888 and is buried with his wife at Greenfield, Ohio.

Dr. Henry Geiger.

Though Dr. Geiger will never be rated high as a preacher, will hardly be thought of at all as a preacher, yet his influence direct and indirect taken together, has perhaps been greater than that of any other member the Philadelphia Church ever had. From the angle of finances he has indirectly done more for the Church of the Brethren than any member on her books. He was active as a trustee, and likely was instrumental in having the Philadelphia Church chartered—the first church to be chartered in the Brotherhood. He it was who brought the Sunday School into the Philadelphia Church. This Sunday School was the seed Sunday School of the Brethren Church, the sower of this seed being James Quinter. The Doctor went out with the city troop in the Civil War, and thus ceased to be a brother. He was an able business man and amassed great wealth. It is his meek, quiet, consecrated wife, who has been and still is turning his wealth into blessing for the church. May God bless Sister Mary S. Geiger! Of her it may be said: "Many daughters have done well, but she has exceeded them all."

Jacob Spanogle.

Though not called to the ministry in Philadelphia, yet Bro. Spanogle was a very useful minister here. He moved to Philadelphia from Perry County, Pa., perhaps about 1860. He was a tanner by trade and in Philadelphia went into the leather business. He was active in the church councils, was a trustee, frequently performed baptisms, and wielded considerable influence in the church. He it was who was instrumental in having Bro. J. P. Hetric come to Philadelphia as pastor. In the church record we find: "Jacob Spanogle, our beloved brother and minister, died suddenly, April 19, 1876; aged sixty-two years. Buried at Germantown."

John Fox.

John Fox was the embodiment of the Philadelphia Church beyond others. He was the mouth-piece of the congregation.

This is well brought out when it came to selling the old Crown Street Church. His remarks set forth the general view of the church. He was a remarkable old man— though he knew the past, had lived in it, was a part of it, yet he had not crystallized in it. He was ready to set aside the past for new things, if they were for the good of the church. Nor did his past prejudice his judgment in respect to the merit of new things. He was trusted. He was interested in all lines of church activity, as can be perceived by reading the history of the Philadelphia Church. And yet he was not in a hurry to invite Christian Custer into the pulpit to preach after the latter's election. He should ever be regarded by the Philadelphia Church as a father in Israel. He was born October 12, 1786. He was elected to the ministry September 28, 1844; and was ordained elder November 16, 1867. He died in 1880 and is buried at Germantown.

The Philadelphia Church has produced some saintly characters.

Catharine Evans

deserves more than a passing notice. We shall leave one who knew her in life, tell us of her.

"'Blessed is the memory of the just,
 Though dead, in their works they live and shine;
And from the silence of the dust,
 Still speak in words divine.'
             Heb. 11: 4; Rev. 14: 18.

"The above words are eminently appropriate to the honored and beloved, Catharine Evans, the subject of the following remarks, called out by her holy death, and the many Christian virtues of her long and saintly life; 'by which she being dead yet speaketh.' The text is peculiarly applicable to her, as we are constantly reminded of it by hearing her words of exhortation and pious counsel, repeated by those around us. Know, too, that they are not without their blessed effects on many.

"Rev. 14: 13 is also beautifully illustrated in the sanctified influence of her many good works. Of her it may truly be said, 'Blessed are the dead that die in the Lord; yea, saith the Spirit, that they may rest from their labors, and their works do follow them.' Her works follow her in the living members she brought into the fold by her religious ministrations, who are trying to walk in the footsteps of her holy example. In every relation in life, as a wife, a mother, and a Christian, she was a pattern of propriety, piety and usefulness.

"Her advantages in the way of pious instruction, in early life were many, for her mother was a Christian of more than usual excellence. Her pastor also, the late venerated Peter Keyser, by whom she was baptized and brought into the church, was to her a Christian minister indeed; and well did she profit by his ministrations, as in after years by those of her beloved pastor John Fox, who stood by her dying bed, still exercising the functions of his holy ministry in her last hours. It was a blessed sight, when her venerable pastor stood by the bed-side with her three daughters, and son-in-law, Jacob Reiff, when she took her last earthly leave of them, giving each a separate charge, as she did to all around her in her last moments. And well and long will her holy words be remembered by all who were privileged to hear them.—A. P. J."

We have spoken of her being the first fruits of the church in Philadelphia. She died June 25, 1866; and is buried at Germantown. Services by John Fox, John Umstad and Jacob Spanogle.

Our church history would be more rich, more sanctifying were more told about the consecrated mothers and sisters in Israel. We might mention *"Kitty" Supplee.* Bro. J. T. Myers tells how she took it to the Lord in prayer when her teeth (for she had artificial ones) were missing next morning. Then she dreamed that she should take up board number so and so of the kitchen floor and she would find them. She insisted on having the board taken up and there were her teeth. A rat had evidently been the robber.

And then old *"Aunt Becky" Yarnall,* the devoted mother who prayed and prayed and prayed, went to the attic after dinner to supplicate for her children, would not give up till she "had them all in the kingdom."

Recent History.

Elder S. R. Zug looked after the Philadelphia Church while he was a member of the Annual Meeting Committee to Eastern Pennsylvania, and was continued after he ceased to be a member of this Committee, until 1906, when T. T. Myers was ordained and took the oversight. September 1, 1907, Bro. Myers moved to Huntingdon, Pa., having accepted the chair of New Testament Theology in the Biblical Department of Juniata College. He had been pastor of the First Church of Philadelphia for sixteen years. He found it a mere handful of members struggling for existence and left it a strong mother church bearing children.

Bro. Charles A. Bame came to Philadelphia following the removal of Bro. Myers. He took up the pastorate, while Bro. J. T. Myers was chosen elder in charge. Bro. Bame continued several years in Philadelphia, and left in the month of February, 1910. The following month D. Webster Kurtz became pastor of the First Church. Bame was rather evangelistic. He was, however, ultra-progressive, progressive beyond possible service. The prevention of a disruption of the congregation was a heavy task to the elder, Bro. J. T. Myers. Bro. Myers refused to continue as elder with Bame in the pulpit. The church to a member stood with Elder Myers. Bame found an opening as pastor of a Progressive Church in Dayton, Ohio. He was ordained an elder in the Progressive Church of Philadelphia, however, before he left.

Bro. Kurtz is an able speaker. The attendance under Kurtz is described as healthy. Kurtz is instructive. Those who come into the church under Kurtz are likely to remain loyal. Kurtz is a scholar. He is one of the few ministers of the Church of the Brethren upon whom has been conferred the degree of D.D.

D. Webster Kurtz was born October 9, 1879, near Hartville, Ohio. His father, Elder John Kurtz, minister and for many years bishop of the East Nimishillen Church, Stark Co., Ohio, was born in 1831 near Reistville, Lebanon Co., Pa. His grandfather was Jacob Kurtz who migrated to Stark Co., Ohio, in 1854. His mother's name was Mary Bollinger, all of whose brothers were ministers in the Church of the Brethren.

He was the youngest of twelve children and was reared

on a farm where he spent most of his time till he was of age. He attended high school and taught three years in a rural school. He attended college at Ada, and Alliance, Ohio, and was graduated at Juniata College in the A.B. course in 1905. After attending Yale Divinity School, he received the M.A. and B.D. degrees together with the fellowship of his class, in 1908. This entitled him to a year's study in European universities. He spent over a year in the study of theology and philosophy at Leipzig, Berlin and Marburg universities.

September 7, 1909, he was married to Ethel L. Wheeler, of Conn. From this time he taught Greek in Juniata College till April 1, 1910, when he accepted the pastorate of the First Brethren Church of Philadelphia. About 100 members were added during the first three years.

He was baptized by his father May 5, 1899; elected to the ministry December 20, 1904; and advanced to the second degree in 1906 at Brooklyn, N. Y. During the summer of 1913 he took a trip to the Holy Land and to the World's Sunday School Convention at Zurich, Switzerland.

Ordained to the Eldership, May 20, 1914.

Resigned at Phila., Aug. 1, 1914 to accept Presidency of McPherson College, Kansas.

B. THE GEIGER MEMORIAL CHURCH.

For some time previous to the founding of this mission some of the workers of the First Church of Philadelphia felt the need of branching out in city mission work. God has always called to the strong churches to give of their wealth and workers for the further extension of the Kingdom. A committee, consisting of the Pastor T. T. Myers, S. S. Brownback and J. W. Cline, was appointed to investigate and report a suitable location for the mission. After a wide investigation this committee decided that the best opening available was in the neighborhood of Lehigh Ave. and 26th St.

The mission was started on November 29, 1896, in the parlor of the residence at 2610 W. Lehigh Ave. with forty-

GEIGER MEMORIAL CHURCH, PHILADELPHIA.

five scholars on the first Sunday and sixty on the following Sunday. Bro. J. W. Cline, who had been recently elected to the ministry, was chosen superintendent and Bro. S. S. Brownback was assistant. Those quarters were soon outgrown, and early in 1897, Bro. Brownback moved into the house on the southeast corner of Lehigh Ave. and 26th St., whose larger quarters served as the home of the mission for over a year. On November 27, 1898, the Geiger Memorial Chapel was dedicated. Dr. M. G. Brumbaugh preached the dedicatory sermon assisted by Brethren T. T. Myers, J. T. Myers and J. W. Cline, the pastor in charge. A commodious parsonage was also erected by its side. Here the mission church and Sunday School had its home until December 29, 1907, when the new commodious church edifice was dedicated. Dr. M. G. Brumbaugh again officiated, assisted by Brethren T. T. Myers, I. N. H. Beahm, C. A. Bame and J. T. Myers, the pastor in charge.

The affairs of the mission were under the immediate direction of the First Church until 1906. On October 19 of this year the little band of workers were organized into the Geiger Memorial Brethren Church, the service being conducted by Bishops S. R. Zug, A. L. Grater, T. T. Myers and J. T. Myers. Since that time the church has had a steady growth, numbering at the present time about 140 members. From the founding of the church to the present time it has had the following pastors:

J. W. Cline, from the beginning to September, 1900; C. O. Beery, November, 1900, to September, 1901; L. M. Keim, December, 1901, to May, 1905; J. T. Myers, September, 1905, to September, 1911; A. J. Culler, September, 1911 to 1914.

The Sunday School has had a continuous growth and success and has an exceptionally good attendance and influence when compared with the size of the church and the surrounding conditions. There are many churches in the immediate neighborhood and fully one-half the resident population is Catholic. It has grown from the small beginnings to an enrollment of 440 and an attendance during the season of about 275. It has maintained every form of

Sunday School activity, Teacher Training, Teacher's Meetings, Cradle Roll, Home Department, Organized Adult Bible Classes, Circulating Library, Socials, Mid-week entertainments, Lectures, various forms of Athletics, and such other activities as the live institutional church finds helpful in winning and holding the young people of the city. Bro. S. S. Brownback has been superintendent ever since the beginning and Bro. E. T. Savidge has for many years been assistant. Great credit is due those who have so well taken charge of the Primary Department which has always been quite large. Sister Thomas had it in charge during the first years followed by Sister Croft, who later with her husband founded the Bethany Mission, then by Sisters Emily Kingdom, Mrs. J. T. Myers and Mrs. A. J. Culler. During many of these years Sister Jessie Rae was assistant superintendent of the Primary Department, always being a most faithful helper. At the present time Sisters Kingdom and McCarty have charge of the department. The present pastor had the pleasure of baptizing some who started as infants in the Sunday School at the beginning, some of whom are now teachers and officers in the same school.

From the early days the Christian Workers' Meeting has flourished. There has also at times been a Junior Christian Workers' Meeting and at other times a Temperance Society for the children.

The Try-Circle (name of the Sisters' Aid Society) was organized about a year ago and has flourished remarkably well, doing much work for the needy, selling garments, and helping the church and Sunday School in many ways.

The Pastors.

The first pastor and one of the organizers of the work was Joseph W. Cline. He was born in the Shenandoah Valley, Va., in 1866, and received his education at Bridgewater College and the Temple University of Philadelphia. He also spent some time in Europe. He was the first superintendent and pastor, and remained with the work for three years. He purchased the ground and directed the erection

THE PHILADELPHIA CHURCHES. 139

of the chapel and parsonage. In September, 1900, he was married to Miss Dora Emma Kuns, of Illinois, after which they moved to California, where they have since resided. During that time he was pastor of the East Los Angeles Church (three years) and of the Pomona Church for one year. He has since then been in business and active in the district and state Sunday School work. He was elected to the ministry and advanced to the second degree in Philadelphia and ordained to the eldership in California. Bro. and Sister Cline have been blessed with two sons and one daughter.

Bro. Chas. O. Beery was the second pastor remaining for one year. He received his early educational training at Mt. Morris College and later in Juniata College. He also took a further course in the Juniata Bible School. He was married to Miss Ella Replogle, of Iowa, in 1898 and came to Philadelphia in 1900. From the work here he was called to the Plum Creek Church, near Elderton, Pa., where he was pastor for four and one-half years. During the past eight years he has been pastor of the Tyrone Church. He writes that he still believes in the Old Book and Its Salvation.

Lewis M. Keim, the third pastor of the church, was born near Harmonyville, Pa., August 2, 1873. His parents were members of the church at that place and all the six children were baptized at an early age, Lewis coming in at fifteen years of age. He was soon a Sunday School worker. He attended Brethren's Normal College at Huntingdon and graduated from its English course in 1894. In July, 1893, he was elected to the ministry in the Coventry Church, after which he spent three years teaching school and preaching in the home congregation with occasional visits to adjoining congregations.

In order to prepare more fully for the ministry he went to Juniata College in the fall of 1897 and was graduated in the class of 1901 with the degree of B.A. In November of the same year he became pastor of the mission. Soon after beginning this work he was married to Miss Mary Myers, of Shirleysburg, Pa.

During his pastorate of nearly four years about forty

applicants were baptized, the morning preaching service was established and plans for the organization of the mission into a church were discussed. After his pastorate here he accepted a call to the pastorate of the Plum Creek and Glade Run churches, where he remained three years. He is now Instructor in Ancient History in the Southern High School of Philadelphia.

Elder J. T. Myers, the fourth pastor of the Geiger Memorial Church, served in that capacity from September, 1905, to September, 1911. He was born in Somerset Co., Pa., in the Brothers Valley Church, September, 1851, and was baptized in February, 1867, in the Middle Creek Church, to which his parents had moved. He was elected to the ministry in 1871. The following year he came to Philadelphia and received a call to become pastor of the Germantown Church. He accepted the call and remained as their pastor until 1877. During this time he studied under a Jewish Rabbi and attended the Lutheran Theological Seminary at Mount Airy. During 1875-6 he had charge of the "Brüderbote" or the "Brethren's Messenger." During the latter year, at the request of Brethren J. H. Moore and M M. Eshelman, he helped to start the publishing of the "Brethren at Work," he furnishing the printing out of both English and German type. He continued with the firm for one year, at the end of which time he sold out his interests to the other members of the company.

In 1877 he was married to Belle Quinter, eldest daughter of Elder James Quinter, and having had a previous call to the Green Tree Church, they immediately moved into the Green Tree Church, where they served in His cause for twenty-eight years. He was ordained to the eldership in 1905. In the fall of 1905 he received a call to this church, where he labored for six years. During his pastorate the church was organized and the new church built. Elder Myers is at present living at his home near Phœnixville, his health not permitting him to engage too actively in ministerial work.[3]

[3] In 1913 he became pastor of the Parkerford church.

The present pastor, Arthur J. Culler, was born of Brethren parentage, March 14, 1883. He was baptized when 12 years of age and at sixteen was superintendent of the Mt. Pleasant Church Sunday School. He graduated from the Louisville, Ohio, High School, and after teaching school for one year, he took a full business course. In the fall of 1903 he became a clerk in the editorial office of the *Gospel Messenger,* where he remained for one year. In 1904 he entered Juniata College, from which he graduated in 1908. In 1906 he was elected to the ministry and in 1907 advanced to the second degree. During the summer of 1907 he was supply pastor of the Altoona Church and during the summer of 1908 he served the Plum Creek and Glade Run churches. During the winter of 1907-8 he was student pastor of the Everett Church. During his college work he visited scores of churches in the interest of the Volunteer Mission Band of the college.

In the fall of 1908 he came to Crozer Seminary and the University of Pennsylvania, during which year he assisted in the work at the Geiger Memorial and preached at the Bethany Mission, baptizing twenty-three applicants at the latter place. The following summer he was supply pastor in the absence of Bro. Myers. He then entered Union Theological Seminary and Columbia University in New York City, remaining there for two years. The summer of 1910 was spent in study and travel in continental Europe. He received the degree of Bachelor of Divinity in the spring of 1911 and accepted a call to the pastorate of the Geiger Memorial Church for the fall of that year. In September, 1911, he was married to Miss Mary Stover, of Warriorsmark, Pa., since which time they have been engaged in the ministerial work of the church. In 1912 he was awarded the degree of Doctor of Philosophy by Columbia University for his work in the Department of Psychology and Religious Education.

Sister Mary S. Geiger.

Widely known and loved throughout the Brotherhood for her devotion and zeal in the Master's cause, and for her interest in all the good movements of the church, Sister Geiger is more closely associated with the success of the Geiger Memorial Church than any one else. More than any pastor her consecration and faith has made the work possible. She still takes a live interest in all its affairs even though at the advanced age of 85 years. She was born February 25, 1828, and was confirmed in the Lutheran Church when fourteen years of age. During her early years she came in contact with the Brethren at Harleysville and was impressed with their teachings. She was married to Dr. Henry Geiger in 1848, moved to Philadelphia in 1852 and was baptized in the Delaware River the same year. Dr. Geiger was elected to the ministry together with David Harley in 1853 and took a great interest in the Sunday School and the work of the young people. During the trying years of the breaking up of the Marshall St. Church and the reorganization of the new Philadelphia Church their support in zeal and gifts went far to make possible the founding of the new church. Dr. Henry Geiger died in 1885, leaving a widow, son and daughter. Since that time she has been found in all good works and it was her thought to found a mission and later a church in his memory. She first supported the mission, later she furnished all the funds for the erection of the chapel and parsonage, and later still for the present commodious church building. She has always borne a large share of the necessarily heavy expense connected with a city church, an expense too heavy to be borne by the mission in these earlier days. The work is very close to her heart and we pray that much good may be accomplished in His cause in this part of His vineyard.

A. J. CULLER.

C. THE FOUNDING AND DEVELOPMENT OF BETHANY MISSION.

Kensington is Philadelphia's manufacturing center. Mills and factories, in this section of the City, are multitudinous and the products are of great variety. There are carpet

HOME OF BETHANY MISSION.

mills, woolen mills, cotton mills, hosiery mills, and other establishments that work in wood and metal. Consequently the residents, for the most part, belong to the laboring class. Again, as Philadelphia has been characterized as the City of Homes, Kensington may be described as that part of the City in which the homes have children in them. A high percentage of the families are young and the children are at an age when they are most susceptible to moral and religious influence. The forms of vice which thrive in every city are equally thrifty in Kensington. Drunkenness probably stands first, followed closely by gambling, sexual immorality and kindred evils. In a sentence, this is the home of great industries, of working people, of numbers of children, and many forms of sin and vice.

It is in the heart of this section that Bethany Mission, of the Church of the Brethren, is located. From the standpoint of the need of the field and the opportunity of touching the youth of the streets, and the masses of laboring people, the location could not have been better selected. The history of the Mission is necessarily biographical because two individuals are responsible for its incipiency and almost wholly responsible for its support. The two persons to whom Bethany Mission owes its existence are Samuel B. Croft and his wife, Julia Croft.

Samuel Croft was born near Covington, Ohio, on June 10, 1857. He was a son of David and Catherine Croft, the latter being a member of the Church of the Brethren.

Julia Croft is a daughter of Larkin and Catherine Younce, both members of the Church of the Brethren, and was born near West Milton, Ohio, on August 29, 1863.

Brother and Sister Croft were married on September 9, 1882, and one year later came to Philadelphia where they have since made their home. On February 27, 1887, they were baptized at the old Marshall Street Brethren Church which now stands at Carlisle and Dauphin Streets and is known as the First Brethren Church of Philadelphia. They were active at the First Church for a number of years and it was here that Brother Croft was called to the office of deacon.

After the building of the Geiger Memorial Church, at the request of the Pastor and others who were interested in the work there, Sister Croft devoted her time to that work for six years, at the end of which time they began work in Kensington.

Brother and Sister Croft had a strong missionary spirit from the beginning of their Christian life and at one time had almost decided to offer themselves to the Mission Board for the foreign field. They always contended that the Brethren as a people were too slow in taking hold of new territory and especially did they believe this to be true of the Philadelphia churches. With the exception of a few individuals, the missionary zeal of our people at that time was exceedingly low.

In the face of discouragements and protests against leaving the other Church, Brother and Sister Croft began to look out a location for a Mission. In doing this, several things were kept in mind. In the first place they looked for a neighborhood that was without a church and in need of religious influence. Furthermore, they desired to locate in territory that was untouched by any other Brethren Church. These two principles have been a great factor in the rapid growth of the Mission. It was thus that their missionary zeal and the crying need of the field conspired together in starting the work in this part of the City.

After some difficulty, a house was rented at 3351 Kensington Avenue. This was a three-story dwelling house. The front room of the first floor had been used as a storeroom. There was a tobacco store on one side of the building and a club (speak-easy) on the other. Both were open seven days in the week and afforded an immediate problem.

At this time the financial problem was perplexing, but Brother Croft had passed through a valuable apprenticeship as bookkeeper in different firms of the City and was now in business as a small manufacturer. He assumed all the financial burden of the work and Sister Croft took on herself the responsibility of pastoral duties. She canvassed the entire neighborhood the very first thing, going from door to door in search of children who were not in Sunday-school. At the same time she distributed the following announcement:

BETHANY MISSION
of the
BRETHREN CHURCH
3351 Kensington Avenue
SUNDAY–SCHOOL 2:30 P. M.
OPENS SUNDAY, June 12, 1904.
A cordial invitation to all.

At the stated time, sixty-seven scholars met in the old store room for the first Sunday-school session. The only minister present was Elder Walter S. Long. His wife was also there. The main audience was made up of boys and girls, many of whom had never been under religious influence either at home or church. Thus the work was launched.

The purpose that Brother and Sister Croft had in view in starting the Mission was to gather the boys and girls from the streets into the Sunday-school and give them plain Bible instructions, and at the same time exert over them the strongest Christian influence. Thus it was hoped to reach, indirectly, the parents at home, for it was evident that they would have to be touched by indirect methods. It is hard to convince a man who loves his beer better than religion that he ought to attend religious service even once during the week. But the desired result came. Sister Croft gained entrance into the homes where, in many cases, the moral, religious and domestic conditions were appallingly abnormal. She plead for a better life, more wholesome home conditions, and for a family religion. She visited the sick, conducted funerals, counciled the perplexed, and told the Christ-story to the sinful. In brief, she superintended the entire work. Brother Croft devoted most of his time to business in order to support the Mission financially. They both spent a great deal of time planning their work in order to do the most in the shortest time, do it efficiently and at the least possible expense.

The children of the neighborhood became greatly attached to the Mission and no less to Brother and Sister Croft, and they flocked together every Sunday to learn God's word and absorb, unconsciously, the Christian influence of the Mission. In a short time, seven rooms of the house were filled with classes and household furniture had to be sold in order to provide room for the school.

Besides the Sunday-school, other branches of work were soon started. The mid-week Prayer Meeting was started for the older boys and girls. A Mother's Meeting was also organized. Thus the influence of the Mission began to touch the homes directly.

It was discovered that many mothers were anxious to attend religious service but could not on account of home duties. This called the Home Department into existence. The home visitation in this work revealed the fact that the mothers were kept from church on account of having to care for small children; hence the Cradle Roll was organized. These two departments have been constant feeding agencies of the main Sunday-school.

One of the greatest problems was that of drink. Beer and other drinks of similar nature were used freely in the homes. It was clear that the first task was to save the children and young people from this awful curse. To do this the Loyal Temperance Legion was organized in 1905. During the lifetime of the Legion 205 boys and girls have taken the pledge against the use of drink, tobacco and profanity. The influence of this little society has been exceedingly wholesome. A number of our young men who have never joined the Church are free from the habit of drink and tobacco.

Up to this time there had been no regular preaching service. The "good seed" had been sown quietly and left to do its work under the influence of the Spirit. On October 6, 1906, the first regular preaching service was held. Charles C. Ellis, now a professor at Juniata College, conducted the first service. He continued to help in the work for several successive weeks and occasionally he preached during his stay at the University of Pennsylvania. Preachers were secured week by week as they could be found. An effort was made to secure consecrated and spiritual men who loved children and young people. For four years ministers were supplied in this way. During this time C. C. Ellis, of the Church of the Brethren, G. B. M. Clouser, of the Baptist Church, and C. D. Rischel, of the Church of God, were the principal preachers, but in all, about forty different men were engaged.

In 1907, three years after the work had been started, twenty-five had been baptized into the Church. The Home Department numbered fifty and the Cradle Roll twenty-five, while the Sunday-school enrollment had reached two hundred with an average attendance of ninety-five. The school needed more room. Every available corner of the old building had been utilized. The neighborhood was not much built up and afforded no larger building than the one in which the school was then housed. Appeals for help to our own people were futile. But the Crofts had been looking ahead. They expected God to bless their work with results. One by one they had purchased three lots side by side at the corner of Willard Street and Kensington Avenue. This gave them a plot of ground 57 by 103 ft. But the hope of a new building seemed Utopian. They did not have the means. Their business was small and profits meager and uncertain. The little congregation made it a matter of much prayer. Finally a business man of some means, acquainted with Brother and Sister Croft, learned of their hopes and anxieties with reference to the work and agreed to loan money for the erection of a new building. This was interpreted as an answer to prayer.

After much careful and economical planning, the contract was let for an $11,000 building. The corner stone was laid on November 17, 1907. Elder J. T. Myers presided, Charles A. Bame and Martin G. Brumbaugh delivered the main addresses. G. B. M. Clouser, President of the Philadelphia Bible College, and M. C. Swigart, of the Germantown Church, were present and took part in the service. The building was pushed rapidly but cautiously in regard to expense. It was planned with reference to the peculiar needs of the work and is entirely removed from ordinary church architecture both inside and out. It is a plain substantial brick building 38 by 76 ft. The main floor has four rooms: The Auditorium, seating about 200 people; the primary and Prayer-meeting room, and two class rooms in which Brother and Sister Croft have lived in order to reduce their expenses. The basement is ten feet deep and has a heater room, two dressing rooms and a large room securely cemented and equipped with swings, sliding-boards, see-saws, etc., where the children are allowed to play and are thus kept off the streets. Special attention was given to the arrangement and location of windows with reference to light and ventilation. The floors are of hard wood and stained; only the aisles are carpeted. These precautions were taken in order that the building might be cheerful and sanitary. In order to reduce the extreme heat of summer, three large electric fans have been installed which add greatly to the comfort of the building and tend to maintain the attendance of church and Sunday-school. In the basement, however, the heaters are run summer and winter in order to make it comfortable for the classes which meet there.

On February 20, 1908, the school moved into the new building. With more room, it began to grow rapidly and with this increase came new and difficult problems. Teachers were needed, efficient officers were hard to get, and a Pastor seemed almost imperative, but the congregation was poor and could not begin to carry the added expense of a Pastor. But in spite of these things the work grew. It grew marvelously. At the close of the fiscal year of 1910 the average attendance of the Sunday-school had reached 186; there had been 80 baptisms, and the average attendance of the Junior and Loyal Temperance Legion Society was about 75. The other departments had grown proportionally.

At this point we must turn aside to account for the rapid growth of the Mission. The thing to be emphasized first is hard work. Brother and Sister Croft are persistent workers. Bethany Mission is their only child and they have given her their undivided attention. Sister Croft has been a real mother to the children of the Mission, a light in numbers of homes, and a power for righteousness in the community. Few can realize the stress under which she has labored. In ill health and against the advice of physicians, she stood by the work and never once slacked in her efforts. Brother Croft has worked for the Mission as few men work for their families. He and Mrs. Croft donated the ground on which the building was erected, borrowed the money which went into the new building, paid the interest, the coal, water, electric and gas bills, and have been responsible for the janitor work. They have not spared themselves, either in work or expenditure, to make Bethany Mission a comfortable place of worship. Back of this labor and sacrifice there has been an ardent love for souls which has made the work joyful and sweet.

The method of work has been a very potent factor in the growth of the Mission. The most effective work has been done in the homes and by house to house visitation. Special effort has been made to keep in close touch with every scholar. Books are kept with the accuracy of any business firm and definite and concise reports given annually. The support of the work is by free will contributions. The spirituality of the membership is not imperiled and the sense of the obligation to support the Master's work willingly and cheerfully is not stifled by church festivals, bazaars and similar functions. The keynote of the work has been evangelism. Rarely has a sermon been preached along with which an invitation has not been given to the unsaved to accept Christ.

Finally, Bethany Mission has met a real community need. This is indispensable to the growth of any institution. Numbers of people in the community did not attend public worship anywhere because they were "just ordinary working people," as they put it, and had a feeling that the larger churches were too cold and formal for them. Bethany Mission, with its free, home-like atmosphere, has always endeavored to provide a congenial place of worship for all classes. It has attempted to be not only the working man's Church but every man's Church.

Previous to the location of the Mission here there was no agency in the immediate neighborhood to comfort and counsel homes in times of distress, and domestic irregularlty. There was no voice that cried out in the wilderness of sin against the saloon, the lewd show, gambling parlors and dens of vice. But the Mission workers have opposed these things in no uncertain sound. It has proven its right to the confidence and support of the community by supplying a vital religious need. These three factors explain, in the main, the rapid growth and development of the work of the Brethren in this section of the City.

Now let us turn to the further developments of the Mission. It was during the summer of 1910 that the membership decided to call a Pastor. The writer of this article was chosen and took up the work in September, 1910, the Church granting the privilege of attending school at Crozer Theological Seminary, and at the University of Pennsylvania. In December of the same year we were organized into a regular congregation. Elders A. L. Grater, J. T. Myers, and J. B. Shisler, conducted the organization which resulted in J. T. Myers being chosen as our Elder and S. B. Croft, Robert G. Jones, and Harvey D. Morton, as deacons. Owing to the inability of the Church to assume the debt on the building, the election of Trustees did not occur until July 1912, at which time the building was transferred to the Church subject to a mortgage of about $8,000. The Trustees, as elected, were William E. Gotwals, President; S. B. Croft, Secretary and Treasurer; Julia Croft, William Angeny and Alexander Dunn.

The present status of the Mission may be gleaned from the 1913 report. The Sunday-school, with Sister Croft as Superintendent, has an enrollment of 481, with an average attendance of 261. The school is divided into three sections and has a total of 30 classes including the primary department which is under the supervision of Sister Myra George. The Home Department is under the direction of Sister Lillian Young and has a membership of 90. Sister Jennie Healey is superintending the Cradle Roll and has 72 infants under her care. The Young People's Prayer-meeting is definitely organized with Brother Herbert Taylor as President. There are about 40 on the roll and they have contributed $50 annually to the Building fund for the last two years besides other benevolences. The Sisters' Aid Society has been doing splendid work under the leadership of Sister Sallie B. Schnell of the First Church. They have just presented to the building fund a check for $100 and have contributed $26.00 to the general funds during the year, besides a contribution to foreign missions. The Junior and Loyal Temperance Legion has maintained an average attendance of 64 for the year and is doing a splendid work for the children of the neighborhood. Our Teacher-Training Class has ten prospective graduates for this coming October (1913). The mid-week Prayer Meeting, and two separate organizations for young men and young women, constitute the remaining activities of our work. The sum total of baptisms since the work started is 187.

The paramount need of the work at this time is a larger building. The Sunday-school attendance has exceeded three hundred several times during the past year and the Church at these times is taxed to its utmost capacity. All space has been utilized from basement to pulpit. There are hundreds of children in the community who ought to be in Sunday-school but the Brethren cannot hope to do much for them without a church large enough to accommodate them. The congregation here is poor but liberal with their meager earnings towards the Lord's work. Last year the contributions to the Building Fund amounted to about $1,100 and the running expenses for the year were about $1,600. The Trustees are beginning a campaign to raise $30,000 to enlarge the building. This is a big undertaking for a congregation so poor and small, but something must be done to save these neglected souls, and we feel that there are those in the Brotherhood sufficiently interested in the Kingdom of Christ to help in this great work.

Bethany Mission will stand as a life-long monument to the devotion and self-sacrifice of Brother and Sister Croft, and scores of men and women will point to this plain little Church as a saving factor in their lives.

I think I could not close this sketch better than to quote from a letter written to me by G. B. M. Clouser, of the Baptist denomination, who did a large part of the preaching during the first years of the Mission.

"PEMBERTON, N. J.
"June 18, 1913.

"*Dear Mr. Bowman,—*

"... It was my privilege to be associated with Mr. and Mrs. Croft from the inception of the work in Kensington, and to watch its growth with keen interest under their patient persevering efforts. ... The audience that I preached to gave me the impression that it was a semi-barbarous community, with moral standards very low, home training and restraint conspicuously absent, parents and children utterly destitute of religious instruction, while the saloon was doing its deadly work—dragging down the home and the tone of the locality, degrading and damning the souls of fathers and brothers.

"The planting of the mission seemed to work a mighty change among the people, and a change in every important sense,—physically, morally, and spiritually. A new light was seen, and a new life imparted to lives of little promise, but time has proved them to be of sterling worth. I have never in all my ministry witnessed such a change wrought in a similar community in so short a time and one of such permanent character. This is to be attributed to the policy of the Mission, and the nature of the ministry fulfilled in the homes of the people by Mrs. Croft. ... The Mission was planted at the psychological moment; it met a great need in the community and remains as a monument to the consecration of two souls who had a vision of service, and followed it.

"Yours Very Sincerely,
"G. B. M. CLOUSER."

PAUL H. BOWMAN.

UPPER DUBLIN CHURCH, AMBLER, PA.

CHAPTER III.

UPPER DUBLIN CHURCH.

The history of the Upper Dublin Church begins with 1840. In this year Bro. John Reiff gave land for a church and free burial ground; and he was likely the chief mover in having the house erected. He was the father of Sisters Anna M. Brunner and Amanda R. Kratz. The deed is dated September 14, 1840. The lot contained ninety-five perches of land. It was deeded to the following trustees: Wm. Jones, John W. Price, John Sperry, Henry Sperry, John H. Umstad, George Price, Joseph Pennypacker and Wm. Price. It was designated that the lot shall be and forever remain a free burying ground.

The meeting house itself was erected in 1840. It is a substantial stone structure, in size about 27×36 ft. (See illustration.)

Upper Dublin is recognized as an offspring of the Germantown Church, is her youngest child. John W. Price, of Fitzwatertown, is regarded as the first minister in charge although the oversight seemed vested in him, John Umstad and Jacob Reiner conjointly, though this must have been subsequent to 1840, for at that date Jacob Reiner was not yet a preacher, and he would not be given immediate oversight after his election. In other words Germantown, Green Tree (then hardly recognized as a separate congregation yet) and Indian Creek were interested in the formation of the new congregation.

John U. Slingluff was about the only preacher who was called from rank and file of the membership to proclaim the Gospel. He represented the church in the District Meetings of 1867, 1868, 1870, 1871, 1872, 1873 and 1875. He later moved to Kansas.

An attempt was made October 28, 1893, to elect a minister from the membership; but the effort resulted in no choice.

Edwin Kirk who frequently represented the church at District Meeting, from 1870 to 1875, preached for the members at Upper Dublin. In 1876 the delegates from Upper Dublin were "rejected on account of being members of a secret society." From this time the name of Edwin Kirk is not found in the minutes. The minutes of the congregation in 1875 state that there was trouble with secret societies.

It was a common thing in the early days for members from adjoining congregations to go to Upper Dublin to worship. It seems this custom was more general then than now, likely because each local congregation now has services every Sunday. In the diary of Abel Fitzwater of Lumberville, near Phœnixville we find this entry, "May 11 (1845) G. D. Price and John Francis preached at Upper Dublin." John Francis, who lived at Shannonville, had at this time regular appointments at Upper Dublin.

The following have been deacons in the Upper Dublin Church:
1. William Jones, born July 7, 1802; died March 18, 1862.
2. Henry Sperry, born January 8, 1791; died July 5, 1859.
3. Henry Slingluff, born January 1, 1799; died February 11, 1881.
4. John D. Gamble, died December 7, 1888; aged 65 years.
5. George Allen, died December 31, 1891, in 84th year. He succeeded Gamble.

William Slingluff was an active deacon. We find him occupying the chair in the council of August 29, 1885.

Casper Slingluff and Howard Ellis were elected deacons August 28, 1886. J. Z. Gottwals was the elder present.

Richard Rayman and John S. Schreiber elected deacons January 25, 1902.

In the minutes of 1902 we read: "Bro. William H. Slingluff one of our Deacons who was always at his place and gave his attention to all matters of interest to the church was called to his home beyond on the eighth of February 1902."

At the beginning we have seen who were the original trustees. February 28, 1885, we find that John D. Jones was elected a trustee in place of Charles Smith resigned.

George D. Price, the one surviving trustee, conveyed the property to George Allen, Charles Smith and Wm. H. Slingluff on August 26, 1879. On the death of George Allen, Henry J. Walton was elected trustee, August 27, 1892.

Friend Henry G. Slingluff was elected a trustee, August 30, 1902. John S. Schreiber was elected to the same office, August 22, 1903.

The first secretary of the church on record at Upper Dublin was J. Howard Ellis, who was elected February 27, 1875. He was a school teacher. February 28, 1885, he resigned and Henry J. Walton was elected in his place. August 27, 1898, Helen Schreiber was elected secretary. She filled the office till August 12, 1908, when Sister Amanda R. Kratz was elected.

We find that J. Howard Ellis was treasurer up to February 23, 1901, when Bro. John S. Schreiber was called to fill the position. Who cared for the funds before Bro. Ellis we have not learned.

The Oversight of the Church.

We have seen that in the early days of the Upper Dublin Congregation she was looked after by Brethren John Price, John Umstad and Jacob Reiner. John U. Slingluff was a resident preacher here until about 1875, when he moved west. Whether or not he had the oversight we cannot at this writing state, but he likely had the principal care of the congregation.

In 1885 Israel Poulson from Amwell, N. J., was received as a minister in the second degree. He had been previously elder in charge of the Amwell congregation. We find him in the chair at Upper Dublin, in the council of February 28, 1885, or some months before his certificate was received, which was on August 29 of the same year. He was recognized rather as the pastor.

Elder Jacob Z. Gottwals was in charge in 1886, and continued to moderate the councils till March 10, 1888. About this time the Upper Dublin Church seems to have turned to the District Meeting to look after her affairs. For in

1889 Jacob Connor, a member of the District Mission Board, was appointed to see to the welfare of Upper Dublin. In the District Meeting Minutes of this year we have the following:

"Brother Jacob Conner reports that he, Brother J. T. Myers and others, visited the Upper Dublin Church and gave them meetings every two week during the year, or nearly so, and find that the great need of the Church there in connection with Germantown, should be supplied with a resident minister, and until that is done, the work there is not likely to prosper."—D. M. Minutes, p. 85.

In the next year's minutes, (1890) we find "Brother Jacob Connor reports that he visited the Upper Dublin church in their semi-annual council and preached for them occasionally. As Brother Connor will not further be charged with the care of the Church, he asks that their wants be considered without delay." —D. M. Minutes, p. 92.

The minutes of District Meeting continue to tell the story. We read of 1891:

"Brother George Bucher was charged to provide during the year that the Upper Dublin Church be supplied with ministerial service. Several appointments failed to be supplied by ministers appointed on account of sickness and rain. At one appointment the minister was present, but there were only two hearers. He reports that this church has warm hearted members who apparently pray for the welfare of Zion, but they are in need of proper and careful instruction by the proper parties on such subjects as the non-conformed principles of the Gospel, and the church visit which latter they seem to have lost sight of."—D. M. Minutes, p. 95.

It would be in place to state here that Bro. Connor, during the two years he had charge, got Bro. E. A. Orr of Philadelphia to come up to Upper Dublin every two weeks to preach, and that he also had had Bro. J. B. Brumbaugh of Huntingdon who was attending Crozier Theological Seminary at Chester, to supply the pulpit for a time. At the council of February 13, 1889, during Bro. Connor's oversight, a committee was appointed to see how much could be raised to support a resident preacher. These were about the first practical steps at Upper Dublin toward a regular pastorate.

We find in one of the councils held by Bro. Bucher that he had taken Elder Frank Cassel of Hatfield along, and also had Bro. Connor "present for friendly counsel."

The District Meeting Minutes fail to tell us anything about the work at Upper Dublin for the next year; but in 1893 we have:

"Elder H. E. Light was placed in charge of the Upper Dublin Church, and he, by the aid of F. P. Cassel, J. H. Price and others held meetings every Sunday until December, after that they had preaching every two weeks. Three council meetings were held, also one love-feast. The meetings of late have been increasing and some more interest manifested than formerly. Since Dec. 4th they paid all the expenses of all the ministers. They have dispensed with the basket collection and the benediction. Two of the members have died during the year."—District Meeting Minutes, p. 108.

February 15, 1893, the congregation decided to make an appeal to the Mission Board for help to support a minister. This appeal was likely to the District Mission Board.

There was something doing at Upper Dublin during the year of 1893-94. For the minutes of 1894 give us a new name in the representation from Upper Dublin—B. F. Kittinger. The minutes of this year have the following report:

"Upper Dublin was placed in charge of H. E. Light, and he, by the aid of F. P. Cassel, J. H. Price, and others, held meetings every two weeks during the year. Three council meetings were held. The pastoral visit was made by H. E. Light.

"At the love feast an election was held for a minister which resulted in a failure. The meetings were somewhat better attended than the year before. Upper Dublin paid all the expenses of the regular appointments, quite recently, through the Home Mission Board, or influence of a part of it. Brother Kittinger, of Marsh Creek Church, Southern Pennsylvania, moved to Upper Dublin. He is a minister in the second degree and was duly installed, and received in his office by the Church in the presence of Elder H. E. Light."—D. M. Minutes, p. 116.

In the light of the foregoing facts it is quite evident that to the administration of Elder H. E. Light is due the credit of putting the Upper Dublin Church on her feet, which fact is further emphasized by developments of the following year.

"Upper Dublin Church was continued under the charge of H. E Light, Brother B. F. Kittinger being the resident minister; meetings were held every Sunday. Of late also a Sunday School was organized. The meetings are still increasing in numbers. Two councils and two lovefeasts were held during the year. Also one protracted meeting. Two were added to the church by baptism. The prospects for reviving the church is encouraging, and by proper and judicious training this church might again be revived to its former strength and spirituality." —D. M. Minutes, p. 121.

From 1895 to 1900 we find Elder S. R. Zug in the chair. The church had made an appeal to the General Mission Board of which Brother Zug was a member. It must have been a special satisfaction to him to look after the interests of this congregation for in the Upper Dublin Church he preached his first English sermon. This was November 25, 1867. It gives satisfaction to the writer to read in the minutes of the congregation during this time, August 27, 1898, " J. G. Francis read scripture." His paternal grandfather had preached in this house more than fifty years in a way that had caused some to marvel, and had not caused him to find favor in the eyes of some; and his maternal grandfather had had the oversight of this congregation for a number of years, during the trying period when it was falling from its early strength to the time it began to look for a modern pastorate. Upper Dublin has a peculiarly warm place in the heart of the writer of these lines.

In 1900 we find Elder Jesse Ziegler in the chair, and in 1901 Elder A. L. Grater. January 25, 1902, the Annual Meeting Committee appointed Jesse Ziegler elder in charge and he continued until 1913, when he was succeeded by Elder M. C. Swigart, of Germantown.

The Pastorate.

Israel Poulson is called pastor in the minutes, but he was hardly what we would now designate a pastor. He came to Upper Dublin in 1881, and returned to New Jersey in 1885. Bro. Poulson seemed to do good work at Upper Dublin notwithstanding his reverses in New Jersey. He baptized eight persons during his sojourn.

The first pastor properly so-called was Bro. B. F. Kittinger. He was received by letter, April 15, 1894. While he was not an efficient organizer, he was a good singer and a good man, one beloved. He remained here a number of years, likely till 1906, when he moved to Germantown. He had an interesting family of children, some of whom joined the church here.

August 25, 1906, it was decided to call Bro. S. F. Myers as pastor at a salary of $300. He was retained year after year till 1911, when Bro. J. M. Booz, the present incumbent, was called. Bro. Myers still lives in the congregation. An Endowment Fund of $200 toward the support of the pastor was created March 28, 1909.

The Membership.

We have not learned the names of the original members at Upper Dublin. There are a few families who have been towers of strength—Slingluffs, the Ellises, and the Reiffs, including Sister Brunner and Sister Kratz. Sister Kratz's husband though not a member was very liberal toward the church, supplying a parsonage free for a number of years. Of late years Bro. John S. Schreiber and wife have been pillars. When we enter the city of the dead we find among others the following names—Smith, Reiff, Gamble, Slingluff, McCool, Jones, Sperry, Fry, Thomas, Spencer, Allen, Haycock, Collom, etc.

Up until 1875, one hundred and fifty persons had been members at Upper Dublin. From 1875 to 1900, twenty-eight were baptized and seven were received by letter, the largest ingathering being in the early part of 1880, when eleven were baptized by J. Z. Gottwals. Since 1900, twenty-three at least have been received by baptism and letter. Thus the total number of persons who have been within the fold at Upper Dublin are more than two hundred. Membership at present twenty-six.

Church Auxiliaries.

The date of the organization of the Sunday School at Upper Dublin has not been exactly ascertained, but there was a Sunday School here in the days of Poulson. Perhaps Harry Walton was superintendent at that time. Other superintendents since have been Bros. Roman, Kittinger, Schreiber, Myers and Booz. A Sunday School library was authorized, January 25, 1902. The present enrollment is seventy-five. In the Home Department there are about twenty, and about a dozen on the Cradle Roll. The second teacher training class has graduated. The class of last year numbered six. Sister Amanda Kratz is the teacher.

Prayer-meeting is now held every two weeks in the church on Wednesday evening. This is now the first time that a prayer-meeting has been authorized.

It was decided, February 25, 1911, to make an effort to organize a Sisters' Aid Society. Sister Anna Brunner was the instigator of the movement. The society was organized August 26, 1911, with the following officers: *President,* Sister Brunner; *Vice-President,* Sister W. H. Brooks; *Secretary,* Sister Shoemaker; *Assistant Secretary,* Mrs. Gamble; *Treasurer,* Sister Schreiber. There are twenty-six members in the Aid Society, but not all are members of the church.

A Missionary Committee was appointed August 31, 1912. An Auditing Committee was authorized in February, 1909.

The Report of the Annual Meeting Committee will likely be of interest. It was submitted a few years ago, perhaps in 1904.

" We, the Committee sent by Annual Meeting, submit to the Upper Dublin congregation the following Report:

" 1st. That all the members of the Official Board work in harmony with the decision of General Conference as to the order of dress and self-denial and to use every endeavor to mould sentiment in favor of Conference decision and non-conformity and to fully instruct applicants for membership in the above.

"2d. We further decide to appoint five or more brethren and sisters to supplement the work of the Official Board to work for the order privately and from house to house.

"Committee John S. Schreiber, Helen Scheiber, Anna M. Brunner, Richard Royan, Harvey Godshall.

"Signed: L. T. HOLSINGER,
P. S. MILLER,
D. HAYS."

Some important Resolutions were adopted at a Meeting of the Committee in Norristown, September 22, 1900. We give them at this place.

"(1) Resolved that lines to be established shall not disturb the present church relationship, in present families of respective churches, nor their children who wish to connect themselves with the church.

"(2) Recommended that the Stony Creek R. R. be the line between Mingo and Upper Dublin.

"(3) Recommended that the line between Upper Dublin and Germantown be the Philadelphia city limits.

"(4) It was moved, seconded and passed that we recommend that Norristown be organized into a separate congregation and to include the borough of Norristown.

"(5) Likewise that Royersford mission be organized into a separate congregation, limits Royersford and Spring City."

The Upper Dublin Church was presented, August 31, 1912, with a beautiful communion pitcher by Bro. and Sister Ellis and family of Norristown, in memory of their departed daughter, Anna Myrtle.

Some improvements have been made to the church property. There has been a general renovation of the church inside and out with the coming of new life. A porch has been built at the front door. Tables were procured for the backs of the benches for love-feasts, in 1894. A heater was authorized placed in the church, August 13, 1901.

There is considerable sentiment in favor of locating the

house of worship in the town of Ambler. The present house is a mile or more out in the country with scarcely any members living in the neighborhood. There was agitation in 1912 favorable to buying the Methodist Church in Ambler, but it was finally decided not to buy; but this does not mean that sentiment favorable to locating in town has in any measure diminished. With a church such as we have been considering, located in a favorable place in Ambler, with her present able, cultured young pastor, the Brethren of the Upper Dublin congregation have a bright outlook, and we expect them to achieve grand success for the Master in their allotted sphere.

Overseers of this Congregation:
1. John W. Price, 1840.
2. John H. Umstad.
3. Jacob Reiner.
4. John U. Slingluff.
5. Israel Poulson, 1881-1885.
6. Jacob Z. Gottwals, 1886-1888.
7. Jacob Connor, 1889-1891.
8. George Bucher, 1891-1893.
9. H. E. Light, 1893-1895.
10. S. R. Zug, 1895-1900.
11. Jesse Ziegler, 1900-1901.
12. A. L. Grater, 1901-1902.
13. Jesse Ziegler, 1902-1913.
14. M. C. Swigart, 1913-.

PART III.

THE CHURCH IN NEW JERSEY

INTRODUCTION.

The history of the Church of the Brethren in New Jersey begins with 1733. In the fall of this year John Naas with four other heads of families, viz., Anthony Dierdorf, Jacob More, Rudolph Harley, and John Peter Laushe, crossed the Delaware River into what is now Hunterdon County, and settled at Amwell, thirty-eight miles northeast of Philadelphia. The heartless bigotry of Christian Libe at Creyfelt, Germany, had for a time made John Naas inactive in the Gospel ministry; but Alexander Mack had gotten him into working trim again before going to Jersey. The missionary zeal which had characterized him in Germany again took hold of him at Amwell. Says Abraham Cassel: "During his life time this church was the spiritual birthplace of more Brethren than perhaps any other in the Union."

The growing work there demanded more preachers. We find John Bechleshammer a seasoned preacher already in 1738, or only five years after the Brethren went to Jersey. He likely was elected a year or two after that event. George Klein was baptized at Amwell in 1739. He was there elected as an assistant in the ministry, perhaps shortly after the death of John Naas, who died in 1741. Klein moved to Northkill in Berks Co., Pa., in 1750, to look after the little flock at that place. Likely shortly after this date Gideon Rouser was called to help in preaching, for Morgan Edwards informs us that Elder Bechleshammer had one Gideon Rouser for his assistant. In 1790 Edwards gives us to understand that up to that date no elder had been ordained in Jersey to take Bechleshammer's place. In 1790 the Amwell preachers, not elders, were William Housel and Abraham Laushe.

So up to 1790, so far as we can learn, the ministers in Jersey were: John Naas, born in 1669 or 1670; died May 12, 1741; elected to ministry at Creyfelt, Germany. John Bechleshammer, elected between 1733 and 1738. George Klein, born October 9, 1715; baptized in 1739; ordained at Northkill in 1757. Gideon Rouser.—. William Housel, born in Newwitt, Germany, 1728. Abraham Laushe, born at Creyfelt, Germany, in 1732.

There is in the " Chronicon Ephratense " a narrative of great interest in connection with the colonial life of the Jersey church. We give it herewith.

"In Dec., 1738, Beissel with many of the solitary made a considerable visit to the Baptists at Amwell, in Jersey. These people, from the time of their first awakening, had a great love for the work of the Lord in the Settlement; whereupon this visit opened the door for the breaking of bread together, which otherwise, because they were united with a congregation of Baptists in Germantown, would not have been looked upon with approval. When the Superintendent returned home, he called together a church council, and announced with what love they had been received in those regions by the children of God. At the same time, he announced how concerned he was for those poor people, and that they would have to be helped out with a Brother from Ephrata.

"These good people in Amwell specially availed themselves of this open Philadelphian church door, and made many a visit of more than a hundred Eng. miles to the Settlement, and built themselves up in the unity of the Spirit on the death of Jesus Christ. Thereby the Superintendent was induced to undertake another visit, on which he was accompanied only by Solitary Brethren. As many of the Baptists there stood in judgment against the work of God in the Settlement, some feared that the two parties might get into each other's wool, whereby the general edification might be hindered. Yea, some sought to bring the visitors to the then Baptist teacher, Bechtelsheimer (Bechleshammer) by name, in hope that then matters might occur over which they might gloat; but they were disappointed in this hope. The Superintendent, who bore in his heart the seal of the redemption of the whole world, started on his visit, and was received with all affection by the teacher referred to and his helpmate. They sat down with him and listened to him for more than an hour, during which there flowed from him in a flood all that the Spirit gave him. And as everybody thought the visitors might now be dismissed in peace, these good people first showed forth their particular love by treating them to a rich collation. . . . So likewise the whole organization helped the visitors across the water again at its own expense. This is mentioned here with the intent that, if any of these dear people should still be living and should read this, they may know that their faithfulness shown towards the work of God has been held in hallowed remembrance.

"Meantime some among them longed that there might be established among them a household, such as they had seen at the Settlement, for they had well-brought-up young people, and hoped that something useful might be accomplished among them. It would indeed have been easy to introduce the form among them, but to fill this effigy with the Spirit was not a human work. At that time there was among the Brethren at the Settlement one by the name of Elimelech, one of the Eckerlins, whom the stars had formed for a priest and redeemer of the bodily life, so that while other Brethren spent their time in hard labor, he sought his own pastures and imposed his priesthood upon people.

"Beissel ordained Elimelech to be teacher at Amwell, and publicly consecrated him with the laying on of hands. From this the latter thought he would be the successor of the former, as he was now his 'right hand.' On his departure Beissel wrote him a letter which contained the following admonition: 'Continue steadfast in prayer and with watchfulness of spirit for the flock of Christ, that thou mayest rightly divide the Word of Truth which hath been sown in you.'

"This letter he took with him to Amwell, where he showed it to everyone as his credentials which he had received from the Superintendent. His people indeed sought to sustain him in his office, but when they noticed it was an imitated affair and not inborn, they lost courage, so that when he wanted to institute midnight meetings, like those in the Settlement, and invited their daughters to the same, they feared that offenses might arise, and dismissed him; whereupon he returned to the Settlement again in disgrace. Thereupon several families in Amwell left, and removed to the Settlement, namely, Dietrich Fahnstick,

Conrad Boldhauser, John Mohr, Bernard Gitter, etc., which added several Solitary ones to the Sister's House, though none of them remained steadfast save one, Armella by name, who ended her course among them."—"Chronicon," pp. 122–125.

In 1790 the Brethren in Jersey were yet so German that Morgan Edwards had difficulty in conversing with them. He tells us a little about their manner of worship. The communion "was administered at no set time; but as often as a brother finds himself disposed to give the feast of charity, then the church is invited to meet at his house (for they have no meeting-house) and when feetwashing is over, and the right hand of fellowship and kiss of charity given, the Lord's Supper is administered, with the usual elements and singing of hymns." While there are things that Edwards evidently did not understand, yet from the above it can be gathered that the kiss between feetwashing and the communion is as old as 1790 at least.

The early Jersey church was very active in missionary work. Already in 1733, John Naas crossed over to Great Swamp, Upper Milford, in Bucks Co., Pa., preached to inquiring souls there, baptized six, thus laying the foundation for the church which was organized two years later, and which became a strong Colonial congregation. The interest taken by the Jersey Brethren in the work in Pennsylvania is shown by George Klein moving to Northkill, Berks Co., in 1750, to look after the flock there. Although Elder Michael Pfautz had administered the Lord's Supper to a few members in Northkill in 1748, yet George Klein is really the founder of the congregation. Klein went out from Northkill into the Little Swatara region, baptized a number, and organized the Little Swatara Church in 1757. So Northkill (now Maiden Creek) may be regarded as a child of Amwell; and Little Swatara as either her child or grandchild, whichever you please.

P. H. Beaver, of Montandon, Pa., in the "Almanac" of 1872, p. 16, says: "Our great-grandfather, Wendel Becker, now Baker, immigrated from Palz, Germany, in the year 1749, to America, and anterior to the Revolutionary War, removed to Buffalo Valley, from the church at Amwell, in

New Jersey. . . . He was, therefore, the first, and for a time, the only member of the Brethren in Buffalo Valley." So here is another child of Amwell. Time fails us to tell of more. There are indications that the Jersey church thinks that she has brought forth so many worthy children that she is now old enough to lie down and die.

CHAPTER I.

AMWELL CHURCH.

When Morgan Edwards visited the Brethren in New Jersey in 1790, there were twenty-eight families of members with a total baptized membership of forty-six. His "syllabus" of the church there, February 2, 1790, is as follows:

Churches of Tunkers in Jersey	1
Members	46
Families	28
Souls (allowing five to a family)	140
Ministers, ordained	0
Ministers, licentiate	2

The two unordained ministers of Amwell in 1790 were William Housel and Abraham Laushe, the latter being a son-in-law of Elder John Bechleshammer, the second and last elder of the church prior to 1790. Bro. Abraham Cassel states in a letter that both of these ministers were ordained: what his proof is I do not know.

In 1790 the German language was still spoken among the Brethren, or at least among the descendants of Bechleshammer, for they could neither speak nor understand English. A great change, however, in the matter of language took place in the next two decades. In 1811 Israel Poulson gave land for a meeting-house. It is likely that at this date already he was elder of the church, for he acted in that capacity for a long, long time. He was unable to speak German, and, being possessed of great influence, he likely swung the church into the use of the English language. By the time of his death, the German had vanished from among the Brethren of Jersey.

A secular historian of New Jersey states that a church house was supposed to have been built about a mile northeast of Headquarters, Delaware Township, as early as 1750.

AMWELL CHURCH, N. J.

OLD AMWELL CEMETERY, N. J.

This is likely a mistake, as Morgan Edwards states in 1790 that the Brethren in Jersey had no meeting-house, the meetings evidently being held in the private houses. By 1811 the Brethren had decided to build a meeting-house. In this year, May 27, as before stated, Israel Poulson, Sr., transferred to the trustees of the Brethren, Gideon Moore, Samuel Faus and Henry Laushe, a tract of land in Amwell township 21/40 of an acre, for the purpose of building thereon a meeting-house. So the first meeting-house of the Brethren in New Jersey, a frame one, was built in 1811, on the same ground on which the present house stands.

April 13, 1839, the church "agreed to take a lot of Gideon Moore for a burying-place." This lot, the present cemetery, is a short distance south of the church. The old, original burial place of the first Brethren in Jersey is at some distance from the present church. The Amwell Church, the present one also frame, was rebuilt in 1856, at a cost of $1,600. The church property in 1880 was valued at $3,500. June 16, 1893, a committee of nine was appointed to procure a parsonage for the Amwell Church. October 10 of the same year it was decided to build a parsonage, and the committee of nine was constituted a building committee. The parsonage in Sergeantsville was the result. J. R. Laushe, Isaac Haines, and Henry Van Dolah were elected trustees, October 31, 1893, who were forthwith instructed to take upon themselves a name of incorporation.

Up until 1849 there was but one congregation of Brethren in New Jersey—the Amwell Church. We have stated that Wm. Housel and Abraham Laushe were the ministers in 1790, and that Israel Poulson, Sr., likely was already before 1811. Bro. Abr. Cassel states that numerous of Abr. Laushe's descendants were in the ministry. In 1835 the Amwell Church began to keep a record of her church councils. We quote:

"At a meeting of the German Baptist Church which is in Amwell township, N. J., held on the 11th of August, 1835, at their meeting-house, for the purpose of transacting business relative to the peace and good order of said church, it was resolved that there be a record made and kept of all important business transacted relative to said church affairs.

"Israel Poulson, *Elder,*
Gideon Moore, } *Deacons,*
Jacob Waggoner, }
Abraham Laushe, *Clerk.*"

In the days of Israel Poulson it was the custom to call all ministers elders. If there were more ministers in the Amwell Church in 1835 than Israel Poulson, this church paper, an important one, does not show it. In 1790 a definite discrimination is made in the degrees of the ministry; when Israel Poulson died in 1856 no such discrimination existed. From this we may form an opinion of his housekeeping. It is thought that Henry Laushe was a minister before Israel Poulson: his son Isaac Laushe certainly was. The son Isaac was unsteady in his walk. He moved to Syracuse, Ohio, where he was killed in a sleigh by being struck by a railroad engine.

Then following, on October 10, 1835, Edmund Dalrymple was elected as an "additional elder." The duties of the office as stated by the minutes of the council of that date were "administering church ordinances, baptism, marriage ceremony, etc." Dalrymple was not much of a preacher, but a good man and eloquent in prayer. He died August 31, 1847. His death paved the way for division in the Amwell Church. John P. Moore had been elected a deacon in 1840 in place of his father, Gideon Moore, deceased. John was elected an "elder," April 13, 1844. When Dalrymple died in 1847, it was stated that an election would be held for some one to take his place. Israel Poulson, Jr., was elected "elder" April 8, 1848. Inasmuch as he was elected to take the place of Dalrymple his seat was above John P. Moore. This gives us another glimpse into the housekeeping of the older Poulson. Here lay the cause of the division which took place the next year.

But let us look for a moment at the other recorded events of note before 1849. We have seen the officials of the church in 1835: Israel Poulson, elder; Gideon Moore and Jacob Waggoner, deacons; and Abraham Laushe, clerk. It was resolved apparently at this same meeting "That Gideon Moore, Henry Laushe, and Asa Moore be the trustees." As we have seen, in 1839 it was agreed to take a lot of Gideon Moore for a "burying place"; and it was agreed at the fall council of the same year that Israel Poulson build a stone wall around it. Agreeable to the majority, Henry Laushe was appointed clerk, April 13, 1839. The election of John P. Moore to the deaconship and later to the ministry we have noted. April 11, 1845, Cyrus Van Dolah was appointed clerk. And April 8, 1848, comes the election of Israel Poulson, Jr., as an elder in place of Dalrymple, deceased. Then follows this minute:

"October 10, 1848. Our elder, John P. Moore, having brought confusion into the church and being a disorderly member and not willing to yield to the requirements of the church, they have thought proper to disown him as a member and to have no church fellowship with him." We need not pass judgment on this action, for we have the judgment of an Annual Meeting Committee more than thirty years later.

April 7, 1849, William Waggoner was elected an "elder" and Enoch Hoffman a deacon. Waggoner likely took the place of Moore, deposed. At the same council "there was a piece of writing brought before the church, and was read by Henry Laushe, containing the following:

"'We, the undersigned, as men and women that feel ourselves accountable before our Heavenly Father, after serious consideration in relation to matters and things concerning the Church in New Jersey to which we once belonged, feel that under the present state of things we cannot feel reconciled at this time, therefore we wish our names taken off until such times as reconciliation can be made. We conclude that you are aware of the reasons.

"'WILLIAM MOORE ASA MOORE
DANIEL MOORE SARAH BREWER
CATHARINE SHEARMAN CAZIAH COWDERICK
SILAS SHEARMAN MARTHA MOORE
ANNA MOORE ELIZABETH TRIMMER
MARY DALRYMPLE HESTER CARSON

CATHARINE DALRYMPLE   WILLIAM MOORE
MARTHA COWDERICK   CATHARINE MOORE
JACOB FAUSS   LUCY ANN SINE.'

"The church took the above in consideration, and granted them their request. As they brought no accusation against the church, the church, from the above writing, has disowned them, and (decides) to have no church fellowship with them."

We must now turn our attention for a time from the "Mooreites," until we have traced some of the subsequent history of the Amwell Church.

Israel Poulson, Sr., died February 14, 1856. The same year a committee was sent by the Annual Meeting to adjust difficulties in the New Jersey church. This committee consisted of Andrew Spanogle and Peter Long of Pennsylvania, and John Kline, J. Wine, and Martin Miller of Virginia. Elder Israel Poulson, Jr., refers to this committee of 1856 when the committee of 1881 investigated the trouble. The seceding members knew nothing of this committee, but it evidently had to do with this trouble. Who had this committee of 1856 come to New Jersey, and what the finding of the committee was, we have not been able to ascertain; but the committee came immediately after the death of the older Poulson. It is not likely that the committee came as a result of his dying request: more likely it came following action by some one who thought that now, as Israel Poulson, Sr., was dead, the seceders might get favorable treatment. The finding of this committee likely suited Poulson, Jr., for his reference to the findings of this committee seems to indicate this. He also refers to the matter having been before adjoining elders. The seceders knew of the trial before "adjoining elders," but claimed that they had not received just treatment. What this finding was we do not know, but it was likely agreeable to the younger Poulson. John Umstad was among those who looked into this trouble. This investigation grew out of a feeling on the part of some of the Amwell Church that the expelled members had not been justly treated. We await the judgment of the Annual Meeting Committee of 1881.

In the meantime the work of the Lord was moving on in Amwell. February 14, 1861, Robeson Hyde and John D. Hoppock were elected "elders"; and Cyrus Van Dolah, William Moore, Paul K. Huffman, and Asa Park were chosen deacons. There seems to have been a reorganization or a replenishing of the organization at this time.

There was quite an awakening in the Amwell Church in 1864. From July 11 to 31 of this year John H. Umstad, John Slingluff, and "E. H." (likely Emmanuel Heyser) held meetings here. As a result, thirty-two persons were baptized by Israel Poulson.[1]

Abram Laushe was chosen a deacon to fill the place of Asa Parks, deceased, September 8, 1866. Thomas W. Brewer was elected deacon, September 10, 1870; and Joseph Haines and Theodore Stevenson, April 15, 1873. These are the last minutes of importance we have of the Amwell Church before the notable reversal of conditions in Jersey in 1880.

We now turn our attention to that field of the Brethren in New Jersey afterward known as the Bethel Church.

The beginning of the work in this section was due to the labors of Israel Poulson, Sr. He had preached in the homes hereabouts before 1848. The fruits of these labors made a church here a possibility. The first house was built in 1848 or 1849. The land had been given by Amos Dilts. This first house was quite small, a frame house, built at a cost of only $300. Outsiders to stigmatize called it the Hemlock house, it being built partly of hemlock. The Brethren gave it no regular name. When the new edifice was put up in 1878 it was christened "Bethel."

The principal members here at first were Joseph Rudabock, Andrew Shepherd and wife, Annie Baker, Joseph Woodruff and wife, Samuel Case and Tunis Case. William Waggoner, elected to the ministry in 1849, lived in this section. Israel Poulson, Jr., became the main preacher here. John Umstad and Jacob Reiner held special meetings with considerable success. And this became for years the main church in the neighborhood.

[1] *Gospel Visitor* of 1864, p. 269.

Bethel seems to have become a separate organization from Amwell with Brother Robeson Hyde as the presiding minister. The first record of minutes of councils held here are dated September 16, 1876.

On this date the church "met at 2½ o'clock. Meeting called to order by Bro. R. Hyde. Prayer by Brother Hyde. The church then resolved to have a church record kept of all the proceedings of council meetings; and for this purpose Amos Chamberlain was appointed secretary." Spring and fall councils, as was the Amwell custom also, were held.

On Saturday, August 3, 1878, the church met " according to previous appointment, at two o'clock, to take into consideration the building of a new meeting-house on the old site. Agreed to take one week to raise more money." On August 10, accordingly, the church again met in council and decided to build. Ephraim Gary, R. Hyde, and H. H. Anderson were appointed a building committee. It was agreed to tear down the old house on Monday the twelfth.

"According to previous agreement the new meeting-house was dedicated to the service of Almighty God on December 5, 1878. Services at ten o'clock by Bro. J. P. Hetric of Philadelphia, Pa., by reading 225th hymn. Prayer by Brother Hetric. Bro. James Quinter of Huntingdon, Pa., preached the dedication sermon from the 27th Psalm, 4th verse."

December 2, 1879, at a special meeting for the purpose, the following five brethren were elected trustees of the Bethel house: Ephraim Gary, H. H. Anderson, Servis Trimmer, Sidney L. Bush and John Heller. The Bethel Church sent Bro. R. Hyde as a delegate to District Meeting of 1880. The New Jersey churches were rather loose in organization, and seldom represented at District Meeting. While Brother Hyde was sent by Bethel organization in particular, he is credited in the District Meeting minutes to the New Jersey Church in general.

Amos Chamberlain was succeeded as clerk by J. T. Gary in 1880, but as the latter did not come into possession of the minute book for some time, minutes are not again recorded till 1884. But we have brought the record of the Bethel Church down to 1880, the beginning of a new era in the Jersey church.

SAND BROOK CHURCH, N. J.

GRAVE OF ELDER ISRAEL POULSON, SR., N. J.

GRAVES OF ELDER JOHN P. MOORE AND WIFE, N. J.

CHAPTER II.

SAND BROOK CHURCH.

The beginning of the Sand Brook Church takes us back to 1848, to the expulsion of John P. Moore from the Amwell congregation. On account of this trouble we have learned that eighteen more brethren could no longer walk with the Amwell Church, and were expelled April 7, 1849. These eighteen, with John P. Moore as their speaker, had organized a separate church already on March 10, or nearly a month before their "expulsion" by Amwell. This church was locally called the "Mooreites," but they called themselves "United Christians." They organized by adopting the following Articles of Association:

"We, the undersigned, after careful and serious consideration, do unanimously agree to stand in union together as professed Christian brethren and sisters, in-as-much as we think it is an all-important matter and privilege that we have the indisputable right to worship God according to the dictates of our own consciences, consistent with His word as we understand it, for which privilege we confess that we have great reason to be thankful; therefore we have concluded that by the assisting grace of God we design to try to keep the ordinances of the Lord's house according to the doctrines and principles of our Lord and Savior, Jesus Christ, and His holy apostles, as they are delivered to us in the Gospel, which our Savior says shall judge us in the coming day. Therefore we feel that we are under obligation, as much as in us lies, to try and live in union together in the church militant (because we feel that it has in time past done much hurt and made sore by being of different minds); and therefore we would that there should be no pre-eminence one above another, considered that in regard to the business that we design to transact of importance we want to be united in, and agreed to have officers in said church, and also did legally appoint as elder John P. Moore, and as deacons William H. Moore and Jacob Bouss (Fauss); and further agreed that our plan of receiving members in said church is that all the members present must be agreed, and, to excommunicate, all must be consulted before and agreed to; which subscribe our names, this tenth day of March in the year of our Lord one thousand eight hundred and forty-nine.

" Signed
" John P. Moore
 William H. Moore
 Daniel J. Moore
 William S. Moore
 Sarah Brewer
 Catharine A. Moore
 Hester Carson
 Keziah Coudrick
 Martha Coudrick
 Elizabeth Trimmer
 Mary Dalrymple
 Catharine Dalrymple
 Asa Moore
 Silas Shearman
 Martha Moore
 Lucy Ann Sine
 Catharine Shearman
 Anna Moore."

While the " Mooreites " nobly refrained from lodging any complaints against any in the Amwell congregation, yet the nature of their sore may be gathered from this agreement. Preëminence of some in the old church, coercion against the dictates of conscience, and forcing measures through council without consulting all the members. They were in rebellion against the arbitrary kingship of Poulson.

The Sand Brook Church began to grow immediately after its organization. By the end of the year 1849, they had received nine members. Their first council was held in the home of Silas Shearman, May 12, 1849. They lost no time in building a house of worship, the present stone one. Their council of April 13, 1850, was held in the meeting-house. At the first council they decided to observe the salutation of the holy kiss at communion. In the first council in the meeting-house, April 13, 1850, William S. Moore was elected clerk. At this council they also decided to receive members only by trine immersion. Councils were held in March and September.

During the first decade, till 1860, thirty-four members had been received. Among these was Charles W. Moore, who was baptized November 24, 1855. He was afterward deacon, preacher and elder. A week before Charles Moore was baptized, the church elected another preacher. We give the account as recorded in the minutes.

"Sand Brook, November 17, 1855.

"The church at this place being met together and duly organized in public meeting, a resolution was passed that the Elder-elect should be subject to the deacons, and Henry T. Trout having received a majority of all the votes cast was elected elder on the day above named.

> "Witnesses present
> "John P. Moore
> Jacob Fauss
> William H. Moore."

September 17, 1864, Charles W. Moore was elected a deacon.

The total number of persons received into the Sand Brook Church from its organization in 1849 to its reëntrance into the Brotherhood in 1880 was fifty-eight. Adding to these the nineteen who formed the original organization, the "Mooreites" as such, in their entire history, had in their communion seventy-seven persons.

The Sand Brook Sunday School was opened in 1875. Charles Moore was elected superintendent; he continued in this office till 1899 at least.

Reëntrance into the Brotherhood. Before the Annual Meeting of 1879, Elder John P. Moore remarked to his nephew, Deacon Charles W. Moore, that he thought of going to Annual Meeting that year, and asked him to go along. The latter, however, received the suggestion with little favor; but on thinking the matter over, decided to go. The elder by this time had given up the idea; but Charles decision was deep-seated and carried the day. Both went.

On the train thither they met a preacher of the Brethren by the name of Daniel F. Good. Good became interested in the work in Jersey. Before reaching the place of Annual Meeting, Good stopped off, but forgot his baggage. As the train pulled out, realizing the situation, Good called out to Charles Moore to take the baggage into his custody. This the latter did. Good met him again at Annual Meeting and regained his possessions. This led to warm friendship.

Some time later Good came to New Jersey, and held meetings at Sand Brook. But this action on the part of a brother was not looked on with favor by the Amwell adherents. A lovefeast was to be held at Bethel. Good persuaded Charles Moore to go with him to the feast. The presence of these two men threw the good brethren of Bethel into a complete muddle. Should they ask Good to take a seat with the other ministers? This question delayed the opening of the meeting for hours. But the decision finally went against extending the courtesy to the strange preacher. An old member of the Amwell Church in those days declares that the Amwell members would as soon have worshipped with negroes as with the "Mooreites." After the Bethel feast, the two visitors made straight for their carriage. For some time Good was silent. Finally he exclaimed: "Well, if this is the union you have in New Jersey, I have enough of it!" On his way home Good stopped off and laid this matter before Elder D. P. Saylor of Maryland. The next year a committee was appointed to look into the matter of receiving the "Mooreites" back into the Brotherhood. This committee consisted of D. P. Saylor, R. H. Miller, M. Miller, C. Bucher, and S. Harley. We give the report of the Committee, which speaks for itself.

"We, the undersigned brethren, a Committee appointed by Annual Meeting of 1880 to visit a number of petitioners of Sand Brook, Hunterdon Co., New Jersey, report as follows:

"According to appointment, we the undersigned (Elder Christian Bucher having failed to come) met with the petitioners in Council Meeting, in the meeting-house at Sand Brook, on Wednesday, August 18, 1880; and upon investigation we found that the petitioners were a remnant of members of the church in New Jersey, who adhered to John P. Moore, who had been expelled from the New Jersey church about the year 1849 or '50, with others who had united with them in maintaining and keeping up a separate organization and worship, up to the present time; but expressing a wish to be in unison with the order of the general Brotherhood, petitions Annual Meeting for a committee, etc.

"We find that John P. Moore was a minister in the second degree, and that a difficulty existed between him and the elder, and that Moore was finally expelled from the church without any elder or minister being present but those belonging to the New Jersey church and they themselves involved in the trouble.

"Such proceedings being contrary to the general order of our Brotherhood, we decide the expulsion of Moore illegal, and hence he was never legally expelled; but inasmuch as he and those members who adhered to him kept up an organization as fully in the order of the Brotherhood as was the church that expelled them, we decide that under the circumstances their worship was in order, and all that were received by baptism should be recognized as members of the German Baptist Church.

"Hence we decide it best to hold this organization, comprised of John P. Moore, those who withdrew and followed him, and those received into their fellowship by baptism, shall be held a church of the Brotherhood, and the present organization be continued as it is till they and the adjoining churches see best to change it; and we advise all to work for peace and union with the other church, and for harmony with the general Brotherhood.

"Signed by the committee—
"D. P. SAYLOR,
R. H. MILLER,
MOSES MILLER,
SAMUEL HARLEY.

"This report was read and explained to all the members of both churches present, and the vote of the Sand Brook church taken, and was by them unanimously accepted; and a copy of these same was given to Elder Israel Poulson to be read to the church where he presides and offered to her members for their acceptance.

"D. P. SAYLOR,
R. H. MILLER,
MOSES MILLER,
SAMUEL HARLEY."

The Sand Brook Church met in her first council after the visit of the Committee on September 18, 1880. John P. Moore presided with Gideon C. Moore as secretary. The report of the visit was satisfactory, and the church agreed to hold her love-feast some time in the future, in the old order. From this time full accounts of councils were kept, heretofore the minutes preserved having been very fragmentary.

On May 11, 1881, a special council was held for the purpose of electing a minister and deacon. Charles W. Moore, the only deacon, being elected to the ministry, two deacons were elected. The choices fell on Gideon Brewer and Asa Moore. All were then installed into their offices according to the order of the Brotherhood, by Elder D. P. Saylor. August 23, 1882, at a special meeting, John P. Moore was ordained to the eldership, and Charles W. Moore advanced to the second degree of the ministry. The officiating elders were Samuel Harley and Christian Bucher.

Re-adjustments in Jersey. In 1881 a protest against receiving the Sand Brook delegation, likely from the Amwell congregation, was sent to the District Meeting. The protest was voted down. A petition for an investigating committee was also sent up to Annual Meeting. The report of this second committee is self-explanatory, and we herewith give it in full.

"We, the undersigned, being a committee appointed by the Annual Meeting of 1881 to meet the Amwell church in New Jersey to investigate and settle certain difficulties between the above named church and the other persons who had been separated from said church a number of years, met with the brethren of the Amwell church in council August 18, 1881.

"The petition for the Committee contained two points. The first was a request to investigate the proceedings of a committee sent by Annual Meeting of 1880 to the Sand Brook church; and, second, to investigate difficulties existing between the Amwell and Sand Brook churches. The work contained in the first point devolved upon the undersigned alone, but that of the second point devolved upon the undersigned and Elders D. P. Saylor and R. H. Miller. These two brethren, having been on the committee whose work the undersigned were appointed to examine, were present at the investigation to present and explain their proceedings as far as was necessary for them to do.

"Bro. I. Poulson, the elder of the Amwell church, being one of the petitioners, represented the following charge and objections to the work of the former committee. We investigated the objections separately with all the testimony we could obtain; but while we investigated the objections of Bro. I. Poulson separately, we give our decision upon them together, as they are closely connected.

"It was plain to us that the proceedings of the church in the council presided over by I. Poulson, Sen., and which resulted in the expulsion of J. Moore and others, were not legal, since the elder and his son, I. Poulson, Jr., were parties in the church trials, and as they had no other elders present. The trial not being legal, the expulsion of J. Moore cannot be considered legal; but it did not seem so plain to us that the seventeen persons who withdrew from the church were not really separated from the church. The testimony that they were really separated or expelled was not as plain as was desirable to prove the fact; the difficulty having occurred over thirty years ago, and many of the witnesses being dead, and others very old, it is difficult to obtain the testimony it is desirable to have to prove the facts in the case. But as the members of the Sand Brook church have manifested a desire to return to our general Brotherhood, and as we are to exercise charity to all, we decide that the testimony brought before us was not sufficient to reverse the former committee's (work), and we therefore accept it, and give it to the Amwell church as the best we can do under the circumstances, and recommend to all the members of both churches Christian forbearance and brotherly love.

"The second point in the petition will be investigated in the proper order and by the full committee, if it is judged necessary. This report was read to the church and explained, and after an exhortation, the *viva voce* vote of the Amwell church was taken; and seventy-one of her members voted to accept the report, and none to reject.

"Signed by the Committee:
"JOHN WISE,
JAMES QUINTER,
CHRISTIAN BUCHER."

"We, the undersigned, being the full committee appointed by the Annual Meeting of 1881 to investigate matters of difficulty existing between the Amwell and Sand Brook churches, according to the petitioners of the Amwell church to the Annual Meeting for a committee, met in the Amwell meeting-house on the 18th of August, 1881, continuing the council which commenced on the previous day.

"The first charge made by Bro. I. Poulson, in behalf of the Amwell church against the Sand Brook church, is the following: The organization of the Sand Brook church, composed of J. Moore and seventeen members who withdrew until they could be reconciled, was illegal; and, they assuming another name, put themselves beyond the jurisdiction of the church. On the above charge, we decide that in changing the name for the purpose of getting rid of the Amwell church they did wrong; and we ask an acknowledgment of them.

"Second, Bro. I. Poulson says they claim that they knew nothing of the committee of 1856, and that they had not a fair trial before the adjoining elders, both of which we deny. In regard to the above charge, we decide in regard to the first item, which relates to the committee of 1856, that the evidence proves a misunderstanding rather than a misrepresentation; and in regard to the second item, we decide that it was not clearly proved that there was a full and satisfactory investigation before the adjoining elders.

"The third charge of Bro. I. Poulson was as follows: We purpose to show that the charge was not that J. Moore was the cause of all the trouble, and that the charge was not brought by my father alone, but that it was the church which brought it. On the first specification in the charge, we decide that the evidence proves that the charge of all the trouble was against J. Moore at the time of his expulsion; but on the second specification we decide that it was not definitely proved who brought the charge against J. Moore at the time of his expulsion.

"Fourth. The charge of Bro. I. Poulson was: 'They said I was elected in Dalrymple's place and to fill his place, and that I was thus installed.' This is not correct. We decide that on this charge there was not sufficient evidence to prove clearly that Bro. I. Poulson was installed in the second degree of the ministry at the time of his election, but it is very evident that there was trouble growing out of his installation."

"This report was read to the church and explained, and a *viva voce* vote taken; and fifty-five of the Amwell members present voted to accept it and two to reject; and of the Sand Brook church twelve members were present, and all accepted it.

"Signed by the committee:
"JOHN WISE,
JAMES QUINTER,
D. P. SAYLOR,
R. H. MILLER,
CHRISTIAN BUCHER."

Other clouds were gathering in the sky for Elder Israel Poulson. He was not as wise in settling up an estate of which he was executor as he should have been. He moved to the Upper Dublin Church in Pennsylvania, and without a church letter.

October 24, 1882, the church appointed a committee to wait on J. M. Smouse, relative to his becoming pastor of the Amwell Church. Smouse was engaged at a salary of $300 per year, and began his labors December 1 of this year. Quarterly councils were instituted at the council of December 8, 1882; and the first church treasurer, Cyrus Van Dolah, also elected. John D. Hoppock was ordained to the eldership December 28, 1882; bishops present, J. Z. Gottwals and J. P. Hetric.

In the council of February 28, 1883, a letter " from the bishops was read advising the church to take immediate action in the difficulty existing between the church and Israel Poulson." There were six charges against Poulson, embodying unfaithfulness to his bond as executor, causing division in the church, and removing without a letter of membership. The church after exhausting in vain all efforts for home settlement, called in a committee, which consisted of Elders Christian Bucher, Samuel Harley, and William Hertzler. This committee seems to have been accepted by Annual Meeting, with the addition of Elder Moses Miller as chairman. Elders Gottwals and Hetric were also advised of the investigation. The committee met August 28, 1883, and found Poulson guilty of procrastination which caused his bondsmen to suffer unjustly, and of carelessness as administrator which led to division in the church, and was condemned for moving away without adjusting difficulties and securing a church letter. He was relieved of the office of bishop, and required to make an humble acknowledgment of his short-comings, after which he was to be granted a certificate of church membership as a minister in the second degree. The church accepted the work of the committee by a vote of fifty-three to twenty-three. Poulson met the conditions, and received the certificate of membership August 29, 1883.

Smouse left Amwell in shame, in the fall of this same year. At a special council January 5, 1884, Amos Haines was called to the ministry—J. Z. Gottwals and J. P. Hetric, elders present.

And still there were troubles. The District Meeting of 1884 was asked to send a committee to settle them. The committee appointed was C. Bucher, J. Z. Gottwals and Samuel Harley. Ten charges were presented to the committee. Among them were the following: Some absenting themselves from public worship, validity of changing time of church meetings, validity of ordination of J. D. Hoppock, irregularity of the election of a brother to the ministry, the opening of the church to an expelled minister, and reporting his meeting in *The Evangelist*. The first and last were not commended; the others, not sustained. Other grievances the committee refused to consider, because they had already been before a committee from Annual Meeting. This committee also decided that the Bethel branch was an organized church, and advised that a line be struck between it and the Amwell congregation. This committee rendered its decision August 26, 1884.

Amos Haines was advanced April 26, 1885. June 13 of this same year, the missionary cause was brought before the church and received approval. The matter was referred to the ministers, J. D. Hoppock and Amos Haines. During the first year $28.12 were collected.

September 8, 1885, Elders Christian Bucher and Samuel Harley, by request, met with the church. This meeting was for the purpose of adjusting a general difficulty, which had its origin in the trial and resignation of Elder I. Poulson. The friends of Poulson, with few exceptions, absented themselves from public worship, after having been repeatedly visited and admonished to attend. A motion to have Poulson come back to Amwell and preach occasionally was lost. As it seemed impossible to accomplish anything, the matter was dropped with a recommendation from the elders that the members try to effect a reconciliation among themselves.

Brother Haines feeling it his duty to prosecute his studies relative to the ministry asked December 30, 1885, to be relieved of his duty as speaker. He was retained till April 1 next. March 13, 1886, the Amwell Church changed from double to single mode of feet-washing. At the same time it was decided to have Brother Haines exchange pulpits with Joel K. Reiner, of Philadelphia, once a month. The Amwell house was repaired in 1887 at a cost of $140.75.

On January 21, 1890, a committee sent by the District Meeting to ascertain wherein lay the cause of lack of harmony in the Jersey Church met at Amwell. The committee was S. R. Zug, C. Bucher, and F. P. Cassel. Nothing seems to have been accomplished.

Juniata College takes up the Jersey Problem. August 10, 1892, Lambert M. Hyde, Clinton B. Wilson, and Henry Van Dolah were elected deacons. "Amidst a most excellent feeling of sympathy and Christian fellowship, the meeting closed with earnest prayer for the newly elected officers and for the congregation, by brethren John D. Hoppock and Amos H. Haines. May God own and bless the work." So writes Bro. W. J. Swigart, of Huntingdon, Pennsylvania.

September 10, 1892, the church certificate of F. F. Holsopple, a graduate of Juniata College, was presented. Brother Holsopple was a son-in-law of Elder James Quinter. On June 8, 1895, an election for a minister was held, and the choice fell on Ira C. Holsopple, brother of the pastor, who for a time had been residing in Jersey. He was installed into the sacred office August 19, by Elder J. D. Hoppock, Elder W. J. Swigart, and Amos Haines.

Brother Frank Holsopple having accepted a call to the pastorate of the church at Parkerford, Pa., it was decided September 7, 1895, to call Bro. William Howe to Amwell. He was received into the church December 7. Brother Holsopple had labored in a judicious manner to bring about proper fellowship between Amwell and Sand Brook; but he and Elder H. E. Light, who had charge at Sand Brook, failed to understand each other.

There was still considerable indebtedness on the parsonage, and June 13, 1896, a mortgage of $1,046.80 was placed on it. Brother Howe was very conscientious, strict in his living, and laid great emphasis on Bible study. He soon began to find more favor at Sand Brook than at Amwell. September 6, 1896, it was decided not to keep him another year. He was called by Sand Brook, which about this time had united with the Bethel congregation.

October 30, 1896, the Amwell Church decided to call in Bro. J. C. Reiff, as a prospective candidate to hold an extra meeting. Brother Reiff was from the Green Tree Church, was attending Juniata College, and while there was elected by the Huntingdon Church to the ministry. He was called to the Amwell pastorate December 19.

To show how Amwell stood in the customs of the brotherhood, a lady, in 1897, being very sick and realizing that her end was near at hand, and feeling a deep interest in our church and Sunday School work, desired to give to the church her organ, to be used in the Sunday School service. The gift was not accepted.

Brother Reiff, though small in stature, at once started to straighten things out in Jersey. In the spring of 1897, Elder Charles W. Moore was informed that because of alleged charges against him certain members of Amwell, prominently the Haines family, would not recognize him as a brother. Brother Moore followed the course outlined in Matt. 18, through the three stages. November 16, 1897, Elder C. G. Lint, of Meyersdale, Pa., presiding, after due notice had been given to all members to attend, this trouble was considered. No charges were brought against Brother Moore, though proper notice and opportunity were given. Brother Reiff submitted the following letter which was accepted by a vote of seventeen to eight. It was decided to have it printed for convenience in sending it out.

" LETTER.
" SAND BROOK, New Jersey,
" Nov. .... 1897.

"*Dear* ....:

" In council on November 16th, the Amwell German Baptist Church finally decided, on condition of his future good conduct, henceforth to recognize Elder C. W. Moore as an elder in good standing, and with whom the church shall, on above condition, be in full fellowship, and not only with him, but also with every member of the body known as the Union Church of New Jersey, now under his care.

"In order that we, the Amwell Church, may know of a surety upon whom we may, in the future, depend for sympathy, co-operation, and support in all the various workings of the church—to the extent only that they shall be in harmony with the spirit of the Gospel—we ask you to certify by letter, to L. M. Hyde, of Sand Brook, New Jersey, either your willingness or unwillingness, in the future, to be one among us—one in Christian fellowship, one who, by the grace of God, shall endeavor to do all in your power to live and work harmoniously, peacefully, and Scripturally, for the glory of God and of Christ in the world.

"If we do not hear from you by letter or otherwise, before Jan. 1, 1898, we will take your silence to mean that you do not desire longer to be with us, and we will drop your name from the church register, to be replaced at any time thereafter, in regular order, at the joint pleasure of yourself and the Amwell Church.

"To be a member of the Amwell Church, from this time on, shall mean to try to live and act as though our past relations with the Sand Brook and Bethel churches had been only pleasant.

"The Amwell Church will welcome with open hearts and arms all present and past members, who shall be willing to remain or to come in the way herein indicated.

"This letter cannot nullify any matter other than the one considered at the council herein specified.

"A copy of this letter shall be sent to every active or inactive member now living, as they are known to the church.

"Only to promote His cause and His glory.
"The Amwell German Baptist Church.
"L. M. HYDE, *Clerk*."

Thus were the long ostracised "Mooreites" vindicated. Those unwilling to accept Brother Moore as designated in the letter, sent to the Progressive pastor of Philadelphia to come up and organize them into a congregation. Thus the old church of Amwell lost about one half of her membership; among them her secretary, treasurer, and a trustee. But Amwell and Sand Brook began to walk together. It was unanimously decided, March 5, 1898, that the Amwell and Sand Brook worship at Amwell Sunday mornings and at Sand Brook Sunday evenings.

March 20, 1899, Brother Reiff resigned as pastor at Amwell, left New Jersey, and joined himself to the 'Doweyites" of Chicago. The Amwell Church now turned to the Annual Meeting Committee to Eastern Pennsylvania.

CHAPTER III.

BETHEL CHURCH.

The District Meeting Committee of 1884—C. Bucher, S. Harley, and J. Z. Gottwals—decided that Bethel was a separate congregation from Amwell, and advised a line being struck between the two. Bethel had been first recognized by District Meeting as a separate organization in the spring of this year, with Robeson Hyde as her delegate.

In 1885 Israel Poulson returned to New Jersey and took up his abode within Bethel limits. It was soon suggested that Brother Poulson relieve Brother Hyde in preaching one half of the Sundays. The church refused to vote on this matter hastily. Herewith is given the action of a committee which met with the Bethel Church in 1886.

The committee's report follows:

"We convened in council October 2, 1886, at the Bethel church, New Jersey, to labor with the church on the propriety of Brother Israel Poulson preaching there for them, according to the advice of the elders of our late District Meeting.

"Having heard all pro and con, we came to the conclusion that Brother Poulson should be a co-laborer with Brother Hoppock and Brother Hyde, working together to build up the church, providing he lifts his membership at Upper Dublin and presents it to this church, helping to work and labor for union in all church affairs, attend council meetings, as it becometh a co-laborer; and then the members promise to attend all meetings, no matter who holds them, if otherwise possible."

"WILLIAM HERTZLER
ISAAC KULP.

"P. S.—By the consent of the church the elders present wrote the above proposition, which was almost unanimously accepted.

"I. K., *Secretary*."

Brother Poulson secured his letter from the Upper Dublin Church, and it was accepted by Bethel. For some cause, however, Bethel seems to have lost interest in the District Meeting, for after this she did not send a delegate until 1892, when C. W. Moore represented her conjointly with Sand Brook. He continued to represent her each year, excepting 1893, till she united with the Sand Brook congregation. A very undesirable condition of affairs existed in the church about 1888. William Hertzler and Samuel Zug were present in council November 9 of this year. They came as a result of a petition to District Mission Board for help. A special hour for private prayer " for a better state of things in the church" was decided upon for November 21. On this date Elders Samuel Zug and Frank Cassel met with the church, when the congregation decided that they were willing to labor for the upbuilding of the church and for the general order of the Brotherhood. The brethren felt themselves in shape to commune, and decided to do so. In the spring of 1891 A. S. Chamberlain, who had previously been clerk, was the means of a Progressive meeting in the neighborhood. A committee of Brethren was appointed to visit him and "kindly admonish him to do so no more." It was decided at the same time to get Brother C. W. Moore to preach every other Sunday if practicable for him to do so. Here we begin to see the coming together of the Bethel and Sand Brook churches. This tendency was furthered by a council held here April 26, 1892, with the Annual Meeting Committee, when it was "Resolved that this church, though keeping its separate organization, is willing to work in union and harmony with the Sand Brook Church and the Brotherhood at large." Elder S. R. Zug, then of the Annual Meeting Committee, was prominent in the councils of the church at this time.

From 1893 to 1895 Elder H. E. Light looked after the work at Bethel. He worked up interest in missionary contributions. In 1894 C. W. Moore was chosen to represent Bethel at both District and Annual Meetings. No lovefeast was held at Bethel in the spring of 1895, out of deference to the one at Sand Brook. In the council of March 28, 1896, C. W. Moore was chairman. How Bethel now honors the man, when less than twenty years before she refused to recognize Bro. Daniel Good as a minister only because he was a companion to him!

We are not now surprised to read the following minute: "This is to certify that at the regular fall council, 1896, Bethel Church agreed to unite or consolidate with the Sand Brook Church, to be known as the Union Church, holding services, councils, and communions alternately between the two churches. Elder S. R. Zug being present and in the chair." During this time Bro. William Howe was preaching at Sand Brook.

According to the list 134 persons were received into the Bethel Church from its beginning till it united with the Sand Brook Church. Not counting officials there were 58 members at the time of their union. The two Poulsons preached here. Robeson Hyde looked after matters, though not ordained, when councils were first held. Amos Chamberlain was clerk and Sunday School superintendent. He was succeeded as clerk by J. T. Gary in 1880, and as Sunday School superintendent by Ephraim Gary in 1891. Other prominent names in the work here are H. H. Anderson, Servis Trimmer, Sidney L. Bush, John Heller, Joseph Trimmer, Israel P. Trimmer, Lambart B. Hann, A. Gary, and Sisters Edith and Caroline Gary.

Sand Brook Recognized and Independent.—At a council, November 11, 1882, in the Sand Brook Church, the "report of the Annual Meeting" was read by Elder John P. Moore, which was satisfactory to all present; and it was urged by Elder John P. Moore that all work with the Annual Meeting and with the order of the Brethren.

From now on the Sand Brook Church kept in close touch with the District Meeting, never failing to send a delegate. C. W. Moore represented her every year till and after the union with Bethel. Sand Brook now begins to fall in line with all church activities. Elder H. E. Light looked after her interests in connection with those of Bethel. Solicitors for the Mission fund were appointed in the spring of 1894.

Councils from 1894–1896 were held in the home of Israel Poulson. First delegate to Annual Meeting was sent in 1894. Jennie F. Green was appointed *Messenger* correspondent in March, 1896.

The Annual Meeting Committee to eastern Pennsylvania now advised the Sand Brook and Bethel churches to unite. The Sand Brook Church in special council May 5, 1896, agreed to this advice. Bethel accepted it later.

About the time of the union, an incident in connection with the work at Sand Brook took place which should not be overlooked. A young girl, a second Syrian maiden, attended services at Sand Brook. After the meeting she came to Brother Moore and inquired why he did not, inasmuch as he was holding services in other school-houses, come to the one on the west side of Sergeantsville. Brother Moore was strongly drawn to hold a series of meetings in this school-house. Though dissuaded by many, he went ahead. As a result of his efforts eleven were added to the church. The influence of these meetings continued to work for a long time afterward.

During this period of sixteen years—from 1880 to 1896—Sand Brook received into fellowship sixteen persons. Her membership at the time of union was thirty-one.

CHAPTER IV.

UNION CHURCH.

Both the Sand Brook and Bethel congregations met in council at the Sand Brook house September 19, 1896, and "unanimously agreed to be known and recognized as the Union Church of New Jersey." At this council there were present Elder S. R. Zug, member of the committee to eastern Pennsylvania, Elder H. E. Light, member of the District Mission Board, and Elder J. D. Hoppock, as adjoining elder.

The elders of eastern Pennsylvania, at District Meeting in 1896, appointed S. R. Zug and H. E. Light to effect, if possible, an ordination for the proposed Union Church of New Jersey. At the above mentioned council, it was unanimously agreed to ordain C. W. Moore, which ordination was effected "according to the rules of the general Brotherhood." O. R. Fauss was elected clerk and John Q. Adams treasurer of the new organization. About this time Brother Wm. Howe was called in as pastor.

The new congregation called for the District Meeting of 1897. The call was honored. The District Meeting of 1897 was held at Sand Brook, May 12-13. In 1896 the plan of the Home for the Homeless was adopted. The lovefeasts were to alternate between the two houses. Single mode of feet-washing adopted March 20, 1897.

Besides the officers there were at the time of union, September, 1896, in the Bethel branch 58 members; and in the Sand Brook 31 members; there were also five officers, two ministers, and three deacons; making a total of 94 members. By July 1, 1899, twenty-one persons had been received into the Union Church, one disowned, making a membership of 114.

Recent History.

In a letter dated September 24, 1913, Bro. M. B. Miller thus sums up the recent history of the Brethren in New Jersey.

"In the nineties (last century) J. C. Reiff of Huntingdon, Pa., took charge of the work in Jersey. Reiff was a strong factor in driving off what are now the Progressives. He lives now in California, having a secular calling, and is connected with some holiness movement. He resigned as pastor of the Jersey churches, March 20, 1899.

"In council, the churches called Tobias Myers to preach for them indefinitely; and at this council, April 5, 1902, he was chosen to represent at District Meeting.

"July 26, 1902, the churches, through the General Mission Board, called Bro. Hiram Forney of Goshen, Ind., to the pastorate. He did not take charge till November, 1902. In the fall of 1904, Brother Forney resigned and left the work.

"During the pastorate of Brother Forney, Elder Charles W. Moore died, June 16, 1903. Brother Moore was next to the last of the old Jersey preachers who had gone through those turbulent times of the Jersey church's history. He was the last of the Moores in the Sand Brook church. He was generally beloved, preached many funerals, and married many.

"Elder Robinson Hyde, who died in 1901, went with the Progressives, about the time the Progressives organized in Jersey, which was about the last of the nineties.

"Elder John D. Hoppock died in 1906. He was the last of the Jersey elders. He was of a genial disposition, of sterling integrity, and used good common sense and wisdom during those trying times through which the church went.

"Seth Myers took charge of the Jersey churches in the spring of 1905, and continued in his work till the fore part of 1907, when he left.

"During Brother Myers' stay, Henry T. Horne was elected to the ministry. He was a nephew of Elder Charles W. Moore. Brother Horne was a member of the Sand Brook church, but was elected by both churches in joint council. He was the only resident minister in Jersey after Myers left, till about July 1, 1907, when Jacob F. Graybill took charge of the work. He stayed till August, 1909. Myers and Graybill were sent by the Mission Board of Eastern Pennsylvania.

"Monroe B. Miller came into the Jersey churches April 1, 1910, as a volunteer minister in the second degree. Brethren Horne and Miller worked together side by side, with Elder James Shisler as elder in charge. This kept up till the division of the District of Eastern Pennsylvania, shortly after which

Elder Shisler resigned. His resignation was accepted September 11, 1911.

"J. Kurtz Miller was then chosen elder in charge. November 5, 1911, H. T. Horne and M. B. Miller were ordained to the full ministry. May 25, 1912, at a special meeting, the Amwell and Sand Brook churches in joint council almost unanimously decided to unite, forming one congregation, the same to be called by the mother name—Amwell Church of New Jersey. Elder H. T. Horne was made resident elder in charge—J. Kurtz Miller retaining general oversight.

"March 29, 1913, in special council assembled, the Mission Board of S. E. Pennsylvania, New Jersey, and E. New York proposed to the church that M. B. Miller take charge as pastor, and that he be supported conjointly by the Amwell church and the District Mission Board. The church accepted the proposal. This is our position today, with J. Kurtz Miller, President of the District Mission Board, as general overseer.

"By the grace of God we have a rather live Prayer-meeting and Ladies' Aid Society; but our people take so little interest in Sunday School and preaching service. A new voice or something entertaining brings people. Oh, for more power to reach the hearts of these lukewarm Christians!"

"The Brethren's Sunday School in New Jersey, near Croton, Hunterdon County, was organized in May, 1873, with Elder R. Hyde, superintendent, and at present (1876) shows an average attendance of about thirty scholars and ten visitors, making a total average of forty, besides teachers and officers. We take thirty copies of the "Children's Paper," and six of our scholars have come into the fold within the present year.

"R. S. Chamberlain."[1]

[1] "Brethren's Almanac" of 1876.

CHAPTER V.

BIOGRAPHICAL.

A. JOHN NAAS.

John Naas was perhaps the ablest preacher of the early church of the Brethren. Libe and Martin might be placed in his class; Naas was born in 1669 or 1670, at Norten, a town of Westphalia, twelve miles north of Emden. "He was among the first fruits of the Brethren in Creyfelt, and on account of his disinterested piety and great natural endowments, he was soon called to the ministry, in which he manifested so much zeal that his fielld of labor at Creyfelt appeared too small for his ardent desire to extend the knowledge of the newly discovered truth. Hence he made several very successful tours through the adjoining provinces as a traveling missionary, in which he suffered many privations, and once narrowly escaped being pressed into the army of the King of Prussia."

Troubles with Christian Libe at Creyfelt caused him to desist from preaching for a number of years. He is reported, but erroneously, to have come to America with the second colony of Brethren in 1729. He arrived in 1733. See Brumbaugh's "History of the Brethren," pp. 108–124, for a lengthy letter which he wrote to his son in Switzerland. He went almost immediately to Amwell, N. J., where he founded an active church, and which remains "his monument" unto this day.

Abraham Cassel, from whom we quoted above, says further of him: "It is said by one of his contemporaries that knew him well, that he was unequalled as a preacher—being a German Whitefield or a Boanerges. Several of his hymns which are still in use by the Brethren also speak well of him as a poet or hymnologist. He is further represented as being very mild and charitable, almost to a fault, insomuch that he occasionally differed with the Brethren in the administration of judgment to offending members. He died ripe in years and full of faith, on the 12th of May, 1741; and is buried amidst many of his spiritual children in the Brethren's graveyard at Amwell." It should here be added that his remains do not repose in the Brethren graveyard near the Amwell meetinghouse.

He had two daughters and at least one son. One daughter was married to Bro. Wilhelmus Graw, in Creyfelt, who never came to America. The other was married to a Hannes Landis, who afterwards joined the Seventh Day Baptists and went to Ephrata. He was not long satisfied here, however, was again reconciled to the Brethren and became a member of the Conestoga congregation. The son remained in Switzerland at least for a time after the father came to America, to whom the father wrote the long and interesting letter concerning his voyage across the deep.

John Naas may also be regarded as the founder of the Great Swamp Church, in Upper Milford, Bucks Co., Pa., as he was the first to preach there and was present at the organization in 1735. During his short life in America, of eight years, from 1733 to 1741, he frequently appears in the work of the church. He was visited by George Adam Martin. In 1736 he accompanied some of the Germantown Brethren on a tour to Ephrata, where for a time he had a daughter living. His attitude toward this work is not so easy of explanation. The "Chronicon" says that he was greatly enamoured of the way of life of the Settlement. Again he is said to have opposed, with Peter Becker, Beissel's "awakening" in Germantown in 1738. He was also still living when Beissel was so hospitably received at Amwell, but does not figure in the visit. Some years later Beissel in his extravagant way refers to the Widow Naas in terms of great Christian love.

Perhaps the truth is something like this. Naas with Becker saw the danger in Beissel and so concurred with Becker in opposition; but not with Becker saw the good in the ultra-mystic. Naas was a big-hearted, tolerant man. We cannot but believe that he was back of Amwell's attitude toward Beissel at the time of the visit. The whole Amwell organization helped the visitors back over the Delaware. But Naas kept himself out of Beissel's sight. Perhaps Beissel's eyes were holden that he saw him not—the state in which Beissel, in his marvelous spiritual pride, regarded Alexander Mack as being at Falckner's Swamp.

The "Chronicon" says they broke bread together in Jersey, which certainly means they communed together. Naas, the tolerant peace-maker, had the spirit of the Brethren. Yet Naas was not Alexander Mack, our founder. Mack would not have kept back from personally meeting Beissel in Jersey. He had the spirit of Him who felt under obligation to lay down his life for the Brethren. This is Brethrenism; this is loyalty to the Church of the Brethren. But John Naas was a grand, noble man, and torture could not make him renounce his Master; and he yielded to the spirit that was in Alexander Mack—he was a brother and a Brethren preacher.

B. Israel Poulson, Sr.

The parents of Elder Israel Poulson are unknown. He was left by them at the age of seven near Centreville, N. J., where he was reared. He is said to have had Indian blood in his veins. He was bound over when a youth to a man named Jerry King, who utterly neglected his education. When he married his first wife, he was unable to write his own name. She taught him to read. She died soon without children. He then married her sister, who was long and lovingly known as Aunt Hannah Poulson. She was the mother of all his children. His home was at Headquarters, now called Grover. In later life he married the widow of old Henry Laushe.

He was greatly beloved by children. His habit was to lay his hand on their heads. He was always a welcome visitor. Every one clung to old "Uncle Israel." A certain false prophet once came into the neighborhood, announcing that the world was about to come to an end. A man not altogether of sound mind was asked what he would do. He replied: "I would hold on to Uncle Israel's coat-tail."

He was always in demand as a preacher; there was always a place for him. In church visiting he always walked, going across fields to cut off corners. His cane and his pipe were his ever-present companions. Unlike most elders in the Brethren Church, he played the fiddle. He was a man of medium height, had straight, black hair, and always wore a pleasant smile. He was not particular in the form of his dress, yet intended to conform to the order of the Brotherhood. Nor were the three degrees of the ministry clearly defined in Jersey in his day. He was a common man and took an interest in public affairs. He built the stone wall around the cemetery at Amwell. Three hundred dollars having been charged for assessing the township, Uncle Israel declared it was too much; it was robbing the people. He said he would do it for one hundred dollars. The work was given to him, and he was assessor for three years.

In the early days, he preached in school-houses and in the private homes. The people flocked to hear him. And so it was decided to build a meeting-house. He gave the ground. If any in the nineteenth century should be called the father of the Jersey church, it was old Israel Poulson. And he belonged to Jersey exclusively. Outside of this state he was little known. In 1846 we find him among the Elders at Annual Meeting.

Like all, he had his failings, which have been seen in the election of his son to the ministry and the expulsion of John P. Moore. But we believe, as in his vision of the scales which we herewith relate, that his good deeds had the preponderance, and that he has found acceptance with the Great Judge of All.

Visions of Israel Poulson, Sr.

(Related to the writer by Bro. Abr. Cassel.)

The Loaf of Bread. Once upon a time he seemed to be in an immense concourse of people, nothing but people as far as he could see. All seemed to be slowly pressing toward a certain point. Looking intently in the direction of the moving, he could discern a large scales erected. Men were continually being lifted into one side. Some would hold their side down; but many, many would go up into the air. They were weighed in the balances and found wanting. Then it dawned on Brother Poulson that they were in the last judgment, and that he too must be weighed. How would it go with him? He hardly knew. Sometimes he thought he might hold his side of the scales down, but then he doubted. They kept pressing closer and closer. Soon he would be weighed. His heart began to fail. Finally he was at the scales. He was placed in the balances. For an instant he seemed to hold his own, then he could feel himself slowly but surely rising. "Weighed and found wanting." He was just being condemned, when the judge was halted by some one running in the distance, frantically waving his hand, and calling at the top of his voice. It was a boy who held something under his arm. On he came, pushing fiercely through the crowd as fast as he could. The judge waited. The boy forced himself under the scales. Taking what was under his arm, in both hands, he gave it a toss up into the scale in which Brother Poulson was standing. Down came the scale in balance. "Accepted," pronounced the judge. Brother Poulson looked down at his feet. There lay a loaf of bread. He recognized it as the loaf he had once given to a poor widow.

The Laborers by the Way. At another time he seemed to be walking along a road. Many men were at work digging a trench. As he drew nearer there seemed to be a great difference among the workmen. They divided themselves into two classes. One class was gloomy and listless. They worked hard but could make little headway. The others were cheerful and singing, and made the ground fly as though it had wings. They accomplished much. Why the difference? He could see no cause for it. They had the same kind of work. It seemed that they might be of equal strength. The gloomy ones were not sick. The sun beat with equal heat on both. The breeze that fanned the cheerful man, fanned the gloomy ones equally. Their tools were equally good. Everything was the same, yet what a difference! Why? He could not solve the mystery. He would inquire of the foreman. "Why the difference in the work of your men?" "The hard workers keep at their task only from a sense of duty; the cheerful ones love their work."

Then Brother Poulson saw that this applied to our work for Christ.

The Old Fiddle. He played the fiddle and "he could get music out of it." Once he seemed to have an old fiddle. He tried to produce music, but none would come. He tried again and again. He bent himself to the task. He vexed himself. But all in vain. He could get no music out of that "darned" old fiddle.

It was a dream, a vision. What did it mean? He believed the Lord showed him the visions, and that they had a lesson for him. What meant the vision of the old fiddle? He could get nothing out of it. The vision was as dry as the fiddle itself. It needed interpretation.

Soon after he was to preach, but could not hit on a subject. Finally he decided to take a subject on which he had preached once before. The sermon was one which seemed to him to have taken very well. He got up to preach, but it wouldn't go. He exerted himself, forced himself, worried himself, yea, even to sweating; but all in vain. It was dry, lifeless. The sermon was a flat failure.

"Trying to play on the old fiddle," he afterward said to himself. God had given him the vision as a warning.

C. Israel Poulson, Jr.

The younger Poulson was born April 14, 1821, at Headquarters, N. J. He received his education in Moore's public school, about a mile from Headquarters. He then clerked for a time in a store at New Hope, in Pennsylvania, but practically his life was spent in the vicinity of the Amwell Church. His occupation was farming, which he began on his own responsibility at the age of twenty-one. About this time, October 6, 1841, he was married. The partner of his new home, immediately north of the Amwell meetinghouse, was Harriet Johnston. His children are Urania and William J.

He was elected to the ministry April 8, 1848. The unbrotherly way in which he suffered himself to be placed above John P. Moore, even to the extent of expelling the unyielding Moore from the church, was a sowing which after thirty years was destined to bring him trouble and humiliation, and the extinction of his family in the church of the Brethren. Yet, during these years he did faithful work as a preacher. The author remembers him yet faintly when he stopped at his grandfather's home on the occasion of love-feasts at Green Tree. Our child heart went out toward him, and from our child impressions we believe he was a good man.

He moved to Upper Dublin in the spring of 1881, immediately following his reverses in Jersey; but he returned to his native state in 1885. He became a member of the Bethel Church, which, with Brother R. Hyde, he continued to serve till death, February 28, 1896. He is said to have been "off hand" in his preaching. The name Poulson stands out big in the history of the Jersey church during, and we might say throughout, the nineteenth century. It is to be regretted that it has not continued prominent into the twentieth. Let us learn the lesson to be learned from these two lives!

D. The Two Moores.

They were not father and son, but uncle and nephew. The name Moore goes back to the beginning of the Jersey Church, Jacob Moore being one of the five original heads of families of Brethren who located at Amwell in 1733. Gideon Moore, father of John P. and grandfather of Charles W., was one of the two deacons of the church in 1835, and a prominent and influential member of the Amwell fraternity. He was a trustee of the Amwell Meetinghouse. In the minute of April 13, 1839, we find these words: "Agreed to take a lot of Gideon Moore for a burying place."

John P. Moore. John P. Moore was elected deacon of the Amwell Church, to fill the place of his father, deceased, November 11, 1840. April 13, 1844, he was elected "elder," or, correctly, to the ministry. October 10, 1848, he was illegally expelled, shortly after the election of the younger Poulson to the ministry.

He then became the founder of the "Mooreites" who built their meeting-house at Sand Brook. It was he who, in 1879, first suggested going to Annual Meeting, which trip, with his nephew, Charles W. Moore, resulted in the readmission of the "Mooreites" into the Brotherhood. At a special council of the Sand Brook Church, August 23, 1882, he was ordained elder—Elders present, Samuel Harley and Christian Bucher.

He showed himself loyal to the Brotherhood. We find him reading the report of the Annual Meeting to his congregation, and urging his flock to be true to it and the order of the Brotherhood. He was also noted for going on the outer borders, into school-houses, to hold meetings. He started meetings in the Rockton school-house, which were kept up for many years.

He lies buried at Sand Brook, which church is his real monument.

Charles W. Moore. Charles W. Moore, in a sense, was the complement of his uncle, John P. Moore. Had it not been for Charles, the "Mooreites" would have fallen short of getting back into the Brotherhood, and would never have secured full vindication. He was an earnest, zealous, patient worker, but not much of a preacher. As he himself stated, his work was more to go out and gather others in that another might preach to them. As seen, he was deacon, preacher, and elder. He organized the Sand Brook Sunday School and was its superintendent for many years.

Brother Moore was a man of faith. He believed that the gift of healing was not a lost gift today. He cited more than one case in his own experience to prove his position.

An infant in the neighborhood was sick unto death. The doctor had given it up, stating that nothing could help it. Brother Moore called at the home. At the close of his visit, in leaving the house, he passed the cradle in which lay the dying infant. He felt a strong inward impulse to kneel at the cradle and to ask God to restore the child. He knelt and prayed. On reaching home he told his wife that the babe would recover. In a short time it was perfectly well.

The hospitality of his home made Sand Brook a sacred spot to at least one heart. He was a good man, and an humble, and to know him was to love him.

E.   John Hoppock and Robeson Hyde.

The leading preachers in Jersey seem to go in pairs. We have had the two Poulsons and the two Moores, and now we come to two preachers who were elected to the ministry on the same day and labored together for many years. Data is not at hand to give sketches of the lives of either. We can do little more here than preserve their names.

John Hoppock and his family, through all the troubles in Jersey, stood by the old church. He was elder of the Amwell Church for many years. For many years he kept storing away in his garret our church papers, and gave to the writer, as a gift, his whole valuable collection for the Brethren's Historical Society. While he was not a specially great preacher, yet to be in his presence was a sermon—you felt that you were with a man who was good through and through.

Robeson Hyde labored chiefly in the Bethel congregation. See the account of that church. He continued with the old church until his end, but his able and useful son Lambert cast in his lot with the Progressives. This family, if any, makes us feel that all the Brethren of Jersey should be one again. There was in Brother Hyde something primitive, a freedom from conventionality, that made his presence very enjoyable.

There is within the Jersey homes, often unpainted on the outside, so much of Christian hospitality, so much of love and good-will, that one is made to wonder how the spirit of schism could ever find entrance. Satan is the author of it all. But as the Jersey Brethren resist him, he will flee from them. And surely the great home missionary spirit of John Naas, the father of the church in Jersey, must revive. As Bro. Frank Holsopple said, the Jersey Church is his monument, and this monument must not be allowed to tarnish.

COVENTRY CHURCH OF TO-DAY.

PART IV.

THE COVENTRY GROUP.

CHAPTER I.

THE COVENTRY CHURCH.

Coventry, the second oldest Brethren Church in America, was organized, November 7, 1724. The charter members were nine: Martin Urner and wife Catharine, Henry Landis and wife, Daniel Eicher, Peter Heffly, Owen Longacre, and Andrew Sell. Martin Urner was chosen the preacher; and his home seems to have been the chief place of meeting. Some time after Alexander Mack arrived in 1729, he ordained Martin Urner to the office of Bishop. An account of the facts leading up to the organization of this old church, only ten months younger than the old Mother Church at Germantown, will be found set forth in the account of the Missionary Tour of 1724.

A love feast was held at Martin Urner's on Whitsuntide, in 1726. Members from both Germantown and Conestoga were present. But Peter Becker was not among the number. Conrad Beissel officiated. "Extraordinary powers of eternity" were manifested; and the followers of Beissel called it the congregation's Pentecost. Says the "Chronicon": "On the first day of the festival everybody in the meeting was as though drunken with wine, and it was noticed that several, who had engaged in prayer, soon afterward married, and so dragged the gifts of the Spirit into the flesh." After the meeting Beissel baptized eleven. This was the largest baptism up to this time in America.

The Brethren were thrown into a quandary concerning Beissel. They had to admire his gifts, yet they looked upon him as a seducer and forbidder of wedlock. Their amazement and perplexity were increased by a meeting on the following day, when "the powers of the new world were again poured out like a river, the singing was Pentecostal and heavenly; yea, some declared they heard angel voices mingling with it." Martin Urner became greatly distressed. He is said to have embraced his wife, exclaiming: "O, my dear wife! I pray you for God's sake, do not leave me!"

Across the Schuylkill from Coventry, in back of Pottstown, is Falckner's Swamp, where already in 1724 families of Brethren had settled, and in this year had the Lord's Supper administered to them by the Brethren on their notable Missionary Tour. Here Beissel did not have to encounter so much the penetrating eye of Martin Urner, and here he was victorious. But in Coventry his way was pretty effectually blocked. Inasmuch as Falckner's Swamp, which later ceased to be a Brethren's settlement, was nearer to Coventry than to any other enduring congregation, we deem it proper at this place to give a brief account of the work there.

Falckner's Swamp.

A few of the Brethren who had arrived in Germantown in 1719, had settled shortly after their arrival at Falckner's Swamp. We have mentioned the love feast there in 1724. Beissel, on being made teacher in Conestoga, soon began to regard himself as General Superintendent of the work in America. Because of several newly awakened ones at Falckner's Swamp, Beissel in the latter part of 1727, sent Michael Wohlfahrt to look after the interests of the work. Wohlfahrt's report was so favorable, that Beissel with three others visited Falckner's Swamp, and on March 8, 1728, baptized eleven persons. In the following May five more were baptized. Through this activity Beissel acquired such a control of affairs at Falckner's Swamp that the Germantown Brethren, later reinforced by Alexander Mack, were unable to dislodge him. Andreas Frey was appointed Elder here. He gave up his office and was succeeded by Michael Wohlfahrt. "He fell from his office with shame and disgrace, and thereupon fell at the feet of the Superintendent, who revoked the judgment and received him again into spiritual communion." Beissel now placed a John Landes, perhaps the son-in-law of John Naas, at the head of the work. But Landes was a novice, became puffed up, and lasted only six weeks.

Beissel was unreconciled with a brother at Coventry and had placed two of the Germantown Brethren under the ban. The Germantown Brethren thought it proper to warn the newly awakened about Beissel. Beissel then wrote a letter to the Brethren at Germantown, sternly rebuking them for the falseness, deceit, and craftiness which they had practised on the newly awakened ones. The Germantown Brethren showed this letter at Falckner's Swamp, and proposed to leave the Brethren judge in regard to the "insult" in the letter, for which purpose they appointed a meeting at which both Germantown and Conestoga were to be represented. Beissel was not minded to be subject to this arrangement. With arch-craftiness he sent six members from Conestoga to forestall it. Beissel's emissaries were received, and they maintained his hold.

In October, 1730, Alexander Mack, who had come to this country the year before, undertook with several of his Brethren a visit to Falckner's Swamp. Be it remembered that Beissel had already in 1728 given back his baptism to the Brethren. Beissel, not knowing of the visit, was at Falckner's Swamp when they arrived. We quote from the "Chronicon," pp. 49–50.

"Alexander Mack made an address and said: 'The peace of the Lord be with you!' The Superintendent replied: 'We have the same peace!' Thereupon Alexander Mack asked why they had put them under the ban; and proposed that both parties should betake themselves to prayer that God might reveal to them which was guilty of the separation. . . . They accordingly fell upon their knees, and after making their complaints to God, they arose, and A. M. asked: 'Where is Conrad Beissel?' They pointed towards him and said: 'There he stands!' He answered: 'I am a stranger to him; I do not see him; let him speak.' It seems that his eyes were holden that he could not see him. This happened several times to the Superintendent, as not less to Christ himself and other holy ones. Thereupon the Superintendent answered thus: 'I am the man after whom you ask.' A. M. then began asking the reasons why such things had been done. The Superintendent answered: Why they came here in so improper a manner to disturb the meeting; they should have chosen a different time for this matter; and then spoke not a word more. Then things became lively. One brother of Conestoga said: 'Alexander Mack, I regard you as a servant of God!' Peter Becker replied: 'What kind of a servant do you consider him? a servant of his righteousness?'"

Alexander Mack, humanly speaking, the great leader of the Church of the Brethren, had in the love of Christ won Beissel and he knew it; but he realized that it would require a long time for the fact to become manifest; but in his longsuffering, he was willing to abide the Lord's revelation of his victory. The author of the "Chronicon" states that those who knew how affairs stood between the two congregations, knew also that a close union between them was impossible; "for they were born of diverse causes, since one had the letter for its foundation, the other, the Spirit; and while both had the same Father, they had different Mothers." Alexander Mack taught that the letter and the Spirit go together.

The Elder at Falckner's Swamp in 1731 had trouble with his wife. This elder himself adhered to Beissel but the wife forsook him to be a solitary one with the Superintendent. The man told his wife that she was his, that he would not give her up, that she must be subject to her husband. Several times he brought her home by force. His outraged feelings carried him to the extent of violently assaulting Beissel, who afterward advised the wife to go to her husband. Once when a love feast was to be held, he tied her fast lest she should run away. After his death she joined the community, and lived with it till her death in 1779.

"In 1734 the awakened at Falckner's Swamp, it being the seventh year of their awakening, began to break up and to move toward the settlement. They bought up the regions around Ephrata, so that in a few years the country for three or four miles around was taken up by them. Wherever there was a spring of water, no matter how unfertile the soil, there lived some household, waiting for the Lord's salvation" (p. 66).

Thus did Ephrata absorb Falckner's Swamp, which gave itself to Beissel. Falckner's Swamp above all other places seems to have peopled Beissel's newly found home on the Conestoga. During the troubles between Conestoga and Germantown when Falckner's Swamp was the bone of contention between them, Coventry though the nearest congregation to Falckner's Swamp, held aloof. Martin Urner held the love of his wife and the allegiance of his flock; but not so the Elder across the Schuylkill at Falckner's Swamp. Beissel carried away some from Coventry but even on them he did not have a lasting hold. The "Chronicon" tells us, p. 67, "After these (those from Falckner's Swamp) the awakened from the Schuylkill (Coventry) also came and settled down at the Settlement. From these the Sister's Convent gained a number; but only two, Drusiana and Basilla, natural sisters, endured till the end."

"The Coventry Church," says Abraham Cassel, "increased fast, and in 1770 would have been a very large congregation had not so many gone away to get better lands elsewhere, as they were mostly husbandmen. Numbers went to what was then called the Conococheague, in Franklin and Perry counties, in Pennsylvania, and some also to Maryland, Virginia, and the Carolinas.

"The old Brethren were opposed to having a meeting-house. They held their meetings in a kind of rotation, at Martin Urner's and at four other places, and the custom then was that where the meeting was, most of the people stayed for dinner, and the afternoons were spent in private conversation, singing, and prayer, which was so edifying to the people that it was the means of drawing many into the church."[1] Up to 1770 the Coventry Brethren were without a meeting-house. Only two years later, however, in 1772,

[1] See "History of the Brethren Coventry Church," by Isaac Urner, p. 20.

they built one of logs, on the old Martin Urner homestead, on or near the site of the present church.

"From corroborative facts known to me," continues Abraham Cassel, "I have no doubt but that the Coventry Church had hundreds of additions between its organization in 1724 and its census of 1770."

There is a blank here in the history of the Coventry Church which we are unable to fill. No church records kept within the church herself, as in the Conestoga Church, have come down to us. Our only sources of information are external—Morgan Edwards' "History of the Baptists" and the "Chronicon Ephratense." Isaac N. Urner, LL.D., previously mentioned, has this to say in the introduction to his "History of the Coventry Church": "We are told that no early records of the Coventry Church were kept. It seems improbable that such a church would have no records, 'all the early preachers being men of talent and ability,' that the reasonable supposition is that the records have been lost."

In 1770 the Coventry Church consisted of about twenty-two families, whereof forty were baptized. We give the names of these forty members in 1770 as given us by Morgan Edwards:

Martin Urner and wife, Barbara, Peter Reinhart, Owen Reinhart, Henry Dasker and wife, Nicholas Harwick and wife, Abraham Grubb and wife, Christian Monsieur, Barbara Miller, Barbara Welty, Frederick Reinhart and wife, Barbara Urner, Elizabeth Ingles, Catharine Grumbacher, Catharine Bach, John Eiker, Jacob Pfautz and wife, Abraham Bach, Andrew Wolff, Esther Switzer (*nee* Urner), Wendel Danfelder, Henry Bear and wife, Jacob Switzer and wife, Maud Reinhart, Jacob Light and wife, Philip Waggoner and wife, Elizabeth Halderman, Anthony Bernard and daughter, John Light and wife.

While records of the doings of the early Coventry Church seem lost, yet we perhaps have a complete list of her ministry. Abraham Cassel says: "The Coventry Church always had a very efficient local ministry, as her early preachers were all men of talent and ability, and were often visited by able preachers of other localities and of other denominations, such as Morgan Edwards, Elhanan Winchester, George De Benneville, Peter Keyser, and others. Coventry has always been quite liberal in receiving good men of other persuasions." The early bishops of Coventry were right at the heart of the church. We find Martin Urner much in evidence in the colonial congregations, being the officiating elder at many ordinations. The second Martin Urner was a very able preacher and an intimate friend of Alexander Mack, Jr. Two years previous to the Revolutionary War the Prices enter Coventry territory. The early Elders of Coventry were leaders at the Annual Meeting.

There is a peculiarity of the Coventry ministry—families produced them in groups. There were the three Urners, the three Reinharts, the three Prices, the two Harleys, the two Keims; and the two Holsopples moved in as pastors.

The eldership of the Coventry Church has been as follows: Martin Urner, Sr., from 1729 to 1755; Martin Urner, Jr., from 1755 to 1799; Jonas Urner, from 1799 to 1810; George Price, from 1810 to 1823; John Price, Sr., from 1823 to 1850; John Price, Jr., from 1850 to 1879; David Keim, from 1879 to 1897; Jesse P. Hetric, from 1897 to 1912; M. C. Swigart, from 1912 to —. Coventry, though now almost two hundred years old, has only her ninth elder; in other words the eight elders who have finished their terms of services have each been housekeeper on an average of almost a quarter of a century. Not only have their terms of service been long, but as intimated they have been exceptionally strong men.

The assistant ministry of Coventry we perhaps have as complete as the eldership. The first bishop, Martin Urner, Sr., had as his assistant one Casper Ingles. All that we know of him is that he filled this position. In 1770 Elizabeth Ingles was the only one in the Coventry membership bearing the name. Likely before Ingles, however, was George Adam Martin. This brilliant but top-heavy man afterward went over to Beissel. He deserves biographical mention at the proper place. Peter Reinhart, Morgan Edwards tells us, was assistant to Martin Urner, Jr. Martin and Abraham Reinhart also preached but there is no reason to believe they were ever Elders. The last of the Reinharts died in 1842.

In this same year died Jacob Harley, the older of the two Harley preachers. John Harley closed his labors in 1895, but we have not learned when he began them. Peter Hollowbush was elected to the ministry in 1842, the year in which as we have seen two of the ministers died. Jacob Connor was elected May 25, 1872.

Concerning the rest of the ministers called out of the Coventry membership we have more definite facts, as their elections are recorded in the minutes. Minutes were first kept in 1872, the year in which Peter Hollowbush died.

December 4, 1875, Isaac Urner Brower was elected to the ministry. Henry Cassel was the elder present who installed him. At the same time Jacob Connor was advanced.

Elder David Keim requested, May 8, 1880, the election of an Elder, a minister, and two deacons. All were elected but the Elder. The election was held August 7, 1880. The choice for a minister fell on J. Y. Eisenberg; and Isaac U. Brower was advanced. Lewis Keim was elected to the ministry July 22, 1893. Elder J. Z. Gottwals installed the newly elected minister. A young man was desired, likely to become pastor. Bro. Keim went to Juniata College to prepare for the new duties devolving upon him. He was advanced to the second degree of the ministry July 25, 1896. He never became pastor at Coventry, although he served two or three other churches in this capacity. He is the last brother to be elected out of the Coventry membership.

January 4, 1902, Bro. Jacob Grater, a minister in the first degree of the Mingo Church, presented his letter at Coventry and was accepted. He had accepted a position in a Pottstown bank. He entered heartily into the Master's work. Soon afterward, the pastorate at Parkerford became vacant, and Bro. Hetric promised to fill the place till a pastor was secured. Bro. Grater then filled the appointments of Bro. Hetric in Coventry. October 4, 1902, Bro. Grater was advanced. September 30, 1905, he was granted a letter, having moved west.

Bro. William Nyce, a minister of Royersford, moved to

the Harmonyville branch of the Coventry Church, in 1905. Here his active aggressive spirit soon began to tell. See the account of the Harmonyville Church.

The First Pastor.

Elder J. P. Hetric was the first pastor of the Coventry Church. He had previously had charge of the Marshall Street Church of Philadelphia. Bro. Hetric was born in Armstrong Co., Pa., December 20, 1843. He had taught school. He was baptized into the Redbank Church by Elder Jas. Quinter in 1864. He was elected to the ministry on June 30, 1866, and advanced to second degree November 3, 1867. He now attended school to fit himself more fully for his high calling, being graduated from Reid Institute in 1870. He had charge of three churches in his home section before coming, in 1874, to Philadelphia, and at the latter place was ordained an Elder in October, 1879. In November, 1882, he moved to Parkerford, Chester Co., as pastor of the Coventry Church. January 8, 1898, he resigned his pastorate with the view of securing a younger man for the place, but still retained the eldership of the church. He ceased to be elder of Coventry in November, 1912, but still has the oversight of the churches at Parkerford and Royersford. His work proclaims him a man of fine mind.

On January 1, 1898, Bro. Hetric had called a meeting of the officers of the church at Coventry and at Harmonyville and had given six reasons why he should be relieved of the burden of regular preaching. The official body appointed a committee of three to act on these reasons and report. Their report was as follows:

"We, the committee apointed by the moderator, beg leave to offer the following as our report,

"1st. We, after hearing the six reasons given by Bro. J. P. Hetric for retiring as the regular pastor of the Brethren's Coventry and Harmonyville churches, think it would be best for the good of the two churches to accept his statements as reasons for procuring more ministerial help;

"2nd. We recommend a young pastor to take charge of the regular services of the two churches."

"Signed by the Committee."

This report was adopted by the church, January 8, 1898. A committee of three was appointed to procure a new pastor.

Nothing has been said of F. F. Holsopple as a pastor in the Coventry Church. It will be noticed in the foregoing action of Bro. Hetric that Parkerford is not included. Bro. Holsopple had become pastor of the Parkerford branch of Coventry already in October, 1895, and under him Parkerford became a separate congregation in June, 1898.

The Coventry pastor committee secured the services of Bro. J. J. Shaffer of the Shade Creek congregation. His letter of membership there was granted him, September 26, 1898. Bro. Shaffer continued with the Coventry Church only about one year. He resigned as pastor, August 6, 1899.

Ira C. Holsopple, brother of F. F. at Parkerford, was now unanimously elected pastor. Bro. Holsopple's letter was accepted at Coventry, October 5, 1899; but he had begun as pastor already on August 25. He married into the congregation and seems at home here. He has given very acceptable service to Coventry during the last fourteen years.

The Deacons.

The names of the early deacons of the Coventry Church we have been unable to secure. August 7, 1880, Jonathan Keim and Stephen Brownback were elected to this office. Sept. 5 of the same year Wm. Y. Eisenberg was also elected a deacon. This election was likely held to fill the vacancy caused by the election of John Eisenberg to the ministry, John having previously been a deacon.

J. B. Reiff and David G. Bergey were elected for the Parkerford field, December 27, 1890. Elder J. Z. Gottwals installed them. The meeting was held in the Parkerford house.

In Coventry W. W. Kulp and John Buckwalter were elected deacons, August 13, 1892. Also at Coventry, J. H. Haldeman and Rudolph Harley were elected, August 4, 1894, the charge being given by Elder J. Z. Gottwals.

OTHER OFFICIALS.

The first clerk of the Coventry congregation was John Y. Eisenberg. Through his efforts and those of Jacob Connor regular councils with authorized minutes were kept. Jacob Connor was made moderator and John Eisenberg clerk. This was in 1872. This first regular council was held November 2 of this year. Bro. Eisenberg's account of the matter is interesting and we record it.

Bro. Eisenberg and Bro. Connor held a sort of caucus between them and concluded that it would be well to have regular councils and to have records kept. It would seem from these words that the councils at Coventry had been like the General Conferences at the beginning—called only when occasion demanded. There were no authorized minutes at this time as yet, says Bro. Eisenberg. John Harley kept a list of the members, but beyond this there were no records, unless individuals jotted down happenings for their own use. We have not been so fortunate as to find any records prior to 1872.

Brethren Connor and Eisenberg presented the matter to the church, and the church decided to have regular councils and a secretary. Unexpectedly to himself, Bro. Eisenberg was chosen secretary; and Bro. Connor was made moderator. Bro. Eisenberg thought there should be some kind of a constitution; so he drew one up, presented it to the church and it was adopted. Bro. Eisenberg now not wishing to thrust himself on the church as secretary resigned. But he was unanimously re-elected. On inquiry how long this was to continue, Elder John R. Price replied: "For life or during good behavior, like the members of the Supreme Court." Bro. Eisenberg continued as secretary till 1894; or one year after his removal to Royersford, when he resigned. He is still the custodian of the old minute book, Coventry seeming no more anxious to preserve them in a vault than she was to preserve her early minutes which Dr. Urner believes to be lost. What a pity! But she is not the only congregation thus minded. Bro. Eisenberg was succeeded as secretary by Bro. J. H. Haldeman, who still fills the position.

The adoption of the regular council and the officering of

it seems to have been a swing from one extreme to another —much elder authority being followed by little. It seems that the Brethren had been looking to the adjoining elders to decide matters for them, inasmuch as it was decided that Bro. R. Harley should hold the documents (a decision of Elders John H. Umstad, Samuel Harley and Henry Cassel) concerning the money coming to the church from Bro. Philip Hoffman's estate, in place of Peter Hollowbush, deceased.

There seem to have been peculiar conditions in the congregation at this time. At the first council meeting the question was asked: "Is it the duty of the church to live out the decisions of the District and Annual Meetings?" This question was repeated again and again in the councils, but each time deferred.

It may here be in place to state that there are strong reasons to believe that Bro. Jacob Connor fully merited the position he received as moderator of the council, though only a minister in the first degree. He seems to have been the embodiment of the missionary life of the congregation. A call for a missionary convention to be held at Myersdale, Somerset county, December 4, 1878, was issued. Notice was given in *The Primitive Christian* and also in *The Pilgrim*. The notice was read to the church on November 10, and it was decided "to send a delegate and to pay his expenses." Bro. Connor was sent. Three or four years later Bro. Connor gave an account of a missionary trip he had made to Lackawanna. It will be here in place to state that beginning with 1887, Bro. Connor served for one term on the District Mission Board and during that time looked after the Upper Dublin Church. Perhaps it was about this time that Bro. Connor moved to Gratersford in the Mingo Church. At his new home quite an interest was awakened. This was also the home of Elder Isaac Kulp and his talented daughter Emma, afterward the wife of the well known evangelist, Elder Isaac Frantz of Ohio. A neat brick church house was built at Gratersford. But the work went down. Bro. Connor now one of our oldest ministers is at present living in the limits of the Parkerford Church.

For twenty-nine years, ending with 1911, Wm. Y. Eisenberg, brother of John, served the Coventry Church with great acceptance as treasurer. In recognition of his long and faithful service, the church presented him with a copy of the New Testament and Psalms, with appropriate resolutions.

Trustees are officials whose services are too often overlooked, but as we have not the names of the earlier ones, the later ones will also be withheld. But April 5, 1902, the Board of Trustees was fixed at five members, with instructions to organize. In 1909 the term of trusteeship was fixed at five years.

The Children of Coventry.

Coventry as a congregation is only a decade less than two centuries old, and she is a mother congregation. The children of her youth are lost to her. To-day she does not know them when she meets them; and it is impossible for us in our present capacity to make known to her her early children—some farther west in the old Keystone State, some in Maryland, some in Virginia, likely some in the Middle West, perhaps some farther west. Some likely died many years ago and to-day have no tombstone to mark their resting-place. And then her grandchildren, and great-grandchildren, and great-great-grandchildren! What a family tree would be hers if constructed! But tangible children, near at home, she has, and she knows them as such.

Coventry's home field was along the Schuylkill River, above being bounded by Northkill and below by Germantown. West of her was her sister, younger than she by only a few days, a sturdy German dame, and perhaps more prolific in offspring than even herself.

The Nantmeal Mission.

In August, 1773, Daniel Price, of Indian Creek, a descendant of Jacob Preisz, the itinerant preacher of the Brethren in Germany, bought land for his son George in Nantmeal Township, Chester Co. In 1774 George's name appears on the list of taxables. George Price lived in Nantmeal till 1794, when he moved to Coventry Township. But during his sojourn in Nantmeal he opened up a Brethren's mission. Although in his later life the eldership of the Coventry church devolved upon him, he continued to look after Nantmeal until his death in 1823. Nor is Isaac Urner altogether correct in stating that the mission there afterward did not prosper, for the Brethren continued to preach there more than fifty years subsequent to that event.

Elder J. Z. Gottwals, who preached the last sermon for the Brethren at Nantmeal, tells us that beside himself David Keim, Peter Hollowbush, John H. Umstad, and David Rittenhouse preached there. Some of these Brethren certainly labored in this field as early as 1850. After the death of George Price in 1823, no doubt his son and grandson took a lively interest in the work of the head of the Price family in the Coventry district.

After Green Tree became a separate congregation, likely about 1845, she maintained a joint interest in the work at Nantmeal, or at West Nantmeal, as the writer so often heard his grandfather call it, and gathered some of the converts into the Green Tree fold. Some of the older members as Samuel Krause and James Guest came to regard Green Tree as more of a home than Coventry, though their membership was never transferred. Those to join Green Tree were Frances Krause, Levi Krause and wife, Emma Shick, Louisa Evans, Mary Boyer, — Witmore, Catharine Shannamon, and John Stover and wife. Among those holding membership at Coventry were John Essig and wife, Samuel Krause and wife, Joel Dillsworth, Daniel Krause's wife and daughter, Samuel Krause's mother, and James Guest and wife. Some of these members were very substantial residents of the community. Some died, some moved away, and some brought reproach on the Brethren name. In 1880 a committee was appointed by the Coventry Church to visit the Brethren in Nantmeal. This committee, no doubt, recommended discontinuing the work, for it was about this time that it was dropped. Opposition on the part of the Methodists seems to have constituted the death blow.

The Lumberville Mission.

The writer was informed by a Mr. Showalter that the "Morgan School-house" in Phœnixville was built by the Mennonites and Brethren as a place of worship, the two peoples alternating on Sundays in using it. The ground was given by the Phœnix Iron Co. As long as they continued to use the house for worship it was theirs, but in case they ceased to use it, it was to revert to the Iron Company. The Mennonites soon built a house of their own, and it is suggested that the Brethren turned their interest to Lumberville. This matter, however, has not been properly investigated.

As early as the beginning of the nineteenth century, Elder George Price had a preaching appointment every eight weeks at Methatchton, about two miles northwest of Norristown. It was a long drive and the old-time missionary would start on Saturday afternoon and stop over night with Daniel Brower, a Mennonite, and the farmer immediately east of John Umstad. After service on Sunday morning, Bro. Price would return to Brower's for dinner. Frequently in the afternoon, he would hold out-of-door services in Brower's meadow. The old brother would preach in German and his son John, who frequently accompanied him, would speak in English. As a result of these labors, Mary and Elizabeth Brower, daughters of Daniel, united with the Coventry Church.

It was not, however, till a number of years later, in 1833, that a permanent mission was started at Lumberville, now Port Providence. At this time Abel and Isabella Fitzwater, Isaac Price and wife, and John Umstad and wife, as the result of an awakening in the neighborhood, joined the Coventry Church. This led to the building of a joint house with the Methodists, at Lumberville, and the establishing of a permanent work in the neighborhood. For a fuller account see the history of the Green Tree Church.

The Mission at Parkerford.

Very few members lived in Parkerford in 1840. Isaac Kulp and wife and Jonas Fisher and wife were among the number. Many members by the name of Frick lived not far away. Sarah Rinewalt is mentioned as an active young sister. She married James Wells. Susan Sidel, "who kept a record," lived here. While these members desired meetings, yet the Coventry Church saw here an opening for a mission. About 1840 meetings were held in the school house. All the Coventry ministers preached here, and these included John Umstad, Isaac Price, and James Quinter of Green Tree, for Green Tree was yet a part of Coventry. Father John Price was the elder. In this early day Sarah Major also preached here.

A notable revival followed these efforts. Perhaps James Quinter did most of the preaching. Peter Hollowbush, soon afterward elected a minister, entered the church. The need of a meeting-house was felt; and the present Parkerford house was built in 1843. Jacob Frick superintended its erection. For a very interesting account of the work at this place see the history of the Parkerford Church by Dr. William Brower.

The Mission at Harmonyville.

The name of Keim stands out above all others in the work at Harmonyville. The Keim home here was purchased already by Hans or John Keim, the great-grandfather of Elder David Keim. David Keim moved from Coventry Township, Chester County, to Harmonyville, Warwick Township, in 1845. He at once began to build up a Brethren interest here. "His labors were blessed, and he lived to see the interest grow and develop into the present Harmonyville Church, with its fine commodious Meeting-house."[1] Harmonyville has recently been organized into a separate congregation. For a full account of the work see the history of the Harmonyville Church.

Efforts in Pottstown.

Pottstown affords to Coventry her city opportunity—an opportunity not yet improved.

Action was taken, February 11, 1888, toward holding

[1] Urner, "History of Coventry Church."

meetings in Pottstown. Out of thirty-seven members then living there notified to be present with the committee appointed to consider the matter, only thirteen came. The committee on its report April 7, 1888, was discharged and no further action it seems was taken. What a pity, for with only thirteen, including himself, Christ started the Kingdom of Heaven.

January 20, 1909, Ira Holsopple spoke relative to starting a work in Pottstown for members there, it being inconvenient for them to attend at Coventry. But nothing seems to have been accomplished. May the Brethren yet have a strong church in Pottstown!

The Coventry Meeting-Houses.

Coventry was only two years behind the old Mother Church at Germantown in erecting a separate house for worship. The first Coventry house was built on the Urner farm in 1772, and was of logs. It stood until 1817, when it was succeeded by a house of stone. The logs of the old church were used to build a residence at Cedarville.

Sister Stover and the Old Log Church should not be forgotten. Rudolph Stover had bought the old Urner farm about 1810, at the time that Jonas Urner moved to Virginia. His wife was a pious old sister, although her husband was not a member of the church. She loved the old log meeting-house. Here she had been fed on heavenly manna; here her thirsty soul had drunk in the water of life; here she had sat in heavenly places in Christ Jesus. The old log structure became dilapidated, unfit for services, but she objected strenuously to tearing it down. The place was dear to her heart For two years or more deference to the pious sister saved the old log church; but finally the day of its doom was set. The evening before the day, at dusk, the aged sister was seen wending her way to the old Bethel. She entered. Curious persons peeped in at the door. Old Sister Stover had gone to her accustomed seat, was kneeling there for the last time to hold communion with her God.

The Second Coventry Church.

This was built in 1817. It was of stone and very substantially built. It was almost impossible to get the stones apart when the walls were torn down. The house though built of stone followed in internal arrangement the frame house built in Amwell, N. J., six years before. The benches had no backs till about 1870. The house was heated by means of two stoves, with pipes coming together in a big drum over the central aisle. This method of heating has been pronounced by some as too hot for the head and too cold for the feet, while others think the comfort given is not discounted by modern appliances. Elder George Price was the overseer of the work of construction, and Bro. James Wells was the carpenter. About 1880 an organ was placed in this church to be used only in the Sunday School. It was then used for evening meetings; and about ten years after its admission, it was used in the morning service.

The Third House.

Methods, means of carrying on the work of the Gospel, may grow old, may not adjust themselves to new conditions, but the truth changeth not. Heaven and earth shall pass away, but the Lord's words shall not pass away. And so even the second Coventry meeting-house, well built of stone, grew old and no longer met the needs of the work. August 4, 1888, it was decided to rebuild once more; but the action caused disorder in the flock. The matter was allowed to rest for a season. March 8, 1890, a plan for rebuilding was adopted without opposition. The side entrances were walled up, and the entrance made through a vestibule at the end toward the road. The interior was brought up to date, with a loftier ceiling and an alcove back of the pulpit. During the rebuilding the Brethren were allowed the use of the school-house at Kenilworth, formerly known as Madison. A Sunday School addition, for some time urged by the pastor, was recently built to the northwest corner of the church. It is 24 × 26 ft. in size.

SECOND COVENTRY CHURCH, FROM PEN SKETCH.

FARM HOUSE WHERE ANNUAL MEETING OF 1790 WAS HELD, COVENTRY.

COVENTRY GRAVEYARD.

The second church handed down the seats with reversible backs, every third one used at love-feast for a table, diminishing the seating capacity one third, and placing one half of the communicants with their backs to the preachers. The new form of communion table, with table fastened to the back of each seat, was adopted, February 1, 1908. In 1892 a quadrupled silver communion set supplanted the old pewter vessels. It was decided to put a baptistry into the church, November 30, 1903. This came after years of discussion. It cost $161.40.

The Graveyard.

We quote from a letter of Dr. Wm. Brower of Spring City: "Martin Urner, Sr., donated the Coventry Brethren Graveyard in 1743. Coventry Church erected their first meeting-house in 1772, *twenty-nine years* after the starting of the burying ground. Unfortunately the site selected for a church house was fully a quarter of a mile away from the graveyard. In this historic burying ground lie buried six of the Elders who served the Coventry Church. I enclose the list.

First Bishop. Martin Urner, Sr., born 1695; died March 29, 1755.

Second Bishop. Martin Urner, Jr., born September 4, 1725; died May 18, 1799.

Third Bishop. George Price, born November 1, 1753; died September 25, 1823.

Fourth Bishop. John Price, born April 12, 1783; died April 4, 1850.

Fifth Bishop. John R. Price, born April 3, 1810; died March 1, 1879.

Sixth Bishop. David Keim, born January 5, 1803; died March 4, 1897.

Dr. Isaac Urner, a descendant of the Urner fathers in Coventry and for many years President of a Baptist College in Mississippi, rehabilitated the old Coventry burial ground. He built a substantial wall around it and erected huge granite monuments to the Urner family. (See cut.) He left a fund of $5,000, the income of which is to be used in keeping up the cemetery. It is one of the best kept cemeteries in the state.

Auxiliary Organizations.

Coventry was the first of our congregations to adopt a modern church auxiliary. Her Sunday School was started in 1842 or 1843. Sister Elizabeth Harley, afterward Stem, and another young sister were at the bottom of this organization for the Brethren. A young Methodist was superintendent, but these sisters soon made it the property of the Coventry Church. It was first held in the school-house across the way. Sister Stem used to tell how she scrubbed up the school-house floor on Saturdays. The faithfulness of these sisters soon caused the church to look with favor on the new movement, and before long it was permitted to move into the meeting-house. But latent opposition now broke forth, and the Sunday School had to find refuge again in the school-house. But again it won its way back into the meeting-house; and this time the Elder John Price came out in its favor and urged that it never again be allowed to go out of the church.

Different Brethren for a short time served as superintendent, but we shall here mention only Jonas Leopold, who served from about 1851 to 1858 or 1859, when he moved to Lancaster County. His missionary zeal led him here within the present bounds of the White Oak Church, to blaze the way for Brethren in Lancaster County to conduct Sunday Schools. Hiram Gibble then a youth attended the school, and here he caught the unquenchable Sunday School flame that has ever characterized him since amid strong, unyielding opposition. Besides zeal, Jonas Leopold brought more than ordinary intelligence to the work; with the result that the school was lifted to a higher standard.

But opposition continued. It was hoped that if a minister were superintendent the opposition would cease. Peter Hollowbush was given charge, but he had no zeal for this new work. The work lagged. Another preacher was tried; John Harley this time was the experiment. He

THE COVENTRY CHURCH.

proved a splendid success. He would preach in the morning at Parkerford, drive to Coventry, feed his horse, eat a cold lunch, and then spend the remaining time in getting things in shape for the Sunday School. He always wrote out notes on the lesson, and Elder J. P. Hetric pronounces them the best he ever saw.

For a term or two a member of the Reformed Church was superintendent, thus calling attention to the union origin of the school.

Subsequent superintendents have been Elder J. P. Hetric, John Buckwalter, R. E. Harley, W. K. Wise, and Charles Henzen, the present incumbent.

The Coventry Sunday School at the beginning had a library. The blue and red ticket system was used. The superintendent and teachers filled all offices. There were no graded lessons, and Sunday School helps were undreamed of. The New Testament, studied chapter by chapter, was the text-book. But the school has kept pace with modern developments. A Home Department, with William Keim as superintendent, and a Cradle Roll, with Mrs. James Huy as superintendent, were organized at a teachers' and officers' meeting at Bro. John Buckwalter's in the fall of 1908. The Home Department at present (1912) has a membership of about 40, with Sister John Buckwalter as superintendent. There are fourteen names on the Cradle Roll; Sister Ira Holsopple has charge. A Teacher's Training Class was organized also in 1908. There are four organized Bible Classes, two for men and two for women. The two sister's classes now look after the Sister's Aid Society work. The Coventry Sunday School has been carrying the front line seal for three years. The present enrollment is 236.

THE SISTERS' WORK.

The Sisters' Home Mission work was approved by the Coventry Church as early as February 9, 1884. This was certainly one of the sisters' first efforts in the Brotherhood. The home mission work was construed to mean this society, to which the home mission funds were to be paid. This society became dormant for a period. It was revived about ten years ago (1902), was active for three or four years, then went to sleep again. As previously stated, the two organized Sisters' Bible classes now look after the Sisters' Aid Society work.

The Christian Endeavor.

A meeting for organizing a Christian Endeavor Society met in the Coventry Church, March 11, 1894. W. W. Kulp acted as chairman. The following officers were elected: President, George Smale; Vice-President, Emma Stauffer; Recording Secretary, Cora Harley; Corresponding Secretary, Ella Miller; Treasurer, Horace Wells.

Three committees were authorized:

Prayer-meeting—J. P. Hetric, chr., W. W. Kulp, Mrs. Harley, and Amy John.

Look-out—J. P. Hetric, chr., Kate Frederick, Carrie Stamm, and Emma Stauffer.

Social—Carrie Stamm, chr., Flora Hetric, and Clara Frederick.

The Society met for the first time on Thursday evening, March 15, 1894. The meetings for a time were during the week; they were then changed to Sunday evening. For a number of years the meetings of the Christian Endeavor Society were the only services on Sunday evening, or until 1899, a short time before Bro. Ira Holsopple came as pastor. The business meetings are held semi-annually. At first the Society represented at the conventions of the general Christian Endeavor, but since 1898 has met with the other societies of the Brethren in the Schuylkill Valley, the first meeting being at Valley Forge, instigated largely by J. G. Francis, then a young preacher at Green Tree.

The Coventry Church has shown herself appreciative of attempts to write up her history. After Dr. Isaac Urner, a descendant of the old Coventry Urners, had compiled a history of the congregation and had had it published in handsome binding, the following resolution, drawn up by Elder J. P. Hetric, was adopted by the church:

"*Resolved,* That as a congregation comprising the Coventry Brethren Church, we recognize the kindness done us by Prof. I. N. Urner, in preparing and publishing so complete and acceptable a history of the congregation, as a church in council assembled do hereby extend to him our most grateful thanks."

Charities.

Coventry has shown the true Brethren spirit in caring for her poor and afflicted members. She has not tried to shove them off on secular institutions. Individual cases could be cited where considerable sums have been expended and have been continued through a long period of time.

Already in 1872 there were two funds in the church—the Hoffman Fund with interest amounting to $2,597.27; and the Amole Fund amounting to $1,077.50. But nearly all of the Hoffman Fund was later returned to heirs, who in reality had forfeited all legal claims to it. The two Hamilton brothers later also left funds. These funds, however, were not alone limited to charity.

Elder J. P. Hetric, soon after he began looking after the Coventry Church, introduced some very wise regulations concerning the charities of the church, which were adopted by the council on February 10, 1883.

The Coventry Church has set about solving this congregational obligation in a systematic manner. The need of a permanent poor fund was realized, and a Poor Fund Committee was appointed, January 6, 1906, to draft plans, for the regulation of such a fund.

Relation to General Conference.

In the troublous times about 1880, tending to division of the Brotherhood, Coventry held aloof from the General Conference. She refrained from sending delegates so as to maintain a neutral position. In 1884 she was unwilling to accept a committee sent from the General Conference. January 27, 1887, a committee from Annual Meeting waited on her to ascertain why she did not represent at Annual and District Meetings. In 1912 Bro. J. P. Hetric, her elder, represented his district[1] on Standing Committee. In 1913, the District Meeting, accompanied by other district movements, was held in the Coventry Church. We thus see the old Coventry Church, after many years of troubles, working fully in accord with the general church machinery.

Coventry was likely the first congregation of those led astray to return from the erroneous double mode of feetwashing to the single mode. An attempt was made to change, February 12, 1876; but the matter was indefinitely postponed. A query was sent this same year to District Meeting, asking if it would be wrong for Coventry to make the change. The change was consummated, August 9, 1877.

Coventry first elected a Correspondent to the Gospel Messenger March 3, 1897, Sister Essie Kulp being called to the work. Sunday morning collections were authorized at the same time. Privilege was extended to each and every member to engage in feetwashing, September 26, 1908.

While some are inclined to regard Coventry as a little too progressive, too ready to fall in line with worldly churches, and we have seen that her Sunday School and Young People's Society were started in conjunction with them, yet deep down in the congregation is a fine conservative element that has ever brought her finally into proper adjustment, and which finds expression in the ready adoption of the following resolutions:

Elder J. P. Hetric presented several resolutions to the official members of the church, which were endorsed by them. The resolutions were presented to the council of July 23, 1898, at the time that Parkerford was about being organized into a separate congregation. They follow:

"*Dear Brethren:* It is with pain of heart and much regret, that we see many members of our congregation depart more and more from the distinctive principles of pure and primitive Christianity in those well defined phases of character and conduct, that we feel it imperative necessity to call attention to the same in a public expression by the church.

"Then, first, there seems to be a disposition on the part of

[1] Southeastern Pennsylvania, New Jersey and eastern New York.

some of our members to attend and patronize festivals of any and every sort gotten up upon the pretext of aiding either religious or worldly enterprises, while pandering alone to the desire for carnal pleasure and ministering to the unrestrained lust of worldly sensualism, thus showing the trend of the heart to be more inclined to be a lover of pleasure than a lover of God, thus departing from the way of the Lord; and by example enticing others in the same way. We earnestly and urgently entreat our Brethren, old and young, to turn from such course of life, and for time to come to refrain from going to, or patronizing any places that are in the least degree of doubtful Christian propriety, and especially since the word of God so plainly and so distinctly forbids it and exhorts us to forsake the same. 2 Cor. 6: 16–18 and Rev. 18: 4, 5.

"Then, second, there is a disposition on the part of many to step still farther aside from the Gospel principles of plainness and modesty in apparel, and to follow more and more in the foot-steps of the wordly fashions and follies in undue decorations of themselves in the matter of dress—many wear the very gayest, most gaudy, and most showy feathers and flowers in their headdress. While some have even so far departed from the simplicity of Gospel apparel as to wear portions or imitations of birds in their headdress, thoughtless of the innocent lives of God's songsters thus wantonly sacrificed to gratify a taste lacking in humane spirit. The Bible enjoins most emphatically and most positively modesty in our apparel as well as in our general tastes of life. 1 Tim. 2:9 and 1 Pet. 3:3.

"We may not, yea, dare not disregard these plain injunctions of the Holy Scriptures, but at the peril of the soul's salvation. Let all them seek to conform more fully to the plain simple Gospel methods of life and conduct and thus fully meet God's approbation."

These resolutions were approved by the church and ordered placed on the minutes.

CHAPTER II.

GREEN TREE CHURCH.

Perhaps as early as 1800, Elder George Price of Coventry, grandfather of Elder Isaac Price, preached at the Methachton meeting-house, about two miles northwest of Norristown. The trip of about twenty miles was made by horse and carriage—rather a long drive before 10 A.M. on Sunday morning. So the faithful preacher would leave home on Saturday afternoon, and stop over night with Daniel Brower, who lived on the old Brower farm adjoining the Umstad farm on the east. Browers were Mennonites. After services at Methachton, five miles away, Elder Price would return to Brower's for dinner. He did not fail to reward this hospitality, for in the afternoon, in the summer time, he would hold open air services in Brower's meadow. Elder George was often accompanied by his son John. The father preached in German and the son in English. It will thus be seen that the original services of the Green Tree Church were German. To-day no German is spoken in the neighborhood.

The first-fruits of this Gospel seed-sowing in Brower's meadow were Mary and Elizabeth Brower, who connected themselves with the Coventry Church. This was a number of years before 1823, the year in which Elder George Price died. Elizabeth Brower became the second wife of Nathan Pennypacker and the mother of Sister Fannie Fitzwater.

The next important step in the history of the Green Tree church was the conversion of Bella Fitzwater, the sister of John Umstad. The Lord laid his hand on her in sickness. Sarah Righter, afterward the wife of Thomas Major, and also a prophetess, was called to see the invalid. Because of Mrs. Fitzwater's illness, her husband objected to her being baptized; but she was determined and declared that she

GREEN TREE CHURCH.

would be baptized though she died in the water. And sick and alone, she was baptized. This was in 1831. In this her determination may be found the faith which brought forth the Green Tree Church.

There was a general revival all over this section of country from 1830 to 1840. It was the spirit of this general awakening that had laid hold on Bella Fitzwater. Later in the fall of this same year, meetings held by the Brethren of Coventry in the neighborhood led to a great awakening. The example and prayers of Bella Fitzwater soon brought her husband, Abel Fitzwater, to the cross. Both John Umstad and Isaac Price were present, but unconverted, at the baptism of their brother-in-law. John Umstad was inclined to get fun out of his sister Isabella's piety. But in two weeks' time both of these two future eminent preachers went down into the baptismal waters. Many more, during this year, were gathered into the fold. Among them were Joseph Pennypacker and wife, George Price and wife, and Samuel Supplee and wife. Though these events are given for the year 1831, there is reason to place them a year earlier, for it seems that Lydia Francis, wife of John Francis of Shannonville, must have been baptized in the early summer of 1831.

So large had become the flock around Lumberville that it was necessary to build a special fold for it. An agreement was entered into with the Methodists, who had also been holding meetings in the neighborhood, to erect a house of worship at Lumberville. It seems that this house was built in 1832. It was of stone, two stories high, the upper story being used for school purposes and the lower for church services. Nathan Pennypacker, noted for liberality, was solicited for aid, much being expected. He gave one dollar. He afterward explained that if it were a "Dunker" meeting-house, or one of another denomination, he would have given much more liberally. Subsequent history bore out the correctness of his anticipation of a union house.

Now occurs an event in the history of this little mission which is destined to lead to great blessing throughout our entire Brotherhood—the conversion of James Quinter. Before the Lumberville meeting-house was finished the newly converted Brethren held public worship in the school-houses and prayer-meetings at their homes. James Quinter, referring to Bro. Umstad's home at this time, calls it the "Pilgrim's Rest," and Abel Fitzwater's home he designates a "Bethel." Among the school-houses utilized for public services was the one at the Green Tree. Writing to a sister in the neighborhood, Bro. Quinter thus describes his conversion: "How distinctly do I remember the meeting in the old school-house (the Green Tree) not far from your residence, where the bow, 'though drawn at a venture,' sent arrows of conviction into my poor heart, which produced pain and sorrow, from which I could find no relief, until I found it in the healing virtues contained in the stream which flowed from the pierced side of the dying Savior." After services were held at the home of Bro. Umstad to a late hour of the night for the comfort and salvation of those under conviction, Bro. Quinter tells of the solemnity to him of that night as he journeyed homeward toward Abel Fitzwater's, alone, "without Christ . . . having no hope and without God in the world." For some time he groped on in darkness, until one day while working in the barn at Fitzwater's, turning the windmill, he suddenly stopped, the light beginning to dawn on his soul. "I've got—I've got it!" he exclaimed, and ran to the house. "I've got it—peace with God!"

The above event must have taken place some time in 1832, for in 1833 he taught his first school at Hobson's school-house, a mile from Royersford. In the spring of 1834, he returned to Lumberville to teach in the newly erected church and school-house. He taught here from 1834 to 1841. Soon after his conversion, he was impressed with a call to the Christian ministry. Although the impression continued to grow stronger, he quietly awaited the time of the Church's call. Finally in 1838, in a council meeting held in the home of Bro. George Price, a short distance west of Green Tree, he was elected to the ministry.

Bro. John Umstad who was elected to the ministry in 1834 took all the interest of an elder in the young preacher and opened doors of usefulness to him. During his four years of ministry in the Lumberville Church he preached considerably in the neighboring congregations. He held the first protracted meeting of the Brethren in Lawrenceville, now Parkerford, at which place his son-in-law, F. F. Holsopple, led for several years the Lord's flock, and where his other son-in-law, Elder J. T. Myers, is now pastor. Bro. J. T. Myers was also for many years pastor and is now Elder of the Green Tree congregation, which was formerly the old Lumberville mission. How remarkable are the ways of the Lord! It seems that he answered the prayers of Bro. Quinter for the welfare of these churches by placing his children at the head.

Bro. Quinter also preached at the Union meeting-house, south of Shannonville, now Audubon. At such times he was the welcome recipient of the hospitality of John U. Francis, who joined the Church of the Brethren about this time, a man liberally educated, but whose wife Lydia had joined the church years before, and whose personal piety received the surpassing praise of Elder John Umstad.

Bro. Quinter also assisted Bro. Umstad in holding a series of meetings in the little Towamencin meeting-house, now of the past, within the present bounds of the Indian Creek congregation. All of this work was not poetical, for in later years of popularity, Bro. Quinter told to the shame of the Green Tree Church, how he was obliged to walk great distances to fill appointments on Sundays while the horses of the Brethren were standing lazily in the stables.

In 1839, he accompanied Bro. Umstad on a journey as far as the churches of Western Pennsylvania. The visit to the George's Creek Church led to his removal to that place in 1842. From this time on, Bro. Quinter labored in other fields. He was ordained by order of Annual Meeting but be it remembered that he is a son of Green Tree; and that Green Tree furnished this able and holy man to the Brotherhood.

Let us return to the old mission at Lumberville. The first love-feast in this section of the country was held in the new barn of Bro. John Umstad, wherein neither hay nor straw had ever yet lain—certainly a good way to consecrate a building to the office of holding God's blessings of the field. Be it here said that in those days it was the custom to hold love-feasts in the barns. It is said that at this love-feast, the project of building the Union meeting-house at Lumberville was started. If so, this love-feast must have been held in the spring of 1832, instead of 1833, as has been given.

The members of the mission were zealous, and God blessed them in increase of both numbers and power. It is claimed by no less authority than James Quinter that the first prayer-meetings and protracted-meetings of the Brotherhood were held in the Lumberville Church. Referring to these prayer-meetings in his last years, Bro. Quinter says: "Our prayer-meetings that were held in the beginning of the church here afforded us very good opportunities for exercising our gifts. While those meetings were excellent promoters of our spiritual life, they were good schools for our improvement in many ways. In these meetings, we exercised somewhat freely, as did the brethren and sisters generally." Of the spirit of the meetings he writes: "And what blessed meetings we had in those days of the planting of the church at Green Tree. How simple and childlike were our exercises! How warm our zeal! How ardent our Christian love to one another! How closely were our hearts drawn together in Christian fellowship! And we loved God because He first loved us. Those were happy times, oases, or green and watered spots in the land of our pilgrimage. Our sky was bright, and our sea, with the exception of some little breezes that would ruffle the surface occasionally, smooth." May the Green Tree Church never depart from her first love, and if she has or does may she speedily return that her candle-stick be not moved out of its place!

There was a good deal of missionary activity in those early days. The Methachton region was in close touch with Green Tree; and before Green Tree's beginning, with Coventry. William Casselberry, formerly of Worcester township, and his family were drawn to Green Tree. The first love feast in Worcester was held at his home. His wife was a member but he was not. She suggested to him how pleasant it would be, if he were a member, to hold a love-feast in their home. Notwithstanding this seeming obstacle, he offered her the home for the purpose, and the first, and perhaps only, love-feast in that section was celebrated. This was about 1820 or a little later. Wm. Casselberry was one of the first deacons at Green Tree; and his two maiden daughters, Mary and Sophia, counted for much in their day in the life of the church here. As to the extent of the territory of the Green Tree Church, when the Sunday School was started in 1869, Sister Maggie Kindy was appointed to solicit east of the Perkiomen Creek. She solicited as far as Worcester.

The Brethren also used to hold meetings at what was once called Krupp's meeting-house at Jeffersonville. The Brethren's effort at Norristown was started by John Umstad.

An effort of some magnitude was made east of the Perkiomen Creek, near Shannonville, at that time largely a mining village, the copper mines being in operation. Members of different persuasions were laboring here with some success. The older Wetherills gave land for a union house of worship. For the erection of the church, money was raised in the neighborhood by subscription. The Episcopalians, Methodists, Presbyterians and "Dunkers" preached in the building.

The Brethren started their work in this neighborhood about 1840, in the shape of prayer-meetings held in the homes of the members. Bros. William Cloward and Christian Dettra, and Sister John U. Francis gave their homes for this purpose. Later the prayer-meetings were carried into the public house of worship. Whether this was Jack schoolhouse or the union church we cannot now say. The meetings led to a series of meetings, which led to the notable revival in this section in 1840 or 1841. A number of miners were converted, and among others was the husband of Lydia Francis.

It has been stated, by old members, as noteworthy that John Umstad held aloof from these meetings near Shannonville. He and John U. Francis were cousins—the latter being the older. Elder John Price, Sr., of Coventry, had the oversight of this whole field. Isaac, his son, preached frequently at this new mission at Shannonville.

The Methodists in their services in the new union church were rather noisy, and by being so gave offense to the younger Wetherills, who were Episcopalians. Isaac Price, being of a somewhat excitable nature, was influenced in his preaching to some extent by the "amens" of the Methodists though the "Dunkers" did not approve much of this excitement. It is said that the Episcopalian services were not so well attended by the neighbors, as were some of the others. It was thought that this fact was not taken in good part by the Wetherills. It was also thought that they did not relish the idea of having the common people on a par in worship, though they did not object to the poor or common attending services under Episcopal control. It seems that they thought the proper thing to do was to have the property transferred to themselves, which transfer was soon brought about. A representative of the Wetherills, we are informed on good authority, arose in the meeting in the church on one occasion and publicly forbade the use of the church for worship to all except Episcopalians. The Brethren and perhaps others then secured Jack school-house, across the road, for services. John Francis especially was strongly exercised against the Episcopalians, but finally forgave his beloved daughter for attending services there against his will.

John Francis was then used for a time as a speaker, but was never formally elected to the ministry. We find him exercising at Methachton and Upper Dublin, where his speaking gave unusual satisfaction. Abraham Cassel tells of hearing him once at Methachton. No minister came and a John Francis, he related, was asked to conduct the service, which he did. Bro. Cassel states that no one was sorry that no preacher was present. Lack of recognition discouraged him from service. He was a grandson of Capt. Arnold Francis of the Providence Militia, who was used by Gen. Washington at Valley Forge to perform difficult missions, and who later was a prominent citizen. Many of the descendants of John Francis are to-day members of the Church of the Brethren, his grandson being the writer of these lines.

GREEN TREE CHURCH.

We have seen how active was the Coventry Church in home mission work. Besides missions at Nantmeal and Lawrenceville, in Chester county, she had missions in Montgomery county at Lumberville and Shannonville and a joint interest in the work at Methachton. The work in Montgomery was rapidly developing into a separate congregation. The Lumberville mission before it was a separate congregation began already to shoot out branches of her own. We find John Umstad very busy before he was the overseer. He had a hand in starting up the work at Upper Dublin. He was instrumental in baptizing the first ten members taken in at Mingo. He held aloof, however, from the work at Shannonville. He was making extended missionary trips out into the Brotherhood, as when he took James Quinter to western Pennsylvania. All these things took place before there was a Green Tree Church. But conditions had ripened for a new congregation. John Umstad had the situation well in hand. He gave the ground for the erection of the new church,—the union house at Lumberville not being satisfactory. The church received its name from an enormous evergreen tree, which stood on the corner of Umstad's lane and the public highway. A tree of the same kind now stands close to the church on the west side. The church, a stone one, with two doors on the east side, was erected in 1845. The house was dedicated June 6, 1845, and this may be regarded as the birthday of the congregation.

Some entries at this time in the diary of Albert Fitzwater, son of Deacon Abel Fitzwater, will be in place and of no small interest.

"April 7 attended a church meeting at George D. Price's in afternoon.

"April 17 went to mill, stopped at new meeting house, helped raise.

"April 27, Sabbath. I heard G. D. Price preach at Lumberville. Afternoon was at prayer-meeting at J. H. Umstad's. Took tea there.

"May 11, G. D. Price and John Francis preached at Upper Dublin.

"June 6, Clear, flying clouds, and not quite so as yesterday. Had meeting morning and afternoon at the Green Tree. The house was dedicated. D. Rittenhouse, G. D. P., W. P., & J. H. U. spoke.

"June 7, Clear, warm. Afternoon meeting at 3 o'clock. J. H. U., J. Price & J. Righter spoke. Evening we had love-feast. J. Reiner and W. P. spoke. We got home from meeting at 12 P. M.

"June 8, Sabbath. Flying clouds, very warm sunshine. Meeting at Green Tree. W. P., J. H. U. & Isaac Price spoke."

G. D. P. stands for George D. Price; W. P., for William Price; and J. H. U., for John H. Umstad.

It will be noticed that the writer of this diary attended a church meeting at George Price's. His was the first farm west of John Umstad's along the south side of the public road. It will also be remembered that at a council held at George Price's in 1838, James Quinter was elected to the ministry. These facts led us to think that Geo. Price's was a common place, if not the regular place for holding church councils. May he have been the original church clerk?

After the church was built at Green Tree and the Brethren began worshipping there, the adopted place for baptizing was the Schuylkill River below Umstad's dam. Down the lane, across the wooden bridge spanning the canal, a hymn and a prayer in the open, through the crowds covering the slope to the riverside, out into the liquid stream, kneeling in the water. "Dost thou believe that Jesus Christ is the Son of God?" . . . A threefold immersion, the laying on of hands, prayer for the bestowal of the Holy Spirit, the salutation of Christian fellowship—the holy kiss—both in the water and on the shore, then back into the world but not of it, a new creature in Christ Jesus! The banks of the Schuylkill below the dam is a place too sacred in the hearts of many for words to express—a scene for the brush of a master for the preservation of primitive Christianity.

If not the first yet one of the first baptisms at this place was performed Nov. 11, 1846. Jacob Gottwals, afterward bishop of the congregation for more than a quarter of a century, and Ann, his newly wedded wife, were at this time and place, buried with Christ in baptism. There were only three on this occasion; and strange to relate the other was B. F. Price, the only son of Elder Isaac Price, and afterward the son-in-law of the other two.

Ingatherings.—The Green Tree Church continued to grow. Just who and how many were baptized in the decade that followed we have not been able to tell with absolute accuracy. From 1856 to 1858 was a time of great ingathering. Bro. Umstad writes in THE GOSPEL VISITOR of May, 1858, p. 159: "We have had quite a revival in some of the churches east where the Brethren believe in protracted effort. . . . At Coventry they have an unprecedented revival. Last Sunday they baptized thirty, and on the 15th of May, there will be forty-one more added to the church. We at the Green Tree get along more slowly, yet we ought not to complain, since there have been about twenty added to the church here this spring, and there seems to be a spirit of religious inquiry among the people much more than usual."

The revival at Green Tree seems to have started with the series of meetings of two weeks held here by James Quinter in December, 1856. Among other things Bro. Quinter says of the meetings: "A more solemn meeting throughout, we never witnessed. The meeting continued about two weeks; during which time, thirty-two were added to the church by baptism. And at the close of the meetings, there were others who offered themselves as candidates for baptism." "The recollection that several of the converts had in former years been our pupils, and that they had often bowed with us in our school-room, while we endeavored to implore heaven's blessing upon them, gave us increased pleasure at witnessing their 'good confession.'" John Umstad then accompanied Bro. Quinter to New Jersey; and after their return to Green Tree, there was another baptism. Another revival in 1858, according to an aged sister, was almost a duplicate of this one. Some of the staunchest members of the church entered at this time.

Preaching in 1876 by J. T. Myers, then the youthful pastor at Germantown, caused quite an awakening, and was the cause of his coming to Green Tree. Again from about

1887 to 1890, under the preaching for four consecutive years of Bro. W. J. Swigart of Huntingdon, Pa., specially large harvests were gathered. In 1887, there were at least fifty-six; in 1889, there were thirty-four.

The Ministry.

We have seen that Elder George Price of Coventry with his son John were the first ministers of the Brethren to preach in this neighborhood; but there was no organized work yet in the days of Elder Price. During the oversight of John Price, the Lumberville, now Port Providence, Church was built. About 1834, an election for a minister was held at Lumberville. Both John Umstad and Isaac Price were elected. Bro. Price objected; he thought that God had not called him. John Umstad had no objections, but entered, as was his wont, into the work with a vim. In those days of the oversight of John Price, Sr., William Price of Indian Creek came frequently to Port Providence to preach. But he was very German. This intermingling of labors of the Green Tree Church with the "church of the Plains," now Indian Creek, Hatfield and Springfield, continued throughout the days of John Umstad and Jacob Gottwals.

An interesting incident in the lives of these two Prices—Elder John, Sr., and Elder William—is told by Bro. Jacob Connor. John and William had been assigned to the same bed; but there was another bed in the same room occupied by other Brethren. John and William were talking about their church troubles. All else was quiet. As to the occupants of the other bed, it seemed that "slumber's chain had bound them"; but they hadn't. John complained to William that in his church (Coventry) he had so much trouble with "pride," i. e. with fashionable attire: "How is it in your church, William?" William's church was Indian Creek. "Well," answered William, "I have no trouble with pride," perhaps feeling that he was a pretty good house-keeper. Whereupon John answered in an undertone, even in the quiet stillness, as though the walls might have ears, "Then, my brother, the Devil must be English."

Graves of Elder Isaac Price and Wife, Green Tree.

Graves of Elder Jacob Z. Gottwals and Wife, Green Tree.

Graves of John U. Francis and Wife, Green Tree.

Graves of Elder John H. Umstad and Wife, Green Tree.

George Price, the brother of Isaac, was elected to the ministry a few years later. He never became prominent as a preacher. He was the last of the Coventry line of Prices to be elected to the ministry. The first was Elder George, then his son John, Sr., followed in turn by his son John, Jr., at Coventry, brother of Isaac and George at Green Tree.

James Quinter was elected in 1838 and in his four years of ministry at Green Tree left a lasting impression for good not only in the neighborhood but also in adjoining congregations. As we have seen, there are grounds, considering the loose methods of the day, for regarding John Francis as a preacher. He was converted about 1840. His abilities are spoken of as of a high order, but in a few years he became discouraged in his labors. By 1845 David Rittenhouse was in the ministry. He was not regarded as able, but was very strict for the so-called order of the church. In the early fifties, he accompanied Jacob Gottwals in a horse and carriage trip to the Publishing House of Henry Kurtz in Poland, Ohio. This seemed to give to him the spirit of migration, for in 1854 he organized a company of Brethren in Eastern Pennsylvania, which migrated to Northern Illinois. There he became the founder of the Hickory Grove congregation. Members of his family founded other churches farther west.

About August 1, 1855, Jacob Z. Gottwals was elected to the ministry. About three or four years later, at the time that Emmanuel Heyser was elected to the ministry, he was advanced. At the Harvest Meeting of 1873, following the death of John Umstad, he, with Isaac Price, was ordained to the eldership. He continued to oversee the Green Tree Church till 1897, when he handed the following letter of resignation to the congregation:

"GREEN TREE, Sept. 26, 1897.
"I hereby kindly request the dear members of the above-named church to release me of the oversight as house-keeper of said church.
"JACOB Z. GOTTWALS."

His request was granted. He also had the oversight of a

number of adjoining churches, and was appointed on several committees by District Meeting to visit churches. His unique distinction is that of being moderator of the first District Meeting in Eastern Pennsylvania.

About 1858, Emmanuel Heyser was called to the ministry. He was the choice of the young men of the congregation. Young people's meetings, rather in the undesirable spirit of opposition to the old members, were held at the time at Green Tree. He was zealous in the work and found favor. After the war he went to Georgia and taught school among the negroes, at the same time preaching the Gospel to them. His work awakened the interest of the entire Brotherhood and offerings for his work were lifted throughout the churches. On the death of his second wife, he remarried outside of the church, and his work seemed to lose its purpose. The last brother to be elected to the ministry from the membership of Green Tree was J. G. Francis. He was born January 13, 1870. After completing the common school work, he entered Ursinus College, from which institution he was graduated in 1891 with the degree of A.B. After a few years in business in Philadelphia, he spent fifteen months in the Mt. Morris Bible School. While working in the slums of Philadelphia, in 1893, the Green Tree Church had empowered him to exhort. Before going to Mt. Morris, he was formally elected to the ministry. After returning, in the spring of 1895, the Green Tree Church installed him into the ministry. He then spent a year in preparation for the ministry in Union Theological Seminary, New York City. The following year he completed his theological studies in the Ursinus School of Theology, receiving the degree of B.D. He also won the Peter's Prize in New Testament Greek. He was advanced in the ministry in 1899, before going to Reading.

January 11, 1900, he married Mary Zug of Lebanon, Pa. He now moved to Reading, but the Mission Board, then in charge, thought it would not be for the good of the cause to employ him, because he thought they should do something toward his support. He later moved to Lebanon, where he engaged in painting and school-teaching.

The new church life, marked by the keeping of church records, laid hold of the Green Tree Church in 1862. The first minute on record tells of the resignation of Elijah Billew (Boileau) as treasurer. The minute is dated April 7, 1862. J. Z. Gottwals was moderator. The Green Tree Church has taken advance steps in the matter of church records.

The following query was sent to District Meeting in 1881. "Would it not be well at our next District Meeting to have a report from each church of the number of accessions, either by letter or baptism, during the past year; and also to have a portion of time set apart to discuss the best means of advancing not only the growth but the spirituality of the Church?"

It was also from the Green Tree Church that the query went asking recognition for the Brethren Historical Society.

In 1899 through the instigation of J. G. Francis, the congregation decided to keep a more complete record of church history. Bro. Francis was appointed the first registrar, and was likely the first member of the Church of the Brethren to hold such a position. He was authorized to secure a specially prepared book in which to keep the records. The names of all members from the beginning of the congregation were with great labor hunted up. Space was allotted in the book for the following information concerning each member: (1) Name; (2) time and place of birth; (3) time, place and performer of baptism; (4) marriage, time, to whom and by whom; (5) death, time of and burial place; (6) names of parents; (7) number of children; and (8) remarks. The record of each individual is kept on one continuous line, extending almost across two long pages. The book is a magnificent one, bound in full morocco.

When J. G. Francis moved from Green Tree in 1900, Isaac G. Price was appointed registrar; two years later when Isaac Price also moved away, Arnold Francis was made registrar. He still retains the position, though the records are looked after largely by the present pastor, C. F. McKee.

It was decided September 3, 1862, that all wearing gold,

etc., should be expelled. The council broke up in confusion. For a decade the church was practically lifeless. The sternness of Jacob Gottwals made him a terror to his children. But in after years he confessed with tears in his eyes: "I am afraid that we have been too severe on our young people." No records were kept of councils for several years.

In the latter part of 1876, Bro. J. T. Myers, then the young pastor of the Germantown Church, was invited to hold a series of meetings. Children of old substantial leaders were converted. January 1, 1877, twelve applicants for baptism were accepted. The church had tasted a new spiritual life. A desire arose to have Bro. Myers as pastor; an invitation was extended to him; and we find him accepted at Green Tree in July, 1877. The pastorate of Bro. Myers here continued till July, 1905, or for a period of twenty-eight years. He continues still to be its elder. After a stay of a few years in Philadelphia, as pastor of Geiger Memorial Church, he again for a short time resided within the limits of old Green Tree. The writer is one of many who would rise and call him blessed because of the work he did as pastor of the Green Tree Church.

In 1880 the Green Tree Church entertained the District Meeting. The Committee of Arrangements was Samuel Griffin, Joseph Griffin, John Harley, Matthias Harley, and John B. Dettra.

Green Tree has ever been in the van in adopting substantial new methods of church work. James Quinter credited her with the first protracted meeting and first modern prayer-meetings. On March 20, 1899, there was presented a query in regard to Young People's Meetings to be sent to Annual Meeting but it failed to pass District Meeting.

October 3, 1881, the Sisters were authorized to organize an Aid Society for the relief of the Huntingdon Orphan Home. Sister Fannie Fitzwater, wife of Joseph Fitzwater, was for a long time at the head of this work.

The matter of omitting the salutation before the communion has been agitating the Brotherhood for years, and the privilege has finally been granted; but Green Tree decided to omit the salutation before communion, October 1, 1883. The first steps toward a new state district were taken here. April 3, 1882, a petition was sent to District Meeting asking for a delegate from the English churches to Annual Meeting; or, in other words, a representative on Standing Committee. March 28, 1904, Green Tree requested plainly, sending a petition to District Meeting, asking that the English speaking churches be organized into a separate district.

While Elder John Umstad was a very strong opponent to Sunday Schools, yet from early Sunday School times, Green Tree has been a staunch and aggressive champion of the cause. The Sunday School here was started in 1869 by Joseph Fitzwater, a nephew of John Umstad. Bro. Fitzwater had great influence with Bro. Umstad and finally secured his permission "to go ahead and do all the good he could." The saving of the young for the Church was Bro. Fitzwater's great argument for Sunday Schools. He was superintendent at the beginning and has been continuously superintendent ever since—a record of forty-five years—a record unique for Sunday School work in our Brotherhood. For orderliness this school attained a reputation far and wide, and outside of the Brotherhood. In April, 1883, this church asked for a reversal of the decision of Annual Meeting against Sunday School conventions.

While on this subject, more should be said about Joseph Fitzwater. His mother was in a very important sense the mother of the Green Tree Church; and her son since has been largely its life. He was always the writer's ideal deacon. He was church clerk. He was at all meetings and ready unto every good work. His liberality was boundless, and his home was ever the home of his Brethren. He was second to none in loyalty to his own church, but not so narrow that he could not see good and would not co-operate with good in others. His soul beaming out through his radiant face was ever an inspiration. He was not a man to be driven, but one whose soul would almost leap out of him in following love. His spirit is revealed by a resolution he offered in a church council: "Inasmuch as there has been some misunderstanding between members of the Church in regard to various matters, we now pledge ourselves to forgive and try to forget the past, and henceforth will commune with and love each other as brethren and sisters." He was a great friend to the young. His cheery, breezy greetings on hot summer days as he entered the church just before Sunday School drew the boys and girls after him like a magnet draws iron filings. His after-teaching talks, always watered with tears, are never forgotten.

At a council in 1898, J. G. Francis inquired if something could not be done in the congregation to further missionary enterprise. A committee of five—J. G. Francis, J. T. Myers, Jos. Fitzwater, John Bechtel and Howard Yocum—was appointed.

In the cause of temperance Green Tree also has an enviable record of loyalty to the order of the Brotherhood. Isaac Price was a bright and shining light. In 1888 J. T. Myers presented a query which was sent to District Meeting, requesting the churches of the District to use unfermented wine. The sisters' organization of the church was imbued with temperance zeal. They frequently had members of the W. C. T. U. to speak in the church.

The doors of the Green Tree Church were thrown open for anti-secret conventions. For many years the Commencements of Upper Providence township were held within her walls. By wise policies Green Tree had made herself the church of the community.

The inner spirit must ever have a formal outward manifestation. The old stone walls which encased the life of the Green Tree Church at the first, built in 1845, was after the model built by Brethren in that day. On the east side were the usual old time entrances. On the opposite side was the table, with its long bench for preachers behind it. The raised pulpit came. The large ingatherings from 1887 to 1890 awakened a desire to remodel and beautify the old church home. A Building Committee was appointed consisting of Joseph Fitzwater, Samuel Griffin, Matthias Harley, Jacob Cassel and John Reiff. The entrance was made from the north side where an ample vestibule was added. The pulpit, with an alcove back of it, was at the opposite end of the auditorium. South of the auditorium, and capable of being made one with it by sliding doors, was erected the Sunday School addition. The aisles were carpeted and the walls papered. Without the walls were plastered and the roof made more peaked. As thus remodeled the cosy country church along the road at Green Tree gives a feeling of satisfaction to the most cultured æsthetic taste.

Again in 1907, the inner walls having been frescoed, the church was repaired and recarpeted at a cost of $455.87. This was really a reception to the new pastor and his wife, Bro. and Sister C. F. McKee, who came September 9, 1907. With such a gracious reception how could the new pastorate be other than it has proved itself to be—one of efficiency and blessing?

In 1899 a pool was built into the church. May 9 of this year was the first baptism. Grace, the daughter of Bro. Myers, was one of the four baptized.

Green Tree has had many faithful members whose names are in the book of life, but we cannot mention all here. Those intimately acquainted at Green Tree will likely feel that the names of Jacob Oberholtzer, the blacksmith, and Joseph Umstad, both of whom long served the church as janitor and sexton, should be mentioned. Wallace Rambo and Lewis Famous also filled these offices for a short period.

Ushers were first appointed in 1889. They were Lewis Dettra and John C. Reiff. Both afterward left Green Tree and were elected to the ministry.

John Dettra, the youngest brother of Lewis, is a consecrated business man at Oaks. He started a small flag factory to the rear of his father's house, and has built it up till to-day it is claimed to be the largest flag factory in the world. Recently he fixed up the basement of the Green Tree Church for church purposes entirely at his own expense.

Trustees.—The trustees of the Green Tree Church to whom John Umstad and Ann his wife conveyed two acres of land for $150, February 15, 1858, were John Conway, Joseph Fitzwater, John Bartholomew, Joseph Pennypacker and Samuel Supplee. Before this there seem to have been no trustees. The land that John Umstad gave in 1845 likely was never legally transferred to the church. Additional land for the cemetery was likely needed in 1858 and at this time the old and new tracts combined in one survey were transferred to the church. The consideration was likely only the price of the new tract.

By 1887 Samuel Griffin had become a trustee, and three of the original board were still serving. If others had been elected in the interval, they had ceased to be trustees by this time. Amos Gottwals and Abraham Landis were elected May 5, 1888. John U. Francis, Jr., formerly the eminently successful and well beloved merchant at Oaks, is also a trustee.

Deacons.—We perhaps have the list of deacons of the Green Tree Church complete from the beginning. The two first deacons were Abel Fitzwater and George Price. Then follow William Casselberry, Elijah Billew, Joseph S. Pennypacker, John Conway, Joseph Fitzwater, Samuel Griffin, Jacob Cassel, John Reiff, John Harley, Amos Gottwals and John Bechtel, elected October 24, 1892. Harry Ellis and Irwin Force were elected September 3, 1900. Howard Yocum, Abraham Landis and George Hallman were elected April 27, 1903.

Abel Fitzwater was the husband of Bella Fitzwater, the mother of the Green Tree Church. James Quinter was living in his home at the time of his conversion. The pious atmosphere of this home did much to direct his thoughts to religion. Bro. Quinter in later years calls it a " Bethel."

George Price afterward became a preacher, but never exercised much in his office.

William Casselberry was the father of the "Casselberry Girls"—Mary and Sophia, who eschewing marriage, devoted themselves to the work of the Lord. They occupied a prominent place in the church work at Green Tree for many years.

Conclusion.—The membership of the Green Tree Church at present is 300 in round numbers. The assessed membership is given in the District Meeting minutes of this year (1913) as only 275; but only the paying members are included in this enumeration. Twenty have been baptized this year without a special revival being held. Eighty-three have been received by baptism since Bro. McKee has become pastor.

The enrollment of the Sunday School is 232. There are three organized Bible Classes, a Teacher's Training Class, a Home Department and Cradle Roll. The Ladies' Aid Society is active. Green Tree still has a Christian Helpers Society. The Green Tree Church is alive and working.

CHAPTER III.

THE PARKERFORD CHURCH.

The history of the efforts put forth by the Brethren at Parkerford dates back almost to the commencement of the last century. As early as 1808 there were then two preaching points established at which meetings were held at intervals of four and eight weeks. One of these places was in the old School House in Parkerford near the mouth of Pigeon Creek. The other was in what was then Davis' School House on the opposite side of the Schuylkill, about two miles from Parkerford. At this early period there were four sisters living in this territory. One on the opposite side of the river near Davis' School House, was sister Catherine March, or as she was then called, old granny March. She was the great-grandmother of Mrs. D. W. Brower, of Spring City. This mother March joined the church in her youth and died in 1848, in her eighty-fifth year. The meetings held in the Davis' School House at intervals varying from four to eight weeks were at her solicitation. Two of these four sisters lived at the "old Parkerford Mill"—an aged sister, Mrs. Mary Parker (nee Hummel), and Mary Wilson, her daughter—mother and grandmother of the late Sister Susan Sidle, of Parkerford. The "old Mill" at which Sister Parker and her daughter Mary Wilson resided was a historic place even in their day —for it was here that Washington, with Generals Greene, Sullivan, Stirling and Armstrong with 8,000 Continental soldiers and 2,000 Militia, crossed the Schuylkill River, September 20, 1777, after the disastrous battle on the Brandywine. The third Sister on the Parkerford side of the river was Mary Shantz—nee Rinehart—wife of old Jacob Shantz, who lived about a half mile north of the Parkerford Mill. The place is now owned by Samuel Pennypacker. In corresponding with Elder Isaac Price in

Union Church (Remodeled), Port Providence.

Parkerford Church.

1882 in reference to the early work of the Brethren at Parkerford, preceding the establishment of the church—I learned that Elder John Price, father of Isaac Price, was the pioneer preacher, both at Parkerford and at Davis' School House across the river. Later on, old Father Price was assisted in this work by Bro. Isaac Price and Bro. John Umstad—and at a still later period Bro. James Quinter was also associated with these Brethren in filling these preaching appointments. The services at the Parkerford School House were held with some regularity about every four weeks.

The School House had been built by the community to serve the double purpose of establishing a pay school and also a place for public worship. The House was built in two apartments, separated by a sliding partition—the front part of the building was fitted up with school desks and seats for the accommodation of children,—the rear of the building was fitted up with pews, each rising higher than the one in front. On preaching occasions the entire house was made use of. In addition to the services held every four weeks on Sabbath afternoons, there were occasions at long intervals when there would be a few night services, when special efforts were put forth to reach the unsaved. But the last of these special evening services was a most memorable one, a great manifestation of the Spirit's presence and power to awaken the unawakened, a truly pentecostal season. I can do no better than to quote the exact language of Dear Bro. Isaac Price. He says: "We had several protracted meetings at Lawrenceville School House. But the last, following which the Church House was built, was a memorable one. We had what we called a 'glorious time'; preaching came easy. House crammed full, and on a certain Tuesday evening, sixteen on invitation came forward. The day before, on Monday, I had to go to West Chester to Court. Father attended Monday night and Tuesday night—who helped him I do not remember—but on Tuesday night I think Bro. Umstad was not there—and sixteen coming out, Father did not know what to do. He had never then been in such a meeting, with such a state of feeling—swearers, drunkards and such like came forward. And a great snow had fallen on Sunday, Monday and Tuesday. The roads were terribly drifted. And Father thought best to close the meeting. It was a painful thing to many of us." To those of us who knew Bro. Isaac Price, we know it must indeed have been a painful thought to have been deprived from participating in a meeting fraught with such power from on High. It was indeed a high day in Zion.

In the spring following the great revival twenty-five or more were baptized. The following summer, 1843, the Meeting House was built. Before entering fully upon this part of our subject, it is proper to add that about 1830 or probably a little later, Sister Sarah Righter preached for some time at Davis' School House and also at the Parkerford School House. When Bro. James Quinter was elected to the ministry, Sister Sarah Rinewalt got him to hold meetings at the old farm house, on the summit of Crab Hill, about a mile south of Parker's Mill. This old house is located near the big elm tree, which from its high elevation has stood for years as a notable landmark for many miles around.

The ground for the new meeting house was bought of David Y. Custer for the sum of $110. The purchased tract had a front of one hundred and ten feet, and embraced one acre of ground. The conveyance was made to Jacob Frick, Peter Hollowbush and Isaac Kolb, Trustees. Deed was dated September 16, 1843, and recorded April 10, 1845. In the construction of the house, the Brethren entrusted the oversight to Brother Daniel Scypes, who did the carpenter work, while Conrad Longacre had charge of the mason work. The house was dedicated with appropriate services on Sunday, September 24, 1843. The membership as constituted at the time the house was built, would necessarily include the entire membership of the Coventry Church at that period, and this condition of the churches prevailed for more than forty years afterwards, for the Lawrenceville or Parkerford Church was so exclusively a branch of the Coventry Church during all these years, that a quarterly conference or a single Communion Service was not held within its sacred precincts. The annual love feast held every autumn in the old Coventry Church, was always the happy occasion for a reunion of the entire membership, not only of the Mother Church but embracing also her two branches at Parkerford and at Harmonyville. The first Communion Service held in Parkerford Church occurred on the fifteenth of May, 1886, just forty-three years after the church was built. Since 1886 Communion Services have been observed regularly in the month of May of each recurring year. The first quarterly conference was held on Saturday, November 14, 1885, and from that time forward they had been alternated every three months with the Coventry Church, until the spring of 1896, when by mutual consent of the Coventry and Parkerford Churches it was agreed that Parkerford Church should conduct its own affairs, have its own quarterly conferences, have a separate treasury and be entirely free from the jurisdiction of the Coventry Church, except the church at Parkerford was to be under the charge of the Bishop of the Coventry Church.

On Sunday afternoon, April 14, 1878, the Brethren of the Parkerford Church met and organized the first Sabbath School held in their church. Bro. David G. Wells was elected the first superintendent, since which time Sabbath School has been maintained regularly every year, and for several years past, the school has been kept open every Sabbath throughout the year. The following persons have served as superintendent for a longer or shorter period: David G. Wells, Isaac U. Brower, Wm. Brower and John B. Reiff. The latter is our present superintendent and has served for quite a number of years.

In the spring of 1889 a special meeting of the Brethren was held, to take into consideration the propriety of reseating and remodeling the Meeting House. A Building Committee of three was appointed to carry out the plans, Committee Joseph Johnson, Samuel Rosen and Aaron Keiter. Upon the completion of the house and the refurnishing of the same at an expenditure of about $1,200 special dedicatory services were held late in the fall of 1889,

Elder J. P. Hetric was in charge, assisted by J. T. Myers, of Green Tree Church. The trustees of the church at that period were: Brethren John Frick, Henry Pennypacker and Aaron Keiter.

The Brethren decided, in the fall of 1895, that hereafter they would have regular services every Sabbath, and, as a consequence of this decision, extended a call to Bro. F. F. Holsopple to become their settled pastor. Upon his acceptance, they deemed it wise to procure a suitable house for a parsonage. On November 13, 1895, the present parsonage was bought for $1,700. This parsonage is near the Pennsylvania depot and within a square of the Meeting House; it occupies the historic site of the old Colonial log school house of 1750 or thereabouts, of which records are still extant, showing that in those early days the length of the school term was far in excess of what it is even today.

Parkerford Church has had several stirring revivals during the last twenty-five years. The first of these was conducted by Bro. J. P. Hetric, while pastor of the Philadelphia Church, about 1880, when many precious souls were born into the Kingdom. About 1882 Brother J. P. Hetric settled at Parkerford and gradually took the oversight of the Parkerford Church as well as of the Coventry Church. He is still the Bishop of our little flock, for we number about one hundred communicants, whereas the Coventry Church has more than two hundred members. Bro. F. F. Holsopple served our church very efficiently for a period of five years. Our next pastor, Bro. T. R. Coffman, is now (at the writing of this article) rounding out his fifth year of very acceptable service in this part of the Lord's vineyard.

The foregoing very valuable account of the Parkerford Church given by Dr. Wm. Brower, of Spring City, a descendant of the Urners, cannot be supplanted. Yet there are a few things that may yet be said about the work at Parkerford.

When the minutes were first kept in 1885, we find that the council meetings were already alternating between Coventry and Lawrenceville, as Parkerford was formerly called. Separate treasuries were authorized for Coventry and Parker-

THE PARKERFORD CHURCH. 255

ford, July 22, 1893. Charles Urner had, however, years before been a treasurer at Lawrenceville. Seventy-seven members in and around Parkerford had signed in 1893 a request for a separate treasury at that place previous to one being authorized. In the matter of sending delegates, Parkerford was to pay one third of the expense.

At the council of July 23, 1898, F. F. Holsopple, pastor at Parkerford, presented the following petition for the Parkerford Brethren:

"PARKERFORD, PA., June 4th, 1898.

"We the Brethren at Parkerford in council assembled this day do petition the Coventry Brethren's Church to grant at July council that the Parkerford Branch of the Coventry Brethren's Church be constituted a separate church to be known as the Parkerford Brethren Church.

"F. F. HOLSOPPLE, *Moderator.*
"DAVID BERGEY, *Clerk.*

"F. F. Holsopple and David G. Bergey were appointed a committee to present the above."

This petition was granted by the Coventry Church, so the Parkerford Brethren Church was born July 23, 1898.

Bro. F. F. Holsopple was the first pastor of Parkerford Church proper. Bro. Hetric had lived here while pastor of the whole Coventry Church. Bro. Holsopple had married Grace, the youngest daughter of Elder Jas. Quinter, and his coming here now to build up the work, makes us think that the Lord still had in mind Bro. Quinter's prayers for the work at Lawrenceville. Bro. Holsopple is of a family of preachers. His father is an elder, and two of his paternal uncles are preachers, his maternal grandfather was the well known Elder Christian Lehman and two of his own brothers are preachers, one being Bro. Ira, pastor at Coventry. But when he entered school at age of six, he believed he would be a school teacher. After teaching a number of years and graduating from Juniata College, he became pastor of the church at Amwell, N. J., September 1, 1892. In October 1895, he came to Parkerford. During his five-year pastorate more than twenty were added to the church. The prayer meeting and Sunday School were revived, a Sisters' Missionary Society and a Young People's Christian Helper Society were introduced and the Parkerford Church was organized into a separate congregation. Then his strong inclination to teaching caused him to accept a chair in Juniata College.

For three years or more Bro. Hetric looked after the pastoral needs of Parkerford. Bro. T. R. Coffman came as pastor, from a pastorate at Tyrone, Pa., on April 3, 1904. He was born June 27, 1873, at Hagerstown, Md. His education and teaching were largely along business lines until he was elected to the ministry in 1897. When he came to Parkerford the membership was a few less than one hundred. It is now one hundred and five. But it should be borne in mind that he has had many deaths to overcome, many of the old burden bearers of the church having passed away in the last few years. A Christian Workers' Society has been organized, the Sunday evening session being spent in the study of Jewish history. The Sisters' Society has been kept active, and the Sunday School, numbering about one hundred, under the efficient superintendency of Bro. J. B. Reiff has come to the " front line." The second teacher's Training Class is ready for graduation at this writing. There is a Home Department of thirteen, and a Cradle Roll of eight. Bro. Coffman was ordained to the eldership, December 10, 1911, J. T. Myers and J. P. Hetric officiating. After the ordination of Elder Coffman, Elder Hetric and he had joint oversight of the church until the resignation of the latter in December, 1912, to take up the pastorate of the Pittsburgh Brethren Church. Elder J. T. Myers, of the Green Tree Church, is the present pastor.

ROYERSFORD CHURCH.

CHAPTER IV.

ROYERSFORD CHURCH.

As it is necessary to have people before you can have a church, we shall first consider the members who moved into this town. But while we speak of the church in Royersford, we must not forget that some of the most active members in building up the work here, lived in the twin town across the river, in Spring City. There were Bro. David Wells, and daughters, Annie and Katie; Sister Mary Taylor; Dr. Wm. Brower, wife and daughter Blanche. These have all lived in Spring City for a number of years. All were members of Coventry.

But we now come to *The First Members in Royersford.*
Wm. Isett and wife were the first. They came from the Mingo Church, in the fall of 1882. In the spring of 1884 the Price family moved here from Mingo Church also. Those members were Mrs. Price, son Wm., who had joined at Huntington in 1883, daughters Elizabeth and Elmira baptized at Parkerford in 1886. In March, 1884, Wm. Dettra and wife of Green Tree Church moved from Oaks Station to the outskirts of the town. They moved into the town proper, September 1 of the same year. Sister Roeller came from the Parkerford Church in March, 1889. Her husband was not then a member. Bro. Joel Freed and wife from Mingo settled down in Royersford. Sister Mary Freed, wife of Samuel Freed, moved here in July, 1890, from Mingo Church. In December of the same year, from the same church, came John Isett and family, consisting of himself, his wife Hettie, and daughters Kate and Sallie. Next came Sister Jos. Johnson from Coventry, in April, 1891. Her husband is a member of the German Reformed Church. David Isett and his wife moved here in March, 1892; and his brother Benjamin and wife, in December of the same year. Both families were from the Mingo Church.

Wm., Benjamin, and David are all sons of John Isett. In May, 1892, Bro. Wm. G. Nyce with his mother came from Norristown; they were originally from the Mingo Church. Early in 1893 came C. F. McKee from the Manor Church, Md. He came to take charge of the books of the Grander Stove Co., of which Bro. Wm. Price, his old schoolmate at Huntingdon, was a member and later president. Bro. McKee was married in 1897 to Sister Iva Kaler, also from the Manor congregation. Rev. John Isenberg came from Coventry in 1893. From the same congregation came the Hunsbergers in 1895, in which year came also Bro. Robert Jones and family from Illinois. Jacob Grater and wife, a deacon and son of Elder A. L. Grater, came from Illinois in 1896. Sister Emma Tyson of Coventry, a school teacher in Spring City, worked here during the school months.

Thus we see that in a period of thirteen years a considerable and very complex membership had gathered here, where before there had been no members. But it was a splendid body of workers, from which at least four ministers were made.

The first form of religious life here was manifested in prayer-meetings held in the homes of the members. After the prayer-meeting had been conducted for some time, some of the members thought it would be well to start a Sunday School. The idea found favor, but great trouble was encountered in finding a place of meeting. Finally the Episcopalians agreed to let the Brethren have the use of their hall, Winter's Hall, on the corner of Main St. and Second Avenue, in the afternoon, they having their Sunday School in the morning. The expenses connected with the hall were to be equally divided, the Brethren's share of the rent being $1.00 per Sunday.

The first meeting of the Sunday School was held on May 3, 1891. This was the same day on which the Dauphin Street Church of the Brethren in Philadelphia was dedicated. The total number present was twenty-nine. There were five classes in the beginning. By 1898 they had increased to sixteen classes with one hundred and seventy-six scholars, making a total enrollment of one hundred and ninety-two.

The first superintendent was Bro. David Wells, who the next year was succeeded by Bro. W. S. Price, who has been the efficient superintendent ever since.

Men who do things were connected with this school. April 5, 1892, W. S. Price, Dr. Wm. Brower and Joel Freed were appointed a committee to purchase a lot on which to build a church. A vacant lot on Walnut Street was bought for $450. W. S. Price, David G. Wells and Joel C. Freed were appointed trustees. Early in the next year, when it was decided to "proceed to build a church at once," this lot was deemed unsatisfactory, and it was sold for $500. The lot on the corner of Third and Washington Streets was then bought. It was decided to build of brick with Wyoming blue stone trimmings. A pool was placed in the church. The general plan of the remodeled Green Tree Church was followed, with the exception that the vestibule was within the main walls. All business was done in the name of the German Baptist Brethren Sunday School. It was necessary to mortgage the property to some extent, but the debt was reduced rapidly. Considerable help was given by neighboring congregations. January 1, 1895, the trustees were increased to five, the new ones being E. L. Markley and Frank Roeller. The first minutes of the Sunday School were kept in 1892. In this same year they purchased an organ, and have a thoroughly up-to-date Sunday School.

The Home Department of this Sunday School, the first work of the kind, was organized, November 5, 1896. Elmira Price was made superintendent.

From the beginning there was preaching, if possible, every two weeks, after Sunday School. Bro. J. T. Myers did most of the preaching and did it free of charge; but Royersford was never lax in giving proper financial aid to those whom she called in to preach. In May, 1894, the mission volunteered to pay $25 toward paying the Parkerford minister if he would preach for them every other Sunday evening. March 6, 1897, it was decided to have regular Sunday morning preaching. The principal ministering Brethren who have assisted the church at this place are J. T.

Myers, J. P. Hetric, John Isenberg, Jay G. Francis, Lewis Keim, Jesse Ziegler, and Abraham L. Grater.

While many members had moved into Royersford, yet revivals did considerable in building up the membership. The first revival lasting one week, was held by Jesse Ziegler. There were no visible results. A year later J. T. Myers held a few meetings. Soon after they closed, Frank Roeller joined the church, placing his membership at Green Tree. He is the first fruits of the Royersford Mission.

In January, 1894, Bro. Myers held a series of meetings for two weeks with the result that nine entered the fold. I. N. H. Beahm held meetings for three weeks in February, 1895. He was assisted by J. G. Francis, who gave Bible readings in connection with the services. Two were added to the church, and were the first from Royersford to place their membership at Parkerford. Bro. Beahm preached some doctrinal sermons which made considerable stir in the town.

J. T. Myers, Jesse Ziegler and Frank Holsopple held a series of meetings in the fall of this same year. Seven were awakened and were the first to be baptized in the baptistry. The baptism took place, January 24, 1896.

In October, 1896, Bro. W. J. Swigart came two weeks. While there was only one accession, he awakened considerable interest and no doubt did much to prepare the church for the harvest that soon followed. This harvest was the direct result of the labors of Bro. F. F. Holsopple, who garnered nine into the fold.

In the fall of 1897 Elder D. F. Stauffer of Benevola, Md., and J. G. Francis conducted meeting. Four were added to the church. The total number baptized at Royersford up to 1898 was thirty-three. The number that had moved in was forty-seven. Deducting two deaths, the membership, January 1, 1898, was thus seventy-eight.

The Christian Helper Society.

On January 2, 1894, it was decided to organize a Christian Helper Society, and W. S. Price, Wm. Nyce, C. F. McKee, Frank Roeller, Annie Wells, Emma Tyson, Sallie

Isett, Elmira Price, and Irene Frock were appointed a committee to get it in shape. The idea was to get a society that would help the church, not one that would run away with it. Finally on May 1 of this same year, after two or three times reporting progress, the committee reported that it had organized. W. S. Price was elected chairman and E. L. Markley, secretary. Two committees—the Sunday School and the Lookout—were immediately appointed. The good that this society did in inspiring the members and in building up the young in Christian work was very great. It proved itself a worthy companion of the Sunday School. A Junior Christian Helper Society was also organized with Bro. W. G. Nyce in charge. Several of the churches of the Schuylkill Valley followed the lead of Royersford and organized Christian Helpers Societies. The name here was changed July 6, 1903, to Christian Worker Society.

A Sisters' Missionary Circle was organized in July, 1897. While clothing was gathered and sent to missions in the cities, flowers to cheer bestowed, and sewing done for the home poor, yet the main object at organization was to assist in paying off the church debt. In 1900 they paid $200 on the mortgage. April 15, 1901, they gave $100 toward paying a note. These facts certainly proclaim that the sisters were doing something.

Royersford Organized.

It was decided, April 2, 1900, to have Elder J. P. Hetric come to conduct the organization of the mission into a separate congregation, with Elders J. Z. Gottwals and A. L. Grater present to assist. The minutes are as follows:

"Royersford, Pa., Jan. 7, 1901.

"Royersford Mission convened in meeting for the purpose of organizing said mission into a German Baptist Brethren Church. Elders present organized by electing J. P. Hetric chairman and Jesse Ziegler as secretary.

"The boundaries of this organization shall be the borough lines of Royersford and Spring City, with the understanding that any modification of such lines as may be deemed necessary shall be possible by the mutual agreement with churches concerned.

"*Name.*—It was decided that the name shall be the Royersford Brethren Church.

"*Officers.*—It was decided further that two deacons should be elected. The choice fell upon Bro. C. F. McKee and Bro. W. S. Price, who were duly installed into their office by Eld. J. P. Hetric. Sister Price not being present she will be received at a later meeting.

"The choice of presiding elder fell on Bro. J. P. Hetric.

"Bro. B. Frank Roeller was elected clerk of the church, and Bro. C. F. McKee was elected treasurer.

"JESSE ZIEGLER, *Clerk.*"

It seems that there was some difficulty over this organization, and the committee from Annual Meeting was called in. So we have the following:

"To all whom it may concern, Greeting. This is to certify that the committee appointed by the Annual Meeting to visit the churches of Eastern Pennsylvania and New Jersey recognize the organization of the Royersford church.

"Respectfully submitted

"W. R. DEETER
"L. H. DICKEY
"D. HAYS

Com."

February 20, 1902, a committee was appointed to see about getting a pastor. In three days' time sufficient money had been subscribed to support one. But subscribing the money was not the only requisite for getting a pastor.

J. Linwood Eisenberg had been elected to the ministry here, and on November 29, 1903, he was advanced. Bro. W. G. Nyce had been elected at Parkerford before the organization of Royersford; and J. Y. Eisenberg had for years been living in Royersford, so the church was well supplied with resident ministers. But there was no pastor. Bro. C. F. McKee was also elected to the ministry here, October 24, 1906. But this was only a step preparatory to his becoming pastor of the Green Tree Church. He was advanced

January 19, 1907, and on April 7 following was given his letter of membership.

Bro. Alva J. Specht, of Ohio, was secured as pastor. He had been teaching. He came to Royersford, July 1, 1908. He was a minister in the second degree. He was well liked, but notwithstanding resigned his pastorate, May 12, 1909. The church accepted his resignation and passed resolutions expressing appreciation of his services.

Bro. A. W. Dupler, of Ohio, was unanimously elected pastor, June 25, 1909; and Bro. Quincy Leckrone was called, October 3, 1910. Bro. Leckrone still serves the charge. He is a clear thinker and able speaker.

It became necessary to increase the body of deacons; and November 29, 1903, Bro. B. Frank Roeller and William Harley were elected to this office. The board of deacons was diminished by one when Bro. C. F. McKee was called to the ministry. So we find that on April 7, 1907, two more were elected—W. J. Wadsworth and Alvin P. Harley.

The first year the work at Royersford cost the Brethren there $53.62. For the nine years previous to 1907, the expenditures amounted to $8,299.79, or a little less than $1,000 a year. In 1908 there was paid out $3,037.47. In this same year the church was chartered.

The present membership is one hundred and two. The Sunday School has but one hundred and ten members but this does not include the Home Department and the Cradle Roll. There is a Teacher Training Class of fifteen. The Sunday School is thoroughly graded.

CHAPTER V.

HARMONYVILLE CHURCH.

Harmonyville is a small village about a mile from the famed Falls of French Creek, in Chester County. It has a graded school and a Brethren's Church. The church was organized, January 25, 1913, with about 70 members, a Sunday School of 159 scholars, thoroughly up-to-date, and a mid-week prayer-meeting. The pastor is Bro. W. G. Nyce; the deacons are Jonathan H. Keim, Leonard Keim, Thomas Brewer and Edgar K. Lloyd; the trustees are Hiram Keim, Jacob H. Stager and Jonathan Keim. At present the church has no elder.

The prominent name in connection with the work at Harmonyville is Keim. Dr. Isaac N. Urner, in his history of the Coventry Church, of which Harmonyville till its recent organization, was a part, says: "Rev. David Keim . . . in 1845 moved to Warwick Township, and soon commenced building up a Brethren interest there. His labors were blessed, and he lived to see the interest grow and develop into the present Harmonyville Church, with its fine, commodious meeting-house. He was a bishop in the Brethren Church."

Harmonyville is only a few miles from Nantmeal, where a Brethren's mission was kept up for many years, but the two were entirely distinct, nor is the Nantmeal Mission in its death known to have given any members to Harmonyville.

Originally the Brethren preached in the old school-house a short distance out from the village. David Keim preached here before he moved up to Harmonyville. In a year or two a new and larger school-house was erected in Harmonyville, likely in 1846, and the services were transferred to the new house. Here the Brethren continued to worship till the meeting-house was built in 1880.

The Sunday School.

The Harmonyville Sunday School is not a new institution. It was started in 1859 as a union school, the Methodists also worshipping in the school-house. The first superintendent was George Wennings, a Methodist, with Bro. Jacob Ehrgood as assistant and Bro. Jonathan Keim as secretary. Other Brethren active at the beginning were Hiram Amole, Keziah Amole and Keziah Keim. The second year Bro. Ehrgood was superintendent. In 1861 Jonathan Keim went west but returned two years later. He was now made superintendent and continued until the Sunday School had been in the church for a few years. The Methodists, having built a church in 1878 at some distance, withdrew and left the Brethren in exclusive control. As superintendent Bro. Keim was succeeded by Bro. Stephen Brownback, a deacon and son-in-law of Elder David Keim. He continued in charge till the spring of 1894, when he moved to Philadelphia, where he became an equally prominent Sunday School worker. Hervey Keim now became superintendent at Harmonyville. He was followed by Leonard Keim. Harry Keim is the present incumbent.

The Sunday School is the strong arm of the church at Harmonyville. As stated, it has an enrollment of 159. There are two organized adult Bible classes, numbering 45 members each. The adult members are drawn from a radius of three miles. The school is graded throughout, there being twelve classes in all. This Sunday School takes an active part in the County Sunday School organization; and District Sunday School conventions have been held here. Harry Dickinson, teacher of the male organized adult Bible Class, is mentioned as a worker worthy of note. There are a Cradle Roll, Home Department and Teacher Training Class. Harmonyville has a front rank Sunday School.

A Christian Helper's organization was started here, January 5, 1900. It labored with the general organization in the Schuylkill Valley. The local organization was discontinued; and a Working Committee of Five was appointed July 21, 1906, to supervise all evening meetings.

As to the church property—the ground was given by

Samuel Keim, father of Jonathan. As stated the house was erected in 1880 at a cost of $1,000 above the generous free labor of members and the ground. It is a stone structure 30 × 40 ft. There is a frame vestibule in front, about 10 ft. × 10 ft. In 1895 a pool was constructed out in the yard, at a cost of $21.74. A stone annex 19½ × 30 ft. was built to the rear, for Sunday School purposes, in 1909, at a cost of a little over $500. The church is lighted by an acetylene gas plant which was installed at a cost of $300. There are twenty jets within the building and one outside. The upkeep averages throughout the year a cost of 35 cents per week. It is said to be the best lighted church for miles and miles around.

When the Sunday School addition was dedicated, September 5 and 6, 1909, there was held a Grand Family Reunion of all who had ever been connected with the work at Harmonyville.

A number of revivals have been held here. The most notable was the one held in 1886 by Bro. J. T. Myers, when 22 were converted. There were ten converts in 1903, when Bro. Chas. Bame of Philadelphia did the preaching.

The first business or council meeting was held at Harmonyville, December 2, 1893, the work being all the time till 1913 a mission of Coventry. From 1893 Harmonyville, however, has had her own minutes. At the outset Elder J. P. Hetric was chosen chairman; H. C. Keim, secretary; and J. H. Stager, treasurer. A Financial Committee of three was appointed: J. H. Stager, J. H. Keim, and David Haldeman.

The Coventry council decided, November 26, 1887, on request from Harmonyville members, to hold a love-feast at Harmonyville. This was likely their first feast.

July 24, 1909, a request was presented at the Coventry council, also from Harmonyville, to allow a separate organization at that place. The Coventry council did not object if the Harmonyville members wished thus to organize. For some cause the organization was not effected, as we have seen, until January 25, 1913.

The Ministry.

As we have seen, the ministry of the Brethren at Harmonyville began with David Keim. The Keim family has been so prominently, so extensively, and so continuously connected with the work at Harmonyville, that a short sketch of the family is in place. We glean chiefly from the History of the Coventry Church by Dr. Isaac Urner.

The first of the Keim family came to America about 1709 and settled originally in Oley Township, Berks Co. Subsequently members of the family moved out in different directions. One branch located in Reading, one in Bucks Co., and a third in Chester Co., at Yellow Springs. The head of this last branch was named Hans or Johannes,— in English, John. Afterwards this Hans settled at or near the present village of Harmonyville, in Warwick township. He had four sons,—George, John, Peter, and Stephens.

George Keim was the grandfather of Elder David Keim. The parents of Elder David were Jacob Keim and Hannah Switzer, daughter of Ulrich Switzer and Hester Urner. The property of Hans Keim, great-grandfather of Elder David, was still in the Keim family in 1898, its owner then being Jonathan Keim of Pottstown.

Deacon Jonathan Keim, whose name has frequently been mentioned in connection with the Sunday School, is a nephew of Elder David and father of Lewis Keim. His father Samuel gave the ground for the church. In his old homestead three generations of Keims have been reared, each consisting of four sons and two daughters.

David Keim was born in 1802 and was evidently elected to the ministry before 1845. He was likely ordained before 1872 as no record of his ordination is given in the minutes which were first kept in 1872. He died in 1897; aged about 95 years. As a preacher he was very conscientious, ever warning against false teachers. He was deliberate, yet earnest in speaking. He was liberal in giving, having started the fund for building the Harmonyville church with a subscription of $100.

Lewis Keim is the second Harmonyville preacher. For his biography see Geiger Memorial and Coventry Churches.

William G. Nyce is really the first pastor of the Harmonyville Church. He was born, October 12, 1869. He was an aggressive church worker in Royersford, with his membership at Parkerford, when in 1900 he was called to the ministry by the Parkerford congregation. He married Lena Keim, daughter of Jonathan, of Harmonyville, and November 1, 1905, moved to this place. When the church was organized here in the present year, he was unanimously elected minister or pastor, with the understanding that his duties were to begin at once. The entire care of the church here devolves upon him.

The Deacons.

The first two deacons of Harmonyville were Jonathan Keim and Stephen Brownback. They were elected at the Coventry council, August 7, 1880, the year in which the Harmonyville house was built.

Brownback moved to Philadelphia in 1894; and Thomas Brewer was elected to fill the vacancy, November 11, of the same year.

The trustees are Hiram Keim, an old stand-by, Jonathan Keim, and Jacob H. Stager. As before stated, Jacob Stager was elected treasurer at the beginning. So acceptable have been his services that on the organization of the church, he was reëlected to the position for life.

The Hamilton brothers—John and Frederick—were bachelors for a long time, finally married, but never had children. They left a sum of money to the Coventry Church, known as the Hamilton Fund. The Fund figures frequently in the worthy doings of the Coventry congregation. They lived in Harmonyville territory, and so are now properly claimed for this congregation.

CHAPTER VI.

BIOGRAPHICAL.

A. Autobiography of George Adam Martin.[1]

In the year 1733, I was strongly moved to repentance and a change of life, and all without any man's intervention, which confused me so that I did not know what to do. For my heart was troubled. Wherever I went or was, my conscience was so disturbed that I avoided all company and felt grieved at any vanity I met with. I was constantly frightened and alarmed, for my conscience smote me everywhere; besides I was young, bashful and timid. I therefore went about like a lost sheep, and thought all people better than myself, which opinion indeed I still have. I never looked for much from men, and if I occasionally listened to some one preaching, I was not frightened by it, because I felt myself more damned than any preacher could damn me; nevertheless some little hope remained, and I thought perchance I might yet be saved. Being in such a condition, I was baptized on my faith in the year 1735. This I did to honor God in Christ Jesus and intended to follow him; but had no further thought about the piety of a community, because my inner troubled state did not permit me to think about other things. All my thinking and striving were only as to how I might enter the kingdom of God.

After my baptism, when alone in the woods, I knelt down behind a tree and prayed. After I had finished, it came into my mind to open the New Testament, and whatever I found under my right thumb that should be my precept during life. Then I turned up: "Study to show thyself approved unto God, a workman that needeth not to be ashamed, rightly dividing the word of truth" (II Timothy 2: 15). This troubled my mind excessively; sometimes I

---

[1] From *The Chronicon Ephratense*.

took it to be a temptation; then, again, as if I had tempted God; and again that the Spirit had mocked me. Taking all together I did not know what to make of it. To become a workman in the church of God, that I dared not harbor in my mind. Soon after I was led into such temptation for about sixteen weeks that I incessantly heard nothing but: "You are damned! You are damned!" This frightened me so that I enjoyed neither sleep, nor eating nor drinking. My father asked me what was the matter with me, but I dared not tell him, for I thought that never before had a person lived on earth in such a damnable state. At last I was delivered out of this bondage, received pardon, and became a recipient of the gracious visitation of my God in Christ Jesus, and of the power of regeneration, of which before I had known nothing. Thus by grace and compassion alone I became one of the redeemed of the Lord. After this I became cheerful and joyous in my Saviour, Jesus Christ, diligently read the Bible, exercised myself in prayer, took pleasure in divine things, and meddled with nothing but what concerned my salvation; besides I held the Brethren in high esteem and had a sacred regard for everything good.

It happened in the year 1737 that my Superintendent (Martin Urner) was called upon to go to the Great Swamp, in order to baptize several persons. When he announced this at the meeting and asked who was willing to go with him, I was willing to go. After our arrival, when the meeting was over, the persons to be baptized were introduced, and a passage from Luke XIV was read to them, about the building of towers and waging war, which also was customary among them even in Germany; for when I was baptized this surprised me, and I did not know what to think of it. It was done as often as persons were to be baptized, so that you did not know whether you were to build or not, to go to war or not, or whether God had 10,000 and the devil 20,000 men. As soon as you came to the water the hymn was usually sung: "Count the cost says Jesus Christ, when the foundation Thou wouldst lay," etc., which A. M. (Alexander Mack) had composed already in

Germany. When these confused transactions were now also enacted here, as was customary, it suddenly seized me so that my limbs trembled, and it flashed like a flame through my whole being, and before I knew it I heard myself speaking in an overloud voice. I was frightened at myself, for I thought of nothing less than speaking. I said that it was not the Lord Jesus' intention to bring such things before candidates for baptism, for their purpose was to enter into their covenant with God by baptism, and to build upon the rock Jesus Christ; those who wished to build a tower besides the temple of God might have such things brought before them. This speech frightened everybody, and all were silent and dumb. At last our Superintendent, M. U. (Martin Urner), of blessed memory, said, "What shall we do then, for something must be said to the people." Without taking thought I answered: "The eighteenth Chapter of Matthew, about exhortation and punishment, might be read"; which proposal was adopted from that hour, and is still customary with them to this day.

This was the first stumbling block I found in their doctrine. But because they adopted my suggestion throughout the whole country, and no person moved against me, but all were surprised and thought that this movement on the part of a young man which they saw and heard was the work of the Spirit of God, I greatly honored them, since they in so childlike a way gave all honor to God. Moreover they now noticed me more, especially did my Superintendent love me until he died, and he was much grieved when he had to lose me. But I did not respect the household of the Congregation, and nothing of the kind touched me; but I was earnest in my calling to gain favor before God by my life and behavior. I took no offence at any person, nor did I seek their esteem; I only endeavored to follow the dictates of my conscience. But it happened by and by that they, contrary to my wish, chose me as their Superintendent, after I had already obediently moved across the waters of the Susquehanna.

Before this occurred it happened that Count Zinzendorf and many of his Brethren came into the country and occasioned a great stir, especially by his conferences. And because all denominations were invited to them, I too was deputed by my Superintendent to attend them. When I arrived at the conference, which was held at Oley, I found there some of our Baptists, Seventh Day men, Mennonites and Separatists. The Count himself was president, and for three days I heard queer and wonderful things there. After my return home I went to my Superintendent and said that I looked upon the Count's conferences as snares, for the purpose of bringing simple-minded and inexperienced converts back to infant baptism and church-going, and of erecting the old Babel again. We consulted with each other what to do, and agreed to get ahead of the danger, as some Baptists had already been smitten with this vain doctrine, and to hold a yearly conference, or as we called it, a Great Assembly, and fixed at once the time and place. This is the beginning and foundation of the Great Assemblies of the Baptists. After this general meeting had been established, the opportunity was offered to speak of various matters whenever we met. . . .

(After referring to disputes in which he took part at the Great Assemblies, he continues:) It may be thought that I have deviated too far from my reasons why I left the Baptists; but no, these are the very reasons, for I took offence at the foundation and origin, because the originators deviated from their aim and basis, which in my opinion is the love of God towards all men, and formed a sect like the Inspired, out of the great awakening which had taken hold of them in Germany, and aroused strife and hatred by their disputes. . . .

Now I return to our yearly meeting, at which the European ban-branch continually became a topic of conversation, so that you always had to contend with these quarrels, until A. D. (Abraham Duboy) and M. F. (Michael Frantz) at last died. Then other and thinner branches came forth, with which it was still more difficult to deal, until at last they put me out. Then I thought the affair would end, but only commenced in earnest; for as quiet as ever I kept they let me have no peace. I was heartily tired of their affairs.

Some, however, still adhered to me and could not leave me. They also were suspected and were avoided on my account, for whoever would not ban me himself had to be banned.

Now I became puzzled, for the wild European ban-branches threw such a shade, mist, darkness and gloom over the eyes of my mind that I could not see the light of the sun in the Gospel. I still lay buried under the hellish ban-doctrine, and my conflict was very great, for I was even afraid to doubt the ban-doctrine. In Germany I should willingly have entered the highest classes of the high schools, but here I had to attend high school against my will, had to learn the language of Canaan, and to begin with A. This, indeed, appeared very strange to me, because nearly everybody who knew me considered me a great doctor of Holy Writ. . . .

(For additional information concerning the life of George Adam Martin, see "The Churches in Southern Pennsylvania," Chapter 9, Part I.)

B. John Umstad.

John Horning Umstad, the founder of the Green Tree Church, was born in Philadelphia, January 1, 1802; and died April 26, 1873. When nine years old, his father moved to the Umstad farm. In 1829 he was married to Ann, daughter of Daniel and Frances Brower. Daniel Brower's farm joined the Umstad farm on the east. Daniel was a Mennonite and in the meadow of his farm the Brethren first preached in the neighborhood, perhaps before John Umstad was born. John H. and Ann Umstad had born to them four children, one son, who died in infancy, and three daughters. One daughter, Sarah, the only child to join the Brethren, died unmarried during the life of her parents. Catharine B. married Louis Detrich, who moved to Baltimore; and Frances B. married Milton I. Davis, who became the owner of the Umstad homestead.

John Umstad in his early days possessed a vivacity bordering on wildness. His spirit is manifested by different incidents told of him. His father owned another farm beyond the Perkiomen Creek. The barn was old and did not appeal at all favorably to John. One day it took fire and was well up in flames when John arrived on horseback. Putting the spurs to his horse he galloped at high speed round and round the barn, swinging his cap in the air and shouting: "Now, we'll have a new barn; now, we'll have a new barn!"

Young ladies were frequently in summer among the Philadelphia boarders on the Umstad farm. They were everywhere, to the extent of being a nuisance; and John likely loved fun for its own sake. There is a large island in the Schuylkill belonging to the farm, reached by a ford, some places upwards of four feet deep. The girls must go along across in the cart. In midstream John slipped out the keystaff. Our young ladies got to the rear of the cart. The picture that followed we leave to your imagination.

He was even inclined to get fun out of his sister Isabella's piety. But the Spirit of God got hold even of him, and made of him a new creature. But we are told that with him, like the rest of us, the old man with his deeds was not all put off at once. He was converted in 1831. This occurred at Coventry. He went there while in a troubled state. In speaking to the elder, "Pappy John Price," as he was called, he was invited to go along home. With characteristic openness, Bro. Umstad replied, "That is just what I expected to do." Soon after his conversion he laid aside his fashionable attire and conformed to the attire common among the Brethren, so says his biographer in a history of Montgomery County, Pa. But there is reason to believe that he became especially strict along this line only after 1860.

He along with Isaac Price was elected to the ministry about 1834; and entered with his accustomed zest into the work. Isaac was inclined in preaching to give the Spirit time to move him. On one occasion, Isaac was not immediately moved, or perhaps he was overcome by feeling, at any rate he stood waiting. Bro. Umstad broke in: "Bro. Isaac if thee hasn't anything to say, thee had better sit down!" Whereupon Bro. Umstad got up and began to preach. After he became a member of the church, he always used the Friends' language: no doubt he had been accustomed to it in his childhood days in Philadelphia.

He was a great man for prayer. Often when away from home, he would arise early on Sunday morning, and, like the Savior, withdraw from men, perhaps into the woods, and pray alone to his Father in secret. A tenant farmer tells that frequently in the barn or elsewhere he would find him in prayer. One night this man was awakened from his slumber by a noise outside. On going to his window he beheld under the large buttonwood tree below the house, Bro. Umstad on his knees. An amusing incident is told. Once while visiting with an earnest Brother, the latter began praying aloud in his sleep. "Brother, pray!" he exclaimed. Whereupon Bro. Umstad got out of bed, down on his knees, and began to supplicate a throne of grace.

As a preacher, Bro. Quinter says of him: "Brother Umstad's labors in winning souls were very successful. He labored not only in the public ministry, but also much in private. He was instant in season and out of season. The cheerfulness of his Christianity, added to his natural vivacity, made him an agreeable companion, and when in private with his friends he seldom failed to use the opportunity of recommending Christ to them, which was often done successfully. . . . In his public preaching he was warm and pointed, and his direct appeals to sinners was often very strong."

On meeting strangers his constant question was, "Do you love Jesus?" A certain unconverted man once said, "I hate to meet that man, for he always says: 'Well, Bub, do you love Jesus?'"

He was both a home missionary and a foreign missionary. He was instrumental in starting several mission points near home. He opened the work in Norristown, did the first aggressive work in the Mingo region. But in those days of the horse and wagon, he did work that may well be called foreign. We find him as far west as Iowa. While at times he went alone, he frequently followed the Gospel method of going two by two. Perhaps his chief traveling companion was D. P. Saylor. We give D. P. Saylor's account of one of these trips.

"MD., Nov. 14, 1855.

"*Dear Brother,*—By these I inform thee of our health and happiness; and also (of) a visit of love Br. U. and myself have performed among the Brethren in Virginia and Maryland. We left my place on the morning of the 5th of September, and returned on the evening of the 17th of October, being out six weeks and one day. During this time we attended twelve lovefeasts, ten in Virginia and two in Maryland, besides many other meetings, (perhaps forty) and traveled nearly 800 miles.

"The next day after our return, being the 18th of October, our lovefeast at Beaver Dam came off, and on the 20th at Meadow Branch in the Pipe Creek Church, which made the number fourteen for Br. Umstad.

"The Lord has remembered Zion, and the refreshing from His presence has been manifested. From a few of the churches we have heard since my return home, stating the number they have baptized since, and when I this evening added the number together, I find them to be *fifty,* nearly all young people. From one church, it is written, that the Lord's day after we had left, they had baptized 18, and among them only one married man; the rest were all young people.—11 young women and 6 young men. The Brethren rejoice greatly; so do I, and no doubt the angels in heaven participate in that joy. . . .

"D. P. S."

John Umstad was away from home so much that he almost became a stranger to his family. Once on leaving home he said to his wife of his sickly daughter: "If Sarah dies bury her." He was comfortably fixed in things temporal, so that hard work was not imperative upon him. His farm was generally turned over to a tenant. He believed in a free Gospel, and so always paid his own traveling expenses. While at home he was always busy. He spent much of his time at home reading. He was a great reader. He was very hospitable, had many visitors. He was fond of fishing, having built a fish pond in his meadow. His father had built a dam in the Schuylkill River, across to the island, at which he had erected a carding mill, and later a grist and saw mill. The story is told that on one occasion

Bro. Umstad had an engagement to preach, but thought that he would have time to go fishing awhile in the morning before services. He became so absorbed that he forgot all about the preaching. Suddenly the thought of his appointment struck him. On entering the church, he found a waiting congregation. Without ado he entered the pulpit and announced his text: "I go a fishing." John 21: 3.

His style as a writer and likely as a speaker may be gathered from the following lines from his pen, on the death of little David Harshberger of Snake Spring Valley, Bedford Co., Pa.

"Yes, that little David is no more; he who seemed to be so lively, and so happy, and so merry, and so pleasing, is no more. Although he ran about his father's house as if all was his, and made for him, and the new mill, and father and mother, and grandmother, all, all seemed to him as his, him to serve, and him to obey. But he is gone to rest. He slept some ten minutes only in the great cold spring and never waked. The mother busy about her domestic duties could not long brook the absence of her darling boy, sends sis to seek him, but O that horrible scream! With a mother's quickened pace she hasted, drew him from his cold, cold bed, clasped him to her more than frozen heart, but oh, the spirit's gone, her little boy does not answer, and the angels shout a new arrival among their heavenly throng."—*Gospel Visitor* of September, 1859, p. 288.

He was very liberal to the poor. On one occasion a poor woman came to his home begging. He gave her five dollars whereupon she went to the house. His wife then came to him and asked what she should give. Not saying anything about what he had done, he replied: "Mother, just give her what you think is right." He carried out to the letter the Savior's command that when one makes a feast he should not invite his rich friends but the poor who could not recompense him again. On a certain Thanksgiving Day, he invited all the poor of the neighborhood to his festive board. He became so liberal that interference was deemed necessary. Unprincipled people would take advantage of his goodness of heart by borrowing money and never repaying. One such once told him that he would never pay till he was sued. "Very well," replied Bro. Umstad, "then you will never pay." The man was afterward converted and paid the money.

He always had family worship. While still young in Christian experience, he found it necessary to build a new barn. The workmen boarded with him. So many strangers in the home made the cross of family worship too severe; so the first morning passed away without the family assembling about the home altar. Bro. Umstad was conscience-smitten. Next morning he called the men together and thus addressed them: "I have been accustomed to having family worship, but thought I would pass it by while you men were here. I am convinced that I was wrong, so we will have our worship." His family worship led to the conversion of at least two of the workmen.

While he was very popular in the Brotherhood, he was never appointed on a committee to look after church government. On one occasion a query came up to the District Meeting from the Green Tree Church, asking what should be done with sisters who insisted on dressing after the worldly fashions. Isaac Price was puzzled. "From the Green Tree Church?" He knew of no such question before a Green Tree council. All eyes were turned to John Umstad for an explanation. He sprang to his feet and pointing his finger at the fashionably attired ladies in the rear, exclaimed: "If those ladies had to dress in those clothes for Jesus' sake, they would not do it!"

But he was used on some very important committees. He was a member of the committee that brought about the re-entrance of the Far West Brethren into the Brotherhood. He was member of a committee to revise the hymnal, though the work finally devolved on James Quinter. He was also a member of the committee of 1859 that advised District Meetings as a method of efficient evangelism.

"His health began to decline a few years before his death, and the winter preceding his departure he did not preach any, being so advised by his physician. As he lived close to the meeting-house, however, he occasionally met with the church and delivered a short exhortation. He preached his last sermon to the people of his charge, to whom he had so long ministered, April 13, 1873, and left home on the fifteenth to visit his daughter and her family at Baltimore, where he arrived on the sixteenth but little the worse for his journey. On the following Sunday night, the twentieth, he was taken with severe pains and paralysis of the lower parts of the body. The disease ran rapidly to a crisis, and he expired on the twenty-seventh, just a week after the attack. He died at the residence of his son-in-law, Louis Detrich, in that city, in the seventy-second year of his age, and after about forty years' devoted service in the ministry.

"His remains were conveyed to his home, and on Thursday, May 1, he was interred in the cemetery of the church he had helped to found so many years before. At his funeral there were in attendance nearly twenty ministers, and an immense throng of sympathizing friends and neighbors." The funeral sermon was preached by Elder Jacob Reiner, it having been agreed between them that the surviving one should preach the other's funeral.

PART V.

INDIAN CREEK GROUP.

CHAPTER I.

"GREATSWAMP."

Among the early congregations organized by the Brethren was that in the "Greatswamp." The history of this church has never been recorded, and it ceased to exist so long ago, that the congregation that now worships in this same territory did not know the former ever existed. This was the first organized congregational activity of the Brethren in this vast territory where are now located the churches of the Indian Creek Group. There is so much that is of interest, and there has been such a far-reaching influence set in operation, that this early church well deserves a careful discussion here, and her history recorded. To write this history required years of research, but the writer feels satisfied that the fruits of these labors, in the facts of a unique history recorded for the first time, will be fully appreciated. Here, as elsewhere, we are indebted to Rev. Morgan Edwards for some of the earliest data and facts, and quote as follows:

"*Greatswamp.* This society is distinguished by the above name, which is a name of a tract of land called the Greatswamp. The meeting is kept at the house of Mr. John Frick in Upper Milford Township, in the county of Bucks, about 40 miles northwest from Philadelphia. The families belonging to the society are about 20 whereof 28 persons are baptized. Thus stood things with them in 1770. Their beginning was in this manner. In the year 1733 one

Salome Miller and Joseph Miller her brother, John Brecht and wife, Peter Longanacre and Peter Rhode were baptized by Mr. John Naass. In 1735 were baptized by Mr. Peter Baker and Mr. Martin Urner, one Hanse Zuk and wife, John Sleifer, and John Frick and wife; and the same time had the Lord's supper administered to them by Mr. Peter Baker. This was the period of their existence as a society; and 11 their number. They have existed for 35 years without any remarkable event, except that Count Zinzendorf took away some of them in the year 1752. At first they were visited by ministers from other parts, and increased fast. Several of the Mennonites joined them. But since that time the increase has been inconsiderable. The first settled minister they had was Rev. Abraham Deboy."

Since his ministry covered a period so early in the history of *Greatswamp,* a brief biographical sketch is in place here. Edwards says of him, "He was born in 1679 at Epstein in Germany. Bred a Presbyterian (Reformed). Embraced the principles of the Baptists (Brethren), in 1712. Came to America in 1728. Settled at Perkiomen; and from thence went to the Greatswamp in 1738, where he died and was buried March, 1748." This brief record forms the outline of his life, but is incorrect as to the date of his coming to America, which should be 1732. See Brumbaugh, page 144. Elder Duboy, it will be noticed by this date, was born the same year in which Alexander Mack, Sr., was, and became his assistant. He joined the church in the Marienborn district, but a few years later joined the mother congregation at Schwarzenau, and seems to have been a minister of considerable prominence. He was a modest man and very pious. He was unmarried. Bro. A. H. Cassel many years ago related to the writer that Bro. Duboy had a strange presentiment of his death. On the morning of the day on which he died, he informed the family in which he lived that the time of his departure had come. He dressed in a shroud prepared for the occasion and invited the family to join him in singing, *"Nun fahr ich hin mit Freuden, ins rechta Vaterland,"* etc., then, after a fervent prayer, he reclined on a couch and breathed his last, as one would fall into a quiet sleep. He was 69 years of age.

Morgan Edwards informs us: "Since that time (1748), Mr. John Frick hath preached to them; but is not ordained" (1770). He gives the following list of members: "John Frick, exhorter, and wife, Laurence Erboch and wife, Andrew Meinzinger, John Demud and wife, John Sleifer and wife, Henry Kun, Philip Goodman and wife, Philip Deal, Frederick Deal, John Redrock and wife, Egite Christian and wife, Lodowick Christian and wife, Jacob Staut and wife, Mary Christian, widow Rinker, Catherine Rinker, widow Olinger, widow Crayling, Freny Trissel."

Reference was made to the baptisms of 1733 and 1735. George Adam Martin makes reference to the baptism of 1737,—"It happened in the year 1737, that my Superintendent (Martin Urner), was called upon to go to the Greatswamp, in order to baptize several persons."[1] As he reports, in the Chronicon, it was at this baptism, in 1737, that Martin suggested the reading of Matthew 18, instead of Luke 14. This suggestion was accepted, and first followed in the Greatswamp, and has been the rule of the Brotherhood ever since.

There are several distinct centers around which the history of Greatswamp clusters. I am greatly indebted to J. G. Francis for information and facts found in his article, "An account of the early Brethren in the Greatswamp, as gathered from John M. Zuck, a great-grandson of Peter Zuck, one of the original members."

"The Brechts or Brights lived about the center of the Brethren settlement near Zion Hill, some four or five miles above Quakertown, on the Philadelphia and Allentown road. North of Brights, were the Sleifers; northwest, the Rothrocks; west, the Fricks; southwest, the Zucks. The Brethren lived here at an early date. They were pioneers. They came here when this was virgin territory. It was then Indian land, and later became a part of the famous Walking Purchase. It is only a few miles from Springtown, in the post-office of which we copied the following: 'Springtown-Route of the Indian Walk, or Walking Purchase, September 19, 1739, led through Springtown. Here the

[1] *Chronicon Ephratense*, pp. 243, 244.

walkers—Marshall and Yates—dined with George Wilson, the first white settler, who located here in 1728, as an Indian trader.'" It will be seen by these dates, that John Naas preached here, baptized members, and that the church was organized and a Lovefeast held a number of years before the Penns had bought this land from the Indians.

Mr. Zuck states, "this land is not swampy and never was. It is rather level, or not hilly, and the soil is good. The name Greatswamp is rather misleading. The Brethren lived in what is now Upper Milford, Richland and Springfield townships, near the intersection of the three townships, close to the Lehigh County line."

Bro. Francis's account further states as follows:

"On the north side of the Brecht farm is the old Brecht cemetery. It is east a short distance from the Philadelphia and Allentown road, just before you come to Zion Hill Lutheran Church, along the road leading down to Shelley's Station. It would have been more correct to have called it the Bright and Rothrock cemetery, for it is right on the line between the two old farms and taken out of both, and in it the Rothrocks buried as well as the Brechts. Other families also buried here. The little cemetery, about 40 feet wide and 60 feet long, is said to be full, but not a stone is marked, the little sandstones being scarcely visible any more. The southern part of the cemetery is surrounded by a crude wall, a wall running almost through the middle. This walled-in section was especially the Brecht cemetery. The whole cemetery is overgrown with trees. See cut. As long as the Rothrocks lived around here, they kept the cemetery fenced, but now it is completely neglected. The Brights have also all moved away, the nearest one lives in Springtown.

"But not all of the Brethren of the old settlement are buried here. A mile, or more, south of this cemetery, along the Philadelphia and Allentown road is the East Swamp Mennonite Church with its city of the dead. The Mennonites have from the first been numerous here. Here lie the remains of Peter Zuck, one of the early Brethren, and also some of the Sleifers who were members. Peter has a well-preserved tombstone. On it are the words: '*Hier lieght begraben Peter Zuck. Er is geboren den 20den August, im Jahr 1728, und is gestorben den 13ten tag May im Jahr 1812.'* His house was a preaching station. He is the second generation of Zucks in America. His father bought the old Zuck homestead in 1727, and it has continued in the family to the persent day. John M. Zug our informant, now in his eighties, being owner of a part of it. There was also preaching in a barn south of Zucks. This old barn when torn down was found to have some very sound logs. A certain rather profane fellow declared that the soundness was due to the preaching of the Brethren."

The Settlement in Sacon Township.—There seem to have been two somewhat distinct settlements in the Greatswamp Church, or possibly one earlier than the other. While we know considerable about this settlement in Sacon Township, which we are now to consider, it is difficult to fix dates, and to locate just where the members lived. Several facts, however, are well established. The membership at one time must have been quite large, and in a large and flourishing community. Some of the families of members, of which we have knowledge, were large and of more than ordinary prominence. Some of these families have continued through succeeding generations, down to the present.

The Old Cemetery.—So limited were all forms of records, that for a time it seemed hopeless to unravel the mysteries of this now historic setlement. The old cemetery was the only known clue, with which this history might be traced, but fortunately it turned out to be the key to the whole situation, and, therefore, because of its importance, a brief description of it is in place here. The first thing that strikes the visitor to this ancient God's acre is the substantial character of the wall, and the large amount of space the wall encloses. This size shows the great importance of the place, to a large community in time past. This large space in this city of the dead is probably fully occupied. There are many small stones, and plenty of evidence of many unmarked graves. There are some larger tombstones, and a few newer ones, and of more recent date, the cemetery itself being much neglected, and little cared for. Except for the

BRECHT AND ROTHROCK CEMETERY, GREAT SWAMP.

MENNONITE CEMETERY, WHERE PETER ZUG AND OTHER EARLY BRETHREN ARE BURIED.

OLD CEMETERY, NEAR HELLERTOWN.

size, one might suppose the place to be of little importance by its neglected appearance inside. But the size, and the substantial enclosure are abundant proof that a community was greatly interested in perpetuating what to-day is not visible. This wall is the crystallized thought of a community, its visible testimony to buried interests within. This walled cemetery is about 100 feet square, and if the ground is fully occupied, as it seems to be, about 400 people lie buried here.

The Old Deed.[1]—Having learned something of the old cemetery, and its importance to the community, it will be of much interest to know something about the deed that established upon a little spot of ground, of which the cemetery is a part, such an important educational and religious center. It was almost three years from the time I began work upon the history of Greatswamp, until I found trace of this important old document. I am greatly indebted to Rev. Jacob Rothrock,[2] a lineal descendant of one of the Brethren families of Rothrocks, of Greatswamp, and whose ancestors are buried in the old cemetery, for the privilege of copying from the *Old Deed*. In copying from this historic paper, I have followed literally the spelling and capitalization, so as not to destroy its unique identity.

To All To Whom These Presents Shall Come John Kram, of lower Sacon township in the County Northampton, and Commonwealth of Pennsylvania, yeomen Peter Kram of the Same Place, yeomen Henry Kram of the Same Place yeomen Sons of Jacob Kram late of lower sacon township, Deceased Susana Kram Catarina Rigel Daughters of the Said Jacob Kram Deceased Send greeting Whereas Jacob Kram aforesaid Shortly before his Death Did order Peter Rhoads to Devide his land to and Among his Sons and to make Respective Draughts thereof and also Did order and Direct the Said Surveyor to Survey off a Certain piece at the Northwest Corner of his mill land Beginning in the graveyard being the Northwest Corner of this land thence extenting by land of Isaac Rothdrock South four degrees and a half East eight perches

[1] The Original in possession Rev. Jacob Rothrock.
[2] Pastor of the Reformed Church, Lansdale.

and four tenths of a perch to a post thence by his other land North Seventy-Seven degrees East ten perches and four tenths of a perch to a post North thirteen Degrees West to a post in in a line Between the Said Kram and Isaac Rothdrock four perches and four tenths of a perch thence by land of Said Isaac Rothdrock North Seventy nine Degrees and three quarters of a Degree ten perches to the Place of beginning Containing Sixty four perches of land which land So Described and Containing Sixty four perches the said Said Jacob Kram being intented by lawful Conveyance to give grant and Confirm unto the menoist and Baptice Societice for to Build a house thereon for Keeping School and Buplic worship therein and also for a graveyard for the Said Societice and other Neighbours which will chose to Burying their Deat (which Diet a Christian Death,) therein and to hold a Burial Sermon in the Said School house.

But whereas the Said Jacob Kram before he could Complete his intention being taken with hard Sickness and made his last will and Testament by which he ordained and Devised all his other land Except the above Discribed Sixty four Perches and also Did ordain and Devise of all his Personall Estate But Did not Mention and Direct anything of the aforesaid Sixty four perches of land it is suposed that he hath forgot by the hart paine of his Sickness and Did Die in Respect to the Said Sixty four Perches of land intested. But whereas all the children then alive of the Said Jacob Kram being Contented with the mind of their father and did Wish that the Said Land might be Confirmed unto the Said Societice.

But being allso Delayed until their two Brothers also Did Die intested.

Now Know Ye all whom May Concern that we John Kram Peter Kram Henry Kram Catarina Rigel and Susanna Kram in Consideration of the love which we bearing to the Said Societice as also for the Desire which we bearing that the intention and mind of our father the Said Jacob Kram might be fulfilled hath Respectively for our Self and our Respective heirs Released Granted and Confirmed and by these present Do Release Grant and Confirm unto Samuel Kauffman of lower Sacon township County and Commonwealth aforesaid in trust and behalf of the Said menoist Societice and unto Samuel Rothdrok of the Same place in trust and behalf of the Said Baptic Societice all our Right title intress Claim and Demand of in and to the above Discribed Sixty four perches of land Hereditaments and Appurtenances to have and to hold the Said

Sixty four perches of land Hereditaments and Appurtenances unto them the Said Samuel Kauffman and Samuel Rothdrock and their Successors in trust of the Said Societice to the only and proper use and behoof of the Said Societice for the use allthough as it is above Declared and Described Being the intention of the Said Jacob Kram Deceased for ever and the Said John Kram Peter Kram Henry Kram Catarina Rigel and Susanna Kram Do testify that their Brothers Jacob and Abraham when they being alive they was of the Same mind with them and would have Done the Same as they themself have Done by these Present In Witness Whereof the Said Peter Kram John Kram Henry Kram Catarina Rigel and Susanna Kram have to these Present Set their Hand and Seal this first Day of April in the year of our lord one thousand eight Hundret and two.

                    JOHANES KRAM (Seal)
                    PETER KRAM (Seal)
                    HENRY KRAM (Seal)
                          her
                CATARINA × RIGEL (Seal)
                       mark
                          her
                SUSANNA × KRAM (Seal)
                       mark

It will be seen by the foregoing deed that the survey was made during the life time of Jacob Kram, and by his direction, and likely the ground was occupied as designed many years before the deed was made. It will be noticed, further, that the graveyard was in existence already when the survey was ordered,—" Beginning in the graveyard, etc." How many years intervened I do not know, but we do know that Jacob Kram and two of his sons died before the deed was finally made.

It is impossible to trace the history of the house, that was used for a long time, for school and church services. It is said it was destroyed by fire, and rebuilt. It seems in time there was no minister living there, and the Brethren from Indian Creek filled the appointments. The house was old and dilapidated, and the membership having nearly died out, the place was abandoned. With the introduction of the public school system, the place was handed over to the school directors, with the provision that the meeting house benches should be stored in the loft of the new school house, and on funeral occasions, the school desks should be removed and the benches brought down for the seating of the funeral assembly. Rev. Rothrock informs me, that as a boy, he assisted twice in making this preparation for funerals. No funeral probably was held here for many years. After the building of churches, funeral services were held elsewhere, and other graveyards located, and the place is little used now. It is a long chapter that extends backward into the forgotten past. The history of these generations is finished, and for the most part it is a sealed volume. A brick school house still stands on this historic spot, a living monument that reflects the light that shines out of past.

INDIAN CREEK MEETING HOUSE.

CHAPTER II.

INDIAN CREEK CHURCH.

Geographically, the early Indian Creek field was of vast extent, without boundaries of any kind, or congregational lines.

The Brethren have lived and labored here for one hundred and ninety-four years, and the field was once exceedingly rich in religious and family history, but much of it has passed into oblivion many years ago. While the Greatswamp Brethren Church was the first organized congregation, the first preaching services by the Brethren were held in the present bounds of the Indian Creek, and when the Greatswamp ceased to exist as an organization, the entire region became Indian Creek territory, and the Indian Creek ministers supplied the preaching that revived the work, which later became the Springfield congregation. It is impossible to say now when the first regular preaching services were held in Indian Creek, or, indeed, when the church was organized. We do know, however, that some of those who constituted the first emigration of 1719, settled in the Skippack region, and were visited by the Germantown ministers even before the Germantown Church was organized.

"Now we must consider the movements of the Baptists at Germantown. Peter Becker, in pursuance of the Superintendent's counsel, with two other Brethren, undertook in the autumn of 1722, a journey to all their Brethren scattered throughout the land, which was their first church visitation in America. They traveled through the regions of Shippack (Skippack), Falckner's Swamp, Oley, etc."[1]

Again, in 1724, after Germantown was organized, when

[1] See *Chronicon,* page 22.

the famous Missionary Journey was undertaken, this same region was visited:

"Now, after God had so manifestly blessed their labors, they sought to work forward to meet the awakening, and resolved to undertake a general visitation to all their Brethren in the whole country. They fixed upon the twenty-third day of October, of the year 1724, as the time for starting on their visitation from Germantown. They first went to Schippack (Skippack), etc."[1]

It is evident, therefore, from these and other records, that the Indian Creek territory early received attention from Germantown, and continued to do so for many years. We know, furthermore, that one of the Germantown ministers[2] settled on the Indian Creek very early, and at the time of the first Lovefeast in Germantown, he is counted one of the members of the Germantown Church. It is not strange, therefore, that Indian Creek seems to have been regarded for many, many years, as a part, or branch, of Germantown.

Although I have continued diligent research for several years, I have been unable to find satisfactory data of the history of the earlier periods of Brethren activity in the Indian Creek. I must be content, therefore, with tracing some isolated facts, and a brief history of the lives of some of the most prominent Elders, and their families. It is altogether likely that some ministers, even prominent in their day, have entirely escaped notice. Little remains of the earliest period after a lapse of one hundred and ninety years. What a wealth of history has perished where death has garnered six generations! The little that remains was far too valuable to be consigned to entire oblivion. Even what seemed to be so barren a field has yielded gratifying results, and I am sincerely thankful for even meager gleanings from many sources. I can only hope that what is here set forth will inspire some one to continue a faithful research for rich rewards that are yet possible, though now covered beneath the dust of a century, and more.

[1] See *Chronicon*, p. 24.
[2] See discussion of the Price family, later in this chapter.

THE PRICE FAMILY.[3]

The history of this noted family for the past two hundred years, if it could be written, would fill a large volume. A brief sketch here is due this family, which has been prominent in the activities of the Church of the Brethren throughout her history in America. Jacob Price, or (John Jacob Preis), was the ancestor of the Price family in America. He was a noted preacher among the Brethren in Europe, almost as soon as the Church was organized. He came to America with the first emigration, in 1719. He settled for a short time in Germantown, where he became acquainted with Dirk Johnson, who about this time had obtained a warrant for 500 acres of land, on or near the Indian Creek. This warrant was granted August 15, 1719, and on February 19, 1720, 500 acres were surveyed for him. On the following 20th of June, 1720, Jacob Price purchased 200 acres from Dirk Johnson and wife, Margaret. This located Jacob Price on the Indian Creek, where his descendants have resided ever since, and the Price homestead has continued in the family until the present time. Jacob Price made considerable improvements on his farm, but he never became a naturalized citizen. He had an only son, whose name was John, who was born in Germany, and was in his seventeenth year when he came to America.

The following published account is quoted in "*Sketches of Lower Salford Township*":

"Aaron, the brother of Moses, was hardly more distinguished as the lineal head of the Hebrew priesthood, than was Jacob Price as the progenitor and head of a line of Elders and ministers among the German 'Baptists, or 'Dunkers' (Brethren), of Pennsylvania, continuing down to the present day. This Jacob Price, who was born in Witgenstein, Prussia, about the beginning of the eighteenth century (earlier), emigrated in 1719, and settled at Indian Creek, Lower Salford

---

[3] We are largely indebted to Abraham H. Cassel for the facts in regard to the earlier history of the Price family. He furnished much valuable information to Jas. Y. Heckler for his "Historical Sketches of Lower Salford Township," a copy of which was kindly loaned me by N. F. Heckler, and I hereby acknowledge my indebtedness to all.—The Author.

Township, Montgomery County, where he took up land. He was small in stature—rather imperfectly developed physically—and not commanding in appearance, but a powerful preacher.

"This man had one son, Johannas, also a minister at an early age. He became noted for his aptness in writing poetry. In 1753, Christopher Sower, of Germantown, published a collection of his hymns, but in spite of his talents he became so weakly that his father feared that he would not live to have issue, and, so anxious was the parent to leave a name and posterity behind him that he encouraged his son to marry while still very young. He did so and was blessed with two sons."

It seems to be a well established fact that the wife of this John was a beautiful Indian maiden who was selected for her physical perfection. One traditional account states that when the Indians removed from the neighborhood this beautiful girl, sick with fever, was left behind. Jacob Price, the father, was out hunting, and discovered the sick girl. He took her to his home, where she was tenderly nursed to health, and became the wife of John the weakly son. Another account says, her people lived in a log house, on the farm, on the other side of Indian Creek. She bore her husband two sons, the second born after the death of his father. When John Price died, it is said, the young widow in her sadness, longed for her own people and joined them, while the grandfather, Jacob, raised the two infant sons, Daniel and John. Certain it is that this woman has infused new life into the Price family, that has continued for a century and a half, and all her descendants may be proud of such blood and vigor.

Jacob, being well advanced in years and bodily infirm, his son, John, now being dead, conveyed his plantation, containing 200 acres, to his oldest grandson, Daniel, with all the power vested in himself, being an alien and no citizen, February 7, 1741, on condition that he would pay to his brother, John, £600 in lawful money of Pennsylvania, or give him his equal half of the 200 acres. To secure the payment thereof, Daniel gave his bond for the said amount, and in case Jacob, their grandfather, should die before John was of lawful age the money was to be given to Jacob Reiff in trust for the said John Price. The £600 were paid to his brother, John, April 3, 1753, when the latter signed a release, acknowledging the receipt of the said sum and renouncing all claim to the land. Daniel Price made application to have the plantation legally conveyed to him by patent which "was obtained from the Honorable John Penn, Thomas Penn and Richard Penn, December 10, 1742." This established Daniel Price on the ancestral homestead, and his male descendants became prominent elders and ministers in Indian Creek, Coventry, Green Tree, Germantown, Upper Dublin, Hatfield, Springfield, and other churches in Eastern Pennsylvania. Some of these will be noticed in proper order, in succeeding pages.

John Price, the younger son before mentioned, in early life removed to Franklin County, Pennsylvania, where he and his family won high esteem and material prosperity. Some of the descendants are scattered throughout the middle west,—Elder D. E. Price, of Illinois, an ex-moderator of Annual Meeting, being one of them. But this branch of the family forms no part of the present history.

Daniel was born December 11, 1723, and he was, therefore, within one day of 19 years, when he received the patent for his grandfather Jacob's farm. Thus was laid the foundation for the material resources that have served the Price family for so many generations. He seems to have been a man of great energy and industry. "He cleared away the forests and brought the land into service, the meadows into grass, and the fields under cultivation." He added to his possessions, until in 1776, he was assessed for 345 acres. He had thirteen children, but only five sons and two daughters raised families. In 1783 he sold to his son John, 130 acres of the farm; and in 1787, 165 acres to his son William. He died in 1804; aged 80 years, and 2 months. This William increased his holdings until he owned 322 acres. He died at the age of 45 years, in 1805. It will thus be seen that some of these early Prices had large and valuable possession in farms, and later became mill-owners and merchants here and elsewhere.

The following is a brief tabulation of ministers in the Price family at Indian Creek, and elsewhere:

Elders and Ministers of the Price Family.

First Generation.—Jacob Price, the great ancestor, was a prominent minister and elder, in Europe and America.

Second Generation.—John Price, son of Jacob, was a minister and poet very young. He died at about 22 years of age.

Third Generation.—There seems to be no record that either Daniel or John, of this generation, was a minister.

Fourth Generation.—John, son of Daniel, son of John, son of Jacob, was for many years the elder of Indian Creek. He died September 7, 1829; aged 77 years, 9 months, and 2 days.

George, of the same generation, and a brother to the above John, moved to Coventry, and was for many years a prominent minister there, and Elder of the Coventry Church from 1810 to 1823.

Fifth Generation.—John, son of the above John, of the fourth generation, was for many years a minister at Germantown and Upper Dublin.

William W., brother of the above John, was a poet, and German hymn writer, a sweet singer, and a celebrated preacher. He was Elder of Indian Creek many years.

John, son of the preceding George of the fourth generation, was the noted "boy preacher," and succeeded his father as Elder of Coventry, from 1823 to 1850.

Sixth Generation.—Isaac, son of the above John, of Coventry, was an active and able minister and elder at Green Tree.

George, brother to Isaac above, was a fellow minister with him at Green Tree.

John, Jr., a third brother, was a minister at Coventry, and succeeded his father, John, as Elder of Coventry, from 1850 to 1879.

Henry A., son of Daniel, son of John, son of Daniel, son of John, son of Jacob, was Elder of Indian Creek. He died in 1906.

Caleb, son of Daniel, son of Daniel, son of Daniel, son of John, son of Jacob, was a minister at Hatfield and Upper Dublin.

Seventh Generation.—Jonas, son of Jacob, son of William W., was for many years one of the leading ministers at Hatfield.

Jacob M., son of Abraham, son of Jacob, is the present Elder at Indian Creek.

Biographies, and creditable notice have been given elsewhere in this volume to the several Price ministers in their respective congregations of this District. For lack of material and information, as well as lack of space, I can not give extended biographies of the ministers in the home congregation of the Price family. I wish to add, however, a few biographical facts, and a few facts of general interest. The Price family has furnished a large number of teachers as well as preachers, during its succeeding generations. Throughout the history of the Indian Creek Church there have almost always been one or more Price ministers, and much of the time a Price has been Elder in charge.

Bro. Abraham H. Cassel, many years ago, wrote as follows:

"As most of the Prices are living in Montgomery County, and being acquainted with them in all their generations, I would say for them in general that they have ever been identified with the most intelligent people of the country, and appear to have been a priestly race of teachers and preachers as far back as we have any knowledge of them."

Of William W. Price he wrote as follows:

"William W. Price was the youngest son of Elder John Price, of the fourth generation. He was born August 29, 1789, on a part of the old homestead at Indian Creek, and early in life while working yet with his father on the farm manifested an eager desire for knowledge, so that he embraced every opportunity to cultivate his mind, occupying all his spare moments in reading and other studies in which he made great progress until his sixteenth year when he was apprenticed to the tailor trade, which he followed till he arrived to manhood; then he was requested to teach a school; he accepted the offer and was for several years a successful teacher. In 1813, being then in his twenty-fifth year, he married Mary Reiff and commenced farming, besides working at his trade whenever he could. They had ten children, nine of which grew to manhood and most of them have families. In 1814 he was elected to the ministry, and about the year 1830, he was advanced to the office of Elder or Bishop, which he filled with untiring zeal and unflinching faithfulness until the day of his death, which occurred August 7, 1849, at the age of nearly sixty years. Of him it may well be said, 'He preached the word; was instant, in season and out of season,' sowing the divine seed on every side. Besides the cares of a large family and the faithful discharge of duties to the church at home, he traveled a great deal as an Evangelist, visiting the surrounding churches and assisting them at their councils, communion seasons, etc. Occasionally he also took far trips as missionary to other states, and visited many of the churches in Maryland, Virginia, and through the interior of Ohio, long before our modern facilities for travel had been established, going in his own conveyance and also at his own expense, thus practically enforcing the precept: 'Freely ye have received, freely give.' . . . He had a powerful voice and a very retentive memory. Besides his fame as a preacher he was also a great vocalist, having a thorough understanding of the science of music and sang with a wonderful command and compass of voice. He was also a poet of considerable ability, and wrote quite a number of German hymns, besides making many translations of popular and favorite English verses, a small collection of which were collected by me and were published by J. E. Pfautz, at Ephrata, Pa., in 1858. He also wrote several sacred poems of considerable length, . . . which were never published; besides miscellaneous matters in prose and verse."

The Harley Family.

Next to the Price family, in importance, is the Harley family. The latter having fewer prominent men, but its history is as old, and it has exerted likewise a very wide influence in Indian Creek and other Congregations of the District.

Rudolph Harley, Sr., came to America in the first emigration of 1719. We have little positive information, but a few points are important. He is the ancestor of the Harley family in America, and he was a minister at Indian Creek. Upon his arrival in America, he settled in Germantown, and about the year 1733, removed to Amwell, New Jersey. This was about the time when the celebrated Elder John Naas established the work in New Jersey. He seems to have removed to the Indian Creek in 1740, and in the year 1744 purchased from George Stump a farm of 182 acres, which he owned until 1784.

This brief information is mainly from his great-great-grandson, Abraham H. Cassel. A little more information will appear under the head of "*Organized Effort.*"

Information is not at hand to trace this family either by generations or by individuals, but a few facts are interesting. Some reference is made to Harleys in the history of other Congregations of the District. The Price and Harley families intermarried, and for several generations the work at Indian Creek was largely carried on by these two families. Rudolph Harley, Jr., married Mary, daughter of Elder Peter Becker; and his son, Samuel, married Catherine, 2d daughter of Elder Christopher Sower. This is how Elder Peter Becker, Elder Rudolph Harley, Sr., and Christopher Sower, 1st, were great-great-grandfathers to Abraham H. Cassel. He, therefore, represents, in himself, four prominent families of Brethren.

There were at least three ministers in later generations, in the family of Rudolph Harley, Sr., viz.: Samuel, Benjamin, and Jonas.

Elder Samuel Harley.

I must close this family by a brief biography of its most celebrated representative. He was "the fifth child of Abraham, born November 26, 1795." He was married to Elizabeth Klein and had two children. Jas. Y. Heckler, in "*Sketches of Lower Salford Township,*" says of him:

"He was a minister and Bishop, or Elder in the Dunkard or Brethren Church, and was one of the most eloquent and influential speakers the church ever had. He became widely known and highly distinguished as a speaker and orator in the German language."

The following is taken from *"Cassel Family, by Daniel Kolb Cassel":*

"Rev. Samuel Harley, son of Abraham, ... was a farmer by occupation, and early in life became a member of the German Baptist or Brethren Church. It was not very long until he was elected to the office of deacon in which capacity he was often requested to offer prayer and to bear testimony to the sermons, which he did with so much ability that he was soon called to the ministry. He was a diligent reader of Scripture, of church history, of the church fathers and of religious authors, and improved rapidly as a speaker and orator. After the death of Elder William Price, in 1849, he was ordained to the position of Bishop by the laying on of hands. He had much magnetic influence and in his preaching had a very persuasive way in declaring his ideas, appealing to sinners, convincing and converting them. He was the most eloquent German minister in the Brethren Church in his time, and wherever he went he drew large crowds of people. He was also very sociable and affectionate in his intercourse with his friends. He often went into other localities to preach, and when it was known that he was coming, the people would flock together to hear him. It was by his preaching that many people were converted to God and a number of churches were started, and eight or more meeting-houses were built under his care. As a minister and an orator he was very successful, and his abilities were of the highest order. ... He died October 20, 1878, aged 82 years, 10 months and 24 days."

Samuel Harley was a son of Abraham, son of Samuel, son of Rudolph, Jr., son of Rudolph, Sr. Benjamin was his brother and Jonas was his son.

OTHER FAMILIES.—There are other families, many of them no doubt, which have entered actively into the work at Indian Creek during these almost two hundred years, whose names are not even known to me. There are some, however, that have furnished prominent workers, ministers and lay members, that deserve brief notice, in fact deserve more extended notice than can be given here.

The Nyce family is likely an old one at Indian Creek, and dates back to Germantown at an early day, and has representative workers in a number of Congregations in the District. This family was represented in the Indian Creek ministry during the past generation by Elder William P. Nyce. See *"Elders of Indian Creek."*

The Cassel family is a very large and influential family, has had a continuous existence in this country for more than two hundred years. Members of this family have been in the Brethren Church for four or five generations. Like the Price and Harley families this one has also given ministers to other congregations.

Abraham H. Cassel.—A conspicuous figure in our church history, and one of the most celebrated laymen in the Brotherhood, was Abraham H. Cassel. His biography has been written many times, and very fully in newspapers and magazine articles, and, also, in "The Cassel Family, by Daniel K. Cassel," and it is not necessary to record here an extensive account of his life. The frequent references to, and quotations from, his writings, in this volume, have already recorded in part his extensive labors of research into the early history of the Brethren. It is necessary, however, to present here some biographical facts that shall give him a proper setting in his home congregation, four of whose prominent families, as stated, he so conspicuously represents. From "Biographies, Men of Montgomery County, Abraham H. Cassel," by Samuel W. Pennypacker (Ex-governor), I quote as follows:

"This remarkable man, whose memory will be cherished as long as the German race exists in Pennsylvania, is a descendant in the fifth generation of Hupert Kassel (Cassel), who came to this county about 1715. . . .

"He was born in Towamencin township, Montgomery county, on the 21st of September, 1820, and reared in an interior German settlement, at such a distance from the outside world that only in recent years has a railroad approached within five miles of his residence; among a people whose highest ambition is the accumulation of land, which they only acquire by hard labor and rugged selfdenial; and whose sole literary food is the Bible or sermon of the Dunker or Mennonite preacher—a farmer like themselves. His immediate ancestors and parents were plain and worthy people, whose views of life were limited to the sowing of the seed and the gathering in of the harvest; and who felt in their consciences that to permit a child to spend his time over books was to start him upon the broad way which leads to destruction. . . .

"His father finding that his fondness for books was increasing, and fearing that it would lead him entirely away from useful labor, sternly endeavored to repress it. Fire, money and light were denied him, and even the rod was not spared in the effort to crush the supposed evil propensity. The boy was therefore compelled to pursue his studies by stealth, as he had opportunity—in the wagonhouse, in the haymow, and late at night while others were asleep. About six weeks' tuition at a country school house was all the instruction he received. . . . He learned to write with a chicken feather, which a kind relative showed him how to split at the point. When a young man he began to teach school, and in this occupation continued for eight years. While boarding around in the farmers' houses, in lieu of salary, as was the custom, he found the opportunity of his life in learning the whereabouts of those rare old tomes, long since neglected and forgotten, which the religious enthusiasts who settled Pennsylvania brought with them across the Atlantic, or reprinted here for their spiritual delectation. In early youth he began to invest his spare earnings in books, and now, at the age of fifty-eight (in 1879), he has a library of over 10,000 volumes, which is in some respects one of the most remarkable in the world, and in its own particular specialties stands entirely alone. It would be impossible within the limits of such a notice as this to give an adequate idea of his valuable collection. It is in the main a theological and historical library in English and German, though not confined to those subjects of language. In the works of the fathers of the Church of the Reformed of the sixteenth century, and in the early printed Bible it is particularly rich. The literature of the Dunker Church (Brethren), specimens of which are difficult to find elsewhere, is here seen entire. It contains much literary *bric-a-brac*.

"On the 1st of April, 1843, he married Elizabeth, daughter of Issachar and Elizabeth Rhodes, and they had eight children.

"In addition to his library he owns a farm of seventy-five acres, and by industry and frugality has accumulated what is considered a competence by the unpretentious people among whom he lives."

Bro. Cassel sold his library principally in three collections, viz.: Mt. Morris College, Mt. Morris, Ill.; Pensylvania Historical Society, Philadelphia, Pa.; and Dr. M. G. Brumbaugh, for Juniata College, Huntingdon, Pa.

He died April 23, 1908, aged 87 years, and is buried in the Harley, or Klein, Burying ground, at Klein's, or Franconia meeting-house.

The Booz family has been identified with the work for several generations and has produced some active workers. Jacob Booz, of the past generation, was a minister for many years,—and his son, Jacob M. Booz, is now an Elder at Upper Dublin.

Elder James Shisler, representing the Shisler family, is a very active minister in the present generation, and has been non-resident Elder of several congregations in the District.

The Heckler family has furnished active workers for several generations, including James Y. Heckler, author of *"History of Lower Salford Township"*; and *"Ecclesianthem, or a Song of the Brethren."*

Jesse Y. Heckler, a brother, was a minister in Nebraska, and Joseph, another brother, is a deacon, at Hatfield.

Many other families might be mentioned in this connection, but I am either not familiar with their history, or they have been sufficiently noticed elsewhere.

Organized Beginnings.

Unfortunately we know but little of the earliest Indian Creek history, except as already noted in the principal workers and their families. We have already stated, however, that services were held by the Germantown ministers from earliest times. Bro. Abraham H. Cassel wrote many years ago, about these times, viz.:

"Several other Brethren soon settled in the vicinity, prominent among them was Johannes Kempfer, Ulrich Stauffer and George Reiff, who with their numerous descendants soon constituted the nucleus of the present Indian Creek Church, for as soon as a goodly number were within convenient distances they instituted public worship in their private houses and barns.

Rudolph Harley and Jakob Preis (Jacob Price) served as exhorters or licensed preachers, and as the members here were mostly the offspring of the mother church at Germantown, they were for many years regarded as a branch of the Germantown Church and were therefore under their fostering care, and frequently visited by the Elders and officials of Germantown."

After the death of his wife, at Germantown, in 1746, Elder Peter Becker moved to the Indian Creek, and resided there, with his daughter, Mrs. Rudolph Harley, Jr., until his death, in 1758. Jacob Price having died, the ministers during this period, resident, were Peter Becker and Rudolph Harley Sr., with frequent visits from Germantown, and Elder Abraham Duboy, of Greatswamp, also assisted for several years, until his death, in 1748. These were indeed the beginnings, but all these workers passed away before there was an organized and separate congregation.

Generations passed away, and a new era dawns. John Price, the great-grandson of the above Jacob Price, " was born in 1751, and became a member early in life, and soon after an assistant in the ministry, and was ordained about 1785. From that time the Indian Creek branch became an independent church."[1]

Eld. John Price was in the Eldership about 44 years, and seems to have had charge of the Church during the entire period, which was evidently a period of considerable expansion of the work. But nothing can be said definitely about the growth, as there seem to be absolutely no records of baptisms for the first one hundred years or more.

Meeting-Houses and Burial Grounds.

INDIAN CREEK.—It is impossible to say when the first meeting-house was built, but it was built on the grounds of the present Indian Creek Meeting-House, on which grounds there have been four houses, the first three being on the same site at the road. *The First House* was a small one, " like a small school-house," a frame structure, built of unfinished boards, painted red and the building was not heated or

[1] Notes, by Abraham H. Cassel.

PRICE CEMETERY, INDIAN CREEK.

GRAVE OF ELDER SAMUEL HARLEY,
INDIAN CREEK.

GRAVE OF ELDER HENRY PRICE,
INDIAN CREEK.

lighted. So tradition tells us, and the story is likely correct enough,—and the picture is, indeed, entirely correct, if this house existed at an early date, as seems to be the case. *The Second House* was also of frame, built on the same site, but larger in size,—indicating the needs of the growing interest in the religious activity on the Indian Creek. I have not been able to find out how long these houses stood, but it is very evident these two served their purpose as a place of worship many years. *The Third House* occupied the same site, and was much larger. It was a substantial stone building, with a basement under a part of the building, and is said to have been erected in 1850, or soon after that date. This house served the congregation for half a century, and, though Mingo, Hatfield and Springfield were cut off, and organized separately, the growing mother congregation could no longer be properly accommodated in the stone house of the fathers, and it was torn down in 1906. *The Fourth House* was built the same year. It had been decided to repair the old stone house but a strong sentiment developed for a new house. Elder Jacob M. Price and deacon Jeremiah Shelly were appointed as solicitors to see if the money could be raised. They started out, and on the afternoon of the third day, the amount, $5,500, had been raised. The stone for the basement wall of the new house of worship was taken from the old stone one. It is built of brick, size 50 $\times$ 70 feet, slate roof, and full basement story, audience room heated by hot air furnace. This splendid new church building was dedicated September 29 and 30, 1906.

Burial Grounds.—There are two burial grounds in this neighborhood. The Price Burial Ground is located on the old Price homestead, within sight of the meeting-house, and is historic, having been used by the Price family for many generations, likely from the beginning. Family connections are also buried here, but not many others. Some years ago a burial ground was opened at the meeting-house, and this is the general public burial place.

Klein.—This place is also called Franconia. The land was taken from the Klein farm, and is located in Franconia township, hence the two names. This meeting-house is less than two miles from Indian Creek, is a small, frame house, not large enough for love feast services. The following account of the dedication, I find in the notes of Abraham H. Cassel:

"Dedication of our new Meeting-House, Franconia, Christmas, 1843. Jacob Wenger and Samuel Gibble with us all night, father sorely afflicted, could not go out. 1st. Meeting, William Price, (preached) John 10:21, of the feast of Dedication,—its origin, and meaning. 2nd by Wenger. Noon, Jacob Reiner, Hosea 11, 'I have written unto him the great things of my law but they were accounted as a strange thing.' 2nd. by Samuel Harley, Morning Jacob Wenger, John 2:5, German, then Berge and Henry Nice (Men.) spoke very well, then William Price concluded with a very appropriate Prayer. House crowded during the whole time."

The Harley Burying Ground adjoins the Klein Meeting-house, and is, of course, very much older; for Elder Peter Becker, who died in 1758, is buried here and it, therefore, may be almost as old as the Price Burial Ground. This farm was owned by Rudolph Harley, Jr., and it is possible that he gave the ground about the time his father-in-law, Elder Peter Becker, died, in 1758. In the old deed, of 1800, "The graveyard, known as Harley's burying ground, located on this tract, was reserved in the conveyance when the farm was sold by Henry Harley to Isaac Klein, and was not sold." According to these facts, the burying ground is about one hundred years older than the meeting-house.

Towamincin, also called *Towamencing,* in many old records. This meeting-house is also known as "Frey's," and "Reiff's," and has a very interesting history, and its locality. John Reiff was a minister among the "*Funkites,*" a branch of Mennonites, and had a meeting-house built on his own land near the Skippack in Towamencin in 1814. Upon the death of John Reiff, in 1826, the farm and the meeting-house passed into the hands of John Reiff, Jr. "By his will, dated August 14, 1830, he devised his farm and his mills to his only son, Henry P. Reiff, and the meeting-house with half an acre of ground, on the Forty-foot road, to the use of the Dunkard church (Brethren) forever."[1]

He was known as John Reiff, the miller, and he has been spoken of by old people who knew him, as a very fine man and a zealous Christian. He was married to Catherine Price, and was a faithful member of the Church of the Brethren. I quote the following from Bro. Abraham H. Cassel's notes, of this old place of worship: *"Protracted Meetings at Reiff's Meeting House on Christmas 1841."* *"Friday Evening,* William Price 1 Mose 49:10 (5 lines quoted in German). James Quinter *Saturday Morning* James Quinter Isaiah 9:6-8 (text quoted in English, and some outline of the sermon). William Price also Isaiah 1:16.

"*Saturday Evening* John Umstad I. Kings 4:21 'Why halt ye, etc.' James Quinter II. Cor. 4:13 'We believe and therefore speak we so earnestly'—both with extraordinary power and ability. 1st. night with Mrs. Reiff and daughter the rest with Bro. M. F. was greatly refreshed and well rewarded for coming. May the Lord grant me his grace and enable me to live up to the resolution I then formed—*John Umstad* sang the Beautiful Hymn 'Hail the blest morn when the great mediator down from the regions of glory descended'—with an effect the like of which I never heard nor seen before, after having made some remarks over it." Without any attempt to change, I have copied these personal notes of a remarkable series of meetings held seventy three years ago. Such a trio of able and godly men could perhaps not have been duplicated anywhere in the Brotherhood. Because these men of spiritual power lived, our inheritance is richer, and our opportunities and responsibilities greater. This meeting-house having served the community so well for several generations, was torn down in 1880, and the new house built almost on the same foundation.

Elders at Indian Creek.—Those who assisted in the work before the organization, 1723 to about 1785, were as follows:

[1] "Sketches of Lower Salford Township."

Elders Jacob Price and Rudolph Harley, Sr., and Peter Becker from 1746 to 1758, were *resident*. Elders Peter Becker, (1723 to 1746), Alexander Mack, Sr., Alexander Mack, Jr., and Christopher Sower, of Germantown, and Abraham Duboy, of Greatswamp, were *non-resident*.

Since the organization, the following are known to have been in charge: Elder John Price, 1785 to 1829. Elder William W. Price, about 1830 to 1849. Elder Samuel Harley, 1849 to 1878. Elder William P. Nyce, about 1886 to 1889. Elder Henry A. Price, 1889 to 1906. Elder Jacob M. Price, 1906 to present.

I have laboriously gleaned in a wide extended field of history, and it may be some of the best I did not find, but I present with joy what I have here brought, in the hope that it may in part be worthy of those who toiled here in the past, and with the prayer that it may inspire the present generation to worthy emulation.

CHAPTER III.

THE MINGO CHURCH.

The history of the Mingo Church in its separate existence dates from the year 1869 when it was first represented by its own delegates to the District Meeting of that year.

Prior to the above date when all its territory was still a part of the Indian Creek Church, there had been much activity by the Brethren in these parts and a strong membership had been built up both around the Mingo and the Skippack houses and also quite a few families lived in the vicinity of Methatchon House and also quite a little band in Norristown where also a house of worship had been built.

So that the territory now known as the Mingo Church, reaching from east of Norristown west to Pottstown touching the Schuylkill River east of Royersford and following that stream for several miles, making the territory covered about twenty miles long and ten miles wide, at that time including Norristown and Royersford (which since have both been organized separately) contained four houses of worship and a membership of approximately one hundred.

At this time there were also the following ministers: Henry Cassel, Abram Cassel, Isaac Kulp, John Gottwals, John Isett, and Benj. Harley. Henry Cassel was an Elder and was placed in charge of the church. Also the following deacons: John Detwiler, Jacob Harley, Jesse Conner, Jeriah Saylor, Samuel Markley.

Outside of these with their families, we should mention Frederick and Samuel Isett, Benj. Keyser, Abraham Alderfer, Joseph Tyson, Philip Stearley, Henry Grater, Fred and John Isenberg, Michael Freed, B. F. Derr, Isaac Grater, Jesse Cassel, Dr. S. B. Detwiler, Harry Ashenfelter, Philip Rosenberger, Abram Zollers, Jacob Markley, Andrew Wanner, Abraham Moyer, Charles Starr, Henry Fry, Samuel Hendricks, Jacob Landis, John Alderfer, John Bean, Elizabeth Brandt, Benj. Reiff, William Spare, R. Scheets, William, Benj. and Jesse Clemmer, and their parents, Brethren Christman and Emery. Eighteen of the 46 families mentioned are represented in the present membership. Fifty-seven of the present members are direct descendants of the original families and 20 of these from one family, that of a deacon. Where are the other families?

There was already about this time and a little before, considerable of an exodus to the west including Samuel Horning, Minister, John Horning, Deacon, Isaac Conner, Samuel Horning, Jacob and Lewis Wasser.

On account of some very local trouble there was some deflection to the River Brethren including among them John Haldeman, Jacob and Christian Haldeman and Daniel Harley.

Henry Cassel, the first Bishop of the Mingo Church, was born July 11, 1814; was elected to the ministry, 1849, twenty years before the date of organization of the church. He had charge of the church from its organization to the time of his death, June 28, 1883. Bro. Cassel was an enthusiastic and forceful speaker, and had good executive ability and the church prospered greatly during his incumbency. It is only after his death, however, that any known records were kept of the church's growth and proceedings. After Bro. Cassel's death the church was without a resident Elder for several years. August 8, 1885, in an effort to have an ordination effected, Abram Cassel and Isaac Kulp were so nearly tie that both were ordained and they both took equal part in looking after the interests of the church without deciding which should be foreman, as is now usually done.

In the spring of 1885 Abram L. Conner, an efficient young minister, with his family moved to Virginia. The following spring Isaac Harley, a deacon, and his family also went to Virginia.

The first action that appears upon the church's records in reference to Sunday Schools was taken in April, 1886, when it was granted that schools might be organized at both Skippack and Mingo. There is a very fragmentary record of a Sunday School that was organized in the spring of 1870 with Isaac Kulp, Dr. S. B. Detwiler, John Reiff, Andrew Wanner, Abram Zollers and others as leaders. After continuing for about five years it seems that it was discontinued for several years and again had a short existence after which all records disappear. Since the year 1886, however, and before our territory was further subdivided, there have been as many as six Sunday Schools in operation at one time.

In the spring of 1888, Jesse Ziegler and his family moved into the congregation and was elected Sunday School Superintendent at Mingo. The same spring the District Meeting was also held at the Skippack House.

In 1889 Jacob Conner, a minister in the second degree, moved into the Mingo Church from Coventry, Chester Co., and helped along in the ministry, which had become considerably weakened through death and emigration and advancing years. Bro. Isaac Kulp especially about this time was so disabled physically that he could not serve the church in any active capacity, and Bro. Abram Cassel, having died, it also left the church without a resident Elder.

On May 10, 1890, the church called Jesse Ziegler to the ministry, and on February 14, 1891, Andrew Wanner was elected deacon. October 11, 1891, Jesse Ziegler was advanced to the second degree of the ministry. October 31, 1891, Samuel H. Price was elected deacon at Norristown. William Johnson, a deacon, from Carroll Co., Ill., having moved into the Mingo congregation, his certificate was accepted, March 21, 1891. May 6, 1893, Bro. Isaac Cassel was elected to the ministry.

Through the personal efforts of Isaac Kulp and his daughter Emma and the members at Gratersford, they had built up there a strong Sunday School and good meetings in a small and uncomfortable chapel. Bro. Jacob Conner and his family also having moved close to the village, they felt justified in making an effort to secure a house of worship. September 9, 1893, the church decided to build a house at Gratersford and appointed Michael Freed, Jacob Conner,

Wilson Brunner, John Detwiler and Jesse Ziegler building committee.

August 17, 1895, Wm. F. Gottshall and Amos Ziegler were elected deacons. Bro. Robert Jones, a deacon from Whiteside Co., Ill., having moved into the community with his family, their certificates were accepted March 14, 1896. In the fall of 1896, Elder A. L. Grater, also from Illinois, moved into this church, and September 4, 1897, he was elected as Elder of the Mingo Church. His son, Jacob Grater, a deacon, was also duly received into his office. The members at Norristown desiring that a greater effort be made in the town to do mission work, the church appointed Sister Elizabeth Grater to take up this work.

December 4, 1897, the church decided to call for next Ministerial Meeting of the District. This meeting, together with a special District Meeting, called to convene at the time of Ministerial Meeting, was held in October, 1898, in the Mingo House.

After making a special effort to build up the work at Norristown it was seen that it was indispensable to the success of the work there to have a minister live there and give the cause much attention. Early in 1898 Bro. William M. Howe came and took up this work. About this time Levi Ziegler and family moved in from Lebanon County.

The church, having decided that more workers were needed, called Brother Jacob Grater to the ministry and Samuel Jones and Samuel Gottshall to the deacon's office, and ordained Jesse Ziegler to the Eldership on May 5, 1900.

At this time the church also adopted a plan to take care of some bequests that had been made for the maintenance of the several cemeteries of the church, as well as some other endowment funds. A considerable fund has thus been gathered and permanently invested to support the work of the church.

About 1890 the members at Royersford began to have services and Sunday School, and in 1900 organized into a church, thus taking a number of the Mingo members at the time and since, as they have moved into the town.

In 1901, Norristown was organized into a separate

church and most of those living in the town and those who moved there since have left the Mingo Church and cast in their lot with the workers there. No less than about sixty members have taken out their certificates in the above two instances.

Daniel P. Ziegler, a minister, with his family moved in from Berks County, and his letter was received, May 18, 1901. In the fall of the same year Bro. Samuel Markley died, aged 67 years. He was a devoted and active deacon for many years and in his departure the church lost one of its most faithful workers.

December 7, 1901, Daniel P. Ziegler was advanced to the second degree of the ministry. It was also decided on account of Jesse Ziegler moving to Reading to elect a minister. March 19, 1902, Levi Ziegler was elected.

The cause around the Methatchon House having weakened through members dying and moving away it was decided, December 6, 1902, to discontinue services there for the time. Some effort was made to revive the meetings, but finally the work was abandoned. Jesse Ziegler and family having moved back from Reading their certificate was accepted, March 5, 1904.

Bro. Joseph N. Cassel moved from Hatfield in 1905 and the following spring was elected Superintendent of the Sunday School at Skippack.

P. A. Smith, a minister, from Reading, with his family having moved into the congregation, their certificate was accepted, March 7, 1906.

Elder A. L. Grater having moved to Norristown, resigned as elder of the church and Jesse Ziegler was elected as Elder and Levi Ziegler and P. A. Smith were advanced to the second degree of the ministry, September 7, 1907.

John Ziegler, a deacon, moved into this church from Berks County and May 5, 1910, the certificates of himself and family were received; at the same meeting, Joseph N. Cassel was elected to the ministry and Reuben Haldeman was chosen deacon.

On Thanksgiving day, 1910, the local missionary and Sunday School meeting was held at Mingo.

The members at Gratersford having nearly all moved away and the work having decidedly lapsed even after repeated efforts to revive it and to keep up a Sunday School, at a Council, December 3, 1910, the trustees were authorized to sell the property, which they did. The Mingo Church now has concentrated its efforts at Mingo and Skippack, the members of late years that have not gone into the larger towns having settled more around these houses.

At the present the church has five ministers,—Elder Jesse Ziegler, Elder in charge; three ministers in the second degree, Isaac Cassel, Levi Ziegler, P. A. Smith, and one in the first, Joseph N. Cassel.

The official board also includes seven deacons, Andrew Wanner, S. H. Price, Wm. Johnson, Wm. F. Gottshall, Samuel F. Gottshall, John Ziegler, Reuben Haldeman, one church clerk, Messenger Correspondent, a missionary committee of three members, and a membership of nearly one hundred and forty.

The Mingo Church furnished the first foreign Missionary sent out by Eastern District of Pennsylvania. In the fall of 1908 Sister Katherine Ziegler, daughter of Daniel P. and Mary Ziegler, left her mother (father having died the same summer) for the India Mission-field as the representative of the Sunday Schools of the District.

Bishops of Mingo Church: (1) Henry A. Cassel, 1869–1883; (2) Abram Cassel and (3) Isaac Kulp, 1885–1890; (4) Frank P. Cassel (non-resident), 1893–1897; (5) A. L. Grater, 1897–1907; (6) Jesse Ziegler, 1907–.

JESSE ZIEGLER.

HATFIELD MEETING HOUSE.

CHAPTER IV.

HATFIELD CHURCH.

It is likely that for a number of years some members were living in this part of the Indian Creek territory, and that services were held once in a while in homes and school houses. As a young man, Abraham H. Cassel taught school in this neighborhood, and it was here that he got his wife, a Miss Rhodes. Among the earliest members here was Caleb Price, who taught school at the Eight-Square School House where the Brethren had preaching. He attended services at Upper Dublin later, was elected to the ministry there, and later moved to Ohio. His sister Mary was also a member early, married Abraham Price of Indian Creek. Among the earliest members, besides Bro. Caleb Price, and his sister, Mary, were:

Old George Fisher and wife, John Kile and wife, Jacob Reiner and wife, Peter Custer and wife, Abel Ballew and wife, and a few other sisters.

The Eight-Square School House.—Here, as in many other communities, in an early day, the Brethren figured prominently in combining the educational and religious activity of the community. There was need of a school house in this neighborhood. The community, or neighbors, proposed that if the Brethren would assist in this work, the school house would be built especially large so that the Brethren could hold preaching services therein. The offer was accepted and the Eight-Square which became such a conspicuous part in the life of this community, was built. I have not been able to fix the exact date when it was built, but events that follow will show the time when history was made in this famous school house; certain it is, that it was built some time before 1840. Bro. Jacob Crauthamel, of Hatfield, says of this period: "I remember going with my parents to the Eight-Square School House to services when

I was a small boy. My grandfather (Hunsberger) was active in building it, one of the main men. He was a Mennonite, but thought much of the Brethren, and invited them to his home for dinner, at time of services. The Brethren had services every two weeks, no one else, but after the Brethren left, the Methodists had services sometimes." Just when these services commenced and when they entirely ceased, I can not say, but it was during this period of preaching at the Eight-Square that the foundation of the Hatfield Church was laid, many of the substantial families of the community constituting the foundation stones.

The Revival Services at Eight-Square School House.—I am greatly indebted to our late Bro. Abraham H. Cassel for a brief record of a few services. It will be noticed that services were held, according to this record, at least as early as September, 1839.

"September 29, 1839. 8 sq. School House, Hatfield, Isaac Lawshe John 5: 14. Sin no more lest worse things come over thee, and other passages of the same Chapter.

"William Price, German.

"March 21, 1840. Saturday evening, Hockers old Free School House, on the cow path Road. James Quinter, John 9: 35–6 (text quoted,) he showed, 1st. what believing in him is, then 2nd. that all are not believers, that pretend to be.

"March 22. School-House, Hatfield, James Quinter Acts 16: 16–40 he showed 1st. How happy man was in every event of his life if he is a Christian and gave a striking example of it from Paul and Silas singing Praises to *God* at midnight when confined in stocks and of their prayer being answered by an earthquake—also of the jailer's question '*What must I do to be saved*' 1st. What *he did do* and how we should take an example of him and do likewise.

"Monday, April 27. School-House in Hatfield. John Price, Sr., I. Tim. 4: 16 (Quoted in English.)

"William Price, Heb. 2: 1–4. Baptismal services, Mary Price, Peter Custer and wife.

"Saturday evening, May 2nd. At Bro. Isaac Lawshe's Worrington Bucks County. *Israel Poulson* I. John 3: 1–3 (Quoted).

"Sunday Morning 3rd. *Israel Poulson,* John 14: 1–2 Let not your heart, etc." "Afternoon, *Israel Poulson,* Rev. 2: 1–8. Quoted.

"Pfingsten, June 8. In School House, Hatfield, William Price, Ps 29. (Quoted in German.)
"July 12, 1840. School House Hatfield, (Saturday evening,) John Umstead, II. Tim. 1 Chap. Jacob Reiner a good exhortation.
"Sunday Morning in woods. John Umstead Rom. 12. William Preis Rom. 12, Ger. Silas Thomas, Baptized.
"Saturday, August 29, evenings at County line School-House near Lexington. John Umstead, 'I am not ashamed, etc.
"Sunday Morning, New School House, Hatfield. James Quinter I. John 5: 8. (Quoted in English.) 4 Baptized.
"April 4, 1841. School House, Hatfield. William Price, Luke 1: 74-75 (Quoted in Ger.)
"(2nd. Day Lovefeast May 22, at Indian Creek,) Sunday Morning—Zuck (Abraham) done the principal Sermon. In the afternoon we held an Election for Ministers, on which occasion the Majority fell upon Jacob Reiner from Line Lexington, and Benjamin Harley of Stone Hill."

Bro. Reiner was for many years the Elder of the Hatfield Church, perhaps until his death in 1889, and was especially active, and the main force in building up, and maintaining Pine Run. Under the head of *"Protracted Meetings,"* by Bro. Cassel, I find the following:

"School-House in Hatfield, Christmas 1839, 5 meetings, evening, *Wm. Price,* John 3: 33-45, (Quoted Ger.), *Jacob Reiner,* Deut. 32: 29, (quoted in Eng.) Forenoon, *James Quinter,* Gal. 4: 4-9, Evenings, *James Quinter,* Phil. 3: 7-9, Forenoon, *James Quinter,* Mark 8: 38. (These texts quoted in English, at length.)
"School-House, Hatfield, April 18, 1840. 1st. evening *John Umstead,* John 14: 6 (text quoted, Eng.) Closed with a very warm Prayer-meeting. Morning *James Quinter* I. Cor. 15: 57-58 (Text quoted.) Noon *James Quinter,* I. Tim. 5: 24-25, (Text quoted in English.) *John Price,* Acts 17: 30-31, (Text quoted, Eng.) Very good. 2d Evening *James Quinter* I. Cor. 1: 23-24 (Text quoted, Eng.) *John Umstead* a short testimony thereto. 2d. Morning *William Price* Ps., 2: 8-12 (Text quoted, Ger.) *John Umstead, Jacob Stover, James Quinter,* no texts. 3 were received and baptized."

These quotations are brief, but I think understood. They are exceedingly interesting from several viewpoints. Many of the important men of all the adjoining churches were engaged in establishing this infant church. The character of the texts used from time to time is characteristic, and instructive. These quotations fix a definite period when protracted meetings, among us, were in their beginnings. It was a formative period of vast influence for expansion, well illustrated in the work at the "*8 square.*" Here were men who became national figures. The results are interesting here, and throughout the territory of the Indian Creek Mother Church, and for this reason I have devoted considerable space to recording these important matters. I hope the long research necessary to gather some details of this earlier period, will be repaid by some permanent interest and value of this record.

The First Meeting-House.—The land was donated by Bro. Geo. Fisher, who afterwards moved to Ohio. After some timber had been hauled, before the house was built, the Brethren made some seats beneath the big white oak trees, and William Hertzler, then a young man in the ministry, and unmarried, preached to the assembled Brethren and their neighbors. This was the first service held upon these grounds, an appropriate consecration service. This first meeting-house was built of brick, about 30 by 40 feet, with preacher's platform and stand. The date seems to be about 1851, when this house was built, and it stood only about 15 years. There were at the time of building about 25 members. The revival services at Eight-Square, often called the "big revival," was the immediate cause for the move to build the meeting-house. Among the converts were: Joseph Crauthamel and wife, and daughter Mary, Isaac Hunsberger and daughter Mary, Caleb Price's mother, Elizabeth, Aaron Wagoner and wife, John Münsinger and wife, and others, 15 in all. When these converts from the revival were taken up, the church met at the home of Jacob Hunsberger, the friend of the Brethren. For many facts of this interesting period, from 1850 to 1865, I am indebted to Jacob and Elder Hilary Crauthamel, sons of Joseph Crauthamel, and grandsons of Jacob Hunsberger, who were prominent figures in these times of the "*building period.*"

The Second Meeting-House.—A meeting was called to consider repairing, when it was found that the foundation had given way, the gable was cracked, and the house was too small for the increasing congregation. It was decided to build a new house at once. The old house was torn down, and the brick used in the new house, which is also of brick, and plastered. Joseph Crauthamel was on the building committee and carried the brick, barefooted. This house served the congregation until 1906, when a large addition was built, and a heater placed in the basement. Regular services commenced in Lansdale, in 1888, and in 1896, the present meeting-house there was built. Regular services are also now held in Souderton. Other church activities, evergreen Sunday Schools at Landsdale and Hatfield, cottage prayer-meetings, teacher training class and teachers' meetings are maintained.

May 7, 1874, the District Meeting convened in the Hatfield Church, and again in 1907.

Minutes have been kept only since 1871, and from them Bro. Geo. H. Light, the present church clerk, kindly furnished some data.

Ministers.—Elders William Price and Samuel Harley of Indian Creek were prominent in the work in Hatfield, in the earlier years, Harley being Elder in charge until the time of organization. Elder Jacob K. Reiner was born Mar. 22, 1807; elected to the ministry May 22, 1841, and ordained to the Eldership about 1864, at the time of the organization of the Hatfield Church, and became Elder in charge. Died Jan. 12, 1889, and is buried at Pine Run. Jonas Price, Sr., moved over from Indian Creek, about the time of the revival, later elected to the ministry, and advanced. Moved to Elizabethtown, where he died, and is buried at Price's graveyard, Indian Creek.

Elder F. P. Cassel was the next minister elected in Hatfield. He was born Dec. 16, 1849, baptized in 1865, elected to the ministry before 1879, ordained to the eldership about 1884.

Elder Hilary Crauthamel was born Nov. 14, 1841. He was elected to the ministry Aug. 9, 1884. Some years later he was ordained to the eldership, and had charge of the church for a number of years, during the time of impaired health of Elder F. P. Cassel. Bro. Crauthamel died February 14, 1914, and is buried at Hatfield. Ministers elected since: W. B. Fretz, May 11, 1889; Jacob M. Booz, Sept. 11, 1909; G. H. Light, May 11, 1912.

Deacons.—The following have been deacons in the Hatfield Church:

James Custer, John Kratz, Jacob Rosenberger, Jonas Cassel, Jacob Detweiler, William Kratz, Joseph Heckler, Peter Frederick, Artemus Rosenberger, Frank Münsinger.

CHAPTER V.

SPRINGFIELD CHURCH.

Just when Greatswamp Brethren Church ceased to exist as an organization can not be determined; but it is probable that a few surviving members were the means of reviving the work that finally led to the organization of the Springfield Church. Certain it is, that several of the prominent Bishops of the Indian Creek Church, of the past generation, preached in the old union meeting house; this region had of necessity become a part of the vast Indian Creek domain.

Territorial Extent.—This territory of the Springfield Church is bounded on the east, by the Delaware River; on the south, by the territory of the Hatfield and Indian Creek congregations; on the west, by the Maiden Creek; and on the north, unbounded by any Brotherhood lines. This is a vast region of territory, for the most part, unorganized, extending east and west, 38 miles, and from the southern boundary indicated, northward as far as the habitation of man, covering thousands of square miles, and containing perhaps more than a million of population. Until about 45 years ago, this was a part of the Indian Creek territory.

History of Organized Effort.—While the Brethren began preaching in this territory in 1733, and continued, perhaps, for a century, it is probable that for a few years, at least, preaching had entirely ceased. When the work was revived, the center of activity seems to have been moved some distance. According to recollections of the older members, the earliest preaching services that were held in the present organized territory, which led to permanent results, were mainly held in the neighborhood of the present Springfield Meeting-house, at the homes of the following members:

Moses Shuler, Harrison Traumbauer, Samuel Kauffman, David Yoder, Abraham Stauffer, Peter Kauffman, Henry Moyer, Benjamin Price.

Purchasing a House.[1]—The next step in the development of the work was the purchase of a private home, with the intention of remodeling the same for the purpose of holding preaching services. But before the remodeling, Abraham Hottel offered an acre of ground nearby, for the purpose of building a meeting-house thereon. This offer was accepted, and the same year, the Springfield Meeting-house was built. Brethren Jonas Harley and Henry Price constituted a committee for at least a part of these transactions by the Indian Creek Church, in what was soon to become *Springfield territory*.

The Stone Meeting-House.—The deed given by Abraham Hottel, and Hannah, his wife, bears date, April 2, 1866, and was made to "Harrison Trumbauer and Abraham Stauffer, Trustees of the German Baptist Congregation at *Springfield,* in the county of Bucks." Brethren Daniel Booz, Peter Kauffman, and Henry Moyer, the latter still living, at this writing 1913, constituted the Building Committee. Daniel Booz was a mason by trade, and as such helped to build the walls, and also his son-in-law, Benjamin Price, and Henry Trumbauer. The house is built of stone, with slate roof, and is 36 × 40 feet, with basement, and an added room, 12 × 12 feet. Much was contributed in lumber and labor by the members, and by some who were not members.

Elder S. R. Zug informs me, that in 1866, he held a meeting at Texas in the home of Elder Moses Shuler, and then held a meeting in the Brethen house in Bethlehem, and the next day he went to Springfield to the dedication of the new meeting-house, and attended the love-feast and communion services held at the same place. This indicates where services were held at this time.

Work in Bethlehem and Allentown.—A meeting-house was also built in Bethlehem, size 30 by 36 ft., frame, with slate roof. While some members were living in the city, the preaching services continued for a number of years. At

[1] This house was re-sold afterwards, and continued to be used as a residence.

SPRINGFIELD MEETING HOUSE.

BRETHREN CHURCH, QUAKERTOWN.

one time there were more than twenty members living here, but some of them proved unfaithful, some died, others moved away. Some years ago, only a few members being left, services were discontinued, and the house is now falling into decay. Perhaps as early as 1850, preaching services by the Brethren, were held in Allentown. All the ministers of the old Indian Creek Church preached here, including Isaac Kulp and Henry Cassel, who later were Elders in Mingo. These services were continued for a period of more than twenty years, and at times much interest prevailed, and about 10 or 15 members lived in the city. It seems, however, there was no effort made at any time to start a Sunday School, or to build a house of worship, the services being held in the homes of the members. Many years ago, the interest was allowed to die out, some of the members proving unfaithful, the services were discontinued, and no effort seems to have been made to revive the work.

Organization.—About two years after the building of the Springfield Meeting-house, the scattered members in this territory were formally organized into the Springfield Congregation, in the year 1868. At the time of organization, Elder Moses Shuler was chosen Elder in charge, with Jacob Booz, minister, he having been elected at the time of the dedication of the meeting-house; and Harrison Trumbauer and David Yoder deacons. Her name, however, does not appear in the District Meeting lists of churches, until 1879; and not until 1881 did her first delegates appear at the District Council. In 1885, and again in 1898, the District Meeting was held in Springfield.

Sunday-School.—In about 1867, a Sunday-school was organized at Springfield, and kept up for some years. Daniel Booz was the first Superintendent, and was followed by Benjamin Price. A feature of this school was a German class, taught by Sister Daniel Booz, some of the members of which committed whole chapters to memory.

After some years this school was discontinued, and no school held for a long time. Some fifteen years ago, the school was reopened, and has continued with much interest, and is at present in a prosperous condition. The Sunday-school in Quakertown is also in a flourishing condition, and both schools seem to be increasing in size and influence.

Prayer-Meeting.—Since much space was devoted in Chapter I, to the Greatswamp Church, much that might be interesting in small detail must of necessity be omitted in the later life of Springfield. I must, however, call attention to the Sunday afternoon prayer-meeting, that is said to have been maintained for many years. I am well satisfied that this is the type of Sunday afternoon worship which has come down through the church-life from former generations, and is the bond of union with the spirit of the past. Around this home altar, all ages meet to worship, just as they used to do in the early days, and the early years, down in Germantown.

The Emigration.—A few years ago a number of Brethren moved into this territory, in the vicinity of Quakertown, from central and western Pennsylvania. In all about thirty members moved in, including several ministers and deacons. This emigration extended influence and interest into a new community, that soon centralized in Quakertown.

A New Church House.—A small building was purchased, and with a spirit of enthusiasm and united effort, the work of enlarging and improving and remodeling made rapid progress. The house is 36 × 52 feet, arranged for holding love-feast services. There is good interest at this preaching point.

Officials, at this writing, 1913, are: Elder Benjamin Hottel, Elder in charge; ministers, William F. Spidle, James F. Ream, John Ackerman; deacons, Henry Trumbauer, Henry Yoder, Allen Mohr, Mathias Steely, Simon Lint, Jacob Fox, Jacob Holsinger, Thomas Norris.

CHAPTER VI.

NORRISTOWN CHURCH.

The earliest preaching services in the vicinity of Norristown were held at Methatchon. When the colonial government confiscated all the property of Elder Christopher Sower, in Germantown, he retired, penniless, with his daughter to this community, and they took up their abode in the spring house loft of some one who befriended him in his distress. During the years of his residence here, he preached somewhere around his home neighborhood, for he preached away from home, during these years. When he died, in 1784, his funeral was held at Methatchon, where he was buried. It is possible that services were held continuously from that early date until a few years ago. For in 1800, and thereabouts, Elder George Price, of Coventry, journeyed more or less regularly from Coventry to Methatchon to hold preaching services.[1] Methatchon has much interesting history, which, however, forms no part of this chapter, except to show that the Brethren interest began about two miles from Norristown.

Elder J. H. Umstad was likely the most active in establishing the Brethren cause in the city of Norristown, and perhaps did the first preaching. Just when these services were first held, and how regularly, I can not say, but the meetinghouse was built in 1869, and services were likely held for several years before that time.

Bro. J. Howard Ellis says of this period: "I remember coming here with Brethren John Umstad, Jacob Z. Gottwals and my uncle John Slingluf three years previous to that time, when services were held in a hall, at the corner of Main and Barbados street."

[1] See "History of Green Tree Church." From other records we also learn that the Brethren from Indian Creek preached here, and this region early became Indian Creek territory, and remained so until it became a part of Mingo upon the organization of that Church. Germantown ministers also preached here.

After the new meeting-house was built, Norristown became one of the centers of activity of the Mingo Church, and continued to be such for almost forty years. About 1896 the members at Norristown desired that a special effort should be made to do mission work in the city, and upon this appeal the Mingo Church appointed Sister Elizabeth Grater to take up this work. "After making a special effort to build up the work at Norristown it was seen that it was indispensable to the success of the work there to have a minister live there and give the cause much attention. Early in 1898, Bro. William M. Howe came and took up this work."[2]

Norristown Church was organized Mar. 12, 1901 with one deacon, J. Howard Ellis and twenty-one members. E. C. Harley was elected deacon on that day. The preaching for several months was mainly by supplies. On Oct. 12, 1904, Leonard Taylor was elected deacon. There is a well-attended weekly Prayer Meeting held. The Sunday School is at present in charge of E. C. Harley as Superintendent and has an enrollment of over one hundred. The present church membership is forty.

Pastors.—William M. Howe was elected the first pastor and served from October 14, 1901 to October 7, 1902. On July 7, 1903 Elder T. F. Imler took charge as pastor and served until July 7, 1907. From Feb. 7, 1911 to March 5, 1912, Elmer F. Nedrow a student of Elizabethtown College was the pastor having preached a few months at Norristown before moving his family. Edgar M. Detwiler the present pastor took charge March 5, 1912.

Elders.—Elder A. L. Grater from October 12, 1901 to January 8, 1906. Elder T. F. Imler from January 8, 1906 to June 10, 1907. Elder James B. Shisler from July 5, 1907 to the present.

[2] Elder Jesse Ziegler in "History of Mingo."

PART VI.

CONESTOGA GROUP.

CHAPTER I.

CONESTOGA CHURCH.

This congregation was organized on November 12, 1724, by Elder Peter Becker of Germantown and was the first organized church of the Brethren in Lancaster County. It was located south of Ephrata.

The original membership consisted of seven members: Conrad Beissel, who was the first minister; Joseph Shaffer, John Moyer and wife, Henry Höhn and wife and Veronica Frederick. The first deacon was John Hildebrand. Peter Becker was their Elder, although non-resident.

Soon trouble arose, caused by Beissel deviating from the customs of the Brethren, especially by observing Saturday for the Lord's Day or Sunday. Much admonition did not help. Alexander Mack came to America in 1729 and the congregation agreed to let this trouble be decided by a vote of the majority of the membership. The vote resulted as follows: six brethren and five sisters voted with Beissel for Saturday, and twenty-four brethren and three sisters favored Sunday with Peter Becker.

J. G. Francis contributes the following account of this division:

"A quotation from Bro. M. G. Brumbaugh's 'History of the Brethren,' pp. 299 and 300 reads:

"'On the authority of Abraham H. Cassel, the following somewhat remarkable method was used September 29, 1734, to determine the loyalty of the members. A great meeting or council of the congregation was held and Michael Frantz placed a rail on the floor of the barn in which the meeting was held.

He then requested all who wished to join the new congregation to step to the right side, he leading the way. He requested all those who desired to follow Conrad Beissel to step to the left side of the rail. In this way a peaceful separation occurred.'

"I also had personally from Abraham Cassel an account of this separation, and it is in my mind that our great antiquarian stated that the rail was placed on the bridgeway leading to the barn floor. But I do not wish to be dogmatic. Following my impression, however, in having a picture of the old barn taken for this history, I placed a fence rail, as will be seen in the picture, in the middle of the bridgeway, where if my impression is correct, Michael Frantz must have placed the original rail. This old barn is within the present bounds of the Akron congregation, near Millway station, and is owned by the Oil Company. Some frame additions have been built to the original barn.

"According to my understanding of the matter the council was held in the barn, while the dividing was consummated in the open."

After the reorganization of this congregation, Elder Becker had the oversight of it until 1734. Conrad Beissel on his own account founded the convent at Ephrata, leaving the Church of the Brethren in 1728.

After Alexander Mack's death at Germantown in 1735, Michael Frantz was elected as minister in the Conestoga Congregation and Johannis Landis as deacon in 1735. From 1729 to 1734, thirty-seven persons were baptized by Elder Peter Becker. Their names appear in a record now in possession of Elder Hershey Groff, of Bareville, Pa. Many of the additions to this congregation by baptism and otherwise, together with elections of deacons, ministers and elders, are also found in said record and generally agree with the list given in Brumbaugh's "History of the Brethren," pp. 299-315. In Brumbaugh's work, p. 313, the statement occurs that from 1755 to 1763 no record was made. From the record above referred to, the following is taken to supplement the record of Brumbaugh:

In 1753 George Miller, John Bengelbach and wife, Rudy Yound, Katie Hartman, Margaret Geib were added and Jacob Stoll elected to the ministry.

BARN WHERE RAIL ON BRIDGE-WAY SERVED TO DIVIDE THE BRETHREN FROM THE BEISSELITES, NEAR MILLWAY.

GRAVES OF CONRAD BEISSEL AND PETER MILLER, EPHRATA.

Saal and Sisters' House, Ephrata Cloister.

Brothers' House, Ephrata Cloister.

In 1754, Christian Stauffer and wife, George Ester and wife, Anna Frick, Elizabeth Frick were added.

In 1755 Peter Wampler and wife, Henry Aller and wife, Christian Lanecker, Jr. (Longenecker), John Lehman, Jacob Hernley, Hanickel Ackerman, Barbara Flory, John Groff were added.

In 1756 were added Henry Ester, Sister Wampler, Elias Ackerman, Lenhard Sebold and wife, Peter Pebel, John Frick, Christian Frick.

In 1757 Sister Margreth, Elizabeth Boser, Maria Nusbaum, Michael Gäll, Margred Byer, John Bock, Susan Bauman, Sister Mosser were added.

In 1758 Brother Keim and Wendel Mynig were added.

In 1759 Balser Specht and wife were added.

In 1760 no baptisms on account of temptation.

In 1761 were added John Bather and wife, Jacob Zug, Abraham Frantz and wife.

In 1762 Maria Zug and Sister Hamacker were added.

In 1763 were added Ann Lanecker and Philip Snell.

DIVISIONS AND SUBDIVISIONS OF CONESTOGA CHURCH.

Elders and Ministers in Conestoga Congregation.

*1. Peter Becker,[1] 1724-35.
 2. Conrad Beissel. Baptized 1724; left church in 1728.
*3. Michael Frantz, 1735-48. Baptized in 1734; elected 1734; ordained 1735; died September 25, 1748.
*4. Michael Pfautz, 1748-69 (21 yrs.). Baptized in 1739, September 29; elected in 1744; ordained September 25, 1748; died 1769, aged 59 yrs. Buried at Middle Creek Church, near Cocalico Creek. 179 persons were baptized under his eldership.
 5. Jacob Stoll. Baptized in 1748; elected in 1753; died in 1822, aged 91 yrs. Buried at Middle Creek graveyard. In ministry 69 yrs.
 6. Jacob Sontag (Sunday). Baptized in 1743; elected in 1748; ordained 1763.

[1] The asterisk (*) means bishop or elder in charge of congregation for time indicated following the name.

*7. Christian Longenecker, 1769-1772. Baptized in 1755; elected in 1764; ordained in 1769. Seven persons were baptized under his eldership, 1769-1772.

FIRST DIVISION OF CONGREGATION WAS UNANIMOUSLY AGREED TO IN 1772.

Ministry at Time of Division.

I. *Conestoga.*

Bishops Peter Eichelberger and Jacob Stoll.

II. *White Oak.*

Bishops Christ. Longenecker; Johannis Zug, baptized in 1749; elected in 1770; ordained in 1780.

III. *Swatara.*

Bishops Han Jacob Beshor, George Kline and others.

*8. Peter Eichelberger, 1772-95. Baptized in 1752. Under Eichelberger and Jacob Stoll's care, 151 persons were baptized.

*5. Jacob Stoll, 1795-1822. Under Stoll's care, 1795-1802, 16 persons were baptized.

9. David Kemper. Baptized in 1791; elected in 1801; died in 1832 at age of 81 yrs. Under Stoll and Kemper from 1802-22, 204 persons were baptized.

*10. Jacob Pfautz, 1823-64. Baptized in 1805; elected in 1815; ordained in 1823. Died in 1864, aged 87. He was the son of Johannes Pfautz and grandson of Elder Michael Pfautz. Served as minister and elder 49 yrs. Buried at Middle Creek graveyard. Under Pfautz's oversight 484 persons were baptized. Congregation numbered 429 members in 1861.

*11. Abraham Zug, 1823-41. Elected in 1815; ordained in 1823; died 1841, aged 69 yrs. Buried at Tulpehocken Meeting House graveyard.

DIVISIONS AND SUB-DIVISIONS OF CONESTOGA CHURCH

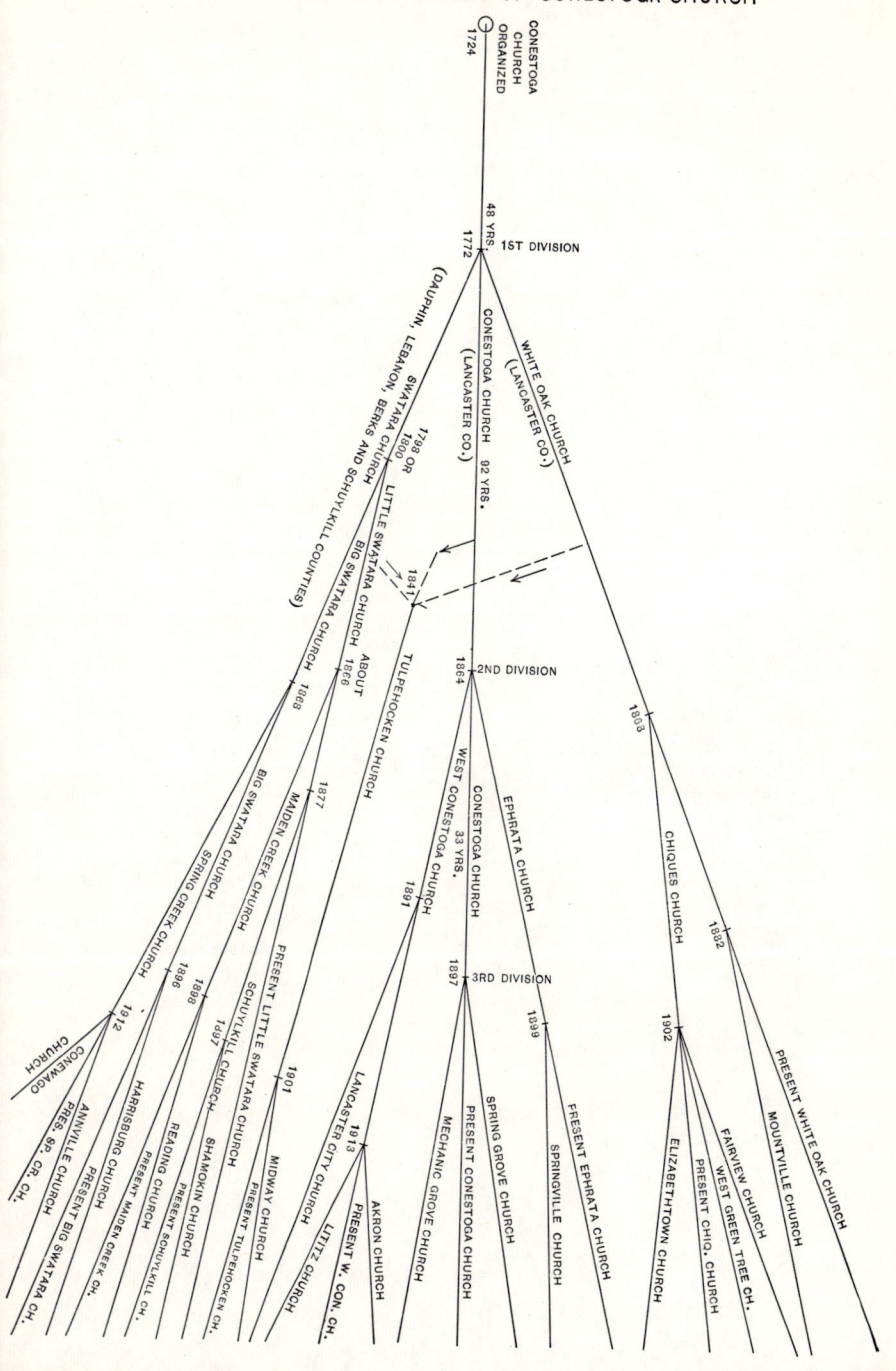

12. Christian Bomberger. Baptized in 1828; elected June 4, 1831; ordained June 4, 1862. Under the oversight of Jac. Pfautz and Bomberger, 1842–61, nearly 500 persons were baptized.
13. Samuel Myer. Baptized in 1816; elected in 1822 or 1824; moved to Ohio in 1842.
14. Michael Landis. Baptized in 1819; elected in 1822 or 1824. Moved to Ohio and left church.
15. Christian Rupp. Baptized in 1834; elected May 28, 1840; ordained in 1867.
16. Joseph Myer. Baptized in 1840; elected August 31, 1844; ordained in 1887 at age of 80; died in 1892, aged 85 yrs. Buried at Myer burying ground one mile south of Bareville.
17. Jacob Reinhold. Baptized in 1844; June 2, 1845, not elected, but was permitted to preach by a majority of Congregation; died in 1885 in Lancaster, aged 70 yrs.
18. Christian Brubaker. Baptized in 1848; elected June, 1855, second acceptance April 25, 1889; advanced April 8, 1895; died 1901, aged 82 yrs. Buried at Longenecker's near Lititz.
19. Israel Myer. Baptized in 1847; elected June 2, 1849; died of dropsy, October 4, 1870, aged 56 yrs. Buried at Mohler's cemetery.

SECOND DIVISION OF CONGREGATION WAS UNANIMOUSLY AGREED TO MAY 5, 1864.

Ministry at Time of Division.

I. *Conestoga.*

Bishop Christ. Bomberger (non-resident); Christian Rupp and Joseph Myer.

II. *West Conestoga.*

Bishop Christ. Bomberger (resident); Jacob Reinhold and Christian Brubaker.

III. *Ephrata.*

Bishop C. Bomberger (non-resident); Israel Myer and Samuel Harley.

*12. Christian Bomberger, 1864-1880. Died May 21, 1880, aged 78 yrs. Buried at Middle Creek. Under the oversight of Bomberger and Rupp, many were received into the church by baptism.

*15. Christian Rupp, 1880-87. Died August 24, 1887, aged 82 yrs. Buried at Rupp family graveyard.

*16. Joseph Myer, 1887-92, father of Samuel R. Myer and of Elder John Myer, of West Conestoga Church.

20. Samuel R. Myer. Baptized in 1864; elected August 9, 1866; died 1876, aged 43 yrs. Buried at Myer family graveyard south of Bareville. Had a daughter who graduated at Millersville S. N. S. and is preceptress and teacher of English and Elocution in Elizabethtown College from 1900 to present time.

21. Rudy S. Reidenbach. Baptized in 1861; elected in 1874; ordained in Spring Grove Congregation on December 18, 1897. Grandson of Elder Jacob Sontag.

*22. John W. Graybill, 1892-99. Baptized in 1875; elected May 22, 1876 or 1877; ordained in 1892; died on October 5, 1899, aged 64 yrs. Was greatly beloved and his death much lamented. Buried at Earlville.

*23. Hershey Groff, 1900-1902, March 20. Baptized in 1878; elected in 1885; ordained July 28, 1900. Resigned eldership in charge March 20, 1902. Has records in his possession of baptisms since 1724, from which these facts have been largely gleaned and compiled.

24. Jacob Pfautz. Baptized in 1880; elected in 1889; advanced to second degree August 5, 1892.

*25. Isaac W. Taylor, 1899-1900; 1902-1911. Baptized in 1880; elected in 1891; ordained in Spring Grove Congregation on May 22, 1899. Non-resident elder of Conestoga Congregation from 1899-1900, and from 1902-1911.

Third Division of Conestoga Congregation in 1897.

Ministry at Time of Division.

I. *Conestoga.*

Bishop John Graybill; Hershey Groff and Jacob Pfautz.

II. *Spring Grove.*

Bishop John Graybill; Rudy Reidenbach and I. W. Taylor.

III. *Mechanic Grove.*

Bishop H. E. Light, residing in Mountville Congregation; and George Bucher, moved in from Tulpehocken Congregation.

26. Abram H. Royer. Baptized on November 15, 1891; elected in 1897; advanced 1900.
27. Martin Ebersole. Baptized in 1892; elected in 1899; advanced in 1906; ordained October 7, 1912.
28. John G. Graybill. Elected in 1900; relieved of ministry at his request in 1910. Reinstated on December 8, 1913.
29. Diller Myer. Baptized in 1898; elected on November 9, 1910.

Deacons in Conestoga Congregation.

1. Henry Mohler, baptized 1809; elected in 1815.
2. Jacob Bollinger, baptized 1811; elected in 1815 or 1824.
3. George Myer, baptized in 1816; elected in 1824.
4. Henry Mohler, Jr., baptized in 1813; elected in 1831.
5. Abraham Graybill, baptized in 1816; elected in 1831.
6. Johannis Myer, elected in 1855.
7. John Mohler, Sr., baptized in 1840; elected 1847, 1844 or 1845, May 26.
8. David Royer, baptized in 1831 or 1834; elected June 2, 1849.
9. Christian Wenger, baptized in 1854; elected June 1, 1855.
10. Michael Weidler, baptized in 1841; elected June 1 or 26, 1855.

11. Samuel Harley, baptized in Montgomery Co.; elected May 8, 1861, afterwards in 1864 elected to ministry, and eldership in 1871.
12. Rudolph Gunkle, elected May 8, 1861.

Deacons After Second Division in 1864.

13. Isaac Shirk, baptized in 1861 or 1859; elected in 1864.
14. Jacob S. Minnich, elected in 1864.
15. Levi Rupp, baptized in 1861; elected May 11, 1866.
16. Daniel Myer, baptized in 1864; elected May 11, 1866.
17. Samuel R. Wenger, baptized in 1883; elected 1885.
18. Isaac W. Taylor, baptized in 1880; elected in 1889. Afterwards elected to ministry and eldership.
19. Christian Groff, elected 1890.
20. Martin Ebersole, baptized June 12, 1892; elected 1898.
21. John G. Graybill, elected 1899.
22. Rife Myer, elected in 1899.
23. Mahlon Myer, elected in 1900.
24. Reuben Myer, elected 1912.

The present Conestoga Congregation numbers 212 members. Its officials are: Elder S. H. Hertzler, non-resident elder in charge, since 1911. The ministry consists of Elder Hershey Groff, Elder Martin Ebersole, Jacob Pfautz, John G. Graybill and Diller Myer. Deacons are Samuel R. Wenger, Rife Myer, Mahlon Myer, and Reuben Myer.

The church houses of this congregation are located as follows: *Eby House,* built in 1860, 40 by 50, of brick at a cost of $762; located at Monterey; *Bird-in-Hand House,* built in 1888, 50 by 80, donated by Adam Ranck and Samuel Denlinger; cost to church $1,500 in money and plenty of trouble; *Intercourse House,* purchased in 1891 from Methodists at cost of $800; size 36 by 55. Preaching services are held at union houses at Earlville, known also as Carpenter's Church (size 40 by 50), and Bareville (size 30 by 50).

The present church activities consist of Sunday School organized at Bareville in 1894 and at Earlville in 1910; also a Sisters' Aid Society organized in 1904.[2]

[2] This congregation held a local Sunday School meeting on November 9, 1912, and a similar meeting November 27, 1913.

BIRD-IN-HAND MEETING HOUSE.

EBY MEETING HOUSE.

In 1887, May 11 and 12, the District Meeting of Eastern Pennsylvania was held in the bounds of the Conestoga Congregation on Bro. Adam Ranck's farm, one-half mile from Bird-in-Hand. On October 28, 29, 1903, a Ministerial and Sunday School Meeting was held at the Bird-in-Hand House.

CHAPTER II.

WEST CONESTOGA CHURCH.

The West Conestoga Congregation was organized May 5, 1864, being one of the three divisions made of the Conestoga Congregation. This occurred near Akron, at the home of Jacob S. Minnich, and was occasioned by the fact that the Conestoga Congregation was getting too large, having a membership of between four and five hundred.

The officials at the time of organization were as follows: Elder Christian Bomberger, as elder in charge; Ministers, Jacob Reinhold and Christian Brubaker. The deacons were Michael Weidler, elected in 1855, and Jacob S. Minnich, elected at the time of the division. (For further particulars, see Conestoga Congregation.)

The following officials have been elected since 1864: Jacob Hackman, baptized in 1862, was elected to ministry, May 24, 1866, and ordained August 1, 1878; George Bingeman, baptized in 1868 or 1869, was elected to the ministry, January 18, 1873; John Myer was elected a minister May 29, 1879, advanced June 3, 1887, ordained, August 1, 1898; Cyrus R. Gibbel, son of John B. Gibbel, baptized 1887, was elected to the ministry, April 25, 1889, advanced April 8, 1895, ordained July 26, 1906; David Snader, baptized 1890, was elected a minister on April 8, 1895, advanced August 1, 1898; Edwin B. Brubaker, baptized 1896, was chosen as a minister on August 6, 1900, and advanced January 1, 1906; John W. G. Hershey's date of baptism is 1891 and of election to ministry is January 1, 1906, advanced January 2, 1911; Adam G. Fahnestock was called to the ministry on January 2, 1911, advanced to second degree on August 2, 1913; Wallace Zook elected to ministry, January 15, 1914. All these ministers are living at this writing except the first two. Elder Jacob Hackman resigned eldership of West Conestoga Congregation in

MIDDLE CREEK MEETING HOUSE.

Grave of Elder Michael Pfautz.

Grave of Elder Jacob Stoll.

Grave of Elder Jacob Pfautz.

Grave of Elder Christian Bomberger.

1900; died October 28, 1903, aged 79 years; buried at Millport. George Bingeman removed to Ohio.

The elders or bishops of the congregation since organization are: Christian Bomberger, 1864–80; Jacob Hackman, 1880–1900; John Myer, 1900–1912; Cyrus R. Gibbel, assistant elder, July 26, 1906 to October 22, 1912; elder, 1912.

The deacons elected since 1864 follow: Joseph Pfautz, elected May 24, 1866; John Myer, baptized 1858, elected January 18, 1873; Jacob L. Minnich, elected May 19, 1879; George D. Schreiner, elected June 12, 1884; Nathan Brubaker, elected May 21, 1891; Samuel N. Wolf, elected October 28, 1895; Henry Balmer, elected August 6, 1900; Andrew Bollinger, elected January 2, 1911; Harrison Steely, elected in Mechanic Grove Congregation, May 13, 1899, and moved to West Conestoga Congregation in 1909; Allen Balmer and Benjamin Bollinger elected January 15, 1914.

The congregation has four church houses described as follows: *Lehn' House*, a brick structure 40 by 50 feet in Manheim township; *Lexington House*, situated at Lexington, is a frame building 44 by 50 feet; *Middle Creek House*, a frame building 50 by 80 feet, built in 1874, is located in Ephrata township, Lancaster Co., two miles west of Lincoln; *Millport House* is a union house built of brick and is located at Disston.

The present activities of this congregation consist of a Sunday School organized at Lititz in 1896; one prayer meeting at homes of members held weekly, and a Sisters' Aid Society organized in 1912.

Other facts of special interest in the history of this congregation may be noted here. The territory of the West Conestoga Congregation was the scene of part of the labors of Elders Michael Pfautz (1710–1769), Jacob Stoll (1731–1822), Jacob Pfautz (1776–1864) and Christian Bomberger (1802–1880). The graves of these four elders are at the burying ground of the Middle Creek House and the photographs of their tombstones are presented herewith.

For more facts concerning these men see Conestoga Congregation.

The West Conestoga Church was divided a second time into three divisions on March 24, 1913: West Conestoga, Akron and Lititz. This leaves the membership of the West Conestoga Church about 260.

During the eldership of Jacob Stoll, the Annual Conference of the Church of the Brethren was held in the bounds of the West Conestoga Church (then called Conestoga) on May 19, 1820, at the home of Bro. Joseph Royer, near the Middle Creek house. In 1873 the District Meeting of Eastern Pennsylvania was held in the West Conestoga Church, and the Ministerial and Sunday School Meeting of said district was held at Middle Creek house, November 12 and 13, 1913.

The present officials of West Conestoga Church are: Elder Cyrus R. Gibbel, elder in charge; E. B. Brubaker and Adam G. Fahnestock, ministers in second degree; and Wallace Zook in the first degree. Deacons: Henry Balmer, Andrew Bollinger, Allen Balmer, and Benjamin Bollinger.

Geistliches
Gewürz-Gärtlein
Heilsuchender-Seelen
Oder kurz-gefaßten
Betrachtungen,
Ueber einige auserlesene Sprüche der heiligen Schrift, in gebundenen
Schluß-Reimen
und
Geistliche Brosamen,
Zur Erweckung, Stärkung und Erquickung, auf das Innere Leben gerichtet, von einem Kinde in de Schule JEsu Christi.

Nebst einem
Anhang,
Bestehend aus Geistlichen Liedern und Andachten, ans Licht gegeben von
J. St—ll.

Ephrata:
Gedruckt und zu haben, bey Johannes Baumann.
Im Jahr 1806.

TITLE PAGE STOLL'S BOOK.

EPHRATA BRETHREN CHURCH.

CHAPTER III.

EPHRATA CHURCH.

(*a*) FIRST EPHRATA.

The Ephrata Congregation came into existence May 5, 1864, being one of three divisions into which the Conestoga Congregation was divided, and named thus on account of the borough of Ephrata being the chief town in the bounds of this newly-formed church. See diagram, page —, and West Conestoga Congregational History for place and cause of division.

The officials at the time of organization were as follows: Elder Christian Bomberger, elder in charge, but residing in West Conestoga Church; ministers, Israel Myer, and Samuel Harley, a deacon of the Conestoga Church, was elected a minister at the time of the division; deacons, David Royer, Rudolph Gunkle, Isaac Shirk and Jacob S. Minnich. (For dates of elections of foregoing officials see Conestoga Congregation.)

The following officers have been elected since 1864:

Ministers.

1. William Price (Preis), baptized 1848; elected 1866; was elected a deacon, May 20, 1865; died November 22, 1892, aged 70 years. Buried near Cocalico at Dissler's Graveyard.

2. Isaac Shirk (being a deacon already in Conestoga Congregation), elected November 19, 1870; died at Akron, 1885, aged 60 yrs. Buried at Brick Church, midway between Ephrata and Akron.

3. Israel Wenger, elected May 11, 1878, and ordained August 8, 1891; died December 2, 1907, aged 63 yrs. Buried at Middle Creek in West Conestoga Congregation.

4. Isaac Keller, elected October 24, 1882; advanced January 25, 1890; died January 12, 1911, aged 75 yrs. Buried at Keller Graveyard in Springville Congregation.

338   THE CHURCH OF THE BRETHREN.

5. John W. Schlosser, elected October 4, 1890; advanced September 12, 1896; ordained August 22, 1908.

6. Elias B. Lefever, elected October 22, 1892; advanced April 9, 1898; removed to California, where he was ordained.

7. Henry Royer, elected September 12, 1896. He was suspended from the ministry on September 4, 1905, by a committee of Elders; then joined the Old Order Church.

Deacons.

1. William Price, elected May 20, 1865; afterwards elected to ministry.

2. John L. Mohler, elected November 19, 1870.

3. Jacob Kilhefner, elected January 1, 1875.

4. Isaac Keller, baptized in 1870; elected May 11, 1878; elected to ministry on October 24, 1882.

5. Hiram Snyder, elected April 24, 1883.

6. Henry Royer, elected October 5, 1885; elected to ministry in 1896.

7. Aaron Gibbel, baptized 1881 in West Conestoga Congregation; elected August 8, 1891; elected to ministry in Springville Congregation.

8. Albert Gelsinger, elected August 8, 1891.

9. J. Bitzer Johns, baptized 1887; elected, October 21, 1896; elected a minister in Springville Congregation.

10. John R. Royer, elected October 21, 1896.

Elders in Charge of First Ephrata Congregation.

1. Christian Bomberger, 1864–1880.

2. Samuel Harley, 1880–1893.

3. Christian Bucher, September 16, 1893 to April 11, 1896.

4. Israel Wenger, April 11, 1896 to August 5, 1899.

The first Ephrata Congregation kept no minutes of its proceedings until 1880. Bro. Edwin Königmacher was the first clerk. In addition to the deaths above noted, the following ministers died in the bounds of the first Ephrata Congregation: Israel Myer (see Conestoga Congregation, page 329) on October 4, 1870, and Samuel Harley on May 6, 1896.

(b) Second or Present Ephrata.

The Ephrata Congregation of the Church of the Brethren as it exists today was organized on September 2, 1899, in Ephrata, Lancaster County. This organization is one of the two divisions into which the first Ephrata Church was divided on August 5, 1899, from the Conestoga Church in 1864, the other being the Springville Congregation.

At the time of the organization, Elder I. W Taylor, residing in Spring Grove Congregation, was chosen Elder. The other officials elected September 2 were: David Kilhefner, minister, and the deacons, R. Gunkle, J. R. Royer, S. W. Kulp. There were one hundred and thirty-two members in the present Ephrata when the congregation was divided in 1899. Since that time the following ministers have been elected: S. W. Kulp, August 1, 1903; George W. Weaver, April 10, 1909; Wm. K. Kulp, August 1, 1912. Three deacons have been elected since the organization as follows: J. M. Miller and J. K. Kilhefner, August 1, 1903, and S. K. Kilhefner, August 1, 1910. David Kilhefner was advanced to the second degree of the ministry, August 9, 1902. S. W. Kulp was advanced, August 3, 1907; George W. Weaver was advanced August 1, 1910; David Kilhefner was ordained to the eldership, August 3, 1907. In the twelve years since its organization one hundred and thirty-four have been received into the church by baptism.

The present officials are: Elder, David K. Kilhefner; minister, S. W. Kulp; deacons, J R. Royer, J. K. Kilhefner, J. M. Miller, H. S. Gibble, S. K. Kilhefner and A. Z. Taylor. George W. Weaver moved to Fairview Church in 1912 and Wm. K. Kulp moved to Mechanicsburg, Pa., in August, 1913. The present membership is two hundred and forty.

This church has one church-house built of brick, 50 by 65 feet, with a seating capacity of seven hundred, located in the town of Ephrata. It was built in 1889 at a cost of $3,000. The following Brethren constituted the building committee: J. B. Keller, A. W. Mentzer and E. Königmacher. The present church activities consist of one Sunday School, organized on June 8, 1889; a weekly Prayer Meeting held in the church; a Christian Workers' Meeting organized August 1, 1909, and a Sisters' Aid Society, organized August 9, 1902. The latter has done much in a practical way and has as its officers: President, Emma Hildebrand; Vice-President, Emma K. Seltzer; Secretary, Gertrude Shirk; Treasurer, Alice Taylor.

The church has a temperance committee consisting of J. K. Mohler, H. G. Mentzer and S. W. Martin. The missionary committee of this congregation consists of J. M. Miller, J. M. Neff and Miles Keller, and in 1912 was instrumental in raising $900 for missions.

Elders in charge of Second Ephrata Congregation: I. W. Taylor, September 2, 1899, to April 10, 1909; David Kilhefner, 1909 to present time.

Ministerial Meetings held in Ephrata Congregation are as follows: November 2, 3, 1904; October 26, 27, 1910. Special District Meeting, September 21, 1910. District Meeting of 1913 was also held here.

BRETHREN CHURCH, LANCASTER.

CHAPTER IV.

LANCASTER CITY CHURCH.

Lancaster City Congregation of the Church of the Brethren was organized on October 29, 1891, from territory and members belonging to the West Conestoga Congregation. On August 19, 1872, the West Conestoga Congregation through and by her trustees, Jacob Minnich, Joseph Pfautz and John W. Byrne, bought a church property located on northwest corner of Mulberry and Grant Streets, Lancaster, Pa., belonging to the Evangelical Association of Lancaster, Pa. The Brethren first held meetings every eight weeks and later every six weeks, largely in the German language until the time of organization in 1891. The elders present at time of organization were: Jacob Hackman, Elder of West Conestoga Church, B. Z. Eby, Wm. Hertzler, H. E. Light, J. S. Newcomer, Samuel Harley, and S. R. Zug. Elder S. R. Zug, of Mastersonville, Pa., was selected as Elder in charge; A. J. Evans, Clerk; J. H. Bushong, Treasurer; Benj. Evans, J. H. Bushong, and J. G. Kline, Trustees.

From October 29, 1891, to September 1, 1892, services were held bi-weekly by such ministers as could be secured. At the latter date, T. F. Imler and wife Sadie, of Waynesboro, Pa., accepted a call to become pastor of the congregation. A Sunday School had previously been started. At a church council held October 19, 1892, it was decided to create a fund for buying or building and the following Soliciting Committee was appointed: T. F. Imler, Benj. Evans, J. G. Kline, A. J. Evans, and Anna M. Shirk. The first lovefeast was held November 6, 1892, about seventy communing.

On July 26, 1893, Valentine Workheiser made a proposition to the Church, offering a church property previously owned by the Western Methodist Episcopal Church in exchange for the one now in use. After investigating, the church accepted this offer, August 16, 1893, making the exchange and paying $700 for church property 64 by 130 ft. The last services in the old house were held August 27, 1893, and the first service in the second house on September 3, 1893. First series of meetings were held by Elder H. C. Early of Virginia, beginning on October 29, 1893, at close of which seven were baptized. Missionary, Sewing and Benevolent Society started April 28, 1894.

The second house soon needed repairs and was too small to accommodate the audiences. A committee consisting of Benj. Evans, J. H. Bushong, and John Prange was ordered to purchase additional ground in the rear of the present lot. This was done for $800, making the entire lot 64 by 270 ft. On January 13, 1897, the church appointed S. R. Zug, T. F. Imler, and J. W. Myer as a committee on plans for a new house. This committee became later also the building committee. The new house, 50 by 80 ft., was built by Wenger & Kreider, of Witmer, Pa., for $5,500, heating and seating excepted. Charter applied for through A. J. Eberly, and granted by Court, February 9, 1897. Closing services in second house held June 27, 1897, S. H. Hertzler of Elizabethtown, Pa., preaching the last sermon. The third and present house was dedicated November 28, 1897, Elder Silas Hoover preached dedicatory sermon; Prof. Geo. B. Holsinger, of Bridgewater, Va., led the song service. The seating of the second story cost $655 and seats were placed July 16, 1898.

The Girls' Sewing School was started in the missionary room on October 8, 1898, with Emma I. Welty as teacher. On July 21, 1899, it was decided to build a parsonage, which was done at cost of $2,200, 18½ by 50 ft., completed January 1, 1900, and occupied by T. F. Imler, the pastor, February 12, 1900.

The following ministers were elected since the organization: John W. Myer, October 7, 1896; John A. Hollinger, May 15, 1901; David W. Weaver, January 14, 1903; Harry B. Yoder, August 15, 1906; Geo. W. Beelman, January 11, 1907. Deacons were elected as follows: Albert J. Evans, October 19, 1892; Uriah C. Fasnacht, January 9, 1895;

Amos P. Dubble, October 7, 1896; Daniel Kautz and Hiram Graybill, on September 14, 1897; John Kline, July 12, 1899; Wm. N. Zobler, April 11, 1900; David W. Weaver, April 11, 1900; Harry B. Yoder, April 11, 1900; Charles Bower, May 15, 1901; Eli Myer, January 22, 1902; J. Albert Seldomridge, January 22, 1902; Wayne W. Felker, Geo. W. Beelman and Ira W. Miller, on October 11, 1905; Nathan Kilhefner and Franklin Byer on January 11, 1907. Advancements in the ministry were made as follows: J. W. Myer, May 15, 1901; D. W. Weaver, April 12, 1905; H. B. Yoder, January 11, 1907. Elders were ordained as follows: T. F. Imler, July 12, 1899; H. B. Yoder, August 8, 1910.

Growth and Development.

In 1902 Elder T. F. Imler was called as Business Manager of Brethren Publishing House at Elgin, Ill., and his resignation as elder in charge was accepted by the church, October 15, 1902. Elder I. W. Taylor was elected as elder in charge, accepting the call, November 20, 1902. On December 9, 1902, the church decided J. W. Myer should occupy the parsonage and take up the pastoral work, which he accepted.

In 1904, the Brethren conducted Sunday School and preaching services in the Clay Street Chapel (colored). This gave practical experience to a number of members in the slum district of Lancaster.

On April 11, 1906, the church chose Sister Kathryn Ziegler from the home congregation to be presented to the Home Mission Board of the District as a missionary to the foreign field. The next District Meeting accepted and recommended Sister Ziegler, encouraging her to prepare for mission work. Sister Ziegler entered the mission field in India in the fall of 1908, after completing the English Bible Course in Elizabethtown College.

In 1906 it was also decided to purchase a tent and work in the various parts of the city during the summer months. This work was continued during the year 1907.

In 1906 it was mutually agreed between the West Conestoga Church and Lancaster City Church to extend the latter's territory. The present eastern line from Conestoga Creek along the road leading to Eden crossing the same road leading to a point near Henry Hess's place on Lancaster and Ephrata pike, and thence in a straight line to the Lancaster and Lititz pike, including this territory from this line to city limits. By this change the Union House at Eden (where the West Conestoga Brethren held services) became part of city church territory. In 1907 regular preaching services were opened at Eden and are continued at this time.

On January 21, 1908, J. W. Myer asked to be relieved from pastoral duties. H. B. Yoder was then called to take up the pastorate and serves in this position, now occupying the parsonage. On July 9, 1913, Elder I. W. Taylor resigned as Elder of the church, and Elder H. B. Yoder was elected as his successor in the oversight of this congregation.

On July 19, 1911, at a special council, it was agreed to open a new mission at 221 Coral St., and the following locating committeee was retained to direct the work: H. B. Yoder, President; Geo. W. Beelman, Secretary; Elizabeth Eby, Treasurer; J. W. Myer and Nathan Kilhefner. This committee appointed Sunday School officers, which were ratified by the church, July 23, 1911, as follows: Superintendent, Ira W. Miller; Assistant, J. W. Myer; Secretary, Hannah Seldomridge: Assistant Secretary, Helen Kline; Librarian, Eva Witmer; Assistant Librarian, Minnie Fisher; Treasurer, Walter Stump; Chorister, Ada Beelman; Mission Visitor, Lydia Baum; Teachers, Ira Miller, John W. Myer, John Baker, Cora Price, Florence Evans, Mary Myer, Catharine Wright. At the dedicatory services on July 30, 1911, there were 108 persons in attendance.

The present officials are: Elder H. B. Yoder, Elder in charge and pastor; ministers, J. W. Myer and Geo. W. Beelman. Deacons: John Kline, Daniel Myer, Eli Myer, J. Albert Seldomridge, Wayne Felker, Ira W. Miller, Nathan Kilhefner, Hiram Graybill, C. Alfred Whisler.

The present church activities consist of a Sunday School, Christian Workers' Meeting, and Sisters' Aid Society. The home department of the Sunday School was organized

September 1, 1908, with H. B. Yoder, Superintendent. The temperance committee is Geo. W. Beelman, Emma Landis and Cora Price.

On April 13, 1904, the church appointed Sister Elizabeth Miller as city home missionary. She has become an active and faithful worker, living out the Savior's teaching in Matt. 25: 34–40. She has brought many little children into the Sunday School with garments which she supplied.

On January 14, 1914, the church elected B. F. Waltz to the ministry and John D. Ebersole and Harry W. Wolgemuth as deacons.

Bishops of this congregation: (1) S. R. Zug, 1891–1899; (2) T. F. Imler, 1899–1902; (3) I. W. Taylor, 1902–1913, July 9; (4) H. B. Yoder, 1913.

CHAPTER V.

MECHANIC GROVE CHURCH.

Before the organization of the Mechanic Grove Church, among the first members living in the territory now constituting this church were the Eckmans, Cyrus Royer, Adam Stoneroad and John Hoake. These lived near Refton and some soon moved to Illinois.

Meetings were held from two to four times a year at the homes of Bro. Eckman, Cyrus Royer, and Tobias Herr, who lived five miles east of Refton. It is said that John Umstad, Wm. Price and Peter Hollowbush were among the early ministers to proclaim the Brethren's doctrine here.

About 1890, the Brethren of the Conestoga Church began to worship at Refton in a meeting house of the United Brethren built in 1879. On March 19, 1896, Bro. Geo. Bucher, a minister of the Tulpehocken Church, residing near Kleinfeltersville, Lebanon Co., moved on a farm near Mechanic Grove. There were then sixteen members living in what is the present Mechanic Grove district. John L. Minnich of near Lititz, Charles Garner and wife, and Harrison Steely soon afterward moved in. Thus fourteen new members were added, and by October, 1898, the membership reached 34.

Bro. Bucher began to hold services in his home and at Bro. Minnich's, so that there was preaching in the neighborhood every month. The first members to be received by baptism which occurred in 1897, were Katie Minnich, aged fourteen years, and Fianna Bucher, aged ten. Katie Minnich soon died and was the first one buried at the Mechanic Grove burying ground.

The first council was held at Bro. Bucher's, April 17, 1897, for the purpose of organizing a new congregation. Elder H. E. Light presided; Elder John W. Graybill was also present. At this council the organization of the Mechanic

Grove Church resulted, being one of the three districts into which the Conestoga Church was divided in this same year. The officials of the organization were: Elder H. E. Light as Elder in charge, but residing in the Mountville Church; George Bucher, a minister in the second degree, and no deacons. Of the thirty-four members, twenty-three were present, nine brethren and fourteen sisters.

The boundary line of this church, as adopted at the first council, was as follows: Beginning at Conestoga Creek, where Pequea and Lampeter Townships join, thence south to Long Lane through Strasburg to Gap (Strasburg to belong to the Conestoga Church). The territory of this congregation embraces the southern third of Lancaster County, being about twenty miles each way.

At this same council J. L. Minnich was elected and installed into the deacon's office and also chosen the first treasurer. A petition to the District Meeting was drawn up, asking to be received into the care of the Home Mission Board, which was granted.

At the second council, also held at Bucher's, George Bucher was ordained to the eldership, September 4, 1897, and given charge of the church. Mary Phillipy was appointed correspondent to the *Gospel Messenger*. The question of building a house of worship at Mechanic Grove was also discussed. It was decided to begin to build with the means at hand, provided the Home Mission Board would assist to the extent of giving $400. This assistance however was refused. A building committee consisting of J. L. Minnich, Cyrus Royer and George Bucher was appointed, the church having decided to build at any rate. Accordingly, a frame structure 50 × 50 ft., suitable for lovefeast purposes, was erected at a cost of $1,836.53 and dedicated October 1, 1898, at which time the first lovefeast was held in the new church. The first lovefeast by this congregation was held at Elder Bucher's home, October 2, 1897.

Next a movement was started to purchase a church building at Refton. After appeals for aid had been made to the Conestoga and Spring Grove churches it was agreed to purchase the Refton House for $775 on January 22, 1898.

Cyrus Royer, John Minnich and Edwin Pehlman were appointed trustees of this house, which is a frame building 30 × 40 ft. The first lovefeast held at this house, which was the second one held by this congregation, occurred May 21, 1898.

About the same time it was decided that the council meetings as well as the lovefeasts alternate between the Mechanic Grove and Refton houses. Preaching services from this time on were held every fourth week at each of these houses with a monthly service at Elim, on another of Bro. Bucher's farms, five miles south of Mechanic Grove. Sunday School was organized in the Mechanic Grove House, April 26, 1903.

The following elections of officials have been held since the time of organization: On May 11, 1901, U. C. Fasnacht and Rufus P. Bucher were elected to the ministry; on November 14, 1909, P. M. Habecker was called to the ministry. The following were elected as deacons: Harrison Steely, May 13, 1899; P. M. Habecker, September 8, 1906; Benjamin Kreider, November 14, 1909; Charles A. Livengood and Cyrus Stauffer, June 10, 1911. On January 19, 1908, U. C. Fasnacht was advanced to the second degree of the ministry. Rufus P. Bucher was advanced in the ministry, December 6, 1908.

At a council meeting held at the Mechanic Grove House in the presence of Elders I. W. Taylor and H. E. Light, a charge against George Bucher was adjusted. At a council meeting held September 21, 1907, at George Bucher's home, where I. W. Taylor, Hiram Gibbel and Hershey Groff were present, George Bucher was charged with having used the law against a brother. He refused to comply with what the church asked of him and stated that he would no longer work with the Brethren, expecting to unite with the Old Order Brethren. A council meeting held at the Refton House at which H. E. Light, Hershey Groff and I. W. Taylor were present (the latter presiding), disfellowshipped George Bucher and wife, they having before this time identified themselves with the Old Order Brethren.

The present officials are: Elder S. H. Hertzler, Elder in

MECHANIC GROVE MEETING HOUSE.

KEMPER'S MEETING HOUSE.

charge, residing in Elizabethtown; ministers: U. C. Fasnacht, R. P. Bucher, P. M. Habecker; deacons; Benjamin Kreider, Charles Livengood, Cyrus Stauffer.

The growth of the work has been slow but steady, the membership numbering sixty-five on September 14, 1913. Of the original 34 members, only four were left on September 14, 1913. In 1901, in the month of October, the Ministerial and Sunday School Meeting of Eastern Pennsylvania was held at Mechanic Grove. The condition of the church in general at this time is good.

Bishops of this congregation: (1) H. E. Light, April 17, 1897, to September 4, 1897; (2) George Bucher, September 4, 1897, to 1907; (3) Samuel H. Hertzler, Jan. 19, 1908.

CHAPTER VI.

SPRING GROVE CHURCH.

The Spring Grove Church of the Brethren was organized April 24, 1897, at the Blueball meeting house, having been a part of the Conestoga Church formerly. On this occasion the following elders were present: H. E. Light, B. Z. Eby, Israel Wenger, John W. Graybill, the last named being chosen as Elder in charge. Aaron W. Martin was elected deacon on the same date, but being absent was installed May 19, 1897.

On December 18, 1897, R. S. Reidenbach was ordained to the eldership and Samuel W. Taylor elected to the ministry. Isaac G. Martin and John Buffenmyer, Sr., were elected deacons. On said date John Graybill's resignation as elder was accepted and R. S. Reidenbach was given charge of the church. May 22, 1899, I. W. Taylor was ordained and by vote elected Elder in charge and served until now. At the same time, Samuel W. Taylor was advanced to the second degree of the ministry. The services of said date were in charge of the Elders, H. E. Light, John Graybill, B. Z. Eby, and John Herr. On April 23, 1907, Amos Taylor was elected deacon, Elders H. E. Light and Hershey Groff having charge of the services. On May 26, 1909, Amos M. Martin was elected minister and Jacob Redcay and Horace Buffenmyer were elected deacons. At this service Elders Hershey Groff, John W. Schlosser and David Kilhefner were present. On September 9, 1913, Samuel W. Taylor was ordained to eldership and Amos M. Martin advanced to second degree of ministry.

From the organization of this congregation to February, 1912, there have been thirty-two deaths and sixty baptisms. Twenty certificates have been received and seventy-six certificates granted. Six members have been disowned and not reclaimed. The present membership is ninety-one. The officials at the time of the organization were R. S. Reidenbach, elder, I. W. Taylor minister, S. W. Taylor, deacon, with a membership of about eighty. The present officials are: Elder, I. W. Taylor as Elder in charge; Elder, R. S. Reidenbach, and Elder, S. W. Taylor, and Amos Martin, minister; Deacons, J. B. Becker, John Buffenmyer, Sr.

The congregation has three church buildings: the *Spring Grove House*, a frame building, 40 by 50 ft., located at Spring Grove, was built in 1892 at a cost of $3,000; the *Blueball House*, 30 by 40 ft., frame, located at Blueball, built in 1875 at a cost of $2,200; *Kemper's Church House*, near Murrell, a sandstone structure, built in 1864 at a cost of $2,000.

The present church activities of this congregation consist of one Sunday School at Voganville, organized in 1905, formerly held at Spring Grove and Voganville, and Prayer Meeting in private homes of members.

Bishops of the Congregation: (1) John W. Graybill, April, 1897, to December 18, 1897; (2) R. S. Reidenbach, 1897-1899; (3) I. W. Taylor, 1899.

CHAPTER VII.

SPRINGVILLE CHURCH.

On May 5, 1864, Conestoga Church was divided into three church districts; namely, Conestoga, West Conestoga and Ephrata. The Ephrata district consisted of the town of Ephrata and also of a large territory in the country north of Ephrata. On August 5, 1899, the Ephrata Church, numbering about three hundred and thirty-five members, was divided into two divisions or congregations. The town of Ephrata constituted the one division, called the Ephrata Church, and the rural section, called the Springville Church, constituted the other division. The newly formed Ephrata congregation consisted of one hundred and thirty-two members in the Borough of Ephrata and some adjoining territory and retained the old name Ephrata Church.

The officials of the Springville Congregation at the time of its organization in 1899 consisted of Elder Israel Wenger, Elder in charge; ministers, Isaac Keller, John W. Schlosser, and Henry Royer; deacons, John L. Mohler, Jacob Kilhefner, Hiram Snyder, Aaron Gibbel, Albert Gelsinger, J. Bitzer Johns. Since the organization the following ministers have been elected: Aaron R. Gibbel, on October 5, 1907; J. Bitzer Johns, on August 27, 1908. The following have been elected deacons since 1899: Reuben M. Hertzog, and John G. Martsall, on August 22, 1908. On the same date Aaron R. Gibbel was advanced to the second degree of the ministry and John W. Schlosser was ordained to the eldership. Mar. 14, 1914, J. Bitzer Johns advanced to 2d degree.

The congregation in 1913 had a membership of two hundred and fifty-seven, with the following officials: Elder in charge, John W. Schlosser; ministers, Abram H. Royer, Aaron R. Gibbel, J. Bitzer Johns; deacons, Hiram B. Snyder, Albert Gelsinger, Aaron H. Royer, Reuben M. Hertzog, John G. Martsall, Jacob Redcay.

MOHLER MEETING HOUSE, NEAR EPHRATA.

The congregation has five church houses: *Mohler's,* a frame building 50 by 80 ft., located near Ephrata, built in 1872, and cost $4,364.34 (this building was destroyed by fire, April 9, 1898, and rebuilt in the same year at an expense of $2,414.44); the last building committee was Aaron Hummer, Samuel Mohler, Michael Keller, Levi Mohler, John L. Mohler; the *Springville House,* brick structure, built in 1854, 36 by 60 ft., at Springville, had an annex built to it in 1889; the *Denver House* built in 1877, 36 by 40 ft., frame; the *Blainsport House* is a frame structure, 36 by 40 ft., built in 1866; the *Cocalico House,* 36 by 50 ft., built of brick, in 1909, at a cost of $1,500, with the following building committee: Daniel Noll, Benjamin Burkholder and Samuel Snyder.

The present activities of this congregation consist of an evergreen Sunday School at Springville, organized in 1904; and two midweek Prayer Meetings held at the homes of members. The following have been elders in charge of this congregation: Israel Wenger, August 5, 1899, to September 4, 1905; John Herr, residing at Myerstown, 1905 to 1908; John W. Schlosser, 1908 to the present.

The Annual Conference of 1846 was held on May 29, at Trout Creek, Lancaster County, in the present bounds of the Springville Congregation, on John Royer's farm, near Springville. The District Meetings of Eastern Pennsylvania were held in the territory of this congregation as follows: at the Mohler House, April 29, 1875; April 30, and May 1, 1890, and May 6 and 7, 1908.

CHAPTER VIII.

AKRON CHURCH.

The Akron Church was organized on April 5, 1913. It was formed from territory belonging to the West Conestoga and Springville congregations. At a council meeting of the Springville Church, held at Mohler's on March 15, 1913, permission was granted the members living in Akron and vicinity to join with part of the West Conestoga Church for the purpose of forming a new congregation, to be known as the Akron Church. Twenty-seven members were in this way taken from the Springville Church.

On March 24, 1913, the West Conestoga Church was divided into three divisions as follows: West Conestoga, Lititz, and Akron. The territory of the Akron Church consists of the Borough of Akron, Lancaster County, and vicinity, and some territory including the Brick Church House (Steinmetz's formerly) of the Springville Church.

Steinmetz's Meeting-house.

Bro. J. G. Francis deserves the credit for the following interesting history of this ancient landmark:

"'Memorandum Book of the German Baptist brick meeting-house, near Isaac Steinmetz's generally called Steinmetz's meeting-house.

Ephrata Township, January the 12th, 1847.
"' Constitution

"'We, the undersigned, having agreed to form a constitution of a meeting house to be erected on the land of Isaac Steinmetz, in the township of Ephrata, Lancaster county, at the crossroads, near Steinmetz's brickyard, as follows, to wit:

"'The said house to be called "German Baptist Meeting-house." It shall be for the use of the religious denomination, called German Baptists, for them to hold religious meetings in the same at any time. Any preacher or preachers of any other

AKRON MEETING HOUSE.

STEINMETZ'S MEETING HOUSE, NEAR AKRON.

GRAVE OF ELDER SAMUEL HARLEY, NEAR EPHRATA.

GRAVE OF LUDWIG MOHLER, ANCESTOR OF THE MOHLERS IN AMERICA.

denomination, or some person for him or them, must obtain permission from all the Trustees of said house before he or they can go into the said meeting house, with the intention of preaching.

"'A part of said house may be occupied for teaching a day school any time it is considered necessary by the surrounding neighbors.

"'No kind of exhibitions or lectures shall be allowed in said house.

"'One half acre of ground shall be given to build the said house thereon, and for the use of a graveyard

"'Three Trustees shall be annually elected by the contributing subscribers to said house, every year on the second Saturday of every March, in the afternoon, between the hours of one and four.

"'The election shall be held by the Trustees then in office.

"'No votes shall be accepted at any of the said elections held as aforesaid, which are handed in by proxy. The election shall be held in said meeting-house.

"'Any man elected Trustee must live within one mile of said house.

"'Witness our hands, the day and year above written.

      ISAAC STEINMETZ
      DAVID MARTIN
      CHARLES BAUMAN
      GEORGE FRANTZ
      SAMUEL WOLF
      JOHN E. PFAUTZ"

"All of those signing the Constitution were members of the Brethren Church but Samuel Wolf, and he later became one. From this constitution there is no evidence of any sharp dealing on the part of any Brethren. And the deed agrees with the constitution. It is dated April 18, 1848. Isaac Steinmetz received $30 for eighty perches of land, deeded by him to trustees David Martin, George Frantz and Isaac Steinmetz. The meeting-house was already erected at the time of drawing up the deed. It was finished in 1847 and was 36 by 50 ft.

"This farm had belonged to Christian Brubecker. It came to Steinmetz through his wife Mary, daughter of Brubecker. The south end part, also by the deed as well as by the constitution, could be used for a school house on consent of the Trustees. This fact reveals very clearly the relation of these old Brethren to the cause of public education. The door at the south gable end was the entrance to the school-room. The place of the old partition, now torn out, is very noticeable. In times of worship the partition could be so removed that those sitting in the school-room part could see and hear the preacher. The top and bottom parts were stationary.

"For building the house $686.87 were subscribed by 206 neighbors, or an average of $3.36 per neighbor, certainly a popular subscription. The heaviest subscribers were David Martin, John E. Pfautz and Isaac Steinmetz. In the list we find old substantial Brethren names—Christian Bomberger, Joseph Myers, Jacob Pfautz, Sr., Christian Rupp, Isaac Shirk and Michael Weidler.

"The first election for Trustees was held March 11, 1848, when David Martin, Isaac Steinmetz and George Frantz were chosen. The following is a list of Trustees up to 1900, when elections ceased:

1. David Martin, 2 yrs.
2. Isaac Steinmetz, 12 yrs.
3. George Frantz, 8 yrs.
4. John E. Pfautz, 19 yrs.
5. Joseph Landis, 4 yrs.
6. John Albright, 4 yrs.
7. Charles Bauman, 9 yrs.
8. Isaac Shirk, 4 yrs.
9. Samuel Wolf, 6 yrs.
10. Jacob B. Keller, 16 yrs.
11. Jacob Kilheffer, 8 yrs.
12. John Kilheffer, 8 yrs.
13. John G. Kilheffer, 10 yrs.
14. Jacob Holsinger, 3 yrs.
15. Aaron Hummer, 18 yrs.
16. Jacob Neff, 5 yrs.
17. Samuel Kulp, 3 yrs.
18. John Lefever, 7 yrs.
19. John Kilheffer, 4 yrs.
20. Wane Culp, 2 yrs.
21. John Klimes, 4 yrs.

"Last election was held in 1900, but the elections were often neglected and then the old Trustees were simply continued.

"The house was variously called Steinmetz's, the Brick meeting-house, and the German Baptist meeting-house. To whom it belonged and the purpose of its erection are evident.

"Shutters were put on the house in 1853. In 1856 it

was unanimously agreed to make some improvements to said house, by filling up, making out stone steps, and putting water spouts in front of said house. Cost $37.77½.

"School seems to have been held right along. In 1866 it was necessary to lay a new floor in the school-room. This cost $66.57. These repairs seem to have led to charging the School Directors for the use of the building, for on March 30, 1867, the Trustees received from the School Directors $25, school rent. This sum or a little more continued to be paid until 1884.

"At a council in Mohler's Meeting-house in 1890, it was decided 'to remodel the German Baptist Brick meetinghouse.' The doors which had been on the side toward the road were now placed on the opposite side; the total cost for remodelling was $245.83—$9.17 more than necessary having been subscribed.

"This is an old house whose history is worthy of preservation. It is perhaps the pioneer brick meeting house in eastern Pennsylvania—logs and stones had previously been used. It is likely the mother of the work at Ephrata as well as at Akron. When the new house was built in Akron many wanted to tear down the old brick structure, but it found a champion in Sister Isabella Smith, who saved it from destruction. She has now over $200 subscribed toward repairing it. Regular services are no longer held here, but it will be convenient for funerals. A large cemetery, surrounded entirely with a neat iron fence accompanies the old church and will for generations afford a beautiful burial place for the Akron congregation."

At the time of organization of this church the membership numbered seventy-seven. The officials then were: Elder in charge, Elder I. W. Taylor, Superintendent and Secretary of the Brethren Home at Neffsville; minister, David Snader in the second degree; deacons, S. N. Wolf, and A. J. Evans. On October 18, 1913, the following officials were elected: minister, S. N. Wolf; deacons, George B. Wolf and Elsworth Wenger.

This congregation has two houses of worship. The *Brick House* above described. The *Akron House* was built in

1898, a frame structure, 44 by 50 ft., and was remodeled for lovefeast purposes with a basement, since the organization of the church. It was rededicated, October 19, 1913. Elder John Herr, of Myerstown, preached the dedicatory sermon. The first lovefeast of this congregation was held November 1, 1913, following a series of evangelistic meetings conducted by Elder J. H. Longenecker, of Palmyra.

The church has a Sunday School at Akron, organized March 26, 1906, with the following officers: Superintendent David Snader; First Assistant, S. N. Wolf; Second Assistant, John P. Snader; Secretary, H. N. Wolf. There is a weekly Prayer Meeting held at the homes of members.

CHAPTER IX.

LITITZ CHURCH.

Lititz Church was organized on January 10, 1914, with a membership numbering 120. Twenty-three of this number were from the White Oak congregation. The West Conestoga congregation, however, furnished the bulk of the membership; namely, ninety-seven of the charter members. Elder I. W. Taylor, superintendent of the Brethren's Home, was chosen elder in charge; J. W. G. Hershey, clerk; and Nathan Brubaker, treasurer. The resident ministers are: Elder John Myer, and J. W. G. Hershey, in the second degree. The deacons are: George Shreiner, Nathan Brubaker and Horace Buffenmyer. The Sunday School of the new organization with an enrollment of 85 has been placed under the superintendency of Henry Gibbel. A Teacher Training Class is maintained. The sisters have an Aid Society of which Sister J. W. G. Hershey is president and Sister Florence Gibbel, treasurer. A plain frame house 40 × 50 ft. built in 1887 is the home of this new congregation.

The organization was preceded by a two weeks' series of meetings conducted by Elder J. G. Royer, of Mt. Morris, Ill. Bro. Royer presided at the organization of the new congregation. His tactfulness likely had much to do with the frictionless evolution of the church.

The Manheim Road and Market Street in Warwick form the northern boundary of the new church; the road from Hess's Mennonite meeting-house to Bushong's Mill bounds it on the east; the southern boundary is an irregular southwestern line to the intersection of Peter's Road and the Lancaster and Lititz turnpike; the turnpike is the western boundary to Macpelah cemetery, thence a line northwest to southwest corner of Lititz borough, then north along borough limits and on to Manheim Road. The Lancaster and

Lititz turnpike had been the old boundary between the two old congregations, so it will be seen that a comparatively small part of the territory was given by White Oak, as was also the case in the membership. So much for the present status of the new congregation.

Deacon Jacob S. Minnich was the first aggressive worker living within the town of Lititz. When the meeting house was built in the extreme eastern part of the town, Jacob S. Minnich and John R. Gibbel were the Locating and Building Committee. Both Bro. Minnich and Bro. John B. Gibbel lived east of town and John R. Gibbel, son of John B., lived also in the eastern part. Since then, the location of the membership has shifted and the church is far removed from the trolley and membership. There is a strong probability, therefore, that a new house of worship more conveniently located will be erected in the not distant future.

In 1888 John B. Gibbel asked permission to hold prayer-meetings in Lititz on Sunday evenings. The request was granted. Then came the agitation for a Sunday School with Jacob Minnich in the lead. The congregation refused the request for a Sunday School; but nothing daunted, the leader went on, declaring that since Annual Meeting upheld Sunday Schools, one would be organized. The school continued for two years, when it was forced to close. After a few years it was revived, the church having later granted the privilege. It was specified, however, that a minister must be superintendent. Cyrus Gibbel was placed over the reorganized school; he was succeeded by E. B. Brubaker, who in turn was followed by J. W. G. Hershey, who continued in office up to the time of organization of the new congregation. The school has been evergreen since the reorganization.

The first effort for a new congregation was made by presenting a petition signed by Lititz members to the West Conestoga council in 1907. This petition was refused. A number of years having passed, the effort was repeated in 1913 and now the members of Lititz rejoice in the realization that all things come to them who wait. A meeting of the members of Lititz as an unorganized body was held on

New Year's Day, 1914. Elder Samuel Hunberger of the Brethren's Home presided. It was decided by a unanimous, rising vote to organize, and also to petition West Conestoga to change the line from the one formerly suggested by a committee to the one which was later adopted. The Brethren west of the pike petitioned White Oak for a line and for the privilege of uniting with the members in the West Conestoga portion of Lititz. The petitions were granted with the happy result which we have noted. The new congregation has a territory of almost four square miles, with a population of about four thousand.

CHAPTER X.

BIOGRAPHICAL.

A. Jacob Stoll.

Jacob Stoll was born in 1731, baptized in 1748, elected a minister in 1753, and died in 1822, in his ninety-second year.

It is not known positively when he was ordained a Bishop, but in an old manuscript the writer of this sketch has seen, it is mentioned that Elder Stoll "was sixty-seven years a Bishop." Whether the author of that manuscript had in view the time he was in the ministry, or whether he was really ordained an Elder two years after his election, we know not, but if the former, he missed it by two years, for from 1753, when he was elected, to 1822, when he died, was sixty-nine years—the longest term of any brother in the ministry in Eastern Pennsylvania we know of. A close second is Samuel Haldeman, now living in Reedly, California, who was born, raised, baptized, and elected a minister, in Montgomery County, Pennsylvania, and afterwards moved to Schuylkill County, and from there to the West. He was born in 1820, baptized in 1840, elected in 1847, and is therefore now (1913) sixty-six years in the ministry. Both he and his wife are living yet. She will be ninety-three next April, and they have been married over seventy-one years. They are both able to attend meeting, and on last August 14, he gave a ten-minute talk in meeting, both edifying, and instructive. (From Eld. D. L. Forney, in *Gos. Mess.*, Vol. 62, No. 39, page 614.)

There was an Esther Stoll baptized prior to 1734, and also Esther Stoll in 1745, who were likely mother and sister of Elder Jacob Stoll.

It was said by the old Brethren who lived contemporary with Elder Stoll that at the time of his call to the ministry, he had an engagement to get married, but after his election he and his fiancee talked the matter over and mutually agreed to cancel the engagement, lest his entanglement in a family relation might be a hindrance to his work for the Master, and so he was never married.

Just where he was born, or where he had his home during his earlier life we know not, but it is known that he always led a simple life, and the probability is that he always lived in the same vicinity, and when he was older he is known to have lived alone over a spring house, on the farm of Bro. Joseph Royer, near where Middle Creek Meeting-house now stands. There he had his loom, he being a weaver by trade, and there he slept and lived, when not engaged in his duties as overseer of a large flock, scattered over a large territory.

By this time some members of Conestoga had moved across the mountain into what is now Lebanon County, where the Brethren would have an occasional meeting at the Brethren's homes, and on such occasions Elder Stoll would take his staff, on Sunday morning early, and walk across the mountain, and preach, and in the afternoon walk home again. On one such occasion, when the meeting was at Brother Henry Royer's, on the farm now owned by a Brother Bucher, east of Reistville, when bidding farewell, sister Royer said she don't know what they will do when Elder Stoll don't come to preach for them any more; then he stamped his cane on the floor and said: "Then you have the same God you now have."

Brother Samuel Gibbel at one time lived in the Conestoga district, and later moved to Lebanon County. One day he went to Elder Stoll and complained about a Brother for being so notoriously untruthful, that the people talk about it, thus bringing disgrace on the church. After waiting a little for a reply, Elder Stoll said: "Make him different." That was all he got. This information the writer has from a son of Gibbel.

Elder Jacob Hollinger, when he lived, told the writer, that Elder Stoll was very simple in his living, that he wore knee breeches made of buckskin, which he wore at all times and places, and that by his trade he became acquainted with a storekeeper in Lancaster, who took such a liking to him that he gave orders that when he dies, that preacher with the "Buckskin breeches" should preach his funeral, and he did.[1]

In conversation Elder Stoll had little to say, and in preaching his sermons were short and pithy, so that when the people were about ready to listen for what comes next, he would sit down, and when he was urged to preach longer sermons, he would say, "We must not preach people weary, but hungry, so that they come again the next time."

When he was old, and knew that at best his life in this earthly house would be brief he gave instructions that he should be buried in the Middle Creek Cemetery, just inside the gate, so that people going in and out would have to walk over him, and when the grave was dug about the proper depth, they came upon a flat rock, on which they placed the coffin.

Some years afterward the cemetery was enlarged which made it necessary to change the place of entry. His grave is marked by a small stone, with J. Stoll, 1822, on it. "Mark the perfect man, behold the upright, for the end of that man is peace." Ps. 37, 37.

Elder Stoll, some time in his active life, wrote a book on religious topics and had it published in German, and with all diligent search so far the writer was unable to find a copy, but remembers having seen it years ago, and all he remembers of the title page is the name of the author, the peculiarity of which made a lasting impression on his mind; viz., "J. St–ll." This proves that he had literary abilities above the ordinary of his time. (See cut of Title Page).

S. R. Zug.

---

[1] When Peter Miller, of the Beissel monastic community died, all the celibates were old and more or less feeble, so that it was determined to invite a clergyman to perform his last rites. Recourse was had to the minister of the nearest Dunker congregation, who was Jacob Stoll, living less than four miles from Peter Miller's residence. It is stated on good authority that Jacob Stoll preached the funeral sermon of Peter Miller on September 28, 1796, taking for his text Rev. 14: 12, 13.—Editors.

B. Abraham Zug.

Abraham Zug was born in Warwick, now Penn Township, Lancaster County, Pennsylvania, and was the youngest son of Elder Johannes Zug.

He was married to Susanna Royer, from Middle Creek. They had four sons and one daughter: John, who afterwards became the Elder of the Tulpehocken Church; Daniel, who moved to, and died in Franklin Co., Pa.; Abraham and David, twins, who lived and died in Lebanon Co.; and Catharine, who was never married.

He was a tanner by trade and lived in Rapho Township, about a mile southeast of Mastersonville, where he carried on his trade for some years. About 1805 they moved to Lexington, Warwick Township, where he had a tannery, and where, in 1815, he and Jacob Pfautz were elected to the ministry the same day. When his sons grew up, and needed work he sold out there, and moved to Lebanon County, where he bought a farm, near where Richland now is. Here he, and his wife, lived their remaining years, and now rest in the Tulpehocken Cemetery, not far away.

They still belonged to the Conestoga Church, though living in another county, so in 1823 he and Jacob Pfautz were ordained Elders, and the same day Samuel Myer, and Michael Landis elected ministers, and Henry Mohler, Sr., and Jacob Bollinger, deacons.

In July 1841 Elder Zug died in his 70th year. In his eldership he was frequently called to Little Swatara to assist in church work. He was a good counsellor, not radical, but firm, wise, and tactful, making few words, well considered, in a kind, mild voice, and always to the point.

He stood well in the community in and outside of the church. At his funeral Thomas Leinbach, a Reformed minister, asked liberty to say something, which being granted, he eulogized the departed as a true model Christian, and his death as an irreparable loss to the community.

S. R. Zug.

C. Christian Bomberger.

Christian Bomberger was born in Penn Township, Lancaster County, Pa., in 1801. Of his parents little is known, but his mother was a daughter of Christian Graybill, a prominent Brother. They were of German descent, and lived on the farm. Christian received a fair education. When he grew to manhood, he chose the profession of medicine.

He was united in marriage to a Miss Fahnestock. Among the Fahnestocks were some prominent physicians, who proved helpful to him in his chosen profession.

To them were born two sons and four daughters. They lived on a farm below Lititz until their sons started out for themselves; then they took to the farm, and the parents moved to Rothsville, where the doctor devoted his time to the church and the practice of medicine. In his medical work he used magnetism and faith cure to some extent and sometimes obtained results that were positively unexplainable by the ordinary laws of *Materia medica*. He never undertook important surgical cases, but recommended them to skillful surgeons in Lancaster.

In 1828 he and his wife united with the church. Three years later, he was called to the ministry. While he made a success of medicine, he had little faith in his ability to preach. So often did he say so to his wife that she grew tired, and on one occasion replied to him that God could open the mouth of Balaam's ass to rebuke his master, why could he not his? This gave him some courage at least to make an effort. From this time his influence grew, and he became a physician for both body and soul. In 1862 he was ordained Elder and given charge of the Conestoga Church. In 1864 the Conestoga Church was divided into three churches—Conestoga, West Conestoga, and Ephrata, with Elder Bomberger in charge of the three for the time being. He was one of the best counsellors of the district, and was therefore called from home frequently to aid in adjusting difficulties in many parts of the district. He was one of a sextette in eastern Pennsylvania, who were leaders in the district, the other five being Samuel Harley, Sr., of Indian Creek, John H. Umstad, Jacob Hollinger, John Zug and David Gerlach. His body is at rest in the Conestoga Congregation (Middle Creek Cemetery) and his labors for righteousness and peace are still felt among the churches where he labored. He fell asleep in 1880, in the 79th year of his age.

S. R. ZUG.

D. SAMUEL HARLEY.

Elder Samuel Harley, the second elder of the Ephrata Church, was born and raised in Montgomery County, Pennsylvania, and came to Lancaster County while he was yet a young man. He was called to the ministry in the Ephrata Church in 1864, after having been elected a deacon in the Conestoga Church in 1861. He was advanced to the second degree of the ministry in 1867 and ordained in 1871.

Elder Harley united with the church in the Indian Creek Congregation in Montgomery County. He was married to Elizabeth Johnson on May 14, 1843, and baptized with his wife the following spring. Their union was blessed with two daughters, the older, Mariette, was married to Yelles Cassel, a son of Abram Cassel, the antiquarian, and the younger was married to Jeremiah Kurtz, of Ephrata. He was married a second time on March 15, 1874, to Sister Catherine Royer, still living.

Elder Harley was a highly respected man in his community. As an elder, having charge of the Ephrata congregation, he was a good housekeeper, watching over the flock. His preaching was mostly in his own district and adjoining districts. He was often called to other churches for counsel. He officiated at three hundred marriages. He served several times on the Standing Committee at Annual Meeting. He was once a member of the Home Mission Board. He was not a fluent speaker but his words were to the point and with power.

During the last few years of his life he retired from active church work on account of both mind and body failing in health and strength. The call to come up higher reached him May 6, 1896, having attained the age of seventy-six years, two days. His funeral was largely attended. Interment was made at Mohler's Church burying ground. The text was Daniel 12:2, 3. The pallbearers were the four ministers of the Ephrata Church. Elders Samuel R. Zug and Christian Bucher officiated.

E. John B. Gibbel.

John B. Gibbel was baptized in White Oak Congregation in 1856, elected to the ministry, October 17, 1866, and later advanced to the second degree of ministry. He moved into the West Conestoga Congregation, March 18, 1873, near Lititz and labored in the latter congregation until the time of his death, January 20, 1889, dying very suddenly of apoplexy of the heart, aged 56 years 7 months 22 days; burial at Middle Creek graveyard. He served 23 years in the ministry and two of his sons, Cyrus R. Gibbel and Aaron R. Gibbel, are ministers in the Brethren Church and his daughter, Elizabeth Gibbel McCann, served as a missionary in India from 1897 to 1903 and 1904 to 1907, as wife of Elder S. N. McCann, of Virginia.

PART VII.

WHITE OAK GROUP.

CHAPTER I.

WHITE OAK CHURCH.

White Oak Church was originally a part of Conestoga, although history informs us that a few members had settled in White Oak Land, prior to 1736, in which year there was a lovefeast held. It was a part of Conestoga Church, and, although a considerable distance from the main body of the church, it was supplied in the ministry from Conestoga.

The first minister who lived within the bounds of what later became the White Oak Church district, was Peter Hummer. He lived on, and owned, a large farm, a part of which is now owned by Allen Hoffer, about three miles west of Manheim. Where he came from, or when he was elected, we have no positive data.

About 1753, or soon after, he bought a farm of 199¾ acres, as aforesaid. It is probable that he was elected to the ministry soon after, for the White Oak settlement had no minister nearer than Jacob Stoll, and he lived at Middle Creek, from ten to fifteen miles away. In 1769 he, and his wife Catharine, sold 62 acres to Stoffel Miller, who, in 1774 sold the same to George Gantz, who started what was long known as Gantz's tavern. In 1770, Hummer and wife sold the balance of said farm to his son-in-law Sebastian Keller, whose wife was Catharine Hummer, of whom more will be said later on. Sebastian Keller passed it to his son, Sebastian 2d, who spent his life there, and then passed it to his son Sebastian 3d, who sold it to his sister's son, John K. Snyder, who sold it to his brother, Samuel K. Snyder, who, about 1875, sold it outside of the family, thus showing that it remained in the family about 120 years. Peter Hummer died in 1784, leaving seven children, four sons and three daughters; viz., Peter (who was married to Barbara, a daughter of the first elder, Christian Longenecker), Jonas, Joseph, Abraham, a daughter Susanna, married to Martin Shuh, one Elizabeth to Casper Lesher, and one Catharine to Sebastian Keller. One daughter Mary had been married to Stoffel Miller, but died before her father, making eight children in all. By a marriage contract, on record in Lancaster, made between Peter Hummer and Susanna, widow of John Spencer, deceased, dated April 19, 1782, it appears he married his second wife. On September 3, 1784, he made his will which was probated September 18, 1784, which shows that he died between those dates.

We may have to draw largely on Dr. Brumbaugh's History of the Brethren, also as we have orally, from such men as Elders C. Bomberger, J. Hollinger, John Zug, and Abraham Gibbel, whose father was Johannas Gibbel, a deacon, and whose mother was a daughter of Hans Hummer, a brother of said Peter Hummer. These old fathers all lived contemporary with the fathers who were in touch, personally, with the work of the church almost from its beginning in White Oak Land, and their testimony can be taken as fairly authentic. In Brumbaugh's history, page 520, etc., we have the statement that Catharine Hummer "made a wonderful stir in the colonial church, that her father Peter Hummer was a minister, and that she would accompany him in his preaching tours, and take part." Her father seems to have had full confidence in her visions, and he would, in his preaching, sometimes remark that God does in such a wonderful way manifest himself in his family, and his daughter would follow it up with relating her visions, and that in her trances she is permitted to commune with the spirits of departed saints.

It was related by those who seemed to have it from good authority that she had these trances for years, off and on, but, as Dr. Brumbaugh mentions four in the fall of 1762, it seems they have become more frequent, and of longer duration.

On May 27 and 28, 1763, there seems to have been a called General Conference (Kurtz's Brethren Encyclopedia, page 136) at which this trouble was considered by the Brethren. This meeting was in the Conestoga Church, of which White Oak was then a part. The decision is as follows:

"The undersigned Brethren from their different places (of abode) have been here assembled in the fear of the Lord, in order to see, in heartfelt and compassionate brotherly love, how we might advise our Brethren, in God beloved, concerning the many woundings and different transgressions that have occurred since the exercises, visions, and doings of, and with the sister Catharine Hummer, in the White Oak country have happened—after we have yesterday heard the accusations of the Brethren against one another and their testimony, that they would not seek any division, but were willing to hear our brotherly counsel of love—we have (in the next place) all, every one of us, carefully heard and considered the mind of each, and every one of us, the undersigned Brethren, has declared his mind and advice freely, one after the other, and then we have further united in the fear of the Lord in this, that we would in union counsel our Brethren as follows: First, we believe and judge, indeed, that Brother Hummer has brought too much of his humanity, (or human nature) into this movement, from which different fruits of disunion have grown. In the second place, however, we consider, that both sides have gone too far in words and judgments against one another, and hence it is our brotherly counsel, that Brother Peter Hummer should needs make acknowledgments, where he might have offended with regard of brotherly obedience, and if there are on both sides conviction and acknowledgment, then we advise, out of brotherly love, that on both sides, all judgments and harsh expressions, might be entirely laid down, though we have not the same opinion of that noted (singular) occurrence, so that those who think well of it, should not judge those who are of the contrary opinion, and those who do not esteem it, should not despise those who expect to derive some use and benefit from it.

"For the rest we advise you, beloved Brethren, receive one another, as Christ has received us, and pardon one another as Christ has pardoned us also, and let us everywhere consider, that all disputing, and judging, and despising should be laid aside, and thus remain, that every one leave to the other his own opinion, in the fear of the Lord, and altogether for conscience sake. Moreover, it is our advice that all unnecessary, and too frequent visiting should cease, and every one should earnestly abstain from all appearance of evil, and aim in all things after truth and uprightness, in order that truth may make us free from all that might still keep us in captivity, and prevent us from coming to a oneness of mind in Christ Jesus according to the will of God. If now one or the other should think we have not sufficiently judged the occurrence, let him consider that we cannot see the least cause for a separation for conscience sake. Hence we have felt constrained not to criticise, or judge this (strange) affair, but rather to advise every one to a godly impartiality and patience that none may judge anything before the time, until the Lord come, who both will bring to light the hidden things of darkness, and will make manifest the counsels of the heart, and then shall every man have praise of God according to his faith and its fruits. Signed by Jacob Myer, Peter Dirdorf, Martin Urner, Nicholas Martin, Lorenz Shrab, Henry Naff, George Schreiber, Christopher Saur, George Etter, Joseph Reutsh, Jacob Stutzman, John Shlipfer, Jacob Mohr, Mattes Schweitzer, Henry Raudenbush, Gideon Rausser, Daniel Letterman, Daniel Arnold, Anton Hartman, Sander Mack, Nicholas Letterman, Stephen Ulrich."

It was further said that when she had those visions, no one could go into her room, lest they disturb her trance, but one young man of her acquaintance. He could go in, and it would not disturb her. In the summer of 1763 it developed that she was not true, and the church took her case up, and dealt with her. Then it happened, as it is often the case when members make mistakes, and are disciplined, they call it persecution. Hence the letter from her to Alexander Mack dated November 6, 1763, in which she says:

"The winter of persecution is here. Contempt and persecution are strong. I am not only persecuted and hated by the world, but also by those that call themselves believers. They say that what has been done by me is idolatrous. They blaspheme whereof they know not."

"Dear Brother Sander, thou hast written me that the heaviest will weigh less than nothing in the end. I am imperfect. May the Lord give his good Spirit into my heart, that when I am weighed I may have the right weight, and may be taken from this sorrowful world, into eternal rest."

May this have been some of the "tribulation" which caused Elder Pfautz to fail to keep a record of baptisms from 1755 to 1763? (Brumbaugh's Hist., page 313.) Many did not believe in those visions, and therefore it caused a lot of trouble. It ended in 1763. The blow of his daughter's fall, in whom he placed so much faith, was so hard, that he did not preach any more (at least for some time) and that in a meeting once, when he was urged (it is said), he got up and quoted the sixth verse of the first chapter of the Song of Solomon, which reads in German: "*Sehet mich nicht an das ich so schwartz bin, denn die Sonne hat mich also verbrannt. Meiner Mutter kinder zurnen mit mir. Man hat mich zur Hüterin der Weinberge gesetzt; aber meinen Weinberg, den ich hatte, habe ich nicht behütet.*" Then he sat down again.

By the way, Catharine Hummer afterwards married the young man who visited her in her trances, and her son became a prominent witch doctor, known far and wide. Catharine Hummer's husband was Sebastian Keller, who got the Peter Hummer farm in 1770. They had six children, viz.: John, who lived in Dauphin County, and had a daughter who was married to a Mr. Shenk and lived near Deodate, and one married to John Ruhl, and lived near Elstonville, Lancaster Co. His second son was Dr. Sebastian the second, who lived on the home farm, and died in 1839. His third child was Esther, married to George Bear. Next was Jacob, and George, and Rosina deceased, leaving a daughter, Magdalena Evans.

Sebastian Keller the first was a member of the state legislature, when Lancaster was the state capital, and it was said he would walk to town, fifteen miles, Monday morning, and home again on Saturday afternoon. He made his will February 4, 1808, which was proven March 14, 1808. Sebastian second had two children; viz., Dr. Sebastian third, who lived, and died, in Elizabethtown, Pa., whose son,

Sebastian fourth, now lives in Steelton. The other was Elizabeth, married to John Snyder, who lived about one mile northeast of Mastersonville at a mill, whose children— four sons and four daughters—are all dead, but the youngest son, Cyrus K. Snyder, who lives in Pasadena, Cal. Sebastian second died in 1839.

Other ministers were Peter Eichelberger and Jacob Stoll, who later became elders in the Conestoga Church. Eichelberger was baptized in 1752, and Stoll was baptized in 1748. Hannes Zug was baptized in 1749, George Miller in 1753, and Christian Longenecker in 1754. Stoll was elected to the ministry in 1753, Longenecker in 1764, Zug in 1770. Of the other two, we have no record. Han Jacob Böshor was baptized in 1747. When elected we know not, but the record which Elder C. Bomberger, of Conestoga Church, had, and now in possession of Elder Hershey Groff, states that "the church district is getting large, and the membership spreading; it was agreed to divide. So they, in 1772, divided into three districts, with Peter Eichelberger and Jacob Stoll, ministers in Conestoga; C. Longenecker and Hannes Zug in White Oak; and John Jacob Böshor and George Kline in Swatara." The line between Conestoga and White Oak is mentioned as "the Lancaster and Schaeferstown road," which is to this day the dividing line between churches. In 1769, C. Longenecker was ordained to the eldership, and in 1780 George Miller and Hannes Zug were ordained by Christopher Sower and Martin Urner. Regarding the other three—or four with Kline—we have no record of their ordination, but considering the time at which they were baptized, and Elder Pfautz having died in 1769, and Jacob Stoll having been elected in 1753, eleven years before Brother Longenecker, it is highly probable that they were ordained, at least, before that division of the church took place in 1772.

Ulrich Zug came from Switzerland in 1727 to his wife's brother, Michael Bachman, four miles northwest of Lancaster, who went to White Oak Valley and preëmpted by warrant about 1,000 acres of land which he afterward had patented. About 1742, he sold to Ulrich Zug 345 acres and

Monument of Ulric Zug, Ancestor of Zugs in America, Erected through the Efforts of Mary Zug Francis, Lebanon.

Grave of Elder Abraham Zug and Wife, Tulpehocken Cemetery.

Grave of Elder John Zug and Wife, Heidelberg Cemetery.

Grave of Michael Zug and Wife, Tulpehocken Cemetery.

allowance, for "£60 and one ear of Indian corn for every 100 acres to be delivered in Lancaster on November 1 for said Bachman yearly to the proprietors forever."

Ulrich Zug had eight children,—six sons and two daughters. According to the best information we have, they came to this country Mennonites but his wife was baptized to the Brethren Church in 1741 and he in 1742, their son Peter in 1747, John in 1749, Magdalena in 1748, Michael in 1752, Jacob in 1761 and Christian in 1769.

In the spring of 1759, the children of Ulrich Zug divided the farm into two equal parts, of 175 acres, one to Jacob, and one to Michael, the others all releasing for their shares, all signing their names in German. The last we know of Peter Zug is in 1762, when he, with others, stood in defense of Elder George Adam Martin, and "opposed his excommunication, and were anxious to reinstate him," etc. (Brum. Hist., p. 331). Whether he was married, or when or where he died, is all a blank to us. Jacob took half of his father's farm in 1759, after the death of both parents, but sold it to his brother Hannes in 1772, and moved to Washington Co., Md., where he died in 1794. One of his daughters was married to a Long, and was the grandmother of Elder David Long, late of near Hagerstown. One to a Wolf, on whose grandson's farm the Annual Meeting was held in 1857. One to Elder Nicholas Martin, who was grandmother of the late Elder Nicholas Martin of near Hagerstown. One son John moved to Bedford Co., Pa., and from there to Indiana. And two sons remained in Welsh Run district, from whom came Elder David Zuck, who lived in Fulton Co., Ill., as also Elders John Zuck of Clarence, Iowa, and David, now elder of Welsh Run Church.

Michael married Maria Wolf, and took a half of his father's farm, but later sold it, and moved to Somerset Co., Pa., where he died childless.

Hannes, or John, and his father Ulrich were engaged in clearing a piece of woodland, when, while at work, he said to his father that he has it in his mind to take a wife. The father then asked him: *"Hast du dann was im Zweck?"* John answered: "Yes, sister Anna Heffelfinger." The father answered, "*Shon recht. Ich will es den Armen diener sagen dasz sie gehen sie fragen ob sie dich auch haven will.* (All right, I will tell the deacons that they go and ask her whether she will have you.) This was quite a different way for trying to get a wife, from that now generally in use.

About 1760 John Zug and wife went with her father to the Beaver Valley, now Dauphin Co., Pa., near Beaver station where he had taken up a large tract of land, and where he promised to give them a farm to clean of brush and timber; but in 1762 the Tuscarora Indians from the valley up the river became so dangerous by murder, and arson, and robbery that by fall they decided to go back to White Oak until life became safe again. So in that fall one morning they started on foot with their two children, each carrying one. After going a little way they saw a man lying in a buckwheat patch dead. He shouldered the man, who was yet warm, and took him along to the next house, not knowing when he might be the next one shot from behind a tree.

Things in Paxtang and Beaver Valleys grew worse instead of better, and in 1763 a number of young and middle-aged men organized themselves into a company, and assumed the name, "The Paxton Boys," for the purpose of revenge. But the Indians learned of it, and went to an Indian town in Manor Township, about six miles southwest of Lancaster, whence the Paxton Boys trailed them, but when they arrived there, the marauders had gotten wind of their coming, and had left. The Indians misdirected the gang, who essayed to follow, so as to give the fugitives time to escape. When the neighbors learned of the trick the Indians played on the Paxton Boys, they had the Manor Indians placed in the Lancaster Workhouse for their protection, but the Paxton Boys came back, burned the Indian village, broke into the workhouse, and killed every Indian. There was a little boy among them, and one man proposed to spare him, but before he had done speaking another one grabbed him by the legs, flung him around, and dashed his brains out against the wall, the bloody mark of which could be seen as long as the old prison remained, which was on the northeast corner of West King and Water Streets.

Hannes Zug had four sons and four daughters; viz., Christian, married to a Miss Rupp, and died young, leaving one daughter who was married to a Frick, two of whose daughters were married to two Swarrs, and lived near Landisville. John, married to a Miss Mohler, was given a part of the home farm, where he lived some years; then sold it to David Sahm; then he moved to Running Pump tavern, about two miles west of Elizabethtown, where he lived ten years; then he bought a farm near Carlisle where he lived, and died, leaving one son, Jacob, who lived in Carlisle, and died there. Joseph, married to Barbara Eby. He got the home farm, where he lived and died, aged 51 years. He had four sons and one daughter, Andrew, Joseph, John, Benjamin, and Catharine, who was married to Peter Eby. Elders S. R. Zug and B. Z. Eby[1] were grandsons, and S. Z. Witmer and J. C. Zug great-grandsons of his. Abraham was a tanner and lived some years in Rapho Township. His wife was a Miss Royer. Later he carried on his trade at Lexington, and from there he bought a farm in Lebanon Co., near where Richland now is. He was elected a minister in 1815, ordained 1823, died 1841, aged 69 years. Of his family more will be said in another chapter. One daughter was married to Jacob Deardorf, and moved to Franklin Co. Another was married to a Mr. Ream, and moved to Ohio. One was married to Jacob Kinsey and lived near Cornwall, Lebanon Co., and one was married to Abraham Shissler, and the last lived, and died, near Bainbridge, Lancaster Co. Hannes Zug was baptized in 1749, elected a minister 1770, ordained by Christopher Saur, and Martin Urner in 1780, and died 1821, in his 90th year.

Christian, fifth son of Ulrich, had a farm near Lititz. He had four sons and several daughters. Jacob lived in Cumberland Co., Pa. He was baptized by Elder Moses Miller at the age of 97 years and his wife at the age of 86. He lived yet about a year. He had several children, among

[1] Elder B. Z. Eby opposed Sunday Schools as long as he could, but after they were introduced into his church, he left, and went to the Old Order.

them a son Christian, living in Pittsburgh, became a multi-millionaire. Christian lived at a place called Papertown, Cumberland Co. Of his descendants we know little. David lived in York Co. Two of his grandsons, Jacob and Peter, lived in Bainbridge some years ago. Abraham had his father's farm, which he gave to his two sons, Christian and Henry. One daughter of Abraham's was married to Joseph Aldinger, one to Joseph Graybill, one to Jacob Stehman, and one died unmarried.

Henry, Ulrich's sixth son, moved to the Potomac River, in Washington Co., Md. From all the information we could gather James Zug, or Zook, who lived near Arcanum, Ohio, was a grandson of Henry. Three of James's daughters are living there now, one a Mrs. Caylor, and two had been married to James and Reuben Gilbert.

Ulrich Zug's oldest daughter Magdalena was baptized 1748. She was afterwards married to Michael Frantz, son of Elder Michael Frantz. He was also baptized in 1748. Shortly after 1770 they moved to Botetourt Co., Va. Elder Isaac Frantz, of Pleasant Hill, Ohio, is a great-great-grandson of theirs, and their descendants are numerous throughout the West.

Christina, the other daughter of Ulrich Zug, married a Musselman, when she was fourteen years old, and they united with the Mennonites. A son of theirs, many years ago, had a fruit tree nursery near Manheim, and two of that nurseryman's children, Jacob, and his sister, about 30 years ago, lived along the state road below Manheim.

Andreas Eby lived about one and one half miles south of Manheim. He and his wife were baptized in 1767. Sometime after 1772 he was elected to the ministry, and the writer heard his grandmother, who was Eby's daughter, relate that when she was eight years old, which must have been 1777, the Revolutionary conscriptors came and took father, and two horses, to the camp in Lancaster, but a man who knew him, one day came to the camp, and was surprised to find him there. He then went to headquarters and obtained his release, because he was a minister, but the horses they kept. When the war was over they brought one horse back, but so poor that his ribs could be counted from a distance. She was then thirteen years old, and said, "Oh, how I pitied that horse!" They said the other horse was dead. Those were troublous times that tried men's souls. Jacob, known as "Jockley" Hirshy, and wife were baptized in 1768, and in war times was a deacon, who lived about a mile west of Andreas Eby. One night the conscriptors came to his place, and brought a neighbor along by the name of Long, whom they caught at his home, a little south of Hirshy's, and he let on as if he would gladly go along, but Hirshy objected, and while they were fussing around with him, Long examined the conscriptors' muskets, which had flintlocks, and slyly shook off the priming from the pans, and then went for the door, and the men ran for their guns, and followed, and snapped, but they missed fire, having no priming, and Long ran, shouting, "Hurrah for King George." That was the last seen or heard of Long by any one that knew him. The supposition was they caught him afterward, and shot him. Hirshy did not go to the war, but how he got off we are not able to tell.

Next we know anything of Andreas Eby was in 1789, when he was on Standing Committee. When he was ordained, we have no date, but he died in 1798.

The church prospered after said division. The list of baptisms contained in the record kept by the Conestoga Church, after 1772, the time of the division, to 1800, is 138, and is mentioned to contain only those of Conestoga, while that in Brumbaugh's history is 68, and most of them, if not all, are known to have lived in the White Oak district. From 1772 to 1799 the two lists have not a single name in common so that it is highly probable that one is the list of Conestoga, and the other kept by someone of White Oak, of which Dr. Brumbaugh got possession. It is remarkable that with all diligent search and inquiry, not a single record, or mention, of any work done by the White Oak Church, from the time of its separation from the Conestoga Church, in 1772, to its subdivision in 1868, could be found, except said list of baptisms, and the trouble between C. Longenecker and J. Zug, which we have in Annual Meeting minutes, and what we have orally, by tradition, from the fathers. So far we see that in 1789 the ministers of the White Oak Church were C. Longenecker, John Zug and Andreas Eby. Elder Eby died in 1798, and lies buried on his farm now owned by S. G. Summy, and his grave is marked by a rough field stone on which is carved A. E., 1798.

In 1759 the farm of Andreas Eby was assessed as 200 acres, and his brother Hans Eby's 150, both adjoining, and constituted their father's farm. Their mother's name was Barbara, who was baptized in 1749. She had two sons, Andreas and Hans, and four daughters, Maria, Elizabeth, Barbara and Regina, all unmarried and members of White Oak Church.

Andreas and his wife Elizabeth had seven children; viz., John who later became the Elder of Codorus Church, York Co.; Elizabeth, unmarried; one, the wife of Yount; and Anna, wife of Christian Myers (the last two of Codorus); Madgalena, wife of Daniel Shumaker, who lived, and is buried on the home farm; Barbara, wife of Joseph Zug; and Maria, wife of Christian Streit. Four daughters lived and died in White Oak district, and the other two daughters, and son John in the Codorus district.

The following minutes partly explain the trouble in the White Oak Church for years. The initials of names of Brethren only are given, and to prepare the reader, I will here give the full names of those signified: Christian Longenecker, Johannes Zug, Alexander Mack, Martin Urner (by J. L. and J. St. we do not know who is meant), Jacob Hershe, and Johannes Gibbel. In ancient times personal matters which could not be settled at home were taken to Annual Meeting, and there considered, instead of sending a Committee, as is now the rule.

"Annual Meeting, 1799, Pipe Creek, Md.

"Article I.—Whereas there has existed for a long time a great difficulty between Bro. C. L. and Bro. J. Z., the overseers of the White Oak Church; and whereas there have been expressed very grave accusations, and hard sayings by C. L.

against some Brethren, who shall be named hereafter, it has come to pass that Bro. C. L. has selected six Brethren, and J. Z. has also selected six Brethren, and they (both) have agreed to obey or submit to the advice or united counsel of those Brethren to which also the members (of the church) have consented. So we have assembled ourselves, we trust, in the fear of the Lord, and with a fervent prayer to God, that he would bless our hearts with wisdom and understanding, in order to be enabled to counsel our dear Brethren wisely, and to come to conclusions evangelical, or according to the doctrine of the Gospel. And after having heard the complaints and accusations (of both sides) we have become entirely agreed, and believe all, that Bro. L. has done grossly wrong against Bro. Z. and also against Brethren A. M. and M. U.'s transactions, and against J. L. and J. St., and whatsoever else might have been done (of the same nature).

"Further, we believe also that wrong has been committed by J. Z. against L. but not so grossly as Bro. L. has done. Hence it is our unanimous conclusion, that when C. L. believes in his heart, and cordially makes acknowledgment before this present brotherly and members meeting, and also before—(his own) meeting, and asks for pardon, and also makes heartfelt confession for the suspicious (and offensive) expressions against the old Brethren, and against J. St., then we will, and it is hoped the members will, bear with him in patience, and he may continue to serve as overseer in W. O. Church. And what concerns Z. we have agreed that when he makes acknowledgment before the members, that he has also done wrong, and asks pardon, he shall also serve as overseer with L., yet so that in important matters, such as baptism, breaking of bread, receiving and excluding (members), he should not go on without L.'s knowledge and consent; but with regard to holding meetings, attending funerals, solemnizing marriages, he shall have equal liberty with Bro. L.

"Now whoever of them will not submit to this above stated counsel and conclusion shall stand still in his office until he is willing to accept it, and when it is accepted of both, there shall be hereafter no more heard of those things which are past.

"Unanimously concluded by us, the subscribers: Martin Urner, Martin Gaby, Henry Danner, Peter Leibert, Jacob Danner, Philip Engler, Michael Pfoutz, Martin Garber, Daniel Utz, Philip Levy, Valentine Pressel, Stephen Ulrich."

It will be noticed that the above minute starts out by saying that "there has existed for a *long time* a great difficulty," etc. Just how long, or when, or from what, it had its beginning, we have no means of knowing, but the following facts may give some light on this point:

In John Winebrenner's "History of all Religious Denominations," on pages 560–565, we have the facts given that William Otterbein, formerly a Reformed minister, and Martin Boehm, a Mennonite minister, have been holding meetings together, and causing quite a stir among their hearers, getting many followers, and that in order to accomplish more and better results, they had their first conference in Baltimore, in 1789. The writer further says, "Big meetings were resolved on, the first was held in Lancaster county, Pa.," and that it was largely attended by Lutherans, German Reformed, Mennonites, and others. They, then, coming together from such various preëxisting orders, and worshiping together, "gave rise to the name 'United Brethren in Christ,' which name was afterward adopted by the church" (namely in 1800).

They "elected William Otterbein and Martin Boehm, as superintendents, or bishops; and agreed that each should act according to his own convictions, as to the mode of baptism." Now this meeting was said to have been held in Donegal Township, and resulted in many conversions. But not all were ready and willing to unite with this new organization, believing that there is but one mode of baptism, that is right, and that is triune immersion. Jacob Nissley, a minister of the River Brethren, who is dead for some time, told the writer, that a delegation of those dissatisfied ones went to the vicinity of Manheim, to confer with Elder C. Longenecker, with a view of uniting with the Church of the Brethren, but that Elder Longenecker told them that the Brethren Church was not any more on the true foundation, that they have the form, but lack life and spirit, and advised them to start a church for themselves, and build on the true foundation. Mr. Nissley said he had his information from the founders of the River Brethren Church. The delegation as abovesaid were: Jacob Engle, Hans Engle, C. Rupp,

WHITE OAK CHURCH.

Hans Stern, a Mr. Heiges, and Schaeffer. Some of them, if not all, came out from the Mennonites, and none from the Brethren Church. The writer in Winebrenner's history, on page 553 says, in a footnote, that "they were sometimes called *River Mennonites* from the circumstance that some of their first ministers had stood in connection with the Mennonites." On the same page, in giving the history of the church, he says: "At a later period some ministers and lay members of the Täufer united with them."

Abraham Gibbel told the writer that Hans Stern, one of the delegation of six, as aforesaid, unhesitatingly told him, that after they went home from Elder Longenecker, they consulted and concluded that they would take the advice, but none of them being baptized, they went across the Blue Ridge, to Elder George Miller, in the Swatara Church; and asked him to baptize them, but told him that they would then organize for themselves, upon which he refused. This must all have transpired before 1798, for in that year Elder Miller died. They then began their church by one baptizing another, and he then baptized the rest. The difficulties in W. O. Church, therefore, must have started early in the nineties, at which time he (Longenecker) published his pamphlet, in which he made rude expressions, derogatory to the church and a number of Elders.

It is reasonable to suppose that if Elder Longenecker had been at peace with the church, and the church with him, and he had done his duty, the River Brethren Church would never have been organized; that is, if they had been honest, and sincere, and the presumption is that they were.

We have no information that anything was done in regard to the said difficulty until four years afterward, in 1803, the case was again taken up in general conference, and the following action taken:

"Annual Meeting, 1803, place unknown.

"Our cordial and united greeting of love to all our beloved Brethren and members of the White Oak Church. We wish much grace, mercy, and blessing from God the Father of our Lord and Saviour Jesus Christ, to all our fellow members, united with us in love and faith, as also especially to our dear Brethren C. L. and J. Z. It is our heart's desire that the good God would make us all faithful laborers in his vineyard; for all that were hired by that householder, were hired to labor in his vineyard, to which we wish you all much grace, blessing, and salvation from God. The cause of our present writing is this: Since we, or some of us, have been informed by our dear Brother Martin Gaby, who, on his journey to us, passed through White Oak, and also had meeting there, that Bro. C. L., since the big meeting, has only been a few times at meeting, and now, for a considerable time has not come any more at all to meeting, so that some Brethren feel oppressed in their minds on account of the word or expression which is found in that conclusion made at that big meeting; viz.: 'That Bro. J. Z. should not go on with baptism, breaking of bread, receiving and excluding without L.'s knowledge and consent'; hereupon we, the undersigned Brethren, have conversed on the matter, and are of one mind on it, and now the same as it was at that time (four years before), and is in part also expressed in said conclusion, though briefly, that we all considered that Bro. L. had done wrong grossly, and if he would believe it from the heart, and confess and make acknowledgment, we, and hoping the members, would bear with him in patience, and then he should serve as overseer in W. O., and thus should Bro. Z., in such important matters not go on without his knowledge and consent. But if Bro. C. L. withdraws from the service, or from the duty of his office, contrary to the doctrine of the Apostle, where he says: 'If any one has an office let him attend to the same,' (Ger. translation Rom. 12: 7) if now Bro. L., withdraws himself from the service of the church, as overseer, so as not to attend the meetings, then he deprives himself of this honor, that Brother Z. cannot counsel with him, if he, Bro. L., does not attend meetings, according to his duty. So it is our unanimous mind, that on this account Bro. Z. should not be bound, or hindered, to go on in his office, and faithfully discharge its duties, and prove himself a faithful laborer. But if Bro. L. acknowledges, according to said conclusion, and endeavors to be faithful in his office, then we desire and hope the members will receive him, and not lay obstacles in his way. We mean on account of things that are past."

(Signed by most of those who signed the other of 1799.)

The following year, 1804, the case was again before the conference at the Pipe Creek, Md., and decided as follows:

"Art. 10. Our cordial and united greeting of love to our beloved Brethren, especially to C. L. and J. Z., and also to Brothers J. H. and J. G. We desire and wish you all that may tend to the glory of God, to the salvation of souls, and in the edification of the church. Inasmuch as it appears that Bro. C. L. assumes more authority in the service of the church than it pleases us and the church, and Bro. J. Z. has given more out of his hands than is pleasing to us and the church, so that it causes pressure and offense; therefore it is our loving counsel to you that you should keep house in the service of the church in union and control so that Bro. C. L. should make the commencement in meeting, (preparatory) to prayer, and then it is all the same who is speaking first, and when the meeting is to be brought to a close, then the beloved brother J. Z. is to make the conclusion. At the next meeting the loving brother J. Z. is to make the beginning, and it is immaterial who may speak first; and when the meeting is to be closed, the loving brother C. L. shall conclude, and so on. In important matters, brother Z. should do nothing without counseling brother L.; and so likewise should brother L. do nothing without counseling with brother Z. so that union is preserved. But he who will not keep house thus and give satisfaction to the church, and will not accept the apostolic counsel of love of the beloved old Brethren, such should be silent, and can not serve the church in his office. Further if a person desires to be baptized, and makes known a preference by which brother he would like to be baptized, then that brother, with the counsel of the church, is to satisfy the candidate, and forward him. With these lines we have given nothing new, but adhere to the conclusion which has been laid down already six (five) years ago, by the beloved Brethren. We have further to notice that there were very rude expressions made by brother L., saying that 'there is gone forth a spirit of Satan, and rules in the church, and of this J. Z. is the head,' etc., and even the church has been compared to the rebellious company of Korah. Such should be acknowledged and recalled by all means."

Two things stand out very prominent in, and through this trouble, which lasted ten or more years; namely, if any one tries to rise in the estimation of the church by pulling another down, he will make a failure; and second, the long suffering, patience, and forbearance the old Brethren had in dealing with erring members.

In 1808 Elder Longenecker died, aged 76 years, and is buried at Longenecker's Church near Lititz, with his son Solomon on one side of him and his grandson, Elder Christian, on the other, and it was said he was not fully reconciled to the church.

His wife's maiden name was Margaret Geib. They had nine children, two of them died young, and the other seven were: First, Solomon, who lived near Lititz, on the farm on which Longenecker's Meeting House now stands, now owned by S. B. Longenecker. He had one son Christian, who later was the Elder of White Oak Church, and was elected about 1828, or 1830, ordained about 1841, died 1855, aged 64 years. His grandson Linn Longenecker is now a minister in White Oak. Second, Abraham, who lived near Linglestown, Dauphin Co. The late noted and well known writer, C. H. Balsbaugh, was a grandson of his. Third, Daniel, who moved to Adams Co., Pa. He had sixteen children, two of whom, Daniel and Samuel, were noted ministers. Fourth, Elizabeth, married to Michael Huber, but died before her father, leaving five children; viz., Barbara, Elizabeth, Christina, Mary and Michael. Fifth, Barbara, married to Peter Hummer, Jr., who also moved to Adams Co. Sixth, Mary, wife of David Ober. She lived near Mt. Hope, and belonged to the Mennonites. Prof. H. K. Ober, of Elizabethtown College, is a great-grandson of hers. Seventh, another, the wife of Valentine Gensel, of whose family we know nothing.

Elder Longenecker was born in 1731, and died in 1808, aged 76. His wife born 1735, died 1796, aged 63. His father Hans Longenecker was born in Europe in 1703, was baptized by Elder Michael Frantz prior to 1739, died in 1767, aged 64, and his wife Elizabeth born 1709, died 1781, aged 72. In 1754 his son Elder Christian was baptized, who in 1764, was elected minister, and in 1769, at the death of Elder Pfautz, was ordained Elder. We have records of four other sons of Hans; namely, Hannes, Jr., Peter,

Henry, and Ulrich, and his descendants are now found in Lancaster, Dauphin, Lebanon Counties, widely scattered, both in location and religious faith.

Elder Longenecker's father-in-law, Conrad Geib, was born in Europe in 1694, and died in 1762, aged 68, and his wife Margaret born 1703, died 1765, aged 64.

The land for two miles on both sides of Chiques Creek from Manheim northward, at some time in the past, belonged to the Longenecker family. The Fretz family also lived near Manheim. And Abraham Longenecker and wife, who was Barbara Fretz, moved from the vicinity of Manheim, across the South Mountain, and had four sons: Peter, Jacob, Daniel and Abraham; and three daughters: one married to Christian Witmer; one to Samuel Oberholzer; and one to Isaac Eshelman.

Elder J. H. Longenecker, of Palmyra, is a grandson of Peter, and as there was but one family of Longenecker's and Fretz's in the vicinity of Manheim in those days, the presumption is strongly that Abraham was a grandson of Hans, Sr., likely a son of Peter. Barbara Fretz, no doubt, was a sister of Hannes and Magdalena Fretz, who were baptized in 1776.

After Elder Longenecker's death, Johannes Zug was the only minister in the White Oak Church. He opposed an election, fearing some brother might be elected with whom there might be trouble again, choosing rather to do all the work alone, though over 70 years old, than go through another experience like that which he had. This lasted several years, when he finally consented to have an election for a minister. When the time came to hold the election he declined all responsibility, even refusing to vote. When the voting was over, the result was a tie, and when it was shown to him, he said, "Jetzt will ich auch stimmen" (now I will vote too), and then voted for Henry Gibbel, thus breaking the tie between him and Joseph Hershy. This election took place about 1810, for in 1814 Brother Gibbel was on the standing committee at Pipe Creek, Md., Annual Meeting. (Min. of A. M., Pub. 1909, page 36.) He is buried in the family graveyard on his farm (late Kreider's farm) near

Kreider's Meeting House, and near Manheim. His grave is marked by a small head stone, on which is carved, "H. Gibbel, 1825."

Between the election of Elder Gibbel and 1822, were elected to the ministry, Daniel Fretz, and Jacob Haller. Just when either was elected or ordained is not known, no records being kept, but it is known that Brother Fretz was Elder in charge in 1822 (Elder Zug having died the year before).

In 1822 Abraham Gibbel was elected to the ministry, about 1828 Christian Longenecker, who was a grandson of the first Elder of White Oak, David Gerlach in 1837, John S. Newcomer in 1841, Peter Werner about the same time, Philip Ziegler in 1845, Jacob Rider about 1847, Samuel Graybill in 1855, Samuel R. Zug in 1865, and John B. Gibbel in 1866. These, so far, were the ministers of White Oak Land from its first settlement, in 1736, in their order of election, to the division in 1868.

About 1841 the White Oak Church was divided into two districts, known as Upper and Lower White Oak, by a line from the Susquehanna river at Marietta, by the nearest road, to Sporting Hill, thence by shortest road to where Union Square now is, thence about one mile, by road, northeast to the next Manheim road, then by that road to Manheim, and from there, by the state road to Schaefferstown. The distance from Sporting Hill to Manheim, by the nearest road, is about two miles, and the way the line was made is about seven. The object of making the line that way was to cut Elder Fretz into the lower district. Who was responsible for it we have now no means of knowing, but the division did not give general satisfaction, and in order to carry it through, it was suggested that members living in one district, who would prefer to have their membership in the other, should have the privilege to do so. With this proviso the division was effected.

About the same time, that part of White Oak Church, extending across South Mountain into Lebanon County, with parts of Conestoga, and Little Swatara, was organized into Tulpehocken Church.

WHITE OAK CHURCH.

By said division the ministers in the lower district were: Elder Daniel Fretz, Christian Longenecker and David Gerlach. Elder Fretz, having the misfortune to be kicked by a horse, fracturing his leg, and being then 65 years old, his memory and voice failing, insisted on having Brother Longenecker ordained, and a minister elected, both which were accomplished, and brother John S. Newcomer elected. The upper district had Elder Jacob Haller and Abraham Gibbel, ministers. The same year Peter Werner was elected to the ministry in the upper district.

Jacob Haller was not given to preach long, or entertaining sermons, but very pointed and instructive. The writer well remembers that at a lovefeast in 1861, when he was 84 years old, and in the presence of a number of strange ministers, he stood up and lifting up his hand, said in German, "I believe that I could guess what you all think. You think I might keep my seat, and let the others talk, but if I can I will try to say much in a few words."

On one occasion when a Brother who was a little forward had consumed much time, and said but little, Elder Haller arose and said: "I will say something too if something comes to me worth saying." Then he stood a little, looking on the table, and again looking up, said: "I believe nothing comes, so I will give the time to others who may have something to say." This, no doubt, was meant as a reproof.

Abraham Gibbel was different. He was a fluent and entertaining speaker and expounder, voluble in conversation, with pleasing address, and his services were much in demand from the beginning. He was elected about 1822. Daniel Fretz was then Elder in charge of White Oak Church, and when the members came before the Elders to vote, one after another said: "Jacob Myers, Jacob Myers." Now Jacob Myers and his brother (not a member) had a store in Petersburg, and kept liquor, as all rural stores did at that time. Then Elder Fretz became excited, and said: "Something must be done. We dare not elect a man to the ministry who sells liquor," and went out among the members and asked them: "Have you been in to vote?" If they said: "No," then he said: "Well, go in, but don't vote for 'Yoke Moyer,'" and when the votes were all in, Brother Gibbel had a majority, and was declared the choice.

It was, of course, not long until Bro. Myers found out how the work was accomplished, and went to Bro. Gibbel and asked him to decline to serve, but he said he has not asked for it, and will not renounce it. The result was that Myers left the church, joined the Universalists, preached for them, and made political speeches, was a ready talker, and lived to an old age. He was an uncle of Elder Grabill Myers, remembered by many now living.

Brother Gibbel prospered in the ministry for about ten years, when, for some mistakes, he lost his membership. Not long after, he was restored again, and also soon reinstated in office, but this proceeding delayed his ordination as Elder.

In the summer of 1846, a lovefeast was held on the premises of Bro. John Groff, where an election was held for a minister which resulted in calling Philip Ziegler. Quite shortly before that meeting it became manifest that Bro. Gibbel had blundered again, and was disowned, and Peter Werner soon after also, so that Bro. Ziegler would have been practically left alone, but he availed himself of the privilege granted at the division, and, with his wife, they claimed their membership below, and from that time on the ministers of the lower district supplied the regular appointments in the upper district.

These incidents, happening one after another, caused many members to change their membership to the lower district, leaving but a small number standing loyal to the upper church.

In 1847 Elder Jacob Wenger, of Little Swatara, and George Hoffer (2d degree) of Big Swatara met with the remnant of the Upper White Oak Church, in council, unknown to Elder Longenecker, who had practical charge of both churches, and held an election, which resulted in calling Jacob Rider to the ministry, and Joseph W. Gibbel, as deacon, and restored Abraham Gibbel and Peter Werner to membership.

This work was recognized by some and by others not,

which created more or less confusion and bad feeling, and resulted in a committee from Annual Meeting consisting of Andrew Spanogle, Peter Long, and Samuel Lehman of Pennsylvania, and Philip Boyle and Daniel P. Saylor of Maryland who met both churches in joint council, on the premises of Philip Ziegler, in 1851, who probed the trouble to the bottom, and by their report wiped away the crooked line made ten years before, and merged the two churches into one again, and ordered that Jacob Rider and Joseph W. Gibbel be recognized and respected in their respective offices, and that Abraham Gibbel and Peter Werner be held as private members, which report was almost unanimously accepted.

In 1855 Elder Christian Longenecker died, in his 64th year of age. In 1856 David Gerlach was ordained, and given charge of the church. About this time Abraham Gibbel and Peter Werner became urgent to be again reinstated in their office as ministers, but the Elders (Fretz, Haller and Gerlach, then living) were slow to make a move, too slow for them, and they began to appoint, and hold meetings so that they were both disfellowshipped again. They had a following of twelve members, including themselves. They held one lovefeast, elected a minister and deacon, and for several years tried to build up a church. In the meantime they baptized one, but their effort was not successful and finally quieted down. In 1862 Gibbel and Werner were again both reconciled and received back into church fellowship, and one after another of their followers came back again, with few exceptions. In 1864 Abraham Gibbel died in his 74th year. The same year Daniel Fretz died in his 89th year. In 1865 Jacob Haller died in his 88th year. In 1867 Peter Werner died in his 74th year. Thus four conspicuous characters were removed from the White Oak Church, by death, in a ripe old age, in less than three years' time.

In 1868 White Oak Church was again divided by a line extending from Marietta via Mount Joy and Sporting Hill to Manheim by nearest road, and thence by nearest road to Mount Hope. The lower district to retain the old name, and the upper chose the name Chiques, after a creek that passes diagonally through the district. At the division in 1868, the ministers in White Oak were: David Gerlach, Jno. S. Newcomer, Samuel Graybill and John B. Gibbel, and the deacons were: Jacob Stehman, Henry Stehman, John Minnich and Jacob Sonon, with about three hundred members. The Chiques' ministers were: Philip Ziegler, Jacob Rider, and Samuel R. Zug, and the deacons were: Benjamin Zug, Samuel Gibbel, and Joseph W. Gibbel, with about two hundred members.

In the winter of 1869 and 1870 Dr. J. M. Dunlap, one of the school directors of Manheim borough, Lancaster Co., brought an old deed to the office of an attorney-at-law, in Lancaster, in presence of the writer of this sketch, and asked advice in regard to selling the property mentioned in the deed, and using the money realized by such sale in a school house then being built. While the doctor and the lawyer were consulting about the matter, the writer read the deed. While he has forgotten the date, and the name of the party who made it, he distinctly remembers the following contents: the deed was made for the use of four religious denominations, viz.: Lutherans, Reformed, Mennonites, and Dunkards (Brethren) for the purpose of building a church, which was specified to be used alternately; namely, one was to have the use of it one Sunday and the week following, another church was to have it the next Sunday and the week following, and so on, so that each church had the use of it every fourth week. The deed was made to four trustees, each church being represented by one: namely, the Brethren by Henry Giebel, the Mennonites by a Mr. Hershy, a Mr. Bartruff was trustee for one of the other churches, and the fourth has been forgotten. The house was often seen by the writer, and was of logs, one story, about 30 X 40 ft. The house was so used by the churches, but as they got houses of their own they gradually dropped out.

In 1772 Baron Stiegel, the founder of Manheim, deeded to the Lutherans the land on which they have their church, and burying ground; later the Reformed, in town, and the Mennonites about one mile north, had their own, and the

Brethren began to have their meetings in their private homes, so that this house ceased to be used. Then it began to be utilized for school purposes long before the free school law was passed, and afterward, until 1870.

It is not likely that the Lutherans would have joined in this union movement after they had one of their own, and Henry Giebel was baptized in 1748 and lived to be 72 years old, so that in all likelihood this house was built between 1762 and 1770. Although we spent time and money in search of that deed, we failed to find it. It is even not recorded. But we found the lot on which the house stood. In February, 1870, the legislature of Pennsylvania passed a special act authorizing the school directors to sell, etc. They sold it to Benjamin Donavon who lived alongside (in whose deed reference is only made to the act of assembly), and he sold a part of it, with the old house, to sister Barbara Manly, who, with her daughter Ann, lived in that house some time, and then razed it and built on the spot a new double dwelling, now owned by the daughter, who was since married to a Mr. Ritter, now dead, and it is nearly in the center of the town.

LATER WHITE OAK CHURCH.

Before the first division of the White Oak Church territory in 1868, it contained all of Lancaster County north and west of Lititz and Lancaster, and extended northward across the Blue Ridge Mountain into Lebanon Co., west of Schaefferstown. In 1841, White Oak ceded the part of its territory in Lebanon Co. to what was then organized into Tulpehocken Church.

In 1868, White Oak Church was divided into two divisions known as White Oak and Chiques. Elder David Gerlach was resident Elder of White Oak after said division and also had charge of Chiques Church until April, 1869, when Philip Ziegler was ordained Elder by Jacob Hollinger and William Hertzler, and given charge. Elder Gerlach continued in charge of White Oak with ministers John S. Newcomer, Samuel Graybill and John B. Gibbel, and deacons Jacob Stehman, John Minnich, Henry Stehman and Jacob Sonon. The membership numbered about 300.

In 1871, Dec. 25, B. Z. Eby was elected minister and B. G. Musser, deacon. In September, 1872, Hiram Gibble was elected a deacon and on January 1, 1873, H. E. Light was chosen a minister in place of John B. Gibbel who intended moving into West Conestoga district. About the same time, Jacob Stehman, a deacon, died.

In 1876, Elder Gerlach had a stroke of palsy while preaching at a funeral, which incapacitated him; so in 1878 at a lovefeast held at Bro. John Hernley's, J. S. Newcomer was ordained by Christian Bomberger and Samuel Harley and given charge of White Oak Church. In 1879 Elder Gerlach died in the sixty-eighth year of his age.

In 1877 Hiram Gibble was elected to the ministry, and Israel Graybill and Tobias Herr to the deacon's office. About this time Samuel Gibble, a deacon, moved in from Chiques Church. In 1880 George Bingeman, a minister, moved in from West Conestoga Church, and Samuel Graybill died in 1881, aged 72 years.

In 1882, White Oak Church was divided a second time by cutting off the southern end, now known as Mountville, with Elder Newcomer in charge, and H. E. Light, minister, and B. G. Musser and Tobias Herr, deacons. The northern division retained the old name White Oak, which constitutes the present White Oak Church. The White Oak Church of to-day is bounded on the north by the Blue Ridge Mountain, on the east by the Lancaster and Schaefferstown Road, on the south by Mountville Church, and on the west by Fairview and Chiques churches, with the exception that the eastern boundary has been slightly moved westward since the organization of Lititz Church on January 10, 1914.

The officers of White Oak Church after the division of 1882 were: ministers, B. Z. Eby, Hiram Gibble, and George Bingeman; deacons, John Minnich, Henry Stehman, Samuel Gibble and Israel Graybill. The membership at the time of this division is not known, but at present it numbers about 465.

In 1883, B. Z. Eby was ordained an Elder and given charge of the White Oak Church. He continued in this

LONGENECKER'S MEETING HOUSE.

position until 1906 when he moved to Fairview Church. In 1900, Hiram Gibble was ordained and succeeded B. Z. Eby as Elder in charge. Other ordinations in this church occurred as follows: H. E. Light in 1888; Israel Graybill and Reuben S. Graybill in 1910; N. B. Fahnestock in 1912. Ministers were elected as follows: Israel Graybill in 1883; Reuben S. Graybill in 1885; N. B. Fahnestock in 1898; Linn B. Longenecker in 1906; Charles D. Cassel in 1907; Israel B. Graybill in 1910. The following were elected as deacons: Reuben Graybill and Nathaniel Minnich in 1883; Abraham Longenecker in 1885; Samuel G. Keller in 1888; N. B. Fahnestock in 1895; T. S. Beck in 1898; Eugene Brubaker and Israel B. Graybill in 1907; Levi Fahnestock and Isaiah G. Gibble in 1911.

Deaths of officials occurred as follows: Elder J. S. Newcomer died in 1902, aged 92 years; Elder Israel Graybill, in 1911, aged 74 years; Elder Reuben S. Graybill, in 1913, aged 74 years.

Prayer meetings are held at private homes. The first Sunday School in this church, after the division of 1868, by authority of the church, was organized in 1902 in Manheim, with Elder Hiram Gibble as superintendent, and T. S. Beck as assistant superintendent. After an existence of several years, it was discontinued on account of opposition. In 1912 the congregation by a good majority decided to organize again and chose N. B. Fahnestock, superintendent.

The building of the first house of worship in the White Oak Church occurred in 1859, when two were erected: one, known as *Kreider's* near Manheim, and the other, *Longenecker's* near Lititz. The latter was rebuilt in 1912 (see illustration) and made much larger than the former one. Other meeting-houses in this congregation were built as follows: *White Oak,* near Elstonville, in 1872; *Graybill's,* near Elm, in 1881; *Manheim,* in 1893. Several of these houses are intended for lovefeast occasions. Prior to 1881, the communion meetings were held in barns of members.

Bishops of later White Oak Church: (1) David Gerlach, 1868–1878; (2) John S. Newcomer, 1878–1883; (3) B. Z. Eby, 1883–1904; Hiram Gibble, 1904, September 19, to the present.

CHAPTER II.

CHIQUES CHURCH.

After the division of White Oak Church in 1868, the part cut off was organized with about 200 members, three ministers, Philip Ziegler, Jacob Rider and Samuel R. Zug, and three deacons, Benjamin Zug, Samuel Gibble and Joseph W. Gibble, under the name of Chiques Church, and in charge of Elder D. Gerlach. In 1869 Philip Ziegler was ordained by Elders Gerlach, Jacob Hollinger and Wm. Hertzler, and given charge of the church.

In 1871 Jacob L. Eshelman was elected to the ministry, and died in 1892, aged 68. In 1874 Elder Ziegler died in his 70th year of age. In 1873 Abraham L. Eshelman was elected a deacon. In 1877 privilege was granted to raise funds to re-build the Chiques meeting house.

In 1880 A. L. Eshelman was elected to the ministry, and B. R. Zug and D. M. Eshelman, deacons.

In 1882 a plan for re-building Chiques meeting house was proposed in council and passed by a vote of 31 to 8, and that summer it was rebuilt, by J. G. Stauffer and M. G. Gibble, building committee. In raising, the framework, from lack of proper support below, and the weight of people working above, broke down, by which two men and a boy, John Shenk, Jacob G. Gibble and John Werner, were killed, and a number injured, which caused some trouble in the church for several years.

In 1875 Jacob Rider was ordained, and in 1883 he died, aged 79 years, whereupon Elder C. Bucher, of Tulpehocken Church, was chosen Elder in charge, until 1885, when S. R. Zug was ordained by Elders Samuel Harley and Wm. Hertzler, in presence of Elders J. Hertzler, C. Bucher, J. S. Newcomer, and B. Z. Eby.

In 1884 Jonas P. Price came from Montgomery Co., Pa., to Elizabethtown, where he married his fourth wife, and

MT. HOPE MEETING HOUSE.

GRAVE OF ELDER DANIEL FRETZ AND WIFE.

Ober 3 Schulhaus (Abraham Mayer) Daniel Widder,	Widwe Herschisin Henrich Herr. alt Sem Grebiel. Daniel Grebiel.	Ober's Schulhaus (Abraham Mayer.) Daniel Widder.	Widwe Herschisin. Henrich Herr alt Sem Grabiel. Daniel Grabiel
Unbi Hernner, Isaac Eschelman. Henrich Reyer	Mount Plesent.	Unbi Herner. John Jung. Henrich Reyer	Mount Plesent
Offen.	John Zug. Christian Kauffman. Jacob Geib.	Offen.	John Zug. Christian Kauffman Jacob Geib.
Mount Plesent Philip Rigler Obers Jacob Bucher	Widwe Herschisin.	Monnt Plesent John Groff Obers. Jacob Bucher.	Widwe Herschinn
John Leman. Samuel Gibbel.	jung Sem Grebiel. Jacob Steman. Mount Plesent.	Jacob Reyber. John Leman. Samuel Gibbel.	jung Sem Grebiel. Jacob Steman. Mount Plesent
Offen (Georg Gibbel)	Abraham Minnig. Sem Schumacher. C. Langenecker.	Abraham Groff. Offen. [Georg Gibbel.]	Abraham Minnig Sem Schumacher. C. Langenecker.
Henrich Gibbel. John Kinsi		Daniel Gibbel. Abraham Gibbel.	

MEETING LIST BEFORE DIVISION OF LANCASTER AND LEBANON CIRCUITS
AND BEFORE THE DAY OF MEETING HOUSES.

lived here until he died in 1895, aged 82 years. He was in second degree, and is buried in the Price grave-yard, near Indian Creek Meeting House.

In 1882 John Gerlach, and 1885 Henry S. Zug, received as deacons, by certificate; and in 1889 H. S. Zug elected a minister and D. M. Hiestand a deacon.

1891. C. C. Madeira, a minister, first degree, received by certificate.

1893. Elder Wm. Hertzler presented his letter from Spring Creek, and in 1896 died, aged 68 years; and same year A. L. Eshelman died, aged 65 years.

1892. Three deacons were elected, viz.: D. R. Forney, Eli Brubaker and Isaac S. Gibble. In 1895 Daniel M. Eshelman was elected to the ministry, and in 1897 S. H. Hertzler was elected a minister. In March, 1899, S. B. Fahnestock was elected a deacon, and D. M. Eshleman advanced to second degree. In December, 1899, S. B. Fahnestock was elected as minister and S. H. Hertzler advanced to second degree.

In the spring of 1902 Chiques Church was divided into four districts, all of which organized soon after, viz.: Chiques, West Green Tree, Elizabethtown, and Fairview.

Chiques Church, at its organization in 1902, had as ministers, S. R. Zug as Elder, and H. S. Zug, second degree; and as deacons, B. R. Zug, D. M. Hiestand and I. S. Gibble.

In September, 1902, P. C. Geib was elected a deacon. In 1903, I. S. Gibble was elected a minister (died 1906, aged 52), and S. S. Eshleman was elected deacon. In November, 1905, John C. Zug was elected a minister. April, 1906, S. S. Eshleman was elected a minister, and H. B. Shearer and S. G. Wenger deacons.

On April 1, 1906, S. R. Zug and John C. Zug moved to Elizabethtown, but by consent of both churches continued their membership and ministerial labor in Chiques Church.

In 1905, H. S. Zug was ordained Elder. In May, 1909, Allen B. Ruhl was elected a minister and advanced to second degree August 24, 1912. In year of 1910 Elder S. R. Zug and John C. Zug moved their membership to Elizabethtown where they lived. In 1912, Henry Hess was elected a deacon. On November 29, 1913, Henry L. Hess was chosen minister and Monroe G. Hollinger, and Benjamin G. Stauffer, deacons.

In 1871 the first Sunday School was allowed and later was organized in Chiques Meeting House, it being the first among the Brethren in Lancaster County.

The officials of the church now are: H. S. Zug, Elder; S. S. Eshleman, and A. B. Ruhl second degree ministers, and Henry L. Hess, first degree. Deacons are: B. R. Zug, P. C. Geib, H. B. Shearer, S. G. Wenger, Monroe G. Hollinger and Benj. G. Stauffer. The membership is 258.

The second Sunday School was organized in 1898, in a leased meeting house, near Mt. Hope. Both schools have been kept up since. The first Chiques Meeting House was built in 1856. It was not arranged for lovefeast, and needed much repairing, hence rebuilding.

In 1910 a new church house was built, suitable for holding lovefeasts, known as Mount Hope Meeting House, into which the Sunday School was moved from the leased meeting house.

A Christian Workers' Meeting was organized in this congregation in February, 1907, with M. G. Gibble, president, and Minnie Ginder, secretary.

Bishops of Chiques Church: (1) David Gerlach, 1868–1869; (2) Philip Ziegler, 1869–1874; (3) Jacob Rider, 1875–1883; (4) Christian Bucher (non-resident), 1883–1885; (5) S. R. Zug, 1885–1910; (6) H. S. Zug, 1910.

MOUNTVILLE MEETING HOUSE.

EAST PETERSBURG MEETING HOUSE.

CHAPTER III.

MOUNTVILLE CHURCH.

The Mountville Church district was taken from the White Oak in 1882, and organized into a separate church with ministers, Elder John S. Newcomer and Henry E. Light. The deacons were B. G. Musser and Tobias Herr. The membership numbered about two hundred.

Since the organization of this congregation, the following ministers were elected: Tobias Herr in 1883, Amos Hottenstein in 1885, Henry S. Sonon in 1890, Milton G. Forney in 1898, Isaiah N. Musser in 1902 and William N. Zobler in 1910. Advancements to the second degree of the ministry occurred as follows: Tobias Herr in 1885, Amos Hottenstein in 1890, Henry S. Sonon in 1898, Milton G. Forney in 1902 and I. N. Musser in 1910. In 1900 Tobias Herr was ordained. His death occurred in 1901 in the seventy-fourth year of his age. Other ordinations to the eldership were made in 1909 when Amos S. Hottenstein and Henry S. Sonon were made elders.

Deacons were chosen by this congregation as follows: Henry Herr and John H. Herr, August 13, 1883; P. S. Hottenstein, November 27, 1890; B. Hershey, April 8, 1898; Henry Bender, May 28, 1902; Benjamin M. Brenneman, December 26, 1905; Elam Weaver and Daniel S. Neff, November 16, 1910.

The present officials are: H. E. Light, Elder in charge; elders, A. S. Hottenstein and Henry S. Sonon; ministers, M. G. Forney, I. N. Musser, W. N. Zobler; deacons, B. G. Musser, John Herr, P. S. Hottenstein, H. Bender, D. S. Neff, Elam Weaver, J. A. Seldomridge. The membership at present numbers three hundred forty-five.

CHURCH HOUSES.

Petersburg House.—The Petersburg House is the oldest place of worship in a special meeting-house in the Mountville congregation. The old log meeting-house, or block house as it was called, is still remembered by many. It stood where the new brick house now stands. It was not built by the Brethren nor for the Brethren. Jacob Hershey, April 2, 1831, conveyed for one dollar "a certain lot of ground situated in the township of East Hempfield" with the purpose in view of "promoting the worship of Almighty God and the Gospel of Jesus Christ . . . to and for the use, benefit and behoof of the society called Mennonists and the meeting-house thereon erected and being for their place and hour of public and divine worship and next after and at all such times when it will actually not be used for that purpose by the said society called Mennonists, that all and every Protestant minister or preacher of the Gospel may hold public meetings therein for divine worship without hindrance or molestation forever."

The father of Jacob Hershey, himself a Mennonite, was Benjamin, Jr., who inherited this land from his father, Benjamin, Sr., in 1790. They were doubtless Mennonites. The log architecture of the old house was prerevolutionary and the house itself was likely built before our independence. In fact tradition tells us that when it was built every settler brought a log towards its erection. Most of the logs were likely brought by Mennonites, but enough of other persuasions to give to the house the union character that was afterwards recognized in the deed given by Jacob Hershey. There can be no doubt that it stood for many years on private property deeded to nobody's trustees.

It was early used as a neighborhood schoolhouse. The fathers of many of the old residents now living attended school here. Among them was the father of Elder Amos Hottenstein, who must have gone to school here as early as 1825. Later, a part of this house was used as a residence. The Lutherans likely worshipped within the old log walls until 1847 when they built their present house of worship in Petersburg.

The Brethren had been worshipping in this neighborhood in private homes, among them that of Brother Jacob Stehman. About 1840 he erected over his spring a house intended especially for worship but only when his turn came for meeting, perhaps every twelve or twenty-four weeks. This was a step in the direction of special houses of worship, which at the time were violently opposed. He lived some distance north of Petersburg and the said spring is one of the sources of the Conestoga Creek. Perhaps the Brethren began to worship in the block house when the Lutherans withdrew. We were certainly in it by 1850. The meetings in Stehman's spring-house ceased when the block house was secured for worship. Jacob Graybill's barn just west of Petersburg was a place long used for lovefeasts.

The Mennonites transferred their remaining claim in this old property to the Brethren, September 29, 1867, likely about the time they erected a new house for their own private use. The tract on which the old log house stood contained one hundred and twenty perches. The new brick schoolhouse was erected on this tract where the driveway now goes in, about 1860. It was erected by the permission of the Brethren and showed the friendly attitude of the Brethren towards public education. The Mennonite interest at this time was waning.

The present brick house, 45 X 60 feet, was erected by the Brethren in 1873 at a cost of $2,674.29. This was the first lovefeast house in the White Oak congregation, and was built amidst great opposition. The Graybills were very anxious to have their old family cemetery incorporated into the new cemetery of the congregation at this place. The liberality of Herman Graybill and his father in giving towards the erection of the new house secured the desired end. The survey for the Petersburg cemetery was made July 31, 1878. Including the Graybill cemetery this church burial place contained 77.7 perches, the ground costing the church $78.25. The tract of land below the church containing 64½ perches was purchased by the Brethren in 1875 at a cost of $657.50. The brick schoolhouse was removed some years after the new meeting-house was built. Sunday School was organized in this house in 1898.

Neffsville House.—On September 28, 1869, Jacob Graver conveyed to Christian Brubaker, trustee for the West Conestoga congregation, and to Henry B. Rohrer, trustee for the White Oak congregation, for $549.37½ one acre and one hundred and thirty-three perches of ground in Neffsville. On this tract perhaps the next year the two congregations erected the present brick structure, in size 40 × 50 ft. The house was built on White Oak ground. April 9, 1901, the West Conestoga congregation for one dollar released her interest to the Mountville congregation. This is the oldest meeting-house now standing in the Mountville district, but in interest it is about the weakest. There are some indications of reviving interest.

Mountville House.—Mountville is a town four miles east of Columbia. While this belonged to the White Oak Church, yet a substantial brick church house, covered with slate, 70 × 40 ft. with basement, was erected in 1881 at a cost of $3,500. The new house of worship was dedicated September 25 in the same year with services morning, afternoon and evening, in the presence of a large congregation. Elder James Quinter, of Huntingdon, Pa., preached in the English language in the morning and evening and Elder Wm. Hertzler of Spring Creek congregation preached in the German language in the afternoon.

A tract of ground consisting of one acre and ninety-eight perches on which this building stands was bought March 31, 1881, for $675. On May 27, 1884, twenty-nine perches were secured in addition. Both of these tracts were donated to the congregations by Joseph Stoner. On March 29, 1886, the church bought two acres and two perches additional at a cost of $600, thus making the church property in Mountville to consist of three acres and one hundred twenty-nine perches. On this ground are a cemetery and a substantial dwelling house for the janitor. Sunday School was organized here in 1899. This house together with the Petersburg house are the main lovefeast houses of this congregation.

Manor House.—The name of Herr stands foremost in the history of this house of worship. On April 22, 1751, Abraham Herr bought from the Penns 424½ acres of land in Manor township. Of this tract, Abraham and his wife

NEFFSVILLE MEETING HOUSE.

MANOR MEETING HOUSE.

SALUNGA MEETING HOUSE.

MOUNTVILLE CHURCH. 403

Anna on May 20, 1751, transferred to Jacob Martin, perhaps their son-in-law, 163 acres. This descended to Jacob's son Isaac in 1783. May 3, 1784, Isaac conveyed this land to John Herr, likely a descendant of the original Abraham Herr. John willed this property to his son Abraham as his portion, Abraham being the oldest son of a family of seven children. Abraham still lived in the original log house but built the large limestone house in 1808. His son, Henry Herr, Sr., as early as 1830 had joined the Brethren Church. This was the first break the Brethren made into this old preëminent Mennonite family. Henry Herr, Sr., had married his grandfather's daughter, and it was some time after this event that he and his wife joined the Brethren.

By 1830 John Gerlach, tenant farmer and brother of Elder David Gerlach and also a member of the Brethren Church, lived in this neighborhood. Whether statements by him set Henry Herr to thinking and reading, we know not; but think and read he did, with the result that he became a member. David Gerlach, Christian Longenecker and John Newcomer were the first preachers of the Brethren in this section. Preaching services were held in the home of Henry Herr as early as 1835. Other families from this strong Mennonite region to join us were the Witmers, Lefevers, Shenks, Brennemans, and Neffs. Tobias Herr was the only minister elected from this section, and Henry Herr, Jr., and Benjamin Brenneman the only deacons.

April 1, 1876, Henry H. Herr, Jr., transferred for one dollar to Benjamin Musser and Tobias H. Herr, trustees for the Brethren, one acre and one hundred and thirty-three perches of land for the erection of a house of worship and for a cemetery. The Manor church-house was built the same year, being a brick structure, 36 × 40 ft.

A Sunday School was organized here in 1910. Henry M. Herr, son of Elder Tobias Herr, was superintendent continuously to 1914. Henry Gerlach succeeds him.

The old Herr homestead descended to Elizabeth Herr Brenneman, now the widow of Deacon Benjamin Brenneman. She recently sold it to Ephraim Gerlach, a Mennonite, whose father Daniel was a member of the Brethren Church.

The Brethren of Manor, however, do not believe that this has cut them off from Heaven's blessings and are ready to push forward with undiminished faith.

Salunga House.—When Bro. John H. Herr and wife moved to Salunga in 1870, there was only one member living here, a sister Mary Ann Hoofstetter who, however, moved away about this time. She had a brother David in Pittsburgh, Pa., who manufactured Hostetter's Bitters, a product made by his father in Salunga. The son became very wealthy. The Hostetter burial ground was located back of the present Salunga church house. The wealthy son offered to give five hundred dollars to the congregation which would build a meeting-house here and keep up the burial ground.

Prayer meetings well attended were held in the home of Brother and Sister Herr who were anxious for Brethren to preach there. Elder Henry Light promised them services if they would open their house for this purpose. Brother Light preached about a week to a crowded house and several united with the church.

Brother Herr was now instructed to buy an acre of land adjoining the Hostetter cemetery which was transferred to the Brethren's trustees April 1, 1887, for $600. John H. Herr, elected a deacon in 1883, was one of these trustees. Mr. Hostetter not only gave his five hundred dollars but also donated to the church in addition the strip of ground on which the sheds stand. Later, another small strip of land was added to the Salunga property.

The house was built in 1887 at a cost of $3,000. It is a frame structure, 40 × 50 ft., and is arranged for lovefeasts. The dedicatory sermon was preached by Elder William Hertzler, December 12, 1887. Sunday School was organized here in 1908 with Bro. Amos Hiestand as superintendent, who is still serving the church in this capacity. The average attendance at the Sunday School is seventy-five. At present twenty-four members live in this village and ten members live in Landisville.

Although this congregation has four Sunday Schools, it has as yet no Christian Workers' organizations.

D. C. REBER.

CHAPTER IV.

FAIRVIEW CHURCH.

Fairview Church, one of the four divisions of the former Chiques Church, was organized June 9, 1902. Elder Hiram Gibble was elected Elder in charge. Other ministers were: C. C. Madeira, second degree, and S. B. Fahnestock, first degree. There were no deacons. The membership numbered 131. In the same year, H. B. Gibble and J. B. Brubaker were elected deacons.

1903. Herman Balmer was elected deacon.

1905. S. B. Fahnestock was advanced to second degree of ministry.

1906. J. B. Brubaker was elected minister, and J. B. Kolp and Elmer Heisey deacons.

1910. Allen G. Baker was elected minister.

In 1912, George Weaver, a minister, moved here from Ephrata.

On August 28, 1913, S. B. Fahnestock was ordained an Elder.

There is only one meeting house in this district, known as Fairview, built in 1894, and originally arranged for lovefeast occasions.

A Sunday School was organized here in 1904.

The officers now in Fairview Church are: Elder in charge, Hiram Gibble; ministers, Elder S. B. Fahnestock, John B Brubaker, Geo. Weaver, and A. G. Baker; and deacons, Henry B. Gibble, Herman Balmer, J. B. Kolp, and Elmer Heisey. The present membership is 134.

CHAPTER V.

WEST GREEN TREE CHURCH.

In 1902, a part of former Chiques Church was organized with a membership of 210, as West Green Tree Church. The officers at that time were: S. R Zug, Elder, D. M. Eshleman, second degree minister; deacons: D. R. Forney, and Eli B Brubaker. In the same year, in September, an election was held for a minister and a deacon. The result was a tie between Hiram E. Kaylor and S. S Shearer, when both were installed as ministers and Abraham L. Frey as deacon. In 1906 N. W. Eshelman, in 1907 H. S. Eshelman, and in 1912 Allen Ober, were elected deacons. In 1911, Nathan Martin brought his letter here from Elizabethtown as a minister in the first degree. In 1910 A. L. Frey, a deacon, was granted a certificate and moved to Elizabethtown. D. M. Eshelman was ordained in 1905, September 5. In 1912, August 17, N. W. Eshelman was elected a minister, and W. S. Longenecker a deacon.

Advancements of ministers to the second degree of the ministry were made as follows: September 5, 1905, Hiram E. Kaylor and S. S. Shearer; March 7, 1911, Nathan Martin.

The first Sunday School in West Green Tree Church was organized at Green Tree House, in 1902, and another in the Rheems House, 1908. The officers of West Green Tree Church now are: D. M. Eshleman, Elder; H. E. Kaylor, S. S. Shearer, and Nathan Martin, ministers in second degree, and N. W. Eshelman, first degree; and deacons: D. R. Forney, E. B. Brubaker, H. S. Eshelman, Allen Ober, and W. S. Longenecker. Membership, 245.

The first meeting-house built in what is now West Green Tree Church was built in 1869, and the next in 1903, at Rheems, both arranged for lovefeast occasions.

In 1912 a meeting-house was bought from the Methodists in Florin.

ELIZABETHTOWN BRETHREN CHURCH.

STEVENS HILL CHURCH.

CHAPTER VI.

ELIZABETHTOWN CHURCH.

Of the beginnings of the Brethren in Elizabethtown, Elder S. R. Zug says:

"About 1870, the Brethren used occasionally to have a preaching service in the old United Brethren Church in Elizabethtown. At that time there were not over a dozen members in town.

"In 1875, the old school house on Mechanic Street was sold and the party who bought it at $425 then offered it to the Chiques Church at the same price, to be utilized as a meeting house which offer was accepted and meetings were held there regularly until the meetings became too large. So then in 1888, Brother Jos. H. Rider, son of Elder Jacob Rider offered to donate a large lot of ground on Washington St. for the church if it would build a meeting house on it large enough to hold lovefeasts in it. This offer the church readily accepted and the same year built a brick meeting house on it 50 × 80 ft. with basement. The other was sold and converted into a dwelling house.

"A Sunday School was started in the old house some years before the new one was built and was then transferred to the new and has since been kept up and has been growing and prospering."

Thirty-two years later than the time referred to in the above quotation, namely on May 2, 1902, the Elizabethtown Church was organized, having been cut off from the Chiques Church. Its membership numbered one hundred and sixty, of whom about one hundred and ten were present at the organization. This was done in the presence of Elders J. H. Longenecker, G. N. Falkenstein, H. E. Light and S. R. Zug. Elder S. R. Zug was elected as the Elder in charge; J. H. Kline was elected Treasurer; I. W. Eshelman was elected Recording Secretary. Jos. H. Rider, Addison Buch and Tobias Hoffer were chosen trustees. Other officials at the time of organization were: ministers, S. H. Hertzler, in second degree, G. N. Falkenstein, an Elder connected with Elizabethtown College as trustee and Principal, I. N. H. Beahm also in second degree; deacons, J. H. Kline and A. W. Martin.

The territory of this church extends from a mile east of the town to the Susquehanna River, being bounded on the east and south by the West Green Tree Church; on the north by the Spring Creek Church. In September 1903, the latter ceded some of its territory to the Elizabethtown Congregation, making the Swatara Creek at Middletown and the Harrisburg pike the boundary line, and at the same time also transferred its interest in the Swatara Hill church house.

The official body of the church has been increased as follows: D. C. Reber moved here as a minister from Brooklyn, N. Y., in July, 1902, having been elected a teacher in Elizabethtown College and at present its President. In 1903 J. H. Kline was elected a minister; in 1904 H. K. Ober; in 1906, Nathan Martin; in 1911, R. W. Schlosser and J. G. Meyer. The last three were called to the ministry in compliance with the advice of Annual Conference of 1890 requesting churches to hold elections from time to time to increase our ministry with a view of using such ministers wherever the church may need them. In 1910 Elder S. R. Zug and his son, John C. Zug, a minister in first degree, placed their membership in this church, but removed to Palmyra in 1912.

In 1903, J. M. Pittenger, a minister, located at the college as a member of the faculty. Other ministers who were teachers at the college were: J. H. Keller in 1904, W. H. Sanger in 1905-6, E. E. Eshelman in 1907-10. In 1909 Elder I. N. H. Beahm and in 1911 Nathan Martin moved away. In 1910, C. C. Madeira, a minister in second degree in the Fairview Church, located here. In 1909 Levi Mohler, a minister in second degree, moved here from Cumberland Co., and his son, Harry B. Mohler, resided here from 1911-13.

On account of the college being located in this congregation a number of ministers have come and gone as students, whose names are omitted here they having been only transient members.

Deacons have been elected as follows: I. W. Eshelman in 1902, Isaac L. Hoffer and Amos G. Longenecker in 1903; John M. Gibble, J. S. Hackman and David B. Kline in 1912.

Advancements to the second degree of the ministry were made as follows: December 15, 1904, D. C. Reber and J. H. Kline; March 12, 1908, H. K. Ober; February 8, 1911, John C. Zug.

On October 20, 1904, S. H. Hertzler and I. N. H. Beahm, then President of the college, were ordained as elders and the former chosen as assistant Elder of the church. Ordination committee was J. H. Longenecker, H. E. Light and John Herr.

The present officials are: Elder S. H. Hertzler, Elder in charge; Elder G. N. Falkenstein; Dr. D. C. Reber, J. H. Kline, H. K. Ober, Levi Mohler, C. C. Madeira, ministers in second degree; and R. W. Schlosser and J. G. Meyer in the first degree; and deacons, A. W. Martin, I. W. Eshelman, I. L. Hoffer, Charles Bower, A. L. Frey, John M. Gibble, J. S. Hackman and D. B. Kline. The membership is over three hundred.

Church Activities.

After the organization of this congregation, preaching services were conducted in Elizabethtown every two weeks in the morning and every two weeks in the evening, preaching in both the German and English languages at the morning service. On April 1, 1904, it was decided to have preaching every Sunday, one week in the morning, and the next week in the evening, and also to have services at the College Chapel every two weeks in the evening while school was in session. After September, 1906, services were held at the College Chapel one Sunday in the morning and the next Sunday in the evening alternating with the services in town, thus giving the congregation two preaching services each Sunday while school was in session.

In addition to the services at college and town, there was preaching at Bainbridge until 1907 every four weeks and also at Royalton in U. B. Church, every six weeks until 1907, and at present at Newville, a union church, every month in the afternoon after the Sunday School. Also preaching services at Swatara Hill every six weeks at ten o'clock A.M. Following the Sunday School, every two weeks there is preaching at the Stevens Hill house. Every eight weeks the Elizabethtown ministers preach at Middletown at 2:30 P.M., alternating with the ministers of the Harrisburg Church. Thus the Lord's Day program is as follows: Sunday School in town at 9 A.M. followed by preaching at 10 A.M. in town or at College at 10:30 and sometimes at Swatara Hill. In the afternoon, Sunday School at Newville at 1:30 and at Stevens Hill at 2 o'clock, preaching at same place at 3 o'clock or at Middletown at 2:30. In the evening Christian Workers' Meeting preceding the preaching in town at 7 P.M. or at the college at 7:30.

The mid-week services are as follows: Monday evening once a month the Sunday School teacher's meeting, Tuesday evening at 7:30 Prayer Meeting, Wednesday evening Teacher Training Class in town and College Prayer Meeting. Every Saturday evening at the college two classes meet for mission study.

The council meetings at first were held semi-annually in March and September. After September, 1903, they were held quarterly on the Thursday evening before full moon in March, June, September and December. In December, 1908, the time for quarterly council was changed to the first Thursday of the afore-mentioned months in the evening, but for the March council, the time is afternoon and evening.

Evangelistic meetings have been held in the Elizabethtown Church since the organization as follows:

1903. W. M. Howe at college.
1904. W. M. Howe at college.
    S. S. Beaver in town.
1905. J. G. Royer at college.

1906. J. K. Miller at college.
    Reuben Shroyer in town.
    David Weaver in town.
1907. F. P. Cassel in town.

1908. Jesse Ziegler in town.   1911. H. K. Ober in town.
1909. J. A. Long at college.   John C. Zug in town.
   I. N. H. Beahm in town. 1912. G. B. Royer at college.
   G. S. Rairigh in town.   R. P. Bucher in town.
1910. G. M. Lauver at college. 1913. W. B. Stover at college.
   B. F. Heckman at college.   S. A. Honberger in town.

Since the organization, about 125 persons have been received by baptism.

Love feasts are held in spring and fall of each year. At first the time for love feast was during the week, beginning at 1:30 P.M. and continuing till the following noon, furnishing meals to the public also. In March, 1911, it was decided to have the spring love feast on Sunday and the fall during the week. Since March, 1912, both feasts are held on Sunday evening with all-day services and closing Monday noon. Visitors are entertained at the homes of members instead of at the church. September, 1910, the church decided that sisters shall break bread and pass the cup during the communion service.

DECISIONS.

On September 6, 1902, Elizabethtown Church decided to use unfermented wine in communion service at love feast. Also ministers are excused from financial contributions for defraying current expenses of the congregation.

On March 24, 1904, decided that an indoctrinating talk of fifteen minutes shall be given to the membership at each regular council meeting. On December 15, 1904, decided to assess members for the purpose of raising funds for church expenses which assessment is made by the official board. At the same time the method of electing the officers of the Sunday School, Christian Workers' Meeting, and Missionary Reading Circle was adopted as follows: A nominating board consisting of the official board, officers and teachers of the Sunday School, the Sunday School Advisory Committee shall nominate the officers of the various church auxiliaries by ballot to be ratified by the council.

In September 1905, the pastoral visit to be made by the Elder was asked for and granted. On March 8, 1906, decided that all members shall hereafter be received on certificate by being asked to promise in open council or to visiting Brethren to be loyal to church as governed by the Gospel and the decisions of Annual Conference. Also that there shall be Prayer Meeting and Bible Reading each week on Tuesday and Thursday evening respectively.

In March, 1907, decided that Sunday School shall open at 9 A.M. and preaching at 10 o'clock. In 1908, the qualifications for Sunday School officers and teachers were adopted as follows: The Sunday School teachers and officers shall have the same qualifications as delegates to District and Annual Meeting. In 1911 decided to have preaching in town morning and evening each Sunday during the college vacation.

Permanent Committees.

The church has four standing committees: (1) A *Lookout Committee,* created in 1904, whose duties are to invite people moving into town to come to our church services. This committee has been abandoned and the work assigned to the Superintendent of the Home Department and its visitors. (2) A *Sunday School Advisory Committee,* of five members, created in 1903. (3) A *Temperance Committee,* of three members, created in 1912. (4) A *Missionary Committee,* of four members, created in 1913.

Church Auxiliaries.

At the initiative of J. M. Pittenger a *Missionary Reading Circle* was organized in June, 1904, while he was a teacher at the college. The circle consists of a Town Branch and a College Branch. The town branch held biweekly meetings for a number of years studying mission books under the direction of a teacher. Their offerings were placed in the Church Fund for the support of a Foreign Missionary. The organization consists of a president, vice-president, secretary and treasurer.

The following have been most actively identified with the town branch: A. G. Longenecker, C. M. Neff and Martha Martin as Presidents; Martha Martin and Elizabeth Hoover as Secretaries and S. G. Graybill as Treasurer. One hindrance to the success of this branch has been the lack of a suitable time for holding its meetings and so it was abandoned December 11, 1913.

The college branch of the Circle holds weekly meetings on Saturday evening during the school year. This branch regularly subscribes for the Missionary Review of the World for the college library. For several years a beginner's class and an advanced class in mission study have been conducted simultaneously studying books on missions. Several members of these classes have volunteered to give their lives to mission work. Elder J. F. Graybill and wife, Elder J. M. Pittenger, B. Mary Royer, Kathryn Ziegler, all of whom are now in foreign mission work, have been active members in the college branch. Also Elmer F. Nedrow and Elder R. A. Nedrow, who are now in the Lake Ridge Mission in New York State. Some of the funds raised by this branch have been used to purchase mission books for the college library and some funds were sent to mission points. During revival services at the school, it coöperates actively for the saving of souls and holds religious services at the homes of aged, or shut-in members in town.

A *Christian Workers'* organization was effected in 1907 by electing the following officers: J. Z. Herr, President; Martha Martin, Secretary; and H. H. Nye, Treasurer, to serve for one year. Others who have since served as president of the organization are M. A. Good, S. B. Kiefer, R. W. Schlosser, and Isaiah F. Basehore.

On March 29, 1900, a *Sisters' Sewing Circle* was organized with the following officers: President, Lizzie Masterson, Vice-President, Lizzie Will; Secretary, Salome Engle; Assistant Secretary, Mary Stauffer; Treasurer, Annie E. Hertzler. Others present were Mary Rider, Annie Hawk, and Amanda Witmer. The present membership is about forty. Meetings are held every other Wednesday afternoon.

The practical work of the Circle consists of making garments, quilts, and cash donations. From 1903 to 1906, sixteen dollars was paid annually for the support of an India orphan. Nine dollars was sent to India sufferers in 1902. Boxes of clothing were sent to Washington, D. C.,

St. Joseph, Mo., Chicago, Ill., Brooklyn, N. Y., Reading, Pa., Mt. Carmel, Pa. About one hundred dollars was donated to Elizabethtown College, and ten dollars to Kansas sufferers.

Mrs. J. H. Rider has been president for twelve years and Mrs. S. H. Hertzler was treasurer from the beginning until her death in October, 1912.

The *Sunday School* has been the strong right arm of the church in Elizabethtown and one of the chief factors in church growth and progress. Before the organization of the congregation, even before the present commodious house of worship was built, the Sunday School was there, not however without considerable opposition. Among the pioneer Sunday School workers in Elizabethtown may be mentioned I. N. S. Will, S. H. Hertzler, Jos. G. Heisey, J. H. Kline, Jos. H. Rider and wife Mary. J. H. Eshelman has been superintendent continuously since 1903. Among the assistant superintendents may be mentioned S. P. Engle, A. G. Longenecker, S. G. Graybill and Chas. Bower.

The Sunday School officers are chosen for one year and assume their duties the first Sunday in January. The officers consist of Superintendent, Assistant Superintendent, Secretary, Assistant Secretary, Treasurer, Assistant Treasurer, Chorister, Assistant Chorister, Superintendent of the Primary Department, Superintendent of the Home Department, Superintendent of the Cradle Roll. The method of choosing these officers is described on page 411.

Outpost Sunday Schools have been conducted at Mount Ober, Newville and Stevens Hill. In the summer of 1906, the Mount Ober Sunday School was superintended by Nathan Martin and conducted two quarters. In 1908 E. E. Eshelman was superintendent and preached every two weeks at the same point.

Newville is a village one mile west of Elizabethtown, where the Brethren have conducted Sunday School in a union house since 1902. W. A. Withers and S. G. Graybill had charge of this Sunday School the first few years. Others who have served as Superintendent at this place are A. G. Longenecker, Daniel V. Shenk, Leah Sheaffer, Martha

Martin, David Kline. Other denominations also conducted Sunday School here at times.

The most flourishing outpost Sunday School is the one at Stevens Hill, about five miles west of Elizabethtown. Here in a school house, Sunday School was conducted almost uninterruptedly since 1904. Those who have labored in this work here are A. G. Longenecker, D. C. Reber, Elizabeth Kline, B. F. Wampler, Mrs. B. F. Wampler, M. A. Good, I. W. Eshelman, Isaac Madeira and wife.

After the house at Bainbridge was sold, April, 1908, and much interest was manifested in preaching services at Stevens Hill, the advisability of erecting a house of worship there was considered in June of 1908. The matter was referred to the Sunday School Advisory Committee, who was instructed to canvass the sentiment of the community, in regard to the project. The community favored the work. Later, plans for a church house adapted for Sunday School purposes were presented by the same committee and on March 2, 1911, the church decided to build a church house 40 by 60 feet frame structure, about a quarter of a mile east of the school house. (See picture of this edifice.) The building committee consisted of D. C. Reber, Chairman; A. G. Longenecker, Secretary, and I. W. Eshelman, Treasurer; John M. Gibble and Jos. G. Heisey. On Thanksgiving Day of 1911 the house was dedicated with services forenoon and afternoon conducted by Elders John Herr and J. H. Longenecker. The cost of the church was $3,191.33 and the land and shed for horses cost $350. A. Z. Witmer, John M. Gibble, and A. G. Longenecker were appointed trustees for this house of worship. When A. G. Longenecker resigned as superintendent in December, 1912, prior to moving to Palmyra, R. W. Schlosser was appointed by the church to have charge of the Sunday School and preaching at this point for the year 1913, and J. S. Hackman was elected trustee in Longenecker's place. Revival services were conducted at this house in August, 1912, by Elder H. B. Yoder, of Lancaster, and several were received into the church by baptism. In 1913, this congregation conducted three evergreen Sunday Schools.

The supervision of these Sunday Schools is given into the hands of the Sunday School Advisory Committee. This committee is organized according to the following constitution:

CONSTITUTION OF LOCAL SUNDAY SCHOOL COMMITTEE.

I. *Object:*
    1. To inspire.
    2. To guard.
    3. To direct.

II. *Field:*
    1. The entire Local District.
    2. With all its resources.

III. *Formation:*
    1. Five members.
    2. Named by official Board, confirmed by open council.
    3. Except the beginning, one to be nominated every year for three years.

IV. *Qualifications:*
    1. Sound in the faith.
    2. Organizing ability.
    3 Same as delegates to Annual Meeting or to accept such.

V. *Duties:*

1. To discern all the Sunday School resources and needs of the district, and to endeavor to meet them.

2. To decide places and number of Sunday Schools, if more than one.

3. To organize any new Sunday Schools where needed, and wisely give any and all necessary assistance.

4. To advise all Sunday School officers and teachers with regard to any improvements that may be made, or thus mutually to consider.

5. To make full report of the Sunday School work, and when properly accepted, such report to be sent to State District Sunday School Secretary.

6. To hold Sunday School meetings quarterly in harmony with Annual Meeting Minutes, Ans. Article 7, p. 158 of A. M. Minutes, 1897.

7. To make the Sunday School a nursery to the Church, endeavoring to further the Sunday School cause, and to keep

the entire work in harmony with the teachings and simplicity of the Gospel.

8. To organize themselves with rules to be confirmed by official Council.

9. To gather and compile statistics.
    a. Giving No. of pupils in each and all schools in church.
    b. Number of members' children not in any of the Brethren's Schools.
    c. Number of members' children in other Sunday Schools.

The following Rules and By-Laws to further govern the work of this committee were adopted in 1908:

RULES AND BY-LAWS OF THE LOCAL SUNDAY SCHOOL COMMITTEE OF ELIZABETHTOWN CHURCH OF THE BRETHREN.

I. *Officers.*

The officers of this Committee shall consist of Chairman, Vice-Chairman, Secretary, and Treasurer.

II. *Duties of Officers.*

1. The Chairman shall preside at all business meetings of the Committee; he shall represent the Committee in general supervision of all the Sunday Schools in the Elizabethtown district, and also serve as a member of the Library Committee of each Sunday School.

2. In the absence of the Chairman, the Vice-Chairman shall perform the duties of that officer.

3. The Secretary shall keep a full record of the proceedings of all business and public meetings, present the same for approval, and when approved, record them in a minute book; he or she shall perform all other duties common to this office.

4. The Treasurer shall have charge of all moneys of the Committee, and shall pay all expenses incurred, when so ordered by the Committee.

III. *Business Meetings.*

1. This Committee shall hold its regular business meetings on the first Wednesday of each month, unless otherwise agreed upon by the Committee.

2 Special meetings may be called at the request of the Chairman.

IV. *Quorum.*

Three members of this Committee shall constitute a quorum, one of the three to be the Chairman or Vice-Chairman.

V. *Order of Business.*

The order of business shall be as follows, subject to such change as the Committee may decide:
1. Prayer.
2. Reading and approval of minutes.
3. Unfinished business.
4. Miscellaneous business.
    a. Report of officers.
    b. Report of out-post Sunday Schools.
    c. Election of officers in January.
    d. Arrangement of programs for the April and October public meetings.
    e. Organization of Sunday Schools.
    f. Reports to be presented at Spring and Fall Councils.
5. New business.

The Sunday School Advisory Committee originally consisted of three persons: a deacon, a lay brother and a lay sister. The first committee appointed, March 6, 1903, was J. H. Kline, H. K. Ober and Elizabeth Myer. In June, 1908, the committee was enlarged to five members without any restrictions. The following have served on this committee:

1. J. H. Kline, 1903–1904.
2. H. K. Ober, 1903–1905.
3. Elizabeth Myer, 1903–
4. A. G. Longenecker, 1904–12
5. Nathan Martin, 1905–10.
6. D. C. Reber, 1908–
7. I. W. Eshelman, 1908–
8. Martha Martin, 1910–11.
9. Elizabeth Kline, 1911–
10. J. G. Meyer, 1912–

This committee makes a statistical and general report of the condition of each Sunday School under its oversight annually and in a large measure deserves credit for bringing about the following marks of progress in Sunday School work:

1. Superintendent of Primary Department since 1907.
2. Teacher Training class since October, 1908.
3. Home Department since September, 1909.
4. System of Grading and Promotion since 1911.
5. Two local Sunday School meetings annually since 1907.
6. Monthly Teachers' Meetings, 1912.

The first class in teacher training, consisting of Martha Martin, Laura Hess and Ada Leicht, was graduated in 1910 with E. E. Eshelman as teacher. The second class consisted of seven ladies taught by Lydia Stauffer and was graduated with public exercises in the church in 1912. The third class taught by Martha Martin consists of eight persons and graduated in 1914. The superintendents of the Primary Department were Mrs. G. N. Falkenstein, Mrs. B. F. Wampler, and Elizabeth Kline. Elizabeth Myer was the first Superintendent of the Home Department and is the present incumbent. There are three organized adult Bible Classes in the Elizabethtown Sunday School.

General Meetings.

The District Meeting of Eastern Pennsylvania was held in Elizabethtown in 1902. The first Ministerial Meeting of the same district was held on November 21–23, 1893. Both these meetings were held while Elizabethtown was yet a part of the Chiques Church. Since the organization of the Elizabethtown Church, the Ministerial, Sunday School and Missionary Meetings of Eastern Pennsylvania were held at Elizabethtown on November 1, 2, 1905, and October 30, 31, 1907. The Local Sunday School and Missionary Meetings of the District were held here July 4, 1907, July 5, 1909, and July 4, 1912.

Missionary Activity.

A healthy missionary sentiment exists in this church fostered by missionary teaching in Sunday School, preaching and Reading Circle. The annual missionary offering ranged from sixty-three dollars to $127, half of which was given to home mission board and the other half to the worldwide work. The total missionary funds thus raised in the twelve years by solicitors amounted to $1,048. This does not include about $200 given toward the building of the Harrisburg Church, nor the Annual Conference offering. The congregation contributed between four and five thousand dollars to the Brethren Home at Neffsville, $450 to the erection of the Orphanage at the same place, and $32,300 to Elizabethtown College.

In 1906 the question was asked, "Will the Church support a foreign missionary if funds can be raised?" The church said, "Yes." In June, 1907, a plan for raising money to support a foreign missionary was adopted. At the close of each council meeting, a collection of envelopes previously distributed to the members is lifted. The matter of supporting a brother or sister in the foreign field by this church after having been repeatedly agitated, was decided December 11, 1913, by authorizing the official board to find a suitable person to be approved by the church at a future time.

Pastoral Visit.

The pastoral visit was made by Elder S. R. Zug from 1905 to March, 1911. Then Elder S. H. Hertzler was asked to make it. The work of the Elder in charge is especially arduous because of the college being located here. Elder Hertzler has been paying an annual pastoral visit to the teachers and students of the college with a view of bringing about coöperation and unity in church and school, and through these means a cordial relation has been established that has been very helpful in maintaining the observance of those practices of the church which most colleges of the Church of the Brethren have lost.

Miscellaneous Matters.

Since the election of J. H. Kline to the ministry, the office of treasurer of the church was ably filled by A. W. Martin.

The temperance committee of the church consists of D. C. Reber, Martha Martin and J. Z. Herr.

The missionary committee is composed of Martha Martin, Elizabeth Hoover, John Buffenmyer, Anna Wolgemuth.

In March, 1913, the following committee was appointed to provide better accommodations for the growing needs of the Sunday School in town: S. H. Hertzler, D. C. Reber, John M. Gibble, J. H. Eshelman, Jos. G. Heisey, Addison Buch and Tobias Hoffer. This committee's plan was adopted December 11 and Jos. G. Heisey, John M. Gibble and D. C. Reber were appointed to execute it.

Bishops of the Elizabethtown Church: (1) S. R. Zug, 1902–1912; (2) S. H. Hertzler, Assistant Elder, 1904–12; (3) S. H. Hertzler, 1912.

On June 4, 1914, C. C. Madeira, Levi Mohler, and D. C. Reber were ordained elders. Ordination commitee: S. R. Zug, J. H. Longenecker, and John Herr.

D. C. REBER.

CHAPTER VII.

BIOGRAPHICAL.

A. Peter Hummer.

Peter Hummer, the first minister living in what later became the White Oak Church, resided about three miles west of Manheim. He had a brother, Hannes Hummer, not a minister, who lived about two miles northeast of him, in a direct line, whose wife was Veronica Heffelfinger, a sister to the wife of Elder Johannes Zug.

We have no data as to when Peter was baptized, or elected, and about all we have of his life and family is given in connection with his work under head of the activities of White Oak Church.

B. Christian Longenecker.

The biography of Christian Longenecker, the next minister in White Oak Church, is given as fully as we can give it, in connection with his work, under White Oak Church, with this exception, that his father, Hans, was a brother in the church in 1739, who had five sons we know of, Hans, Jr., Peter, Christian, Henry and Ulrich, who were all members, except Peter we know not, but his wife was.

C and *D.* Johannes Zug and Andreas Eby.

The biographies of these Elders are given so fully under the head of the White Oak Church, that we deem it superfluous to add much more.

These are all the ministers the White Oak Church district ever had prior to 1800, and were elected in the order here named. Andreas Eby died in 1798, age unknown, and Elder Zug died in 1821, in his 90th year, and is buried in the family graveyard, on the home farm, where his father and mother were buried, about 60 years before, and where his son Joseph, in the fall of 1821, and his grandson Andrew, in 1824, were buried,—four generations. The inscriptions on the gravestones are almost entirely worn away by age and weather, so that some of their descendants erected a new wall around the graveyard, now belonging to them by deed, on record about 40 years ago, and erected a large granite stone, with the inscription of all on, in memory of loved ones gone before. An illustration of said new granite stone, which weighs about 2½ tons, is herewith given, all in the rough, but on the side of the inscription.

E. Henry Gibbel.

Henry Gibbel lived a little south of Manheim, and was elected to the ministry about 1810. When he was ordained we know not, but he served on Standing Committee in 1814. He died in 1825, and is buried on his farm.

He had no children, but they adopted his brother's daughter, who was married to Andrew Hoerner, who got the farm. After them, their son-in-law, Cornelius Kreider, had it, and after his death, their son John Kreider had it, and is living there now. Andrew Hoerner was a deacon in the church.

F. Daniel Fretz.

Sometime between 1812 and 1822 the White Oak Church had two elections for ministers, just in what years we know not, but the result was the election of the following, in the order named:

Daniel Fretz and Jacob Haller.

Elder Fretz had charge of the church in 1822. He was married to Jemima Sullivan, of Scotch descent. He lived about 2½ miles northwest of Manheim, adjoining land with Elder C. Longenecker, and he, in connection with Abraham Longenecker, a son, were the executors of Elder Longenecker, who died in 1808.

He was a shop carpenter, turner, and undertaker. He

wrote many wills, always in German, which, when probated, had always to be translated. He had three sons and three daughters, all dead now, and all died outside of the father's church. They belonged to other churches, but had faith in their father, as a Christian, and at his funeral selected Dan. 12: 3 as a text.

Elder Fretz was a devout Christian, a ready and fluent speaker, always in German. In council he was ready to give expression to his views, but always in a mild way, so that he had many friends, and few enemies.

When he became older his mind gradually failed him. He said some things, and after a few moments he would repeat the same, having forgotten that he had said it, and so in his preaching. His voice was naturally weak, and in his preaching his sympathies were sometimes aroused, which caused him to weep. Then his voice was hardly more than a whisper.

In the spring of 1864, the writer, with another Brother, paid the church visit to Elder Fretz. He was sitting up in his room. His youngest son lived with him, in a small one-story house, which, with the surroundings, and no doubt the attention he received, was not at all inviting. Yet he was, like John on the Isle of Patmos, "in the Spirit," and did not notice material things around him; for he repeatedly said: "There is nobody in the world that has it as good as I have. When I need anything, it is brought to me, and I need not worry about anything." He often repeated the poet's language: "Ich weisz ich musz von allem los, eh' ich in deinem Friedenshoosz, kann bleiben ohne wanken."

In going away from his place our conclusion was, that while his mind and body were strong, he worked himself, through the merits of his Redeemer, into Heaven, and now, when both fail him, he is there, waiting for his transition into the spirit world, there to enjoy the full fruition of his labor in life.

In his preaching he would often say: "We have three principal enemies to contend with, viz.: The Devil, the world, and self; and when we have once conquered self, then the other two cannot affect us much."

In the summer of 1864 he died in his 89th year, and is buried in the family graveyard, by the side of his wife, who preceded him about 20 years.

When he was about 65 years old, he and his son Daniel were out riding on horse-back, and they had occasion to go through a field, when the son got off and opened the bars. The father rode through. When the other horse was led through, he turned around and kicked, fracturing Elder Fretz's leg below the knee, which was not set properly, and healed crooked. This caused him to limp, and made walking a task for him all the rest of his life.

G. Jacob Haller.

Elder Jacob Haller lived about a half mile east of Manheim, on the same little farm where his father, Jacob Haller, lived. He was born, and elected to the ministry, and died, in each case, but shortly after Elder Fretz, and always lived and labored in the same church, except a few years when it was divided, and afterwards merged again. This is our reason for taking the two together in giving their biographies. Each of them labored in the ministry for about 50 years, nearly the whole time together. They lived only about three miles apart, and were never known to disagree.

Elder Haller was not a fluent and entertaining preacher, but his remarks were always to the point. He was sometimes hard to understand, and would frequently use parables and allegories, so that many hearers might have had occasion to say, like the people in the Savior's time, " explain unto us the parable."

When Elder Haller was old, he related, in conversation, his experience in the ministry. When he was elected it made him feel good that the church had so much confidence in him; but when he came to meeting, he was expected to preach, and when he had made the attempt in the morning, he would go home, and in looking over his effort, and seeing the many imperfections, he would be placed upon the rack of torment all that afternoon, because of which he knows that he stayed away from meeting more than a hundred times; but when he was older he got over that, and said he would try to redeem some of his lost time.

He had a sister, married to a man named Smith, whose son Joseph was married to Elizabeth, a daughter of Elder Haller (first cousins), who both lived in the Lost Creek Church, in Juniata County, Pa., about 80 miles from Elder Haller's home, to whom he made frequent visits, always on foot, having no horse. He made those visits when over 80 years old, so on one visit a brother of Lost Creek Church said to him: "You are reputed to be rich, and we cannot understand why you always walk so far." His answer was: "Yes; I am rich, but I own no horse. I am content, and godliness with contentment is great gain,—the greatest wealth a man can have in this life." On his trips he visited and rested along the way.

He was twice married. His first wife was Elizabeth Gibbel, a daughter of Jacob Gibbel, and she died young. He afterwards married Polly Kinsey, who also died long before his death. She was a daughter of Jacob Kinsey, and a granddaughter of Johannes Zug.

He had one son Joseph (who was weak-minded, but entirely harmless) and four daughters, viz.: Elizabeth, before mentioned; Mary, married to Jesse Heslet; Barbara and Katie, both single, who kept house for him until he died.

When he was old, he related his experience in his conversion. He and his wife were under conviction sometime, but labored against it in different ways, to no purpose. So one Saturday evening they went to a dance in Manheim and spent the night in a frolic. This only made matters worse, so they yielded, and in two weeks later they were baptized, having in the meantime changed their mode of dress to the order at that time prevailing in the church. This they did as a precaution against drifting back again into their former life.

Sometime in the late summer of 1865, he was bitten by a dog, in the hand, which developed into blood poisoning, which, after much suffering, caused his death in November, 1865, in his 88th year, and is buried in the Gibbel graveyard, less than a mile southeast of Manheim where his two wives are buried. Thus ended the lives of two (the other being Elder Fretz) of the most noted, as well as the most consecrated Christian Elders of the Church of the Brethren of their time. Peace to their ashes!

H. CHRISTIAN LONGENECKER, SECOND.

He was born in Warwick Township in Lancaster Co., in 1791. He was a grandson of Christian Longenecker, the first Bishop of White Oak Church, and the only child of his father, Solomon. He was married to a Miss Becker, with whom he had four sons and four daughters, viz.: Peter, Christian, Emanuel and Abraham; Elizabeth, married to John Minnich, who afterward became a deacon; Barbara, married to Christian Brubacher, who was later elected minister; Leah, married to Henry Zimmerman; and Rachel, married to Abraham Kreider,—all dead now. He was elected a minister about 1828.

In conversation once, in a company of Brethren, he said he never was angry. When the others expressed surprise, he said there was one occasion when he had a horse that balked, and refused to work, he felt a little different. If that was not anger, then he was never angry.

He was the only Brother in all the surrounding churches, that wore a full beard, at that time, and when he was urged to change, he said it cost too much. He explained the cost this way. His conscience required him to wear a full beard, for some time, but he did not want to appear odd from his Brethren; so one day a choking spell came on him, without any known cause. He thought he was dying. There he vowed that if God would spare him, he would obey his conscience. The spell passed, and now it was up to him to pay the vow. He was ordained about the year 1841, and in 1855 he died in his 64th year. He is buried by the side of his wife, who preceded him, and on the same block with his father and mother and grandfather, in the cemetery at Longenecker's Church, near Lititz.

I. David Gerlach.

David Gerlach united with the church young, and was elected to the ministry in 1837. Some years later, he married Sister Catharine McGinn, and moved to Mount Joy, where they lived all their subsequent life.

He was one of a family of five sons and one daughter that we know of, viz.: Henry, John, Jacob, David, Samuel, and Mattie; three of the sons, and the daughter, were members of the church. It is not known whether the parents belonged to any church.

Elder Gerlach was ordained in 1856, and immediately placed in charge of the White Oak Church, rather under Elders Fretz and Haller. The latter said: "Another may willingly have the line, if he is allowed to keep a hold of the brakes."

He was an eloquent preacher of the whole truth, yet he would handle his subjects in such a way as to give no offense, even though some would disagree with some of his views. He was known to say that he cannot eat, or sleep well if he knew that some truth-loving soul was grieved by anything he did, or said.

His kindheartedness sometimes would lead him to do evil, that good may come. As an instance, the church decided a case by a large majority, according to advice of Annual Meeting, but some Brethren were sorely displeased. At the next council he brought it up again for reconsideration. The result was the same as before, but still failed to satisfy all; so he brought it up the third time with the same result, when he stood up in council, declaring that under the circumstances he cannot carry out the decision, because of opposition, not because he was opposed, but because he could not muster up courage enough to quell the opposition, though he had the body of the church to back him up.

During the first ten years of District Meeting, from 1867, he served six times as Moderator, and five times on Standing Committee.

In 1879 Elder Gerlach died in his 68th year, and is buried at Kreider's Church near Manheim. The text used at his funeral was his own selection, I Cor. 15: 58.

J. John S. Newcomer.

Elder John S. Newcomer, of Mountville, Lancaster County, died May 20, 1902, aged 92 years and 20 days. The deceased was blind for over three years. In his younger days he served several years as a deacon in the Church of the Brethren and was then elected to the ministry which office he held for about fifty-seven years. However, during his later years he could not serve owing to his advanced age. Funeral services were conducted by Elder B. Z. Eby and the home ministers from 2 Tim. 4: 5–8.

H. E. Light.

K. Samuel R. Zug.

Ancestry.—Ulrich Zug and wife, whose maiden name was Bachman, came from Switzerland about the year 1727 and settled in Lancaster Co., Pa., where they raised a family of six sons and two daughters.

They were Mennonites, but in 1742 he was baptized to the Brethren Church. He died in 1758.

John or Hannes Zug, one of his sons, was born in 1731, and was baptized in 1749. He married Anna Heffelfinger about 1758, was elected to the ministry 1770, and was ordained as an Elder in 1780 by Martin Urner and Christopher Saur. He died in 1821 in his 90th year. They had four sons and four daughters. One son Joseph, about the year 1821, while overheated took a cold plunge bath, took sick, and died, aged about 51 years. He was married to Barbara Eby, and they had four sons and one daughter. One of his sons Benjamin Zug was born July 12, 1802. He married Elizabeth Ruhl in 1824. They were baptized about the year 1828. He was elected to the office of deacon in 1848, and died in 1886, aged 83 years. She died in 1892 at the age of 90. They had five sons and two daughters.

Birth and Early Life.—One son, Samuel Ruhl Zug, the subject of this sketch, was born February 29, 1832, and was reared on the farm. As was customary in those days, farmers' boys were not expected to go to school before the holidays, especially not when they were old enough to work.

When frost set in, causing other outside farm work to cease, then getting in the winter's supply of firewood was in order. This was made ready for the stove, by hand with ax and saw. Threshing at that time was not finished in a few days by steam and separator, but by the slow process of treading out the grain on the barn-floor by four and six horses guided by a little fellow that sat astride the leader. This continued for weeks, Saturday being the cleaning up day. Rye usually was thrashed with flails.

School Privileges.—From the above it is easily understood that his school privileges were meager indeed. In 1850 Samuel asked his father for the privilege to learn the trade of blacksmithing. The father said: " No, not this summer; we want to build a house, but if you stay at home, and help us until fall, you may either learn a trade, or go to school at Lititz, Pa." This came to the young man as a genuine surprise; especially so, since the Brethren at that time were opposed to high schools.

On the 1st of October, he went to Mr. Beck's school at the above named place, and the following March, he was taken sick with typhoid fever and never went to school afterward. After this, he taught school for four winters in succession.

His Marriage.—In 1852, he was united in marriage with Fannie W. Shelly, and in 1861 he and his wife were converted, and were received into the Church of the Brethren by baptism at a lovefeast on the farm of Samuel Graybill near Manheim, Pa.

Ministry and Eldership.—He was called to the ministry, October 11, 1865. In the year 1868, the Chiques Church was cut off from the old White Oak congregation, and organized with about 200 members and 3 ministers, viz.: Philip Ziegler, Jacob Rider, and S. R. Zug. The new organization received 89 accessions during the year. In 1871 Brother Zug was advanced to the second degree, and in 1885, on Thanksgiving Day, ordained to the Eldership, and was given the oversight of the church. The older ministers at this time had died. The membership now numbered about 400. In the fall of 1867 through the effort of Brother Zug, the first series of meetings were held in the Chiques house, this being the first among the Brethren in the county, and continued every year since.

Sunday School.—In 1878, he asked permission to organize a Sunday School, which privilege was granted, but not to be held in the church. In the spring of 1879 he renewed his request when the use of the meeting-house was granted, and the first Sunday School among the Brethren in the county was organized.

New Organizations.—As time went on, the membership of the Chiques congregation grew until they numbered over 700. The subject of dividing the same was agitated for years. Several efforts having failed, Elder Zug by request of the church finally submitted a plan at a special council held March 28, 1902, recommending that the church be divided into four congregations, which plan was adopted. This gave to each church a good lovefeast house, and to the weakest church numerically 125 members. The four churches were formally organized and named as follows: Chiques, West Green Tree, Fairview, and Elizabethtown, all except Fairview retaining Elder Zug as their Elder in charge.

When S. R. Zug was elected to the ministry, there were but two organized churches in Lancaster County, three ordained Elders (one of those dying three weeks later), and ten ministers in first and second degree, with a membership of about 1,000. At this time (1913) there are 14 organized churches, 20 Elders, and 38 ministers in first and second degree and over 3,000 members.

At the time when Bro. Zug was called to office, there were no series of meetings, no Sunday Schools, no English preaching, except at funerals and by special request. The members generally were opposed to more than a common school education, but a marked change has come. The above named things, which as a rule were regarded as innovations, are not only tolerated now, but are regarded as indispensable to the cause. Elder Zug held the oversight of the Chiques Church until 1910, when he resigned, and was relieved, and the charge given to Elder Henry S. Zug.

In 1912 he resigned the charge of Elizabethtown congregation. In 1905 he was also relieved of the care of the West Green Tree Church.

Other Organizations.—On July 23, 1891, the West Conestoga Church, of which Lancaster City was a part, concluded that the city should constitute an organization of its own. October 29, 1891, the church was organized with a membership of 31, without a resident official. On this date, Elder S. R. Zug was chosen as their Elder in charge. For a time he had to depend on ministerial help from other churches. By solicitation of the Elder, T. F. Imler, of Waynesboro, moved to Lancaster and by the united effort of these two good men many people were added to the Lord and a fine, large, substantial church building erected, which was soon paid for.

On July 12, 1899, T. F. Imler was ordained, and the church placed in his care, thus relieving Elder Zug. The church at this time numbered about 140.

July 20, 1895, the York City Church was organized with a membership of about 160, Elder Zug being chosen as their Elder. This charge he held until 1899, when Jos. A. Long was ordained to the Eldership, and was chosen as Elder in charge. So in two days, Elder Zug was relieved of the charge of two city churches. The York congregation at this time had about 230 members, and a project was set on foot before Elder Zug left, to erect a large new house of worship, which was since built.

On the evening of November 19, 1895, the church at Harrisburg was organized, with 15 members and no resident official. Elder S. R. Zug was chosen to take the oversight. Here as at Lancaster the Elder had to depend on ministerial help from other churches, holding their services in rented halls. In 1899, a lot was bought with a one story dwelling for $3,000. This was converted into a place of worship and was used until 1904, when a large new brick building was erected, and was dedicated in May, 1905. Several ministers moved in temporarily but did not stay more than about a year each. On January 7, 1901, Brother A. L. B. Martin was elected to the ministry. Elder Zug resigned in 1911, when Elder G. N. Falkenstein became his successor by choice of the church. The membership at this time was 92.

Elders Wm. Hertzler, S. R. Zug and others had been engaged in evangelistic work at Ridgely, Md., for several years, and in the fall of 1883, Brother Zug attended the first love-feast ever held on the eastern shore of Maryland, said service being held in an old saw mill.

On August 2, 1884, the above-named Elders assisted in organizing the Ridgely Church, with a membership of 22. The oversight was placed in the hands of Elder Zug, which charge he held for a number of years. About the year 1901, he was also chosen as Elder of the congregation in Philadelphia under the supervision of the Committee from Annual Meeting.

Mission Board and Missions.—From its incipiency, Elder S. R. Zug was a leading spirit in missionary effort in eastern Pennsylvania. In 1879, he was elected a member on the Home Mission Board, and was re-elected from time to time, continuously, with the exception of one year until 1894. During this time he rendered much valuable help by his wise counsel and active service in the field. At this time he resigned from the Home Mission Board, giving as his reason his appointment on the General Missionary and Tract Committee, he being chosen as a member of said committee in 1893, and two years later, was reappointed for a term of three years. During this time the India Mission was established.

District and Annual Meeting.—The first District Meeting was held in 1866, where Elder Zug was present, and he has attended every District Meeting ever since without a break, covering a period of 47 years. This is remarkable indeed. He was also elected either as Writing Clerk, Reading Clerk, or Moderator of the meeting for upwards of twenty years in succession. Four times he was sent as a member of standing committee, and represented the local church at Conference for many years. He attended 11 Annual Meetings prior to 1883, and every one since.

Ministerial Meetings.—He was the prime mover for the

first Ministerial Meeting in eastern Pennsylvania, which was held in Elizabethtown in 1893. These meetings have been held annually ever since with the exception of the year 1894,—all of which he attended.

Home for the Homeless.—Through his efforts and those of Elder B. Z. Eby of Manheim, Pa., who enlisted others in its favor, after obtaining permission of District Meeting of 1895, the Home for the Homeless was established with considerable opposition. He was a Trustee of the institution from the beginning until 1912, being relieved at this time on account of age. A farm of 75 acres was bought near Manheim, for $4,500. Additional buildings were put up at an expense of about $7,000. In 1909, the location of the Home was changed, and a large substantial brick building erected near Neffsville, Pa., in which Elder Zug took a prominent part.

Financial Reverses.—Financially, Elder Zug had his misfortunes. From 1889 to 1894, he lost about $10,000 in different ways, principally the result of misplaced confidence in a friend who failed, which almost made him bankrupt; which, in addition to his church work, was enough to unnerve, and even unbalance, an ordinary man; but by the help of God, and his wife, and children, he survived it all; and has as he believes sufficient to keep him the short time yet allotted to him on earth.

Brother Zug was blessed with a good wife and helpmeet in his ministerial duties. She traveled with him over 53 years in wedded life; over 40 in the ministry. He recognizes that she is entitled to much credit for any good or success that has come to the church and the world through his instrumentality and labors.

In times of sorrow, trouble, or trial, she would always encourage him not to pout, or show any signs of displeasure, but to deport himself in a way that is characteristic of Christ, our elder Brother. On July 10, 1905, she passed over into the spirit world. Together they had four sons. Since her departure, he has had his home with the youngest son, John C. Zug, who was born April 26, 1866, elected to the ministry in the Chiques congregation, November 25,

1905, and advanced to the second degree at Elizabethtown, February 8, 1911. At the earnest solicitation of Elder J. H. Longenecker, he moved to Palmyra in the fall of 1912, where he was ordained to the Eldership on September 6, 1913. Here the aged father now lives, is well cared for, and is contented and happy, still rendering acceptable service in the ministry.

Method of Work.—Of Elder Zug it may appropriately be said, " he was a good man and full of the Holy Ghost, and of faith, and much people was added unto the Lord." He is a born leader, a wise counselor, and a man of strong convictions, but always open for better light. His spirit of aggressiveness (as is always the case) has often brought him enemies.

His method of church work, however, was not to rule with a rod of iron, " neither as being lords over God's heritage." Possibly he had the spirit of forbearance and leniency almost to a fault. The writer often heard him remark that he would rather err on the side of mercy, than on the side of enforcing rigid discipline, and in meting out justice. When his views would not prevail in a council, he made special effort to exercise a forbearing spirit toward those who may have differed with him, only asking similar treatment when the majority came to vote his way.

His long self-sacrificing life has been crowned with great blessings, and with marked success. May many stars be added to his crown!

One of these days it will be said of Elder Zug, he has passed away, and many of us will say what Jonathan said to David: " Thou shalt be missed, because thy seat will be empty."

J. H. LONGENECKER.

PART VIII.

SWATARA GROUP.

CHAPTER I.

BIG SWATARA CHURCH.

At the time of the separation of the Swatara Church from the main body of the Church of the Brethren north and northwest of, and including Lancaster County, in 1772, it included as elders and ministers: Han Jacob Boeshor and George Klein, in the eastern settlement of members, at Little Swatara and North Kill Creeks, respectively; and George Miller and Adam Hamacher, in the western settlement at Conewago and Big Swatara Creeks.

George Miller was baptized in 1753. He lived and raised his family near Conewago Creek, and his was the only family of members known to have lived on the Lancaster County side of Conewago, belonging to Swatara Church.

The families of Jacob Metzger and Christopher Brauser lived on the northwest side of Conewago, below Middletown. These are the only members known to have lived near Conewago at that time, prior to Elder Miller's death, which occurred in 1798, aged 76 years, 9 months, and is buried on his farm by the side of his wife, who died two years previous, aged 69 years, 6 months, about two miles northwest of Elizabethtown. A more extended account of his work, and family, will be given in connection with that of Elder George Klein under the head of Little Swatara Church, because Henry Miller, a son, married into the Klein family, thus bringing the two families, and their work, into a closer relationship.

Nothing is known of Adam Hamacher, or his work in the church, since 1770, when Morgan Edwards mentions

HANOVERDALE MEETING HOUSE.

Wendle Henry
Welker & Monshine
Frederick Baker
George Stauffer
Wendle Henry
John Berst

John Gerber
Henry & Hoffer
Michael Blauch

Samuel Fox
Henry Balsbach
Wendle Henry
Ziegler

John Shoop
Wendle Henry
Benjamin Kline
Hoffer
Peter Balsbach

BIG SWATARA MEETING LIST.

him, and his wife and daughter, as a minister, and members of the church. We have a record which states that about 1798 or 1800, the Swatara Church was divided into two parts: the one, called Big Swatara; and the other Little Swatara, from the fact that the one is traversed by the main stream of Swatara Creek, and the other by a branch of the same, called Little Swatara. The Heffelfingers, Hamachers, Balsbaughs, Henrys, Etters, and others lived in the Swatara Valley, on both sides of the Creek; hence the settlement received the name Swatara Church.

No records being kept in many of the churches, in ancient times, much of what is now known of their work is from hearsay, and from results that followed.

What became of Adam Hamacher, or when he died, is not known; but it is known that Valentine Balsbaugh, a son of Bro. George Balsbaugh, and grandfather of the late C. H. Balsbaugh, the noted writer, was married to Elizabeth, a daughter of Elder George Miller, and was forty-three years old at his father-in-law's death, and has long been the Bishop of the church; the presumption is that he was elected to the ministry in Miller's lifetime, as assistant, and after his (Miller's) death had charge of the church.

In 1811 George Basehore moved from Little Swatara to a farm near Hornerstown, in Big Swatara, where he lived, and in 1841, died and is buried on the farm on which he lived. He was married to a Fackler from that locality, which may have had something to do in his moving there. He was a minister before coming there, and was a son of Jacob and Christina Basehore. He was born in Schuylkill Co., Pa., in 1775, and was in his 67th year when he died. He had a brother, Benjamin, who was born in 1768 and moved to the valley of Virginia. Where he lived, in Virginia, we failed to find, but we found a German poem the heading of which states it was composed by him, while in jail, in Virginia, and, by request of his children, printed, as follows:

Ein Schönes Geistliches Lied,

welches von einem Mann namens Benjamin Boeshor, im Staat Virginien, aufgesetzt wurde, während er im gefängnisz schmachtete, und welches nunmehr auf verlangen seiner Kinder gedruckt worden ist.

1 Bewahre mich O Gottes Sohn,—
In dieser bösen Zeit,
Und shau herab von deinem Thron,
Auf die Unbarmherzigkeit,
Und verlasz uns nicht.

2 Erhalt uns doch zu deiner Treu,
Und mach in uns doch alles Neu,
Und mach uns von der Sünden frei,
Dasz wir zu deinem Lob und Dank
Dienlich sei, wie es der Herr begehrt.

3 Nimm von uns Herr du treuer Gott,
Die schwere Straf, und grosze Noth,
Die wir mit Sünden ohne Zahl,
Verdienet haben alzumahl,
Dasz wir dir dienen Treu.

4 Ja nimmer gehe falsch im Handel,
Noch im reden, noch im thun,
Willt du für den Herren wandeln,
Dermaleins auch seelig ruhen,
Vater hilf mir doch.

5 'Ach wollst du Gott bewahren,
Rein vor diesem argen geschlechte,
Und lasz uns dir befohlen,
Dasz sichs uns nicht fehle
Der Gottes Hauf im Volk erhaben.

6 Mein vertrauen stets zu dir,
Mach mich an meiner Seelen reich,
Reichthum Zeitlich Gut das währet
Nur ein kleine Zeit
Und hilft doch nichts zur Seligkeit.

7 Es liesz auch nicht der treue Gott,
Die drei Männer im Feuer ohne Noth,
Sein Engel sandt' er hin,
Bewahrt vor des Feuer's Gluth,
Und half ihnen aus aller Noth.

8 Nun weil ich doch verurtheilt bin,
  Durch Bosheit und verdrisz,
  So schafft doch Gott gewisz dahin,
  Wie es endlich bleiben musz,
  Und kanns kein Mensch verhindern.

9 Wie ich verspert in starker Mauer,
  Und eiserne Thür und Fenstern dran,
  So kann ich doch dem Herren vertraun,
  Dasz ers gewisz doch ändern kann, Halleluja!

10 Es wird gewisz doch ärger sein,
   Die ewige Grub und Finsternisz,
   Wo Finsternisz und ewige Pein,
   Der verlorne leiden musz unendlich da.

11 Solche art der Schalkheit Brüder,
   Welches Gott verboten hat,
   Schändet alle meine Glieder
   Und beraubt mir was ich hab—
   Herr vergib es doch.

12 Himmel Schreiend sieht es aus,
   Wann man hilft in gröster Noth,
   Und der falsche Bruder geht voraus,
   Scheriff und Layer nimmt doch Rath,
   Schweisz und Blut ist Preis.

13 O was Greul finden wir,
   Hier in diesen guten Zeit,
   Ach was Geitz und Wucher hier,
   Mit grosser Unbarmherzigkeit,
   Und denket nicht an sein End.

14 Recht getreu ist hoch zu preisen,
   Heuchelei ist Gott ein Greuel,
   Will man Gottes Kindlein heissen,
   So verscherze doch nicht dein Heil,
   Zur ewigen Freude zu gehen ein.

It was learned from Samuel Basehore, a grand nephew of said Benjamin Basehore, that his imprisonment was for debts which he was unable to pay, and that after his release he returned to Lebanon County, Pa., and lived, and afterwards died, near the Union Canal water works; but it is not known when he died, or where he was buried. In 1815 he was a member of Standing Committee It is not known whether George Boeshor was ever ordained, but the presumption is he was not.

Elder Balsbaugh was a son of George Balsbaugh and wife, who came to America from Germany, in company with George Henry and wife, and others, in 1754, and took a farm, jointly, on Spring Creek, where Spring Creek meeting-house now is on their farm. There is where Valentine Balsbaugh was born, in 1755, on St. Valentine's day, February 14.

Sometime after, on account of some disagreement, the Balsbaugh family moved to the west side of Swatara Creek, on a farm, about a mile east of Hanoverdale, where George Balsbaugh lived the rest of his days, and where he died in 1802, and is buried at Spring Creek, in his 66th year of age.

On this farm his son Valentine lived, and died November 26, 1851, in his 97th year of age, and where his remains lie buried in the family graveyard, on the farm.

He had a daughter Elizabeth who was married to Lorenz Etter, who was born April 2, 1787. He was a minister, but when elected we have no record, neither of his ordination, but it is known that he was ordained, and given charge of the church, when Elder Balsbaugh became too old and feeble to attend to the needs of the church, probably between 1836 and 1840. He died November 9, 1853, and is buried in the Balsbaugh graveyard.

Jacob Hollinger was born in Lancaster County in 1797, and died in 1877, in his 80th year. His wife Catharine died same year, in 84th year, both buried at Spring Creek.

They moved to Dauphin County about 1826, where shortly after he was elected to the ministry. He was married to Catharine Shumaker and raised two sons and six daughters. The sons, Joseph and Daniel, were both ministers, and ordained elders. Joseph died some years ago, in Illinois, and Daniel now lives in Conewago Con-

BIG SWATARA CHURCH.

gregation, recently organized, having been a part of Spring Creek district, and he being over 80 years old.

Sometime between 1835 and 1840, George Hoffer was elected to the ministry, but some years after, he began to preach a doctrine different from the way the Brethren did, and after several years' trial to get him to desist, he was silenced, and about 1857 he left the church, and united with the Zion Children, commonly known as Brinserites, and preached for them the rest of his life. The doctrine in dispute was Acts 2: 38, Hoffer maintaining that baptism is not essential to remission of sins.

In 1851, William Hertzler moved from Tulpehocken Church, Lebanon Co., where he was elected to the ministry in 1847, to his father-in-law, John Hoffer's farm in the Big Swatara Church district, in Dauphin Co., about 3 miles northwest of Elizabethtown, where he lived until 1894, when he moved to Elizabethtown, where he died of cancer, in 1896, and is buried in the Spring Creek Cemetery, Dauphin Co., in his 69th year of age.

David Etter was elected to the ministry in 1867.

In the fall of 1868 the Big Swatara Church was divided into two districts, by making Swatara Creek the line between them. The meeting for that purpose was held in the old Spring Creek meeting-house. At the same meeting, John Etter and William Hertzler were ordained to the Eldership by Elders John Zug, and David Gerlach, Bro. Etter to have charge of the district northwest of Swatara Creek, under the old name of Big Swatara; and Bro. Hertzler as assistant to Elder Hollinger, but he practically had charge of the church.

Benjamin Kline, a minister, had moved from Little Swatara into this district in the vicinity of Hilemandale, and was ordained an Elder after Jacob Hollinger, but at the time of the division of the district, he was fallen asleep.

The Big Swatara Church, under this new organization, had about 200 members, and ministers: Elder John Etter, who was elected in 1853; Jacob Kiefer elected in 1858; and David Etter in 1867; and deacons: Peter Balsbaugh and

David Smith. In the following year, this church had a very successful revival, and over 60 accessions by baptism.

In 1869, David Smith was elected to the ministry, and Isaac M. Gibble, John Kiefer, Samuel Reed, and Benjamin Basehore, deacons.

In 1871, Samuel Reed was elected a minister, and Adam Shope and Abram Balsbach, deacons.

In 1877, John H. Witmer and Christian Hernly were elected deacons.

In 1882, John H. Witmer and Adam J. Shope were elected ministers, and Abraham Fackler and Andrew Miller, deacons.

In 1889, Samuel Balsbaugh and John Aungst were elected deacons.

In 1904, Emanuel Kline and Isaac Baker were chosen deacons, and in 1908 Clayton Miller and Josiah Gingrich were elected deacons.

In 1899, John A. Landis, and in 1901, Thomas Patrick and David Etter, Jr., in 1904, Amos M. Kuhns, and in 1912, Clayton B. Miller, were elected ministers, and in 1910 George Aungst and David Baker were chosen deacons.

In 1884, Elder John Etter died in his 65th year.

In 1887, David Etter was ordained an elder, and in 1899, he died in his 80th year.

He died while he was baptizing his granddaughter. When he had immersed her the second time, he fell over, and when he was brought out on the shore, he was dead. This caused a wonderful stir, and ended the baptismal service for that day. It caused the question to be raised whether that girl should be baptized as if no effort had been made, or whether the ceremony should be finished from where it was broken off. It was made a question to Elders at District Meeting, and discussed from both angles, and was decided according to the latter view.

In same year Samuel Reed and John H. Witmer were ordained elders, so was David Smith. Elder Smith died in 1900, in his 83d year, and Elder Reed died in 1901, in his 68th year. The four elders, John and David Etter, David Smith and Samuel Reed are buried in the Hanoverdale Cemetery; also Jacob Kiefer who died in 1884, in his 80th year.

In 1905, Adam J. Shope was ordained an elder.

The officials now are: Elder J. H. Witmer, who has charge of the church, and Elder A. J. Shope, and John A. Landis, Thos. Patrick, David Etter, A. M. Kuhns and Clayton B. Miller, ministers; and Abm. Fackler, S. Balsbaugh, Jno. Aungst, Emanuel Kline, Josiah Gingrich, Geo. Aungst and D. Baker, deacons, with a membership of 310.

On November 19, 1896, a council meeting was held in the Hornerstown meeting-house at which, by request, Elders S. R. Zug and J. H. Longenecker were present, where a petition, signed by eighteen members of Harrisburg and its suburbs, was presented, asking to be organized into a church, which was granted, making the city limits the line between this new organization, and the mother church, from which it was taken. More of this organization will appear under the head of the Harrisburg Church.

In 1905, some of the rural territory of Big Swatara Church was ceded to Harrisburg, including Steelton, Highspire, and Middletown.

Sunday School.—The first Sunday School in the Big Swatara Church was held in the Conewago meeting-house, about 1865. It was a union school, and its first superintendant was Elder Wm. Hertzler, but the first Sunday School held in Dauphin, Lebanon, Lancaster, or Berks County, by authority of the Church of the Brethren, was organized in 1876, in the Hanoverdale House, and proved a success, in spite of opposition. They now have four Sunday Schools: at Hanoverdale, East Hanover, Hornerstown and Paxton.

In March, 1905, a Sisters' Aid Society was organized in this congregation.

Meeting Houses.—The first church house built by Big Swatara Church was built on land then of Wendel Henry, in 1848, of limestone, 38 × 42 feet, and was known as the Spring Creek House, after a stream passing nearby.

The next church house was built in Conewago Township,

not far from a creek of that name, a brick house, in 1854, known as Conewago House.

The third meeting-house built by this church was in Hanover Township, known as Hanoverdale House, built in 1860. This was larger than the others, intended for lovefeast occasions. For up to this time lovefeasts were held in barns, and always in summer.

The fourth was built in Paxton Township, known as Paxton House, in 1865. These four meeting-houses were built before the division in 1868, and by that division, the two first came on the side, called Spring Creek, of which more later, and the two last named, in the Big Swatara Church. We now continue with this church after the division. In 1869 a church house was built in East Hanover Township, and is known by that name, located about 5 miles east of Hanoverdale.

In 1878 another house was built at Hornerstown, and in 1881, one was built, across the mountain, in Fishing Creek Valley.

By a hurricane at night in September, 1896, the Hanoverdale House was partly demolished, so that the church decided to take it down entire, and rebuild, which they did, and after the division, the East Hanover House was built in 1869, the Hornerstown House in 1878, and the Fishing Creek Valley House in 1881. The Hanoverdale House is the only one arranged in which to hold lovefeasts.

Bishops of Big Swatara Church.

1. Valentine Balsbaugh, 1798–about 1840.
2. Lorenz Etter, about 1840 to about 1853.
3. Jacob Hollinger, about 1853–1868.

Bishops of Later Big Swatara.

4. John Etter, 1868–1884.
5. ———————.
6. David Etter, 1887–1899.
7. John H. Witmer, 1899–

MOYER MEETING HOUSE.

CHAPTER II.

THE LITTLE SWATARA CHURCH.

"In 1745, George Besher, Michael Frantz, Peter Heckman, John Frantz and others settled in this district. They were baptized by Elder George Kline of the Northkill congregation. Elder Kline was the first elder (in charge, ordained in 1750), assisted by Peter Heckman, who was ordained soon after 1770. On August 12, 1780, the above-named Michael Frantz was ordained elder by Elders Sower and Urner, and George Beasher (Bäszhaar) and Jacob Moyer were ordained deacons (ministers). As early as 1770, there were forty-five active communicants. Their names follow: Peter Heckman, minister, and wife, John Heckman and wife, Michael Frantz and wife, Nicholas Gerst and wife, Jacob Moyer and wife, George Beasher, David Marge and wife, Simon Merrich and wife, John Frantz and wife, Christian Frantz and wife, Rose Schnables, Jacob Smith and wife, Eliza Kentzel, Adam Henrich, Mrs. Cryder, Philip Ziegler and wife, Jacob Breneisen and wife, David Kleine and wife, Widow Benedict, Elizabeth Benedict, Sophy Kish, Leonard Sebalt and wife, John Grove, Jacob Baker and wife, Jacob Deal and wife, Hans Stohner and wife, Jacob Beashör and wife."[1]

It is unfortunate that there is no record of this historic church that we know of from 1780 to 1858,—a space of 78 years, excepting statement in account of Big Swatara Church. Nevertheless, by strenuous research, we were enabled to find data to fill up this gap, at least so far as elders are concerned. We do not claim accuracy in every detail, but in the main, facts are obtained from reliable sources.

Elder Hans Jacob Beashör (Bäszhaar) was the son of Hans George Beashör, who immigrated to America prior to

[1] Brumbaugh's History, p. 320.

1738, and settled a few miles northwest of Millersburg, Dauphin Co., Pa.

He was married to Christine Alderfer, and had a family of nine children.

Elder Hans Jacob Beashör is without doubt the Jacob Beashor who signed the Annual Meeting minutes of 1790 and 1814.

Elder Hans George Beashör, son of Elder Hans Jacob Beashör, was born February 8, 1775, and was married to Christine Fackler, of Big Swatara, and no doubt it was this marriage that caused his removal later to Big Swatara.

Elder Joseph Merkey was born November 28, 1782. It will thus be seen he was about 30 years of age when Elder Hans George Baeshör moved to Big Swatara about 1812. It is stated by Dr. Basehore, of Palmyra, that Hans George Baeshör was Elder in charge of Little Swatara at the time he moved away. Joseph Merkey being 30 years of age may at this time already have assumed considerable of the burdens of the ministry. He was a small man and rather weak physically. His talk was good, and to the point, but there was not much of it. He died March 12, 1869; buried at Merkey's Cemetery.

David Merkey was born May 11, 1795. He was the youngest brother of Joseph, and Elder before John Hertzler, but John moderated the council meetings before David died, and before his ordination, being better adapted to the work. David Merkey died December 2, 1873; buried at Merkey's Cemetery.

Elder Jacob Wenger, son of Christian Wenger, was born March 10, 1801. He was elected to the ministry in the Brethren Church about 1835. He was ordained by 1850, his Eldership coming in between that of Joseph and David Merkey. He was a big, strong man, and had a powerful voice. He was a man of high standing, of pleasant approach, and was regarded as a strong preacher. It is thought by his daughter that he was preaching as early as 1835. He was associated with Joseph Merkey, who was about 20 years older. The question arises whether Joe

THE LITTLE SWATARA CHURCH. 447

Merkey was Elder before Wenger? But Wenger was the controlling and leading spirit in the church.

"Watch and pray" was not duly observed on his part. The tempter was on his track, and lo, behold, he made a misstep, which he at first confessed, and afterwards denied, and of course, he was disowned by the church. Because of his denial, it was impossible for him to return to the Brethren. This occurred between the years 1854 and 1856. Afterwards he first held meetings of his own, but during this time baptized but one person—a woman, who said she was deceived, thinking Wenger a minister of the Brethren.

She wished to come to the Brethren later, and would have been admitted, without re-baptism, had it not been for the presence of ———— who, though a young minister, insisted on the order of the Brotherhood being read to the congregation.

She then joined the Brinsers, and afterwards came back to the Brethren by re-baptism. Wenger also joined the Brinser Church, and quite a large number of Brethren went with him, but practically all came back.

Truly this was a trying time for the Little Swatara Church. At times the clouds rose so black and thick that there was apparent danger of the church being disrupted, but the tide turned, the storm was subdued, there was a great calm, and Israel again prevailed.

He died January 6, 1881. He was married to Lydia Frantz, who was born February 27, 1801, and died October 14, 1853. It was the year after her death he made the misstep.

He and his wife, his father and grandfather, with their wives, are all at rest in the Wengert graveyard, near Jonestown. His son, Jacob F., was a preacher of the Brethren. He was elected late in life, and never attained to fluency of speech. He was born 1831, and is buried at Jonestown. His son David had also belonged to the Brethren, but while yet young joined the Brinsers, among whom he became a preacher in his old age.

Benjamin Kline was born July 12, 1791, and was elected to the ministry in the Little Swatara Church. Inasmuch as

Benjamin Kline was 10 years older than Jacob Wenger, he may have been preaching as early as 1825. He moved away from the Little Swatara congregation, during the time of supremacy of Jacob Wenger, to the Big Swatara district, where he was later ordained to the Eldership. This was not far from 1865. Kline was a good talker. He died September 11, 1868, and is buried at Kauffman's meetinghouse, 2 miles north of Annville.[2]

The following elections for officers were held in this church: 1858, John Hertzler was elected to the ministry; 1860, Abraham Pfautz was elected to the ministry; date of advancement unknown; ordination a few years before his death. April 24, 1875, John Hertzler was ordained; Jacob W. Myer, Senior, was elected minister, and Henry Lentz and Elias P. Ziegler, deacons. Elders present: Samuel Harley, John Etter, and Christian Bucher. June 7, 1876, Jacob W. Myer, Senior, was advanced to second degree, and Daniel R. Kline and Jacob F. Wenger were elected ministers. At the same time, Benjamin Balsbaugh was elected deacon. April 7, 1883, at Frystown House, Samuel Myer was elected minister, Samuel Z. Gettel, deacon, and Daniel R. Kline advanced to second degree of ministry. January 1, 1890, Samuel Myer was advanced to the second degree of the ministry and William Oberholtzer elected deacon. Present: S. R. Zug, and David Etter. October 13, 1894, Edward M. Wenger was elected minister, and Jacob Pfautz, deacon. August 8, 1898, Edward Wenger was advanced and J. W. Myer and John Ziegler, who moved to Montgomery County in 1910, were elected deacons. December 11, 1899, Jacob Pfautz was elected minister. December 10, 1900, J. W. Myer, Junior, was elected minister, and Elias W. Edris and Alfred M. Lentz, deacons. May 1, 1901, Jacob W. Myer, Sr., was ordained to the full ministry, and Jacob Pfautz advanced to the second degree. June 10, 1902, Elias W. Edris was elected minister. December 8, 1902, Ira D. Gibble was elected deacon. August 8, 1904, E. M. Wenger was ordained to the Eldership, and J. W.

[2] For much of the foregoing information, the writer is indebted to the extensive genealogical writings of Michael Zug, late of Lebanon, Pa.

THE LITTLE SWATARA CHURCH. 449

Myer, Jr., advanced to the second degree. August 14, 1905, Ira D Gibble was elected minister and Samuel Sherman, deacon. April 14, 1911, Henry Z. Ziegler was elected to the ministry, Ira D. Gibble advanced to the second degree, and Jacob Merkey and Samuel Ziegler elected deacons. August 13, 1906, Jacob Pfautz was ordained, Elias Edris advanced to the second degree, and Henry Ziegler elected deacon. January 2, 1892, John H. Lentz was elected deacon.

Officials that Served in the Church that Are Not on Record.—Elders: Joseph Merkey, David Merkey, and Jacob Wenger; Jonathan Hunsicker, Benjamin Kline, and Samuel Gettle, ministers; and deacons: Samuel O. Myer, George Gibble, John Crouse, Peter Gettle, and John Merkey.

Present Officials of this Church.—Elder E. M. Wenger, who has charge of the church; Elder Jacob Pfautz, Jacob W. Myer, Elias W. Edris, Ira D. Gibble, all in the second degree, and Henry Ziegler in the first degree; and deacons: John H. Lentz, Alfred M. Lentz, Samuel N. Sherman, Jacob Merkey, and Samuel Ziegler.

Obituaries of Ministers.—John Hertzler, born September 10, 1826; died August 27, 1901. Buried at Frystown. Abraham Pfautz, born June 17, 1826; died February 2, 1906. Buried at Frystown. Jacob W. Myer, born January 29, 1832; died May 1, 1906. Buried at Myer Homestead. Samuel Myer, born May 21, 1857; died April 19, 1894. Buried at Myer Homestead. Jacob F. Wenger, born October 7, 1831; died December 15, 1881.

Houses of Worship.—This church at present has six houses of worship the oldest of which is the Merkey House, near the Blue Mountains. This house was built in the year 1848, stone building, having a seating capacity of about 500. Valuation $1,500.

The Ziegler House, near Rehrersburg, was a brick building having a capacity of seating about 300. This, however, was rebuilt in the year 1875, placing in its stead a new frame building 50 × 70 feet, seating about 900. Valuation $4,000.

Frystown House, a frame building erected in the year

1875, having a capacity of about 700. Valuation $2,500. Thus we notice that in one year two houses of worship were built. Hereby we can see what may be done where there are willing minds to promote the cause of Christ and His Church. The Moyer House is a brick building erected in the year 1860, having a capacity of about 500. This was rebuilt in 1884, brick, 50 ✕ 72 ft., capacity about 900. Valuation $4,000. Light's Meeting House was built in 1877, a frame building, capacity about 700. Valuation $2,500. Fredericksburg House is the last built in the year 1910, a brick building, capacity about 600. Valuation $2,500. In the Moyer and Ziegler Houses, lovefeasts are held alternatively. Other houses, not belonging to the Brethren where regular worship is held, we may name— Union House, Kutztown, and Shuberts.

Union Meeting House.

This is one of the old landmarks of Bethel Township, and deserves more than a passing notice. This meeting-house land was given by Rudy Hunsicker, who died in 1768. More land was given by his son, Jacob Hunsicker, for the only use, purpose, and benefit of the different congregations in that part of the country.

"*This Indenture* Made the Fifth day of August in the year of our Lord one thousand, eight Hundred and twenty-six, etc."

On the land donated by Rudy Hunsicker, a school house and dwelling house, combined, was erected. On funeral occasions this building was used for preaching services. In 1812, this building was repaired. After serving its usefulness, a new meeting-house was built in the year 1859.

At this time there was considerable friction. The Church of the Brethren desiring to have a church of their own, built suitable for lovefeast purposes, is what brought about the commotion. Preparations were made to build a church, on the opposite corner where the Union Church stands, which again was reconsidered, and decided to build a house, about a mile further east, and thus we have the Moyer House built in 1860.

THE LITTLE SWATARA CHURCH. 451

The Brethren have regular services at both houses, although close together, and the attendance is good at both places.

The meeting-house built in 1859 again had served its usefulness, and a new house was built in its stead in the year 1913, 40 by 60 feet, 14 feet high, with a basement 40 by 40 feet for Sunday School, and 20 by 40 feet for preparing meals on funeral occasions if wanted. Building Committee, E. W. Edris, W. H. Hunsicker, and Sol. Meyer. The house was dedicated August 30 and 31, 1913. The following ministers representing the different denominations officiated, viz.: Saturday afternoon, Alfred Gingrich and Henry Kreider; Saturday evening, Ammon Brubaker and Geo. Lentz; Sunday forenoon, Jacob Longenecker, Jacob Pfautz and E. W. Edris; Sunday afternoon, A. J. Bachman and Oliver Bitner; Sunday evening, Rufus Bucher, Henry Light, John H. Bicksler and Emanuel Garis. Preaching in main room and basement. All the services were well attended. E. W. Edris, Moderator.

UNION HOUSE CEMETERY.

The first land given for a burial ground was first owned by Christian Brightbill and Christian Lantz. Christian Brightbill purchased his land from Thos. and Richard Penn, then Bethel Township, Lancaster County, dated the 6th day of February, 1738, and Christian Lantz purchased his land from the Commonwealth of Pennsylvania, then Bethel Township, Dauphin County, dated the 19th day of September, 1752. It is believed that the first land was given by the said Christ Lantz, and the executors of the said Christian Brightbill, somewhere between the years 1750 and 1769. But no deed was given that time. It was given free. The next land was also given free without a deed by Abraham Lantz, son of the said Christian Lantz, and Christian Brightbill, son of the said Christian Brightbill, somewhere between the years 1769 and 1798, and the land was given again free by Abraham Lantz, and John Brightbill between the years of 1833 and 1840. Then it again being necessary to have land, when John Brightbill, son of John

Brightbill, and Michael Wolf, son-in-law of Abraham Lantz, gave or sold land and gave each a deed to Joseph Hunsicker, Abraham Lantz, and John Light, appointed trustees for the said graveyard, or burial ground, dated 25th day of March, 1853. They each gave a deed for all the land given by their forefathers, so there is a full right for the property, as the deeds will show. It was again necessary to have land; accordingly, land was purchased in the year 1886, from Adam Brightbill, son of John Brightbill, by A. G Gettel, H. M. Lentz, and Wm. H. Hunsicker, trustees. A deed was given dated April 23, 1886. This last bought land was laid out in blocks, and sold from five to ten dollars each. At this time also a committee was appointed to frame rules to govern the association. As to the name it was decided that this association shall be known and styled by the name of "The Union Cemetery Association" of Bethel Township, Lebanon County, Pennsylvania.

The present officers of the Association are: President, E. W Edris; Secretary, W. H. Hunsicker; Treasurer, Monroe Wolf.

This city of the dead is nicely located, and many, many, have been laid to rest there, awaiting the general resurrection in the last day.

The following clipping from a certain periodical dated January 5, 1900, sets forth the Union Meeting House in its true light:

"A LIBERAL CHURCH
*Bethel Township Landmark's
Wide Open Doors
Union Meeting House*

Successor of a Haven of Religion and Education—Large Enough to Take in Those of All and No sects—The Graveyard.

"At a cross-roads in Bethel township, half way between Mt. Zion and Fredericksburg stands what is known as the 'Union Meeting House.'

"On its site stood fifty years ago one of the first schoolhouses of the country, which served both as dwelling house, and school house, as was generally the case in ye olden time.

"When the free schools were forced on Bethel and on most of the other Townships of the County, a brick building was erected on an opposite corner of the cross-roads, and the old structure, having served its time and uses, was torn down.

"In its stead was built the above-mentioned 'Union House.' The name was a good and expressive one, for it was erected by a veritable union among the good folk of the vicinity, a union of purpose—the purpose of having a convenient, common, liberal place of worship for all Christian creeds and beliefs, and the doors have always stood wide open to all who accept the Bible and the doctrine of the New Testament as the foundation of their religious belief. Close by is a graveyard, where repose the remains of some of the early settlers of the countysite, among whom are numerous members of the old and respected Grove family, now almost extinct; the Hunsickers, the Wolfs, the Moyers, the Brightbills, the Lights, the Lentzs, and many others.

"The Burial Ground.

"Burial lots are for sale to all on reasonable terms, to Jew and Gentile, Baptists and Lutheran, High Church and Low Church, and within its consecrated precincts may lie down together, the infidel with the orthodox believer, the one with the privileges of the other.

"Among the sects that make use of building as a place of worship, are the 'German Baptists,' the 'River Brethren,' and the 'United Brethren in Christ,' though a number of other denominations have conducted services in it.

"The German Baptists have preaching every four weeks, and their services are conducted by Revs. Jacob W. Moyer, Abraham Pfautz and Edward Wenger.

"The River Brethren, another branch of the Baptists, hold meetings only four times a year—every twelve weeks. The latter held a protracted series of meetings, lasting a week, in the latter part of December, conducted by Revs. Jacob Martin, and Jacob Brubaker, both of Lancaster County, Pa.

"The U. B. people also have at different times, more or less regularly, held church services, but were on several occasions grievously annoyed by the beastly rowdy element among the big boys, which exist to a more or less disgraceful extent in even the quietest and most Christian community.

"Color and a Name.

"The church building bore for many years the name of the 'Brown meeting house,' owing to the color of its paint, but last summer it underwent some necessary repairs when it was painted white, and it will of necessity lose that cognomen. It is also known as Wolf's meeting house.

"A Union Sunday School is held during the warmer seasons of the year; most of the officers being German Baptists, because they are the most numerous in the neighborhood. The books used are in the English language, but the singing is unaccompanied by instrumental music. The German Baptists are opposed to organs.

"The affairs of this Union Church are managed by a Board of Control elected annually. The regular election was held on New Years day, with the following result: President Elias W. Edris; Treasurer, Edward Wolf; Secretary, Wm. H. Hunsicker; Trustee, Adam H. Hunsicker; Janitor, Ezra Hummel.

"It is a fact significant of the wide-open-door policy of this organization, that at least two of the above named officials are not connected with any Church as members.

"E. G."

Sunday Schools.—The church is alive along the different lines of church activities. At present it has four organized Sunday Schools. The first Sunday School was organized at Frystown in the year 1887. In 1898, it was divided into four different schools at different places, viz., Frystown, Merkey's, Ziegler's, and Union House. All these schools are fairly well attended. Frystown Sunday School is an evergreen.

The present superintendents are, viz., Frystown: Henry M. Frantz; assistants, Geo. Miller, and William Ziegler. Ziegler's: Jacob Merkey; assistants, Samuel Ziegler, and Elias Frantz. Merkey's: Samuel Sherman; assistants, Calvin Boeshore, and Frank Ebling. Union House: Adam L. Light; assistants, Elias Myer, and Levi Wenger.

District and Annual Meetings.—The District Meeting of the Eastern District of Pennsylvania was held twice in this church, the first time in the Frystown House in the year 1881, and the second time in the Moyer House in the year 1901.

THE LITTLE SWATARA CHURCH.

In the year 1871 the Annual Meeting was held in this church on the farm of John Merkey, 9 miles from Myerstown, the nearest railroad station. The delegates and all those that came by railroad were taken to the place of meeting by private conveyance. Quite a contrast to present facilities at our Annual Meetings. Forty years have made a wonderful change in our Brotherhood. Who would now think of locating Annual Meeting 9 miles from a railroad station?

Prayer Meetings, Etc.—The church has its weekly prayer meetings the year round, and during the summer at three different places, making actually three weekly prayer meetings. During this last winter (1912) a revival meeting was held at Frystown; during these meetings 39 expressed their desire to embrace their Savior, and to be joined to the body of believers. The church is in a fairly healthy and prosperous condition, yet not without their trials and adversities which meet the faithful ones on the way. The present membership reaches about 350. May the future become brighter and brighter for this old historic church! Little Swatara Church held a local Sunday School meeting afternoon and evening, November 2, 1912, and a similar meeting in 1913.

Elders in Charge of this Church.

1. George Klein, 1757–1783.
2. Han Jacob Beshor, —— ——.
3. Hans George Beshor,   –1812.
4. Joseph Merkey,   –1869.
5. Jacob Wenger, —— ——.
6. David Merkey, about 1869–1873.
7. John Hertzler, 1875–1901.
8. J. W. Meyer, Sr., 1901–1906.
9. E. M. Wenger, 1906–

Obituaries of Officials of Little Swatara Church. Not on Record.—Ministers: Benjamin Kline, born July 12, 1791; died September 11, 1868. Buried at Kauffman's meetinghouse, north of Annville. Joseph Merkey, born November

28, 1782; died March 12, 1869. Buried at Merkey's Cemetery. David Merkey, born May 11, 1795; died December 2, 1873. Buried at Merkey's Cemetery. Philip Ziegler, born January 25, 1764; died ———. Buried at Ziegler farm. Jacob Wenger, born March 10, 1801; died January 6, 1881. Buried near Jonestown. Jonas Hunsicker, born January 27, 1813; died December 12, 1869. Buried at Union House. Samuel Gettle, born April 20, 1828, elected 1867; died August 17, 1874. Buried at Ziegler House. Daniel Kline, born August 20, 1837; died November 1, 1899. Buried at Ziegler House. Deacons: John Merkey, born January 10, 1803; died January 22, 1885. Buried at Ziegler House. Peter Gettle, born October 21, 1817; died February 12, 1892. Buried at Union House. William Ziegler, born January 1, 1825; died January 29, 1875. Buried at Ziegler House. Elias P. Ziegler, born May 18, 1835; died October 9, 1882. Buried at Ziegler House. Henry L. Lentz, born December 22, 1830; died July 7, 1904. Buried at Union House. John Crouse, born November 3, 1820; died April 18, 1901. Buried at Frystown. Benjamin Balsbaugh, born November 14, 1821; died November 1, 1905. Buried at Merkey Cemetery.

CHAPTER III.

TULPEHOCKEN CHURCH.

The history and record of the Tulpehocken circuit of the "Church of the Brethren," Lebanon County, Pennsylvania, follows:

Abraham Zug's moved from Warwick Township, Lancaster County, as members of the Conestoga circuit, to Jackson Township, Lebanon Co., near to where now Richland Station is, in the month of April, 1813,—there being already three families, as members there, which made them four families—nine members. In October or November, 1815, Abraham Zug was elected to the ministry by the Conestoga circuit, this territory was yet a part of the Conestoga circuit. Jacob Pfautz was elected to the ministry the same time, he living near the Middle Creek meetinghouse, Lancaster Co. In the year 1823, the said Abraham Zug and Jacob Pfautz were ordained to the full ministry, or as Elders, or Bishops of and for the Conestoga circuit. The said Abraham Zug died July 18, 1841, aged 69 years, 4 months and 22 days, in the above-mentioned home. At the death of Elder Abraham Zug, there were about fifty members in the Lebanon Valley, holding their membership in the three following circuits: Conestoga, White Oak, and Little Swatara.

Adjoining Elders advised an organization, to be known as the *Tulpehocken* circuit, which advice the members holding their membership in the Conestoga and Little Swatara circuits accepted, and an organization was effected on the 5th day of October, 1841, electing John Zug, son of aforesaid Abraham Zug, to the ministry; and Daniel Royer and Jacob Oberholtzer as deacons. About 35 votes were cast. The following Elders were present to officiate: Jacob Pfautz, Daniel Bollinger, William Price, John Price, and David Shallenberger.

In September, 1842, Moses Pfautz was elected to the ministry. Elders Jacob Pfautz and John Price officiated.

In the fall of 1844, those members which held their membership in the White Oak circuit, also agreed to hold their membership in the Tulpehocken circuit. (In the spring of 1844 the White Oak circuit held their lovefeast at Jacob Bucher's, near Cornwall.) May 27, 1846, John Gibble and Jonathan Hertzler were elected deacons. May 29, 1847, Daniel Royer and William Hertzler were elected to the ministry, and John Zug advanced to second degree. Elders Jacob Pfautz and Daniel Bollinger, present. September 18, 1853, Isaac Brubaker was elected to the ministry. Elders Daniel Bollinger and Christian Longenecker, present. June 5, 1860, at lovefeast at Elder John Zug's, Christian Bucher and Samuel Kurtz were elected deacons. June 10, 1861, at lovefeast on farm of Samuel Kurtz, tenant to Samuel Loose, Jr. (Graybill's old farm), Christian Bucher was elected to the ministry. Elders Jacob Hollinger and Daniel Keller, present. John Zug was ordained to the full ministry in the year 1861. Elders Jacob Hollinger and Joseph Merkey, present. September 21, 1865, at the home of George Bollinger, near Reistville, George Bucher was elected to the ministry, and John Kline to the deaconship, and Christian Bucher advanced to second degree. Elders Jacob Hollinger, and David Gerlach, present. May 18, 1871, at Heidelberg House, George Bucher was advanced to second degree, John Herr was elected to the ministry and Abraham Myer, deacon. One hundred and sixty-eight votes were cast. Elders Jacob Hollinger, and John Etter, and ministers, John Hertzler, Abraham Pfautz, Joseph Hollinger, and S. R. Zug, present. April 3, 1875, at Heidelberg House, Christian Bucher was ordained, John Herr advanced to second degree, and Abraham Myer elected to the ministry, and Jacob Nissley to the deacon's office. Only 119 votes cast, roads very bad. Elders William Hertzler, and John Etter, present. May 27, 1879, at lovefeast at Heidelberg House, Martin Heisey was elected to the deacon's office. Elders Jacob Rider, and John Hertzler, present. April 30, 1881, council meeting in Heidelberg House.

HEIDELBERG MEETING HOUSE.

Jacob Nissley was elected to the ministry, and Benjamin Smith and Cyrus Bucher, deacons. Elders Samuel Harley, and John Hertzler, present. April 29, 1882, at Heidelberg House, Reuben Royer was elected deacon. Elders Samuel Harley, and John Hertzler, present. April 25, 1885, George Gibble received as deacon by letter from Little Swatara Church. Accepted April 27, 1885. October 20, 1885, at lovefeast, Heidelberg House, Martin Heisey was elected to the ministry. Elders William Hertzler, Samuel Harley, and John Hertzler, present. January 30, 1886, council at Heidelberg House, Nathan Gibble, Ephraim Brubaker and Levi Bollinger were elected deacons. Only two were intended, but the last two were tie. Elder Samuel Harley, present. In April, 1891, Deacon George Hess from Maiden Creek, and Deacon William Oberholtzer from Little Swatara Church, moved into our circuit, and were received as deacons by letter July 25, 1891. December 21, 1896, William H. Oberholtzer was elected to the ministry, and Martin Heisey advanced to second degree. Elders H. E. Light, J. H. Longenecker, and Israel Wenger, present. In Heidelberg House. December 20, 1897, in Heidelberg House, John Herr was ordained, Joseph Wilhelm and Edwin Kurtz elected deacons; one was intended, but these two were tie. Elders John Hertzler, J. H. Longenecker, and Israel Wenger, present. August 20, 1900, at Heidelberg House, Jacob Nissley was ordained; William H. Oberholtzer was advanced to second degree; Joseph L. Wilhelm was elected to the ministry; and Mohler Bucher, a deacon. Elders J. H. Longenecker, John Hertzler, and Israel Wenger, present. Two hundred and fifty votes cast. March 16, 1903, at Heidelberg House, John L. Royer was elected to the ministry. All the adjoining Elders were present. August 21, 1905, at Heidelberg House, Benjamin Zug was elected to the ministry; Harry Hacker and John Gibble, deacons; John L. Royer, advanced to second degree. Elders present: C. Bucher, Jacob Myer, and E. M. Wenger. July 15, 1906, S. Z. Gettle was received as deacon, by letter from Little Swatara Church. March 28, 1911, at Heidelberg House, Michael Kurtz was elected to the ministry,

Jacob Wenger to the deacon's office, and Benjamin Zug advanced to the second degree. From the time of organization, 1841, up to January 1, 1912, there were 17 Brethren elected to the ministry and 21 to the deacon's office.

Official Force, January 1, 1913.—Ministers: Elder John Herr, Elder Jacob Nissley, Elder W. H. Oberholtzer, J. L. Royer, second, B. F. Zug, second, Michael Kurtz, first. Deacons: S. Z. Gettel, Harry Hacker, John Gibble, Jacob Wenger.

Obituaries of Officials.—Elder John Zug died July 19, 1873, at 8 o'clock, at the advanced age of 76 years, 2 months and 5 days. Interment and funeral services at the Heidelberg House, July 23, in presence of the largest funeral gathering ever witnessed in this part of the county. The last night he lived on earth, he desired that those by his side should sing the hymn:

> Meine Seele lobe Gott.
> Meine Seele lobe Gott.
> Der ein mächtig heilig wesen,
> Gans volkommen auserlesen,
> Der dir hilft aus aller Noth,
> Meine Seele lobe Gott.

Moses Pfautz died December 29, 1845, aged 33 years, 6 months and 11 days. Buried at Tulpehocken House. Jacob Oberholtzer died November 14, 1865, aged 60 years, 9 months and 10 days. Preaching in mansion, buried in Gibble's graveyard, now Heidelberg House. Daniel Royer died August 11, 1862, deposed from the ministry about one year, aged 55 years, 2 months and 6 days. Buried at Millbach House. William Hertzler moved to Big Swatara circuit, now Spring Creek, Dauphin Co., in 1851. John Gibble died June 25, 1881, aged 78 years, 3 months and 14 days. Funeral Tuesday, June 28, at the Heidelberg House. Jonathan Hertzler died December 25, 1887, aged 86 years, 6 months less 2 days. Funeral Friday, December 30, at Tulpehocken House. Isaac Brubaker died April 8, 1866, aged 50 years, 3 months and 24 days. Services in mansion, buried in family graveyard. Samuel Kurtz died October

25, 1897, aged 70 years and 8 months. Buried at Heidelberg House. George Bucher, left with family for Conestoga Church, March 18, 1896. John Kline disowned September 25, 1880. Abraham Myer expelled from the church January 29, 1891. Cyrus Bucher moved to Astoria, Illinois, in spring of 1882. Reuben Royer moved to Newton, Kansas, in spring of 1886. George Gibble again moved to Little Swatara in spring of 1893, died August 7, 1894, aged 88 years, 3 months and 23 days. Buried at Heidelberg House. Benjamin Smith died June 18, 1898, aged 50 years, 5 months and 9 days. Buried at Cornwall House. George Hess died January 22, 1902, aged 78 years, 10 months and 21 days Edwin Kurtz resigned March 19, 1906. Ephraim Brubacher died May 16, 1913.

There is no record of names of members, at the time of organization of the church. However, among the earlier members, we would mention the Zugs, Bollingers, Widders, Gibbles, Royers, Buchers, Geibs, Brubachers, Klines, Weavers, Oberholtzers, Hertzlers, etc.

In our church record we find 23 Bollingers, 23 Klines, 24 Buchers, 25 Gibbles, 25 Weavers, 27 Brubachers, 32 Geibs, 56 Royers.

Division of Tulpehocken Church District.—March 18, 1901, Elder Christian Bucher asked to be relieved of the charge of the church on account of age and failing health; the church granted it, and gave Elder John Herr the charge of the church. The church numbered 483 members. December 16, 1901, the church agreed to divide into two districts, making Crowstown road the line. East of said road retains the name of Tulpehocken, with a membership of about 300, having John Herr as their Elder, Jacob Nissley and W. H. Oberholtzer as ministers; Ephraim Brubaker, Levi Bollinger and Ed. H. Kurtz as deacons. In the spring council of 1903, it was unanimously agreed by both districts that the line be changed from Crowstown to Prescott road, with the exception of Elder C. Bucher, and deacon N. P. Gibble and their household, who shall hold their membership in the Midway district. June 7, 1842, it was agreed that the line between the counties of Lancaster and Lebanon, shall be the line between Conestoga and White Oak circuits in Lancaster Co., and Tulpehocken circuit, Lebanon Co., in the presence of Elders David Pfautz, Christian Long, Joseph Rothrock, Daniel Bollinger, and John Price. April 30, 1887, the Tulpehocken Church agreed with the Little Swatara Church, that the line between the two circuits shall be one mile north of the Reading and Harrisburg turnpike, and run parallel with it. On the east, the Tulpehocken Church extends to the city limits of Reading.

Houses of Worship.—Five houses of worship, viz.: Tulpehocken, Millbach, Heidelberg, Myerstown, and Richland.

Tulpehocken House (Royer's) was built in the year 1840. Building Committee: Daniel Zug, Johan Weber, Jacob Royer. Seating capacity 600. Valuation $3,000. Stone[1] building, 30 × 40 ft. This being the oldest house, we herewith present copy of conditional part of deed, Jacob Royer and wife to German Baptist Church.

This Indenture made the 7th day of December, 1840, Between Jacob Royer of Jackson Township, Leb. Co., Pa., and Catharine his wife, of the one part, and Jacob Bollinger, of Township, County and State aforesaid, Trustee of the German Baptist, who call themselves Old Brothers Society Meeting house, and the lands and burying grounds belonging thereto, and Abraham Zug, Jr., and Jacob F. Diener of the same place, Trustees of the School Department to be established in the above named Meeting house, and the School room, wherein the School is to be held, of the other part; Whereas John Lantz and Anna his wife by their Indenture &c. did grant &c. unto said Jacob Royer &c. &c. And whereas the members of the said Old Brothers Alias German Baptist Society of the Conestoga family, them belonging thereto, do view the necessity of a meeting house for public worship, or divine service for themselves their own use and behoof of the said German Baptist, Alias Old Brothers, which is to say and them who belong to the Conestoga Family, have agreed amongst themselves & for their heirs and successors to build and erect a meeting house for the

[1] About 25 years later, an annex 24 by 30 feet of brick was made.

TULPEHOCKEN MEETING HOUSE.
BASEMENT DOOR ENTERS INTO OLD SCHOOL ROOM.

RICHLAND BRETHREN CHURCH.

purpose aforesaid, and whereas others of the neighborhood which do not belong to the same Society; However stand in need of a Burying ground and a School house. Now compromise with the members of the said Old Brothers Alias German Baptist Society belonging to the Conestoga family, therefore the said Jacob Royer and others the members of the said Congregation belonging to the Conestoga family, with others, their neighbors also view the necessity of a good Education as essential to the rising generation and to the form of our Republican institutions as forming the only true political and moral basis of the same. Now have agreed to build, and did erect and build the said meeting house, on the following described piece or parcel of land, for the purpose of Public worship in the second Story, and for a School to be taught in the first Story of said house as aforesaid, Agreeably to their written and verbal contract made as follows, in writing, says that the said Jacob Royer Sr. Give the following described lot of Ground for a Burying Ground, to erect a house thereon for a School and meeting house to the Old Baptist Brotherly Society belonging to the Conestoga family, On the following Conditions agreed upon: Every person, or persons who die a natural and honest death be it a member of said Society, or any body else, is and shall be admitted and allowed to be buried on the said burying grounds, no matter to what Society they belong, without hindrance or molestation, and the funeral sermon to be held in the meeting house by such persons, as he, or they who have the funeral shall choose to have for to Preach the funeral Sermon, and that the meeting and School building be erected, the meeting room for Divine Service to be in the upper part, or second Story in said house, and the School room to be in under, in the lower part, below the meeting room, say in the lower Story of said house, And that every person, or persons, who was helping to erect or supported, or taking part, or hath taken part or share, or do take part or share at the said School house and School by supporting the same, shall have a right to the rules and regulations of the School and School room, which the same shall require as a member to vote for trustees, as far as respecting the School apartment, in lower Story, &c. &c.

There are a few living yet, who remember that they went to school in the basement of Tulpehocken Church before the public schools were fully inaugurated. There were only two desks, one on either side; but they extended through the whole length of the building, and the teacher's desk at the end. Among the teachers were—Hoffman, Levi Carver, William Killinger, Jacob Kline, and William Hertzler. The school term was four months in the year during the winter. It was a subscription school, 3 cents a day, only when present, and children came from near and far, and many are the fond recollections of the fathers and mothers yet living, of the school in the basement of the church.

Even when public schools were fully established in the township, several terms were yet held in this church under the supervision of the school board, after which a separate building was procured close by, and today there is a newly-built school house only about fifty feet from the church. Truly church and school go together.

Millbach House was built in the year 1850, with Daniel Zug and Daniel Royer as Trustees. Seating capacity, 350. Valuation $2,000; brick building.

Originally Seth Royer and Isaac Gibble, of the neighborhood of Kleinfeltersville, thought that a church should be built in their neighborhood, and offered to give very substantially towards its erection. Their action led to the erection of the brick house, 36 × 46 ft. The original cost of erection was $1001.72, of which there was paid

> By members, excepting Isaac Gibble....$ 321.82
> By Friends 200.93
> By Isaac Gibble 105.00
> By Seth Royer 373.97
> $1001.72

The Building Committee consisted of Seth Royer and Isaac Gibble. In former years there was considerable confusion and contention about this meeting-house, when on the 17th day of April, A. D. 1861, an Act of Assembly was passed authorizing Daniel Zug and Daniel Royer, the trustees, to sell the aforesaid meeting-house. This was done by public vendue on the 6th of July, A. D. 1861. The property was purchased by Seth Royer and Isaac Gibble, for the use of a meeting-house and graveyard for the sum of twenty-five dollars. May 9, 1875, Seth Royer died; and on July 8, of same year, Allen W. Mentzer was elected trustee in his place. In 1876, the house was blown down. The cause given was that the carpenter work was not sufficient. Besides gratuitous labor, the cost of repairs was $449.31. Money was raised by subscription—117 subscribers. April 2, 1878, A. W. Mentzer moved to Ephrata, and John Erb was elected in his place. Isaac Gibble, undoubtedly a trustee since 1861, died in 1881; and April 7, 1882, Reuben Bollinger was elected to the office. After his death Ephraim Erb filled the place. February 23, 1889, one fourth acre of ground was bought of George Bucher for $50, for burial purposes. In 1910, land was given by Ephraim Erb, on which sheds were erected. At present we have abundant shedding at all of our meeting-houses, to shelter the horses, during our worship. "A righteous man regardeth the life of his beast."

Richland House was deeded to Adam Schaeffer in trust for the use of the German Baptist Brethren, German Reformed and Lutheran congregations September 9, 1870. In 1896, the Lutheran members disposed of their undivided third to the other two. In 1901, the Brethren received sole control and ownership of the house. Seating capacity, 300. Valuation, $2,000. Brick building.

RICHLAND HALL CONVERTED INTO A HOUSE OF PUBLIC WORSHIP.

Rules and Regulations.

RICHLAND, June 3, 1870.

Your committee to whom was referred the duty of drafting suitable rules and regulations for the control and government of the joint ownership and use of the Hall after its purchase and conversion into a house of public worship and for Sunday School purposes—beg leave to present the following as the result of their deliberations:

1st. The property shall be conveyed to the use of the German Baptist, German Reformed, and Lutheran denominations of Richland, and shall be owned and controlled by the members of said three denominations exclusively—each denomination to pay its proportionate share of the purchase money for the building.

2nd. Whenever circumstances should render it necessary to promote the cause of religion and preserve the peace and good ends of these several denominations that either the one or the other should prefer to withdraw its claims to worship in said building, in such case the party withdrawing shall effect an amicable settlement with the parties remaining in possession of said building for such consideration in money to be paid the party withdrawing as their interest in said building and Justice may demand, provided that such money paid to the denomination withdrawing must be again invested for a house of public worship within the limits of Richland.

3rd. The limits or boundary within which these regulations shall exist and operate shall be known as follows, viz.: Commencing at dwelling of Jacob K. Landis thence to George Stief —thence to Adam Loose—thence to tenant house of John Smaltz—thence to John Kreitz—thence to Peter Forry—and thence to Jacob Landis the place of beginning—including all those named but none beyond, and none shall be chosen a Trustee whose residence is not within these prescribed limits unless no member capable of serving of either one of said denominations should be found within, in which case the nearest resident of said denomination may be chosen.

4th. The time for occupancy of the house shall be amicably divided by weeks into three equal parts, and each denomination shall have its allotted and regular week for worship, but should any one denomination not fully occupy its time, it may be allotted to another on application to the proper trustee. The Sabbath School shall be conducted on the Union System which heretofore existed in this place. Ministers in good standing of other religious denominations shall be permitted for special and funeral occasions to preach in said building when not engaged by regular or previous appointment—Funeral occasions are to take special precedence.

5th. As soon as convenient after the adoption of these regulations—and at a meeting of which due notice shall be given, each of said denominations shall elect one of its own members a Trustee and elect their successors annually on the second Tuesday in May of each year. The qualification of voters for said Trustee shall be prescribed by each denomination as it seems fitting. In case of death, removal, or resignation of any member serving as a Trustee, the vacancy shall immediately be filled by the denomination in which it occurs.

6th. The said Trustees shall immediately after their election, organize by designating one of their number for President, one for Secretary and one for Treasurer.

7th. The President shall call all meetings and preside at same. Sign all orders for money drawn and attested by the Secretary.

8th. The Secretary shall keep correct account of all business of the board.

9th. All money collected and received shall be promptly paid over into the hands of the Treasurer, who shall charge himself therewith—and keep strict accounts of all moneys received and paid out.

10th. The duty of Trustees shall be to complete the purchase of the building, and without delay attend to making all necessary alterations, and repairs in manner following—Have the stage now in the room taken down, and lay an even floor through—excepting an ordinary sized platform raised eighteen inches above the floor with common pulpit fixtures and arrangements, and good close backed seats for the whole room somewhat similar to those few now in the Hall. Have substantial steps put up at front door, and pavement laid in front of building, and make such improvements as a majority of the board of Trustees shall deem necessary. Provide fuel and light, allow regular and special appointments, and have general supervision over the building.

11th. All expenses incurred by the Trustees for alterations, repairs, fuel and light, shall be defrayed with money collected at dedication of building, and by general contribution.

12th. No one of these three denominations shall act arbitrarily, or independent of the others respecting any matter involving the rights of all. Nor shall any voting or election be had, except as already provided, for Trustees, who in the discharge of their duties shall respect the wishes of a majority of contributors.

RICHLAND, June 3, 1870.

Pursuant to public notice previously given, the members of the several denominations, met at the depot office,—and on

motion Abraham Zug was called to preside—After a free discussion and interchange of opinions—the foregoing regulations were unanimously adopted.   C. E. HOFFMAN,
DANIEL HOSTETTER,
WILLIAM BECKER.

September 9, 1870, a deed was tendered by Edwin W. Landis and Malinda his wife, Levi D. Landis and Amelia his wife, to Adam Schaeffer in trust for the use of the German Baptist, Reformed, and Lutheran congregations. March 28, 1896, the Lutheran members of the church at Richland disposed of their one undivided third part of, or interest of, said church conveyed by deed to Jacob Dillman and Isaac F. Landis in trust for the German Baptist and Reformed denominations. On October 12, 1901, the German Reformed members of the church at Richland disposed of their one undivided one-half part of or interest of said church conveyed by deed to deacons of the German Baptist Brethren in trust for Tulpehocken Church. Thus ends the *Union* Church. The house now belongs wholly to the Brethren. However, for want of more room, the probabilities are that in the near future the Brethren will follow suit, and dispose of the whole, and invest the money in a new church building, at a new place where there is more space.[3]

Myerstown House was built in the year 1876. Seating capacity, 500. Valuation $3,000. Brick building.

Heidelberg House was built 1867. Original size, 50 × 70 ft. In 1900 an annex of 12 feet in length. Present seating capacity, 900. Valuation $4,500; stone building. The first meeting was held November 23 and 24, 1867, Saturday afternoon and evening and Sunday forenoon. The first hymn that was sung was " Lobe den Herrn den Mächtigen König der ehren." The first Scripture was read by Bro. Jacob Reinhold, reading Hebrew 3: 1–9, taking the 4th verse for his text. In the evening Bro. William Hertzler took for his text Heb. 4: 12–13, followed by Brethren Hollowbush and Kiefer.

[3] In 1913 the old church was sold and a new church was built on Race St., 50 by 80 feet, brick, which was dedicated February 1, 1914.

First Lovefeast Held in Heidelberg House.

Extract from Elder John Zug's record:

"1869, October den 15, und 16$^{ten.}$ Wurde zum ersten mal Liebes und Abendmahl gehalten in dem Heidelberg Versamlung Haus, von der Tulpehocken Gemeinde von Lebanon und Berks Co. Es war schön angenehm Wetter während der ganzen Zeit, und Freitag Abends bei dem Abendmahl herschte eine angenehme Stille bei der Volksmenge im Haus und zusehende und der Herr war mit uns.

Die predig Brüder die gegenwärtig waren von den angrenzenten Gemeinden und Districten der Brüderschaft, waren Elder und Bruder David Merky, Elder und Bruder David Eshleman von Maiden-Creek, Elder und Bruder William Hertzler von Conewago, Dauphin Co Bruder Samuel Graybill von Weiseichen land, Lancaster County, Bruder Samuel R. Zug, von Mastersonville, Bruder Jonas Price, von Hatfield, Montgomery County, Bruder Daniel und Jacob Hollinger von Ober Cumberland, Bruder George Smith von Schuylkill Co. und Bruder Joshua Koenig von Berks Co. Maidencreek District. Diese oben erwehnten Brüder predigten aus dem Wort des Herrn zu den Menschen während der Zeit das die Versamlungen im gang waren, welche anfingen Freitag Morgens den 15$^{ten.}$ October um 9 Uhr, und Samstags Mittag um 12 Uhr zu ende ging als den 16$^{ten.}$

Des Herrn Abendmahl und Brod brechen wurde geleitet durch den Eltesten und aufseher Bruder von der Tulpehocken Gemeinde. Die lehr Brüder John Hertzler und Abraham Pfautz, von der Kleine Swatara Gemeinde, waren auch gegenwärtig, aber sie entschuldigten sich weil sie so wie einheimisch und nahe bei uns sein, und üeberliesen es den vorerwehnten Brüder.

Im ganzen genommen, waren die Versamlungen gesegnet mit Gnade und Liebe Gottes. Demselbigen Gott der allein weise ist, sei ehre durch Jesum Christ in ewigkeit. Amen. Römer, Cap. 16. v 27

Das vorhergehende ist geschrieben für Unterricht und Andecken für die Nachkommeschaft in der Tulpehocken Gemeinde, und soll aufbewahrt bleiben in der Gemeinde bei den vorgesetzten Brüder. So viel von mir, einem geringen alten Bruder von etwa mehr als 72 Jahr alt

JOHN ZUG.

Sunday Schools.—The first Sunday School was organized by George Bucher in the Cornwall House (now Midway district), in the year 1880. This was kept up for several years. In 1881, Bro. Cyrus Bucher organized the first Sunday School in the Heidelberg House. This also was of short duration, owing to the fact that following year, Bro. Bucher moved to Astoria, Ill. At present, there are four schools, viz.: Heidelberg, Tulpehocken, Myerstown and Richland. These schools owe their existence to the Heidelberg school, which was reorganized in the year 1891, with John Herr as superintendent, and N. P. Gibbel, assistant superintendent, Ed. H. Kurtz, secretary, and S. G. Spayd, treasurer. At this time very few of the members took an interest in Sunday Schools. There were no members as teachers, and even the officers, aside from the superintendents, were outside of the church. However, by the grace of God, in the course of a few years nearly all became members of the church. In 1897, the Tulpehocken and Midway Sunday Schools were organized, W. H. Oberholtzer, superintendent, and F. L. Reber, assistant of the Tulpehocken, and Benjamin Smith, superintendent, and Joseph Wilhelm, assistant of Midway. In 1901, a Sunday School was opened in Richland for the winter months, with Isaac King, superintendent, and Jacob M. Gettel, assistant. This was kept up for two winters. Second year Jacob Dillman was superintendent. In 1911, this school was reorganized for the year round, with Harry Hacker as superintendent, and Michael Kurtz, and Jacob Wenger as assistants. The Myerstown Sunday School was organized in fall of 1910, with W. H. Oberholtzer as superintendent, and Peter Phillippy, assistant. Each of the respective schools have an enrollment of 100 and over. The present superintendents are, viz.: Heidelberg: H. F. King, C. R. Bucher; Tulpehocken: Samuel Wenger, David Layser; Myerstown: W. H. Oberholtzer, Peter Phillippy; Richland: F. L. Reber, Jacob Wenger.

In the fall of 1911, the Tulpehocken Sunday School was closed, and not reopened in the spring, on account of its close proximity to Myerstown and Richland, being only about one and one half miles distant from either. In the spring of 1912, a Sunday School was organized in the Millbach House, with J. L. Royer as superintendent, and Baron Heisey and Harry Dubble as assistants. This seems to be a very promising field for Sunday School, having over 100 enrolled, with an average of about 80. On November 16, 1912, a local Sunday School meeting was held at the Tulpehocken House, and November 8, 1913, a joint Sunday School meeting of the Tulpehocken and Midway Churches was held at Myerstown. In December, 1911, a Sisters' Aid Society was formed with headquarters in Richland, Mary Hess Reber, President; Mary Brubaker, Secretary; and Lydia King, Treasurer. There are in progress three weekly Bible classes, viz., Myerstown, Richland, and Reistville. Under the blessing of God, there was a steady growth in the Tulpehocken Church. At the time of organization, 1841, there were 50 members. Under the Eldership of John Zug, and Christian Bucher up to 1901, the church grew to the number of 483. After the division of the district, December 16, 1901, under the Eldership of John Herr, up to 1911, the church grew from 300 to 400, the present membership. Praise God from whom all blessings flow!

Bishops of Tulpehocken Church.

1. Jacob Pfautz, 1841–
2. John Zug, 1861–1873.
3. Christian Bucher, 1875–1901.
4. John Herr, 1901–

CHAPTER IV.

SPRING CREEK CHURCH.

At the division of Big Swatara Church in 1868, Spring Creek Church had as officers: Jacob Hollinger and William Hertzler, Elders; and Joseph Hollinger, minister; and Abraham Balsbaugh, Samuel Gibble and Daniel Hollinger, deacons. About 250 members. Elections for deacons: 1869, Joseph Witmer and Isaac Struphaar; 1873, M. R. Henry and J. H. Longenecker; 1881, Henry S. Zug; 1885, Daniel Struphaar and Benjamin Longenecker; 1890, S. Z. Witmer and Jacob Heagy; 1895, John Booser and Allen D. Bucher; 1900, J. H. Gingrich and Jos. B. Aldinger; 1904, Andrew Clendenen; 1903, Harvey S. Gibble; 1906, George Hoffer.

Election of Ministers.—1869, Geo. S. Becker and Daniel Hollinger; 1876, J. H. Longenecker; 1878, Cyrus Bomberger; 1881, John Ensminger; 1887, D. Struphaar and Alfred B. Gingrich; 1894, H. B. Hollinger and S. Z. Witmer; 1900, Allen D. Bucher; 1906, Daniel K. Kreider; 1909, Jacob H. Gingrich; 1910, Aaron H. Hoffer.

Ordinations Since 1868.—1893, Geo. S. Becker and Jacob H. Longenecker; 1903, Cyrus Bomberger; 1905, Alfred B. Gingrich; 1909, H. B. Hollinger and S. Z. Witmer. Elder George S. Becker died December 4, 1904, in his 76th year, and his wife the day following, in her 78th year, buried in one grave, in the Spring Creek Cemetery.

The old Spring Creek meeting-house, near Hershey, on the late Henry farm, was built in 1848, of limestone, 38 × 42 feet. In this house the meeting was held which divided Big Swatara district in 1868. In 1854, the Conewago meeting-house was built, less than two miles north of where Elder George Miller was buried in 1798. In 1869, a meeting-house was built, known as South Annville, 2½

SPRING CREEK MEETING HOUSE.

OLD SPRING CREEK MEETING HOUSE.

miles south of Annville. This was the first house built after the division. In 1886, the first lovefeast house was built near the old Spring Creek House, and known by the same name, 50 × 80 feet, with basement, and the old house was converted into a dwelling for the janitor.

The Palmyra House was erected in 1892, and is 40 × 50 feet; and the Annville House, built in 1906, 48 × 78 feet, was the second lovefeast house in the Spring Creek district.

Another lovefeast house was built in 1911, known as the Bachmanville House, 40 × 55 feet, and dedicated May 16, 1912. John Herr and Rufus P. Bucher preached the dedicatory sermons. The Building Committee consisted of J. B. Aldinger, A. H. Hoffer, J. F. Booser, Wm. Gruber, A. Y. Gruber. All these meeting places are well supplied with shedding for teams, and their aggregate cost is over $30,-000, free of debt.

The first Sunday School, organized by authority of the church, was in the Spring Creek House, in 1889, and was kept up ever since; that at South Annville in 1891; Conewago in 1893; Palmyra in 1894; Bachmanville in 1908; and Annville in 1907. All these schools have been reorganized from year to year ever since.

The Missionary Committee of the Spring Creek congregation consists of Frank S. Carper, Aaron Grubb, and Harrison Gipe. The Sunday School Advisory Committee is composed of Geo. W. Henry, A. G. Longenecker, Aaron Grubb, W. E. Glasmire, and Benj. Ebersole.

In the spring of 1912, Spring Creek Church district was divided into three separate churches, which were all organized soon thereafter, viz.: the one retaining the name Spring Creek, having the Spring Creek and Palmyra Houses, and ministers: J. H. Longenecker, Elder; and deacons, Andrew Clendenen and Geo. Hoffer. A few weeks after organization, Frank S. Carper was elected minister, and Harrison Gipe and Milton Basehore, deacons. In the fall of the same year, Elder S. R. Zug, and J. C. Zug, a minister, moved here from the Elizabethtown Church. On September 6, 1913, J. C. Zug was ordained to the Eldership by Elders

S. H. Hertzler and John H. Witmer. The membership is 254.

BISHOPS OF SPRING CREEK CHURCH.

1. Jacob Hollinger, Elder, } 1868–1877.
2. Wm. Hertzler, Assistant Elder,
3. Wm. Hertzler, 1877–1893.
4. J. H. Longenecker, 1893–

CHAPTER V.

MAIDEN CREEK CHURCH.

Maiden Creek Church is located north and east of the city of Reading. It contains territory that is of historic note in the Church of the Brethren. Northkill congregation, Falkner's Swamp, and Oley are within its bounds. As early as 1724, Peter Becker preached at Oley, and a lovefeast was held. A number of members joined the church. The church was from the first a prey for Moravian and Ephrata missionaries, and that spirit has not died out to this day. Elder George Kline ministered to them for many years.

In 1770 about twelve families were identified with the Oley congregation. Twenty persons were in communion, as follows: Martin Gaby, minister, and wife; John Yoder, minister, and wife; Conrad Price and wife, David Price and wife, David Kinsey and wife, Christian Kinsey and wife, Peter Kleine, Elizabeth Ellis, Margaret Harpine, Catherine Plank, Daniel Kleine and wife.[1]

August 12, 1780, at a meeting held at Little Swatara, Elders Christopher Sower and Martin Urner ordained Martin Gaby as Elder, and Bro. David Kinsey as minister, in the Oley congregation.

Owing to frequent removals, and being a hotbed of sectarianism, the church did not prosper. Even to this day, there is no church in our district that is making less progress, although lawful efforts have been made to revive the work, but in vain. Pricetown meeting house is the second or at most third meeting house built in this country by the Brethren. At this time it is the only original house standing without being remodeled, in a fairly good condition.

The deed to this property is well preserved by the church, given in the year 1807, by Elder Martin Gaby.

[1] Brumbaugh's History, p. 298.

"This denture made the 16th day of Sept. in the year of our Lord One thousand eight hundred and Seven, *Between* Martin Gaby of Ruscombmanor Township in the County of Berks, and State of Penna., the Elder, and Susanna his wife of the one part, and the Society called Old Baptist Society, in and about the Township of Ruscombmanor Aforesaid, of which the said Martin Gaby, David Kinsey, John Beyler and Christian Kinsey are the present Trustees of the other part Witnesseth, that the said Martin Gaby and Susanna his wife for the promotion of the Gospel, and for and in consideration of the sum of Five Shillings to them in hand paid by the said, etc., etc.

It is a fact, however, that the house was built about thirty years before the deed was given, as may be seen by an article which appeared in The Reading Eagle of August 18, 1894. This article in the main is correct. It is herewith given in full:

"At Pricetown, on an eminence near the fork of the road, leading to the ruins of the Oley Furnace, stands the old stone church of the German Baptist denomination, popularly known as Dunkers. This is said to be the oldest building of the kind in the United States. It was erected in 1777. In its architecture it has not been changed a particle since, though its walls show the wear of the elements.[2]

"Ministers of the denomination who have traveled all over the country, occasionally visit the building, and these say that while there were churches of this kind built sometime before the date just mentioned, all these have disappeared or were remodeled to such an extent as to make it impossible to see what the original building looked like. But the one at Pricetown remains unchanged and will probably stand as it does today for many years to come, since good care is taken of it.

"It is a plain 30×25 one story building with a 16×16 addition, both parts being constructed of rough stone. The walls are nearly two feet thick and have outworn several shingle roofs. In the early part of the last century, love feasts were held in this building regularly.

"The cooking was done in the addition for which purpose it was erected, and the sisters then brought the food into the main building, where the feast was held. In those days, a culinary

---

[2] The Germantown house was erected in 1770, but has been altered.

PRICETOWN MEETING HOUSE.
THE OLDEST UNALTERED MEETING HOUSE IN THE BROTHERHOOD.

MOHRSVILLE MEETING HOUSE.

MOHRSVILLE CEMETERY.

department was distinctly necessary here. People from all over the country and from many beyond its borders attended these feasts. There was no other Dunker Church then within a radius of 40 miles, and with the exception of the Wertz and Spies churches there were no other houses of worship for a great distance. Services held in the old Dunker church were always well attended, no matter how bad the weather. But now at least a dozen churches have sprung up in the territory formerly covered by this one.

"The first members of this denomination who reached America landed in 1719, having emigrated from Holland and Germany. The greater number settled in Germantown, but a few reached Oley Township and Lebanon and Lancaster counties. From 1730 to 1745, they were numerous in Oley, but by 1760 many had moved away. In 1724, a general meeting which was attended by members from all over the colonies was held in Oley in one of the large farm houses. There was no house of worship in that section at this early date. In the same year that this big meeting was held in Oley, an extended pilgrimage was made by 14 brethren to all parts of America where there were Dunkers. This was called an 'Apostolischer Kreutzung.' Seven of these Brethren were on foot and seven on horseback. At all points they passed where there were Dunkers living, they stopped several days to preach the Gospel. In many places the whole party of fourteen stopped at one place. In 1742, another well attended conference[3] of this denomination was held in Oley.

"About the year 1766, Martin Gaube,[4] one of the most enthusiastic of the Oley Dunkers, became of the opinion that the church could do much more work if it had a regular building in which to worship. By this time there were quite a number of Dunkers in what is known as Ruscombmanor and Alsace townships, so Mr. Gaube decided to move to the former place and build a meeting house on his own account. He purchased a number of acres of land of Conrad Price, who then owned all the land on which the present village of Pricetown stands, and about the year 1775, erected a dwelling on his tract.

"Two years later he built the meeting house. From 1778 to the opening of the last century services were held here about 7 times a year by itinerant ministers. Between 1775, when Gaube

---

[3] This was not a Brethren conference but one of the several instituted by Zinzendorf.—EDITORS.

[4] Gaby.

moved to Ruscombmanor into his newly erected house, and 1778 when their meeting house was finished, services were held during the summer under a large oak tree that stood alongside the Gaube residence, and in winter in his house or barn. It is traditionary that these open air services always attracted such large crowds that, although the tree's shadow was large, many had to stand in the sun, which was considered a great concourse in those days of widely separated homes. The meeting house was afterwards erected quite near this tree, and the house of Mr. Gaube.

"This tree[5] stands today. It must be considerably over 150 years old, but its appearance suggests a tree in its prime. It casts its big shadow over its old companion, the meeting house, and far beyond into the graveyard which is just back of the house of worship. Its height is over 60 ft. and the trunk has a diameter of about 5 feet.

"The lower part of the tree appears to be solid, which promises many additional years of life for the historic old oak. As is shown by the picture accompanying this article the tree is not gnarled or scantily branched, but it exhibits all the vigor of a young tree.

"In 1807, Martin Gaube conveyed to the Baptist Society, composed of members in Ruscombmanor and the surrounding townships, a one Acre lot of ground and the house of worship erected thereon, together with the burying ground bounding the church on the west side. Outside of the private burial places, this was the first graveyard in that section of the country. Before the erection of the numerous other churches all people who had no burial places of their own interred their dead here irrespective of denomination.

"The trustees of the society at the time Mr. Gaube gave the church and ground were: Martin Gaube, David Kinsey, Christian Kinsey and John Beyler. Among the principal members were the Kenzie, Rublemoyer, Faint and Price families.

"Between 1807 and 1830, the church flourished but then many of the members gradually moved away. Shortly after 1832, it is said that there was not a single member living in the township. There were, however, a few in Alsace, who kept their eye on the property and gave Lutheran and Reformed ministers the privilege of using the building occasionally.

[5] The old oak tree has since given way to the elements, and is no more, but one very big maple tree still remains on the south side of the grounds.

"They also allowed a Union Sunday School to be held in the Church. This Sunday School has been kept up every year ever since, and, outside of Reading is the oldest in the county. Among the early ministers who occasionally preached in the meeting house were: George Price, John Price, Henry Kassell, (Cassel), John Tzug (Zug) Samuel Harley, Jonas Price, William Hartzell (Hertzler) and Christian Bucher.

"Sometime before 1846, Samuel Fox moved from Alsace to Ruscombmanor. Mrs. Fox, who was a very enthusiastic worker, of the denomination, was instrumental in getting Dunker ministers to visit the place more frequently.

"On Christmas eve, 1846 Rev. Tzug held services, and from that time on ministers paid regular visits to the place, and the church commenced to assume a more thriving aspect. Jeremiah Rothermel, of Temple, was the first regular minister of the church. Since his election, services have been held every six weeks. He delivered an occasional sermon up to a short time before his death, which occurred a few years ago. Subsequent preachers were: Augustus Hoch, of Pricetown, Jacob Yoder of Centreport, David Eshleman of near Centreport who was made a bishop while preaching here; Joshua and Israel Koenig, Chas. Madeira, Henry Kline, of Muhlenberg, and Jonathan G. Reber of Centreport. The last two are serving at present (1894).

"To this day, the meetings are in most cases well attended by people who are not members. Protracted meetings are held nearly every winter. Services are always attended by members of the church from distant parts of the county, even during inclement weather, when the carriages of the members can be seen going through the village. They use only the very plainest pattern of carriage, and they are very nearly all alike, durability and strength being the primary consideration. When the writer visited the church on a recent beautiful Sunday forenoon, the services were opened by the singing of a familiar German hymn by the congregation, the preacher reading off line after line to his audience.

"The interior consists of a plain room. The walls are entirely free of paper, paintings, fresco or kalsomine. The windows are without ornament or decoration of any kind. The seats are plain wooden benches with a straight board for a back. There is no pulpit or pulpit furniture. The preacher is not even given the prominence of having a raised platform on which to stand while addressing his audience. His bench is no softer than that of any of his hearers. He has a long table in front of him, on which is placed his Bible and hymn book. Back of the table stands a long bench. His bench and desk face the audience, and this is the only distinction that his office affords. The graveyard just back of the church, the wall of which can partly be seen in one of illustrations accompanying this article, presents an appearance as plain and unassuming as the edifice. There is a high and substantial wall around it. None but the very plainest of tombstones are allowed to be erecected here, not a particle of ornamentation being tolerated, high stones and monuments being out of the question, as are also ornamental fences. In this burial ground there are no family plots, but all rest side by side like members of one family. Around the church are scattered a number of big trees, and under these hitching posts were formerly planted. One of the finest of these trees was struck by lightning several years ago and subsequently had to be removed. Since then a comfortable and substantial shed has been erected along the side of the graveyard wall.

"Martin Gaby died in the year 1812, and was buried in the Pricetown Cemetery. The inscriptions on the tombstone are in German and somewhat hard to decipher. As nearly as can be made out it is as follows:

> Hier ruhet
> Martin Gaby
> Er wurde geboren
> den 9ten tag May, 1742
> und Starb
> den 20ten January, 1812
> Er war ein lehrer der
> Deutschen Täufer Gemeinde
> Wurde Alt 69 yr. 8 mo. 10 tag"

Elections held before Organization.—April 8, 1864, an election was held at the house of Bro. Jacob Yoder for two deacons, but after the election, three were declared elected viz.: A. Godwalt, V. Hartman, S. Klein. Present: Elder John Zug, Joseph Merkey, David Merkey, Jacob Kline, John Hertzler, George Gibble, and John Merkey. May 15, 1865, an election was held at the house of Bro. Valentine Hartman for a minister, in the presence of Christ. Bomberger and John Zug. The lot fell on Bro. Augustus Hoch; at the same time, Bro. Jacob Kline was advanced to the second degree. 30 votes were cast. Bro. Hoch refused to serve. He was admonished time and again, but still refused, and also blasphemed the Brethren and ministers, and was finally disowned.

April 28, 1866, an election was held for a minister at the house of Jacob Yoder, and the lot fell on Jeremiah Rothermel. At the same time, three deacons were elected, viz.: Jacob Yoder, John Kemerer and Emanuel Yoder, in the presence of Elder John Zug and officials of Little Swatara Church.

Apparently about this time a separate organization was effected. The minutes were lost.

The above elections were all held in this district while yet identified with the Little Swatara Church.

There are two church houses: Mohrsville and Pricetown. Mohrsville House, built 1867, brick, capacity 400, valuation $2,000, and Pricetown House previously described.

Mohrsville House Remodeled.

April 15, 1899, it was decided to remodel the Mohrsville meeting house so as to be suitable for lovefeast occasions.[6] Considerable work had to be done to get the basement into a proper condition. New benches were placed in the main room, a platform was erected, with other minor changes.

Lovefeasts were held before this meeting house was remodeled at the following places, viz.: Elias Geib's near Fleetwood; George Hess's, near Fleetwood; Mary Levan's, near Pricetown; 1887, Daniel H. Reber's, near Bernville; 1888, John Kline's, near Bernville; 1890, Friend William Ernst's; 1891, Daniel H. Reber's, near Bernville; 1892, Henry Miller's, at Bern; 1893, Harrison Stoudt's, near Centreport; 1894, Sister Rachel Fox, Stoudt's Ferry Bridge; 1895, Isaac Degler's, south of Bern.

Elections after Organization.—Joshua King was baptized in July, 1868, and within one year was elected to the min-

[6] Up to this time lovefeasts were held at private homes, in the barn.

istry. Later on, he moved to the eastern shore of Maryland. About the year 1874, Israel King was elected to the ministry. After serving a number of years, he died.

George Hess and John Kline were elected as deacons at the same time. Date unknown.

David Eshleman moved into this church, and was received as a minister. Later on was ordained. Died and buried at the Mohrsville graveyard.

November 26, 1887, Henry S. Kline and Charles Madeira were elected to the ministry, and Elias Kemerer and Daniel H. Reber as deacons. Elders present: Samuel Harley and John Hertzler.

April 18, 1891, a certificate was granted to Charles Madeira and wife, who moved to Chiques Church; also to George Hess (deacon) and wife, who moved to Tulpehocken Church.

April 18, 1891, Jonathan G. Reber was elected as minister; advanced in 1900.

April 24, 1898, Nathaniel Yoder was elected to the ministry. Believing his ministry was not edifying, he forwarded a petition to Elders' Meeting of the District for a committee to relieve him of his office. Said committee, with the church, granted his request, and he was relieved of his office September 25, 1909.

Spring of 1900, Elder C. Bucher resigned as Elder in charge. His resignation was accepted, and John Herr was elected to take charge of the church.

March 16, 1904, Elias G. Reber was elected as deacon. A certificate was granted to him and his wife in 1907, for Elizabethtown. However, before he left, he took sick and died.

April, 1902, Henry S. Kline moved to Reading Church.

October 19, 1907, lovefeast was held at Mohrsville House. Brethren Edwin Ernst and Benjamin Fox, Junior, were elected to the office of deacon. At the same time John Herr handed in his resignation as Elder in charge, which was accepted, and William H. Oberholtzer was elected in his stead.

MAIDEN CREEK CHURCH. 483

In the spring of 1909, Elder Spencer Beaver and wife were received in their office by letter.

The present officials of the church are: Elder W. H. Oberholtzer, Elder in charge, assisted by Elder Spencer Beaver, and Jonathan G. Reber in 2d degree; deacons: Edwin Ernst, and Benjamin Fox. The present membership is 45. The church is not making much progress; however, the little band of members seem to be in earnest in the cause of the Master, having their regular worship at the Mohrsville House, and also at Pricetown, and occasionally at the home of members. They have their weekly prayer meetings and a Sunday School at the Mohrsville House with an average attendance of about 30. This Sunday School was organized April 14, 1901, with J. G. Reber as Superintendent and Absalom Yoder, Assistant. A sister, whom the Lord has blessed with considerable means, having the welfare of the cause of Christ at heart, especially the Maiden Creek Church, bought a property close to the Church, erected a double brick building thereon and donated the whole to the church. At present Elder Spencer Beaver and wife occupy one part of the house, and the other part is rented by the church. Would there were many more members so

OBITUARIES OF OFFICIALS OF MAIDEN CREEK CHURCH.

Names.	Born.	Died.	Buried.
Deacons:			
(1) Adam Godwalt...	Moved to Ohio.		
(2) Valentine Hartman	Dec. 7, 1807	Aug. 16, 1867	Mohrsville.
(3) Samuel Kline.....	Sept. 3, 1819	Sept. 9, 1865	Becker's premises, near Hamburg.
(4) John Kemerer....	Oct. 3, 1801	Jan. 27, 1882	Mohrsville.
(5) Emanuel Yoder...	Feb. 19, 1819	Feb. 18, 1886	Mohrsville.
(6) John Kline.......	Oct. 28, 1837	Oct. 15, 1894	Mohrsville.
(7) Elias Kemerer....	Aug. 22, 1827	Jan. 14, 1902	Mohrsville.
(8) Daniel H. Reber..	Apr. 28, 1836	July 6, 1912	Reber Cemetery, near Bernille.
(9) Elias G. Reber....	Dec. 6, 1864	Mch. 28, 1907	Reber Cemetery, near Bernille.
Ministers:			
(1) Jeremiah Rothermel............	May 17, 1822	Feb. 12, 1890	Hinnershitz Church.
(2) Jacob Yoder......	May 2, 1818	Sept. 26, 1881	Mohrsville.
(3) David Eshleman..	June 22, 1798	Oct. 4, 1873	Mohrsville.
(4) Israel King.......	Apr. 10, 1844	Jan. 29, 1888	Mohrsville.

fully consecrated to the Lord, as to do service unto Him, that will speak after our bodies moulder in the earth!

In 1883 the district meeting of Eastern Pa. was held at the Mohrsville House.

Elders in charge of this church: 1.   2. Jeremiah Rothermel, –1890; 3. Christian Bucher, 1890–1900; 4. John Herr, 1900–1907; 5. Wm. H. Oberholtzer, 1907–.

CHAPTER VI.

SCHUYLKILL CHURCH.

The Schuylkill Church occupies the southwestern part of Schuylkill Co., that section lying between the Blue Mt. on the south, and Second Mt. on the north. It is bounded on the west by the Big Swatara congregation, the line being near Inwood. It extends indefinitely east, its horizon in that direction apparently being Cressona. Tower City (now Shamokin) Mission bounds it on the north; on the south it is bounded by the Little Swatara Church, of which it was originally a part, until 1877, when by mutual agreement it became a separate church, and organized under the present name, with Elder Geo. Smith as the housekeeper, and Bro. Joshua Struphaur as one of the ministers, and John Haldeman, Levi Butz, and David Yothers as deacons.

Bro. Smith had charge of the church until 1885, when for some gross charge he was disowned. He was a man of considerable talent, and before he became identified with the Church of the Brethren, he was a prominent minister in the U. B. church. About the year 1879, Bro. Michael Haldeman was elected to the ministry, in which capacity he served until 1899, when he left the church, and became identified with the Old Order Brethren.

In the fall of 1893, D. C. Kutz was elected to the ministry. After the disowning of Bro. Smith, Elder John Hertzler became the Elder in charge, which place he filled until his death in 1901.

In the fall of 1901, Elder J. W. Myer was chosen as their Elder, serving in said capacity until he resigned on account of ill health. Since then Elder E. M. Wenger had charge. Elias Kintzel also served the church in the office of deacon, but is deceased. Other Brethren serving in the deacon's office are Edward Herring, Samuel Zerbe, John Neidlinger, and Frank Haldeman. William Kintzel was elected to the ministry in the year 1904, while still unmarried. Another election was held in the spring of 1911, which resulted in the electing of Elias Morgan to the ministry and Frank Haldeman as deacon.

Samuel Haldeman moved to Schuylkill Co. in 1852 and later on moved out west. He was elected to the ministry in the Indian Creek Church in 1847. He was born October 25, 1820, and was married to Harriet Horning August 14, 1842. His wife was born April 24, 1821, being younger by six months. Both have attained the age of ninety-three years. On Aug. 14, 1913, they rounded out seventy-one years of married life. Few, if any, have attained to the age of Elder Samuel Haldeman and wife, who at present are living at Reedley, Cal. He has been in the ministry sixty-six years. For some years, Bro. Haldeman has been able to use his voice but little in public speaking, but his occasional short talks are much appreciated by the congregation, and few are more regular in church attendance than our aged brother and sister. The Wednesday evening prayer meeting finds them often in their accustomed places.

John Holdeman moved here in 1853. The next year he taught school. In 1854 he was married to Sarah A. Struphaur, whose grandfather, Michael Struphaur, was the first preacher of the Brethren in Schuylkill County.

George Smith was the first Elder of the Schuylkill Church. He joined the Brethren Church about 1870. He was received without re-baptism, having been immersed thrice, in entering the United Brethren Church, where he had formerly been a minister, preaching at Highspire, Pine Grove, and other places. He was an excellent German preacher, well versed in the Scripture, and widely read.

All is well that ends well, but to be true to history we are obliged to put on record that he did not die as a brother. Because of misconduct on his part (see Romans, 1 : 27), he was disowned by the church.

Meeting Places.—In the early part of this church's history, the meetings were principally held in Struphaur's meeting house. Later meetings were held in several school houses, and some private homes. The church in council

Reedley California october 6. 1913 Dear Brother Elder S R Zug we received a letter from Brother John Haldeman & he wanted me to write a letter to you to let you know when I was born what year I was born october 25. 1820 Baptised in 1840 & Elected to the Ministry in 1847. Baptised & Elected in the Indian Creek Mountgumery County Pensylvania. & all our Comfort is in our old days to be faithful to the end & we know not how to be thankful enough for the health we have enjoyed & we wish you the blessing of the Lord from your well wishing Brother Elder Samuel Haldeman.

SAMUEL HALDEMAN LETTER.

HARRISBURG BRETHREN CHURCH.

SCHUYLKILL CHURCH.

decided to build a meeting house in Swope's Valley in the summer of 1911. This church was dedicated April 14, 1912.

In the absence of suitable church houses, the lovefeasts were so far held in barns. The principal places for the lovefeasts were: John Haldeman's, William Kintzel's, Widow Elias Kintzel, and Jacob Morgan's. This is the only church in the district where lovefeasts are yet held in barns.

Houses of Worship.—*Old Struphaur,* built about 1865, frame, about 24 × 30; cheaply built. *New Struphaur,* built in 1888. Cost $836, frame, 34 × 36. *Swope's Valley,* built in 1911–12, frame, about 32 × 38. Bro. Wolf undertook to build it if church gave $250.

Sunday Schools.—The church early became interested in Sunday Schools. Having at present an interesting Sunday School, a number of the Sunday School pupils united with the Church. Visiting members always feel at home with the saints at Schuylkill. They are especially noted for their hospitality and good will. Probable size of membership is 85,

Bishops of this Congregation: (1) George Smith, 1877–1885. (2) John Hertzler, 1885–1901. (3) J. W. Myer, Sr., 1901–1905. (4) E. M. Wenger, 1905–.

CHAPTER VII.

HARRISBURG CHURCH.

This church was organized from a part of Big Swatara Church, at a council held in the house of brother and sister Joseph C. Eshleman, No. 340 S. 14th Street, Harrisburg, on the evening of November 19, 1896, by Elders David Etter, Jacob H. Longenecker, and Samuel R. Zug, with three Brethren, and about twelve Sisters.

After the members present had unanimously voted in favor of an organization, with the approval of the Elders present, Elder S. R. Zug was chosen to have charge of the church.

There being then no minister or deacon in the city, it was decided that the officials of Big Swatara Church should be asked to supply them until they are in a condition to help themselves, which was kindly accepted.

The first meetings were held in a hall, on the third floor, at the corner of 13th and Market Streets, but in the spring of 1897, Studebaker Hall, on the second floor, on north 3d Street was leased, where Sunday School and meetings were held, until 1899, when the lot, with an old one story frame dwelling, on Hummel Street, was bought for $3,000. This house was changed, by removing partitions, into a meeting house, and was so used until 1904 when the new church was built, at a cost of over $8,000, on the same lot, large, with movable partitions, which is expected to last for some time, and is all paid for.

In 1897, Frank Haas, minister, moved here, but left again in 1898.

In 1898, Brother John M. Mohler was engaged as Pastor, and labored and cared for the spiritual needs of the little flock for a year or more. After he left, his son-in-law Harry Spanogle came for some time, and by the combined efforts of all concerned, there were soon some additions by baptism, and removals from neighboring churches.

In 1898, A. L. B. Martin was elected a deacon, and in 1900, J. C. Eshleman and A. H. Maugans were elected deacons.

In 1901, A. L. B. Martin was elected a minister, and Aaron H. Hoffer a deacon.

In 1903, J F. Graybill was elected a minister, and in 1906 D. H. Widder.

In 1906, D. E. Miller was elected a deacon, also in 1906 Addison Hoffer. In 1909, Isaac Baker, a deacon, moved here.

In 1906, D. E. Miller, a deacon, in 1907, J. F Graybill, a minister, in 1908, A. H. Hoffer, a deacon, and in 1911, A. L. B. Martin, a minister, all moved away. In 1912, Adam Hollinger and Abraham K. Hollinger moved in.

In May, 1906, a Mission Sunday School was started in the northwestern part of the city, which was kept up since.

In 1905, more territory was ceded by Big Swatara Church to Harrisburg, including Steelton, Highspire and Middletown, and in 1907, August 4, a regular meeting once a month, in the old Lutheran Church in Middletown, was established, and has been kept up since.

In 1911, Elder S. R. Zug resigned as Elder in charge, and pressed its acceptance which was granted, with the proviso that he be retained as advisory Elder, and Elder G. N. Falkenstein was elected to have charge.

The officials now are G. N. Falkenstein, Elder in charge; the ministers are D. H. Widder, Adam Hollinger and Abm. K. Hollinger, and the deacons J. C. Eshleman, Addison Hoffer and Isaac Baker, and the membership numbers 90.

CHAPTER VIII.

SHAMOKIN CHURCH (FORMERLY TOWER CITY MISSION).

The work of the Tower City[1] Mission, now known as the Shamokin Church, was organized as early as the year 1889. Of course the field had been canvassed a number of years previous to this time by a number of ministering Brethren, Brethren Hiram Gibble and D. P. Ziegler having labored more extensively than any other of our Brethren. Bro. Hiram Gibble, as we will notice later, was Elder in charge for a number of years.

Among some of the first Elders that took an active part in this mission were William Hertzler, John Hertzler, David Etter, J. H. Longenecker, H. E. Light, John Herr, Hiram Gibble, and some Brethren in the second degree. Elders William Hertzler, John Hertzler, and J. H. Longenecker were among the first to have charge of the mission, followed by H. E. Light, Hiram Gibble, and E. M. Wenger. The last named having charge of the church at the present time, by authority of the church and Home Mission Board.

Bro. D. P. Ziegler was elected as early as 1891, as one of the ministers located in this territory. Later on Bro. William Kopenhaver was elected to the ministry, followed by placing their choice on Bro. Geo. H. Miller, now located at Mt. Carmel, about 8 miles from Shamokin, where his services are rendered. Bro. Kopenhaver is at the present located at Pottsville. The Brethren that served the Church in the capacity of deacons were Bro. Lucas, George Tobias, Geo. B. McKinney and William Forry. The first two named have died, and the last two in recent years moved to the Midway Church, in Lebanon, Pa.

[1] Since there are no members now living at Tower City, from whence the name was derived, it was decided by District Meeting of 1911, to so change the name of the Mission, that hereafter it will be known as Shamokin Mission, or Shamokin Church.

The importance of the work of the Sunday School too was not overlooked by the Brethren, having organized a Sunday School as early as 1896. In the year 1906, the Mission Board decided to locate S. S. Beaver and wife at Shamokin to act as pastor and missionaries, which position they filled for nearly three years. During the greater part of this time, the services were held in Schleif's Hall, at a rental of five dollars a month. Part of this was formerly paid by the Mission Board, but now it is self supporting for the last five years.

This territory formerly belonged to the Schuylkill Church, that is, it was regarded as such. In the year 1897, by a committee appointed by the Schuylkill Church and the Mission Board the Shamokin Church was cut off from the Schuylkill Church, by making as its southern boundary the Sharp Mt., and not making a special line to the east and north.

CHAPTER IX.

READING CITY CHURCH.

While yet belonging to the Maiden Creek Church district, quite a number of members living in the city of Reading, application was made to have regular worship. To this end the old Quaker Church on North 6th Street was rented where for a number of years regular services were held, a Sunday School organized, and other church auxiliaries, giving new life and impetus to the work. Finally the Quaker Church could no more be rented, and the Brethren succeeded in renting the old Baptist Church on Chestnut Street where the work was carried on a few years.

Church House Built.—Through the instrumentality and liberality of Bro. Percival C. Nyce, a lot was bought, and a house built on Church Street, near Greenwich, in the year 1897. The building committee consisted of Elder C. Bucher (who at this time had charge of the Maiden Creek Church), Percival Nyce, and George Sherman.

The church house is a brick building, having a capacity to seat about 400. Valuation $4,000.

A debt of $1,600 remained on the house, due P. C. Nyce, one third to be paid in 1898, one third in 1899, and one third in 1900. The Eastern District of Pennsylvania took hold of the matter and the debt was canceled January 1, 1899. The canceling of the debt of sixteen hundred dollars ($1,600) resting on the Reading Church must be credited to Bro. P. C. Nyce, as may be seen by the following proposition:

At a Special District Meeting held in the Mingo Church, October 27, 1898, called by Annual Meeting Committee, the following proposition by P. C. Nyce was presented to the Meeting:

READING BRETHREN CHURCH.

"READING, PA. Aug. 29, 1898.
"TO THE MISSIONARY BOARD OF THE EASTERN DISTRICT OF PENNSYLVANIA, GREETING:

"Believing that it is the will of God that the Reading Church should be credited with a donation of ($500) five hundred dollars to the Home for the Homeless at Manheim, Pa.; ($500) five hundred dollars to the General Missionary and Tract Committee as endowment for World wide missions; ($500) five hundred dollars to the Missionary Work of Eastern District of Pennsylvania, and ($100) one hundred dollars to the Brooklyn Mission in New York, care of Alice Boone, therefore upon the condition that these amounts above named, be all paid and receipted on or before Jan. 1, 1899, the claim of ($1600) sixteen hundred dollars, now held by me against the Missionary Board of the Eastern District of Pennsylvania shall be cancelled in full."

"The above proposition was unanimously accepted by the above named Special District Meeting, and a quota of thirty cents per member suggested to be forwarded to Treasurer H. E. Light, and it was also resolved that the above be placed on the District Minutes of 1899.

JOHN HERR, *Clerk*."

"Treasurer H. E. Light now reports the money was paid to the Home, and Several Missions, and settlements made with Bro. P. C. Nyce, on Dec. 31, 1899, who gave a receipt for the four receipts, and cancelled his claim as per said proposition.
"Accepted."

The wisdom and prudence of Bro. Nyce, and the unassuming manner in which this proposition was made, is verily to be admired. He did not wish to have the credit to himself, but rather that the struggling Reading Church should have the credit for these valuable, and highly appreciated donations, "believing that such was the will of God." The Spirit of Christ "Who gave His life for the church."

Organization.—The Reading City Church was organized January 1, 1898. An election was held for a minister and two deacons. The result was no minister, the neutrals having the majority. A. H. Longenecker and Daniel M. Stouffer were elected deacons. John Herr was elected as

Elder in charge. Elders present: C. Bucher, Israel Wenger, John Herr. April 8, 1898, the church was placed under the care of the Home Mission Board. At the same time also the single mode of feet washing was adopted. The first love-feast was held May 14 and 15, 1898.

Ministers.—April 5, 1901, John Herr resigned as Elder in charge, which resignation was accepted. However, as the church failed to procure an Elder in charge, Bro. Herr kept the oversight of the church, and finally Elder Jesse Ziegler was induced to move into Reading as a resident minister and took charge of the church. His certificate was accepted March 28, 1902. In the course of a few years, Elder Ziegler again moved out of Reading, and his resignation was accepted September 10, 1903.

July 5, 1904, John Herr was again elected Elder in charge.

April 1, 1905, Bro. Herr again resigned and E. M. Wenger, the present Elder in charge, was elected.

July 7, 1902, George Sherman was elected deacon. April 10, 1903, Peter Smith was elected to the ministry. Henry H. Moyer was elected a minister, June 17, 1912. In 1913, Daniel I. Trutt and John King were elected to the office of deacon.

The only resident ministers were: Jesse Ziegler, Peter Smith, Jay G. Francis, and David Weaver. Each one served only for the course of a few years and then moved away again. The remainder of the time the church was supplied by ministerial aid from adjoining churches, as is the case at the present time. Bro. David Weaver held out longest. He was received with his office as minister by letter October 13, 1906. Resigned April 10, 1911. The church granted him leave of absence for one year. Because of having a large family of children, he thought it advisable to move into the country. His heart is still in the work at Reading.

Church Activities.—The church has regular preaching services, morning and evening, each Lord's day ever since its organization. At first the services were conducted in the German language in the morning, and in the English in the evening. At present the services are mostly English, very seldom that a German sermon is delivered. There is a prosperous Sunday School with an average attendance of about 50. Christian Workers' Society meets every Sunday previous to evening worship. There is a Sisters' Aid Society, and also an organized Bible class and a Cottage Prayer Meeting. Thus we see that the church is alive and at work. At times dark clouds gathered over it, but as often disappeared and again the sun shone in all its brilliancy. The present membership is about 75. Not all are active members, but as is the case in all churches, too many only are honorary members. The active members have stuck to the old ship Zion, through good and evil report. To know the members of Reading means to love them for their zeal and devotion to the Lord's house and cause. I think we are justified in saying that there is hardly a church in the District that is making more sacrifices financially than the members in Reading. Very few are blessed with this world's goods. Bro. Nyce is one of them, and to his honor be it said that he devotes much of his means to the glory of God.

Occasionally when questions arise in the Church requiring money, Bro. Nyce makes the proposition: "I will pay one half if the remainder of the members pay the other half." Many of the members who are employed and work as day laborers pay monthly into the church treasury, and pay more annually than many Brethren in other churches valued by the thousands. At present they are giving full support to two poor members at the "*Brethren Home.*" During 1912, while having a series of meetings more than a dozen confessed Christ and united with the church. This occasioned new life and inspiration in the church, looking for still greater things in the future. What is most needed at the present time is a resident minister, to be a shepherd to the sheep. Truly, "Thou Bethlehem in the land of Juda, art not the least among the princes of Juda."

The present officials are: Elder in charge, John C. Zug of Palmyra; ministers: Elder D. W. Weaver, Henry H. Moyer, in the first degree of ministry; deacons: Allen Longenecker, George H. Sherman, Daniel I. Trutt, John King. The following constitute the trustees: Emerson Wickle, Allen Longenecker, George Sherman, Henry Kline and Lovington Royer.

CHAPTER X.

THE MIDWAY CHURCH.

The Midway Church was organized March 24, 1902, at the Midway House. Prior to this, the Midway Church formed a part of the Tulpehocken Churcn, and owing to the strength of the membership who could not all be accommodated with seats at the lovefeasts any more and the extent of territory to be worked, it was decided at regular council at the Heidelberg House, December 16, 1901, to divide the congregation; hence the above organization.

The officials at the time of organization were as follows: Elder in charge, Christian Bucher; ministers, Martin Heisey and Joseph L. Wilhelm; deacons, Nathan P. Gibble and Mohler Bucher; clerk, J. L. Wilhelm.

There were 195 members in the new church, the names of which will all be found in the history of the Tulpehocken Church prior to the division.

Ammon H. Brubacher was elected to the ministry March 28, 1904; Jay G. Francis was received by letter as a minister, June 13, 1905; Abraham Z. Brubaker was elected August 30, 1909; John H. Smith was elected deacon March 23, 1903; Henry M. Patches, August 30, 1909. William A. Forry was received by letter as a deacon August 24, 1908, and George McKinney, July 23, 1911.

Martin Heisey was ordained and A. H. Brubacher advanced to the second degree of the ministry August 30, 1909.

April 2, 1912, at a Council Meeting held in Lebanon William A. Forry was elected to the ministry and Allen Edris to the deacon's office. Jan. 18, 1913, Samuel Wenger and Howard Weiss were elected to the office of deacon.

August 25, 1913, A. H. Brubacher was ordained to the eldership, and A. Z. Brubaker advanced to the second dgree of the ministry.

MIDWAY MEETING HOUSE.

LEBANON BRETHREN CHURCH.

July 17, 1912, Joseph Wilhelm was relieved of his office.

September 7, 1912, John H. Smith was relieved of his office, and on January 18, 1913, disowned by the church.

August 30, 1909, J. G Francis was silenced.

February 16, 1913, George McKinney moved to Shamokin.

Mar. 23, 1914, J. G. Francis was reinstated to the ministry.

The church has been growing steadily since the organization with Elder C. Bucher and later John Herr, elders in charge. Notwithstanding the church's difficulties at times, there was a goodly number of accessions. Instead of services at the several churches every four weeks, there are services every two weeks, and since the church owns her own house of worship in Lebanon, there are services in the forenoon and evening every Sunday. The Sunday Schools have both become evergreen and have each been supporting an orphan in India and also contributed to the orphanage work in the district. About 50 of our Sunday School pupils have become members of the church.

The present officials are as follows: Elder Jno. Herr, Elder in charge, non-resident; C. Bucher, Martin Heisey, and A. H. Brubacher, Elders; J. G. Francis, A. Z. Brubaker and William A. Forry, ministers; N. P. Gibble, Mohler Bucher, Henry M. Patches, Allen Edris, Samuel Wenger and Howard Weiss, deacons.

The present membership is 246.

The Midway Church has three houses of worship, one at Midway, one at Cornwall, and one on south Ninth St. in Lebanon. All are frame buildings. The size of the Midway House is 80 ft. by 50 ft., built at a cost of $3,850.65, in 1895; building committee, Benjamin Smith and Jeremiah B. Light. Bro. Smith took sick during the time of building when Elder C. Bucher with Bro. Light acted as building committee. The house was dedicated October 27, 1895, with preaching on Saturday evening, October 26, Sunday morning and evening, October 27. Brethren Amos S. Hottenstein and Reuben Graybill were the officiating ministers.

The size of the Cornwall house is 40 ft. by 60 ft., built in

1871, at a cost of $2,957.29. The building committee consisted of Jacob Bucher, Samuel Brubacher, and Jonathan Geib.

The size of the Lebanon house is 28 ft. by 40 ft., built by the "Followers of the Living God" in 1903 and purchased from them by the Brethren in 1908. Brethren N. P. Gibble, A. H. Brubacher and J. G. Francis, purchase committee, bought it for $2,400. With later purchase of more ground and improvements made, the church cost about $3,000.

Midway Church has a Sunday School at Midway house organized March 28, 1897, and one in Lebanon organized on Easter Sunday, April 2, 1899. There are weekly prayer meetings in Lebanon and vicinity,—in the church when no fire is needed, and in the homes of those who call for them, at other times. A Christian Workers' Society was organized in Lebanon in 1907. Quite a number take an active part. The Sisters' Aid Society in Lebanon was organized in 1909 and is under the control of the Sunday School there.

The church in general is in a fairly prosperous condition at present.

A. H. BRUBACHER.

The foregoing account of the Midway Church is supplemented by sketches of the work done at Cornwall and in Lebanon. Elder John Herr gives the following history of

"EARLY MEETINGS AROUND CORNWALL.

"Before the Cornwall House was built, there was preaching at the houses of members in the neighborbood. The following are at least some of the places where there was preaching: Samuel Brubaker's, Isaac Brubaker's, a preacher, where his grandson Abraham now lives; at Jonas Geib's, at Jacob Bucher's; at Abraham Geib's; at Henry Horst's, Sr., the present mill property; at Peter Heisey's where Bro. Martin now resides; and at Cyrus Brubaker's. At some of these places there were meetings only in the summer time; but Jacob Bucher, Isaac Brubaker, and Abraham Geib had meetings all the year round, every twelve weeks, making regular preaching every four weeks. The other Brethren had meetings only in the summer time and held them in the barns. But when visiting preachers came around, they also had preaching in their homes in the winter. Among these visiting preachers were Graybill Myers, Wm. Hertzler, Christian Brubaker, Jacob Reinhold, Adam Hollinger, Jacob Hollinger, Daniel Longenecker, Jonas Price, Adam Brown, and Solomon Sieber, of Juniata Co. These Brethren would hold series of meetings, going from one house to another evening after evening, and sometimes holding meetings during the day. Lovefeasts were held at Cyrus Brubaker's, Samuel Brubaker's, Isaac Brubaker's, Jacob Bucher's, and at Abraham Geib's. These were held just before hay making, when the barns were empty."

Bro. Abram Z. Brubaker furnished the following history of *Bucher's Meeting House,* now called *Cornwall House:*

"Prior to the year 1871, religious services were held by the Brethren in private houses and barns in the vicinity of Bucher's Meeting House. There are several graveyards in this locality. One known as Bucher's graveyard is on a hill near the town of Rexmont; the other, known as Brubacher's graveyard, is on the farm of Cyrus Brubacher east of the former place. When burials took place at these places, the funeral services were held either at the house or in a near-by school-house which often proved inadequate.

"As necessity is frequently the mother of invention so inconvenience was the mother of our meeting house. The idea of a union house was frequently discussed by the neighborhood's thinkers but no active steps were taken until the summer of 1870 when by chance it happened that Mr. A. Wilhelm, manager of the Coleman estate, of Cornwall, Pa., Ezra Bucher, and J. H. Bucher in conversation drifted to this subject. Mr. Wilhelm, who had the reputation of being a far-sighted man and also of a philanthropic disposition, grasped the situation and said: 'I see the necessity of such a church building and I will give $100 towards building such a house; and I will see to it that Robert and Anna Coleman will also give $100 each.'

"A little later Henry Dohner promised to give one acre of land on the northwest corner of his farm for $300 and to contribute $50 towards the building, provided he could be buried there when he died.

"During the winter of 1870 and 1871, the Brethren took

hold of the matter. J. H. Bucher, of near Rexmont, is the owner of a little book in which the subscriptions were entered. The subscriptions are headed by the following:

"TULPEHOCKEN CHURCH, Feb. 8, 1871.

"Whereas, we the members of the Tulpehocken Church of the Brethren sometimes called German Baptists and citizens of South Lebanon and Cornwall Townships, Lebanon Co., Pa., are seriously impressed with the necessity of a suitable house for holding religious services at funeral and other occasions, have, therefore, come to the conclusion to erect such a house on a lot of about one acre of land on the northwest corner of Henry Dohner's farm on the old Schaefferstown road in South Lebanon Township aforesaid, which building shall be erected under the supervision, and remain under the control, of the Brethren.

"At funerals the house and graveyard shall be open for all persons, who may choose to bury their dead there, who have died a *natural death* and get ministers of any persuasion to officiate at such occasion but at all other times of religious services shall be only for the use of the said Church of the Brethren. Any person wishing to hold a funeral in said house whether they bury in graveyard attached or at some other place shall apply to the trustee living nearest to the house, provided more than one is appointed who shall also designate where to dig the grave.

"The said trustees to be appointed by the aforesaid church and to be members of the church. All persons using the graveyard are entitled to contribute towards keeping the fence around it in order and repair.

"Now know all men that we the undersigned have agreed to pay the amounts set opposite our names respectively for the purposes above mentioned."

"Then follows a list of the contributors, of which I will name a few: Jacob Bucher, Sr., $100; Jonas Geib, $100; Samuel Brubacher, $200; A. Wilhelm, $100; Robert Coleman, $100; Anna Coleman, $100; W. G. Lehman, then County Superintendent of Schools, $5, and a host of others. Jacob Bucher, Jonas Geib, and Samuel Brubacher were the first trustees. The last named soon resigned when Cyrus Brubacher was appointed in his place. Samuel Yeagley, C. R. Bucher, and a few others were the carpenters.

"Later, an additional acre was bought from Wm. Yeagley, so the property now consists of two acres. The building is a 40 × 60 frame structure. A substantial shed was also erected. In 1880, a Sunday School was organized under the leadership of Bro. Geo. Bucher."

Geo. Bucher gives the following account of The Brethren's Sunday School at Cornwall:

"The first Sunday School in the Tulpehocken Church was organized at Cornwall, by the Brethren on September 5, 1880, by selecting Bro. George Bucher, superintendent and treasurer, and Bro. Benjamin Smith, assistant superintendent. Twenty females and twenty-three males expressed their intention to attend. The instigation of this first Sunday School came from the heart and mind of the writer. The object was not to substitute the S. S. for proper family training; neither for a stepping-stone to the church in place of the drawings of the Father (see John 6: 44). But I thought by my much absence from home, our children, and others, would have a good place to go, where there were some prospects for them to learning something of Jesus.

"We used nothing but the New Testament, the fount of truth. The Brethren's Hymn Book was used. Thus they learned church service music. We had neither tickets nor pennies.

"The school was partly evergreen. During the winter we had it only on meeting Sundays,—every four weeks. After running two seasons, it stopped for want of support,—not in money, but in officers and teachers. I found it impossible to be present at two places at one and the same time,—at Sunday School and also at church service, and no one else would do it. After the Sunday School's demise, I, as a father, had but one alternative with the children on Sundays—to take them along to church service, if possible. To this and proper family training, the divine record bears ample witness."

Bro. J. G. Francis contributes the following about

The Brethren in and around Lebanon.

"The Brethren first began work in the city of Lebanon on the invitation of Mr. Shomo, associated with Mr. Fauber, proprietor of the Union House of Prayer on South 7th

Street, and of Mr. Young, publisher of a German paper in Lebanon. It was soon after the Cornwall meeting-house was built. These two gentlemen had attended services there and invited Bro. Christian Bucher to preach for them in Lebanon. He entered the open door. At first the preaching was irregular and was done only on invitation; but before long the Brethren rented the house for preaching every four weeks. This was about 1873. Bro. Bucher now began to send Bro. John Herr and George Bucher to fill appointments. The preaching was about all German at first, now and then a visiting English preacher would exercise. Bro. Wm. Oberholtzer preached English once or twice.

"By permission of the church, the Brethren Sunday School of Lebanon was opened Easter Sunday, April 2, 1899, in the house of Bro. Michael Zug, 138 Cumberland St., Lebanon, Pa. The school was opened through the efforts of Sister Martha Eckert, who was anxious to have her boys attend a Brethren's Sunday School. Sister Mary F. Zug was made superintendent and her sister Martha Eckert, assistant. The school was opened at 10 A. M. by singing 'Come Holy Spirit, Heavenly Dove.' There was a total attendance of 20.

"Sister Mary Zug was married the beginning of the following year to J. G. Francis, a minister from Green Tree. They moved to Reading. The Sunday School was reorganized on April 1, 1900, with Bro. Peter A. Smith as superintendent. But the school did not seem to prosper and was closed July 1. Late in the summer of 1901, Bro. and Sister Francis returned from Reading, and others had moved into Lebanon, notably Ella and Anna Biever. The Tulpehocken Church gave consent to reopen the school. December 27, 1901, a meeting with Bro. John Herr in attendance was held at Michael Zug's. The school was reorganized with Peter Smith as superintendent. An Advisory Board consisting of teachers and officers was authorized. It was also decided to have prayer-meetings every Sunday evening at the homes of the members. An effort to secure the Union House of Prayer for the Sunday School was successful, and from thenceforth till the house was bought on South 9th St., the Sunday School was held there. Superintendents of the Lebanon Sunday School following Bro. Smith have been: J. G. Francis, Grant Yeagley, George Keeney, Emory Trimmer, William Forry and Allen Edris. A Home Department of the Sunday School was authorized Aug. 3, 1902. October 5, 1902, marks the beginning of the library of the Lebanon Sunday School, which has attained to a fair size and is considerably used. Since 1903, the Sunday School has been supporting an orphan in India. The Sunday School has also an Infant Roll and maintains Teacher's meetings, and has taken several classes through a teacher's training course.

"The first revival meeting in Lebanon was held by Bro. Edward M. Wenger in March, 1903. One joined the church —Bro. Dana Eckert; and the mother who was the instigator of the Sunday School in Lebanon had the joy of seeing one of her sons brought into the fold. In 1905, J. G. Francis preached for two weeks in his own home. Two were received into the church. A series of meetings was arranged by Bro. Francis, acting under Elder John Herr, to be held in our present house on S. 9th St. David W. Weaver of Reading was secured. Twenty-one came out on the Lord's side. Within a year, Bro. Levi Mohler held another revival, with a result of ten converts. Thus within the space of one year thirty-one were awakened. The Lord was blessing the work abundantly. The most noteworthy revival in the last five years was held by Bro. Rufus Bucher when ten precious souls declared for Christ.

"Following the revival in 1908, by Bro. Weaver, a Christian Workers' Society was organized in place of the previous organization known as Christian Helpers. The first president of the Christian Workers' Society was Dana Eckert, who ably looked after the work till his recent removal to Pittsburgh. Through its offerings taken on Sunday evening the Christian Workers have been able to give financial aid on a number of occasions.

"Under the Sunday School superintendency of Bro. Emory Trimmer, a Sister's Aid Society, formerly agitated, was organized with the unique distinction of being a part of the Sunday School. Bro. Francis was instrumental in having a Bi-Centennial meeting in Lebanon in 1908.

"Finally when the series of meetings by Bro. Weaver in the South 9th St. house proved so successful, that house was bought. It cost $2,400. Additional ground was added to both sides. The building is frame and capable of seating about 300 persons. The property has been further improved and some souls have been garnered."

CHAPTER XI.

ANNVILLE CHURCH.

The congregation known as the Annville Church of the Brethren was organized on March 25, 1912, from territory and members formerly belonging to the Spring Creek Church. Elder John H. Witmer and Elder S. H. Hertzler were present to assist in the work of organization. The election for officials resulted as follows: Elder A. B. Gingrich, Elder in charge; John H. Gingrich, Treasurer; Jacob Heagy, Clerk.

The boundary line of the territory of this congregation is described as follows: Beginning on the Conewago Hill about midway between Colebrook and Lawn, the line runs in a northern direction to the Swatara Creek to a place formerly known as Maulfair's Mill, thence east along Swatara Creek to a point near Jonestown (the line not fully known at Jonestown), thence south to 16th St., Lebanon City, thence in a bee-line to the road past Henry Herr, deceased, thence by said road to the Horse Shoe pike to the farm known as the Zimmerman farm, thence south in a bee-line across the mountain to a point close to Mt. Gretna, thence west along the Conewago Hill to the place of beginning, leaving Colebrook in the Annville district. It is bounded on the north by Big Swatara Church and Little Swatara Church, on the east by Little Swatara and Midway Churches, on the south by the Chiques Church and on the west by the Conewago and Spring Creek Churches.

The present official body of this church consists of Elder A. B. Gingrich, Elder in charge; ministers: Elder H. B. Hollinger, A. D. Bucher (2d degree), and Jacob H. Gingrich (1st degree), and deacons: Jacob Heagy, John H. Gingrich, H. H. Gingrich, and Cyrus Winters, the last two having been elected since the organization. The membership at time of organization was 134.

ANNVILLE BRETHREN CHURCH.

The congregation has two houses of worship: Annville and South Annville. At the Annville house, preaching serices are held three Sundays out of four. The Sunday School here organized on May 5, 1907, meets every Sunday in the year. The first Superintendent was A. S. Kreider. For 1914, the following are the officers: Superintendent, C. H. Winters; Assistant Superintendent, Jacob Heagy. The average attendance is 86. There is a Cradle Roll with an enrollment of 30 and a Teachers' Meeting which meets occasionally.

At the South Annville house, services occur every two weeks with Sunday School during the summer since 1891. A. B. Gingrich was the first superintendent. In 1914, the officers were as follows: Superintendent, B. H. Gingrich; Assistant Superintendent, H. H. Gingrich, with an average attendance of 50. A singing school was conducted at this place in 1912 by A. H. Brubacher.

A Sewing Circle with 12 members was organized in 1912 with Katherine Basehore as President and Annie Minnich as Vice President. For the year 1913, the average attendance at weekly meetings was six. The work of the Circle consists of making clothing and sending money to missions and needy causes. Clothing valued at $50 was sent in 1913 to Neffsville Orphanage and Brooklyn Mission. Ten dollars was sent to Bro. Warstler, Grand Rapids, Mich., and thirty dollars was given to procure carpet for the Annville house of worship. The officers for 1914 are: President, Leah Hollinger; Vice President, Anna Minnich; Secretary, Susan Ziegler; Treasurer, Emma Yake.

This congregation has a weekly prayer meeting at the homes of members. The first temperance committee appointed in 1912 consisted of Cyrus Winters, Elmer Minnich, and Aaron Gingrich. Isaac J. Kreider appointed as the first correspondent to the Gospel Messenger still serves in that capacity. The 1914 Temperance Committee is: Cyrus H. Winters, Aaron Gingrich, and B. H. Gingrich. Florence Keller and Cora Kettering are the missionary solicitors.

D. C. REBER.

CHAPTER XII.

CONEWAGO CHURCH.

In the spring of 1912, Spring Creek Church with a membership of 475 was divided for the first time into three divisions: Spring Creek, Annville and Conewago. On March 27, 1912, one hundred and twenty members thus cut off from the original Spring Creek congregation and residing in the southern part of Dauphin Co. were organized into a separate congregation known as the Conewago Church. Elders S. R. Zug and S. H. Hertzler were present to assist in the organization.

The organization resulted in selecting Elder S. Z. Witmer, Elder-in-charge; J. S. Baker, Clerk; Jacob W. Brandt, Treasurer. The official body at the time of organization was as follows: Elders Samuel Z. Witmer and Daniel Hollinger; Aaron H. Hoffer, minister in first degree; deacons: John F. Booser, J. B. Aldinger, and Jacob W. Brandt, the latter having been elected on the day of organization.

The boundaries of the Conewago Church are as follows: The Conewago ridge in northern Lancaster Co. forms the southern boundary line. Starting at Wagner's Park on this ridge, the line runs northwest to Running Pump, thence along the Lancaster and Harrisburg pike to Royalton; thence in a northern direction toward Hummelstown along Swatara Creek about two miles; thence almost due east leaving Stoverdale and Fishburn Church south of the line and Campbellstown north of it, to the western boundary line of the Annville Church; thence following that line south to a point on Conewago Hill about midway between Colebrook and Lawn. It will be seen then that Conewago Church is bounded on the north by Spring Creek Church; on the east by the Annville Church; on the south by Elizabethtown Church, West Green Tree Church and Chiques

CONEWAGO MEETING HOUSE.

BACHMANVILLE MEETING HOUSE.

Church; on the west by Elizabethtown and Big Swatara Churches, and that its territory lies partly in Dauphin, partly in Lebanon, and partly in Lancaster County.

On November 27, 1912, an election was held for a minister at the Bachmanville house just before lovefeast. As a result, John S. Baker was elected. Since the organization, eighteen persons have been received into the membership by baptism and two have been reclaimed.

The present officials of this church are: Elder Samuel Z. Witmer, Elder-in-charge; ministers, Elder Daniel Hollinger, Aaron Hoffer in first degree and John S. Baker in first degree; deacons, John F. Booser, Jos. B. Aldinger, and J. W. Brandt.

The congregation has two houses of worship, namely, Conewago and Bachmanville. At each of these places a Sunday School is maintained. At Conewago, J. W. Brandt is the superintendent and the average attendance is 60. At Bachmanville, the superintendent is Thomas Geib and the attendance averages 50. Special efforts are made to bring the Sunday School officers and teachers to the highest state of efficiency by conducting Sunday School meetings or institutes. In this way the teachers are instructed in the principles of education pertaining to correct methods of teaching and to successful management of children.

This congregation is active in the temperance cause. During 1913, four temperance meetings were held, which were previously advertised in the local newspapers. The temperance committee is composed of Joseph B. Aldinger, Aaron H. Hoffer, and Eli Boozer.

A weekly prayer meeting is conducted at the homes of members, one week at the Conewago end and the following week in the vicinity of Bachmanville.

Brethren John Booser, Jos. S. Risser and Hiram Gibble constitute the missionary solicitors for 1914. Edgar M. Hoffer is the Gospel Messenger correspondent. A charter has been granted for the cemetery at the Conewago house, which is known as the "Conewago Cemetery of the Church of the Brethren."

The home and chief scene of the labors and activities of Elder George Miller and Elder William Hertzler was the territory now constituting the Conewago Church. And the work of these notable pillars in the church is a constant inspiration to the members of the Conewago congregation.

D. C. REBER.

CHAPTER XIII.

BIOGRAPHICAL.

A. GEORGE KLEIN.[1]

Elder George Klein was born in Zweibrücken, Rhenish Bavaria, South Germany, October 9, 1715, and came to America in 1738, in the ship *Glasgow,* with 384 other passengers. Walter Sterling was master of the ship. They sailed from Rotterdam, and later from Cowes, England. He landed in Philadelphia, and settled at Amwell, New Jersey.

He was married to Miss Dorothy Rebman. They are buried on a plot near where the North Kill Brethren Church was located, now owned by Percival Troutman. Here lie the remains of Elder George Klein, together with his faithful wife Dorothy, and many of his descendants— pioneers, evangelists, and missionary workers. (See Illustration.) The burial ground, graves, etc., were on the verge of destruction, when Jerome I. Kline, of Reading, Pa., and A. S. Kline, of Upper Bern, Pa., took the matter in hand and got possession of the property. Elder George Klein died January 2, 1783. His wife, Dorothy Rebman, died August 24, 1777. Common plain field stones mark their resting place. On the one are the words "Anno Jan. 2, 1783." On the opposite side is the one word, *Vater* (father). On the other stone are the words "Anno, Aug. 24, 1777." On the other side is the word *Mutter* (mother).

[1] For this sketch the committee is greatly indebted to the "Elder George Klein Association," and more especially to Prof. A. S. Kline, Upper Bern, Pa., secretary of said association.

OFFICERS OF THE ELDER GEORGE KLEIN ASSOCIATION.
President, DR. W. F. KLEIN, Lebanon, Pa.
Secretary, W. B. KLINE, merchant, Berks P. O., Pa.
Assistant Secretary, A. S. KLINE, teacher, Upper Bern, Pa.
Treasurer, NEWTON KLINE, cashier National Bank, of Pottstown, Pottstown, Pa.

Since the wife of Elder George Klein died first, no doubt he carved the inscription on his wife's grave stone, which inscription indicates that the engraver was very accurate, as the three sevens (7) are so exactly engraved that there can scarcely be seen any difference in the execution of the sevens.

Elder George Klein lived 12 years at Amwell, New Jersey, where he received his Christian training under the noted preacher Johann Naas, who fled to this place from Germany, and found at Amwell, New Jersey, a place of religious safety. Elder George Klein made visits as early as 1745 and 1747 to Berks Co., Pa., and it is supposed he had 4 more brothers in America. One settled near the boundary lines of Bucks and Montgomery counties. One of his brothers is supposed to have settled in eastern Berks Co., Pa.; one, about 4 miles west of Reading, Pa., and one, at Bernville, Pa. No doubt while being a minister, Elder George Klein visited the struggling Brethren churches as a missionary minister along the route from Amwell, New Jersey, to Bernville, Pa., where he purchased lands in 1747. He owned considerable lands near the Old Northkill Church. His trade was no doubt carpentry and turning, as his sons and grandsons were among the best turners and grain cradle makers. Some of his descendants are still following the same trades. While at Bernville, he was laboring under difficulties as this region was then settled by those of different church inclinations. There seems to have been religious dissatisfaction existing among the people, and his own members were constantly leaving for the western sections of Pennsylvania. His labors in the Christian ministry were confined to western Berks, Lebanon, and Lancaster counties.

He had six sons and one daughter. The daughter was married to Joseph Sollenberger, who took up his abode somewhere near Carlisle, Pa. His son George Klein settled near Broadway, Virginia. Here the martyred Elder John Klein, who was a great grandson of Elder George Klein, was raised. Two sons settled in Lancaster Co., Pa., and

KLEIN CEMETERY.

GRAVES OF ELDER GEORGE MILLER AND WIFE.

the other sons in Berks Co., with the exception of Joseph Klein who has not yet been located.

The descendants of Elder George Klein have built a fine wall around the graveyard, and propose to erect a suitable monument to his memory. The present resting place is on a gently sloping hill near the Northkill Church, about one and a half miles northwest of Bernville, Pa., where Elder George Klein served so faithfully. After a long and useful career in the ministry, he was gathered home into the garner of the Lord. Now the graveyard is being properly put in shape by some of his offspring.

The descendants of Elder George Klein have been diligently at work for over eight years in gathering facts to print or publish a history, and upon the completion thereof, the offspring expect to hold a reunion at the Old Northkill Church.

B. George Miller.

We have no data as to where George Miller was born, or who his ancestors were, but he united with the Church of the Brethren in 1753. He lived, and raised his family, about two miles northwest of Elizabethtown, Pa., near the Conewago Creek. It is not known when he was called to the ministry, but Morgan Edwards, in his history, says that in 1770, George Miller and Adam Hamacher were the ministers of Big Swatara. Brother Hamacher lived near Hummelstown, and the last account we have of him, either oral, or written, is 1772, and the presumption is that he died not long after.

Elder Miller was ordained Bishop, by Elders Christopher Sower and Martin Urner, in 1780, and died in 1798, aged 76 years. He is buried on his farm, by the side of his wife, who preceded him in death two years.

A fuller biography of Elder Miller, and his family, furnished by the late Elder Moses Miller, of Cumberland County, Pa., who was a grandson of Elder Geo. Miller and a great-grandson of Elder Geo. Klein, and procured for this history by Elder John Herr from the Secretary of the Elder George Klein Association follows next.

S. R. Zug.

C. Who My Ancestors Were; and What I Know about Them.

By Elder Moses Miller, of Mechanicsburg, Pa.

Having frequently been asked whether I was related to such and such a Miller family, and generally would have to say no, not to my knowledge, at least not according to flesh, and as my mother was a Kline, and many of our kindred are scattered over a number of states, it may be a great satisfaction, to some at least, to know who their ancestors were and what they were. I will here say that, both sides being German, both names have been changed, or altered; Miller was formerly written Muiller, and Kline, which some write Cline, was formerly written Klein.

First, then, my grandfather, Geo. Miller, was born in Switzerland (if I am rightly informed) in January, 1722, and emigrated to America when a boy. His father's name was Michael. Of the latter I know nothing. Grandfather settled near Elizabethtown, Lancaster County, Pa., and not far from the line between Lancaster and Dauphin counties. Here he became a member of the Church of the Brethren and also a minister in the church, his field of labor being principally in Dauphin Co., and was the first preacher in the Big Swatara Church. He would take his staff on Saturday and walk fifteen miles to the place of meeting; next day after preaching return home, and that without dinner, save a piece of dry bread by the way, frequently stopping, or visiting by the way; saying that if we stop but five or ten minutes, the Brethren can see that we have not forgotten them.

In council with the church, he would stand back so that the members should not talk after him; consequently not a great speech maker. Although he carried on farming, like many others at that time, he was also a weaver by trade, and when people brought yarn, he would hear how they wanted their work done, etc. As soon as that was said, he began to speak on the subject of religion. When some were willing and glad to hear, others said, "Yes I must go; I have not time to stay." I have also from good authority, that he had an ox stolen from him. He knew where the ox was, but lived what he preached, "If any man take away thy goods, ask them not to return them again." But his neighbors had the thief arrested, and lodged in the Lancaster jail. Being yet under the British law, he feared his neighbor would be brought to the whipping post, and pitied him very much. He also feared he might not have a bed in jail, and the weather being cold, he went to Lancaster, over twenty miles, to see, intending if he had none, he would bring him one.

He was beloved by many. One reason for this was, when he would hear anything bad about his neighbors, he would tell no one, but if he heard anything good, he would tell everybody. He died in September, 1798, aged 76 years, and 9 months, and is buried on the farm where he had lived, near the old road which leads from Hummelstown to Elizabethtown. Peace to his ashes!

He left ten children behind,—three sons and seven daughters. Abraham moved to Mifflin County, Pa., was a minister in the church, and instrumental in building the Lewistown Church. Died September 28, 1843. George was also a Brother, at one time, but moved to Erie County, Pa., where there were no Brethren. There he joined in with the Baptists, and also became a preacher of that faith. Barbara was married to Jacob Smith. Eve was married to Daniel Keefer, who was the fourth preacher in the Big Swatara Church. Elizabeth was married to Valentine Balsbaugh, fifth preacher of Big Swatara Church, who was in his ninety-seventh year when he died. He was the grandfather of C. H. Balsbaugh. This was the first preacher the writer heard. Catharine was married to George Minnich; Maria to George Fackler; Magdalena was married to Abraham Snyder. Fanny died single. My father raised fourteen children, nine sons and five daughters, myself being the youngest, and the only one who has the solemn charge upon him to watch over the flock, yet three of my brothers are deacons in the church.

Secondly, my mother's side. From manuscripts in possession of my cousin and Bro. David Kline, of Stonersville,

Berks Co., Pa., I have learned that my great-grandfather, Elder George Klein, was the first minister of the church at North Kill, now Little Swatara, the church in which our last Annual Meeting was held. He was born in Zwei-Bruicken in Germany, on the 9th of October, A.D. 1715. He emigrated to America and settled near Amwell, N. J., where he soon became acquainted with the Brethren, and was baptized to their faith in 1739, by Johann Naas, who was at that time presiding Elder at that place. He was soon after chosen an assistant in the ministry. In 1750 he removed to North Kill, on the Tulpehocken, to take charge of said Church, where he was ordained in 1757, by Elder Michael Pfautz, and Martin Urner. Of his family I know not much, but I do know that our deceased Bro. John Kline's (of Va.) grandfather was a son of this George Klein, and my mother's father was also a son of his. His name was David, and he was also a minister in what is now called Little Swatara Church. He had a number of children, nine of whom I was acquainted with. Their names were: David, Jacob, Abraham, Benjamin, Esther, Christiana, Catharine, Sally, and Elizabeth, the latter being my mother. Benjamin was also a minister in the same church as his grandfather and father were, but moved into Big Swatara Church, where he died a few years ago. Christiana was married to Joseph Merky, who was a minister and lived and died on the farm where the last Annual Meeting was held (see photograph) and where his daughter now lives. Sally was married to Lorentz Etter, who was a minister, and long a faithful servant in the Big Swatara Church.

So I have a little to glory in the flesh. One great-grandfather, two grandfathers, and at least six uncles, with a number a little further off, who ministered in holy things, though I be nothing. But I am well aware that it is written, "He that glorieth let him glory in the Lord," and again, "Let no man glory in men, etc."

I hope that many who may read this, not only those who are akin to those whose names are in this article, but even others, who were acquainted with some of those names, will rejoice with me, and my friends, for the blessed hope we can have for our ancestors, who are gone before us; for we have more inducements to meet with our friends, than if they had lived and died out of Christ, and their prayers, or some of them at least, were for us, who are now in the warfare. May we then, by God's grace, be enabled to meet not only our fathers and friends who have proved faithful, but all God's children and with them rest from our labors, and sing the glad song of deliverance in eternal bliss. Amen.

D. VALENTINE BALSBAUGH.

George Balsbaugh and his brother Peter, and brother-in-law George Henrich, came from Europe, in 1754 or 1755, and settled in Pennsylvania. George Balsbaugh and George Henry settled on the same farm, near where the town of Hershey now is, which farm was, until recently, still in the Henry name, where Valentine was born February 14, 1755. A few years later, Henry and Balsbaugh had some misunderstanding and Balsbaugh went to near where Linglestown now is, and bought a farm, and made a small payment on it (it being the farm now owned by Dr. Charles Smith). But when he came back and told his wife, she said: "I am not going there. The Indians will kill us." It was the time when the Tuscarora Indians from the valleys up the river, had been very troublesome. So he bought another on Manada Creek, about a mile east of Hanoverdale where he moved with his family, and where Valentine always lived and died. George Balsbaugh and his wife were baptized in 1763, and George Henrich and wife in 1766. Valentine was married to Elizabeth Miller, a daughter of Elder George Miller, who died in 1798, at which time Valentine was 43 years old.

We now give our conclusions after bringing together all we have on record, and the reader can take it for what he thinks it is worth. We conclude that Adam Hamacher died not long after 1772, the last we know of him; that Balsbaugh was elected a minister before Elder Miller's death; and that from that time he was the only minister in the Big Swatara settlement of members, until 1811, when George

Beshor moved in from Little Swatara, unless his son-in-law, Lorenz Etter, was elected prior to that, which is not likely.

We know that Elder Balsbaugh had three sons:—John, Henry, and Peter, and three daughters,—Elizabeth, a Mrs. Reichard and Christina. There may have been more. Peter succeeded his father on the old farm, where he was born, lived, died and is buried, and where he raised his family of five sons,—Valentine, Benjamin, Abraham, Christian H., the noted writer, and Samuel, and one daughter, Elizabeth Zortman. He was a deacon, and so were three of his sons. His wife was Elizabeth Longenecker, a granddaughter of the first Elder Christian Longenecker, of White Oak Church.

Elder Valentine Balsbaugh's father, George, died in 1802, aged 65, and the mother in 1798, aged 55, and his Uncle Peter in 1796, aged 58, all buried in Spring Creek cemetery. In his preaching he was in earnest, entering into the spirit of his subject with feeling, sometimes with weeping, thereby arousing his congregation into a feeling of sympathy, causing many to weep with him. There was a man named Fishburn, living about 5 miles away, of about the same age. When they came to be over 90 years of age, they would sometimes send greetings to each other. When he was nearly 97 years old, in 1851, one evening, he said to his son Peter that he prayed God to take him away suddenly without making trouble, and he believes that his prayer will be answered.

The next day he was repairing his chair, and in the adjoining room he was heard to hammer. Then there was a thud as of some one falling. Hastening in they found him lying on the floor, conscious, but unable to speak. All he could do was to nod, or shake his head to anything they said; and in thirty minutes he had fallen asleep. Thus ended a long, useful, and venerable life, and his remains now repose in the Balsbaugh family graveyard, and his grave is marked by a stone erected to his memory.

S. R. ZUG.

GRAVES OF ELDERS VALENTINE BALSBAUGH AND LORENZ ETTER.

GRAVES OF ELDER JACOB HOLLINGER AND WIFE (p. 518).

GRAVES OF ELDER WM. HERTZLER AND WIFE (p. 523).

GRAVE OF C. H. BALSBAUGH (p. 516).

E. Lorenz Etter.

Lorenz Etter was married to Elizabeth Balsbaugh, a daughter of Elder Valentine, and lived about a mile due northwest of his father-in-law. He was born April 2, 1787, and comes from the Etter stock, who were prominent in the church from its beginning in this country. We find the name of a "sister Eter" who was baptized prior to 1739. Again George Eder and wife in 1753, and at the general conference held in Lancaster County, in 1763, among the committee having that meeting in charge, we find the name George Etter, no doubt the same, baptized ten years before, only spelled differently. In 1770 there was a Jacob Etor living in Big Swatara, who, with his wife, were members of the church. They lived at the place where Brother Aaron Grubb now lives, with a larger scope of land to the farm, near Palmyra. It is known that the farm of over 200 acres belonged to Samuel Etter, over a hundred years ago, and after him, to his son Samuel for whom it was sold by the Sheriff, in 1859, to Geo. Tice. It is not known when Elder Etter was elected to the ministry. Neither is it known when he was ordained, but likely sometime from 1835 to 1840. He was married to his second wife, who was Sally Klein. A large portion of the Etter biography is given in connection with the history of the Big Swatara Church.

Elder Lorenz was a fluent speaker, and his services were often required on funeral occasions, far and near. He died in 1853, in his 67th year, and is buried in the Balsbaugh graveyard.

F. George Beshor.

The biography of the Beshor family (pronounced Basehore) is partly given in the history of Big Swatara Church, but we may here add that the great-grandfather of George, we are told, came from France, and settled in New York state, by his French name Jacques Milne la Baseaur. From there he, and others, came to Pennsylvania, and settled in the middle Swatara region, in 1724. He had a son Mathias who is said to have been an Indian fighter, and fond of liquor. Mathias had a son Jacob, who and his wife, we learn, were members of the church in 1770. The record of Conestoga Church informs us that in 1772, when the church district was divided, Han Jacob Beshor and George Kline were in charge of Swatara Church.

We hereto give a copy of the inscription on Elder George Beshor's grave stone.

"Hier ruhen

"Die gebeine von Georg Beshor Wird gebohren 8ten Hornung im Jahr 1775, and starb den 14ten October 1841, und brachte sein alter auf 66 Jahr 8 monat und 6 tag.

Jacob Beshor und seine Frau Christina ist eine Tochter zur welt gebohren.

Anna Maria	born	Aug 11 : 1767
Benjamin	"	Nov 16 : 1768
Christina	"	July 28 : 1770
Elizabeth	"	July 31 : 1772
Georg	"	Feb 8 : 1775
Lydia	"	Mar 14 : 1780
Michael	"	Sept 13 : 1782
Margretha	"	May 3 : 1785
Catharine	"	May 7 : 1787."

The writer has seen one of this list, Michael, when he was said to be over 90 years old, at Little Swatara. Elder George Beshor had five sons, viz.: George, John, Abraham, Daniel and Wendell; and many of the descendants of Elder Han Jacob Beshor are now active members of the Church of the Brethren.

G. Jacob Hollinger.

Elder Jacob Hollinger and wife, who was Catharine Schumacher, were both born, raised, and married in Lancaster County. In 1826 they moved to Dauphin County, west of Campbellstown. Soon afterward he was elected to the ministry. At that time the ministers of Big Swatara were Elder Valentine Balsbaugh, Lorenz Etter, and George

Beshor (pronounced Basehore). Brother Hollinger was put to work right away. The territory was large and the membership scattered, and the meetings held in houses and barns. His preaching was always in the German language.

He was a strong man, both physically and mentally. His motto was: First be sure that you are right, then persevere. He often visited and preached for the churches in adjoining counties.

He had two brothers, John and Daniel, and one sister, married to David Landis, living in southwestern Ohio. Abraham Minnich, who was also married to one of the Schumacher daughters, had a brother, and other relatives, living there; so they decided to pay them a visit. About 1840, or soon thereafter, they made the trip, and all went fairly well going out, and while visiting, but when they were getting ready to start home, intending to make the trip on horse back, Brother Minnich took sick so that he could not ride horse back. After much planning, and consultation, it was decided to sell their horses, and take the hack to where they could get a railroad that would take them east, for railroads did not go to every village then.

Elder Hollinger sold the horses and took the money and they took the hack in the evening, making some kind of a berth for Brother Minnich, Elder Hollinger, and one other man, a stranger, sitting up, and the driver on the outside. After going some distance, with the road on both sides skirted by timber, and the night very dark, the stranger took something out of his baggage, that seemed like a large knife, and with it reached out through a little ventilator hole, and rattled, as if giving a signal, whereupon the driver whipped up his team and drove like Jehu. Then turning to Hollinger, he said: "Take your leg over that way." He answered, "My leg is not in your way." Again in a harsh voice he repeated: "Take your leg that way." Upon this he thought the crisis had come, and jumped up, and ran against the door in the rear, forced it, and rolled out. By the time the vehicle had stopped, and returned, he had scrambled up, and turned into the woods. They called him, but he did not like their company, and did not answer.

He continued to walk, until he came to a hollow, which was filled with water; he pulled off his boots, and waded through some places knee deep, and so he met several ponds, until he reached an opening. Then he considered what to do next; and while he was thinking, all at once he saw a light some distance away. He started for it. When he came there it was two o'clock, and the people were getting ready to go to the Dayton market. They took him along, and there he found Minnich, safe, and the stranger of the 'bus, who approached him, and said, "Why did you run away last night." He answered him: "I think you know, and if this is the way you treat people when they come here, we would better prepare to meet such emergencies," and went across the street to a hardware store, as if to buy some weapon of defence. They took the same hack, minus the stranger, and reached home safe and well, and both lived to a ripe old age, all through life believing they had been among robbers, and that God had protected them.

He was a ready speaker, and in his preaching was emphatic, so that people could always know where he stood on any subject. The writer heard him say in his preaching that he never voted at a political election; that in fifty years he has not taken more medicine than he could bear in his eyes; and that he has never taken a penny for his services as a minister. Elder Hollinger was the grandfather of Elder Jacob H. Longenecker, of Palmyra, who has charge of Spring Creek Church, and also great-grandfather of Elder H. B. Hollinger, of near Annville, Lebanon Co., Pa.

Much of the biographies of the Etters and Hollingers is given in connection with the history of Big Swatara Church.

S. R. Zug.

H. John Zug.

John Zug was born in 1797 in Rapho Township, Lancaster County, Pa. He was the eldest son of Elder Abraham and Susanna Royer Zug and worked for his father in the tannery, and later on the farm until he was over lawful age.

He was married to Eva Margaret Lehn, and they had

eight children,—five sons and three daughters. Abraham, the oldest son, died many years ago—before his father—aged 44, leaving one son and two daughters, one of them the wife of our dear brother, Elder John Herr, of Myerstown. The second son Israel moved to Illinois, where he united with the church, but later left and united with a people called Soul Sleepers, and died at Franklin Grove, Ill. The third son, Nathan, went west, on a visit, single, and took sick and died 1854, aged 22 years. His fourth son, John, lived between Lebanon and Myerstown, where now his son Ephraim lives, on the Pike, whose brother Benjamin, now a minister, lives near Myerstown, and a daughter Lizzie lives where their father lived before he bought the pike farm. The fifth son, Reuben, lived on his father's farm near Reistville. He had five children,—one daughter, Lizzie, and a son, Morris, died single; another, Mary, was married to J. H. Gingrich, and dying, left several children. His son Lane has his father's farm, and Aaron lives in Richland. One daughter Mary died single, aged 24 years. Rebecca was married to Henry Bollinger, and died, aged 25, leaving two sons, Cyrus and Nathan, and Catharine married to David Yingst, died aged 29, leaving one daughter, Margaret, married to Samuel Royer.

Elder John Zug and his wife were baptized in 1826, and he was elected a minister in the fall of 1841, shortly after his father's death, and the same day Daniel Royer and Jacob Oberholzer as deacons. This election was held with the object in view of forming a new organization out of parts of Conestoga, White Oak and Little Swatara territory. Then in 1842, the following Elders, viz.: Jacob Pfautz, Daniel Bollinger, William Price, John Price, and David Schallenberger, met with the members of the proposed new district, and organized them into a "separate congregation under the name Tulpehocken, and that they shall now keep house, with the counsel and assistance of the Conestoga Brethren." Two years after the organization of the new church they had a large ingathering of souls, mostly young people. The writer heard Elder Zug himself say, they had meeting every Sunday somewhere, and it was never safe for him to go to a meeting without a change of clothes, for they had applicants for baptism at nearly every meeting, and sometimes quite a number.

Thus seeing the need of more workers, they had an election in 1847, and elected Daniel Royer and William Hertzler as ministers. Brother Hertzler moving away in 1851, Isaac Brubacher was called to the ministry, but he dying not long afterward, Christian Bucher was elected in 1861, and George Bucher in 1865. Thus the work was kept up in earnest as long as Elder Zug lived.

He was a very alert housekeeper, and left the church in good condition to his successor, Elder Christian Bucher, both spiritually and numerically, so that the church has since been divided, and Midway formed, and organized, of a part of it, and Elder John Herr, whose wife is a granddaughter of Elder Zug, is now in charge of both, and the membership of both together now numbers about 660.

On July 19, 1873, Elder John Zug fell asleep, at the age of 78 years, 2 months, 5 days, and his remains repose by the side of his wife, who preceded him a few years, in the Heidelberg Cemetery, there awaiting the sound of the last call on the resurrection morn, to receive the reward of their labor in life.

In disposition Elder John Zug, and his father, Elder Abraham Zug, were vastly different. The father was cautious of his words, both in public and private, weighing them well, before uttering, and in dealing with erring members, though they manifested an obstinate disposition, he had forbearance, so that on one occasion, when he was censured for being too easy, he quoted part of 2 Cor. 5, 11: "derweil wir denn wissen dasz der Herr zu fürchten ist, so fahren wir schön mit den leiten." He was reserved, with little visible difference whether in joy or sorrow, while the son, under similar circumstances, manifested the extremes, ready to speak, both in public and private; it did not take him long to show on which side of any question he was. In dealing with erring members, when penitent, he was as ready to forgive as any one, but if they were obstinate and rebellious, he soon lost sympathy. They were both honest and sincere, but being so differently constituted, they used different methods to accomplish the best results to the honor and glory of God.

S. R. Zug.

I. Philip Zeigler.

The Ziegler family is one of the Brethren families. The original Ziegler, Philip by name, was a member of the Little Swatara congregation in 1770. He was born in 1734 in Bern, Switzerland. He came to America in 1746, and before 1758 settled on the farm, on which the present Ziegler meeting house is built. A large part of his descendants have belonged to the Church of the Brethren; not a few have been ministers, some have attained to eminence.

His son Philip, born January 25, 1764, was for a time Elder of the Little Swatara congregation. Philip, Jr., married Elizabeth Smith. They lived on the old homestead. They had seven children. He lies buried in the private cemetery of the Zieglers on the Ziegler farm, but his grave is unmarked. His son Jacob was the grandfather of Elder Jesse Ziegler. His son Philip moved to Lancaster County and became the first elder of the Chiques congregation.

John Ziegler, a grandson of the original Philip, married Elizabeth Kline, moved to Rockingham County, Virginia, and became the ancestor of the Rockingham County Zieglers prominent among whom is Elder D. H. Zigler, of Broadway, Va., author of the "History of the Brethren in Virginia."

J. G. Francis.

J. William Hertzler.

Elder William Hertzler was born near Myerstown, Lebanon County, Pa., December 30, 1827. He was second of a family of sixteen children, seven sons and nine daughters, born to Jonathan and Elizabeth Royer Hertzler. His parents were Germans of that substantial type that imparted good ideals to each of their children.

William enjoyed a common school education, worked on

his father's farm till twenty-one, and then started out for himself. In 1848 he married Mary Ann Hoffer, and by this union three sons and two daughters were reared, Elder S. H. Hertzler, of Elizabethtown, Pa., being the third child of the family. In 1851 William moved upon a farm in Big Swatara congregation, about three miles from Elizabethtown, where he resided till his children were grown. In 1894, he moved to Elizabethtown, where he lived a retired life until its close.

When sixteen years old he united with the church. In 1847, when but nineteen years old, he and Daniel Royer were elected to the ministry, in the Tulpehocken Church, on the same day. In 1868 he was ordained, first to assist Elder Jacob Hollinger in the care of the Spring Creek congregation. and later he was given the full oversight, and retained it till 1895.

In 1865, he, with some others, started a Sunday School in the Conewago house. He served a number of years as superintendent, and was a strong advocate of such effort long before the Conference recognized Sunday Schools. He served for a number of years on the District Mission Board of Eastern Pennsylvania, frequently was appointed Moderator of District meeting, and served several times on Standing Committee of the General Conference. His judgment and manner of church work were so good that he was often called to visit churches in the District. He was a peacemaker, an earnest worker, and very considerate of the feelings of others.

He was a man of convictions, and was willing to maintain them, not in an overbearing, but modest, quiet way. It took good, sound reasoning to move him from his opinion, but when convinced of an error he would yield like a man, and not try to defend his error against better knowledge. If he noticed trickery or deception in any one concerning church work, he was not slow to reveal it, and in that way encountered the enmity of some who should have stood by him. When called to the ministry he was young and his mind active, so what he lacked in school, he made up in reading. He used his spare moments to read his Bible, and commit select portions to memory, rehearsing them while at work on the farm, until he had fixed them in his mind. It was his understanding with his fellow laborers, when any minister misquoted or misapplied a scripture, that the one noticing it should go to him in love and call his attention to his mistake.

His closing years were full of pain and suffering caused by cancer, which at last caused his death, February 10, 1896, in his 69th year. He is buried in Spring Creek Cemetery, where his wife was since laid by his side.

S. R. Zug.

K. John Hertzler.

Elder John Hertzler, brother of Elder William Hertzler, and son of Jonathan and Elizabeth Hertzler, was born September 10, 1826, in Jackson Township, about one mile east of Myerstown, along the Berks and Dauphin turnpike.

He was the oldest of a family of sixteen. He was married to Catharine Myer, sister of Elder Jacob Myer. They had no children. He was elected to the ministry in the Little Swatara Church in the year 1858, and ordained to the eldership April 24, 1875.

He was a man of more than ordinary intelligence. Although he had no high school education, yet he was well read, and knew his Bible well. In delivering a sermon, there was quite a contrast between the two brothers, John and William. The latter was considered as one of the most prominent and able ministers in the District, powerfully appealing to his audience with tears in his eyes, touching many a sympathetic heart. Yet some said they would rather hear John preach, who did not have that sympathetic strain, but rather used sound logic, enlightening the mind and judgment. Very little wee chaff in his sermons. Every word counted, and when he got fired up, he made the chips fly, irrespective of where they landed. His one weakness was, he was too reserved or backward. It was thought that sometimes he managed to get to meeting late, so as to avoid leading off in the services. He was a good housekeeper. Along with Little Swatara Church he also had in charge

Schuylkill Church. He died August 27, 1901, not far from Millersburg, Berks Co., and his remains were laid at rest in Frystown Cemetery.

JOHN HERR.

L. JACOB W. MEYER, SR.

Elder Jacob W. Meyer was the son of Samuel O. Meyer. He was born January 29, 1832, on the old Myer homestead, which has been in the Myer family since 1732. The present owner is the ninth generation. He was married October 28, 1853, to Sarah Wenger, daughter of Elder Jacob Wenger, who for some time was an Elder of this congregation. He was elected to the ministry April 24, 1875, advanced to 2d degree June 7, 1876, ordained to the full ministry, May 1, 1901.

He was unassuming in his manners, was much beloved by his flock, and enjoyed the high esteem and entire confidence of his neighbors and friends. He preached the old time Gospel, in an old-time way, and the audience never got tired of listening to him. It was not stuck up so high that the sheep could not reach it. The congregation could not help but feel that it was not him, but the Lord by his Holy Spirit that brought the message.

He had six children, one of whom died in infancy. All of the five were members of the church. Two of the sons —Samuel and Jacob—were elected to the ministry. Samuel was born May 21, 1857, on the old homestead. After leaving public school, spent several sessions at Millersville, and taught school seven terms. Elected to the ministry in March 1883. Married to Anna Gibble, October, 1877. Died April 19, 1884.

Thus ended the short career of this useful, talented young minister. "What I now do, thou knowest not, but shalt know hereafter."

Elder Jacob W. Myer died May 1, 1906, and was peacefully laid to rest in the family graveyard, on the old homestead.

"Though dead yet he speaketh."

JOHN HERR.

M. ABRAHAM PFAUTZ.

Abraham Pfautz, son of Jacob, son of Michael, who was the brother of Conrad, the sons of John Michael Pfautz, the first, who was born and raised in Switzerland, Europe; but a persecution drove him and others to the Palatinate. From thence he emigrated to America, and landed at Philadelphia. Here he settled, lived, died, and was buried at Germantown, near Philadelphia, Pa. His birthday, time of death, and age could not be ascertained.

Abraham Pfautz was born June 17, 1826, in Lancaster County. He was the second youngest of a family of 13. He was married to Elizabeth, a daughter of Henry Royer, of Reistville, Lebanon Co. They only had one child—a son, Jacob by name, who also is in the ministry, and an Elder in the church. They moved from one mile south of Myerstown, to Little Swatara Church about 1853. Abraham Pfautz was elected to the ministry in 1860, and ordained a few years before his death.

He was widely known in the District. Occasionally he officiated at series of meetings in various churches. The writer remembers having accompanied him on a preaching tour about 40 years ago, in York County. At that time it was the custom for two ministers to travel together, and have services morning and evening during the week.

Only one or two meetings at one house, and then proceed to the next, until the whole territory was covered. Protracted meetings were then unknown. One morning being Bro. Pfautz's time to preach, and not having much inspiration, after speaking about 15 minutes, said: "You cannot make good flour, unless you have sufficient power," and sat down. After services a Brother came forward and said: "Bro. Abe, I am a miller by trade, and if I do not have sufficient water power, to make flour, I go to work and make chicken feed. That also is of use."

The hint was well taken. Bro. Pfautz fell asleep February 2, 1906. His remains rest in Frystown Cemetery.

JOHN HERR.

N. Christian Bucher.

Christian Bucher was born November 4, 1833, on the old Bucher homestead in South Lebanon Township. He is the son of Jacob and Veronica (Brubaker) Bucher. His great-grandfather was Dr. Benedict Bucher, who was born in Switzerland in 1717. He settled on the present site of Denver Station, Lancaster County, in 1759, and died in 1787. His grandfather was also Dr. Benedict Bucher, who was father of eleven children, and died in May, 1830. Jacob Bucher, the father of Elder Christian Bucher, was born in 1807. Married Veronica Brubaker in 1830, and died in 1871. They had eight children: Lydia, Christian, Anna, Jacob, Susanna, Veronica, George, and Elizabeth.

C. Bucher, as he modestly prefers to write his name, was reared on the farm, and was educated in the public schools. He taught school from 1853 to 1861, and won the distinction of being one of the six best teachers in the county. He was afterward always concerned in getting the best of teachers for the school to which he sent his children.

In 1851 he married Eliza Dohner, daughter of John and Katharine (Smith) Dohner, of South Lebanon Township. They have had seven children, all living: Mohler and Alice, twins, the former a deacon, and farmer, the latter married to Jonas Brubaker; Allen, a minister of the Brethren, and a farmer; Esther, wife of Isaac Heagy, Clara, wife of Samuel Lentz, Ada and Amy, twins, the former wife of Monroe Keller, and the latter unmarried. All his children are members of the Church of the Brethren.

He bought the ninety-acre farm of John Funk, deceased, of Heidelberg Township, and worked it a number of years. He also did surveying and conveyancing. After some years he moved to Schaefferstown, where in partnership with Allen Mentzer he engaged in mercantile pursuits. After a time he returned to his farm. He was also appointed to superintend some iron-mining operations in the vicinity. In 1887, he left his farm in the hands of his son Mohler, and retired across the road, on a place of a few acres. Here he lived till, with his wife and unmarried daughter, he took up his home with his son-in-law, Samuel Lentz, near Midway.

Here his wife died and is buried in the Cornwall cemetery. Bro. Bucher was elected to the office of deacon June 5, 1860, at the lovefeast held at Elder John Zug's, having been baptized August 6, 1854. He was elected to the ministry June 10, 1861, at the lovefeast held on the farm of Samuel Kurtz. He was advanced September 21, 1865; and was ordained to the eldership in the Heidelberg House April 3, 1875. He had the oversight of the church, however, two years before his ordination.

As a preacher Bro. Bucher was much in demand. He brought things new and old out of the treasury of God's word. To listen to him was to learn something. He was liked none the less for hewing close to the line. When called to the ministry, he was impressed with the responsibility of being a watchman, and ever strove to warn of danger. His blunt way of putting things made him enemies. He was ever anxious to keep his hands from being tied. He was used very much at funerals, not only at home, but also in adjoining churches. He preached 728 funeral sermons that he had jotted down; some were sure to have escaped unrecorded.

He became known at home as a very efficient housekeeper. He was also much used away from home to adjust difficulties. He served on the following committees to churches: To Philadelphia in 1875; to carry out Art. 16 in 1879; to Ephrata in 1880; to Sandbrook, N. J., in 1880; to Amwell, N. J., in 1881; to Berlin Church, Pa., in 1881; to Amwell, N. J., in 1883. A number of times he was elected by District Meeting on the Standing Committee.

He figured largely at our District Meetings, and also to some extent at our Annual Meetings. One of his hardest lessons to learn was, that when decisions were made contrary to his way of thinking, to submit to them. This weakness could be less overcome, in his declining years, and he lost courage, became dissatisfied with many of his co-Elders in the District, and became inactive in church work.

JOHN HERR.

PART IX.

MISSIONARY GROUP.

CHAPTER I.

PEACH BLOSSOM CHURCH.

In September, 1875, Brother S. C. Rittenhouse and family moved to Talbot County, Maryland, from Ohio. Also his father, Elder Joseph Rittenhouse and his wife came with them. Early in the spring of 1876, Elder Rittenhouse began to preach in a schoolhouse near Easton, Maryland, services being held every two weeks. A Sunday School was opened and held every Sunday with good attendance. One was baptized that summer. On account of his wife's health Brother Joseph and his wife returned to Ohio that fall. Shortly after that time Brother N. C. Rittenhouse and family, a brother to S. C., also moved from Ohio.

In March, 1877, Joseph D. Wingard, a deacon, and family moved in from Ohio. These members who had come in up to this time, six in number, presented their letters of membership to Pipe Creek Church, Maryland, the ministers of which church preached for them at intervals until 1880. During that time a union meeting house was built at the river called the Peach Blossom.[1]

Elder William Hertzler and J. T. Myers, of Pennsylvania, came and preached in the new house, October 16, 1881. They at this time organized the Peach Blossom Church. Brother J. D. Wingard was elected to the ministry, and S. C. Rittenhouse was elected deacon. During these meetings ten were baptized. The Peach Blossom house was built by four denominations: Methodist, Reformed, Lu-

[1] It is said the first peach tree in Maryland was planted near this stream; hence the name.

UNION CHURCH, TALBOT COUNTY, MARYLAND.
WHERE THE BRETHREN FIRST PREACHED ON THE EASTERN SHORE.

theran, Swedenborg and the Brethren. Each denomination was to have services every fourth Sunday. But as the others did not have services regularly the Brethren soon had preaching every two weeks.

February, 1882, Caleb Secrist and family—a minister in the second degree—moved here from Kansas.

October 13, 1883, Brother Francis Schwaninger, one of the ten baptized at the organization, was elected to the office of deacon.

In 1885, Joseph Longanecker and family came here from Western Shore of Maryland.

In 1887, Brother Daniel Geib and family moved here from Lebanon County, Pennsylvania.

Also in same year, Brother H. E. Sanger and family, a deacon, came from West Virginia.

In 1888, a dividing line was fixed between this and the Ridgely congregation by a joint committee representing both congregations and locating the same as follows: Beginning at Federalsburg, Dorchester County, running direct to the mouth of Tuckahoe Creek; thence up the creek to Hillsboro bridge; thence by the public road to Centreville, Queen Anne County.

In fall of 1891, Brother James A. Hutchison, a minister in second degree, and family moved in from West Virginia.

The Fairview Meeting House, near Cordova, was built in 1893 and dedicated December 24, of same year. Seating capacity 300 or more. Estimated cost $2,000.

August 30, 1894, Brother Aaron Royer was elected deacon.

In 1896, Brother Allen A. Oberlin, a minister in second degree, and family moved here from Indiana. A Sunday-School was organized at Fairview House, March 18, 1897, with Brother Oberlin as superintendent. August, 1897, J. Roy Rittenhouse was elected deacon.

In 1898, Elder Isaac Barto moved here from Pennsylvania, and shortly afterward took charge of the church. About this time the church passed from under the District Mission Board, under whose care it had been up until this time. April 11, 1901, Elder Barto resigned, and Elder

J. Y. King of the Ridgely Church took charge, which position be held until his death in November, 1906. Following Elder King's death the oversight of the church passed to our present Elder in charge in 1907, Elder S. K. Fike, who with his family moved here from Garrett County, Maryland, in April, 1906.

In 1897, with aid from the Mission Board, a house of worship was built for the colored people, a number of whom had united with the church.

September 19, 1902, a building was purchased, in Easton, which after remodelling was dedicated as a house of worship on September 13, 1903. Seating capacity about 225. Finished cost for house and lot about $2,000.

November 1, 1902, Wm. E. Sanger was elected a deacon. One of our deacons, Brother A. H. Royer, moved to Pennsylvania. May 21, 1904, Brethren F. H. Rittenhouse and M. J. Hutchison were elected deacons. April 2, 1908, W. F. Snively, a deacon, and family moved in from Ohio. On September 3, 1908, Wm. E. Sanger was elected to the ministry and advanced to second degree September 1, 1910. On September 5, 1912, Brother O. S. Miller was elected a deacon. November 23, 1912, during a series of meetings nine were baptized, all Sunday-school scholars.

On December 31, 1912, the membership numbered 85: 1 Elder, 3 ministers in second degree and 7 deacons.

In closing we feel inclined to make special mention of our indebtedness to the Mission Board of Eastern Pennsylvania for their interest and care and financial assistance in building church houses, during the earlier years of our history. And we acknowledge the care and grace of our Father above, and feel that a more earnest purpose and a stronger missionary spirit obtain at this time with our little band than ever before.

Caleb Secrist, Wm. E. Sanger.

CHAPTER II.

RIDGELY CHURCH.[1]

The official record of the organization of the Ridgely Church is as follows: "Ridgely, Caroline County, Maryland, August 2, 1884. The Ridgely Church, Caroline County, Maryland, was this day organized, (with the understanding that they, with the Peach Blossom Church, decide what the line shall be between them, before long), with Conrad Imler as their minister, being in the second degree, and Geo. Brumbaugh and Jos. D. Snowberger as deacons.

The private members now living here are: Elizabeth Brumbaugh, Peter Bechtel, David S. Stayer, Trusanna Stayer, Mat. McDaniel, Sister McDaniel, Sarah Catharine Imler, Susan Imler, Annie Bechtel, Alex. Dasher, Hannah Smith, Hannah Snowberger, Levi R. Brumbaugh, D. B. Stayer, Barbara Stayer, C. O. Biddle, Babara Biddle, Annie Ober, Agnes Blackburn."

(See Part X, Chapter IV.) *"Missionary History,"*— for history *Eastern Shore of Maryland Mission.*

This organization was effected at the Boonsboro Schoolhouse near Ridgely, with the following Elders present: Solomon Stoner and Geo. Hoover in behalf of the District of Eastern Maryland; William Hertzler and S. R. Zug in in behalf of the District of Eastern Pennsylvania. The Elders organized by electing Elder Stoner, Moderator of the meeting, and Elder Zug, Clerk. The Elders decided that the members composing this new congregation should decide by vote, their preference as to which state district they would belong. The vote was as follows: 15 for Eastern Pennsylvania, 3 nays, 1 neutral.

At the first council held October 24, 1884, Brother Matthew McDaniel was appointed clerk, and Brother Jos.

---

[1] I am indebted to Elder T. F. Imler for much information contained in this sketch.

Snowberger treasurer, and decided that the love-feast and communion service shall be held at the home of C. H. Imler, and adopted the single mode of feet washing. The two deacons were appointed a committee to look up a location for a church building and cemetery, and on January 31, 1885, submitted two locations, but neither was accepted by the congregation. Some time later, ground was secured near the schoolhouse, where the organization was effected, and afterwards a frame church building was erected thereon, 40 × 40 feet, and a 14 foot ceiling.

On July 27, 1889, a second house was ordered built, size 36 by 40 feet, the former to be known as the Boonsboro, and the latter as the Bethel house.

Officials Received by Letter.—The work of the Brethren on the Eastern Shore is largely the result of emigration in the earlier years, and the first members there had all emigrated. On April 23, 1885, the certificate of Elder J. Y. King and wife was received, and Brother King became the assistant to Elder William Hertzler, who had charge since the organization. Other officials were received as follows: December 29, 1896, Elder Geo. S. Rairigh; March 20, 1897, William Shimer, deacon; March 29, 1899, Benjamin Stewart, deacon; September 27, 1899, D. R. Heddings, deacon; March 28, 1900, Brother Levi Spicher, deacon; March 29, 1905, J. H. Beer, Elder, and Milan H. Spiker, minister in second degree; September 27, 1905, E. F. Clark, a minister in the second degree, and O. P. Pherson, deacon; March 28, 1906, Edward Steel and George Steel, deacons; August, 1907, Elder T. F. Imler; May 12, 1908, J. W. Arnold, deacon; July 14, 1909, Solomon Longenecker, deacon; September 20, 1909, A. R. Kitchen, a minister in the second degree.

Elections.—November 1, 1890, L. R. Brumbaugh was elected to the ministry, and D. B. Stayer and D. K. Crouse, deacons. August 26, 1897, L. R. Brumbaugh was advanced. July 4, 1902, John P. Holsinger and Aaron C. Reber were elected deacons. March 30, 1904, Milton F. King and Harry R. Holsinger were elected deacons. January 16, 1911, Levi K. Ziegler was elected to the ministry.

RIDGELY BRETHREN CHURCH (INTERIOR).

On October 22, 1909, the Ridgely Church was divided by an Elder from an adjoining state district. The irregularities of this move were called to the attention of District Meeting, and after careful consideration a committee of three Elders was appointed to go to Maryland, and investigate the case. The Committee met the members of the former Ridgely Church in joint session, May 3, 1910. After a long and careful investigation the committee pronounced the work illegal, because of the irregularities, but recognizing the fact that conditions seem to make a division desirable, proceeded in a regular way to divide the Church, the one part retaining the name Ridgely, and the other being called Denton. Each part accepted the decision of the committee. The Ridgely Church had about 150 members before the division, and the line of division was so fixed as to divide the membership about equally.

The new Ridgely Church is fully organized and active in all the church auxiliaries, Sunday School, prayermeeting, Christian Workers, missionary and temperance committees, and efficient work is done. The following have been Elders in charge of Ridgely: William Hertzler, J. Y. King, Geo. S. Rairigh, S. K. Fike, T. F. Imler, the latter being the present Elder.

On November 11–12, 1914, the Annual Ministerial Sunday School, and Missionary Meeting was held in the Ridgely Church.

Note.—The Denton Church without being released by the Eastern District of Penna., made application to be received into the Eastern District of Maryland and was received by that district. See Minutes of District Meeting, 1913.

CHAPTER III.

BROOKLYN CHURCH.

Mission Work in Greater New York City.—The beginning of mission work by the Church of the Brethren in Greater New York City dates back to the year of 1892. Several of Brother Hope's converts of Malmö, Sweden, came to America and making this city their home appealed to the General Mission Board for services. Pastor T. T. Myers, of Philadelphia, Pa., was empowered by the Board to come here and conduct the first services. He baptized several young people and as the outlook for a Mission seemed hopeful, the General Board took steps to open a Mission by appointing Brother J. Kurtz Miller and wife to pioneer the work.

It is worthy of mention that Sister Alice Boone rendered valuable assistance in work amongst the children for a year or so. The first Sunday School was opened April 2, 1897. Also Bro. J. Edson Ulery and wife who succeeded Sister Boone gave much valuable services to the Mission work in its early struggle. The Mission Church was organized October 4, 1899, consisting of five brethren and five sisters. This organization was effected by the General Mission Board. On account of failing health, Brother Ulery withdrew from the work in the fall of 1901 and Bro. J. Kurtz Miller then took full charge of the Mission, November 24, 1901.

At the Harrisburg (Pa.) Conference (1902) Bro. Miller made a strong plea before the Mission Board to take definite steps toward building a Mission Home and Church. The Board granted him the privilege to solicit funds to this end. By January 10, 1905, he had sufficient funds to buy a plot of ground 66 × 100, for which he paid $4,300, spot cash. At the Springfield (Ill.) Conference (1906) he presented plans for the proposed Mission buildings which were adopted by

BROOKLYN BRETHREN CHURCH.

the Mission Board. Brother Miller threw all the "Caleb blood" that he possessed into the good cause, and after having many, "never-to-be-forgotten-experiences," he broke ground for the Mission buildings on April 29, 1908. Seven months later the buildings were dedicated, on November 29, 1908. It is worthy of note that this was our Bi-Centennial year, and was a worthy event in a great year for us as a Brotherhood. The General Mission Board was represented at the dedication in the person of Charles D. Bonsack who with a number of ministers from adjoining congregations took part in the dedicatory services. The Mission Church property was dedicated free of debt and Bro. Miller had $400 (left over after all obligations were met) which he turned over to the General Mission Board for World Wide Mission work.

At the day of the dedication the Mission Church numbered thirty members but doubled its membership by a year later. At this writing (1913) the membership is 115, with a growing Sunday School numbering (in all departments) about 275. The Italian Sunday School numbers about 150 in addition to the English school. The Italian Mission is one of the activities of the Brooklyn Church.

Ministers elected so far in the Brooklyn Church were: D. C. Reber (1902), M. B. Miller (1904), J. H. Hollinger (1906), John G. Caruso (1907), A. M. Dixon (1909), A. P. Geib (1910). Ministers advanced to the second degree: J. E. Ulery (1899), M. B. Miller and D. W. Kurtz (1906), G. C. Myers (1910), A. P. Geib (1911).

Ministers ordained: J. Kurtz Miller (1903) by Elders S. R. Zug and F. P. Cassel. M. B. Miller was ordained (1912) by Elders J. Kurtz Miller and P. B. Fitzwater. The ordination of A. P. Geib is proposed and ratified by the Elders of the southeastern Pennsylvania, New Jersey and New York Conference.

PAUL ROBERT MILLER.

The foregoing account of the Brooklyn Church may be supplemented with additional data gleaned from various sources.

The first systematic work done by the General Mission

Board to open a mission in Brooklyn was the appointment of Sister Alice J. Boone on February 8, 1897. She was assisted by T. T. Myers in organizing the above-mentioned Sunday School, which consisted of twelve scholars at the beginning. During the same summer, the General Mission Board sent Bro. Christian Hope to Brooklyn to help establish a mission. He remained only two months, baptized one, and held the first communion with seven members. In August, 1897, the Board recalled Bro. Hope to the west, asked Sister Boone to visit the churches to raise a fund for more aggressive work and closed the work till the next spring. Then Bro. J. Kurtz Miller was appointed to the work but he declined to accept on account of wishing to complete his preparation for city mission work.

Sister Boone withdrew from the work in the spring of 1899, and in June of that year J. Edson Ulery and wife assumed charge. In October following, Elders S. F. Sanger and A. B. Barnhart representing the Board, organized the congregation known as "The First Church of the Brethren" in Brooklyn. Elder George S. Rairigh of Maryland was chosen bishop and he had the oversight of this church, until the ordination of J. Kurtz Miller in 1903. The other officials were: J. Edson Ulery who was now advanced to the second degree of the ministry; and Ephraim Strayer, deacon. The names of the charter members are: J. Edson Ulery, Sylvia Ulery, Ephraim Strayer, Hannah Strayer, Lewis B. Flohr, Anna E. Flohr, Mrs. Goff, Agnes Texiere, Anna Gran, Martin Texiere, Jacob Texiere.

In September, 1900, Lewis B. Flohr was elected to the office of deacon at the time Bro. Adam Eby and wife, and Eliza Miller first sailed for India. In February, 1900, Sister Elizabeth Grater came to assist Bro. and Sister Ulery in the Mission. In September, 1901, Bro. and Sister Ulery left Brooklyn Church to enter other fields of church activity. Bro. J. K. Miller was then invited to become the pastor again and accepted, preaching his first sermon, November 29, 1901. Beginning with 1901, D. C. Reber was elected treasurer of the church and assisted in the Sunday School and other forms of church work until June, 1902. In the early struggles of the work in Brooklyn, two attempts were made to have the Eastern District of Pennsylvania take supervision of the newly organized congregation, viz.: in Feb. 1900, and in Sept., 1903, but they were unsuccessful.

Sister Grater withdrew from the mission work in the summer of 1902 and was succeeded by Sister Elizabeth Howe. Sister Howe did several years' earnest and effective work here. Other assistants to Bro. Miller in the work were: Sister J. Kurtz Miller, Sister L. Margaret Haas, Amos P. Geib, and Densie Hollinger.

John Caruso, an Italian, united with the church in 1900 and immediately dedicated his heart to the service of the Lord. His zeal and effort, seconded by the Board, resulted in opening a mission at 207 21st Street, Brooklyn. Sunday School was carried on here and up to this time about 30 Italians have been received into the church by baptism including a number of Bro. Caruso's relatives. Bro. Caruso sacrificed time and money for the success of the Italian Mission, and was called to the ministry in 1907. He is still loyal and active in the work.

The mission under Sister Boone was opened in South Brooklyn on 52d St between 2d and 3d Avenues. During her stay, it was moved to the corner of 3d Ave. and 60th St. While Bro. Ulery had charge, it was changed to the corner of 3d Ave. and 59th St. As above stated, to Elder J. Kurtz Miller the Brooklyn Church and the Brotherhood at large is in a great measure indebted for his efforts in devising ways and means for the erection of the present commodious church and parsonage located at 354 60th St.

The committee on plans which also served as building committee consisted of Chas. D. Bonsack, J. Kurtz Miller and M. B. Miller. The total cost of ground, church and parsonage was $29,300. This has been truly a church home not only for the members residing in the city but also for members coming into the city on short visits or for study in New York City. It has been a resting and waiting place for outgoing and returning missionaries while in New York. In 1911, the new state district known as Southeastern Pennsylvania, New Jersey and New York, was formed and the

Brooklyn Church with its large field was transferred to the care of the mission board of this district, May 31, 1912. The present officials are: Elder J. Kurtz Miller, Elder-in-charge; Elder A. P. Geib, minister; deacons, Ephraim Strayer, Benjamin Biershing, J. C. Maugans, Martin Texiere, and Horace Gould.

Besides the preaching services and two Sunday Schools, the Brooklyn Church has a Sewing Circle, Prayer Meeting, Christian Workers' Meeting, and a Missionary Committee. On January 25, 1914, Elder J. G. Royer, of Mount Morris, Ill., began a series of evangelistic services in this congregation. A. P. Geib was ordained to the eldership in 1914.

D. C. REBER.

PART X.

MISCELLANEOUS.

CHAPTER I.

ANNUAL MEETINGS.

A. Those Held in Eastern Pennsylvania.

There were eighteen yearly meetings, or more properly, general conferences, held in Eastern Pennsylvania, since the Brethren were first organized into churches in America that we know of. If the conference of 1742, held presumably in the Coventry Church, was "The beginning of Annual Meeting," as is stated in Brumbach's "History," page 490, we must infer that there were such conferences every year. Might it not have been the custom for some time after that date that, when a church had a case, or a trouble that, after repeated efforts, they could not adjust, and threatened to disrupt the church, and scatter the members, for some of the elders who were aware of the case, to call for a general conference to meet in the church where the trouble was? If it was from the beginning held every year, then it was east of the Susquehanna River, often, of which we have no record.

After twenty-one years from the first such conference, namely on May 27 and 28, 1763, there was such a conference held in the Conestoga Church, which, at that time, embraced all of Lancaster, Dauphin, Lebanon, and part of Berks counties. We have no record to show on whose farm it was held, but pointers indicate it was on the farm of Christian Longenecker, several miles west of Manheim. A full account of the minutes, and names of its signers, is given under the head of "White Oak Church."

By reference to Brumbach's "History," page 503, we have the first intimation of another great meeting, but no place or minute given, but the year was 1775. In 1777 in Conestoga Church, Lancaster County, Pa.

From this time on, if not before, it seems these meetings were annual, but of quite a number it is not known, where held, or the work done, up to about 1830, since which we have the report pretty full. In 1779 it was in Conestoga Church.

The next Big Meeting as called in those days, in Eastern Pennsylvania, was in 1780, and another in 1781, both in Conestoga, and another in 1785 and in the same church, two again in 1788 and 1789; and in 1790, at the home of John Bach, in Coventry, and again in Coventry Church, in 1813, probably again at the home of John Bach, as before. In 1815, the conference was in White Oak Church, on the farm of Joseph Hershey, between Manheim and Junction.

The following letter, translated from the German, has never been printed, and would be of interest to some. The letter was addressed to this meeting.

Morrison's Cove, April 9, 1815.

Heartily much beloved Brethren in council of the Great Meeting.
We, the Brethren in Morrison's Cove, wish to you, with all fellow members in your vicinities, much grace, love and peace from God the Father, and our Savior Jesus Christ, with the comforting communion of the Holy Spirit, to a life and conversation devoted to God so that we may together be faithful professors, and true followers of Jesus Christ, so long as we are yet here in the Church Militant, who hold fast to the once known and confessed truth, so that we may walk in one Spirit and mind of the Truth of the Glorious Gospel, to the end, Amen!

The reason of our writing is this: Because we noticed that there is not that oneness of Spirit according to the Truth, prevailing among you, for we hear there is a disturbance among you, on account of the New Mennonites, that you have too much fellowship with them, contrary to the resolution passed at the council meeting at Conecocheague, not to have any fellowship with them, because they introduce doctrines, and confess that which is not according to the Gospel, so that we in our

PLACE OF ANNUAL MEETING, 1815.
FARM THEN OWNED BY BROTHER JOSEPH HERSHE.

PLACE OF ANNUAL MEETING, 1820.
Joseph Royer Farm.

churches in Morrison's Cove have no fellowship with them, and with such as have, we cannot break bread, because the calling is so much in our time, lo here is Christ, and lo there—Oh, how needful it is for us to hold fast to God from our heart, that He, by His Spirit, may lead us in all truth, as Christ has promised!

We wish for you, beloved Brethren, light and grace, wisdom and prudence, you and us, that we may, with our mind's eyes, look unto Jesus, the Author and Finisher of our faith, and to the advice of Paul, "as ye have received Christ, so walk ye in him," and be grounded in him. For if, we, in oneness of mind and belief, hold fast to the teachings of Christ, and live and walk in love and peace, and union of the Spirit of Christ, according to God's counsel and will, we will depart, and keep ourselves free from all strange spirits and their deceptions.

Therefore the Lord speaks by the prophet Jeremiah (15, 19): "If thou hold thyself to me, so will I hold myself to thee, and thou shalt be my preacher, and if thou teach the righteous to be separate from the wicked, thou shalt be my teacher, and before thou shalt fall to them, they must come to thee" [Lit. from Ger.]

It is our well meaning advice to you, beloved Brethren, to warn you from harm, while they teach that the word of God is a dead word, but Christ says that "the words that I speak are Spirit and Life," and the Apostle writes to the Hebrews: "The word of God is quick and sharper than any two edged sword, etc.," and John writes: "Many spirits are gone out, judge the spirits whether they be of God," and if we shall judge the spirits, we must necessarily judge them by the word, and not by their magnificent speeches.

For many shall come in that day, and say, have we not prophesied in thy name, cast out devils, and done many works, but the answer to them was, depart from me, I know not whence ye are.

Further, beloved fellow members, we commend you heartily unto God and the word of His grace. So much from us weak pilgrims and fellow travellers to the heavenly Fatherland.

       CONRAD BRUMBACH,
       SAMUEL ULRICH,
       CHRISTIAN HUBER,
       MICHAEL ETTER,
       JOHANNES HOLSINGER.

The action of the meeting on this letter is lengthy and can be found in the minutes, published in 1909, page 38.

The Great Meeting held in Eastern Pennsylvania was in Conestoga Church, on the farm of Joseph Royer, in 1820. In 1827, at the home of Daniel Schumacher, in White Oak, formerly the Andreas Eby farm, now S. G. Summy; in 1831, in Conestoga Church; in 1846, in Conestoga Church, at the home of John Royer, on Trout Creek.

In another place of this work will be given a full account of this meeting, taken from a diary of brother A. H. Cassel, who was an eye witness.

The next meeting in Eastern Pennsylvania was on the farm of John E. Merkey, later his son Joseph, in Little Swatara Church in Berks County, in 1871. The next was at Harrisburg in 1902.

SUMMARIZED.

Year.	Church District.	Place.
1742	Coventry	Probably Martin Urner.
1763	Conestoga (now White Oak)	Probably Christ. Longenecker.
1780	Conestoga (now White Oak)	Unknown.
1781	Conestoga (now White Oak)	Unknown.
1788	Conestoga (now White Oak)	Unknown.
1789	Conestoga (now White Oak)	Unknown.
1790	Coventry	John Bach.
1813	Coventry	John Bach.
1815	White Oak	Joseph Hershe.
1820	Conestoga	Joseph Royer.
1827	White Oak	Daniel Schumacher.
1831	Conestoga	Unknown.
1846	Conestoga	John Royer.
1871	Little Swatara	John E. Merkey.
1902	Harrisburg	Paxtang Park.

Standing Committees of the aforesaid meetings, so far as known, were as follows:

1742. Unknown.

1763. Jacob Myer, Peter Dirdorf, Martin Urner, Nicholas Martin, Lorenz Shrab, Henry Naff, George Schreiber, Christopher Saur, George Etter, Joseph Reutsh, Jacob Stutzman. John Schlipfer, Jacob Mohr, Mattes Schweitzer, Henry Raudenbush, Gideon Rausser, Daniel Letterman, Daniel Arnold, Anton Hartman, Sander Mack, Nicholas Letterman, Stephen Ulrich.

1780. Unknown.
1781. Unknown.
1788. Unknown.

PLACE OF ANNUAL MEETING, 1827.
DANIEL SCHUMACHER FARM.

PLACE OF ANNUAL MEETING, 1816.
JOHN ROYER FARM. (See p. 568.)

1789. Daniel Letterman, Martin Urner, Jacob Danner, Heinrich Danner, Jacob Stoll, Johannes Funk, Heinrich Naff, Conrad Brumbach, Nathaniel Schreiber, Daniel Utz, Andreas Eby, Samuel Gerber Herman Blässer, Jacob Läshet, Abraham Oberholzer.

1790. George Preiss, Martin Myer, Michael Frantz, Daniel Bollinger, John Landes, Christian Lawshe, Justus Frichs, Martin Gaby, Peter Keyser, Sander Mack, Nathaniel Schreiber, David Kuntze, Martin Urner, Peter Leibert, Jacob Boeshor, Jacob Danner, Abraham Lawshe.

1813. Unknown.

1815. Johannes Zug, (?) George Price, Samuel Gerber, Jacob Stoll, Herman Blässer, Nicholas Martin, Daniel Stober, George Petry, Daniel Gerber, Benjamin Beshor, Michael Schlothauer, Valentine Balsbach, John Price, Johannes Eby, Andreas Mayer.

1820. Unknown.
1827. Unknown.
1831. Unknown.

1846. David Pfautz, George Hoke, Jacob Pfautz, Christian Long, John Bowman, Daniel Bollinger, Andrew Spanogle, Peter Nead, Dan Miller, Dan Bernhart, Jacob Fahrney, John Funk, Peter Long, Dan Fretz, John Price, John H. Umstad, James H. Tracey, David Shallenberger, Henry Kurtz.

1871. John Zug, Moses Miller, John Wise, D. P. Saylor, David Long, Peter Crumpacker, Solomon Garber, Martin Cossner, David Derrick, F. W. Dove, D. J. Peck, John P. Ebersole, H. D. Davy, J. Miller, Jacob Karns, George Hoover, D. Fry, John Metzger, John Harshey, Benjamin Beeghly, James Quinter.

1902. Tennessee, North Carolina, Florida, S. J. Bowman; First District of Virginia, T. C. Denton, D. A. Naff; Second District of Virginia, Daniel Hays; First District of West Virginia, Jeremiah Thomas; Eastern Maryland, E. W. Stoner; Middle Maryland, Absalom Mellott; Western Maryland, W. T. Sines; Eastern Pennsylvania, J. H. Longenecker; Southern Pennsylvania, Isaac Barto; Middle Pennsylvania, T. B. Maddocks; Western Pennsylvania, Jos. Holsopple; Southern Ohio, J. C. Bright; Northeastern Ohio, Samuel Sprankle; Northwestern Ohio, C. L. Wilkins; Southern Indiana, L. T. Holsinger; Middle Indiana, Daniel Snell; Northern Indiana, W. R. Deeter; Northern Illinois and Wisconsin, C. P. Roland; Southern Illinois, S. W. Garber, J. C. Stoner; Southern Missouri, Northwestern Arkansas, C. Holderman; Middle Missouri, E. E. John; Northern Missouri, L. H. Eby; First Arkansas and Southeastern Missouri, J. H. Neher; Southern Iowa, C. M. Brower; Middle Iowa, F. M. Wheeler; Northern Iowa, Southern Minnesota and South Dakota, A. P. Blough; North Dakota and Northern Minnesota, Levi Mohler; Michigan, Isaiah Rairigh; Nebraska, Uriah Shick; Northeastern Kansas, George Manon; Southeastern Kansas, M. O. Hodgden; Northwestern Kansas and Northern Colorado, C. S. Holsinger; Southwestern Kansas, Southern Colorado and Northwestern Oklahoma, M. Keller; Texas and Southwestern Louisiana, Jos. Minix; Oklahoma and Indian Territory, Samuel Edgecomb; Oregon, Washington and Idaho, George Wise; Denmark, D. L. Miller; Sweden, A. B. Barnhart; First District of India, W. B. Stover; D. L. Miller, Moderator; L. T. Holsinger, Reading Clerk; L. H. Eby and W. B. Stover, Writing Clerks; Wm. Oberholzer, Doorkeeper.

B. Those Held Elsewhere.

We have now given about all that we have at hand concerning Annual Meetings, held east of the Susquehanna River. We shall now proceed to give what we have of those held by the Brethren elsewhere, south and west. We regret very much that we cannot give a full account of them all. From 1742 to 1763 we have no account of any General Conference held anywhere—a space of twenty-one years—and from that time to 1775, again twelve years, we have no data. From 1775 we have no record of any Big Meeting till 1778, but from that time on we have reason to believe that the meeting was held annually; prior to that, probably only when called to consider special work, which could not be adjusted by the home church.

All we know of the 1775 conference is from a letter written by Elder A. Mack to John Price, dated March 11, 1775, in which he says: "I have duly received thy dear little letter, but I cannot know yet if I shall be able to come to the next Great Meeting. I have been speaking to Brother Christopher Sower, to ask if he meant to go. He then had no mind to go, but if I should succeed to persuade him I

ANNUAL MEETINGS.

would gladly stay home myself this time, according to the body, but according to the spirit I would be there in heartfelt love and well wishing. But if it should happen that he insists on his refusal to go, and if it should be convenient for me to go, I would first like to have his own, and the Brethren's consent before starting on the journey," etc.[1]

It would seem from this letter that the meeting was to be held at some point remote from Germantown, which would make the trip quite a task. Following will be a list of Annual Meetings, outside of Eastern Pennsylvania, the year when, the place where, and the names of Standing Committee, where we have them, omitting the minutes, which would make a book in itself.

1778. Pipe Creek, Md.
1779. Conewago, York Co., Pa.
1782. Place unknown.
1783. Pipe Creek, Md.
1785. Big Conewago, Pa. Jacob Saur, Valentine Pressel, Michael Bosserman, Martin Reinhart, David Studebaker, Peter Dirdorf, Martin Urner, Jacob Stoll, Christian Longenecker, Henry Neff, Lorenz Beckner, Philip Lewig.
1793. Conewago, York Co., Pa. Standing Committee unknown.
1794. Shenandoah, Va. Unknown.
1797. Blackwater, Va. Unknown.
1798. Conewago, York Co., Pa. Unknown.
1799. Pipe Creek, Md. Martin Urner, Martin Gaby, Henry Danner, Peter Leibert, Jacob Danner, Philip Engler, Michael Pfoutz, Martin Garber, Daniel Utz, Philip Levy, Valentine Pressel, Stephen Ulrich.
1800. Place unknown, also Standing Committee.
1803. Place unknown. The minute says: " Signed by most of those who signed in 1799."
1804. Pipe Creek, Md. Standing Committee unknown.
1805. Place and Standing Committee unknown.
1810. Antietam, Franklin Co., Pa. Heinrich Danner, Wilhelm Stober, David Long, Martin Gerber, Johannes ———, Peter Keyser, Nicholas Martin, Herman Blässer, Christian Long, Mathias Schneider, Jacob Künsel, Christian Huber, George Preis, Daniel Stober.

[1] Brumbaugh, " History," p. 503.

1812. Place and Standing Committee unknown.

1814. Pipe Creek, Md. Samuel Garber, Benjamin Bowman, George Preis, Daniel Stober, Nicholas Martin, Jacob Beshor, Samuel Arnold, Martin Garber, David Pfautz, John Eby, Christian Long, John Schleifer, Daniel Long, Daniel Garber, Michael Etter, Henry Gibbel, Herman Blässer, George Petry, Daniel Arnold, David Albaugh, John Diel, Jacob Shenefelt, John Price, Isaac Long.

1817. Place or Standing Committee unknown.

1818. Place or Standing Committee unknown.

1819. Conewago, York Co., Pa. Daniel Stober, Christian Long, Jacob Mohler, Benjamin Bauman, Samuel Arnold, Daniel Gerber, Daniel Seiler, Johannes Glück, Abraham Gerber, Johannes Gerber, Michael Pfautz, David Engler, Jacob Price, Johannes Stauffer, Benjamin Eby, John Trümmer, Heinrich Lescher, Peter Aschenbach, Henry Etter, David Vogelsanger, Jacob Hollinger, Frederick Klein, Daniel Jund, Philip Engler, Daniel Reichardt.

1821. Glade, Somerset Co., Pa. Standing Committee unknown.

1822. Canton, Ohio. Standing Committee unknown.

1825. D. Mohlers. Cumberland Co., Pa. Standing Committee unknown.

1826. Daniel Reichard, Washington Co., Md. Michael Myer, Daniel Gerber, Samuel Arnold, Johannes Flory, Christian Long, Daniel Bollinger, Johannes Gerber, George Brumbaugh, Daniel Seiler, Nicholas Martin, Johannes Brumbaugh, Daniel Arnold.

1828. Bro. Gungles, York Co., Pa. Standing Committee unknown.

1829. Geo. Royer, Antietam, Franklin Co., Pa.

1830. Pipe Creek, Md. Unknown.

1832. Rockingham Co., Va. Unknown.

1833. Lost Creek, Juniata Co., Pa. Unknown.

1834. Stark Co., Ohio. Unknown.

1835. Cumberland Co., Pa. Unknown.

1836. Cumberland Co., Pa. Unknown.

1837. Linville Creek, Rockingham Co., Va. Daniel Gerber, David Pfoutz, George Hoke, John Gerber, Jacob Holsinger, David Engler, Sr., Abraham Yundt, John Funk, John Brower, Christian Johnson, Jacob Pfautz, Daniel Arnold, Christ. Long, John Price, John Royer, Lorenz Etter, John Fahrney, John Beeghly.

1839. Huntingdon Co., Pa. Standing Committee unknown.

1840. Morrison's Cove, Bedford Co., Pa. Daniel Gerber, David Pfoutz, Daniel Arnold, Jacob Holsinger, Christian Long, George Hoke, John Price, Abm. Yundt, Daniel Reichard, Michel Dickey, Peter Kober, Isaac Shoemaker, Henry Kurtz.

1841. Somerset Co., Ohio. (Wm. Miller's.) Daniel Gerber, David Pfoutz, Christian Long, Daniel Arnold, George Hoke, Abraham Yundt, John Hart, John Price, Daniel Reichard, Henry Kurtz.

1842. Beaver Dam, Md. Daniel Gerber, Christian Long, John Beeghly, John Price, Dan Bollinger, David Pfoutz, Jacob Pfoutz, Christian Janson, David Ecker, John Sprogle, George Hoke, Jacob Long, And. Spanogle, John Gerber, James Tracey, Henry Kurtz.

1843. Mohican Church, Wayne Co., Ohio. George Hoke, John Brower, John Hart, George Shively, Henry Metzger, Joseph Showalter, Isaac Beery, John Cable, Daniel Miller, John Shoemaker, James Tracey, Henry Kurtz.

1844. Peter Deardorf, Conewago, York Co., Pa. David Pfoutz, Christian Long, John Price, And. Spanogle, of Pennsylvania; George Hoke, George Shively, Henry Kurtz, of Ohio; John Bowman, Benjamin Bowman, Daniel Miller, of Virginia, John Gerber, Jacob Long, of Maryland; and the following other Brethren; Peter Nead, John Mineely, Peter Long, John H. Umstad, Jacob Pfoutz, Jacob Brubacher.

1845. Daniel Barnhart, Roanoke Co., Va. George Shively, Abraham Crumpacker, Peter Frantz, John Bowman, Benjamin Bowman, Daniel Barnhart, Peter Miller, Peter Nead, Christian Bowman, Samuel Garber, Austin Hylton, John Gerber, John Kline, Henry Kurtz.

1845. Special Annual Meeting in Indiana. By reference to the minutes of 1845, as published in 1909, pages 87 and 88, we find that there was a special general conference held that year, on September 26 and 27, in Elkhart County, Ind., in which query 6 was relative to admitting such as are not members, in our church council. We know of no record of any other business of that meeting, and believe it was probably of a local character.

Prior to 1849 the general conference did not work by committees in local churches, since which date there was no special general conference held, but prior to that, frequently.

1846. A special conference was held in Tennessee, September 4, at meeting-house near Jos. Bowman's, in Washington Co.

1847. Isaac Deardorf, Franklin Co., Pa. David Pfoutz, John Price, George Hoke, Daniel Bollinger, Jacob Holsinger, Jacob Pfoutz, John Funk, Jacob Fahrney, John Molsbaugh, Philip Boyle, Samuel Miller, David Hartman, John H. Umstad.

1848. This year there were two general conferences held; the first, June 12, in Wayne Co., Ohio, at Jac. Kurtz's. Standing Committee—George Hoke, Joseph Gerber, John Hart, Henry Kurtz, Philip Boyle, Peter Nead, John Kline, ———— ————, James H. Tracey, Michael Moyer, John Metzger, John Molsbaugh, George Shively, Joseph Showalter, Benjamin Bowman, John Shoemaker, George Rarigh, John H. Umstad, Jacob Myer, ———— ————, David Shoemaker, Daniel Miller, John Shively, John Holsinger. The other was held September 23–25, at the house of Bro. John Koontz, near Delphi, Carroll Co., Indiana. Standing Committee—George Hoke, George Shively, Joseph Showalter, Henry Kurtz, of Northeastern Ohio; Joseph Gerber, Peter Nead, of Southwestern Ohio; Dan. Cripe, of Elkhart, Indiana; J. Molsbaugh, D. Miller, J. Hart, H. Metzger, J. Metzger, Jac. Brower, etc.

1849. Somerset Co., Pa. George Hoke, J. Showalter, Henry Kurtz, Peter Nead, A. Spanogle, J. Molsbaugh, Peter Long, John Kline, Jacob Sayler, Samuel Wampler, Peter Kober, Jacob Meyer, Daniel Yundt, George Shafer, John Holsinger, J. Stutzman, D. Shoemaker, Jos. Arnold, Thos. Clarke.

1850. Bear Creek, Montgomery Co., Ohio. George Hoke, Peter Nead, James Tracey, Samuel Gerber, Joseph Gerber, John Brower, Benjamin Bowman, Daniel Yundt, Daniel Barnhardt. Other Elders, Jacob Miller, George Hoover, David Hartman, John Myer, J. Leatherman, John Shively, Henry Neff, John Hart, Jos. Harter, David Miller.

1851. New Hope, Augusta Co., Va. George Hoke, John Bowman, John Leatherman, Christian Longenecker, John Kline, D. P. Saylor, Dan. Brower, James H. Tracey, Jacob Meyer, Henry Kurtz.

1852. Turkey Creek, Elkhart Co., Ind., June 1. George Hoke, George Shively, Jos. Emmert, John Kline, Dan. Barnhart, D. P. Sayler, Ben Bowman, D. Miller, H. Kurtz.

1853. Beaver Dam, Md. George Hoke, Daniel Miller, Elias Dickey, of Ohio, Benjamin Bowman, David Miller, of Indiana, Joseph Emmert, of Illinois, Ben. Bowman, John Kline, of Virginia, Christ. Longenecker, Peter Long, of Pennsylvania, Jacob Leatherman, Jacob Sayler, of Maryland, Henry Kurtz, Clerk.

ANNUAL MEETINGS.

1854. Ashland Co., Ohio. (Elias Dickey's.) For Ohio, George Hoke, George Shively; for Virginia, John Kline, Joseph Arnold; for Maryland, Philip Boyle, Dan. P. Sayler; for Pennsylvania, Christ. Longenecker, John Berkley; for Indiana, Jacob Miller, George Hoover; for Illinois, Joseph Emmert, Christian Long.

1855. Aughwick, Huntingdon Co., Pa. For Ohio, George Hoke, John Molsbaugh; for Indiana, J. Leatherman, John Metzgar; for Illinois, Daniel Fry; for Virginia, John Kline, Daniel Brower; for Maryland, D. P. Sayler, George Bear; for Pennsylvania, Daniel Bollinger, J. H. Umstad, John Berkley, Andrew Spanogle; Henry Kurtz, Clerk, James Quinter, Assistant Clerk.

1856. Waddams Grove, Stephenson Co., Ill. George Hoke, George Shively, Jacob Long, John Leatherman, Peter Nead, James Tracey, Joseph Emmert, John Berkley, Andrew Spanogle, John Kline, Joseph Arnold, Daniel Miller.

1857. Manor Church, Washington Co., Md., May 31. John H. Umstad, Andrew Spanogle, John Wine, Christ. Keefer, Abraham Neff, J. P. Ebersole, George Hoke, John Metzger, Abraham Moss, Jos. Emmert, Samuel Gerber.

1858. Bachelor Run Church, Carroll Co., Ind. George Hoke, John Brower, Peter Nead, Daniel Miller, of Ohio, John Berkley, of Pennsylvania, John Kline, Peter Nininger, of Virginia, Isaac Pfoutz, of Maryland, John Moyer, George Shively, John Metzger, of Indiana, John Emmert, of Illinois.

1859. Elk Creek Church, Somerset Co., Pa. For Virginia, John Kline, Jacob Thomas; for Maryland, D. P. Sayler, Isaac Pfoutz; for Ohio, J. P. Ebersole, H. D. Davy, James Quinter; for Indiana, Jacob Miller, John Metzger; for Illinois, Samuel Layman, David Rittenhouse; for Pennsylvania, J. H. Umstad, Peter Long, John Berkley. D. P. Sayler, Moderator, D. P. Sayler and J. Quinter, Clerks.

1860. Lime Stone Church, Washington Co., Tenn. For Ohio, Peter Nead, J. P. Ebersole; for Maryland, Henry Koontz, D. P. Sayler; for Virginia, John Kline, Daniel Barnhart, Abraham Neff, Peter Nininger; for Indiana, John Metzger; for Illinois, Christian Long; D. P. Sayler, Moderator; D. P. Sayler and J. Quinter, Clerks.

1861. Beaver Creek Church, Rockingham Co., Va. Joseph Arnold, Geo. Shaver, P. Crumpacker, Martin Miller, Dan. Miller. John Kline, Moderator; B. F. Moomaw, Clerk.

1862. Erbaugh Church, Montgomery Co., Ohio. John

Berkley, John Zug, of Pennsylvania; D. P. Sayler, Maryland; John Kline, John Wine, Virginia; John Brower, Henry Kurtz, Joseph Showalter, Ohio; John Metzger, Jacob Miller, Indiana; Sam. Garber, Dan. Sturgis, of Illinois; John Brower, Kansas; John Ogg, Minnesota; Abraham Replogle, Iowa. J. Kline, Mod.; D. P. Sayler, J. Quinter, Clerks.

1863. Clover Creek Church, Blair Co., Pa. Virginia, John Wine, John Kline, Moderator; Maryland, D. P. Sayler; Illinois, Sam. Layman, Christian Long; Pennsylvania, And. Spanogle, Isaac Meyer, John Holsinger; Ohio, H. D. Davy, Daniel Miller; Indiana, John Metzger, F. P. Loehr; Iowa, David Brower; H. Kurtz, James Quinter, Clerks.

1864. Hagerstown Church, Wayne Co., Ind. For Virginia, John Kline, John Wine; for Maryland, D. P. Sayler; for Pennsylvania, Leonard Furry, D. Gerlach; for Ohio, H. D. Davy, James Quinter; for Indiana, John Bowman, Daniel Bowman, David Miller; for Illinois, Sam. Gerber, Christian Long; for Iowa, Jacob Brower; for Kansas, John Bower.

1865 Rock River Church, Lee Co., Ill. For Maryland, D. P Sayler; for Virginia, Joseph Arnold; for Pennsylvania, John Wise, J. R Hanawalt; for Ohio, Peter Nead, H. D. Davy; for Indiana, Jacob Miller, Hiel Hamilton; for Illinois, Isham Gibson, John Metzger; for Michigan, F. P. Loehr; for Iowa, David Brower; for Kansas, John Bower; H. D. Davy, Moderator; James Quinter, Clerk.

1866. Antietam Church, Franklin Co., Pa. For Pennsylvania, Daniel Keller, John Wise; for Ohio, H. D. Davy, J. P. Ebersole; for Maryland, Christian Keefer, Henry Koontz; for Virginia, John Wine, Daniel Thomas; Jacob Miller, Jno. Knisely, of Indiana; for Illinois, C. Long, S. Gerber; for Tennessee, D. Derrich; H. D. Davy, Moderator.

1867. Pipe Creek Church, Md. For Ohio, Joseph Riser, H. D. Davy, James Quinter; for Indiana, Dav. Miller, Jac. Metzger, Jesse Meyers; for Illinois, Christ. Long, John Fitz; for Pennsylvania, Peter Long, And. Miller, John Holsinger; for Virginia, P. Crumpacker, Dan. Thomas, John Wine; for Iowa, David Rittenhouse, John Murray; for Michigan, F. P. Loehr; for Maryland, Henry Koontz, Isaac Pfoutz, D. P. Sayler; H. D. Davy, Moderator; J. Quinter, D. P. Sayler, Clerks; J. Weybright, Doorkeeper.

1868. Jacob Berkey, Elkhart Co., Ind., June 23. J. P. Ebersole, Daniel Miller, H. D. Davy, James Quinter, B. F. Moomaw, Daniel Thomas, Jacob Wine, D. P. Sayler, Isaac

Pfoutz, David Long, C. G. Lint, D. M. Holsinger, Joseph Rohrer, David Bechtelheimer, Jacob Miller, Dan. Bowman, F. P. Loehr, C. Long, John Metzger, Sam. Layman, J. Wise, Jacob Brower, A. Replogle, H. Brubaker, H. Kurtz, Peter Nead.

1869. Peters Creek Church, Roanoke Co., Va. Abm. Neff, John Wine, Peter Nead, J. P. Ebersole, H. D. Davy, Robert H. Miller, Jacob Flory, Jacob Berkey, John Metzger, Sam. Layman, D. Brower, E. K. Buechly, John Wise, Grabill Meyers, David Gerlach, Isaac Pfoutz, D. P. Sayler, Dav. Long, A. Malsby, F. W. Dove, James Quinter.

1870. Waterloo, Black Hawk Co., Iowa, June 7–9. J. D. Trostle, D. Long, D. Gerlach, Isaac Myers, John Wise, H. D. Davy, D. Brower, D. J. Peck, F. P. Loehr, P. Nininger, Jacob Wine, J. Quinter, Christ. Wenger, Jacob Metzger, Hiel Hamilton, E. Eby, M. Sissler, John Metzger, Jac. Hauger, G. R. Baker, A. Replogle, G. Witwer, Wm. Gish.

1872. Wayne County, Ohio. H. D. Davy, Jacob Garver, John Brown, D. B. Sturgis, Jacob Metzger, R. H. Miller, S. Layman, John Metzger, E. K. Beeghly, Christian Long, Daniel Zook, William Gish, Sam. Mohler, A. Malsby, Abe Naff, Solomon Garber, Martin Cosner, D. Long, D. P. Sayler, Jacob Riner, J. R. Hanawalt, J. Wine and J. Quinter.

1873. Myersdale, Pa., June 2–4. Henry Garst, B. F. Moomaw, S. Garver, M. Cosner, D. P. Saylor, D. Long, D. Gerlach, Jacob Price, John Wise, H. D. Davy, John Brillhart, Jacob Garver, D. B. Sturgis, John Baker, Jos. McCarty, E. Eby, John Metzger, Henry Strickler, Rob. Badger, C. Harader, J. Quinter.

1874. Macoupin Co., Ill. Henry Swadley, B. F. Moomaw, Martin Cosner, D. P. Sayler, D. Long, D. Gerlach, J. Myers, Jas. Quinter, Jacob Garver, J. P. Ebersole, H. D. Davy, J. Lichty, George Long, D. B. Sturgis, Jacob Flory, R. H. Miller, D. Rittenhouse, Rufus Gish, David Wolf, E. K. Beeghly, C. Long, C. Harader, G. Witwer, J. Hershey, Jesse Studebaker, Enoch Eby.

1875. Covington, Ohio, at Brother Cassel's, May 17. A. H. Senseney, Em. Slifer, Wm. Hertzler, Jos. R. Hanawalt, J. Quinter, H. B. Hylton, Jacob Wine, Elias Auvil, Jacob Garber, J. P. Ebersole, H. D. Davy, D. B. Sturgis, Jesse Meyers, Hiel Hamilton, Enoch Eby, John Metzger, James R. Gish, Tobias Musser, C. Long, J. Brower, S. S. Mohler, Sam. Stump, Isaac Miller, J. W. Brumbaugh.

1876. De Graff, Logan Co., Ohio, June 5-7. D. P. Sayler, D. Long, Samuel Harley, Moses Miller, J. Quinter, E. Fleshman, Isaac Long, D. B. Arnold, Geo. Irvin, J. Brown, H. D. Davy, M. Shotts, J Flory, R. H. Miller, E. Eby, D. E. Price, J. Metzger, Joseph Ogg, Abm. Stamy, Daniel Zook, Wm. Gish, Isaac Miller.

1877. New Enterprise, Pa., May 21-23. Jonathan Lichty, G. R. Baker, J. A. Murray, E. Eby, D. E. Price, J. R. Gish, D. B. Sturgis, J. S. Snowberger, R. H. Miller, Moses T. Bare, S. Garber, Jos. Kauffman, John B. Mishler, Henry Swadley, Samuel A. Fike, J. H. Lemon, Solomon Garber, John Wise, J. Quinter, S. Harley, D. Long, D. P. Sayler, J. D. Trostle.

1878. North Manchester, Ind., June 10-12. S. Harley, Moses Miller, C. G. Lint, D. K. Sayler, Jer. Beeghly, C. Wertz, Martin Garber, D. B. Arnold, Elias Auvil, Geo. Irvin, J. P. Ebersole, Samuel Garber, John Knisely, David Neff, R. H. Miller, Enoch Eby, J. R. Gish, Joseph Hendricks, J. F. Ikenberry, R. Badger, D. D. Sell, John Hershey, Jonathan Lichty, Isaac Miller; Enoch Eby, Moderator; J. Quinter, Writing Clerk; R. H. Miller, Reading Clerk; S. R. Zug, Doorkeeper.

1879. Broadway, Va., June 2-4. And. Hutchinson, Michael Sisler, E. K. Bueghly, Edm. Forney, Jos. Hendricks, J. R. Gish, Jesse Calvert, Jos. Amick, R. H. Miller, Isaac Miller, J. P. Ebersole, S. Z. Sharp, Abm. Flory, Mark Minser, Moses Miller, C. Bucher, E. Auvil, Sol. Buckalew, J. H. Lemon, Isaac Long, Jac Thomas, Jos. Wine, David Long; R. H. Miller, Moderator; J. Quinter, Writing Clerk; E. Eby, Reading Clerk; Wm. Hertzler, Doorkeeper.

1880. Lanark, Ill., June 1-3. C. Bucher, J. Quinter, L. Kimmel, D. P. Sayler, D. Long, P. Nininger, J. H. Lemon, J. Thomas, P. J. Brown, J. P. Ebersole, J. Kauffman, J. Calvert, R. H. Miller, D. Bechtelheimer, E. Eby, D. Deardorf, J. Wise, J. S. Snyder, J. Thomas, C. C. Root, S. S. Mohler, J. Lichty, M. T. Bare, I. Miller, J. Berkey; E. Eby, Moderator; J. Quinter, Writing Clerk; J. Wise, Reading Clerk; J. Flory, Doorkeeper.

1881. Ashland, Ohio, June 6-8. J. S. Flory, C. C. Root, R. Badger, E. Forney, J. Rife, D. Sturgis, R. H. Miller, C. G. Lint, S. Harley, J. D. Trostle, D. B. Arnold, J. H. Lemon, Isaac Miller, A. Hutchinson, J. Thomas, E. Eby, J. Wise, D. E. Wolfe, D. Brower, Jos. Kauffman, Moses Miller, D. P. Sayler, D. Stouffer, Isaac Long, C. Bowman, D. Hays; E. Eby, Moderator; J. Quinter, Writing Clerk; J. Wise, Reading Clerk; S. Myers, Doorkeeper.

1882. Arnolds, Kosciusko Co., Ind., May 29–31. Jesse Crosswhite, Joel Naff, John Eller, D. Baker, D. B. Arnold, J. Reiff, Joseph Leedy, Jere Gump, Isaac Miller, D. E. Price, D. P. Sayler, D. Long, Nich. Martin, C. Bucher, J. Quinter, J. I. Cover, G. Irwin, J. C. McMullen, Jos. Kauffman, G. W. Studebaker, D. Vaniman, J. Wise, S. S. Mohler, S. A. Honberger, John Thomas, M. Sisler, A. Hutchison, Henry Brubaker, L. Hillery, J. Forney. Officers same as 1881, except John S. Holsinger for Doorkeeper.

1883. Bismark Grove, Douglas Co., Kan., May 11–13. Abm. Molsbee, B. F. Moomaw, Jacob Thomas, Samuel Myers, S. A. Fike, J. D. Trostle, David Long, C. Bucher, James Quinter, J. S. Holsinger, Noah Longenecker, R. H. Miller, J. C. McMullen, John Smith, Jacob Reiff, W. R. Deeter, John Brillhart, Daniel Deardorf, John Wise, T. D. Lyon, Geo. Bollinger, G. Barnhart, C. C. Root, Isaac Barto, W. Wyland, John Earley, D. Bechtelheimer, W. Gish, M. T. Baer, G. W. Fesler; Moderator, Enoch Eby; Writing Clerk, James Quinter; Reading Clerk, John Wise; Doorkeeper, J. S. Flory.

1884. Miller's Crossing, near Dayton, O., May 30, etc. Eli Renner, John Forney, M. Sisler, W. B. Sell, D. Vaniman, D. E. Price, J. H. Miller, Hiel Hamilton, L. H. Dickey, C. G. Lint, J. Quinter, David Long, S. Buckalew, B. F. Moomaw, H. Garst, Sydney Hodgen, D. Bechtelheimer, S. Flory, S. S. Mohler, Edm. Forney, E. Bosserman, R. H. Miller, Jacob Garber, N. Longenecker, S. Harley, G. Leatherman, Isaac Long, J. W. Eller, D. D. Derrick; Enoch Eby, Moderator; J. Quinter, Writing Clerk; John Wise, Reading Clerk.

1885. Mexico, Juniata Co., Pa., May 22, etc. Samuel Molsby, J. S. Holsinger, M. J. McClure, J. Crosswhite, Sam. Garver, P. E. Whitmore, John Eller, J. C. McMullen, Isaac Barto, Daniel Hays, J. N. Kauffman, Rob. Badger, Jacob Thomas, J. W. Metzger, H. P. Strickler, D. B. Arnold, R. Fisher, J. S. Snowberger, Sol. Stoner, W. R. Deeter, J. D. Trostle, John Brindle, E. Bosserman, M. M. Eshelman, Wm. Hertzler, G. D. Zoller, J. S. Mohler, J. F. Oller, Daniel Deardorf, John Wise; John Wise, Moderator; J. Quinter, Writing Clerk; W. R. Deeter, Reading Clerk.

1886. Pittsburg, Darke Co., O., June 11, etc. Hen. Brubaker, J. R. Gish, Wm. Howe, John Hollinger D. Vaniman, S. Harley, Wm. Davis, I. Billhimer, D. R Sayler, Wm. Wyland, David Neff, C. Cassel, S. S. Mohler, Jere Gump, Asa Harman, C. C. Root, Isaac Miller, Daniel Hays, John Thomas, L.

H. Dickey, John B. Naff, S. M. Goghenour, David Young, Dan. Peters, S. H. Miller, John Smith, G. C. Bowman, D. E. Price, C. G. Lint; D. E. Price, Moderator; D. Hays, Writing Clerk; D. Vaniman, Reading Clerk; John Flory, Doorkeeper.

1887. Ottawa, Kans., May 27, etc. Standing Committee: F. W. Dove, J. D. Trostle, Jacob Thomas, Isaac Barto, Sol. Buckalew, Geo. Barnhart, David Long, Enoch Eby, James Quinter, M. M. Eshleman, I. D. Parker, B. F. Mommaw, Jesse Stutzman, S. H. Myers, L. W. Teeter, E. W. Stoner, Edmund Forney, Wm. Hertzler, M. J. McClure, J. C. Johnson, S. M. Loose, J. H. Miller, R. H. Miller, J. R. Gish, Daniel Chambers, D. E. Brubaker, S. B. Shirkey, C. Holdeman, J. E. Hilkey, B. F. Flory; Enoch Eby, Moderator; M. J. McClure, Writing Clerk; R. H. Miller, Reading Clerk; Samuel Driver, Doorkeeper.

1888. North Manchester, Ind., May 18, etc. Isaac Studebaker, J. G. Royer, Lemuel Hillery, David Eby, George Myers, Benj. Fryfogle, George Stambaugh, Peter Long, C. C. Root, Daniel Snell, Fred. Culp, Wm. Harshberger, J. S. Gable, Landon West, A. M. Dickey, L. H. Dickey, Marcus Fowler, D. N. Workman, Thos. D. Lyon, J. Holsinger, C. L. Pfoutz, C. Bucher, N. Martin, W. Franklin, Jonas Graybill, Jacob Thomas, J. W. Eller, D. B. Arnold, Geo. C. Bowman, C. Hope; Enoch Eby, Moderator; J. G. Royer, Writing Clerk; D. N. Workman, Reading Clerk; S. S. Mohler, Doorkeeper.

1889. Harrisonburg, Va., June 7, etc. John Brubaker, Jesse Stutzman, Samuel Flory, J. W. Eller, N. Longenecker, S. B. Shirkey, Isaac Long, L. H. Dickey, S. S. Mohler, S. H. Myers, L. W. Teeter, W. M. Harvey, D. B. Arnold, J. W. Wright, John Wise, Geo. Leatherman, A. B. Peters, J. A. Root, S. Stoner, E. Bosserman, J. Hollinger, D. F. Stouffer, D. B. Gibson, B. F. Flory, S. R. Zug, Dan. Deardorf, M. M. Bashor, Jac. Hollinger, J. F. Ikenberry, J. S. Flory, Val. Blough, Steph. Johnson, C. Hope; S. S. Mohler, Moderator; J. G. Royer, Writing Clerk; John Wise, Reading Clerk; Enoch Eby, Doorkeeper.

1890. Pertle Springs, Johnson Co., Mo., May 23, etc. S. S. Barklow, W. R. Deeter, J. S. Flory, David Neff, B. B. Whitmer, L. T. Holsinger, John Forney, John Smith, Enoch Eby, S. Driver, D. Bechtelheimer, I. D. Parker, S. H. Miller, Hiram Musselman, J. S. Snyder, Wm. Howe, Hiram Berkman, C. Bucher, W. B. Sell, David Long, A. Hutchison, Uriah Bixler, C. Holdeman, John B. Naff, Geo. W. Cripe, Jonas Graybill, S. Buckalew, Daniel Hayes, D. E. Price, Aaron Fike,

Dan. Chambers, J. B. Bowman, C. Hope; Enoch Eby, Moderator; J. G. Royer, Writing Clerk; John Wise, Reading Clerk.

1891. Hagerstown, Md., June 2, etc. M. M. Bashor, Thos. D. Lyon, William Hertzler, Daniel Vaniman, D. L. Miller, Jere. Beeghly J. Ikenberry, Isaiah Rairigh, E. A. Brunner, J. S. Mohler, J. H. Miller, D. R. Sayler, John Gable, Jacob Rife, D. J. Miller, John Zuck, R. H. Miller, John C. Frantz, John Early, John Smith, Isaac Long, J. E. Ellenberger, J. C. Whitmore, S. H. Myers, Jac. C. Whitmore, George Worst, Jonas Graybill, Samuel Click, J. C. Johnson, Geo. C. Bowman, M. J. McClure, J. F. Oller; Daniel Vaniman, Moderator; D. L. Miller, Writing Clerk; M. J. McClure, Reading Clerk.

1892. Cedar Rapids, Iowa, June 2, etc. G. C. Bowman, Steph. Johnson, Robert Goshorn, Daniel Peters, J. J. Hoover, J. C. Murray, Geo. S. Arnold, B. B. Whitmer, E. Forney, D. F. Stouffer, John Wise, David Troxel, James A. Sell, I. M. Gibble, David Bowman, Edward Loomis, D. L. Miller, Samuel Flory, I. J. Rosenberger, John B. Naff, J. W. Trostle, Jacob S. Snell, Daniel Hays, Wm. Davis, Isaac Rairigh, E. W. Stoner, J. H. Neher, D. B. Eby, S. R. Zug, Henry Brubaker, C. Holdeman, J. C. Johnson, Samuel Barklow, Chas. H. Brown, L. H. Dickey; Daniel Vaniman, Moderator; D. L. Miller, Writing Clerk; M. J. McClure, Reading Clerk.

1893. Muncie, Ind., May 23, etc. Sydney Hodgden, Samuel Edgecomb, Frank McCune, J. S. Flory, J. S. Mohler, John Gable, Jac. Appleman, Uriah Shick, S. B. Shirkey, John Wise, Isaiah Rairich, M. T. Bear, C. S. Holsinger, W. G. Cook, W. M. Harvey, John Harshberger, N. Longenecker, Samuel H. Utz, D. E. Price, Henry Frantz, Jere. Thomas, Geo. D. Zoller, J. S. Holsinger, D. J. Miller, W. R. Deeter, H. B. Brumbaugh, P. S. Miller, D. P. Shively, Jacob Hollinger, S. F. Sanger, L. W. Teeter, C. Bucher, J. P. Zeigler, S. A. Walker, David Long, J. G. Royer; D. E. Price, Moderator; J. G. Royer, Writing Clerk; John Wise, Reading Clerk.

1894. Myersdale, Pa., May 29, etc. John W. Eller, Tobias Kreider, S. M. Miller, W. H. Naff, Samuel Sprankle, John Zuck, Levi A. Wenger, L. H. Dickey, Abm. Wolf, D. B. Arnold, Wm. Harshberger, I. F. Rairigh, W. A. Gaunt, D. Bechtelheimer, S. M. Forney, E. W. Stoner, A. H. Puterbaugh, Geo. E. Wise, G. K. Sappington, S. Buckalew, Chas. M. Yearout, S. A. Miller, Jos. Amick, B. B. Whitmer, F. P. Cassel, J. H. Moore, Enoch Eby, C. L. Pfoutz, J. Rufus Gish, Abm. Molsbee, H. B. Brumbaugh, M. T. Bear, John Metzger, David

Hildebrand, G. W. Clemens, L. W. Teeter; Enoch Eby, Moderator; J. H. Moore, Writing Clerk; L. W. Teeter, Reading Clerk.

1895. Decatur, Ill., June 4, etc. D. L. Miller, S. B. Shirkey, C. G. Lint, P. S. Myers, Fred. Culp, Jas. A. Sell, A. W. Austin, C. Holdeman, E. D. Book, Jacob Whitmore, Sol. Buckalew, C. Bucher, John Hollinger, M. J. McClure, D. F. Stouffer, W. B. Sell, D. B. Eby, Ed. S. Brunner, I. H. Crist, J. H. Miller, Z. Annon, Owen Peters, S. Leckrone, T. S. Fike, Daniel Chambers D. F. Hoover, L. A. Wenger, J. A. Murray, Christ. Krabill, S. F. Sanger, J. W. Diehl, F. B. Weimer, G. W. Hutchison, John Gable, Henry Frantz, C. H. Diehl; Enoch Eby, Moderator; D. L. Miller, Writing Clerk; M. J. McClure, Reading Clerk.

1896. Ottawa, Kans. Henry Sheets, W K. Simmons, John M. Follis, W. H. Naff, Tobias Hoover, Stephen Johnson, P. S. Miller, L. H. Dickey, Harvey Ikenberry, J. P. Zigler, G. L. Studebaker, Isaiah Rairigh, G. S. Arnold, S. S. Ullery, J. L. Snavely, E. W. Stoner, I. D. Parker, Archy Vandyke, S. H. Utz, D. E. Price, W. B. Sell, Eli Yourtee, P. R. Keltner, C. S. Holsinger, F. P. Cassel, D. B. Gibson, John Wise, Jas. Hollinger, Geo. Barnhart, M. M. Ennis, Jas. A. Sell, D. M. Mohler, J. W. Metzger, G. S. Rairigh, J. E. Ellenberger, C. Hope; D. E. Price, Moderator; I. D. Parker, Writing Clerk; D. L. Miller, Reading Clerk.

1897. Frederick, Md., June 8, etc. G. E. Studebaker, D. B. Eby, S. R. Zug, John Wertz, Henry Martin, Nich. Martin, S. Hodgden, J H. Miller, W. S. Reichard, J. D. Trostle, Dorsey Hodgden, Sol. Stoner, Isaac Rairigh, L W. Teeter, Z. Annon, J. E. Ralston, S. M. Loose, B. W. Smith, J. D. Haughtelin, Edw. Loomis, Daniel Hays, L. M. Kob, Hen. Frantz, J. P. Zigler, D. Hildebrand, Jasper Barnthouse, P. S. Miller, D. M. Mohler, H. B. Brumbaugh, G. C. Bowman, C. Holdeman, John Lehner, J. H. Moore, Conrad Fitz; L. W. Teeter, Moderator; J. H. Moore, Writing Clerk; D. Hays, Reading Clerk.

1898. Burlington Park, Napierville, Ill., May 31, etc. John Brubaker, Henry Keller, S. H. Miller, W. H. Naff, C. L. Wilkins, J. C. Seibert, S. Crumpacker, J. W. Rarick, Dan. Chambers, L. A. Wenger, J. H. Wright, S. M. Forney, Jere. Thomas, W. R. Deeter, Wm. Davis, G. W. Annon, P. R. Keltner, Caleb Fogle, G. K. Sappington, S. Buckalew, S. L. Myers, Eli Yourtee, M. Flory, Michael Keller, J. H. Longenecker, F. W. Dove, A. Molsbee, E. D. Book, M. T. Bear, S.

Edgecomb, S. J. Swigart, J. E. Ellenberger, A. Hutchison, W. A. Gaunt, John P. Bailey, D. L. Miller, J. C. Bright, G. A. Shamberger; W. R. Deeter, Moderator; D. L. Miller, Writing Clerk; P. R. Keltner, Reading Clerk; G. N. Falkenstein, Doorkeeper.

1899. Roanoke, Va., May 23, etc. C. Hope, John Zuck, W. K. Simmons, John Bonewitz, C. M. Brower, Jas. A. Sell, J. S. Flory, G. W. Ellenberger, Jac. Hollinger, A. W. Austin, David Bowman, J. Y. King, J. A. Miller, Henry Brubaker, I. W. Abernathy, Enoch Eby, M. J. McClure, A. B. Barnhart, I. S. Lerew, J. H. Baker, Thomas J. Kolb, W. B. Sell, I. B. Trout, D. J. Miller, Geo. F. Wise, A. H. Puterbaugh, G. S. Arnold, J. B. Moore, L. T. Holsinger, J. P. Zigler, S. M. Smith, D. C. Campbell, D. A. Naff, J. L. Thomas, L. H. Dickey, J. B. Pence, O. J. Beaver, H. M. Shutt; L. T. Holsinger, Moderator; J. H. Moore, A. H. Puterbaugh, Writing Clerks; I. B. Trout, Reading Clerk.

1900. North Manchester, Ind., June 5, etc. Jos. B. Bowman, C. L. Wilkins, Jos. Myer, P. S. Miller, L. W. Teeter, I. F. Rairigh, W. H. Naff, J. H. Wright, A. D. Sollenberger, Daniel Hays, J. C. Murray, R. A. Yoder, Jere. Thomas, D. E. Price, E. M. Wolf, Albert Hollinger, C. P. Rowland, L. E. Keltner, W. S. Reichard, John Arnold, A. F. Miller, S. K. Fike, Samuel Weimer, J. F. Neher, John Herr, G. W. Lentz, J. Appleman, Wm. C. Koontz, S. B. Shirky, P. S. Myers, H. B. Brumbaugh, J. H. Neher, Geo. C. Carl, Jasper Barnthouse, John P. Bailey, D. L. Miller, J. C. Bright, S. M. Gochenour, S. R. Zug, N. Longenecker, Harvey Eikenberry; D. L. Miller, Moderator; Daniel Hays, H. B. Brumbaugh, Writing Clerks; L. W. Teeter, Reading Clerk; David Hollinger, Doorkeeper.

1901. Lincoln, Neb., May 28, etc. Daniel Vaniman, John Zuck, Tobias Hoover, Thos. Barklow, J. M. Follis, I. J. Rosenberger, Stephen Yoder, B. E. Kesler, C. G. Lint, N. S. Cripe, J. E. Shamberger, W. J Swigart, J. A. Miller, D. M. Mohler, Jos. A. Long, John Wise, J. P. Harris, J. Y. King, G. M. Throne, J. H. Baker, D. Asherman, John Sherfey, I. B. Trout, Uriah Bixler, I. L. Hoover, John Heckman, G. S. Arnold, Conrad Fitz, I. L. Berkey, H. G. Miller, John M. Lair, Dorsey Hodgden, H. C. Early, J. A. Weaver, D. F. Hoover, G. W. Hutchison, S. M. Miller, L. H. Dickey, M. Nead; Daniel Vaniman, Moderator; I. B. Trout, I. J. Rosenberger, Writing Clerks; H. C. Early, Reading Clerk; S. P. Van Dyke, Doorkeeper.

1903. Bellefontaine, O., June 2, etc. G. J. Fercken, John

P. Bailey, E. D. Book, D. C. Campbell, H. J. Lilly, John Herr, A. C. Wieand, J. D. Hildebrand, John T. Green, J. U. G. Stiverson, C. M. Yearout, David Zuck, Edm. Forney, Geo. Barnhart, Uriah Bixler, Henry Brubaker, J. H. Baker, E. L. Lockard, G. W. Weddle, I. B. Trout, T. S. Fike, J. W. Jarboe, S. F. Sanger, H. G. Miller, Salem Beery, David Dilling, J. P. Zigler, Wm. Davis, D. F. Hoover, W. H. Naff, Conrad Fitz, L. H. Dickey, Jacob Wine, S. M. Smith, W. F. England, Geo. A. Branscom, H. C. Longenecker, L. A. Bookwalter, John Zuck, W. H. Lichty, C. G. Lint, S. J Swigart, Sol. Buckalew; S F. Sanger, Moderator; A. C. Wieand, Writing Clerk; I. B. Trout, Reading Clerk; J. D. Mishler, Doorkeeper.

1904. Carthage, Mo., May 23, etc. John C. Woodie, Jasper Barnthouse, E. G. Rodabaugh, N. B. Sherfy, J. C. Bright, I. W. Brubaker, P. S. Miller, D. M. Garber, J. E. Rolston, C. D. Hylton, C. J. Workman, J. A. Weaver, Daniel Hays, David Lytle, C. L. Wilkins, H. C. Early, L. W. Teeter, S. M. Forney, G. S. Arnold, I. D. Parker, R. A. Yoder, Z. Annon, L. H. Eby, E. M. Wolf, Samuel H. Utz, W. R. Deeter, A. C. Daggett, A. B. Barnhart, I. L. Berkey, G. E. Studebaker, W. T. Sines, John Heckman, J. A. Miller, I. W. Taylor, S. W. Garber, N. S. Gripe, J. H. Longenecker, F. W. Dove, S. E. Yundt, W. A. Anthony, G. W. Lentz, J. H. Stover, H. B. Brumbaugh, M. E. Stair, D. L. Forney, D. H. Walker, Ira P. Eby; H. C. Early, Moderator; H. B. Brumbaugh, Writing Clerk; I. D. Parker, Reading Clerk; W. C. Hanawalt, Doorkeeper.

1905. Bristol, Tenn., June 6, etc. C. A. Williams, H. J. Lilly, James A. Sell, G. F. Chemberlen, D. A. Miller, E. X. Miller, A. L. Boyd, D. Bowman, Tobias Myers, M. H. Peters, Wm. Harvey, John Herr, J. J. Yoder, D. J. Blickenstaff, W. S. Reichard, I. S. Lerew, D. E. Price, Thos. J. Kolb, John Sherfy, W. B. Neff, Z. Annon, Geo. Manon, A. G. Crosswhite, Jere. Thomas, D. G. Wine, D. F. Hoover, H. G. Miller, S. M. Smith, G. W. Sellers, J. M. Kagey, Levi Mohler, Wm. Dessenberg, Wm. H. Naff, H. F. Maust, I. J. Rosenberger, T. C. Denton, John Zuck, D. S. Filbrun, S. J. Bowman, C. M. Brower, C. G. Lint, H. M. Griffith; John Zuck, Moderator; A. G. Crosswhite, Writing Clerk; D. F. Hoover, Reading Clerk; J. S. Geiser, Doorkeeper.

1906. Springfield, Ill. S. P. Jones, D. H. Walker, J. Q. Goughnour, A. E. Nead, J. C. Bright, O. J. Beaver, P. S. Miller, Jesse Stutzman, D. M. Shorb, C. M. Yearout, James Murray, A. W. Hawbaker, H. C. Early, D. D. Thomas, Geo. Mishler,

Daniel Hays, L. W. Teeter, R. F. McCune, D. B. Arnold, Frank Fisher, E. E. Joyce, D. W. Kirk, S. F. Sanger, D. A. Crist, E. A. Brunner, I. B. Trout, S. J. Miller, A. B. Barnhart, Sol. Buckalew, M. H. Peters, S. K. Fike, J. B. Hylton, A. J. Smith, J. H. Longenecker, M. S. Mohler, J. W. Trostle, I. W. Taylor, John Mason, L. E. Keltner, C. L. Baker, J. W. Gephart, Peter Brower, J. B. Brumbaugh; S. F. Sanger, Moderator; I. B. Trout, Writing Clerk; H. C. Early, Reading Clerk; J. Kurtz Miller, Doorkeeper.

1907. Los Angeles, Cal., May. J. H. Stover, H. C. N. Coffman, W. J. Swigart, Edm. Forney, J. H. Keller, W. A. Anthony, David Snyder, G. W. Lentz, J. T. Myers, S. Edgecomb, F. W. Dove, John Herr, A. A. Sutter, D. J. Blickenstaff, D. V. Long, M. Keller, John Heckman, G. K. Sappington, T. E. George, I. L. Berkey, H. G. Miller, S. E. Lantz, Daniel Snell, A. S. Thomas, Wm. Davis, L. T. Holsinger, J. A. Dove, N. B. Wagoner, L. H. Dickey, H. Ikenberry, Geo. Stryker, N. Longenecker, John H. Garst, J. E. Ralston, D. M. Garber, J. H. Peterson, S. N. McCann, I. J. Rosenberger, L. W. Brubaker, S. S. Blough; L. T. Holsinger, Moderator; S. N. McCann, Writing Clerk; John Heckman, Reading Clerk; J. W. Lear, W. C. Hanawalt, Doorkeepers.

1908. Des Moines, Ia., June 9, etc. C. H. Diehl, James Murray, A. C. Snowberger, P. S. Miller, G. A. Snyder, W. H. Lichty, W. H. Naff, L. W. Teeter, J. E. Joseph, H. C. Early, Frank Fisher, J. B. Moore, D. C. Flory, J. H. Wright, George Manon, Jere. Thomas, S. F. Sanger, George Eller, Z. Annon, Manly Deeter, B. E. Kesler, T. J. Kolb, C. L. Wilkins, J. E. Crist, John A. Myers, A. C. Wieand, J. C. Minix, J. H. Longenecker, J. W. Harshberger, A. J. Smith, I. W. Taylor, H. J. Lilly, H. F. Maust, E. S. Miller, A. Killingsworth, D. A. Norcross, James A. Sell, E. E. John, Geo. C. Carl, P. J. Blough, J. E. Ellenberger, Adam Ebey, J. C. Bright, D. F. Sink, David Hollinger; H. C. Early, Moderator; A. C. Wieand, Writing Clerk; S. F. Sanger, Reading Clerk; John C. Zug, Doorkeeper.

1909. Harrisonburg, Va., June 1, etc. H. Eikenberry, M. Keller, J. S. Secrist, J. A. Miller, John H. Utz, John Herr, Wm. Eisenbise, John Rowland, F. P. Cassel, D. T. Wagoner, W. T. Sines, H. B. Brumbaugh, D. J. Lichty, J. M. Smith, H. Beelman, A. G. Crosswhite, G. W. Lentz, Albert Hollinger, S. S. Ullery, J. S. Kline, J. Barnthouse, J. W. Kitson, Noah Oren, J. J. Shaffer, I. L. Berkey, Levi Snell, P. M. Correll,

J. W. Rarick, G. A. Branscom, H. M. Peters, John Zuck, D. F. Landis, D. N. Eller, Silas Gilbert, N. Longenecker, C. D. Hylton, H. C. N. Coffman, J. W. Keiser, Daniel Hays, I. L. Hoover, D. M. Garber, D. H. Zigler, D. A. Crist, D. S. Filbrun, Emra T. Fike, Chas. A. Miller, W. P. Bosserman, Z. Annon; D. M. Garber, Moderator; A. G. Crosswhite, Writing Clerk; G. W. Lentz, Reading Clerk; Ira Kreider, Doorkeeper.

1910. Winona Lake, Ind., June 7–9. J. F. Ross, D. B. Eby, R. A. Yoder, A. W. Arnold, I. H. Miller, J. D. Brower, J. M. Kagey, J. C. Bright, A. P. Blough, H. C. Early, David Hollinger, W. E. West, S. A. Sanger, G. A. Snyder, L. W. Teeter, H. G. Miller, A. S. Workman, Eli Roose, P. S. Miller, Isaac Miller, Daniel Wysong, W. H. Naff, James Gish, A. L. Wright, P. D. Reed, R. F. Bowman, G. E. Swihart, J. C. Minix, E. G. Rodabaugh, Jesse Emmert, D. H. Walker, D. L. Mohler, J. W. Lear, J. F. Dietz, P. B. Messner, G. B. Royer, C. L. Baker, J. T. Green, S. Z. Sharp, E. S. Miller, Caleb Long, W. F. England, J. A. Sell, C. D. Bonsack, J. H. Stober, J. C. Swigart, J. J Yoder, H. J. Lilly, I. W. Taylor, W. C. Watkins, A. C. Daggett, Jesse Ziegler; H. C. Early, Moderator; J. W. Lear, Writing Clerk; G. B. Royer, Reading Clerk; A. L. B. Martin, Doorkeeper.

1911. St. Joseph, Mo., June 6–8. W. T. Price, S. E. Lantz, L. E. Keltner, D. L. Forney, John E. Crist, J. H. Longenecker, W. Q. Calvert, Geo. S. Harp, John Herr, J. E. Bryant, J. C. Garland, J. Kurtz Miller, P. R. Keltner, W. T. Sines, John Bennett, Henry Lilligh, J. E. Ullery, J. A. Long, J. M. Blough, Chas. A. Lentz, W. A. Anthony, D. B. Garber, S. B. Shirkey, W. M. Howe, David Dilling, Rufus Wyatt, Silas Hoover, Manly Deeter, Geo. Mishler, J. A. Miller, Frank Kreider, G. A. Branscom, D. N. Eller, D. F. Hoover, J. H. Brubaker, D. C. Naff, C. B. Rowe, James Murray, A. S. Thomas, Sam. Bowser, B. F. Snyder, I. A. Miller, H. C. N. Coffman, D. M. Garber, D. H. Zigler, H. F. Crist, D. S. Filbrum, D. Hays, D. A. Crist, J. H. Gordon, E. T. Fike; D. M. Garber, Moderator; J. M. Blough, Writing Clerk; P. R. Keltner, Reading Clerk; Edgar Rothrock, Doorkeeper.

1912. York, Pa., June 4, etc. J. W. Deardorf, H. C. Early, Brice Sell, J. P. Dickey, D. M. Zuck, J. P. Hetric, J. H. Graybill, I. W. Abernathy, C. R. Oellig, I. B. Trout, C. L. Wilkins, D. A. Foust, J. W. Lear, T. J. Simmons, J. H. Cassady, I. S. Long, G. W. Ellenberger, H. S. Replogle, A. L. Wright, J. B. Hylton, A. M. Laughrun, Frank Fisher, D. G. Wine, K. G.

Tennison, Dav. Metzler, D. F. Landis, P. S. Miller, E. L. Heestand, N. Longenecker, D. A. Naff, L. T. Holsinger, L. H. Dickey, H. G. Miller, W. I. Buckingham, J. C. Bright, S. A. Sanger, J. F. Souders, B. F. Petry, P. S. Thomas, G. W. Burgin, A. L. Boyd, J. A. Garber, H. L. Brammell, Geo. C. Carl, M. F. Woods, A. C. Daggett, F. P. Cassel, Jere. Thomas, John S. Clark, I. W. Taylor, A. C. Auvil, M. Keller, T. T. Myers; H. C. Early, Moderator; J. W. Lear, Writing Clerk; I. B. Trout, Reading Clerk; W. Carl Rarick, Doorkeeper.

1913. Winona Lake, Ind. H. J. Lilly, D. R. Holsinger, Geo. H. Bashor, Salem Beery, C. Fahrney, O. F. Shaw, Geo. W. Miller, W. B. Stover, J. H. Wright, David Dilling, Frank Kreider, W. R. Deeter, L. W. Teeter, W. E. West, J. Q. Goughnour, D. F. Sink, O. O. Button, Geo. Eller, F. G. Edwards, J. J. Yoder, T. S. Fike, John Rowland, S. M. Smith, Geo. W. Lentz, S. B. Shirkey, D. W. Teeter, D. G. Wine, G. A. Branscom, J. W. Shively, R. R. Shroyer, D. M. Garver, J. W. Fidler, B. F. Snider, Jacob Appleman, H. H. Keim, M. C. Swigart, J. H. Longenecker, John Herr, W. J. Swigart, John Bennett, C. L. Baker, Albert Hollinger, P. J. Blough, Levi Rogers, D. F. Bowman, M. H. Peters, I. A. Miller, D. C. Naff, D. H. Zigler, J. M. Kagey, A. S. Thomas, S. N. McCann, L. A. Bowman, D. B. Eby, Emra T. Fike, J. F. Ross; D. M. Garver, Moderator; G. W. Lentz, Reading Clerk; S. N. McCann, Writing Clerk; M. R. Wolf, Doorkeeper; O. P. Haines, Assistant.

C. Changes in Holding Annual Meetings.

In 1849, a brother with his family moved from Lancaster County, Pa., to northwestern Ohio. After a lapse of thirty-seven years, he made his first visit east, and, when brought from the station to his brother's home, the place where both were born and raised to manhood, he at first would not believe that it was the place where father had lived, but when assured that it was, and taking another look, he said yes, there is the creek that used to flow through the meadow, now a tilled field, and there stands the pear tree that stood at the corner of the old house, and the slope of the land is the same, but the buildings, fences, and fields were all changed, timber cleared away, and the land under cultivation, and other new houses built in the vicinity, all of which made a great change in the landscape, and all these changes seemed to be an improvement for the farm.

We were wondering if the Macks, Peter Becker, the Urners, Prices, Saurs, Elder Michael Frantz, the Pfautzs, Longeneckers, Zugs, George Miller, and more recently, the Harleys, Peter Keyser, Daniel Fretz, Jacob Haller, David Gerlach, Valentine Balsbach, Lorenz Etter, the Beshores, Klines, Hollinger, all of Eastern Pennsylvania, and many others beyond the Susquehanna River, who are dead forty, fifty and more years, and who have attended Annual Meetings of long ago, could now attend one of ours, whether they might not have a feeling akin to that of the visitor from the West, when told that this now holds the place of the "Big Meeting," which they used to have in their time.

The first General Conference that we have any record of was a called one, and likely held at the home of Martin Urner, in Coventry Church, near where Pottstown now is, in 1742. It appears that this meeting was called to more firmly establish the members in the principles and doctrines of the church, as contained in the New Testament, and to protect them from the erroneous and misleading teaching of Count Zinzendorf and others, in an effort to unite the Protestant churches.

The next General Conference we have any record of was held in Lancaster County, in 1763, on account of trouble arising from the claims of Sister Catharine Hummer, that she had trances, frequently, for years, and while under their spell she had visions, and communication with departed saints. Some of the members had faith in her claims, and some had not, and her father, Peter Hummer, being a minister, would give her liberty in public meetings to relate her visions, which was so objectionable to some, that, according to the decision of the conference, the church was at the point of division, as in the Conrad Beissel case.

It was the rule of the Brotherhood from the beginning until 1848, when a church had trouble that could not be adjusted at home by the aid of adjoining elders, to take it to the "Big Meeting," and there if not always, at least often, it was taken up in open council and decided.

It is not known when the conferences began to be held on Pentecost, but that of 1763 was May 27 and 28. I was wondering whether the meeting in Germantown, mentioned in Brumbaugh's "History," page 504, held on June 11, 1791, was not one, since in the list of conferences that year is left blank; because he says there "many brethren from near and far came together; several Elders from other congregations were also present." The question considered at this meeting pertained specially to Germantown, and the meeting was held at the time the conference was usually held, *i. e.,* June.

On October 30, 1794, a conference was held at Shenandoah, Va., and in the autumn of 1797, at Black Water, Va. These may have been special meetings, and the regular meetings unknown, the same as in 1846, the regular meeting was at John Royer's, in Lancaster Co., Pa., and the same year was a special held at the Meeting House near Joseph Bowman's, Washington Co., East Tennessee, on September 4; and on June 12, 1848, the regular meeting was held at the house of Bro. Jacob Kurtz, Wayne Co., O., and September 23 and 24, same year, a special was held at the house of Bro. John Koontz, near Delphi, Carroll Co., Ind. The business of these special meetings, the minutes inform us, was largely of a local character.

The first commitee sent by Annual Meeting consisted of Peter Long, Andrew Spanogle, John Holsinger, of Pennsylvania, Jos. Arnold, Jac. Byser, of Virginia, Geo. Hoke, H. Kurtz, of Ohio, in 1849, to go to the Glade Church, Somerset Co., Pa., and assist them in dividing their territory into four or five districts. The following year two committees were sent to adjust troubles, one to Eel River, Ind., the other to Mansfield, O. This was the beginning of sending committees to churches, authorized to settle difficulties, and if they were successful this ended the trouble; if not, they were to report back to the next Annual Meeting, and this is the rule yet. Since this rule is in force, personal matters are not accepted at the conference, unless committees fail to adjust the same.

Prior to 1866, the Standing Committee was appointed by

the elders of the church where the meeting was held, they to receive all papers sent up by the churches, and to supply them with answers to be considered by the meeting in open Council, but the membership, and the number of churches increasing, which naturally increased the amount of work at the conference, made it necessary to make some change; therefore in 1848 we find the following on the minutes: " Whole number of delegates was 95, and among them were ordained elders 24, elders 31, teachers 14, deacons 15, private members 11, churches represented 59, and though as fully represented as ever before, it is believed that only about one third of the churches had sent messengers. The number of papers handed in amounted to 63. Considering that the reading of all the papers by one committee would take up too much time, it was concluded to distribute them among ten committees, which were to examine them and report thereon to the meeting. These committees were appointed from the delegates," etc. In 1862 we find the following: " It was ascertained that there were represented at this council meeting 136 congregations by about 240 delegates. The General Committee, having received the papers addressed to the meeting, distributed such as contained queries to twenty sub-committees," etc. There were this year seventy-two papers brought to the meeting.

The plan of appointing sub-committees was continued until 1866, when there was a radical change made in holding Annual Meeting (see minutes of that year), but appointing Standing Committee was left the same way until 1868, after which each state district was to appoint one Elder to serve on the committee, and one Brother to accompany him as a delegate, and that local church delegates be discontinued.

In 1885 it was decided that no elder shall serve on Standing Committee more than two years out of four, and in 1897, that no officer, or member of the committee shall serve two years in succession, which is still the rule.

In 1879 and 1880 the districts having the meeting were permitted to charge for boarding the people. Before that it was expected that board be furnished free.

In 1883 the local churches were allowed to represent,

those having two hundred members, or less, by one delegate, and those over two hundred by two, and the accompanying delegate from District Meeting be discontinued.

In 1903 it was decided that state districts having over 3,500 members shall be entitled to two members on Standing Committee.

The first time the Sunday-school question was before the conference was in 1838, and the decision was "Considered most advisable to take no part in such things." In 1857 the question was up again, and the answer was: "We know of no scripture which condemns Sunday-schools, if conducted in gospel order," etc. From that time on it was frequently before conference on some point connected with the Sunday-school question, and at this time it is considered indispensable to the church, and has a prominent place at every conference.

In 1852 the mission question was first considered and sanctioned, but no plan adopted. The question was up several times afterwards but nothing came of it to set the work in motion for some time, until 1884, when a missionary plan was formulated, and a committee consisting of E. Eby and C. P. Roland for one year, D. Vaniman and S. Riddlesberger for two years, and D. L. Miller for three years, were appointed, to carry out the plan. In 1885 a Committee on Book and Tract Work was appointed, viz.: S. D. Royer and S. W. Hoover, three years, Adam Minnick and B. F. Miller, two years, J. Hepner, Saml. Bock, one year; and in 1893 the two works were consolidated under the following committee, viz., D. L. Miller and E. Eby, three years, S. F. Sanger and S. R. Zug, two years, and S. W. Hoover, one year. The plan thus adopted, with some amendments added since, now forms the basis on which mission work is carried on by the brotherhood, both home and foreign.

In 1831 it was decided not advisable for a Brother to send his son to college. In 1853, "Considered that we would deem colleges a very unsafe place for a simple follower of Christ," etc. In 1888, "it is conforming to the world," etc. In 1871, "allowed to engage in college work, yet not as a church school," and in 1883, "forbearance is urged," etc. More recently our colleges are nearly all under the supervision of the conference.

Brethren's Homes and Children's Aid Societies are of more recent introduction, and have had little change.

Fifty years ago and more there was little or nothing done at our Annual Meetings concerning Sunday-schools, mission work, colleges, brethren's and orphans' homes, but matter pertaining to church polity, while more recently this is manifestly changed and reversed. The temperance question was always a live question with our church, but only as touching the members, but in recent years the Church has broadened out.

If any one wishes to know how the Annual Meetings were conducted sixty or seventy years ago, read the description of one in another part of this work, held in 1846, at John Royer's in Lancaster Co., Pa., where the people met Thursday, had council Friday and Saturday; after that a lovefeast. Preaching Sunday morning, commenced at seven o'clock, and continued until 12.30, without intermission, where twenty Brethren would preach, one after the other, each on an average, occupying about fifteen minutes, both in German and English, while the people sat five and one-half hours, on improvised seats, made of rough boards, without backs, listening to men of mature age and experience, whose dress, hair and beards would make them recognizable as Brethren anywhere. It was required in those days that ministers, especially elders, should be fully in the order, and not be without beard. Oh, what a change from then to now!

D. Abraham H. Cassel's Account of Annual Meeting, 1846.

Friday morning May 22, 1846, to yearly meeting with the Rev. Samuel Harley and wife and Samuel M. Harley, passed through to Boyerstown and Reading to Bro. Isaac Smuckers. Next morning through Adamstown and Reamstown to Samuel Landes for dinner. From there through Ephrata and Lititz to Bro. Christian Longenecker's all night. Met many Brethren there from Franklin County and elsewhere. Had meeting there next morning. Samuel Harley spoke about the woman of Samaria; after him old Jacob Haller, Daniel Fretz and David Gerlock. Through Manheim to Philip Ziegler's. But I went from Longenecker's with Bro. John Young near Mt. Joy, eighteen miles. Conversed till near 3 o'clock in the morning, principally concerning the Essenes whether they were Christians or not, and the Millenium. Next morning, he took me to Elizabethtown where we had meeting in a Winebrenarian Church. Our horses were all ungeared and stabled at the tavern and hay and water ordered and paid for by Bro. Jacob Rider. Went with him from meeting for dinner to Bro. Isaac Eshleman's. For tea and all night at John Keyser's. Meeting there next morning where Harley spoke from Hebrews 2:3. Ziegler and Hoffer also spoke a word of testimony. From there we all went to John Young's over night. Had meeting next morning in a school house close by. Text Phil. 2. In the afternoon we had a large Council Meeting at his house concerning the affairs of Abraham Gibble. Next morning to Sister Shoemaker's where many Brethren, ministering and others met us from Maryland, Virginia and other places. Had a very interesting meeting there in the barn. Jacob and Daniel Saylor were also there and spoke with such power and energy that I never heard its equal in my opinion. From there to old Bishop Pfoutz's and next morning to Königmacker's in the vicinity of the Yearly Meeting. Left our horses and baggage there during the meeting which commenced on Friday morning 8 o'clock. Present about twenty-five bishops, one hundred and twenty-six preachers and perhaps 10,000–15,000 hearers. Regular worship lasted till noon. Then the Council commenced which lasted till Saturday dinner when regular worship began again and the balance of the queries were decided by the Standing Committee in a private room after which two candidates were baptized in Royer's Meadow. Then began the preparation for the lovefeast. They erected a large canvas tent for an eating saloon with five tables for two hundred and forty to sit up at a time. The cooking was performed in a large wash kitchen where they had two fifty-gallon kettles over the fire to heat water for coffee and to boil meat and broth for the communion supper which was partaken of by at least two or three thousand communicants. Next morning (Sunday) public worship began at 7 o'clock and closed at half past twelve during which time twenty sermons were preached from different texts. The principal speakers were George Hoke from Ohio, John Kline from Virginia, James Tracey from Ohio, Israel Poulson from New Jersey, Peter Nead from Staunton, Virginia, Henry Kurtz, Ohio, Adam Brown from Missouri, James Quinter, Philip Eshleman from Chickahog Valley, Christel Funk from Greencastle, Pa., the two Saylors from Maryland, Henry Koons from Washington, Andy Miller, old Spanogle, old David Shollenberger, Peter Long, Lorenz Etter and Jacob Brown and Samuel Harley. From there we went that afternoon yet down to Isaac Smucker's. From there home the next day. Arrived at about 8 o'clock in evening; absent thirteen days and traveled about two hundred miles—was much refreshed and well pleased with the journey—been well all the time and had very favorable weather.

The questions discussed in my presence were as follows:

1st. About making different arrangements for holding yearly Meeting. Ans. Laid by.

2d. Whether private members should have the privilege of bringing difficulties before the Y. M. before consulted at home. No.

3d. Whether imposition of hands should be observed in electing deacons. Ans. Left undecided.

4th. Whether one elder or bishop should be vested with more than another. Ans. No.

5th. When an offensive member should be ex-communicated public before all—or received—or privately before the members only. Ans. Left undecided, as circumstances may require different.

6th. Whether conjugal embraces between promise and marriage should be considered and punished as whoredom. Ans. Yes, with certain restrictions.

7th. Whether a gross transgressor can be received upon again confession only without visible marks of a true and thorough repentance and humility for the crime committed. Ans. Under certain circumstances.

8th. Whether a member upon commission of a gross sin must be formally excummunicated if he shows satisfactory marks of repentance and contrition of heart for his guilt. Ans. Undecided.

9th. Whether a Brother may work in a distillery for wages and whether a Brother farmer or miller may sell and grind to and for a distiller. Ans. Best not.

The rest were decided privately for want of time.

E. REPORT OF THE ANNUAL MEETING, HELD IN BERKS CO., PA., ON TUESDAY, WEDNESDAY, AND THURSDAY, MAY 30, 31, AND JUNE 1, 1871[1]

The meeting was held on the premises of brother John Merkey, in Berks county, this state, about nine miles north of Myerstown station on the Lebanon Valley Railroad.

Brother Merkey's large commodious barn was fitted up—well arranged—with the design of holding the meeting in it; but as the congregation was large and constantly increasing, and as Tuesday morning gave promise of a beautiful day, it was concluded to move to the pleasant grove not far distant. The action was suited to the word, and in due time the necessary arrangements were made, and the council assembled.

The exercises were introduced by Elder John Zug, by lining and singing the 108th hymn, in the new German hymn book commencing:

"Komm, O Komm, Du Geist des Lebens."

Elder John Wise then proposed to open in one language and close in another. Accordingly Elder Samuel Lehman proceeded to open the meeting by exhortation and prayer in the German. Wise then read the 15th chapter of Acts.

Elder Henry Davy remarked in substance as follows: As Acts 15th has been read as a basis for our meeting, we

[1] Contributed by J. G. Francis.

are together in the name of God; and therefore we ought to be very solemn. That in so far as doctrinal points were involved, there would not be much occasion for such councils: this was also the case in the chapter read.

Lehman recapitulated in German what Davy had said in English: especially regarding the small matters that so often divide the Brotherhood. He exhorted to humility, and carefulness, and a proper premeditation of what we say.

The following officers were elected:

Elder Henry Davy, Foreman; Elder D. P. Saylor, Ass't foreman; Elder John Wise, Reading Clerk; Elder James Quinter, Writing Clerk; Elder F. P. Loehr, Interpreter, to read queries and answers in the German. D. M. Holsinger was also called as interpreter.

The delegates from Eastern Pennsylvania were David Gerlach and S. R. Zug.[2]

The speeches of the first day were taken down by a stenographer sent by the Phila. Press. This is likely the first Annual Meeting of which a stenographic report was ever given. The first day's speeches are given in the Christian Family Companion of June 27, and July 4, 1871.

The question discussed at greatest length was that of a plan of amending the method of holding Annual Meetings —that each state district send one delegate to represent it on Standing Committee, that each congregation send one representative, and that these compose the Annual Council, and all questions be decided by that body alone. The chief champions of the old way were D. P. Saylor and Jacob Miller; of the new way as proposed, H. R. Holsinger and Joseph Hanawalt.

We are told that the meeting closed at 3.30 P.M. Thursday, and that before night the vast concourse of people had dispersed.

The "General Remarks" of H. R. Holsinger are as follows:

[2] Holsinger in his report says that David Gerlach and S. R. Zug were the delegates from Eastern Pennsylvania. This is an error. The delegates were David Gerlach and John Zug. S. R. Zug was serving on the Committee of Arrangements in place of his father, Deacon Benjamin Zug.

PLACE OF ANNUAL MEETING, 1871.
MERKEY FARM.

PLACE OF ANNUAL MEETING, 1902.
PAXTANG PARK.

"There was nothing unusual connected with the meeting. The attendance was about the average. There was provision in abundance for all. The accommodations were as good as could have been expected. The place was well adapted to the holding of such a meeting, having four pumps on the premises; but we regard it as a great mistake to have such a meeting so far from the railroad, and we heard very severe censures expressed for that part of the arrangements. It was certainly very imprudent to compel so many persons to travel so far over rough roads, on rough conveyances, and spend their time and money, when there was no occasion for so doing.—Hundreds of dollars might have been saved to the brethren and sisters, if the meeting had been near the railroad. We hope this will be taken into consideration in selecting locations for future meetings.

"Among the peculiarities of the meeting, may be mentioned that there was more German speaking, both public and private, than at any previous meeting we attended. There were many persons present that understood scarcely any English. Another was that there was less tobacco smoking. This was remarked by several persons on the ground. It is certainly a hopeful indication. Only occasionally you would see a Brother so imprudent as to come among the people with burning tobacco; and we saw but one 'smoking union' among the sisters, and they had the prudence to retire to themselves."

Holsinger also states that he " obtained the notes of the first day's doings from one of the Associated Press Reporters, who was on the ground the first day; but left on the second day for want of proper accommodations, and on account of annoyance from impertinent inquirers. . . . Had he received the courtesies of the meeting, in the shape of a few square feet of our rough board table, we might have been permitted to lay before our readers the entire proceedings of the Annual Meeting, to the joy and satisfaction of thousands who could not attend the meeting," etc. It would be no small satisfaction to have the great speech of Isaac Price which is described as passing Beecher in eloquence.

This Annual Meeting seems to have blazed the way for full reports, and also to have blazed the way for our modern system of district and congregational representation at Annual Meeting.

We have also words from one of those who bore the burdens and responsibilities of the Meeting, who felt the fears and anxieties, Elder F. P. Loehr. He writes: "But I have digressed, and must return and say, that on Monday I returned to the place of Annual Meeting, where I enjoyed a season of extraordinary refreshing; especially as those queries most dreaded were disposed of without much excitement; and I trust we are all more confirmed that the Lord has not forsaken them that put their trust in him. We have had again lessons of self-denial and submission to one another for Christ's sake, thereby to become more and more combined as members of one body; and such as have dreaded a disruption of the brotherhood, may take courage, and begin anew to work in the vineyard of the Lord with redoubled zeal to keep up the unity of the spirit in the bond of peace."

"Sketches Outside," by Bro. P. H. Beaver, will tell us things we should like to know.

"Annual Council,
May 29, 1871.

"*Dear Brother:* We propose giving you a few familiar sketches of our impressions and emotions, as well as some of our experience in getting here. Some of our Brethren took the first forenoon train from Lewisburg this morning, and some of us took the second or eleven o'clock train and beat the rest of the company to Harrisburg by about five minutes. Here we found an excursion train making up to take the Brethren to Myerstown the place of A. M. which would be ready to move out of the Lebanon Depot at 2 o'clock, one hour after our arrival, so we had a very agreeable hour for interchange of greetings amongst Brethren, and the formation of new acquaintances. Then at the appointed hour we sped away in the direction of Myerstown through as beautiful and fertile a valley as ever our good Father laid down anywhere in America, or elsewhere. This was our first experience upon a R. R. train overflowing with Brethren and our reflections soon resolved into poetry of music. One hour brought us to our stop-off—Myerstown. Here we found about forty wagons of all conceivable patterns from the lightest to the most heavy and capacious. We learned that there were ten miles of country road lying ahead of us to the place of Annual Meeting, which is being held at the house and upon the spacious premises of Brother John Merkey, near the village of Bethel, in Berks Co., Pa. Our trip from the railroad station to this place was full of unusual experience to a north Pennsylvanian. In many respects it was pleasant. Perched high upon the top of an old fashioned wood and (l)eather spring four-horse stage coach, we enjoyed a fine view of the magnificent country through which we passed, to the grateful emotions to our great good Father, which a sight of these golden grain fields inspire in our hearts; But darkness —deference. So we delay our scribbling until morning, and look about for quarters over night, which at first appear to be a discouraging undertaking, judging from the dense mass of human figures moving about in the twilight. As the shadows of night crept over the landscape, a sense of loneliness appeared to settle down upon our heart—loneliness in the midst of a multitude, the first thought appears like a paradox yet when you are a stranger in a strange place, your affections naturally reach out in quest of familiar evening scenes and evening customs, and faces at home.

"In the midst of our mental reveries, we hear a welcome voice, and we have room for some more Brethren, who are willing to sleep on the garret. This was a good 'show' and was gratefully accepted. We were soon decoyed into the arms of Nature's Sweet Restorer, balmy blessed sleep. Two ranks thirty feet long and very sensibly to the heat of a warm garret. This is true without any controversy; but the whippoorwill in an adjacent tree did his utmost to make us forget the rough grating of untoward circumstances.

"'The morning bright with rosy light' and the familiar feathered songsters of Summer mornings waked us out of sleep and back into the world to serve out our probationary state. After the morning ablutions, the morning service to the Father of all, and the morning meal, we again ply our pencil and now the Brethren announced that they want help to move the seats out of the barn into the grove, a most beautiful and delightful grove, a very 'nature bower,' canopied all over with stately widespreading oaks, that is indeed agreeable to the sweltering mass. Thither we resort by and by. Here comes the Standing Committee, and occupies the stand erected for it. O the scene and the occasion. Proceedings open by singing 'Komm, O Komm, du Geist des Lebens.' Exhortation by Brother S. Lehman, followed by prayer. What an impressive occasion. Truly numbers add eloquence and inspiration to such a meeting. It being no part of my design to report the regular proceedings we will here rest till noon.

"Here come the dinner hour and summons; and so we repair to the tent of refreshments, with no disposition to play reporter of the regular proceedings again. Now let us look through this tent constructed of fine boards, about ten hundred feet having been consumed in its construction. One hundred and ten feet long and about forty-feet wide; extending from the pump and back porch of the dwelling house eastward to a large open wagon shed. In this latter building were stowed away when not in use all the table paraphernalia—dishes almost by the cord, knives, forks, spoons, literally by the bushel baskets full. Three tables through the entire length of this tent accommodated from three fifty to four hundred persons, and on Tuesday at noon very nearly two thousand Brethren and Sisters were supplied with dinner. The number of persons attending the council on this day reached three thousand. The floor of the boarding tent was nicely carpeted with tan bark which answered well for wet or dry weather. A brick cooking range, about six feet square, covered with four square cast iron plates each having a circular opening sufficiently large to receive a large iron kettle, such as is commonly used to render lard, all of which were used at times, to their utmost capacity in the preparation of meat, soup and coffee. Nine churches furnished the labor of cooking and serving tables, forty males and fifteen females. This labor was furnished on Monday and Tuesday by the Lancaster churches; and on Wednesday and Thursday, by the Berks, Lebanon and Dauphin churches. Three thousand dollars were contributed toward defraying the expenses of holding this meeting, which is supposed to be ample to cover the bills. From the way the Brethren have gone about this work, it is clearly presumable that they either have money in sufficient abundance, or that they are not seriously cursed with 'the love of money.'

"On Wednesday morning the sky looked lowering, with a light sprinkling of rain, and threatening more; so the congregation 'took up' their boards and benches, as well as their 'line of march' to the spacious barn upon the premises.

"The council was held in the Little Swatara congregation, about a mile from their meeting house, and here as well as at all other accessible points in the neighborhood, the Brethren held meeting for public preaching every evening at 6 o'clock, which arrangements had the effect of very materially scattering the members and securing for them comfortable quarters to lodge at night.

"We supposed that on Wednesday the general attendance would not be so large, but the falling off, if any is very slight. The Peanut and Panacea venders are also still on hand. Just here let us notice a circumstance which proves the influence for good that the discussion of the tobacco question has exerted. We saw some Brethren, and a number of our always dear Sisters literally hid themselves for the purpose of enjoying and regaling themselves with the peculiar sweets to be extracted from cigars and 'meerschaums' after their kind.

"Now we will again look in upon the council and see what we can see there. Evidently there are some 'characters' whose 'points' and foibles, as well as other peculiar traits might be sketched with telling zest and relish, if it were considered profitable to do so; but to faithfully delineate 'Points of character,' with the mention of names are matters too personal to be edifying to the more conservative portion of the Brethren, of whom a majority of this council is evidently composed; but the liberalists have still an immense advantage, because they hold within their ranks a greater amount, height, and depth, and width of intellectual grasp—not to put too fine a point on it—and questions are not decided by numbers, but by weight of council. So we find some of the Brethren to be great sticklers for technical formalities of the most minute, not to say trifling character upon the one hand, and upon the other side the opposite extreme. Those liberal, easy, indulgent and sometimes impulsive, who look much less to form than substance, these are mostly the zealous, earnest evangelists or revivalists of the church, who carry their points and their audiences by a storm of eloquence and fervent pathos.

"Here we must conclude our sketches and get ready to leave for 'Home, sweet home,' before the meeting is over. Good by.

"P. H. BEAVER."

CHAPTER II.

HISTORY OF DISTRICT MEETINGS.

A. THE FIRST DISTRICT MEETING OF EASTERN PENNSYLVANIA.

The honor of originating our District Meetings is claimed for Virginia by Elder D. H. Zigler, of Broadway, that state, author of "The History of the Brethren in Virginia." The Virginia Brethren from their "General Council" of 1856 sent a query to Annual Meeting on the proposition to district the churches, and have general council meetings in those Districts. Art. 23 of A. M. Minutes is no doubt the answer to this query. It reads as follows: "A proposal of forming districts of five, six, or more adjoining churches for the purpose of meeting jointly, at least once a year, settling difficulties, etc., and thus lessening the business of our General Yearly Meetings; we believe this plan to be a good one, if carried out in the fear of the Lord." This is a conditional approval.

A plan to district the churches, attributed to a Virginia pen, was presented to the Annual Meeting of 1858.

General Councils were not alone confined to Virginia. One was held in Milford, presumably Indiana, in 1857. In the same year there are indications that a similar meeting must have been held in Maryland. In 1859, likely at Annual Meeting, the Brotherhood was divided into eleven districts, for the purpose of raising money to pay Bro. Samuel Garber for expenses incurred in a lawsuit growing out of his preaching against slavery. Elder J. H. Umstad represented Pennsylvania east of the Susquehanna river. Elder D. P. Saylor was the dominant figure in this work.

It should not be overlooked that the "Western Brethren" held a general council, November 22, 1851, in Adams Co.,

Illinois. The object of the meeting was to consider differences between themselves and the Eastern Brethren. But this was not intentionally a District Meeting subject to Annual Meeting, though these Brethren later became subject to Annual Meeting.

In order to help missionary work the District Meeting plan of 1858 was brought before the Conference. It was not thought good to adopt the proposition, but was recommended to the prayerful consideration of the Brethren.

When the Conference in 1859 says, "This Meeting recommends and gives liberty to any of the Districts or States to make a move on the subject of spreading and sustaining the Gospel," etc., we have a recognition of District Meetings.

Then in 1859, this same year, because the missionary work continued to be urged, the Conference appointed a committee "to propose some plan by which the Brotherhood in general may take a part in this good work." The committee which was to report at next Annual Meeting, consisted of D. P. Saylor, John Kline, John H. Umstad, Samuel Layman, John Metzger, and James Quinter. The committee in its report gave the following advice: "That the churches of the Brotherhood form themselves into districts, . . . that each of said districts have its treasury," etc. The report of this representative committee was cerain of adoption sooner or later; but because of the slim attendance at the Annual Meeting of 1860, which, with the war spirit in the air, was held in Tenn., the report was only spread on the minutes.

Elder John Umstad, whether he regarded the report as practically adopted, which was the case, whether he looked upon the missionary cause as of sufficient importance to run ahead of formal adoption or whether prompted by the spirit of leadership, but certainly not without authority from Annual Meeting, called a District Meeting in the Green Tree Church, September 22, 1860. We give the minutes as reported by the secretary to *The Gospel Visitor.*

"Pursuant to the advice or suggestion of the committee appointed by the Y. M. (Yearly Meeting) of 1859, who reported to the Y. M. of 1860, Bro. J. H. Umstad of Green Tree Church, Montgomery Co., Pa., issued a call to the Brethren of the churches East of the Susquehanna river, to send delegates or letters to a meeting of delegates to be held at Green Tree Church on the 22d of September, to consider those suggestions for the furtherance of the Gospel in the work of Evangelism.

"The meeting was organized by appointing Jacob Gottwals, Moderator, and Isaac Price, Secretary.

"The following named churches were represented on said day at said place:

Green Tree, Montgomery Co., Pa.
  Delegates, John H. Umstad and Jacob Gottwals.
Indian Creek Church, Montgomery Co., Pa.
  Delegates, Samuel Harley, Jacob Price and Jacob Reiner.
    William Nyce and Abraham Cassel, volunteers to the call.
White Oak Church, Lancaster Co., Pa., was represented by letter.
Conestoga Church, Lancaster Co., Pa., by letter
Big Swatara, Dauphin Co., Pa.
  Delegates, William Hertzler and Wendell Henry.
Tulpehocken Church, Lebanon Co.
  Delegates, Christian Bucher and John L. Zug.
Little Swatara Church, Lebanon and Berks Co.
  John Hertzler and George Gipple.
North Coventry Church, Chester Co., Pa.
  Delegates, John R. Price, A. Grubb and William Perches.
Philadelphia Church.
  Delegates, John Fox. Christian Custer, volunteer.
Germantown Church.
  Delegate, John Price.
New Jersey Church.
  Delegates, Israel Poulson and Enoch Hoffman.

"If there be organized churches East of the Susquehanna river of the Brethren not named in the above, we desire that they may report to the next meeting.

"On motion, it was resolved that the deliberations of the meeting be open to participation to all the above named Brethren, but in any vote of action taken, each church be entitled to two votes.

"There was expression of desire on the part of all the churches to do what was best for the cause of the Master. All appeared burdened with a sense of the responsibility we are resting under to promote Gospel truth and Gospel life.

"There was, however, a fear manifested in relation to the pernicious effect that might result from the new feature of a treasury provided for that purpose.

"To provide money funds to promote gospel truths struck the minds of many as a new and dangerous feature. And it was feared that there was a disposition to pattern after other than gospel examples.

"There was unity of thought or voice, that the responsibility of spreading the Gospel rested on each individual member. But whether a few should give all their time and effort, and be supported by the remainder, while all that other portion of the church should each cast in a mite in pecuniary form or whether each should be an evangelist in life, teaching by practice how to obey the gospel—and such only go forth as felt deeply impressed with the duty relying on the faithfulness of the body of the Brethren to sustain them as aid was needed, were the points upon which a diversity of opinion obtained. There were strong fears expressed by several, perhaps by a large majority, of the pernicious tendency of a treasury. Yet all were anxious that more effort should be made. Those discussions arose under the consideration of the text referred to in the minutes of Y. M. on 1 Cor. 16: 2. That store, it was argued, was for the poor. Some thought for a special occasion. But manifestly, the majority appeared to think it was not for evangelism in the way now proposed, though it might be for evangelism in the indirect mode of reaching needy souls by supplying their most pressing wants—and thus proving the spirit of Christ in the donor. There was life in the meeting—love manifested—amidst strong zeal, and a tenacity that the ancient characteristics of the Brethren be maintained. If we have departed from the humility, zeal, self-sacrificing spirit of our old Brethren who have gone before us, let us labor to get back from whence we departed, rather than mark out new modes of evangelism, seemed to the reporter to be the burden of many minds. Yet all felt a strong call for action, and midst the discussion, the following resolution was offered:

"'Resolved that the churches of the Brethren east of the River Susquehanna constitute a district for the more efficient promotion of the work of evangelism.'

"There were a few who desired no other organization than heretofore,—while others in argument favored the district effort, yet none seemed to be prepared for any definite action acceptable to the whole. And some of the delegates desired to return home to receive more definite instruction.

"Near the setting of the sun, it was resolved that we adjourn to meet on Friday, the 26th of October, at the same place, at the hour of nine, A. M., for worship—and at 10 A. M. enter again into further deliberations on the same subject.

"Further resolved, that these proceedings be offered to the Gospel Visitor for publication.

"ISAAC PRICE, *Secretary*.
JACOB GOTTWALS, *Moderator*."

As looked at from many points of view, this was a regular District Meeting of the Brotherhood. It was called pursuant to action of Annual Meeting, and professes to have been so called. It was called by one who in a way had been placed by Annual Meeting over the district in question. It had a regular official representation from its churches either by delegates or letter. It was organized by having a moderator and secretary and thus preserved a record of its doings. It was the first to send a report of itself to the church paper. It will also be noticed that a record of this meeting was taken some time before the Annual Meeting for a short time forbade District Meeting from so doing; hence no violation of Annual Meeting decision.

This District Meeting stood out through the *Visitor* as an example to the whole Brotherhood. The District Meetings, however, held the following year in Northern Virginia and in Middle Pennsylvania, did not wholly follow this example.

Some would make it appear that the action of the Annual Meeting of 1856 was a recommendation of District Meetings (see Minutes of 1862, Art. 58) but this is putting too much into Annual Meeting's action at that time. Her first recommendation for District Meetings was the recommendation of her committee of 1859 made in 1860 after Conference had practically given recognition to District Meetings. The open unequivocal recommendation for District Meetings did not come till 1866 (see A. M. Minutes).

At the beginning of this article we stated that Elder D. H. Ziegler, of Broadway, Va., claimed for Virginia the honor of originating our District Meetings. But a new claim presents itself in the Brethren Almanac of 1913. On page 13, Elder James A. Sell makes the following claim for Graybill Myers: "It may not be generally known that the plan of dividing the church into State Districts originated with him. Wherever he went in his frequent visits among the churches of Pennsylvania he talked about it, both in private and in public. To him belongs the honor of bringing to pass the system of State Districts throughout the Brotherhood. He lived to see his plans fully adopted and never, while health permitted, failed to attend and take an active part in the District meetings of Middle Pennsylvania. And such was his inbred modesty that he never referred to the work he did in giving to the church this new order of things. It is also worthy of notice that this departure was adopted with little opposition."

Elder Sell sets aside the claim of Elder Ziegler for Virginia without producing a single reason for so doing. Elder Sell mistakes the Middle District of Pennsylvania for the Brotherhood, a mistake which has also been made for Virginia in Virginia, as may be readily seen by comparing the Conference in Virginia in 1861 with the one in Middle Pennsylvania of the same year. We are ready to acknowledge that Graybill Myers gave to Middle Pennsylvania her District Meeting, and that the honor claimed for him above is true of him as regards that state district; but here the correctness of these claims end.

We shall now give the facts in the case as read beefore the Annual Meeting in 1910 at Winona Lake. The first District Meeting held after the one at Green Tree in 1860, of which we have learned was the one in Middle Pennsylvania in 1861. We give the announcement of Graybill Myers in regard to it in *The Gospel Visitor* of April, 1861, p. 126. It is headed in *The Visitor,*

"A GENERAL COUNCIL MEETING.

ALTOONA, PA., March 12, 1861.
"EDITORS OF THE GOSPEL VISITOR:
Dear Brethren: I hereby inform you that the Middle District of Pennsylvania has appointed a council meeting for

said district, at the Aughwick meeting-house, Huntingdon Co. Mt. Union on the Pennsylvania R. R. is the nearest station. This district lies between the Susquehanna river on the east and the Allegheny mountains on the west. The north and south boundaries are the boundaries of the state. The meeting will commence on the 9th of May, at 10 o'clock in the morning. It is expected that each sub-district will hold a council meeting and be represented by delegates or letter to the district council meeting above named. It is further expected that each sub-district will take the Oregon and home missions into consideration, and present their plans for operation. The proceedings of this council meeting will then be presented to the annual meeting for confirmation of amendment. A hearty invitation is given to all the churches comprised in the district in which the council meeting is held."

"Graybill Myers."

We shall yet add our remarks on this announcement of Graybill Myers, and shall then leave the matter to the consideration of our intelligent, fair-minded readers.

This announcement of Graybill Myers is a thorough, practical, statesmanlike one. If not in the lead like John Umstad, yet with steady continuance when started. It was a wise thing to call attention to the Oregon Mission which was then agitating the Brotherhood. It gave the meeting something to take hold of. It is not likely that a District Meeting was held before to determine on holding this one. Elder Graybill Myers, the leader, had likely conferred with the elders of the district.

J. G. Francis.

B. District Meetings.

[It will be noticed that the foregoing article of a District Meeting was concerning a Meeting wholly in the interest of evangelistic work.—Editors.]

At the Annual Meeting of 1866, in Franklin County, Pa., a radical change was made in holding the Annual Meeting. Among other things, it was decided " that states should form themselves into convenient districts, as follows: We recommend that each state form itself into convenient District Meetings. These meetings shall be formed by one or two representatives from each organized church, and we recommend that each church be represented in District Meeting, either by representative or by letter. We think it best to hold those meetings in simplicity, and as much like the common council meetings are held, as possible. A record of the District Meetings may be kept, but not published. They should endeavor to settle all questions of a local character, but those of a general character, or those that concern the Brotherhood in general, should be taken to the Annual Meeting. And all questions that cannot be settled at the District Meetings should be taken to the Annual Meeting," etc., as appears in Minutes published 1909, page 246.

The Middle District of Pennsylvania had already several years before, held a District Meeting, yearly, including all the churches between the Susquehanna River on the east, and the Alleghany Mountains on the west, thus leaving all the churches east of the Susquehanna unorganized. Therefore, some of the Elders in eastern Pennsylvania called a meeting in the Tulpehocken Church, in Lebanon Co., in the fall of 1866, notifying all the churches in East Pennsylvania, of the time and place and purpose of the meeting to organize one or more districts. This being something new, the Elders also invited Elder D. M. Holsinger, of Blair Co., Pa., to be present, because they had several years' experience.

The date of the meeting is not at hand, but it was either in September, or October. The churches were well represented, and Brother D. M. Holsinger, and his son, Henry R., were there.

The Elders prevailed on Elder Holsinger to preside at the meeting. Elder C. Bomberger was appointed clerk, and he appointed S. R. Zug his assistant.

The meeting being now organized, and the purpose of the call of the meeting being stated, and declared open for remarks, it soon developed that there was a difference of opinion as to forming one, or two districts. Those favoring two were, as a rule, from the German churches, and the strongest pleas for one district came from the English.

The arguments for two was the difference in language, and the laxity of discipline of some churches on the matter of dress, while on the other side, it was argued, and that with tears, by some that by staying together, the influence of the plain churches might have a salutary effect on those dressy churches, by mingling together. It may be in place here to state that the difference in language at that time was much more marked than it is now.

All business brought before the meeting had to be presented in both German and English, and the minutes had to be printed in both languages. The outcome finally was a decision, unanimously, to organize, into one district, all the churches east of the Susquehanna River.

The next matter taken up was: when and where shall the first District Meeting be held for church business? Elder David Gerlach offered to take it in the White Oak Church, Lancaster County. The offer was accepted, and it was decided that it shall be held on Ascension Day, 1867, to meet the evening before to organize, and get things in shape for business next morning.

Ascension Day in 1867 coming on May 30 the delegates from the churches met at the Chiques Meeting-house, in the White Oak District, on May 29, 1867, at 6 o'clock P. M.

Following is a copy of the officers and delegates of that meeting, viz.:

"Elder Samuel Harley, Moderator.
Elder C. Bomberger, Clerk.
S. R. Zug, Assistant Clerk.
Jos. Myer, Interpreter.
"The churches comprising said district are:
1. White Oak, Elder D. Gerlach, J. S. Newcomer, Philip Zigler.
2. West Conestoga, Elder C. Bomberger, J. Reinhold, C. Brubaker.
3. Ephrata, Israel Myers, Samuel Harley.
4. Conestoga, Christian Rupp, Jos. Myer.
5. Big Swatara, Elder Jacob Hollinger, Wm. Hertzler.
6. Tulpehocken, Elder John Zug, S. Kurtz.
7. Little Swatara, Elder D. Merkey, S. Gettle, Levi Light.
8. Coventry, Peter Hollowbush, Jacob Conner.

9. Green Tree, Isaac Price, Jacob Gottwals.
10. Germantown, John Price.
11. Upper Dublin, John U. Slingluff.
12. Philadelphia, Jacob Spanogle.
13. New Jersey, not represented.
14. Indian Creek, Elder Samuel Harley, Henry Cassel."

After receiving the credentials of delegates, the meeting adjourned to meet to-morrow morning at 7.30 A. M."

It will be noticed that there were then fourteen organized churches in the district, and the officers and delegates numbered 27 of whom only two are yet living (in 1914) namely Jacob Conner and S. R. Zug. There were at that time only 9 ordained Elders in the district. Now, at the time of our District Meeting of 1911, there were 47 Elders, 76 officers and delegates, and 43 organized churches, with about 7,600 members. Lancaster County alone has about 3,200 members, 18 Elders, and 15 organized churches. Prior to 1872, the Elders present at the District Meeting, organized the meeting by appointing its officers, and that year, for the first time, the delegates, with the Elders present, elected them by vote, the delegates and Elders going before the tellers and giving their votes private, while quite recently (it was decided) that all elections shall be by ballot.

At the beginning, the time of meeting was the evening before Ascension Day. In 1871 it was made one week earlier. In 1887 two weeks before Ascension Day, and more recently another week was added, so that now the time is the third Wednesday after Easter, the Elders at 9 A. M., delegates at 3 P. M.

In 1896 it was decided that none but regular delegates shall have a right to vote. The Elders in 1866 were C. Bomberger, D. Gerlach, Jac. Hollinger, David Merkey, John Zug, J. H. Umstadt, Benj. Harley, Saml. Harley, and Jac. K. Reiner, and but one brother in the District who has so far attended every Dist. Meeting, both regular and special and largely on his own expense. Years ago some churches considered it wrong to give a preacher money, even for travelling expenses, as a delegate.

A list of District Meetings is hereto attached, giving the

HISTORY OF DISTRICT MEETINGS. 589

TABLE OF DISTRICT MEETINGS OF EASTERN PENNSYLVANIA.
By Elder J. H. Longenecker.

	Moderator.	Writing Clerk.	Reading Clerk.	Church Where Held.	Members on S. C.	Delegates.
1867	Eld. S. Harley	Eld. C. Bomberger	S. R. Zug	Chiques house		D. Gerlach.
1868	" S. Harley	" C. Bomberger	S. R. Zug	Green Tree		Wm. Hertzler. Wm. Hertzler.
1869	" Wm. Hertzler	" C. Bomberger	S. R. Zug	Tulpehocken	D. Gerlach	S. R. Zug.
1870	" D. Gerlach	" C. Bomberger	S. R. Zug	Mingo	D. Gerlach	S. R. Zug.
1871	" John Zug	" C. Bomberger	S. R. Zug	Big Swatara	John Zug	D. Gerlach.
1872	" D. Gerlach	" C. Bomberger	S. R. Zug	Coventry	Jacob Reiner	
1873	" D. Gerlach	" Wm. Hertzler	S. R. Zug	W. Conestoga	D. Gerlach	J. K. Reiner.
1874	" D. Gerlach	" Wm. Hertzler	S. R. Zug	Hatfield	D. Gerlach	Jno. R. Price.
1875	" D. Gerlach	" Wm. Hertzler	S. R. Zug	Ephrata	D. Gerlach	C. Bucher.
1876	" D. Gerlach	" Wm. Hertzler	S. R. Zug	Mingo	D. Gerlach	Jacob Rider.
1877	" Wm. Hertzler	" S. R. Zug	Geo. Bucher	Spring Creek	S. Harley	Wm. Hertzler.
1878	" Wm. Hertzler	" S. R. Zug	C. Bucher	Indian Creek	S. Harley	S. R. Zug.
1879	" S. Harley	" S. R. Zug	C. Bucher	White Oak	C. Bucher	
1880	" J. K. Reiner	" S. R. Zug	Wm. Hertzler	Green Tree	C. Bucher	S. Harley.
1881	" Wm. Hertzler	" S. R. Zug	Geo. Bucher	Little Swatara	S. Harley	
1882	" Wm. Hertzler	" S. R. Zug	Geo. Bucher	Coventry	C. Bucher	S. Harley.
1883	" Wm. Hertzler	" S. R. Zug	Geo. Bucher	Maiden Creek	C. Bucher	
1884	" Wm. Hertzler	" S. R. Zug	Geo. Bucher	Hatfield	S. Harley	
1885	" Wm. Hertzler	" S. R. Zug	Geo. Bucher	Tulpehocken	Wm. Hertzler	
1886	" Wm. Hertzler	" S. R. Zug	Isaac Kulp	Springfield	S. Harley	
1887	" S R. Zug	" Geo. Bucher	Jno. B. Gibble	Conestoga	Wm. Hertzler	
1888	" C. Bucher	" S. R. Zug	John Herr	Mingo	C. Bucher	
1889	" S. R. Zug	" Geo. Bucher	H. E. Light	Chiques	S. R. Zug	
1890	" C. Bucher	" S. R. Zug	Geo. Bucher	Ephrata	C. Bucher	
1891	" Wm. Hertzler	" Geo. Bucher	F. P. Cassel	Big Swatara	Wm. Hertzler	
1892	" S. R. Zug	" J. T. Myers	Geo. Bucher	Ridgely, Md.	S. R. Zug	
1893	" Wm. Hertzler	" Geo. Bucher	F. P. Cassel	Indian Creek	C. Bucher	

590   THE CHURCH OF THE BRETHREN.

	Moderator.	Writing Clerk.	Reading Clerk.	Church Where Held.	Members on S. C.	Delegates.
1894	Eld. S. R. Zug	Eld. John Herr	J. H. Longenecker	Mountville	F. P. Cassel	
1895	" C. Bucher	" J. H. Longenecker	John Herr	Hatfield	C. Bucher	
1896	" F. P. Cassel	" J. Y. King	Hiram Gibble	Spring Creek	F. P. Cassel	
1897	" J. H. Longenecker	" Geo. Bucher	John Herr	Sand Brook, N. J.	S. R. Zug	
1898	" J. Y. King	" John Herr	Geo. Bucher	White Oak—	J. H. Longenecker	
1899	" J. H. Longenecker	" Geo. Bucher	J. Y. King	Springfield	J. Y. King	
1900	" John Herr	" I. W. Taylor	G. N. Falkenstein	Conestoga	John Herr	
1901	" J. Y. King	" Geo. Bucher	Jesse Zeigler	Little Swatara	J. H. Longenecker	
1902	" J. H. Longenecker	" I. W. Taylor	G. N. Falkenstein	Chiques, Eliz't'wn	J. H. Longenecker	
1903	" John Herr	S. H. Hertzler	Jesse Zeigler	Indian Creek	John Herr	
1904	" I. W. Taylor	Eld. G. N. Falkenstein	I. N. H. Beahm	Tulpehocken	I. W. Taylor	J. H. Longenecker.[1]
1905	" John Herr	" S. H. Hertzler	Jesse Zeigler	Ridgely, Md.	Tobias Myers	John Herr.
1906	" J. H. Longenecker	" I. W. Taylor	G. N. Falkenstein	Lancaster	J. H. Longenecker	I. W. Taylor
1907	" John Herr	" S. H. Hertzler	Jesse Zeigler	Hatfield	John Herr	J. T. Myers.
1908	" I. W. Taylor	" G. N. Falkenstein	I. N. H. Beahm	Springville	I. W. Taylor	J. H. Longenecker.
1909	" John Herr	" S. H. Hertzler	Jesse Zeigler	West Green Tree	John Herr	F. P. Cassel.
1910	" I. W. Taylor	" G. N. Falkenstein	H. K. Ober	Spring Creek, Anville	I. W. Taylor	Jesse Ziegler.
1910	" P. S. Miller	" G. A. Snyder[2]	J. M. Kagey	Ephrata	Special D. M.	
1911	" J. H. Longenecker	" S. H. Hertzler	Jesse Zeigler	White Oak	J. H. Longenecker	John Herr.
1912	" John Herr	H. K. Ober	G. N. Falkenstein	Big Swatara	F. P. Cassel	I. W. Taylor.
1913	" I. W. Taylor	Eld. S. H. Hertzler	Jesse Zeigler	Ephrata	J. H. Longenecker	John Herr.
1914	" J. H. Longenecker	H. K. Ober	G. N. Falkenstein	Midway	I. W. Taylor	S. H. Hertzler.

[1] Since and including the year 1904 the District was entitled to two members on Standing Committee.
[2] G. N. Falkenstein, Writing Clerk for the District.

place where held, the year, the Moderator and Clerks, and the Delegates to Annual Meetings, and members on Standing Committee from the District.

The first two years 1867 and 1868, the Districts did not appoint Standing Committee, and so our District had two delegates. After that until 1882, inclusive, the District appointed one member on Standing Committee, and a delegate. From that time on it had only one member on Standing Committee, and in place of the accompanying delegate, the local churches could represent.

CHAPTER III.

MINISTERIAL, SUNDAY SCHOOL, AND MISSIONARY MEETINGS OF EASTERN PENNSYLVANIA.

Place.	Date.	Moderator.	Clerk.	Treasurer.	Program Committee.
1. Elizabethtown	Nov. 21-23, 1893	S. R. Zug			
2. No meeting	1894				
3. Spring Creek	Nov. 26-28, 1895	F. P. Cassel	Geo. Bucher	J. H. Longenecker	S. R. Zug, H. E. Light, J. H. Longenecker.
4. East Petersburg	Dec. 1-3, 1896	S. R. Zug	Geo. Bucher	J. Y. King	H. E. Light, J. Y. King, John Herr.
5. Ephrata	Nov. 23-25, 1897	S. R. Zug	Geo. Bucher	J. Y. King	H. E. Light, J. Y. King, John Herr.
6. Mingo	Oct. 25, 26, 1898	A. L. Grater / J. H. Longenecker	John Herr		H. E. Light, John Herr, G. N. Falkenstein.
7. Ridgely, Md.	Aug. 15, 16, 1899	Geo. S. Rairigh	Geo. Bucher		John Herr, G. N. Falkenstein, I. W. Taylor.
8. Lancaster	Oct. 3, 4, 1900	S. R. Zug	Jesse Ziegler	T. F. Imler	G. N. Falkenstein, I. W. Taylor, J. H. Witmer.
9. Mechanic Grove	Oct. 9, 10, 1901	John Herr	G. N. Falkenstein	S. H. Hertzler	I. W. Taylor, J. H. Witmer, Jesse Ziegler.
10. Hanoverdale	Oct. 8-10, 1902	J. H. Longenecker	I. W. Taylor	Hiram Gibble	J. H. Witmer, Jesse Ziegler, I. W. Taylor.
11. Bird-in-Hand	Oct. 28, 29, 1903	F. P. Cassel	Geo. Bucher	H. E. Light	Jesse Ziegler, I. W. Taylor, J. H. Longenecker.
12. Ephrata	Nov. 2, 3, 1904	J. H. Longenecker	S. H. Hertzler	E. M. Wenger	I. W. Taylor, J. H. Longenecker, I. N. H. Beahm.
13. Elizabethtown	Nov. 1, 2, 1905	J. H. Witmer	I. N. H. Beahm	S. Z. Witmer	J. H. Longenecker, I. N. H. Beahm, S. H. Hertzler.
14. Meyers, Lebanon Co.	Oct. 30, 31, 1906	I. W. Taylor	H. K. Ober	A. S. Hottenstein	I. N. H. Beahm, S. H. Hertzler, T. F. Imler.
15. Elizabethtown	Oct. 30, 31, 1907	J. H. Longenecker	G. N. Falkenstein	D. Kilhefner	I. N. H. Beahm, T. F. Imler, G. N. Falkenstein.
16. Heidelberg, Lebanon Co.	Oct. 28, 29, 1908	F. P. Cassel	I. N. H. Beahm	Hiram Gibble	T. F. Imler, G. N. Falkenstein, H. K. Ober.
17. Indian Creek	Oct. 27, 28, 1909	J. H. Longenecker	T. F. Imler	John C. Zug	G. N. Falkenstein, H. K. Ober, Jesse Ziegler.
18. Ephrata	Oct. 26, 27, 1910	John Herr	S. H. Hertzler	H. K. Ober	H. K. Ober, Jesse Ziegler, D. Kilhefner.
19. East Petersburg	Nov. 8, 9, 1911	J. H. Longenecker	J. C. Zug	S. Z. Witmer	Jesse Ziegler, D. Kilhefner, J. C. Zug.
20. Spring Creek	Nov. 13, 14, 1912	John Herr	G. N. Falkenstein	R. P. Bucher	D. Kilhefner, J. C. Zug, R. P. Bucher.
21. Middle Creek[3]	Nov. 11, 12, 1913	J. H. Longenecker	H. K. Ober	A. S. Hottenstein	John C. Zug, R. P. Bucher, S. H. Hertzler.

[3] Stenographic report of meeting for first time.

CHAPTER IV.

MISSIONARY HISTORY.

INTRODUCTION.

The first missionary effort by the District was made a number of years before a Mission Board existed in the District.

A request came from the state of Maine, whereupon in the year 1872, District Meeting passed the following resolution, viz.:

"Resolved, That the request of John Dennis and his Brethren in the State of Maine, in regard to a ministering Brother being sent to them to preach the Gospel, and make known to them the order of the Brethren, should not be slighted but prayerfully considered by the Annual Council, and measures adopted to carry the same into effect."

Whereupon Brethren Daniel Holsinger, and Daniel Longenecker were proposed to look up this field. They being of Middle Pennsylvania District, the following resolution was passed in 1873:

"Resolved, That if the Middle District of Penna. feels willing to send missionaries to Maine this summer, this District will bear part of the expenses, if requested; if they do not, this meeting requests Brethren D. M. Holsinger and D. Longenecker, or two other Brethren, to be sent there, and the expenses be borne by this District."

Middle District not taking any action, the Eastern District sent the above named Brethren on their mission in the summer or fall of 1873.

On their return, their report was not very favorable, and there the mission ended.

The following from manuscript of Elder Christ. Bomberger who was clerk of District Meeting during this time, may be of interest:

"Assessment made for all the churches of the East Penna. District to pay the expenses to the Brethren Daniel Holsinger, and Daniel Longenecker who will go to the state of Maine to preach as follows:

Chiques Congregation	$ 12.00
Conestoga Congregation	12.00
Conestoga West Congregation	12.00
Coventry Congregation	10.00
Ephrata Congregation	12.00
Green Tree Congregation	10.00
Germantown Congregation	5.00
Hatfield Congregation	10.00
Indian Creek Congregation	12.00
Maiden Creek Congregation	6.00
Mingo Congregation	10.00
New Jersey Congregation	10.00
Philadelphia Congregation	10.00
Spring Creek Congregation	12.00
Swatara Big Congregation	12.00
Swatara Little Congregation	15.00
Tulpehocken Congregation	15.00
Upper Dublin Congregation	5.00
White Oak Congregation	12.00
Amount	$202.00

"Hier kennet ihr sehen wie viel vor die gemeinschaften gelegt ist. Es ist besser zu viel, als zu wenig Geld. Wann es nicht alles nimt dann wird es wieder Zurück gegeben und wann ihre Weiber mit gehen dann wird es alles nehmen.

"Sie däten gleichen eine Schwester, eins von ihren Weibern mit nehmen oder alle beiden, von wegen wann sie Weibspersonen taufen wollen, wegen handreichung im aufnehmen. Sie wollen sterten bis den 20 oder 25 October, wann der Herr will, 1872. Ich will das Geld furnishen, aber es ist mir gans recht wann ihr eüer Theil geben woltet auf die Zeit. Es ist 12 Dollar.

"Die Gemeinschaften haben alle eingewilliget das ihre zu bezahlen im Eastern District.

"So ist es meine Pflicht es zu sagen zu alle Gemeinden. Ich will sorgen vor das Geld, wann ich es nicht bekommen kann, dann lehne ich es auf den District.

"CHRIST BOMBERGER."

The foregoing statement was forwarded to all the churches of the District.

History of Home Mission Board of Eastern Pennsylvania.

In the year 1878, the first effort was made to carry on mission work in the District. To this end a committee was appointed. In 1879, the following plan was adopted, viz.:

(*a*) Two Brethren to be chosen, one an ordained Elder, and one may be a minister in the second degree,—All the ministers in the District being candidates.

(*b*) They are to be chosen for one year—from one District meeting to the other.

(*c*) All openings to be at their discretion.

(*d*) All reasonable expenses to be borne by the District.

(*e*) They to report to the ensuing District Meeting, both giving an itemized bill of expenses, and of success.

(*f*) All expenses to be raised by voluntary contribution.

(*g*) All housekeepers to urge the contribution on the members of their Church.

(*h*) That the District treasurer also act as treasurer of the Mission Board.

Elder Wm. Hertzler and S. R. Zug were elected. In 1880, the number was increased from two to three, and Bro. J. T. Myers was added. In 1885, it was decided that being the present plan for carrying on Missionary work was thought not to be as effective as it could be, our present plan was adopted, viz.: (*a*) That the board of missionaries shall consist of six ministers, two to be chosen each year and to serve for three years, to be chosen by the District Meeting. At least two of them shall be ordained Elders. (*b*) That said board so chosen shall be styled as required by Annual Meeting, "The Church erection and Missionary Board of the Brethren of Eastern Pennsylvania," etc.

In 1900, the manner of electing members on the Mission Board was so changed, that the Board nominate two Elders, two ministers of either first or second degree, and two deacons and that the delegates elect two of the six by vote. No member of the board shall serve two terms in succession.

First Report of Missionaries.

In 1880, filled a call at Smithville and Conestoga Centre, Lancaster County. Also filled a call from Tomkinsville,

Lackawanna Co., Pa. This last mission was kept up for 6 years. Two were baptized.

Eastern Shore of Maryland Mission.—In 1881, a Missionary effort was made in Eastern Shore of Maryland, by J. T. Myers. Reported good prospects.

In 1882, Elder Wm. Hertzler and Bro. J. T. Myers report[1] having labored in Talbot Co. over three Sundays, baptizing 10 and organizing a church of 18 souls. Held an election for one speaker, and one deacon, under the name of Peach Blossom Church.

At the time our Brethren first came to Eastern Shore, they found some six members there without a preacher, and unorganized.

[1] In connection with this, the following remarkable circumstance may be of interest, as related by Bro. J. T. Myers, viz.: "While we were holding a series of meetings together in the Peach Blossom Church, on the Eastern Shore of Maryland, having been sent there by the Eastern District of Pennsylvania, we went home with a man, not a member of the Church, and took dinner with the family in the early stage of the meeting. Bro. Hertzler felt a little discouraged over the meeting, not being well at the time. He asked about going back home, saying he was but of little account to me in the meeting—I said to him: 'No, Bro. Hertzler, you stay with me. Your company is help to me, and you can pray for the meeting, and help along in that way.'—Lo, on a certain day, in the early stage of the meeting, I missed Bro. Hertzler near dinner time, at the place where we were staying. I looked around for him about the barn, here, and there, but could not find him. Near by was a large forest. I walked out toward it. As I got near, I heard a voice that interested me. I walked closer, and closer towards the place of the voice, it became more and more distinct, as I got closer. By and by, I got nearer to the place in the woods from which the voice came. I stood awhile and listened intently. At last, I discovered it to be Bro. Hertzler's voice. I stood and listened, and watched. At last I saw Bro. Hertzler behind a large oak tree, on his knees, praying in all the earnestness of his heart for the meetings, and for me. I walked away and never said a word to him about it.

"That night we had a larger attendance at meeting and quite a stir in the meeting, several coming forward to give their hearts to God.

"We continued the meetings for about ten days or so, when a number were baptized, and we organized the Peach Blossom Church on the Eastern Shore of Maryland, the result largely, or mainly, through the earnest prayer of Bro. Hertzler, beside the oak tree in the woods. Truly, Bro. Hertzler was a man of God, and I hear his earnest prayer in the woods beside the oak tree every day I think of him. 'Though dead, yet he liveth,' can truly be said of this great and good man of the Eastern District of Pennsylvania—Bro. William Hertzler."

In 1883 and 84 about 20 members from Middle Pennsylvania, moved into Caroline County, among them one minister and two deacons.

In 1884, a committee from Eastern Maryland, and Eastern Pennsylvania, met to decide on representation. The Peach Blossom Church decided not to change her representation.

The Brethren in Caroline Co. decided by a vote of 15 yeas, to 3 nays, and one neutral to belong to Eastern District of Pennsylvania, and forthwith our Brethren proceeded to organize them into a separate church with one resident minister, and two deacons. Name: Ridgely Church.

While under the care of the Home Mission Board from 1882 to 1897, there were 66 received into the church by baptism, and quite a number received by letter.

Expenses of Board for Ministerial Aid from 1882 to 1903, $613.14. Besides donated towards building meeting houses $1,725,00 as follows: Ridgely Church, Two houses, $875; Peach Blossom, Two houses, $650; Peach Blossom, Colored, $200.

Tower City Mission.—In 1886, Bro. Wm. Hertzler went to Tower City, Schuylkill Co., Pa. and held three meetings. Reported interest good. Left another appointment.

In 1887, once a month a brother went to Tower City, Pa., during the year, and once two went together. One visit was made to Auburn, Pa. A brother also went to Englewood, near Newark, N. J.

In 1888, a lovefeast was held in Tower City Church.

In 1889, the church was organized.

In 1890, meetings were held in Tower City, Clark's Valley, Pine Valley, and Tremont.

1892, Two new openings were effected, one in Mohontonga Valley, and the other at Williamstown. Meetings were also held at Mahonoy Valley, and Minersville.

1898, Advised to rent hall at Shamokin to hold services in.

1911, The name was changed from Tower City Church to Shamokin Church, where the meetings and Sunday School are still held in the hall. At present an urgent request to have a new church building.

From 1886 to 1911, there were 70 received into the church by baptism. Expenses for Min. Aid, hall rent, and support for poor $5,085.73.

Mission efforts were made as follows, viz.:

(a) *Clarence, New York.*—In 1891, about 35 meetings were held by different brethren. A report not so favorable. Expenses from 1891 to 1893, for Ministerial Aid, $149.13.

(b) *Pine Run Mission.*—In 1898, a series of meetings was held, in all 15 sermons were preached.

(c) *Montreal (Canada) Mission.*—In 1899, a call came from Montreal, Can., to which the board responded.

In 1900, some 40 meetings were held besides the regular appointments. 9 were received into the church by baptism. Forthwith an organization was effected.

In 1901, Montreal, Can., Church was given over to General Missionary Board, as a foreign Mission point. Expenses for Min. Aid and hall rent $575.48.

(d) *Lakesville, Md., Mission.*—In 1906, meetings were held once a month in the home of Bro. J. Roy Rittenhouse, usually in the yard, among the shade trees. Three meetings each trip. One week protracted meeting. Good interest reported. Expenses for Ministerial Aid $67.73.

(e) *Alderson, Luzerne Co., Mission.*—In 1907, a mission was opened at Alderson. One was baptized. There were some hindrances but at present the outlook is more favorable. Expenses for Ministerial Aid from 1907 to 1911, $550.94.

Aid given to weak churches, viz.:

(a) *Bethel Church, N. J., and Upper Dublin, Pa.*—In 1888, a request came to the board from these churches for help to revive them and help them along.

In 1889, Elders visited Bethel Church 5 times during the year, met them 3 times in council meeting, held one Lovefeast, besides preaching for them several weeks in the aggregate.

Same year Brethren visited Upper Dublin Church and gave them meetings every two weeks during the year.

"For a number of years, ministers were located in these churches by Home Mission Board, assisted by General Mission Board. Five were received into the church by baptism in New Jersey. Paid for Ministerial Aid out of Home Mission Board fund, from 1889 to 1910, $1,044.11.

Paid for Ministerial Aid to Upper Dublin from 1889 to 1902, $324.58.

(b) *Philadelphia Northern Church.*—In 1892, Mission Board was asked to take charge of it.

In 1894, The Phila. Northern Church was supplied with Ministerial Aid during the year. Had meetings every Lord's Day.

One was baptized. Expenses for Ministerial Aid from 1892 to 1896, $189.22.

(c) *Reading Church.*—Jan. 1, 1898, Reading Church was organized with 46 members, and received into the care of the Home Mission Board.

In 1902, the Board was relieved from the care of the church. While under the care of the Board, 26 were received into the church by baptism.

Expenses for Ministerial Aid from 1895 to 1903, $263.04.

(d) *Mechanic Grove Church.*—In 1897, a request to be received into the care of the Home Mission Board was granted.

In 1900, Board was relieved from care of church. Paid for Ministerial Aid, $15.20.

(e) *MaidenCreek Church.*—Received Ministerial aid from 1905 to 1911. 4 were baptized. Expenses $550.94. During this time church paid towards Home Mission, $410.05.

(f) *Norristown Church.*—Received from Home Mission Board for Ministerial Aid from 1895 to 1911, $419.50. Recd. into the church by baptism 7; by letter 30.

(g) *Harrisburg Church.*—Support given to a Sister to do Missionary work in Harrisburg, from 1898 to 1900 amounting to $146.

Mission Board donated to the following churches towards building houses of worship, viz.:

(a) Ridgely Church, E. Shore Maryland, for two houses....$ 875
(b) Peach Blossom, Md. 650
(c) Peach Blossom, Colored 200

(d) Mechanic Grove 100
(e) Harrisburg 500
(f) Schuylkill 200
(g) Reading 1,600

Members Elected on Mission Board by District Meeting from 1879 to 1914.

1879. Wm. Hertzler and S. R. Zug.
1880. J. T. Myers.

These three were re-elected up to 1885.

1885. I. Kulp, 3 yr., S. Harley, 3 yr., J. Conner, 2 yr., Geo. Bucher, 1 yr., S. R. Zug, 1 yr., Wm. Hertzler, 2 yr.
1886. S. R. Zug and Geo. Bucher, re-elected.
1887. Wm. Hertzler and J. Conner re-elected.
1888. John Hertzler, F. P. Cassel.
1889. Hiram Gibble, Geo. Bucher.
1890. S. R. Zug, J. H. Longenecker.
1891. F. P. Cassel, J. H. Price.
1892. Geo. Bucher, Hiram Gibbel.
1893. S. R. Zug, J. H. Longenecker.
1894. Geo. Bucher and S. R. Zug resigned; elected, H. E. Light, F. P. Cassel, J. T. Myers, John Herr.
1895. H. E. Light, Hiram Gibble.
1896. J. H. Longenecker, John Herr.
1897. J. Y. King, J. T. Myers.
1898. H. E. Light, I. W. Taylor.
1899. John Herr, John Witmer, Jesse Ziegler, unexpired term of J. T. Myers, resigned.
1900. J. H. Longenecker, Hiram Gibble.
1901. Jesse Ziegler, S. Z. Witmer.
1902. I. W. Taylor, Wm. Oberholtzer.
1903. John Herr, E. M. Wenger.
1904. John Witmer, J. W. Myer.
1905. J. H. Longenecker, David Kilhefner.
1906. L. R. Brumbaugh, Jeremiah Shelly.
1907. S. H. Hertzler, Amos Kuhns.
1908. I. W. Taylor, John Herr.
1909. Jesse Ziegler, David Weaver.
1910. J. H. Longenecker, H. B. Yoder.
1911. S. H. Hertzler, David Kilhefner.

HOME OF LAKE RIDGE MISSION.

1912. Rufus P. Bucher.
1913. J. H. Longenecker, H. B. Yoder.
1914. David Kilhefner, 5 yrs.; E. M. Wenger, 1 yr.

By the foregoing list we find that from the time of the organization 1878 up to 1911, 27 different Brethren served on the Board.

A number of Brethren have made considerable sacrifice to labor in the various fields, and although the results may not have met our anticipations, yet we feel that some good has been accomplished. May a great door and effectual be opened in the future for the Board, to the salvation of sinners, and the advancement of His cause.

In 1912, the Board had in charge the following missions, viz.: Shamokin, Alderson, Oley Valley, and Tompkins Co., N. Y., called Lake Ridge Mission.

The Board at this time gives support to the following Evangelists, viz.: Bro. Wm. Fretz, who has the work in hand at Alderson. Elder D. W. Weaver and wife, located at Oley, east of Reading. Bro. E. F. Nedrow and wife who have charge of the work in Tompkins Co., New York, on the east side of Lake Cayuga.

Lake Ridge Mission.

On April 3, 1912, Bro. E. F. Nedrow and family moved from Norristown, Pa., to Lake Ridge, N. Y., to take charge of the work in this new territory. After much patient work and some opposition an old Baptist Church at this place was secured as a house of worship. Conveyance of the same was made October 1, 1912. The place had been very much neglected, but by the aid of the Mission Board and the help of the people of the community we succeeded in making the place presentable and comfortable, much to the satisfaction of all.

On February 2, the house was dedicated. Elder Jesse Ziegler, of Royersford, Pa., delivered the address. An encouraging number was in attendance and regular services have been held each Sunday since.

On April 1, 1913, Elder R. A. Nedrow and family moved

into our midst from Fredrick City, Md., and are very helpful in the work here.

On Sunday, April 6, Sunday School was organized and has continued to the present with an average attendance of thirty-eight. The work here is encouraging, since a number of families of members have moved in, making the total membership 13.

Annual Missionary Contributions of the District.—H. E. Light.

Year.	Home.	Foreign.	Charity.	Tract.	Total.
1889	230.64	295.49	Charity and church houses etc. Brethren Home 62,000.00 not included	25.07	601.00
1890	193.71	211.39		61.20	466.30
1891	97.63	128.80		11.15	237.58
1892	338.88	121.75		40.30	500.93
1893	321.70	300.34		77.54	699.58
1894	324.16	178.64		112.29	615.09
1895	387.27	342.44		25.79	755.50
1896	277.69	623.91		24.00	901.60
1897	298.48	625.56	....	....	924.04
1898	384.99	780.54	....	....	1,165.53
1899	226.79	959.40	....	26.19	1,212.38
1900	577.75	1,064.34	2,704.89	....	4,346.98
1901	383.97	1,071.35	1,435.49	....	2,891.81
1902	804.89	1,191.49	....	6.00	2,002.38
1903	657.30	1,494.46	1,245.82	....	3,397.58
1904	715.83	1,118.58	1,246.65	....	3,081.06
1905	615.57	1,216.72	2,005.25	34.60	3,872.14
1906	633.07	1,095.90	992.54	....	2,721.51
1907	718.85	2,149.65	201.30	....	3,069.80
1908	1,800.41	2,407.43	1,377.50	....	5,585.34
1909	884.46	2,870.60	57.64	....	3,812.70
1910	871.81	1,918.45	964.26	....	3,754.62
1911	926.84	3,042.49	910.17	....	4,879.50
1912	874.45	1,699.12	1,079.46	....	3,653.03
	11,847.14	26,778.85	14,220.97	444.13	55,249.09

Members[1] of the Mission Board of Eastern Pennsylvania.

1. Elder William Hertzler.........served 11 years; elected first 1879.
2. Elder S. R. Zug..............served 13 years; elected first 1879.
3. Elder J. T. Myers............served 9 years; elected first 1880.
4. Elder Isaac Kulp.............served 5 years; elected first 1883.
5. Elder Samuel Harley..........served 3 years; elected first 1885.
6. —— Jacob Conner............served 5 years; elected first 1885.
7. Elder George Bucher..........served 9 years; elected first 1885.
8. Elder John Hertzler..........served 3 years; elected first 1888.
9. Elder F. P. Cassel...........served 9 years; elected first 1888.
10. Elder Hiram Gibble..........served 12 years; elected first 1890.

[1] Compiled by J. H. Longenecker.

MISSIONARY HISTORY.

11. Elder J. H. Longenecker.......served 17 years; elected first 1890.
12. —— J. H. Price.............served 3 years; elected first 1891.
13. Elder H. E. Light.............served 7 years; elected first 1894.
14. Elder John Herr..............served 14 years; elected first 1894.
15. Elder J. Y. King.............served 3 years; elected first 1897.
16. Elder I. W. Taylor ....served 9 years; elected first 1898.
17. Elder Jesse Ziegler............served 6 years; elected first 1901.
18. Elder S. Z. Witmer...........served 3 years; elected first 1901.
19. Elder Wm. Oberholtzer........served 3 years; elected first 1902.
20. Elder E. M. Wenger..........served 3 years; elected first 1903.
21. Elder J. H. Witmer............served 3 years; elected first 1904.
22. —— Jno. W. Myer..........served 3 years; elected first 1904.
23. Elder D. Kilhefner............served 4 years; elected first 1905.
24. —— L. R. Brumbaugh.......served 3 years; elected first 1906.
25. —— Jeremiah Shelly.........served 3 years; elected first 1906.
26. —— A. M. Kuhns............served 3 years; elected first 1907.
27. Elder H. B. Yoder............served 2 years; elected first 1910.
28. Elder S. H. Hertzler..........served 4 years; elected first 1907.
29. Elder David W. Weaver.......served 3 years; elected first 1909.
30. Elder Rufus P. Bucher........served — years; elected first 1912.

This covers a period of 33 years.

MISSION BOARDS OF EASTERN PENNSYLVANIA.

Mission Board, 1879: Eld. Wm. Hertzler,
S. R. Zug,
} 1 year.

Mission Board, 1880: Wm. Hertzler,
S. R. Zug,
J. T. Myers,
} 1 year.

Mission Board, 1881: Wm. Hertzler, 3 years.
S. R. Zug, 2 years.
J. T. Myers, 1 year.

Mission Board, 1882: Wm. Hertzler, 2 years.
S. R. Zug, 1 year.
J. T. Myers, 3 years.

Mission Board, 1883: S. R. Zug, 3 years.
J. T. Myers, resigned.
Isaac Kulp in his stea 2 years.
Wm. Hertzler, 1 year.

Mission Board, 1884: Wm. Hertzler, 3 years.
S. R. Zug, 2 years.
Isaac Kulp, 1 year.

Mission Board, 1885: S. Harley,
Isaac Kulp,
} 3 years.
Wm. Hertzler,
J. Conner,
} 2 years.
S. R. Zug,
Geo. Bucher,
} 1 year.

Mission Board, 1886: S. R. Zug,
　　　　　　　　　　Geo. Bucher, } 3 years.
　　　　　　　　　　Samuel Harley,
　　　　　　　　　　Isaac Kulp, } 2 years.
　　　　　　　　　　Wm. Hertzler,
　　　　　　　　　　Jacob Conner, } 1 year.

Mission Board, 1887: Wm. Hertzler,
　　　　　　　　　　Jacob Conner, } 3 years.
　　　　　　　　　　S. R. Zug,
　　　　　　　　　　Geo. Bucher, } 2 years.
　　　　　　　　　　Samuel Harley,
　　　　　　　　　　Isaac Kulp, } 1 year.

Mission Board, 1888: Jno. Hertzler,
　　　　　　　　　　F. P. Cassel, } 3 years.
　　　　　　　　　　Wm. Hertzler,
　　　　　　　　　　Jacob Conner, } 2 years.
　　　　　　　　　　S. R. Zug,
　　　　　　　　　　Geo. Bucher, } 1 year.

Mission Board, 1889: Geo. Bucher,
　　　　　　　　　　Hiram Gibble, } 3 years.
　　　　　　　　　　Jno. Hertzler,
　　　　　　　　　　F. P. Cassel, } 2 years.
　　　　　　　　　　Wm. Hertzler,
　　　　　　　　　　Jacob Conner, } 1 year.

Mission Board, 1890: Eld. S. R. Zug,
　　　　　　　　　　J. H. Longenecker, } 3 years.
　　　　　　　　　　Geo. Bucher,
　　　　　　　　　　Hiram Gibble, } 2 years.
　　　　　　　　　　Jno. Hertzler,
　　　　　　　　　　F. P. Cassel, } 1 year.

Mission Board, 1891: F. P. Cassel,
　　　　　　　　　　J. H. Price, } 3 years.
　　　　　　　　　　S. R. Zug,
　　　　　　　　　　J. H. Longenecker, } 2 years.
　　　　　　　　　　Geo. Bucher,
　　　　　　　　　　Hiram Gibble, } 1 year.

Mission Board, 1892: Geo. Bucher,
　　　　　　　　　　Hiram Gibble, } 3 years.
　　　　　　　　　　F. P. Cassel,
　　　　　　　　　　J. H. Price, } 2 years.
　　　　　　　　　　S. R. Zug,
　　　　　　　　　　J. H. Longenecker, } 1 year.

Mission Board, 1893: S. R. Zug,
　　　　　　　　　　J. H. Longenecker, } 3 years.
　　　　　　　　　　Geo. Bucher,
　　　　　　　　　　Hiram Gibble, } 2 years.
　　　　　　　　　　F. P Cassel,
　　　　　　　　　　J. H. Price, } 1 year.

MISSIONARY HISTORY.

Mission Board, 1894: S. R. Zug and
    Geo. Bucher resigned.

Mission Board, 1894: F. P. Cassel,   3 years.
    H. E. Light,   1 year.
    J. H. Longenecker,   2 years.
    Hiram Gibble,   1 year.
    J. T. Myers,   3 years.
    John Herr,   2 years.

Mission Board, 1895: H. E. Light,
    Hiram Gibble,   } 3 years.
    F. P. Cassel,
    J. T. Myers,   } 2 years.
    J H. Longenecker,
    John Herr,   } 1 year.

Mission Board, 1896: J. H. Longenecker,
    John Herr,   } 3 years.
    H. E. Light,
    Hiram Gibble,   } 2 years.
    F. P. Cassel,
    J. T. Myers,   } 1 year.

Mission Board, 1897: J. Y. King,
    J. T. Myers,   } 3 years.
    J. H. Longenecker,
    John Herr,   } 2 years.
    H. E. Light,
    Hiram Gibble,   } 1 year.

Mission Board, 1898: H. E. Light,
    I. W. Taylor,   } 3 years.
    J. Y. King,
    J. T. Myers,   } 2 years.
    J. H. Longenecker,
    John Herr,   } 1 year.

Mission Board, 1899: Jno. Herr,
    J. H. Witmer,   } 3 years.
    H. E. Light,
    I. W. Taylor,   } 2 years.
    J. Y. King,
    J. T. Myers,   } 1 year.

Mission Board, 1900: J. H. Longenecker,
    Hiram Gibble,   } 3 years.
    John Herr,
    J. H. Witmer,   } 2 years.
    H. E. Light,
    I. W. Taylor,   } 1 year.

Mission Board, 1901: Jesse Ziegler,
    S. Z. Witmer,   } 3 years.
    J. H. Longenecker,
    Hiram Gibble,   } 2 years.
    John Herr,
    J. H. Witmer,   } 1 year.

Mission Board, 1902: I. W. Taylor, } 3 years.
Wm. Oberholtzer,
Jesse Ziegler, } 2 years.
S. Z. Witmer,
J. H. Longenecker, } 1 year.
Hiram Gibble,

Mission Board, 1903: Jno. Herr, } 3 years.
Ed. M. Wenger,
I. W. Taylor, } 2 years.
Wm. Oberholtzer,
Jesse Ziegler, } 1 year.
S. Z. Witmer,

Mission Board, 1904: Jno. H. Witmer, } 3 years.
Jno. W. Myer,
Jno. Herr, } 2 years.
E. M. Wenger,
I. W. Taylor, } 1 year.
Wm. Oberholtzer,

Mission Board, 1905: J. H. Longenecker, } 3 years.
David Kilhefner,
J. H. Witmer, } 2 years.
Jno. W. Myer,
Jno. Herr, } 1 year.
E. M. Wenger,

Mission Board, 1906: L. R. Brumbaugh, } 3 years.
Jeremiah Shelly,
J. H. Longenecker, } 2 years.
David Kilhefner,
J. H. Witmer, } 1 year.
Jno. W. Myer,

Mission Board, 1907: S. H. Hertzler, } 3 years.
Amos M. Kuhns,
L. R. Brumbaugh, } 2 years.
Jeremiah Shelly,
J. H. Longenecker, } 1 year.
David Kilhefner,

Mission Board, 1908: I. W. Taylor, } 3 years.
John Herr,
S. H. Hertzler, } 2 years.
Amos M. Kuhns,
L. R. Brumbaugh, } 1 year.
Jeremiah Shelly,

Mission Board, 1909: Jesse Ziegler, } 3 years.
David Weaver,
I. W. Taylor, } 2 years.
Jno. Herr,
S. H. Hertzler, } 1 year.
Amos M. Kuhns,

Mission Board, 1910: J. H. Longenecker, } 3 years.
H. B. Yoder,
Jesse Ziegler, } 2 years.
David Weaver,
I. W. Taylor, } 1 year.
Jno. Herr,

Mission Board, 1911: S. H. Hertzler, } 3 years.
D. Kilhefner,
J. H. Longenecker, } 2 years.
H. B. Yoder,
Jesse Ziegler, } 1 year.
David Weaver,

Mission Board, 1912: Rufus Bucher,
S. H. Hertzler, } 2 years.
D. Kilhefner,
J. H. Longenecker, } 1 year.
H. B. Yoder,

Mission Board, 1913: R. P. Bucher,
S. H. Hertzler,
David Kilhefner,
J. H. Longenecker,
H. B. Yoder.

Mission Board, 1914: R. P. Bucher,
J. H. Longenecker,
David Kilhefner,
E. M. Wenger,
H. B. Yoder.

CHAPTER V.

BENEVOLENT ACTIVITIES.

A. Brethren Home.

It has always been the rule of the Church of the Brethren to provide for the poor, aged, and infirm members of the church, and not suffer them to become a public charge. And as it was sometimes almost impossible to find a home for them except with strangers, and even sometimes they were placed in homes isolated from church services, where the church would pay for their support, and they would only be taken for the money that could be made out of it, they were often neglected both from a temporal and spiritual point of view, so much so that they felt that people would be glad if they were out of the way.

Circumstances being such caused some of the leading Elders of the Eastern District of Pennsylvania to agitate the project of establishing a home somewhere in the District where such homeless members could be placed and properly cared for. The result of this agitation was a query coming to District Meeting in the spring of 1893, as follows:

"Art. 12. After maturely considering the propriety and necessity of establishing somewhere in the district a Home for the aged, who require the support of the church, we heartily invite and entreat the District Council to consider this proposition in the light and principles of the life and Gospel of Jesus Christ.

"Ans. F. P. Cassel, Geo. Bucher, and H. E. Light were appointed a committee to inquire into this matter, and to report to next year's District Meeting."

In the spring of 1894, the following report was presented to District Meeting:

"7. REPORT OF COMMITTEE FOR HOME FOR THE AGED

"We, your Committee, appointed to inquire into the propriety and necessity of establishing a home for the aged and poor, beg leave to present the following report:

"After prayerfully and maturely considering the matter, we unanimously give, as the result of our investigation, that such a home, when properly conducted, has spiritual and temporal advantages for its inmates, which they do not have when supported as they are now, which we conclude is in harmony with the spirit of the Gospel, and for these reasons we recommend such a home."

"Ans. The report of the Committee is respectfully received, but as there seems to be a difference of opinion, we deem it best for the union of the District to defer the matter for one year."

The District Meeting of 1895 took up the case again as unfinished business and decided as follows:

"The report of committee to inquire into the propriety and necessity of a 'Home for the aged and poor' (see minutes of 1894, art. 7) was adopted with the understanding that it is only to be considered as granting the privilege and liberty of getting up such a home by a free will offering."

April 16, 1896, a meeting was held at Manheim at which a number of churches were represented, and at which meeting the following committee on location and plan was appointed, viz.: Nathaniel Minnich, B. G. Musser, S. R. Wenger, H. E. Light, B. Z. Eby, S. R. Zug, T. F. Imler.

"At this meeting it was also agreed to call a meeting later of all church members of the District friendly to such a Home."

This meeting was called to be held at Kreider's Meeting House, in the White Oak Church to be held on August 4, 1896, when and where the following plan, offered by Elder S. R. Zug, was adopted, upon which to draw for the construction of the Charter and By-laws, by which the Home is to be conducted, viz.:

"1. The Home is to be located near Manheim, within the bounds of Chiques Church on the farm of Brother Adam S. Basehore, if the farm can be bought on fair terms.

2. The Home shall be known as "The German Baptist Brethren Home for the aged, infirm, poor and homeless of the church, for the Eastern District of Pa., and for such others as may hereafter be determined upon, and its corporate name shall be the "Home for the Homeless."

3. The funds to buy and furnish the Home shall be raised by free-will offerings and any member contributing from one to twenty-five dollars as hereinafter specified shall be entitled to a vote for Trustees, which sum shall be considered a share, or interest and will entitle any brother or sister holding such share or interest, or interests to as many votes as they hold shares.

4. The Home shall be under the control of seven competent Trustees who shall be elected as follows: One shall be the Elder of the church in which the Home is located, and shall be a member of said Board ex officio, and the other six shall hold their office for three years, except at the first election, when two shall be elected for three years, two for two years and two for one year, after which two shall be elected every year for three years.

5. Said Trustees shall, every year, soon after such election, meet and organize by electing a President, a Secretary, and Treasurer, and shall meet as often as is found necessary for properly maintaining the Home.

6. Said Trustees shall appoint a Steward and a Stewardess to superintend the Home under the direction of the Trustees to whom they are amenable.

7. The services of the Trustees shall be free of charge, and they shall fix the wages of their employes.

8. Whatever, if any, lack of funds from free will offerings, may be supplied by loans of not less than twenty-five dollars each, without interest, for not less than five years, which will make such lenders shareholders as aforesaid while such loan lasts.

9. The fiscal year shall be from New Year to New Year, and the annual election of Trustees shall be at the Home, on the first Tuesday of February, and the six to be elected as aforesaid, shall be two Elders, two ministers and two deacons.

10. The Trustees, Treasurer, and Steward shall keep proper records of all their work, and their books shall be open for inspection by any contributor.

11. The use of tobacco or opiates shall be prohibited, if possible; if not, it shall be so regulated as to reduce it to a minimum.

BENEVOLENT ACTIVITIES.

12. The President shall have power to call a meeting at any time, and all needs and suggestions shall be reported by the Steward to the President.

13. The number of inmates shall be regulated by the capacity of the buildings or the funds on hand, and shall consist of the homeless members of the churches, and who are without means of support except from the church, and none shall be received except recommended by the church, which is expected to pay actual cost of keeping and supporting such members.

14. Persons of means, yet homeless, may be taken into the Home upon them paying for boarding, etc., as may be agreed upon by said Trustees.

15. Said Board of Trustees shall use their discretion as to who should be taken in, even if they are recommended by the church.

16 The Trustees shall engage a Physician to be called on in case of sickness, and in case of death, the friends or church of such inmate shall immediately be notified, and if they wish to do so, they can remove them, and see to the funeral, and all, and if they do not take charge of them, they shall have a decent Christian burial by the Home, and expenses paid by the church from whence they came.

17. In case of a vacancy in said Board of Trustees, by death or otherwise, the Board has authority to fill said vacancy for the unexpired term thereof.

18. Both Treasurer and Steward shall make report to said Board of Trustees, at all their regular meetings of all money received, or paid, and of all the work performed by them, by virtue of their office, and said Board shall make a full report of the Home, yearly, to the share-holders, at their meeting the second Tuesday of February.

19. Visitors at the Home, staying for meals, and horse feed, are expected to pay for the same, for the benefit of the Home, as said Board may direct.

20. All churches of the E. District of Pa., N. J. and E. Shore of Maryland may enjoy the benefit of this Home on equal terms, if they, by action of the church, decide to do so. Others will come under section 14.

21. The Trustees shall provide to have regular religious services for the benefit of the inmates.

22. There shall be power by a two thirds vote of the shareholders present at the election of Trustees to change the foregoing plan, or any part thereof."

This plan was adopted by the meeting, practically unanimously.

August 20, 1896, Nathaniel Minnich resigned as one of the committee on location, which was accepted, and the Basehore farm viewed by the committee, for the last time, September 17, 1896, and decided to take it on the following terms, viz.: about 65 acres $4,200, payable April 1, 1897, and $300 five years after, without interest. John W. Grabill appointed to fill vacancy on committee made by resignation of N. Minnich.

October 27, 1896, resignation of B. G. Musser accepted, and M. R. Henry appointed to fill vacancy.

According to announcement, a meeting was held in the Brethren Church in Manheim January 1, 1897, at which the first Board of Trustees was elected, viz.:

For 3 years S. R. Wenger and I. W. Taylor, for 2 years H. E. Light and B. Z. Eby, for one year T. F. Imler and M. R. Henry.

S. R. Zug being a Trustee by virtue of being the Elder in charge of the Chiques Church, in the bounds of which the Home is to be located.

The Board organized by electing Elder B. Z. Eby, Chairman; H. E. Light, Secretary; S. R. Wenger, Treasurer.

February 15, 1897, a charter was granted to T. F. Imler, H. E. Light, B. Z. Eby, S. R. Zug and S. R. Wenger.

Brother and Sister Jonathan Weaver were appointed Steward and Stewardess, and moved to the Home about April 1, 1897, and one or two days afterward, the first inmates arrived, namely, Lizzie Weaver and Annie Adams.

April 16, 1897, besides the two already there, the following were accepted as inmates: Levi Moyer, Martha Fullerton David Troup, Henry Willower, Sister Miller, with several not accepted for want of room.

At this meeting the project of building an annex was first discussed, and deferred.

July 22, 1897, the Board of Trustees decided to build an annex 34 × 36 feet and at a called special meeting of the shareholders, held at the Home on August 5, 1897, the meeting passed the following paper by more than a two third vote.

"Whereas there are no less than seven applicants to enter the Home this fall for whom there is no room, and whereas the charter and by-laws do not give authority to build except by consent of the shareholders, Therefore, Resolved that we give our consent to the Trustees to build addition or additions to the Home this fall. And if the funds by donation cannot be fully raised in time, we authorize them to borrow the balance."

August 19, B. Z. Eby, T. S. Beck and S. S. Graybill appointed as building committee.

September 16, resignation of S. R. Wenger, as Treasurer, accepted, and T. F. Imler appointed in his stead.

January 11, 1898, resignation of S. R. Wenger, as Trustee, accepted, and D. M. Hiestand appointed for unexpired term.

The building of annex has cost $2,621.78.

About this time there was a debt on the Home of over $3,000, Sister Geiger having at the start given $500, and now promised to give $1,000, if the balance is raised by April 1, 1899. It was raised and the debt paid. In the Spring of 1899, J. Weaver and wife left as Stewards, and Amos L. Brubaker and wife succeeded them.

On February 6, 1900, at the organization of the Board of Trustees Elder I. W. Taylor was elected Secretary, and has been re-elected every year since.

April 9, 1902, a plan was presented to again enlarge the Home by an addition of 32 × 60 feet, which was accepted, and S. R. Zug, T. F. Imler and Samuel Keller appointed as building committee.

In the spring of 1901, Brother and Sister Brubaker, retired from the stewardship, and Elder B. Z. Eby and wife succeeded them.

Elder Eby same time resigned as Trustee, and Elder Hiram Gibble, was appointed to succeed him and S. R. Zug was appointed President in place of Elder Eby, and has held that position ever since, and John Herr, of Lebanon Co., was appointed to fill the vacancy as Trustee, occasioned by the resignation of Elder Eby.

During the summer of 1906 the Trustees purchased five springs on the farm of Abraham Hernly, about a mile north of the Home, and also right of way of Mr. Hernly and Milton Nauman, to lay pipe to convey the water from those springs to the Home by gravity. The Trustees were about ready to begin ditching for laying the pipe that fall, when an injunction from the Court was obtained by the Manheim Water Company, against the Home, preventing them to proceed.

That injunction was answered by the Trustees, and the following spring a hearing had by the Court, which decided in favor of the Home, and dissolved the injunction at the cost of the water company.

Simultaneous with the water trouble the Manheim people circulated a report that the Home is polluting the stream from which they get their supply of water, about a half mile below the Home, in view of which the following committee was appointed to consider the legality and advisability of changing the location of the Home, viz.: John Herr, I. W. Taylor and H. S. Gibble, and report later.

The committee looked at a number of places in Lancaster and Lebanon Counties, and finally selected Elizabethtown, as the most suitable site, and the Trustees so recommended to the shareholders, February 4, 1908, but the vote was 19 in favor and 23 against instead of 2/3 in favor.

John Herr was re-elected a Trustee, but declined to serve, and Ammon H. Brubacher was appointed in his stead.

A public meeting of shareholders and friends of the Home was called by the Trustees, to be held in the Brethren Church in Manheim, October 22, 1908, to discuss the propriety of a change of location, which meeting was largely attended, and the sentiment seemed strong in favor of a change. So, at the next shareholder's meeting February 2, 1909, their vote was taken as to giving the Trustees authority to select, and secure a proper site, build thereon, and sell the old home, and the result was 25 for, 6 against, 1 neutral. The option on the Elizabethtown site having expired, and the Masons having since obtained one, we had to look elsewhere; and after viewing different places at Columbia, Mountville, Landisville, and Neffsville, the Board of Trustees decided on a site near Neffsville, where Nathan Brubaker offered to give 10 acres of land, along the Lancaster and Lititz Pike and Trolley, without money, provided the Home pay him, and his wife, during life, an annuity of fifty dollars every six months. One of the seven Trustees held out for Columbia for a while, but finally withdrew his vote, that the choice is unanimous.

In the Spring of 1909, B. Z. Eby and wife left the Home as Stewards, and Elder I. W. Taylor and wife were appointed in their stead.

April 26, 1909, on Plan and Specification, and as building Committee I. W. Taylor, Jacob Heagy, H. S. Gibble, Nathan Brubaker and Nathaniel Minnich were appointed.

The building committee organized: I. W. Taylor, Chairman; H. S. Gibble, Secretary; N. Brubaker, Treasurer; and D. M. Rothenberger, of Lancaster, was appointed architect.

Plan of Building.

Main building 200 × 36 feet. Rear building 78 × 32 feet, with basement under the whole, two and a half stories, with dormer windows on third floor. The two houses are 12 feet apart, with gangway 12 feet wide from cellar to attic, so as to make it practically one house.

The basement wall is solid concrete, as is also the floor. The basement contains the hot water heating arrangement, by which the whole house is heated, and also the laundry, ironing apparatus, cellar, etc.

The first floor in the main building has an office, two sitting rooms, and the rest is divided into guest and toilet rooms. The second floor is entirely used for guest and toilet rooms, and the third floor can also be made into guest rooms, several of which are already prepared. The rear building, first floor, is entirely used for a chapel, dining room and kitchen, and the second floor as an infirmary.

The amendments to the Charter are:

1. "The name shall be the 'Brethren Home of the Church of the Brethren.'

2. "The place where the business of said corporation is to be transacted is at the Home, along the Lititz Pike, near the village of Neffsville, in Manheim Township, Lancaster County, Pennsylvania.

3. "The Board of Trustees shall consist of six members, and any member of the Church, in good standing, over twenty-one years of age, may be elected a Trustee, and the member ex-officio shall be discontinued.

4. "The election of Trustees shall be held on the first Tuesday in November, instead of February."

The new Home was occupied on November 3, 1910, and dedicated November 17, 1910, Elder D. L. Miller of Illinois, being on a visit here, and Elder John Herr, of Lebanon Co., Penna., preached the dedicatory sermon, and Elder S. R. Zug gave a historical sketch. The new Home, with fixtures and furnishings, cost about $48,000, and the old Home was sold to H. H. Cassel for $6793.42.

The financial condition of the Home in 1912 is as follows: It is paid for with the price realized for the old Home, and by donations, of which $24,439.97 was donated on which the Home is to pay to the donors annuities during life, aggregating $948.91 yearly and the Home has an endowment fund of $12,600, loaned out, for which they receive $490 interest, thus leaving a difference between annuities paid, and interest received, of $458.91, which must be raised by charging more to keep guests and inmates. As the donors die the annuities cease, but it will be a long while until the last one is gone.

We still hope to raise the endowment to an amount, the income of which will be sufficient to provide our poor members of the whole District, free of charge, which now includes the Southeastern District of Pennsylvania, New Jersey, and Eastern New York; and that some of our members, and others, who are philanthropically inclined, will come to our aid by donations and bequests.

In the spring of 1912, Elder S. R. Zug, being over 80 years old, spoke of resigning as Trustee, but was urged to stay on to the end of his term, which would be December 31, 1912.

BRETHREN HOME.

DETENTION HOME OF THE CHILDREN'S AID SOCIETY.

On November 5, 1912, at the annual meeting of shareholders he was relieved, and Nathaniel Minnich elected in his place, Jacob Heagy being re-elected. At the organization of the Board of Trustees, after that election, Jacob Heagy was appointed President; I. W. Taylor, Secretary; and Ammon H. Brubacher, Treasurer.

B. History of the Children's Aid Society Movement in the Church of the Brethren in the Eastern District of Pennsylvania.

For a number of years several of the Elders in the Eastern District of Pennsylvania felt that there was a great field open for doing effective and far-reaching work in the way of caring for homeless and orphan children. This conviction grew and among those who first agitated the matter may be mentioned Elder Jesse Ziegler of Royersford, Elder I. W. Taylor of Vogansville, Elder David Kilhefner of Ephrata and Elder H. E. Light of Mountville. After the Annual Meeting held at Bristol, Tennessee, in 1905, had endorsed this kind of work as it was then carried on in the State District of Oklahoma and Indian Territory and further recommended that the several State Districts over the Brotherhood awaken to this important work (see Annual Meeting Minutes, page 6, Art. 2) the matter was more fully agitated, so that the Ephrata Church and the Spring Grove Church each came to the District Meeting of Eastern Pennsylvania of 1906 with similar queries asking that the District Meeting carry out the recommendations of Annual Meeting on this point. This resulted in the appointment of a committee of three Brethren consisting of H. E. Light, Jesse Ziegler and David Kilhefner with instructions to prepare a plan and present the same to the next District Meeting (See District Meeting Minutes, 1906, page 2.) This committee presented the following report to the District Meeting of 1907 which was ordered to be spread on the minutes for one year:

"Report of Committee to Care for Homeless Children.

"We your committee, appointed by District Meeting of 1906 to prepare plans for organizing the work of saving orphans and homeless children, after much deliberation and investigation, desire to submit the following report:

"'The word of God and observation teach us that here lies a large field of useful and commendable work, which has hardly been touched by us as a church.

"'First. We are convinced that to undertake this work simply upon the plan of an agency would be altogether impracticable and unsatisfactory, and that in order to succeed in the undertaking we would need a detention home, where no less than twenty children could be cared for at a time.

"'Second. In order to reach this we would recommend that the District Meeting appoint one or two Brethren to visit the churches of the District in behalf of this work, with the following points in view:

"'(a) To create sentiment in favor of a work of this kind,

"'(b) To secure some guarantee of regular financial support.

"'(c) To have a delegate elected from the official body (Brother or Sister) of each local Church to represent such church in affecting an organization for carrying forward this work.

"'Third. As soon as a majority of the churches shall respond by taking action favorable to the movement, then the delegates elected above described shall be called to meet by the Brother or Brethren appointed by District Meeting to visit the churches, and shall elect twelve Trustees who shall have authority to incorporate and elect a manager and transact such business as may be needful to carry forward this noble work.

"David Kilhefner.
"H. E. Light,
Jesse Ziegler, *Clerk.*'"

The District Meeting of 1908 took up this report and after some discussion decided that the report be adopted except Section *C* of Article 2 and Article 3 and appointed a committee of two Brethren consisting of T. F. Imler and H. K. Ober who were to canvass the district with a view of finding out what sentiment exists for pushing this noble work. This committee came up to District Meeting of 1909 with the following report:

"Report of Committee on Orphanage.

"To the Brethren of Eastern Pennsylvania in District Meeting, Greeting:

"We, your committee, offer the following report: Shortly after District Meeting of 1908, the home duties of the elder member of the committee were so confining as to make it impossible for him to do any active work in the field. And as the other member did not have time except some Saturdays and Sundays the District was not thoroughly canvassed; however, at such times and places as opportunities presented themselves, the matter was taken up, largely with individual members of congregations. In the opinion of the commitee, a healthy, favorable sentiment to the project of establishing an Orphan Home exists over the District, with the proposed idea that such a home should be a place of detention for any orphans until a proper, permanent home has been secured with some family. The committee believes that the Christian home is the best place in which a child can mature and that our District has many homes who are ready to assume the responsibility of caring for orphans as soon as there is a definite point to which they may apply. Therefore, we feel that this matter ought to take definite shape, and that such arrangements ought to be made so as to make the project possible and practical, and as such we humbly submit this as our report.

"T. F. Imler,
"H. K. Ober."

The above report was thoroughly discussed and a committee of five were appointed to carry out the committee's recommendations as they appeared in the above report. The committee consisted of T. F. Imler, Samuel Z. Witmer, H. K. Ober, H. B. Yoder, and Henry R. Gibbel.

This committee organized and a fairly complete report of their first year's work is found in the minutes of the District Meeting of the Church of the Brethren of Eastern Pennsylvania of 1910, as well as a number of recommendations. The District Meeting of 1910 passed a resolution that this committee be continued another year and that they present to the next District Meeting a Constitution and By-laws for adoption, rejection or amendment and that meanwhile the committee be instructed to carry out the recommendations in their report.

Immediately after the adjournment of the District Meeting of 1910, the committee organized and during the year five regular meetings were held, besides a number of subcommittee meetings and presented to the District Meeting of 1911 a Constitution and By-laws which were adopted. This Constitution and By-Laws will be found on pages, two, three, four, and five of the minutes of the District Meeting of Eastern Penna. of 1911. As this Constitution provided for a Board of Trustees, the District Meeting of Eastern Pennsylvania of 1911 at once elected a Board of the following five Brethren for the Eastern District of Pennsylvania: T. F. Imler, H. B. Yoder, H. K. Ober, H. R. Gibbel, and Jacob W. Meyer. At this District Meeting there were steps taken and provision made to divide the Eastern District of Pennsylvania.

The new District which was thus formed adopted the name of Southeastern Pennsylvania, New Jersey and Eastern New York and elected five trustees as follows: Mary S. Geiger, Amanda R. Kratz, C. F. McKee, Ira Holsopple and Quincy Leckrone to serve in connection with the five members elected by the Eastern District of Pennsylvania.

On the third Monday of July, A. D. 1911, these ten trustees met in the First Brethren Church in Philadelphia and organized as a full board.

During the year 1911, plans were studied and perfected for building a detention Home. Sites and locations were carefully considered. The District Meeting minutes of the Church of the Brethren of Eastern Pennsylvania for 1912 contain a report of the said Board of Trustees which shows that the work has been actively carried on. A beautiful location adjoining the Brethren Home at Neffsville, Pa., was finally selected as the place for erecting this building. This site was donated by the Board of Trustees of the Brethren Home. A substantial brick building was erected upon this site during 1912 and completed in the spring of 1913. Subsequently the building was furnished and is now fully occupied and is named " Home for Orphan and Friendless Children." The dedicatory services for the same were held on the afternoon of October 16, 1913, when the following program was rendered:

Devotional Exercises ....Elder S. R. Zug.
Dedicatory Services:
    (a) ....Elder M. C. Swigart.
    (b) ....Elder J. H. Longenecker.
Brief Report of Board of Trustees by H. K. Ober, Secretary.
Offering.
Closing Exercises ....Elder S. Z. Witmer.

Elder I. W. Taylor in connection with his duties as Superintendent of the Brethren Home has been elected Superintendent of this Home for the children. Brother and Sister Heagy, of Ephrata, are serving as the first steward and matron of same.

The Children's Aid Society in addition to being fully authorized and owned by the two State Districts is also incorporated under a charter issued by the Court of Common Pleas of Lancaster County. Up to this time the Society has received and placed eighteen children. The work is now fully organized and eternity alone will reveal the very important work which the church is carrying on through its servants in rescuing young lives and training them with a view of saving them for useful lives of Christian service.

                                H. K. OBER,
                                    Secretary.

CHAPTER VI.

HISTORY OF ELIZABETHTOWN COLLEGE.

I. The Founding.

For some years before the formal opening of Elizabethtown College, there was felt a need in eastern Pennsylvania for a school where the children of the members of the Church of the Brethren might have opportunities for a more extended education than it was possible to get in public schools and at the same time make it possible for them to remain loyal to the Brethren Church, chiefly along the line of nonconformity to the world. It was furthermore decided to extend the privileges of higher education to such members as would obtain the same at State institutions unless afforded by schools in the church of their choice where they would be surrounded by a Christian environment, free from atheistical and other influences that tend to make shipwreck of their religious life. Withal there existed many good schools so far as intellectual training was concerned, but upholding wrong ideals and tolerating, if not fostering, pernicious features such as intercollegiate athletics, hazing, students' fraternities, class rushes, etc. Those interested in the school were moved by a lofty purpose which may be concisely stated thus: to found and establish a school where Christian education was obtainable under the fostering care and in the interest of the Church of the Brethren. This purpose, more formally stated in the Constitution, adopted by the Board of Trustees and friends of the school was as follows: " The object of this school shall be such harmonious development of the physical, mental, and moral powers of both sexes as will best fit them for the duties of life and promote the spiritual interest of its patrons. While under the control and management of the Church of the Brethren and primarily intended for the education of our own child-

Memorial Hall. ELIZABETHTOWN COLLEGE. Alpha Hall.

ren, the school shall be open to all such as desire to avail themselves of its privileges."

In response to a widely-extended written call issued by J. G. Francis, of Oaks, Pa., to meet at Reading, November 29, 1898, to discuss the advisability and feasibility of starting a new college in eastern Pennsylvania, there met in the Church of the Brethren in Reading on said date twelve Sisters and twenty-two Brethren. The meeting was called to order by Brother Francis and the following organization was effected: Elder John Herr, of Myerstown, Moderator; Elder G. N. Falkenstein, of Germantown, Secretary. After devotional exercises conducted by Brother Wm. Howe, of Norristown, the object of the meeting was stated by the moderator. Brother Francis then read some correspondence from a number of prominent Brethren expressing favorable sentiment for a school in Eastern Pennsylvania and tried to show the need of a school in our District that was of a higher standard. Brother Francis then moved that we in the fear of God proceed to establish a school in Eastern Pennsylvania. This motion was seconded by Bro. F. F. Holsopple, of Parkerford, Pa. At Elder Falkenstein's suggestion this motion was not put to a vote in order that there might be a fuller discussion of this important movement. Brother Francis then argued the necessity of a school by presenting statistics of 'members' children at other schools, chiefly schools outside of our church, and said there was need of facilities for preparing ministers in our church. Elder J. H. Longenecker, of Palmyra, said that he was in favor of education, but our State District was not united on this question and this was shown by the small representation at this meeting. He said that much prejudice exists against higher education in our Church. Elder H. E. Light, of Mountville, expressed himself favorable to the movement of starting a school. He said we do not have too many schools and cannot educate too much, but our children need to be educated in our own schools and especially in a school that is loyal to the Church. There was considerable pressure in the meeting to decide at once upon the building of the proposed school. Brother Francis read a paper from

Ephrata inviting the school to locate here. Brethren E. B. Lefever and Samuel Kulp, of Ephrata, were representing the people of that town and stated a number of advantages that the place offered for the new school.

This meeting had both a forenoon and afternoon session, and after considerable discussion, a motion was passed that a committee of five be elected by ballot to take preliminary steps for finding a location for establishing a Brethren school in this District and report at a future meeting. The committee elected by ballot was as follows: John Herr, J. H. Longenecker, H. E. Light, G. N. Falkenstein, Elias Lefever. The meeting instructed this committee to decide a time and place for the next public meeting. This committee organized by electing John Herr, Chairman; G. N. Falkenstein, Secretary.

The locating committee appointed by the Reading meeting underwent some important changes. The chairman, John Herr, resigned on account of ill health. In his stead the committee elected S. H. Hertzler, of Elizabethtown. J. H. Longenecker also handed his resignation to the committee, but the reasons seemed insufficient to grant it. The committee agreed to meet at Mountville on March 6, 1899, the object being to visit school sites. Four members of the committee met there and organized as follows: Chairman, H. E. Light; Secretary, G. N. Falkenstein; S. H. Hertzler and E. B. Lefever being the other members present. Mountville, Columbia, Pottstown, Ephrata, Norristown, and about a month later Elizabethtown, were visited by this committee. Permission was given by Elder S. R. Zug, of Mastersonville, to have a public meeting of the Brethren interested in this movement in the Brethren Church in Elizabethtown on April 5, 1899. All churches of the District were notified of this meeting on March 23. The meeting convened at the time and place stated at 9:30 A. M. and was opened with devotional exercises by the Secretary. A committee of five Brethren offered the following nominations for officials for this meeting which were ratified by it: Chairman, S. R. Zug; Secretary, G. N. Falkenstein; Treasurer, S. H. Hertzler. Elder Zug made a brief address and then called for the report of the locating committee which was read by the Secretary. Representatives of the following places presented sites for the new college: Mountville by H. E. Light, Columbia by H. E. Light and B. G. Musser, Ephrata by A. W. Mentzer, Norristown by letter, Pottstown by J. G. Francis, Elizabethtown by F. H. Keller who read a paper from the town council.

At the afternoon session, Elder George Bucher called for information by what authority this meeting is called. J. G. Francis stated that it originated in his mind. The Secretary, G. N. Falkenstein, spoke of the sentiment for a school throughout the District. The meeting then was declared open for further discussion of the following questions: first, Shall we have a school? second, What kind of a school do we want to establish? A number of speeches were made on these questions. George Bucher said: "I am in favor of a Brethren school on Gospel principles, but it must be subject to the Church and located in a loyal congregation." S. H. Hertzler said if some schools are improperly managed, we need one that is properly managed. After further discussion George Bucher moved that we have a school. This was seconded by Elder Jesse Ziegler, of Royersford and passed unanimously. The next question to be decided was What kind of a school shall it be? S. R. Zug said "coeducational for young people." George Bucher said "for the old ones too. We want a higher school. A college to compare favorably with any in the country. A safe school." J. G. Francis said: "We want a school in which the Bible is the text book, also offering scientific and classical courses." L. M. Keim said: "The new school shall have an agricultural department." Jesse Ziegler favored this also. G. N. Falkenstein said a commercial department was also needed. After further discussion G. N. Falkenstein moved that we establish a school of such a character that compares favorably with any of our schools including Bible, academic, and collegiate departments,—a school to be at the same time a home and a church. The motion was passed by the meeting.

The meeting then decided that a committee of ten be

appointed to be fully authorized to select a site for the location of the school. This committee consisted of H. E. Light G. N. Falkenstein, S. H. Hertzler, George Bucher, Jesse Ziegler, S. R. Zug, J. G. Francis, Abram Royer, Benjamin Hottel and William Oberholtzer. The committee named was also to draft a Constitution and By-laws for the new school and present the same at a future meeting. The committee decided to meet at District Meeting for organization on April 20. The organization resulted as follows: Chairman, H. E. Light; Secretary, G. N. Falkenstein; Treasurer, S. H. Hertzler. All towns offering sites were to place their proposals in the committee's hands not later than May 10. Meantime the offer of Lititz was to be investigated.

The locating committee met again at the Annual Conference at Roanoke, Virginia, May 24, 1899. Of the committee of ten the following were present: H. E. Light, S. R. Zug, George Bucher, S. H. Hertzler, G. N. Falkenstein, and J. G. Francis. William Oberholtzer resigned. H. B. Holhinger was elected in his stead. After devotional exercises and the purpose of the meeting having been stated, it was moved and seconded that sealed offers for the new school be read, and that a majority of the committee be required to decide its location. There were only two offers presented; namely, Ephrata and Elizabethtown. The advantages offered by these places were considered with reference to the following points: drainage, railroad facilities, money, church, water. Three ballots were cast without any decision. The places voted for were Mountville, Elizabethtown, and Pottstown. Following some speeches made in favor of Pottstown and Elizabethtown it was unanimously voted to locate at Elizabethtown. The following subcommittee was appointed to prepare a Constitution and By-Laws for the school: G. N. Falkenstein, Jesse Ziegler, J. G. Francis. The committee decided that the next public meeting shall be at Elizabethtown on June 7.

The committee on Constitution and By-laws met at Royersford, Pa., June 1 with all present. This committee recommended that the name of this school be Conestoga College. After a day's work, the work of the committee was completed. The locating committee met at Elizabethtown, June 6, at noon, the following being present: H. E. Light, Chairman; G. N. Falkenstein, Secretary; S. H. Hertzler, Treasurer; S. R. Zug, George Bucher, Jesse Ziegler, Abram Royer and J. G. Francis. A formal protest was received from Ephrata in regard to locating the school at Elizabethtown and an informal protest was made in behalf of Pottstown. It was then moved and decided to reconsider the location. It was also decided not to admit new offers for the school unless open to all upon due notice. Three minutes' time was allowed each representative for presenting each site. H. E. Light spoke in favor of Mountville, S. R. Zug for Elizabethtown, Abram Royer for Ephrata, and J. G. Francis for Pottstown. On the third ballot eight votes were cast in favor of Elizabethtown.

The committee then adjourned to view several sites about Elizabethtown, after which they met at the home of S. H. Hertzler at 2:30 P. M., where the citizens' committee also met the locating committee. Many speeches were made in favor of two sites, one at the east end of town and the other at the west end. After some balloting which did not decide the location, many warm speeches were made and the matter was left undecided until the public meeting on the following day. The committee then took up the report of the committee on Constitution and By-laws. The name proposed by the Committee on Constitution and By-laws provoked considerable discussion. The name Mack College was presented by J. G. Francis. George Bucher opposed this name on account of it being the name of a man, but liked Conestoga College. H. E. Light thought that Conestoga College was too local a name for the school. Jesse Ziegler presented the name East Penn College. A motion to adopt the last name failed to pass. Finally the name Conestoga College was passed by the locating committee. There were slight changes made in the statement of the object of the school, but in the main the Constitution and By-laws were adopted by the locating committee. On Wednesday morning, June the seventh, the locating committee had another session prior to the public meeting which convened at 9:30

in the Brethren Church. Devotional exercises were conducted by George Bucher. The minutes of the former public meeting having been read, the decision of the locating committee as to the site of the new school was announced. The Constitution and By-laws were also presented for the consideration of the meeting. After an extended discussion on the name question, the meeting decided to adopt Elizabethtown College instead of Conestoga College as the name for the proposed college. Each section of the Constitution and By-laws was then taken up and after considerable discussion it was adopted. The meeting proceeded to elect trustees, Brethren and Sisters voting by ballot. The following persons were nominated by the locating committee to serve as trustees: from Lancaster County, S. H. Hertzler, J. H. Rider, H. E. Light, George Bucher, C. R. Gibble, I. W. Taylor, T. F. Imler; from Berks County, P. C. Nyce; from Montgomery County, Jesse Ziegler; from Lebanon County, F. L. Reber; from Chester County, Nathan Hoffman; from Philadelphia, T. T. Myers, G. N. Falkenstein; from Maryland, L. R. Brumbaugh, J. Y. King; from Dauphin County, M. R. Henry, John Landis. While the votes were being counted for trustees, George Bucher moved to insert a clause in the Constitution and By-laws prohibiting instrumental music. The meeting, however, decided to leave this matter in the hands of the trustees. The By-laws were then read and adopted and the tellers made the following report of the election of trustees: for three years, G. N. Falkenstein, Jesse Ziegler, S. H. Hertzler; for two years, J. H. Rider, Nathan Hoffman, M. R. Henry; for one year, P. C. Nyce, T. F. Imler, and L. R. Brumbaugh. It was then decided by motion that the trustees be authorized to call a meeting of the contributors whenever deemed necessary.

After adopting the Constitution and By-laws as a whole unanimously, the meeting closed at five o'clock. The committee on location, Constitution and By-laws was then formally discharged and the meeting closed with devotional exercises. The writer is indebted to Elder G. N. Falkenstein of Elizabethtown for the minute details setting forth how Elizabethtown College was founded, he having been

Secretary of all the committees and of the three public meetings that were held until the school was formally established.

Elizabethtown had two good locations for the school but the spot where the newborn college was finally to rear its walls was on a beautiful elevation at the eastern end of the borough on the farm of Brother B. G. Groff, a business man. The deal for ten acres of land as a nucleus for a campus was made by Royer S. Buch. He secured the land for the college at $150 per acre by the following proposition: Royer S. Buch and his brother J. Harvey Buch guarantee to pay for 1/3 of this tract, their father Addison Buch guarantees another third and B. G. Groff donated the remaining third. This original tract was increased later by the purchase of four acres from Bro. Groff.

The first board of trustees held its first meeting at Pottstown at the home of Nathan Hoffman on June 16. The organization of the board resulted as follows: President, Jesse Ziegler, of Royersford; Vice President, T. F. Imler of Lancaster; Secretary, G. N. Falkenstein of Germantown; Treasurer, S. H. Hertzler, of Elizabethtown. Elder Imler soon resigned and Brother J. H. Rider, a hardware merchant of Elizabethtown, was elected Vice President in his stead.

On September 23, 1899, a charter was secured. The incorporators were: S. H. Hertzler, J. H. Rider, S. P. Engle, J. H. Eshleman, Jos. G. Heisey, all of Elizabethtown. The trustees at once set out to raise funds for the erection of a building. The ground was broken for the first school building on July 10, 1900.

Arrangements for a Faculty preceded the erection of the first building. Elder I. N. H. Beahm, of Lordsburg, California, was elected the first head of the school with the title of Principal. Elder G. N. Falkenstein, Secretary of the Board of Trustees, appeared second on the Faculty as published in a blue sixteen-page catalogue issued in August, 1900. Miss Elizabeth Meyer, of Bareville, was the first lady in the faculty and had charge of the lady students.

November 13 had been set and announced as the time for the dedication of the first building, since called Alpha Hall, but the building was not completed by that time. Nevertheless school was formally opened on November 13, 1900, in the Heisey Building, corner of Market and Bainbridge streets, Elizabethtown, with six students and three teachers. The students were all boys as follows: Kurvin Henry, of York County, Warren Ziegler and Walter Kittinger, of Montgomery County, Rufus P. Bucher, John Boll and Willis Heisey, of Lancaster County. Professor Beahm was not able to assume his duties when school opened, being confined to bed with nervous prostration. The principal's duties were performed the first year by Professor Falkenstein. The other teachers were Elizabeth Meyer and J. A. Seese, of Virginia.

The first week school work was conducted in the Heisey Building, third floor. Then for two months school was held in J. H. Rider's private dwelling on Washington Street, which was bequeathed to the Elizabethtown Church of the Brethren at Brother Rider's death. On January 2, 1901, the school was moved to College Hill in Alpha Hall which was not yet fully completed at the time. On March 4, 1901, the building was dedicated with appropriate exercises.

II. Experimental Stage.

The educational work so auspiciously though modestly inaugurated was not without trials, difficulties, and obstacles. The fate of the institution so untried and young was unknown and its future success not fully assured as yet. It passed through a period of development that may well be characterized as its experimental stage. In this critical period, who were the makers of Elizabethtown College? These may be classified as consisting of certain staunch trustees, some sacrificing teachers, and numerous fast friends.

A brief record of the early trustee meetings will furnish the names of the leading trustees who have been found true and tried in this educational project. At the first meeting at Pottstown, P. C. Nyce, of Reading, resigned his trusteeship. George Bucher was elected in his stead. At this meeting the following were appointed a committee to secure a charter and also a seal for the new institution: Jos. H.

HISTORY OF ELIZABETHTOWN COLLEGE. 631

Rider, S. H. Hertzler, and T. F. Imler. The Secretary, G. N. Falkenstein, was instructed to have Constitution and By-laws of the Board of Trustees printed. At this meeting the Eastern District of Pennsylvania was divided among the different trustees for the purpose of soliciting funds to erect a school building. The following reported success in their work: Geo. Bucher, Jesse Ziegler, J. H. Rider and S. H. Hertzler. The total pledged was $4,815, of which $3,150 was subscribed by Elizabethtown and community. This report was given at the second Board meeting at Ridgely, Md., at District Meeting on August 15, 1899. The third meeting was held at home of J. H. Rider, October 3, 1899, seven trustees being present. Here a petition circulated by J. G. Francis to change the location of college from Elizabethtown to Ephrata was presented but not favorably considered. A committee was appointed to secure an architect. This committee consisted of T. F. Imler and S. H. Hertzler. The fourth meeting of the Board was at John Herr's home at Salunga October 18, 1899. The following building committee was appointed: T. F. Imler, S. H. Hertzler and George Bucher. At the fifth meeting held at S. H. Hertzler's home in Elizabethtown on Dec. 14, 1899, T. F. Imler was excused from building committee at his request. At the sixth meeting on April 12, 1900, at J. H. Rider's home, A. A. Richter of Lebanon was employed as architect. At this meeting steps were taken to elect the first principal. I. N. H. Beahm was provisionally elected to this position. At the seventh meeting which was held at the Middle Creek Church in West Conestoga Congregation on May 2, 1900, there were seven trustees present. Nathan Hoffman's resignation was received, but not accepted till a later meeting. On June 11, 1900, at S. H. Hertzler's the eighth meeting convened when I. N. H. Beahm and Elizabeth Myer were formally hired as members of Faculty. Also G. N. Falkenstein was elected as teacher. B. G. Groff was awarded the contract to build the first building, the price to be $14,250. J. G. Heisey, of Elizabethtown, was appointed on Building Committee instead of T. F. Imler, resigned. At the ninth meeting held August 16,

1900, the officers of the board were reelected for one year. The following were elected trustees for three years: George Bucher, T. F. Imler, D. Kilhefner. L. R. Brumbaugh was elected for one year. Isaac Royer of Reistville was elected a trustee but refused to accept. The following were appointed a committee on catalogue and also to prepare a program for Opening Day: G. N. Falkenstein, Jesse Ziegler, Elizabeth Myer and I. N. H. Beahm. Sister I. N. H. Beahm was elected as matron.

At the tenth meeting held October 2, 1900, a vault was purchased. Ed. Wenger was elected a trustee. The Opening Day occurred on November 13, 1900, at which time the 11th Board Meeting was held. At S. H. Hertzler's the twelfth meeting was held January 8, 1901. Trustees Kilhefner and Bucher resigned. The first Bible term was appointed for March to be conducted by J. Kurtz Miller. At this meeting a loan of $9,000 was made with the Lancaster Trust Co. Total cost of Alpha Hall, the first building was $14,318.71. Other trustees of the earlier history were M. R. Henry, Benjamin Hottel, Isaiah Musser, S. P. Engle, B. G. Groff (did not accept), A. S. Kreider, S. G. Graybill. In addition as trustee, S. H. Hertzler served as business manager in 1902. I. N. H. Beahm was business manager in 1903-04. Mrs. Beahm was matron from 1903-07. The management of the school was assumed by an administrative committee consisting of I. N. H. Beahm, President; D. C. Reber, Vice President and Registrar; H. K. Ober, Secretary and Treasurer in 1904 for three years.

The faculty for the second year's work consisted of G. N. Falkenstein, Principal; Elizabeth Myer, C. F. Weaver, J. H. Keller, Mrs. G. N. Falkenstein. In 1902, D. C. Reber and H. K. Ober entered the faculty. Professor Falkenstein resigned as Principal in October, 1902. For 1903-04, D. C. Reber was elected as acting Principal. Elizabeth Myer and H. K. Ober also remained in faculty. J. M. Pittenger, of Ohio, an A.B. graduate of Juniata College became teacher of Latin and Science, in 1903. In 1904, Professor Beahm was elected the first President of the school, and D. C. Reber, Vice President. Besides Professor Ober and Miss Myer, the following were employed to teach in 1904: P. S. Davis, W. H. Sanger and Flora H. Good, the latter as the first instrumental music teacher. In 1905, B. F. Wampler, J. G. Meyer and J. Z. Herr, the latter two being Alumni of the school, were employed as teachers. In 1906, E. C. Bixler, A.M., was employed to teach Greek and Latin and continued with school two years. Luella G. Fogelsanger, after completing the Pedagogical Course in 1906, entered the faculty as a full teacher and remained till 1910. In 1907 the first regular Bible teacher was secured in the person of E. E. Eshelman of Waynesboro. He taught in the institution three consecutive years. In the earlier period to the close of the active administration of President Beahm, the following served as assistant teachers in the school: M. Alverda Stayer, S. B. Kiefer, I. E. Shoop, Luella G. Fogelsanger, Nathan Martin, L. Margaret Haas, L. D. Rose.

Of the teachers of the earlier experimental period, five may be mentioned for their efficient and faithful services, which laid a strong foundation for the permanence of the school. Professor G. N. Falkenstein, a graduate of Brethren's Normal College in 1882, and a student for two years in Mount Morris College and the University of Michigan, acted as chief executive during the first two years of the school's existence. Under many trying and discouraging circumstances, he conducted the school while the principal-elect, Professor I. N. H. Beahm, was ill and unable to teach. His health necessitated a change of occupation and the Vice-principal, D. C. Reber, a graduate of Juniata College in 1897 and of N. Y. University in 1902, performed the duties of acting Principal the third year and was eleced Principal of the school the fourth year.

In 1904, Professor I. N. H. Beahm, a graduate of Bridgewater College in 1889, formerly Principal of Prince William Academy, Va., and President of Lordsburg College, Cal., was able to assume the duties of President of Elizabethtown College and remained actively in charge of the institution for three years, a part of the third year of his administration being devoted to travel in Palestine and Egypt. During his term of office, the instrumental music department was opened. Also a two year's course in agriculture was outlined. During his trip abroad Vice President Reber presided over the institution. In 1905, need of a second building became apparent. This was completed in 1906 and dedicated on March 4 of that year.

H. K. Ober entered the faculty as commercial teacher in 1902 after graduating at the Millersville S. N. School in 1898 and from Penna. Business College at Lancaster in 1902. In 1903 he was elected Vice Principal of the school in addition to his duties as commercial teacher. In 1904 he became one of the administrative committee, filling the responsible position of acting treasurer of the institution. He also served as the first business manager of our College Times, and as Principal of the Commercial Department from 1904-1907. As chairman of the Physical Culture committee he was largely instrumental in shaping the future policy of the institution regarding athletics.

Miss Elizabeth Myer, a graduate of the Millersville Normal School in 1887, has held her position in the faculty from the school's inception. She taught reading, grammar, elocution, literature and rhetoric during the first seven. years of the school. She has given excellent service not only as teacher but also as preceptress and as a member on the discipline committee. To her loyalty to the principles of the church along the line of non-conformity and to her influence over the lady students who were members of the church, the school owes a large debt for its position of loyalty to the church in its student body. She also served as Editor of Our College Times for five years in which she wielded a widespread influence for the welfare of the school. She also had a supervisory and stimulating influence over the literary organizations of the school.

Outside of the Board of Trustees, and teachers, there have been many substantial friends whom space forbids to mention. Of those who have subscribed liberally in money, time and influence may be mentioned B. G. Groff, Mrs. J. H. Rider, Mrs. Mary S. Geiger, Joseph Oller, Jos. G. Heisey, Addison Buch and his sons, Royer and Harvey, and others whose names appear as electors on the second page of the annual catalogue of the college. B. G. Groff built all the buildings on the campus up to the time of his death in 1907. He also served as Superintendent of the Grounds and Buildings as long as he lived. As contractor of the first building he donated nearly a thousand dollars of contract price. He was a member of the building committee for Memorial Hall, and showed a constant interest in the college by his presence at educational and religious gatherings at the school.

The largest donor of this early period is Jos. H. Rider. His donations amount to about $10,000 and in his memory the second college building has been named Memorial Hall. As Vice President of the Board of Trustees Bro. Rider rendered valuable services to the College.

With a very meager equipment the school began to do its work. But through the kind assistance of teachers and students this increased from year to year. The first building had modern equipment such as electric light, steam heat, bath rooms, electric program clock, and well-lighted class rooms. Later increased supply of black-boards, hydrant water, three pianos, six typewriters, laboratory stand and fixtures, science cabinet, maps, globes, a second building with increased facilities for library, a physical culture room, and beautifully furnished chapel were secured in this experimental period of the school's history. To this may be added a double cottage, a large shed, and a small stable.

III. Growth and Development.

The enrollment of students increased gradually from year to year. The first gentleman student was Kurwin D. Henry, of Big Mount, York Co., Pa., and the first lady student was Anna Brenneman, of New Danville, Lancaster Co., Pa. The table on next page shows the enrollment by years.

With the beginning of the eighth school year, a change in administration was made and this marks the beginning of a new epoch in the history of the school. Professor I. N. H. Beahm was retained as the nominal head of the institution with an advisory relation to the management of affairs. He devoted much time to preaching and representing the school

	Students.	Faculty.	Graduates.	Bible Term.
1900–1901	27	3	0	115
1901–1902	64	5	0	173
1902–1903	108	5	3	210
1903–1904	106	6	7	334
1904–1905	128	9	26	334
1905–1906	148	11	15	323
1906–1907	177	12	18	312
1907–1908	196	15	25	305
1908–1909	183	17	21	356
1909–1910	188	16	30	232
1910–1911	204	15	32	160
1911–1912	178	15	26	220
1912–1913	195	17	34	323
1913–1914	182	19	29	325

in the field, teaching only during the annual Bible term. The Vice President, D. C. Reber was made Acting President in 1907 and served under this title for three years. In 1910 he was elected President of the college to succeed President Beahm, who resigned his position in 1909.

In addition to his duties as the executive, D. C. Reber continued in charge of the Department of Pedagogy and developed the Pedagogical Course of the school as it exists at this writing. In 1909, he received the degree of Master of Arts from Ursinus College. It was the policy of the new President to make the school a college in fact as well as in name. In 1907 the first students enrolled in the Classical Course. Then this course was revised and began to attract students who had finished the Pedagogical Course. A few college students attended the Ursinus College summer term in 1908 and thereafter and in this way the advanced work of Elizabethtown College received some recognition so that the school became affiliated with Ursinus College, which accepted the work done by this school under college or university graduates. Among the teachers whose work helped to gain this recognition were President Reber, E. C. Bixler, Mary E. Markley and E. E. Eshleman. The Classical Course is operated since and other college teachers such as J. S. Harley, J. G. Meyer, and R. W. Schlosser have helped to maintain the required standard of teaching.

The College Preparatory Course was revised at this time and is beginning to attract more students. A number who completed this course have entered Lebanon Valley College, Juniata College, State College, Oberlin College, Franklin and Marshall College and the University of Penna. without entrance examinations.

The framing and correlation of literary courses has been the work of Pres. Reber. Under his administration the first class in the Classical Course was graduated in 1911. The growth in material equipment has not been so marked during the last six years, but there has been an internal development of various departments of the school's work.

Under the new administration the library has been greatly enlarged and improved partly by means of conducting a lecture course. The museum has been classified under the curatorship of M. A. Good and C. E. Resser. In 1911 an advanced literary society was formed for classical students. The Bible Department was fully organized by revision and addition of courses and the employment of a regular Bible teacher. Under the tuition of E. E. Eshelman and Lydia Stauffer this department is doing a work that has a helpful religious influence in the school.

The Commercial Department organized and developed by H. K. Ober lost his services in 1907 and he thenceforth devoted his energies to the Science Department. After several years of effort, the equipment was greatly increased both for teaching physics and biology. And as an outgrowth of the science work, he also took charge of the Agricultural Department in 1910 upon his election to the Vice Presidency of the school. At the same time at the direction of the management he outlined a course in Sewing. Professor Ober continued as treasurer of the school from 1904–1910. In all these years he continued his scholastic studies partly in Elizabethtown College, and at the Millersville Normal School finished the regular Normal Course and received the degree Master of Pedagogics in 1910. He also spent a summer session at the University of Pennsylvania. As a member of the discipline committee and as field worker and financial secretary to the trustees he has rendered efficient services to the school.

Another department that was developed under the Reber

administration is the vocal and instrumental Music Department. This was under the competent direction of B. F. Wampler from 1905-11. His assistants at various times were Mrs. B. F. Wampler, Leah M. Sheaffer, Elizabeth Kline and W. E. Glasmire. The three last named are alumni of the school. Although these teachers labored under prejudices against instrumental music among the membership of the church yet they succeeded in a measure to disarm criticism from this source and a large percentage of the student body were enrolled in the department. This department is well established and continues to render good service under competent teachers.

The Commercial Department was several years without a principal until J. Z. Herr who had been H. K. Ober's assistant in this work for two years became principal in 1910. The new principal revised the courses of study, reorganized the work on a broader and more modern basis until it is a well-equipped and well-patronized department of the school. Professor Herr was also Professor Ober's successor in the office of treasurer of the faculty.

At the urgent suggestion, solicitation and aid of H. K. Ober, six acres were purchased on the southwest side of the campus by the trustees, a number of them making themselves personally responsible for the purchase. The campus with its growing maple trees planted on April 6, 1901, makes a fine appearance and is a source of gratification to all who contributed money or trees to this project. The campus now consists of twenty acres, a part of which is utilized for orchard, garden or farm purposes.

Trustees of recent period not heretofore named are J. W. G. Hershey, H. B. Yoder, A. G. Longenecker, J. H. Keller, R. P. Bucher, J. Kurtz Miller, John M. Gibble, D. K. Kilhefner, W. H. Holsinger.

Other teachers of this later period were M. A. Good, L. Margaret Haas, W. K. Gish, Anna Wolgemuth, Laura Hess. first teacher of Sewing, and Kathryn E. Miller. Some student teachers were Daisy P. Rider, C. E. Resser, H. H. Nye, I. Z. Hackman, L. W. Leiter, J. D. Reber, I. J. Kreider, Carrie Dennis, Gertrude Miller, Lilian Falkenstein, Laura M. Landis. Mrs. E. G. Reber was matron from 1907 to this writing.

IV. ELIZABETHTOWN COLLEGE IN THE EYES OF EDUCATORS.

The pedagogical senior class is required to take a final examination before graduation. Since 1905 the following city or county superintendents served in this capacity and spoke in praiseworthy terms of the work of the school: M. J. Brecht, of Lancaster Co.; H. J. Wickey, of Middletown; J. Anson Wright, of Bedford Co.; H. V. B. Garber, of Dauphin Co., J. Kelso Green, of Cumberland Co.; L. E. Smith, of Franklin Co.; H. M. Roth, of Adams Co.; Daniel Fleisher, of Columbia; Edgar Reed, of Lebanon; L. E. McGinnes, of Steelton; C. W. Stine, of York Co.

On November 13 and March 4 annually anniversary programs are rendered commemorating the founding and dedication of the school buildings. On such occasions the following educators have delivered addresses at Elizabethtown College: Hon. N. C. Schaeffer, E. O. Lyte, R. N. Roark, A. S. Martin, H. C. Early, Wm. Wine, D. W. Kurtz, T. T. Myers, J. L. Eisenberg, George L. Omwake, George W. Hull. At Opening Day or other occasions the following distinguished speakers have lectured at the college: D. L. Miller, L. S. Shimmell, M. G. Brumbaugh, A. A. Willets, Henry Houck, H. M. Rowe, H. Frank Eshelman, F. J. Stanley, A. B. Van Ormer, George P. Bible, R. M. McNeal, Lawrence Kiester, C. A. Bowman, C. A. Spangler, J. P. McCaskey, W. U. Hensel, R. C. Schiedt, J. G. Royer, H. H. Apple, J. S. Stahr, J. Kurtz Miller. Not only by educators but also by a number of colleges in Pennsylvania has the work done at Elizabethtown College been recognized as being meritorious. From four institutions this recognition has come unsolicited.

V. THE SCHOOL OF THE PRESENT.

Elizabethtown College stands as the exponent of Christian education. Compared with similar institutions, she is one of the youngest institutions in Pennsylvania that are striving to afford opportunities for higher education. Because a number of good friends have stood by her in her infantile struggles she is on a fair footing to fill the mission of her founders. Its supporters are to be congratulated on past progress and achievements and may entertain sanguine hopes for the future. While there has been opposition to its founding and growth, while there have been obstacles to surmount and discouragements to overcome, yet Elizabethtown College thus far had no serious reverses due to epidemics, fires, or immoral conduct on the part of officials or teachers. She has a splendid record of achievement to which we may call attention.

A thousand young people (in 1913) have been students of the school and have been touched to live a life of usefulness. Nearly 200 (1913) of these have finished one or several courses and are out molding the lives of those they influence for good. Scores of young people have been converted to the religion of Jesus Christ through the influence set in motion at the school. Thousands have been inspired in Bible study and at lectures, educational or missionary programs to make the most of themselves—these all will rise and call the school a blessing to themselves and their posterity.

There is a movement on foot to transfer the College to the Church as the property of the two state districts. At the District Meeting of 1913 held at Ephrata, the Ephrata Church petitioned the District Meeting to have a committee appointed to consider the advisability of taking over Elizabethtown College as the property of the church. The following committee was elected: John Herr, F. P. Cassel and J. H. Longenecker. This committee was to represent the Eastern Pennsylvania District in its conference with representatives from the college.

Is the school fulfilling its mission? The record thus far is cause for rejoicing, and convincing to the doubters of the project thirteen years ago. But the College continues to have needs which must be supplied sooner or later. The financial problem needs serious consideration. A $10,000 debt is now being discharged. An endowment fund of

$100,000 is a potent need. Many strong educational institutions are her competitors. She needs ever to be loyal and true to the ideals of her founders. With a resourceful and devoted board of trustees, with an earnest and self-sacrificing corps of teachers, with a loyal and prosperous alumni to pray and push forward the work, the prospect of Elizabethtown College is bright. Long live our College in Eastern Pennsylvania!

CHAPTER VII.
STATISTICAL TABLES.
A. Table of Churches.

Name of Church.	Location.	Date of Organization.	First Bishop.	Bishop in 1913.	Membership in 1914.	No. of S. S.
I. Germantown Group:						
1. Germantown	Germantown, Pa.	1723	Peter Becker	M. C. Swigart	125	1
2. First Brethren	Philadelphia, Pa.	1813(?)	Peter Keyser	J. T. Myers	375	1
3. Geiger Memorial	Philadelphia, Pa.	1906	J. T. Myers	J. T. Myers	140	1
4. Bethany	Philadelphia, Pa.	1910	J. T. Myers	J. T. Myers	115	1
5. Upper Dublin	Montgomery Co., Pa.	1840	John W. Price	M. C. Swigart	35	1
II. Jersey Group:						
1. Amwell	Hunterdon Co., N. J.	1733				
2. Sandbrook	Hunterdon Co., N. J.	1849	Johannes Naas	J. Kurtz Miller	80	1
3. Bethel	Hunterdon Co., N. J.	1876				
4. Union	Hunterdon Co., N. J.	1896				
III. Coventry Group:						
1. Coventry	Chester Co., Pa.	1724	Martin Urner	M. C. Swigart	164	1
2. Green Tree	Montgomery Co., Pa.	1845	John H. Umstad	J. T. Myers	275	1
3. Parkerford	Chester Co., Pa.	1898	J. P. Hetric	J. P. Hetric	100	1
4. Royersford	Montgomery Co., Pa.	1900	J. P. Hetric	J. P. Hetric	100	1
5. Harmonyville	Chester Co., Pa.	1913	J. P. Hetric		60	1
IV. Indian Creek Group:						
1. Indian Creek	Montgomery Co., Pa.	1785	John Price	Jacob M. Price	189	1
2. Mingo	Montgomery Co., Pa.	1869	Henry Cassel	Jesse Ziegler	130	2
3. Hatfield	Montgomery Co., Pa.	1864	Jacob Reiner	F. P. Cassel	145	2
4. Springfield	Bucks Co., Pa.	1868	Moses Schuler	Benj. Hottel	90	2
5. Norristown	Montgomery Co., Pa.	1901	A. L. Grater	Jas. B. Shisler	42	1
V. Conestoga Group:						
1. Conestoga	Lancaster Co., Pa.	1724	Peter Becker	S. H. Hertzler	212	2
2. West Conestoga	Lancaster Co., Pa.	1864	Christian Bomberger	C. R. Gibbel	287	1
3. Ephrata	Lancaster Co., Pa.	1864	Christian Bomberger	David Kilhefner	233	1
4. Lancaster	Lancaster Co., Pa.	1891	S. R. Zug	H. B. Yoder	225	2
5. Mechanic Grove	Lancaster Co., Pa.	1897	H. E. Light	S. H. Hertzler	70	1

STATISTICAL TABLES.

Name of Church.	Location.	Date of Organization.	First Bishop.	Bishop in 1913.	Membership in 1914.	No. of S. S.
6. Spring Grove	Lancaster Co., Pa.	1897	John W. Graybill	I. W. Taylor	82	1
7. Springville	Lancaster Co., Pa.	1899	Israel Wenger	John W. Schlosser	270	1
8. Akron	Lancaster Co., Pa.	1913	I. W. Taylor	I. W. Taylor	72	1
9. Lititz	Lancaster Co., Pa.	1914	I. W. Taylor		120	1
VI. White Oak Group:						
1. White Oak	Lancaster Co., Pa.	1772	Christian Longenecker	Hiram Gibble	466	0
2. Chiques	Lancaster Co., Pa.	1868	David Gerlach	H. S. Zug	252	2
3. Mountville	Lancaster Co., Pa.	1882	John S. Newcomer	H. E. Light	350	4
4. Fairview	Lancaster Co., Pa.	1902	Hiram Gibble	Hiram Gibble	170	1
5. West Green Tree	Lancaster Co., Pa.	1902	S. R. Zug	D. M. Eshelman	250	2
6. Elizabethtown	Lancaster and Dauphin	1902	S. R. Zug	S. H. Hertzler	310	3
VII. Swatara Group:						
1. Big Swatara	Dauphin Co., Pa.	1798 or 1800	George Miller	J. H. Witmer	290	3
2. Little Swatara	Lebanon and Berks	1798 or 1800	George Klein	E. M. Wenger	330	4
3. Tulpehocken	Lebanon and Berks	1841	Jacob Pfautz	John Herr	367	3
4. Spring Creek	Dauphin Co., Pa.	1868	Jacob Hollinger / Wm. Hertzler	J. H. Longenecker	280	2
5. Maiden Creek	Berks Co., Pa.	1866	John Zug (?)	Wm. H. Oberholtzer	43	1
6. Schuylkill	Schuylkill Co., Pa.	1877	George Smith	E. M. Wenger	98	2
7. Harrisburg	Dauphin Co., Pa.	1896	S. R. Zug	G. N. Falkenstein	80	2
8. Shamokin	Northumberland Co.	1897	John Hertzler	E. M. Wenger	23	1
9. Reading	Berks Co., Pa.	1898	John Herr	E. M. Wenger	84	2
10. Midway	Lebanon Co., Pa.	1901	Christian Bucher	John Herr	263	2
11. Annville	Lebanon Co., Pa.	1912	A. B. Gingrich	A. B. Gingrich	125	2
12. Conewago	Dauphin Co., Pa.	1912	S. Z. Witmer	S. Z. Witmer	120	2
VIII. Missionary Group:						
1. Peach Blossom	Talbot Co., Md.	1882	Wm. Hertzler	S. K. Fike	75	2
2. Ridgely	Caroline Co., Md.	1884	S. R. Zug	T. F. Imler	85	1
3. Denton	Caroline Co., Md.	1910	G. S. Rairigh	G. S. Rairigh	75	1
4. Brooklyn	Long Island, N. Y.	1899	Geo. S. Rairigh	J. Kurtz Miller	115	2

B. Elders of Church of the Brethren in Eastern District of Pennsylvania before 1800.

Name.	Date of Birth.	Date of Baptism.	Election to Ministry.	Ordination.	Date of Death.	Name of Church.	Place of Burial.
1. Peter Becker	1687	1714	...	1	1758	Germantown	Kline's graveyard in Indian Creek Church.
2. Valentine Balsbaugh	2/14 1755	...	...	...	1851	Swatara	Balsbaugh's graveyard.
3. John Beckleshammer	...	...	about 1735	...	...	New Jersey	...
4. Hans George Beshor	2/8 1775	...	...	...	1841	...	...
5. Han Jacob Beshor	...	1747	...	before 1772	...	...	...
6. Abraham Duboy	1679	1712	...	...	1748	Greatswamp	Greatswamp
7. Andreas Eby	...	1767	...	...	1798	White Oak	S. G. Sumny's farm.
8. Peter Eichelberger	...	1752	...	before 1772	1801	Conestoga	...
9. Andreas Frey	...	...	...	...	...	...	...
10. Michael Frantz	...	1734	1734	1735	1748	Conestoga	Near Cocalico Creek.
11. Martin Gaby	5/9 1742	...	...	1780	1812	Maiden Creek	Pricetown.
12. Peter Heckman	...	...	...	about 1770	...	...	...
13. George Klein	1715	1739	before 1750	1757	1783	Swatara	Near Bernville.
14. Christian Longenecker	1731	1754	1764	1769	1808	White Oak	Longenecker's, near Lititz.
15. Alexander Mack, Sr.	1679	...	...	...	1735	Schwartzenau (Ger.)	Germantown.
16. Alexander Mack, Jr.	1712	...	...	1753	1803	Germantown	Germantown.
17. George Adam Martin	1715	1735	1739	1739	...	Coventry	Stony Creek.
18. George Miller	1722	1753	...	1780	1798	Swatara	near Elizabethtown.
19. Johannes Naas	1669 or 70	...	...	...	1741	Amwell, N. J.	Amwell, N. J.
20. Michael Pfautz	1710	1739 or 43	1744	1748	1769	Conestoga	Middle Creek.
21. John Price	1751	...	...	1785	1829	Indian Creek	...
22. Jacob Sontag	1700	1743	1748	1763	1822	Conestoga	Middle Creek.
23. Jacob Stoll	1731	1748	1753	1755?	1784	Conestoga	Middle Creek.
24. Christopher Sower, Jr.	1721	1737	1748	1753	1813	Germantown	Methacton Meeting House.
25. Jonas Urner	1772	...	...	...	1755	Coventry	Wolfe graveyard, Md.
26. Martin Urner[2]	1695	1723	...	1729	1799	Coventry	Coventry.
27. Martin Urner the 2d	1725	...	...	1756	1821	Coventry	Coventry.
28. Johannes Zug	1731	1749	1770	1780	...	White Oak	Zug family graveyard.

[1] No record of ordination.

[2] First Elder of Church of the Brethren ordained in America by Alex Mack, Sr.

N.B.—Johann Jacob Preis and Rudolph Harley, Sr., belong also to above list.

B. Elders of Church of the Brethren of Eastern District of Pennsylvania since 1800.

Name.	Date of Birth.	Date of Baptism.	Election to Ministry.	Advancement.	Ordained.	Date of Death.	Place of Burial.
Beahm, I. N. H.	5/14 1859	1879	1881	1883	1904		
Beaver, S. S.	3/9 1845	1865	1887	1890	1908		
Becker, Geo. S.	1829		1869		1893	1904	Spring Creek.
Bomberger, Christian	1801	1828	1831		1862	1880	Middle Creek.
Bomberger, Cyrus	8/25 1839		1878	1884	1903	1908	S. Annville M. H.
Booz, Jacob M.	8/22 1878	1897	1909	1912	1914		
Brubacher, A. H.	3/16 1871	1898	1904	1909	1913		
Bucher, Christian	11/4 1833	1854	1861	1865	1875		
Bucher, George[3]	7/21 1845	1862	1865	1871	1897		
Cassel, Abram	11/27 1811				1885	1891	Skippack.
Cassel, Frank P.	12/16 1849	1865	before 1879		1884		
Cassel, Henry	7/11 1814		1849			1883	Mingo.
Coffman, T. R.	6/27 1873	1897	1897	1900	1911		
Crouthamel, Hillery	11/14 1841	1866	1884	1889	1901	1914	Hatfield.
Ebersole, Martin	7/18 1862	1892	1899	1906	1912		
Eby, B. Z.[3]	9/28 1835	1858	1871	1874	1883	1913	Kreider's.
Eshelman, D. M.	6/18 1845	1869	1895	1899	1905		
Etter, David	1798		1867	1873	1887	1873	Mohrsville.
Etter, John	1826		1853		1868	1899	Hanoverdale.
Etter, Lorenz	4/2 1787				between 1836-40	1884	Hanoverdale.
						1853	Balsbaugh graveyard.
Fahnestock, N. B.	4/26 1850	1878	1898	1903	1912		
Fahnestock, S. B.	7/29 1853	1884	1899	1905	1913		
Falkenstein, G. N.	7/16 1859	1879	1892	1893	1899		
Fike, S. K.	3/8 1864	1878	1895	1896	1900		
Fox, John	10/12 1786		1844		1867	1880	Germantown.
Fretz, Daniel	1776		between 1810-22		before 1822	1864	2½ mi. N. W. Manheim.

[3] United with Old Order Brethren.

Elders of Eastern Pennsylvania District since 1800 (*Continued*).

Name.	Date of Birth.	Date of Baptism.	Election to Ministry.	Advancement.	Ordained.	Date of Death.	Place of Burial.
Geib, A. P.	2/28 1887	1904	1910	1911	1914		
Gerlach, David	11/11 1809		1837		1856	1879	Kreider's.
Gibbel, Cyrus R.	4/27 1859	1887	1889	1895	1906		
Gibbel, Henry		1777	1810		before 1814	1825	Near Kreider's.
Gibble, Hiram	1/6 1841	1863	1877	1883	1900		
Gingrich, A. B.	10/25 1861	1881	1887	1895	1905		
Gottwals, J. Z.	9/11 1812	1846	1855	1858 or 59	1873	1903	Green Tree.
Grater, A. L.[4]	9/12 1844	1871	1880	1884	1893	1912	Mingo.
Graybill, J. F.[5]	6/10 1874	1897	1904	1906	1911		
Graybill, John W.	1835	1875	1876 or 77		1892	1899	Earlville.
Graybill, Israel	8/13 1836	1862	1883	1884	1910	1911	Graybill's.
Graybill, Reuben S.	3/11 1841	1863	1885	1891	1910	1913	Graybill's.
Groff, Hershey	3/29 1845	1878	1885	1889	1900		
Hackman, Jacob	4/29 1824	1862	1866		1878	1903	Millport, Calif.
Haldeman, Samuel[5]	10/25 1820	1840	1847	1863	1866 or 67	1914	Gibbel graveyard near Manheim.
Haller, Jacob	1778		between 1810–22		before 1822	1865	
Harley, Benjamin							
Harley, Samuel (of Indian Creek)	11/26 1795				1849(?)	1878	Kline's graveyard in Indian Creek Church.
Harley, Samuel (of Ephrata)	5/4 1820	1844	1864	1867	1871	1896	Mohler's.
Heisey, Martin	12/9 1844	1862	1885	1896	1909		
Herr, John	2/10 1848	1869	1871	1875	1897		
Herr, Tobias	4/30 1827		1883	1885	1900	1901	Manor Church.

[4] Only baptized in Eastern Pa., elected and ordained in Illinois.
[5] Elected in Eastern Pa., but not ordained in this district.

Elders of Eastern Pennsylvania District since 1800 (*Continued*).

Name.	Date of Birth.	Date of Baptism.	Election to Ministry.	Advancement.	Ordained.	Date of Death.	Place of Burial.
Hertzler, S. H.	9/24 1853	1881	1897	1899	1904	1901	Frystown.
Hertzler, John	9/10 1826	......	1858	......	1875	1896	Spring Creek.
Hertzler, Wm.	12/30 1827	1843	1847	......	1868	......	......
Hetric, J. P.	12/20 1843	1864	1866	1867	1879	......	......
Hollinger, Daniel	7/8 1831	......	1869	1873	1885(?)	1877	Spring Creek.
Hollinger, Jacob	1797	......	about 1826	......	......	......	......
Hollinger, H. B.	7/26 1864	1875	1894	1900	1909	......	......
Hoppock, J. D.	......	......	1861	......	1882	1906	......
Horne, H. T.	1866	1888	1906	1908	1911	......	......
Hottel, Benj.	5/22 1850	1870	1878	1883	1893	......	......
Hottenstein, A. S.	10/31 1850	1880	1885	1890	1909	......	......
Imler, T. F.	7/8 1851	1870	1885	1892	1899	......	......
Keim, David	1/5 1803	......	......	......	1879	1897	Coventry.
Keyser, Peter	11/9 1766	1784	1785	......	1802	1849	Germantown.
Kilhefner, David	12/11 1861	1887	1899	1902	1907	......	......
King, J. Y.	12/13 1847	1868	1869	1870 or 71	1888	1906	Denton, Md.
Kline, Benj.	7/12 1791	......	about 1825	......	about 1865	1868	Kauffman's M. H. near Annville.
Kulp, Isaac	1830	......	......	......	1885	1901	Skippack. (Mennonite Graveyard.)
Kurtz, D. Webster	10/9 1879	1899	1904	1906	1914	......	......
Light, H. E.	3/3 1848	1864	1873	1877	1888	1855	Longenecker's.
Longenecker, Christian	10/31 1791	......	1828 or 30	......	1841	......	......
Longenecker, J. H.	3/3 1852	1868	1876	1881	1893	......	......
Madeira, C. C.	12/25 1867	1884	1887	1895	1914	......	......
Merkey, David	5/11 1795	......	......	......	......	1873	Merkey's.
Merkey, Joseph	11/28 1782	......	1875	1883	1901	1869	Merkey's.
Meyer, J. W., Sr.	1/29 1832	......	1891	1893	1903	1906	Meyer Graveyard.
Miller, J. Kurtz	9/26 1865	1877	......	......	......	......	......

Elders of Eastern Pennsylvania District since 1800 (*Continued*).

Name.	Date of Birth.	Date of Baptism.	Election to Ministry.	Advancement.	Ordained.	Date of Death.	Place of Burial.
Miller, Monroe B.	11/21 1864	1902	1904	1906	1911	....	....
Mohler, Levi S.	8/20 1845	1872	1889	1896	1914	....	....
Moore, Chas. W.	1838	1855	1881	1882	1896	1903	Sandbrook, N. J.
Moore, John P.	1811	....	1844	....	1882	1889	Sandbrook, N. J.
Myer, John.	10/13 1828	1858	1879	1887	1898	....	....
Myer, Joseph.	1807	1840	1844	....	1887	1892	Near Bareville.
Myers, T. T.	3/29 1865	1884	1886	1887	1906	....	....
Myers, J. T.	9/13 1851	1867	1871	1872	1905	....	....
Newcomer, J. S.	4/30 1810	....	1841	....	1878	1902	Mountville.
Nissley, Jacob.	3/7 1843	1866	....	....	....	....	....
Nyce, William P.	5/22 1822	....	1881	1885	1900	1889	Price's Graveyard in Indian Creek Church.
Oberholtzer, Wm. H.	10/20 1849	1877	1896	1900	1907	....	....
Pfautz, Jacob. (of Lancaster Co.)	1776	1805	1815	....	1823	1864	Middle Creek.
Pfautz, Jacob. (of Lebanon Co.)	7/24 1852	1877	1899	1901	1906	....	....
Pfoutz, Abraham.	6/17 1826	....	1860	....	1898	1906	Frystown.
Poulson, Israel, Sr.	....	....	....	....	before 1846	1856	Amwell, N. J.
Poulson, Israel, Jr.	4/14 1821	....	1848	....	....	1896	Prospect Hill, Flemington, N. J.
Price, George. (Coventry)	11/1 1753	....	....	....	1797	1823	Coventry.
Price, Henry A.	3/20 1827	....	....	....	....	....	....
Price, Jacob M.	11/4 1843	1862	1891	1897	1906	1906	Indian Creek.
Price, Isaac. (Green Tree)	1802	1831	1834	....	1873	1884	Green Tree.
Price, John, Sr. (Coventry)	4/12 1782	....	....	....	1823	1850	Coventry.

Elders of Eastern Pennsylvania District since 1800 (Continued).

Name.	Date of Birth.	Date of Baptism.	Election to Ministry.	Advancement.	Ordained.	Date of Death.	Place of Burial.
Price, John R. (Coventry)	4/3 1810				1850	1879	Coventry.
Price, Wm. W.	8/29 1789		1814		1830	1849	Price's Graveyard in Indian Creek Church.
Quinter, James[6]	2/1 1816	1832	1838		1856	1888	Huntingdon.
Rairigh, Geo. S.[7]	3/31 1854	1875	1878	1880	1892		
Reber, D. C.	2/20 1872	1889	1902	1904	1914		
Reed, Samuel	1834		1871		1899	1901	Hanoverdale.
Reidenbach, Rudy S.	8/27 1827	1861	1874	1876	1897		
Reiner, Jacob K.	3/22 1807		1841		about 1864	1889	Pine Run in Hatfield Church
Rider, Jacob.	1804		1847		1875	1883	Near Elizabethtown.
Righter, John.	1784	1809	1841			1860	Germantown.
Rothermel, Jeremiah	1822		1866			1890	Hinnershitz's Church.
Rupp, Christian	1805	1834	1840		1867	1887	Rupp family graveyard.
Schlosser, J. W.	1/8 1862	1890	1890	1896	1906		
Schuler, Moses							
Shisler, Jas. B.	4/23 1856	1879	1897	1903	1906		
Shope, A. J.	2/19 1844		1882	1889	1905		
Smith, David	1818		1869		1898	1900	Hanoverdale.
Smith, George[8]					1877		
Sonon, Henry S.	1847	1871	1890	1898	1909		
Swigart, M. C.	12/28 1868	1890	1894	1900	1912		
Taylor, I. W.	2/20 1856	1880	1891	1894	1899		
Taylor, S. W.	11/21 1850	1874	1897	1899	1913		
Umstad, John H.	1/1 1802	1831	1834			1873	Green Tree.

[6] Elected in Eastern Pa., but not ordained in this district.
[7] Elected and ordained in Western District of Pa.
[8] Disowned in 1885.

Elders of Eastern Pennsylvania District since 1800 (*Concluded*).

Name.	Date of Birth.	Date of Baptism.	Election to Ministry.	Advancement.	Ordained.	Date of Death.	Place of Burial.
Weaver, D. W.	1/23 1875	1894	1903	1905	1912		
Wenger, E. M.	8/28 1854	1876	1894	1898	1904		
Wenger, Israel	1844		1878		1891	1907	Middle Creek.
Wenger, Jacob	3/10 1801		about 1835		1850	1881	Jonestown in Wenger Graveyard.
Witmer, John H.	1848	1869	1882	1887	1899		
Witmer, S. Z.	11/15 1860	1885	1894	1900	1909		
Yoder, H. B.	4/19 1870	1894	1906	1907	1910		
Ziegler, Jesse	7/18 1856	1877	1890	1891	1900		
Ziegler, Philip (Chiques)	1804		1846		1869	1874	Chiques Hill.
Ziegler, Philip (Little Swatara)	1/25 1764						Ziegler farm.
Zug, Abraham	1772	1826	1815		1823	1841	Tulpehocken.
Zug, John	1797		1841	1847	1861	1873	Heidelberg M. H.
Zug, Henry S.	7/9 1860	1879	1889	1895	1905		
Zug, John C.	4/26 1866	1888	1905	1911	1913		
Zug, S. R.	2/29 1832	1861	1865	1871	1885		

C. SUNDAY SCHOOL HISTORY.[1]

The Annual Conference of 1898 advised that "each State District appoint a Sunday School Secretary whose duty it shall be to inspire the Sunday School work of the district and also to supply the Sunday School Advisory Committee with such statistics and other information as that Committee may ask."

The Eastern District of Pennsylvania in the same year appointed Samuel H. Hertzler as the first Sunday School Secretary of said district. He served until he resigned in 1901. E. M. Wenger was his successor in this office serving until 1905. Then George W. Henry was appointed. After serving a year he was appointed for three years and the term of office thereafter was fixed at three years. Bro. Henry is the only lay brother serving in this office thus far.

Name of Secretary.	Term of Office.	Assistant Secretary.	No. of Schools.	S. S. Enrollment.	Conversions.
1. S. H. Hertzler...	1898–1901	none			
2. Edward M. Wenger......	1901–1905	none	55	5,000	188 (1905)
3. Geo. W. Henry..	1905–1906	none	57	5,054	148
4. George W. Henry	1906–1909	none	55	16,051	421
5. H. K. Ober.....	1909–1912	Geo. H. Light, 1911–1914	55–74	19,155	505
6. Nathan Martin..	1912–1915	Abram A. Price, 1914–1917	64	13,262[2]	323[2]

[1] For history of local Sunday Schools, see history of local churches.
[2] For first two years only.

THE CHURCH OF THE BRETHREN.

D. Local Sunday School and Missionary Meetings.

Name of Church.	Place.	Date.	Chairman.	Clerk.
1. Ephrata	Ephrata	July 4, 1904		
2. Lancaster	Lancaster	July 4, 1905		
3. West Conestoga	Lititz	July 4, 1906	Hiram Gibble	
4. Elizabethtown	Elizabethtown	July 4, 1907	G. N. Falkenstein	
5. Ephrata and Springville	Mohler's	July 4, 1908	J. W. Schlosser / David Kilhefner	
6. Elizabethtown	Elizabethtown	July 5, 1909	I. W. G. Hershey / I. W. Taylor	
7. Tulpehocken	Myerstown	July 4, 1910	J. H. Longenecker	
Mingo	Mingo	Nov. 24, 1910		
8. Lancaster	Lancaster	July 4, 1911	I. W. Taylor	
Hatfield	Hatfield	Nov. 30, 1911		
Spring Creek	Hershey	Aug. 27, 1911	John Herr	
9. Elizabethtown	Elizabethtown	July 4, 1912		
West Conestoga	Lititz	Sept. 14, 1912		
Indian Creek	Vernfield	Nov. 23, 1912		
10. Mountville	East Petersburg	July 4, 1913	I. W. Taylor	
Midway	Midway	Aug. 7, 1913	S. H. Hertzler	Amos Kuhns.
Norristown	Norristown	Nov. 22, 1913	Jesse Ziegler	Geo. H. Light.
11. Conestoga	Earlville	July 4, 1914	H. B. Yoder	R. P. Bucher.
Big Swatara	Hanoverdale	Aug. 13, 1914	H. K. Ober	J. C. Zug.

INDEX

Ackerman, John, 322
Akron Church, 326, 336
   Organization, 354
   Steinmetz's meeting house, 354
Albertus, 28
Albrecht, Count Heinrich, 1
Aldinger, Joseph B., 472, 473, 506, 507
Allen, George, 154
Amwell Church, 55, 168, 188, 202, 297
Annual meetings, 272
   In Eastern Pennsylvania, 541-544
   Those held elsewhere, 546
   Changes in holding, 563
   Cassel's account of, 568
   Report of 1871 meeting, 571
Annville Church, 506
   Organization, 504
Antietam Church (Franklin Co.), 74
Arnold, Daniel, 372, 544, 548
Arnold, J. W., 534
Aungst, George, 442, 443
Aungst, John, 442, 443

Bach, John, 542
Baker, Allen G., 405
Baker, David, 442, 443
Baker, Isaac, 442, 489
Baker, J. S., 506, 507
Balmer, Allen, 335, 336
Balmer, Henry, 335, 336
Balmer, Herman, 405
Balsbach, Abram, 442, 472
Balsbaugh, Benjamin, 448, 456
Balsbaugh, C. H., 386, 437, 513, 516
Balsbaugh, Peter, 441
Balsbaugh, Samuel, 442, 443
Balsbaugh, Elder Valentine, 440, 444, 513, 517, 518, 545, 643, 644
   Biography, 437, 515
Bame, Charles A., 135, 137, 147, 266
Ban, 272, 273
Bangor, Timothy, 110, 111, 112
Baptists, 79, 492, 513
Baptists, German, 92, 116, 117, 186, 272, 281, 291, 298, 453, 454, 462, 465, 468, 476, 500

Baptists, Seventh Day, 74, 82, 164, 197, 272
Barnhart, Elder A. B., 538, 546, 561
Barto, Elder Isaac, 531, 545, 555, 556
Basehore, Benjamin, 542
Basehore, Elder Benjamin, 437, 439, 545
Basehore (Beshor), Elder Hans George, 78, 445, 446, 455, 519, 644
   Biography, 437, 517
Bashore, Milton, 473
Basehore (Beshor), Elder Hans Jacob, 328, 374, 436, 445, 446, 455, 518, 545, 644
Bauman, 29
Beahm, Elder I. N. H., 129, 137, 260, 408, 409, 411, 590, 592, 629, 630, 631, 632, 633, 635, 636, 645
Beaver, P. H., 166, 574, 578
Beaver, Elder S. S., 410, 483, 491, 645
Bechleshammer, Elder John, 163, 164, 168, 644
Bechtel, John, 248
Beck, T. S., 395, 613
Becker, Elizabeth, 76
Becker, Elder George S., 472, 645
Becker, J. B., 351
Becker, Mary, 76
Becker, Elder Peter, 6, 10, 14, 17, 20, 38, 52, 53, 65, 69, 74, 75, 76, 78, 98, 102, 197, 205, 208, 281, 289, 297, 302, 304, 306, 325, 326, 327, 475, 564, 642, 644
   Chosen elder, 20
   Missionary tour, 26-30
   Relation to Beissel, 39, 47
   Biography, 76-78
   Character, 70, 77
Beelman, George W., 342, 343, 344, 345
Beer, Elder J. H., 534
Beery, C. O., 137, 139
Beissel, Conrad, 19, 30, 31, 45, 54, 73, 101, 197, 205, 207, 208, 209, 325, 326, 327, 364, 564
   Biography, 32-43
   In New World, 38
   At Germantown, 39, 63

INDEX.

Beissel, in Conestoga Country, 40, 65
    Baptism, 43
    Ordination, 46
    Manner of preaching, 46
    Doctrines, 47
    Attack on Becker, 47
    Baptism renounced, 48
    Relation to Alexander Mack, 49, 52, 56, 163
    Destructive policy, 52
    In New Jersey, 164
    At Falckner's Swamp, 206
Bender, Henry, 399
Benson, Charles M., 94, 104
Bergey, David G., 214
Berleburg, 1, 2
Bermudian Church, 73, 74, 79
Bethany Mission Church, 142-152
Bethel Church, 189
Biershing, Benjamin, 540
Billew, Elijah, 248
Bingeman, George, 334, 335, 394
Bixler, E. C., 633, 636
Boehm, Martin, 382
Boehme, Jacob, 15
Bohemian Manor, 40, 41
Bollinger, Andrew, 335, 336
Bollinger, Benjamin, 335, 336
Bollinger, Elder Daniel, 457, 458, 462, 521, 545, 548, 549, 550, 551
Bollinger, Jacob, 331, 365, 462
Bollinger, Levi, 459, 461
Bomberger, Elder Christian, 329, 330, 334, 335, 337, 338, 356, 370, 374, 394, 481, 586, 587, 588, 589, 593, 594, 642, 645
    Biography, 366
Bomberger, Elder Cyrus, 472, 645
Bonney, Andreas, 90, 91
Bonsack, Elder Charles D., 537, 539
Boone, Alice, 493, 536, 538, 539
Booser, John, 472, 473, 506, 507
Booz, Jacob, 321
Booz, Elder J. M., 159, 301, 318, 645
Boyle, Philip, 391
Bower, Charles, 343, 409, 414
Bowman, Paul, H., 150, 152
Brandt, Jacob W., 506, 507
Brecht (Bright), 282, 283
Brethren Home
    Early history, 608; locations, 609, 615
Brenneman, Benjamin M., 399, 403
Brewer, Gideon, 180
Brewer, Thomas W., 173, 264, 268
Brooklyn Church
    Early history, 536

Brooklyn Church
    Elections, 537
    Italian mission, 539
Brower, Daniel, 230, 250, 273
Brower, Elizabeth, 230
Brower, Isaac U., 212, 253
Brower, Mary, 230
Brower, Dr. William, 220, 223, 253, 254, 257, 259
Brown, Adam, 499
Brown, George, 73
Brownback, S. S., 136, 137, 138
Brownback, Stephen, 214, 265, 268
Brubacher, Elder Ammon H., 451, 496, 497, 498, 505, 614, 617, 645
Brubaker, Abraham Z., 496, 497, 498, 499
Brubaker, Christian, 329, 334, 355, 401, 427, 499, 587
Brubaker, Edwin B., 334, 336, 360
Brubaker, Eli B., 397, 406
Brubaker, Ephraim, 459, 461
Brubaker, Eugene, 395
Brubaker, Isaac, 458, 460, 497, 499, 522
Brubaker, J. B., 405
Brubaker, Nathan, 335, 359, 615
Brumbach, Conrad, 543, 545
Brumbaugh, George, 533, 548
Brumbaugh, Elder H. B., 558, 560
Brumbaugh, Elder J. B., 156, 561
Brumbaugh, L. R., 533, 534, 600, 628, 632
Brumbaugh, Dr. M. G., VI, VII, 9, 12, 27, 60, 66, 67, 76, 78, 98, 102, 105, 107, 110, 120, 128, 137, 147, 196, 281, 301, 325, 326, 370, 379, 445, 475, 541, 542, 547, 565, 639
Brunner, Anna, 153, 159, 160, 161
Bucher, Allen D., 472, 504, 528
Bucher, Elder Christian, 178, 180, 181, 182, 183, 184, 185, 189, 203, 338, 368, 396, 398, 448, 458, 459, 461, 471, 479, 482, 484, 492, 494, 496, 497, 502, 522, 554, 555, 556, 557, 558, 581, 589, 590, 643, 645
    Biography, 528
Bucher, Elder Cyrus, 459, 461, 470
Bucher, Elder George, 156, 157, 162, 346, 347, 348, 349, 458, 461, 465, 470, 501, 522, 589, 590, 592, 600, 608, 625, 626, 627, 628, 630, 631, 632, 645
Bucher, Mohler, 459, 496, 497, 528
Bucher, Elder Rufus P., 348, 349, 411, 451, 473, 503, 592, 601, 630, 638, 652
Buckwalter, John, 214, 225

INDEX. 655

Buffenmyer, Horace, 350, 359
Buffenmyer, John, Sr., 350, 351
Butz, Levi, 485
Byer, Franklin, 343

Carper, Frank S., 473
Caruso, John G., 537, 539
Casimir, Count, 2
Cassel, Abraham H., 129, 163, 168,
   169, 196, 210, 211, 236, 281,
   291, 295, 297, 301, 302, 304,
   305, 313, 314, 325, 326, 367,
   544, 568, 581
   Biography, 299
Cassel, Elder Abram, 307, 308, 309,
   312, 645
Cassel, Charles D., 395
Cassel, D. K., 9, 298, 299
Cassel family, 299
Cassel, Elder F. P., 127, 157, 185,
   190, 312, 317, 410, 537, 557, 558,
   561, 562, 563, 589, 590, 592, 600,
   608, 640, 642, 645
Cassel, Elder Henry, 212, 216, 307,
   308, 312, 321, 479, 588, 642, 645
Cassel, Isaac, 309, 312
Cassel, Jacob, 248
Cassel, Jonas, 318
Cassel, Joseph N., 311, 312
Casselberry, William, 234, 235, 248
Catholics, Roman, 8, 11, 49, 51, 137
Children's Aid Society
   Early history, 617
   Detention home, 620
Chiques Church, 392, 393, 394, 407,
   418, 430, 431, 482, 504, 506,
   523, 594, 609, 612
   Organization, 396
   Divisions, 397
Christian Family Companion, 572
Church of Brethren, 7
   Origin of, 52, 57
   A missionary church, 6
   Persecution of, 7
   No creed, 52
Clark, E. F., 534
Clendenen, Andrew, 472, 473
Cline, J. W., 128, 136, 138
Clouser, Rev. G. B. M., 147, 152
Codorus Church, 72, 73, 79
Coffman, Elder T. R., 254, 256, 645
Colonial churches
   Southern Pennsylvania, 73
   Maryland, 71–72
   In Pennsylvania in 1770, 79
Conestoga Church, 52, 55, 73, 75,
   79, 197, 350, 352, 367, 369,
   371, 379, 457, 461, 518, 521,

   541, 542, 544, 594
Conestoga Church, First lovefeast,
   31, 44
   First division, 47
   Account of early, 81–87
   Early baptisms, 81–87, 326
   Organization, 325
   Elders and ministers, 327
   Subdivisions, 328, 329, 331
   Deacons, 331
   Present officials, 332
Conestoga country, 29, 31, 40, 45, 207
Conestoga Church, West, 329, 344,
   352, 354, 359, 360, 361, 401, 594
   Organization, 334
   Elders and ministers, 335
Conewago Church (Dauphin Co.),
   440, 504
   Organization, 506
Conewago Church (York Co.),
   73, 79
Conewago Church, Little, 72, 73, 79
Conner, Abram L., 308
Conner, Jesse, 307
Connor, Jacob, 156, 157, 162, 212,
   215, 216, 240, 309, 587, 588, 600
Conococheague, 71, 209, 542
Constitution
   Of Philadelphia church, 112–115
Coventry Church, 28, 44, 65, 75,
   79, 120, 139, 239, 253, 274,
   293, 323, 541, 594
   Organization, 205
   Elders of, 211
   First pastor, 213
   Deacons, 214
   Children of, 217
   Meeting houses, 221
   Graveyard, 223
   Auxiliary organizations, 224
   Charities, 227
Conway, John, 248
Crauthamel, Elder Hillery, 316, 318, 645
Crefeldt, 5, 6, 11, 12, 15, 18, 39,
   44, 65, 76, 163, 164, 196, 197
   Congregation at, 7, 9, 10
   Place of refuge, 9, 10
   Emigration from, 13
   An asylum, 39
Croft, Julia, 138, 143–152
Croft, Samuel B., 143–152
Crouse, D. K., 534
Crouse, John, 449, 456
Culler, A. J., 137, 141, 142

INDEX.

Custer, Christian, 107, 111, 112, 118, 133, 581
Custer, James, 318

Dalrymple, Edmund, 170
Danner, Henry, 381, 545, 547
Danner, Jacob, 381, 547
Davy, Elder Henry, 552, 553, 554, 571, 572
Declaration of Trust, 92, 93
Deeter, Elder W. R., 262, 545, 555
Denton Church, 535
Dettra, John, 247
Dettra, Lewis, 247
Detwiler, Edgar M., 324
Detwiler, Jacob, 318
Detwiler, John, 307
Dickey, L. H., 262
Dierdorff, Andrew M., 122, 163
Dirdorf, Peter, 372, 544, 547
District meetings
  A district meeting, 579
  History of, 585
  Table of, 589
Dixon, A. M., 537
Dompelaers, 12
Donner, Elder Jacob, 72, 73, 78, 545
Douglass, Susan, 96
Dubble, Amos P., 343
Duboy, Elder Abraham, 6, 78, 272, 302, 306, 644
  Biography of, 281
Dunkers, 231, 235, 236, 297, 299, 300, 305, 364, 392, 476, 477
Dunlap, Dr. J. M., 392
Dupler, A. W., 263

Early, Elder H. C., 342, 559, 560, 562, 639
Eberbach, 32, 35
Ebersole, John D., 345
Ebersole, Elder Martin, 331, 332, 645
Eby, Elder Adam, 538, 561
Eby, Elder Andreas, 378, 379, 380, 422, 544, 545, 644
Eby, Elder Benjamin Z., 341, 350, 377, 394, 395, 396, 429, 434, 609, 612, 613, 615, 645
Eby, John, 380
Eckerling, Michael, 6, 34, 165
Eckstein, Christian, 70
Eckstein, Elizabeth, 70
Eder, 2, 19
Edris, Allen, 496, 497, 503
Edris, Elias W., 448, 449, 451, 452, 453

Edwards, Rev. Morgan, 56, 74, 75, 79, 166, 168, 169, 210, 211, 280, 281, 282, 429, 511
Eichelberger, Elder Peter, 328, 374, 644
Eicher, Daniel, 29, 53, 205
Eisenberg, J. L., 262, 639
Eisenberg, J. Y., 212, 215, 258, 260, 262
Eisenberg, W. Y., 214, 217
Eisenhower, John, 113, 114, 118
Elders, before Revolution, 78
  Before 1800, 644
  Since 1800, 645
Elizabethtown Church, 431, 506
  Organization, 407
  Church activities, 409
  Church auxiliaries, 412
  Missionary activity, 419
Elizabethtown College, 324, 343
  Founding, 622
  Experimental stage, 630
  Growth and development, 635
Ellis, C. C., 128, 146, 147
Ellis, Harry, 248
Ellis, J. Howard, 154, 155, 161, 323
Endt, Theobold, 92
Engler, Philip, 381
Ensminger, John, 472
Ephrata Church, 330, 352, 367, 594, 617
  First Ephrata, 337
  Present Ephrata, 339
Ephrata Community, 34, 41, 65, 68, 69, 76, 77, 79, 89, 164, 197, 209
Episcopalians, 235, 236, 258
Epstein, 5
  Congregation at, 7, 9
Ernst, Edwin, 482, 483
Eshelman, Abraham L., 396, 397
Eshelman, Elder Daniel M., 396, 397, 406, 643, 645
Eshelman, E. E., 408, 414, 419, 633, 636, 637
Eshelman, H. S., 406
Eshelman, I. W., 407, 409, 415, 418
Eshelman, Jacob L., 396
Eshelman, Nathan W., 406
Eshelman, M. M., 140
Eshelman, Elder S. S., 397, 398
Eshleman, Elder David, 479, 482, 483, 645
Eshleman, J. C., 488, 489
Etter, Elder David, 441, 442, 443, 444, 448, 488, 490, 645
Etter, David, Jr., 442
Etter, George, 372, 544
Etter, Elder John, 441, 442, 444, 448, 458, 645

INDEX. 657

Etter, Elder Lorenz, 440, 444, 514, 516, 518, 548, 570, 645
  Biography, 517
Etter, Michael, 543
Evans, A. J., 341, 342, 357
Evans, Catherine, 111, 133

Fackler, Abraham, 442, 443
Fahnestock, Adam G., 334, 336
Fahnestock, Alpheus, 105
Fahnestock, Levi, 395
Fahnestock, Elder N. B., 395, 645
Fahnestock, Elder S. B., 397, 405, 645
Fairview Church, 431
  Organization, 405
Falkenstein, Elder G. N., V, VII, VIII, IX, 105, 407, 408, 409, 433, 489, 559, 590, 592, 623, 624, 625, 626, 627, 628, 629, 630, 631, 632, 633, 643, 645, 652
Falckner's Swamp, 15, 28, 63, 198, 206, 207, 208, 289, 475.
Falkner, 20, 37
Fasnacht, Uriah C., 342, 348, 349
Fauss, Jacob, 175, 177
Felker, Wayne W., 343, 344
Fike, Elder S. K., 532, 535, 643, 645
Fitzwater, Abel, 154, 219, 231, 237, 248
Fitzwater, Isabella, 219, 230, 231
Fitzwater, Joseph, 244, 245, 246, 248
Fitzwater, Elder P. B., 537
Flohr, Lewis B., 538
Force, Irwin, 248
Forney, Elder D. L., 362
Forney, D. R., 397, 406
Forney, Hiram, 194
Forney, Milton G., 399
Fox, Benjamin, 482, 483
Fox, Jacob, 322
Fox, Elder John, 109, 111, 112, 121, 123, 124, 131, 581, 645
  Biography, 132
Forry, Wm. A., 490, 496, 497, 503
Francis, J. G., V, VIII, IX, 158, 226, 242, 243, 246, 260, 282, 283, 325, 354, 494, 496, 497, 498, 501, 502, 503, 523, 585, 623, 625, 626, 627, 631
Francis, John, 154, 231, 233, 235, 236, 237
Francis, Mary Zug, 242, 502
Frantz, Elder Isaac, 216, 378
Frantz, Elder Michael, 78, 81, 83, 272, 325, 327, 378, 386, 445, 545, 564, 644

Frantz, Michael, Jr., 378
Frederick, Isaac, 30
Frederick, Peter, 318
Frederick, Veronica, 30, 325
Fretz, Elder Daniel, 388, 389, 391, 423, 424, 425, 427, 428, 545, 569, 645
Fretz, Elder William B., 318, 601
Frey, Elder Andreas, 206, 644
Frey, A. L., 406, 409
Frick, John, 281, 282
Friends, 275
Friesland, West, 50

Gaby, Elder Martin, 381, 384, 475, 476, 477, 478, 480, 545, 547, 644
Galliond, Stephen, 29
Gantz, George Balser, 6, 17, 20
Gantz, Johanna, 20
Garber, Martin, 381
Geib, Elder A. P., 537, 539, 540, 645
Geib, P. C., 397, 398
Geiger, Dr. Henry S., 107, 111, 112, 114, 116, 117, 119, 120, 132, 142
Geiger, Mary S., 128, 132, 141, 613, 620, 634
Gelsinger, Albert, 338, 352
Gerlach, Elder David, 369, 388, 389, 391, 392, 393, 394, 395, 398, 403, 441, 458, 552, 553, 569, 572, 586, 587, 588, 589, 643, 645
  Biography, 428
Gerlach, John, 397
Germantown, 13, 20, 27, 37, 39, 44, 48, 58, 63-70, 75, 76, 77, 79, 197, 239, 289, 298, 323, 476, 594
  Arrived at, 14
  Church organized, 17
  Reaction at, 67
  Sunday afternoon meetings, 69
  A divided congregation, 69
  The exodus, 70
  Changes at, 75
  History of church property, 89-93
  Old Folks' Home at, 93
  Stone meeting house, 94-96
  Parsonage, 96
  Old cemetery, 97
  Prominent bishops, 97-103
  Later history, 103
  Recent pastors, 105
Germany, 1, 7, 8, 10, 15, 19, 25, 31, 36, 37, 38, 47, 270, 272, 273, 281, 291, 440, 477, 514

43

658   INDEX.

Gettel, Peter, 449, 456
Gettel, Samuel Z., 448, 449, 456, 459, 460, 587
Gibbel, Aaron R., 338, 352, 368
Gibbel, Abraham, 370, 383, 388, 389, 390, 391, 569
Gibbel, Elder Cyrus R., 334, 335, 336, 360, 368, 628, 642, 645
Gibbel, Elder Henry, 84, 387, 388, 392, 393, 423, 548, 645
Gibbel, Henry R., 359, 619, 620
Gibbel, John B., 334, 360, 388, 392, 393, 394, 589
  Biography, 368
Gibbel, John R., 360
Gibbel, Johannas, 370, 380
Gibbel, Joseph W., 390, 391, 392, 396
Gibbel, Samuel, 392, 394, 396
Gibble, George, 449, 459, 461, 480
Gibble, H. B., 405
Gibble, H. S., 339, 472, 614, 615
Gibble, Elder Hiram, 224, 348, 394, 395, 405, 490, 590, 592, 600, 613, 643, 645, 652
Gibble, Ira D., 448, 449
Gibble, Isaiah G., 395
Gibble, Isaac M., 442
Gibble, Isaac S., 397
Gibble, John, 458
Gibble, John, 459, 460
Gibble, John M., 409, 415, 421, 638
Gibble, Nathan P., 459, 461, 470, 496, 497, 498
Gibson, I. M., 126
Gingrich, Elder Alfred B., 451, 472, 504, 505, 643, 645
Gingrich, H. H., 504, 505
Gingrich, Jacob H., 472, 504
Gingrich, J. H., 472, 504, 521
Gingrich, Josiah, 442, 443
Gipe, Harrison, 473
Glick, John L., 122
Godwalt, A., 480, 483
Goebel, 11, 14
Gommere, John, 17, 18, 20, 22, 24
Good, Daniel F., 177, 178, 191
Gorgas, Widow, 70
Gorgas, Miriam, 70
Gospel Messenger, 312, 347, 362, 505, 507
Gospel Visitor, 239, 276, 580, 583, 584
Gottshall, Samuel, 310, 312
Gottshall, William F., 310, 312
Gottwals, Amos, 248
Gottwals, John, 307
Gottwals, Elder Jacob Z., 127, 155, 159, 162, 183, 184, 189, 212,
  214, 218, 238, 240, 241, 243, 244, 261, 581, 583, 588, 645
Gottwals, Jacob Z., baptism, 238
  Election to ministry, 241
Gould, Horace, 540
Graff, Johannus, 29
Grater, Elder A. L., 137, 150, 158, 162, 258, 260, 261, 310, 311, 592, 645
Grater, Jacob, 212, 258, 310
Graybill, Abraham, 331
Graybill cemetery, 401
Graybill, Israel B., 395
Graybill, Elder Israel, 394, 395, 645
Graybill, Elder J. F., 194, 413, 489, 645
Graybill, Hiram, 343, 344
Graybill, John G., 331, 332
Graybill, Elder John W., 330, 331, 346, 350, 351, 612, 643, 645
Graybill, Elder Reuben, 395, 497, 645
Graybill, Samuel, 388, 392, 393, 394, 469
Greatswamp Church, 55, 75, 79, 197, 270, 280, 289, 319, 322
  Early history, 282
  Brecht cemetery, 283
  Sacon Township, 284
  Old cemetery, 284
  Old deed, 285
Green Tree Church, 202, 259, 293, 580, 581, 594
  Early preaching, 230
  Ingatherings, 239
  Ministry, 240
  Trustees, 247
  Deacons, 248
Green Tree Church, West, 431, 506, 594
  Organization, 406
Griffin, Samuel, 248
Groff, B. G., 629, 631, 632, 634, 635
Groff, Christian, 332
Groff, Elder Hershey, 326, 330, 331, 332, 348, 350, 374, 645
Gumre (Gommere), Anna, 20
Gunkle, Rudolph, 332, 337, 339

Haas, Frank, 488
Habecker, P. M., 348, 349
Hacker, Harry H., 459, 460, 470
Häcker, William, 10
Hackman, Elder Jacob, 334, 335, 341, 646
Hackman, J. S., 409, 415
Haines, Amos H., 183, 184, 185

INDEX. 659

Haines, Joseph, 173
Haldeman, Frank, 485, 486
Haldeman, John, 485, 487
Haldeman, J. H., 214, 215
Haldeman, Michael, 485
Haldeman, Reuben, 311, 312
Haldeman, Elder Samuel, 646
   Biography, 362, 486
   Letter of, 486
Haller, Elder Jacob, 388, 389, 391, 425, 426, 428, 569, 646
Hallman, George, 248
Hamacker, Adam, 436, 437, 511, 515
Hamilton, John, 268
Harley, A. P., 263
Harley, David, 107, 111, 112, 142
Harley, Elder Benjamin, 297, 298, 307, 315, 588
Harley, E. C., 324
Harley family, 296
Harley, Isaac, 308
Harley, Isaiah G., 112, 113, 114, 116, 122, 124
Harley, Jacob (Mingo), 307
Harley, Jacob (Coventry), 212
Harley, John (Coventry), 212, 215, 224
Harley, John (Green Tree), 248
Harley, Jonas, 297, 298, 320
Harley, Rudolph (Coventry), 214, 216
Harley, Rudolph (Philadelphia), 116, 117, 118
Harley, Rudolph, Jr., 76, 297, 298
Harley, Elder Rudolph, Sr., 163, 296, 298, 302, 306, 644
Harley, Elder Samuel (Ephrata), 330, 332, 337, 338, 341, 394, 448, 459, 587, 646
   Biography, 367
Harley, Elder Samuel (Indian Creek), 122, 178, 179, 180, 183, 184, 188, 203, 216, 304, 306, 317, 367, 479, 482, 554, 555, 568, 570, 581, 587, 588, 589, 600, 646
   Biography, 297
Harley, William, 263
Hartman, Anton, 372, 544
Hartman, J. H., 127
Hartman, Valentine, 480, 483
Harmonyville Church, 213, 253
   Mission, 220
   Organization, 264
   Sunday School, 265
   Ministry, 267
Harrisburg Church, 410, 420, 443
   Early history, 488

Harrisburg Church, election, 489
Hatfield Church, 240, 293, 303, 594
   Organization, 313
   Eight-Square school house, 314
   Revival services, 314
   First house of worship, 316
   Second house of worship, 317
   Ministers, 317
Hays, Elder D., 161, 262, 545, 554
Heagy, Jacob, 472, 504, 505, 615
Heckler, James Y., 291, 297, 301
Heckler, Jesse Y., 301
Heckler, Joseph, 301, 318
Heckler, N. F., 291
Heckman, B. F., 411
Heckman, Elder Peter, 445, 644
Heddings, D. R., 534
Heffly, Peter, 29, 205
Heidelberg, 33, 34, 35, 36
Heisey, Elmer, 405
Heisey, Elder Martin, 458, 459, 496, 497, 646
Heisler, John, 109, 111, 112
Henry, M. R., 472, 612, 628, 632
Henrich, James, 73
Henry, Prince, 2, 4, 50, 51, 57
Hermits, 21, 45
Hernly, Christian, 442
Herr, Elder John, V, VIII, IX, 350, 353, 358, 409, 415, 421, 458, 459, 460, 461, 470, 471, 473, 482, 484, 490, 493, 494, 497, 498, 501, 503, 511, 521, 522, 526, 527, 529, 559, 560, 561, 562, 563, 589, 590, 592, 600, 613, 614, 616, 623, 624, 640, 643, 646, 652
Herr, Henry, Jr., 399, 403
Herr, John H., 399, 404
Herr, Elder Tobias, 346, 394, 399, 403, 646
Herring, Edward, 485
Hershey, B., 399
Hershey, Jacob, 379, 380
Hershey, J. W. G., 334, 359, 360, 638, 652
Hershey, Joseph, 542
Hertzler, Jonathan, 458, 460
Hertzler, Elder John, 396, 446, 448, 449, 455, 458, 459, 469, 480, 482, 485, 487, 490, 581, 600, 643, 647
   Biography, 525
Hertzler, Elder S. H., 332, 342, 348, 349, 397, 408, 409, 414, 420, 421, 474, 504, 506, 524, 590, 592, 600, 624, 625, 626, 627, 628, 629, 631, 632, 642, 643, 647, 651, 652
Hertzler, Elder William, 127, 183, 189, 190, 316, 341, 393, 396,

397, 402, 404, 433, 441, 443, 458, 459, 460, 464, 468, 469, 472, 474, 479, 490, 499, 508, 522, 525, 530, 533, 534, 535, 553, 554, 555, 556, 557, 581, 587, 589, 595, 596, 597, 600, 643, 647
Hertzler, Wm., biography, 441, 523
Hertzog, Reuben M., 352
Hess, George, 459, 461, 481, 482
Hess, Henry L., 397, 398
Hetric, Elder J. P., 111, 125, 126, 132, 174, 183, 211, 212, 213, 225, 226, 227, 228, 254, 255, 256, 260, 261, 262, 266, 562, 642, 647
Heyser, Emmanuel, 173, 241, 242
Hiestand, D. M., 397, 613
Hildebrand, Johannes, 20, 47, 53, 69, 70, 81, 325
Hildebrand, Maria, 20, 81
Hoch, Augustus, 479, 481
Hochmann, Ernest Christoph, 57
Höcker, Heinrich, 70
Höcker, Louis, 70
Höcker, Maria, 70
Höcker, Margretta, 70
Hoech, Bastian, 92
Hoech, Johanna, 92
Hoerner, Andrew, 423
Hoffer, Aaron H., 472, 473, 489, 506, 507
Hoffer, Addison H., 489
Hoffer, George, 390, 440
Hoffer, George (deacon), 472, 473
Hoffer, Isaac L., 409
Hoffman, Enoch, 171
Hohn, Henry, 29, 30, 31, 54
Hollinger, Adam, 489
Hollinger, Abraham K., 489
Hollinger, Elder Adam, 499
Hollinger, Elder Daniel, 440, 469, 472, 506, 507, 647
Hollinger, J. H., 537
Hollinger, J. A., 342
Hollinger, Elder H. B., 472, 504, 520, 626, 647
Hollinger, Elder Jacob, 363, 367, 370, 392, 441, 444, 458, 469, 472, 474, 499, 524, 587, 588, 643, 647
 Biography, 440, 518
Hollinger, Monroe G., 398
Hollowbush, Peter, 212, 216, 218, 220, 224, 252, 346, 468, 587
Holsinger, Elder D. M., 122, 123, 553, 572, 586, 593
Holsinger, George B., 342
Holsinger, Harry R., 534
Holsinger, H. R., 572

Holsinger, John P., 534
Holsinger, Jacob, 322
Holsinger, Johannes, 543
Holsinger, Elder L. T., 161, 545, 546, 559
Holsinger, Elder W. H., 638
Holsopple, Frank F., 185, 204, 211, 214, 233, 254, 255, 260, 623
Holsopple, Ira C., 185, 211, 214, 221, 226, 255, 620
Holtzappel, Henry, 6, 20
Hoover, George, 533
Hoover, Elder Silas W., 342, 562
Hope, Elder Christian, 536, 538
Hoppock, Elder John, 173, 183, 184, 185, 193, 194, 647
 Biography, 204
Horne, Elder H. T., 194, 195, 647
Horning, John, 308
Horning, Samuel, 308
Hottel, Elder Benjamin, 322, 626, 632, 642, 647
Hottenstein, Elder Amos S., 399, 400, 497, 592, 647
Hottenstein, P. S., 399
Housel, William, 164, 168, 169
Howe, Elder William M., 185, 191, 193, 310, 324, 410, 562, 623
Huber, Christian, 543
Huffman, Paul K., 173
Hummer, Catherine, 369, 370, 371, 372, 373, 564
Hummer, Peter, 369, 370, 371, 373, 422
Hunberger, Samuel A., 361, 411, 555
Hunsicker, Jonas, 456
Hunsicker, Jonathan, 449
Hutchison, James A., 531
Hutchison, M. J., 532
Hyde, Lambert M., 185, 187, 204
Hyde, Elder Robinson, 173, 174, 189, 191, 194, 195, 202
 Biography, 204

Imler, Elder T. F., 324, 341, 342, 343, 345, 432, 533, 534, 535, 592, 609, 612, 613, 618, 619, 620, 628, 629, 631, 632, 643, 647
Imler, Conrad, 533, 534
Indian Creek, 76
Indian Creek Church, 153, 240, 287, 296, 319, 594
 Earliest preaching, 27, 28
 The Price family, 291
 Elders and ministers, 294
 The Harley family, 296
 Other families, 298
 Organization, 289, 301

Indian Creek Church
  Meeting houses, 302
  Burial grounds, 303
  Towamincin, 304
Indian maiden, 292
Ingles, Casper, 211
Inspirationist, 34, 35, 36
Isett, John, 257, 307

Johns, J. Bitzer, 338, 352
Johnson, William, 309, 312
Jones, Robert, 310
Jones, Samuel, 310
Jones, William, 154

Kagey, Elder J. M., 590
Kalklöser, John H., 6, 68, 69, 70
Kampfer, Johannas, 20, 301
Kautz, Daniel, 343
Kaylor, Elder Hiram E., 406
Keim, Elder David, 211, 218, 220, 223, 264, 265, 267, 647
Keim, Jonathan, 214, 264, 265, 267, 268
Keim, Leonard, 264, 265
Keim, L. M., 137, 139, 212, 260, 267, 625
Keim, Samuel, 266
Keller, Daniel, 458
Keller, J. H., 408, 632, 638
Keller, Isaac, 337, 338, 352
Keiler, Samuel, 395, 613
Kelpius, 21, 36, 37
Kemerer, Elias, 482, 483
Kemerer, John, 481, 483
Kemper, David, 328
Keyser, Abraham, 96
Keyser, Hannah, 118
Keyser, Elder Peter, 101, 107, 109, 110, 134, 211, 545, 547, 642, 647
  Biography, 103, 129
Kiefer, Daniel, 513
Kiefer, Jacob, 441, 443, 468
Kiefer, John, 442
Kilhefner, Elder David, 339, 340, 350, 592, 600, 601, 617, 618, 632, 638, 642, 647, 652
Kilhefner, Jacob, 338, 352
Kilkefner, J. K., 339
Kilhefner, S. K., 339
Kilhefner, Nathan, 343, 344
King, Israel, 479, 482, 483
King, John, 494, 495
King, Elder Joshua Y., 469, 479, 481, 532, 534, 535, 559, 590, 592, 600, 628, 647
King, Milton F., 534
Kinsey, David, 475, 476, 478
Kinsing, Martha, 70

Kintzel, Elias, 485, 487
Kintzel, William, 485, 487
Kitchen, A. R., 534
Kittinger, B. F., 157, 158, 159
Klein Association, Elder George, 509, 511
Klein, Elder George, 78, 328, 374, 436, 445, 455, 475, 514, 518, 643, 644
  Baptism, 163, 164
  Founder of congregations, 166
  At Little Swatara, 436, 445
  At Maiden Creek, 475
  Biography, 509, 512
Klein, S., 480, 483
Kline, Elder Benjamin, 441, 447, 448, 449, 455, 514, 647
Kline, Daniel R., 448, 456
Kline, David B., 409, 415
Kline, Emanuel, 442, 443
Kline, Henry S., 479, 482, 495
Kline, Jacob, 480, 481
Kline, John (Lancaster), 341, 343, 344
Kline, John (Maiden Creek), 481, 482, 483
Kline, John (Tulpehocken), 458, 461
Kline, Elder John (Virginia), 172, 510, 514, 549, 550, 551, 570, 580
Kline, John H., 407, 408, 409, 414, 418, 420
Klingin, Anna Margaretha, 57
Koch, Jacob, 20
Koch, Stephen, 6, 11, 20, 65, 66, 70
  Visions of, 66, 69
Kolb, J. B., 405
Kopenhaver, William, 490
Köster, 37
Kratz, Amanda, 153, 159, 160, 620
Kratz, John, 318
Kratz, William, 318
Kreider, Benjamin, 348, 349
Kreider, Daniel K., 472
Kuhns, Amos M., 442, 443, 600, 652
Kulp, Elder Isaac, 189, 216, 219, 307, 308, 309, 312, 321, 589, 600, 647
Kulp, S. W., 339, 356, 624
Kulp, W. K., 339
Kulp, W. W., 214, 226
Kurtz, Elder D. W., 2, 3, 50, 537, 639, 647
  Biography, 135–136
Kurtz, Edwin, 459, 461, 470
Kurtz, Elder Henry, IX, 75, 87, 241, 371, 545, 549, 550, 565, 570
Kurtz, Michael, 459, 460, 470

662 INDEX.

Kirtz, Samuel, 458, 460, 587
Kutz, D. C., 485
Labadists, 40, 41, 49
Lake Ridge Mission, 413
Lancaster City Church
   Organization, 341
   Growth and development, 343
Landert, Sigmund, 31
Landis, Abraham, 248
Landis, Henry, 18, 20, 29, 205
Landis, Johannis, 326
Landis, Michael, 329, 365
Lang, Frederick, 18, 20
Laushe, Abram, 173
Laushe, Abraham, 164, 168, 169, 170, 545
Laushe, Henry, 170, 171, 198
Laushe, Isaac, 170, 314
Laushe, John Peter, 163
Lauver, G. M., 411
Lawrenceville, 237, 251, 252, 254, 255
Leatherman, Elder Daniel, 72, 73, 78
Leckrone, Quincy, 263, 620
Lefever, Elder Elias B., 338, 624
Lehman, Christian, 255
Lehman, Samuel, 391, 571, 580
Leibert, Peter, 77, 92, 112, 381, 545, 547
Leinbach, Rev. Thomas, 365
Lentz, Alfred M., 448, 449
Lentz, Henry, 448, 456
Lentz, John H., 449
Leopold, Jonas, 224
Letterman, Daniel, 372, 544, 545
Letterman, Nicholas, 372, 544
Levy, Philip, 381
Libe, Christian, 6, 18, 163, 196
   Minister at Crefeldt, 10
Light, George H., 317, 318, 651, 652
Light, Elder H. E., 127, 157, 158, 162, 185, 190, 191, 193, 341, 346, 347, 348, 349, 350, 394, 395, 399, 404, 407, 409, 429, 451, 459, 490, 493, 589, 592, 600, 602, 608, 609, 612, 617, 618, 623, 624, 625, 626, 627, 628, 642, 643, 647
Lint, Elder C. G., 186, 553, 554
Lint, Simon, 322
Lititz Church, 336, 354
   Organization, 359
   First efforts, 360
Livermore, Harriet, 97
Livengood, C. A., 348, 349
Lloyd, Edgar K., 264
Long, Elder Christian, 122, 462, 547, 548, 549

Long, Elder J. A., 411, 432, 559, 562
Long, Elder Peter, 172, 391, 545, 550, 565
Long, Elder Walter S., 105, 128, 145
Longacre, Owen, 29, 205
Longenecker, A. G., 409, 412, 414, 415, 418, 473, 638
Longenecker, Abraham, 395
Longenecker, A. H., 493, 495
Longenecker, Benjamin, 472
Longenecker, Elder Christian (first), 86, 327, 328, 370, 374, 379, 380, 381, 382, 383, 384, 385, 387, 423, 516, 541, 544, 547, 643, 644
   Biography, 386, 422
Longenecker, Elder Christian (second), 388, 389, 390, 391, 403, 458, 550, 551, 568, 647
   Biography, 386, 427
Longenecker, Daniel, 499, 593
Longenecker, W. S., 406
Longenecker, Elder J. H., VI, 358, 387, 407, 409, 415, 421, 435, 443, 451, 459, 472, 473, 474, 488, 490, 520, 545, 558, 560, 561, 562, 563, 589, 590, 592, 600, 601, 602, 621, 623, 624, 640, 643, 647, 652
Longenecker, Linn B., 386, 395
Longenecker, Solomon, 534
Lovefeast
   First in America, 18
   First in Philadelphia, 110
   In barns, 234
Lowman, Henry, 74
Lucas, 490
Lumberville, 233, 234, 237, 240
Lumberville Mission, 219
Lutherans, 9, 34, 36, 49, 51, 63, 67, 382, 392, 400, 401, 453, 465, 468, 478, 530
Lynd, James, 108, 109, 111, 112, 114, 130

Mack, Alexander, Sr., 3, 5, 6, 21, 31, 49, 51, 52, 55, 75, 77, 78, 98, 163, 198, 205, 206, 207, 208, 270, 281, 306, 325, 326, 644
   Biography, 56–61
   Life work, 57
   Character, 58–60
   Seal, 60
   Removal, 61
   Arrival, 51, 64
Mack, Elder Alexander, Jr., 57, 68, 78, 92, 112, 211, 306, 372, 380, 544, 545, 546, 644

INDEX.

Mack, Elder Alexander, Jr., leaves Germantown, 70
  Returns, 78
  Elected to ministry, 78
  Biography, 98
  Baptisms of, 99
  Mack family, 102
Mack, Ann Maria, 57, 102
Mack family, 102
Mack, Hannah, 100, 102
Mack, Christina, 57
Mack, Johannes, 57, 90, 91, 96
Mack, John Valentine, 57, 69, 70, 102
Mack, Maria Hildebrand, 70, 102
Madeira, Elder C. C., 397, 405, 408, 409, 421, 479, 482, 647
Maiden Creek Church, 166, 319, 469, 492, 594
  Early history, 475
  Houses of worship, 476, 481
  Elections, 480, 481
  Obituaries, 483
Major, Thomas, 111, 112, 131, 230
Major, Sara Righter, 131, 220
Mannheim, 33, 56
Marienborn congregation, 5, 7, 9
Markley, Samuel, 307
Martin, A. L. B., 432, 489
Martin, Amos M., 350, 351
Martin, A. W., 350, 351, 408, 420
Martin, Elder George Adam, 73, 74, 78, 196, 211, 282, 375, 644
  Autobiography, 269
Martin, Nathan, 406, 408, 409, 414, 418, 633, 651
Martin, Elder Nicolas, 72, 73, 78, 372, 375, 544, 545, 547
Martsall, John G., 352
Maryland (see Bohemian Manor), 71, 72, 73, 80, 209, 217, 276, 296, 380, 387, 530, 533, 535, 569
Maugans, A. H., 489
Maugans, J. C., 540
Mayer, John, 30
Mayle, Jane, 18, 20, 48
McCann, Elder S. N., 368, 561, 563
McCann, Elizabeth Gibbel, 368
McKee, C. F., 243, 247, 249, 258, 260, 262, 620
McKinney, George B., 490, 496, 497
Mechanic Grove Church
  Early preaching, 346
  Organization, 346
Mennonites, 9, 10, 29, 40, 219, 230, 272, 273, 281, 283, 299, 304, 314, 375, 378, 382, 383, 386, 392, 400, 401, 403, 429

Merkey, Elder David, 446, 449, 455, 456, 469, 480, 587, 588, 647
Merkey, Jacob, 449
Merkey, John, 449, 455, 456, 480, 544, 571, 575
Merkey, Elder Joseph, 446, 449, 455, 458, 480, 514, 647
Methatchton, 219, 230, 234, 236, 237, 307, 311
Methodists, 224, 231, 235, 236, 265, 314, 323, 332, 341, 407, 530
Metzger, Elder John, 551, 552, 553, 554, 580
Meyer, J. G., 408, 409, 418, 633, 636
Meyer, Elder Jacob W., Sr., 448, 449, 453, 455, 459, 485, 487, 525, 647
  Biography, 526
Midway Church, 461, 471, 490, 504
  Organization, 496
  Early meetings, 498
  Lebanon work, 501
Miller, Abraham, 513
Miller, Andrew, 442
Miller, Clayton B., 442, 443
Miller, D. E., 489
Miller, Elder D. L., 3, 546, 557, 567, 616, 639
Miller, Eliza, 538
Miller, Elder George, 374, 383, 437, 472, 508, 564, 644
  Biography, 436, 511, 512
Miller, George H., 490
Miller, Howard, 126
Miller, Ira W., 343, 344
Miller, J. M., 339, 340
Miller, Elder J. Kurtz, 195, 410, 536, 537, 538, 539, 540, 561, 562, 632, 638, 639, 642, 643, 647
Miller, Martin, 172
Miller, Elder M. B., 193, 194, 195, 537, 539, 648
Miller, Elder Moses, 178, 179, 183, 377, 511, 512, 545, 554
Miller, O. S., 532
Miller, Peter, 54, 67, 69, 74, 364
Miller, Elder P. S., 161, 590
Miller, Elder R. H., 178, 179, 180, 182
Mingo Church, 237, 257, 275, 303, 323, 492, 594
  Early membership, 307
  Present officials, 312
Ministerial meetings
  Table of, 592
Minnich, Jacob L., 335, 341
Minnich, Jacob S., 332, 334, 337, 360
Minnich, John, 392, 394, 427

664 INDEX.

Minnich, John L., 346, 347, 348
Minnich, Nathaniel, 395, 609, 612, 615, 617
Missionary activity, 24, 31
 Tour, 26–29, 290
 Early history, 593
 Organization, 595
 Members of board, 600, 603
 Offerings, 602
 Table of meetings, 592, 652
Mohler, Harry B., 408
Mohler, Henry, 331, 365
Mohler, Henry, Jr., 331
Mohler, John, Sr., 331
Mohler, John L., 338, 352, 353
Mohler, Elder John M., 488
Mohler, Elder Levi S., 408, 409, 421
Mohr, Allen, 322
Mohr, Jacob, 372, 544
Moore, Elder Chas. W., 176, 180, 186, 190, 191, 193, 194, 648
 Biography, 203
Moore, Elder John P., 170, 171, 175, 177, 178, 180, 181, 182, 648
 Biography, 202
Moore, Asa, 180
Moore, Gideon, 169, 170, 179
Moore, Elder J. H., 140, 558
Moore, William H., 173, 175, 177
Moravian, 475
More, Jacob, 163
Morgan, Elias, 486
Morrison's Cove, 74, 542, 543
Mountville Church, 394
 Organization, 399
 Church houses, 399, 401, 402, 404
Moyer, Henry H., 494, 495
Moyer, Jacob, 73
Mühlbach, 29, 40, 41, 43, 48
Mühlenberg, 72
Münsinger, Frank, 318
Musser, B. G., 394, 399, 403, 609, 612, 625
 Biography, 429
Musser, Isaiah N., 399, 632
Myer, Abraham, 458, 461
Myer, Daniel, 332, 344
Myer, Diller, 331, 332
Myer, Eli, 343, 344
Myer, George, 331
Myer, Israel, 329, 330, 337, 338, 587
Myer, Jacob, 372, 544
Myer, Johannis, 331
Myer, Elder John, 330, 334, 335, 359, 648
Myer, Elder Joseph, 329, 330, 356, 587, 648

Myer, J. W., 342, 343, 344, 600
Myer, Jacob W., Jr., 448, 449, 526, 620
Myer, Mahlon, 332
Myer, Reuben, 332
Myer, Rife, 332
Myer, Samuel, 329, 365
Myer, Samuel O., 449, 526
Myer, Samuel R., 330
Myer, Samuel (Little Swatara), 448, 526
Myers, Christian, 380
Myers, G. C., 537
Myers, Elder Graybill, 122, 123, 390, 499, 553, 584, 585
Myers, Elder J. T., 104, 105, 124, 134, 135, 137, 140, 147, 150, 156, 233, 239, 244, 246, 254, 256, 259, 260, 266, 530, 561, 589, 590, 595, 596, 600, 642, 648
Myers, S. F., 159, 194
Myers, Elder T. T., 8, 105, 126, 128, 135, 136, 137, 536, 538, 563, 628, 639, 648
Myers, Elder Tobias, 194, 560, 590
Mysticism, 34, 36, 39, 40, 44, 45, 47, 64
Mystics, 9, 15

Naas, Elder John, 6, 10, 12, 69, 78, 163, 164, 166, 204, 207, 281, 297, 510, 514, 642, 644
 Biography, 196
 Son of, 12
Nagele, Hans Rudolph, 29
Nantmeal mission, 217
Nedrow, Elmer F., 324, 413, 601
Nedrow, Elder R. A., 413, 601
Neff, Daniel S., 399
Neff, Henry, 73, 372, 544, 545, 547, 550
Neidlinger, John, 485
Newcomer, Elder J. S., 341, 388, 389, 392, 393, 394, 395, 396, 399, 403, 587, 643, 648
 Biography, 429
New Jersey churches, 594
 Origin, 163
 Colonial life in, 164
 Amwell Church, 75, 82, 168, 169, 175
 Sand Brook Church, 175
 Bethel Church, 189
 Union Church, 193
Nissley, Elder Jacob, 458, 459, 460, 461, 648
Norris, Thomas, 322
Norristown Church, 275
 Early preaching, 323

INDEX. 665

Norristown Church
  Organization, 324
Northkill Church, 75, 79, 217, 475, 509, 510, 511, 514
Nyce family, 298
Nyce, Percival C., 492, 493, 495, 581, 628, 630
Nyce, William G., 212, 258, 260, 261, 262, 264, 268
Nyce, Elder Wm. P., 299, 306, 648
Ober, Allen, 406
Ober, H. K., 386, 408, 409, 411, 418, 590, 592, 618, 619, 620, 621, 632, 634, 637, 638, 651, 652
Oberholtzer, Jacob, 457, 460, 521
Oberholtzer, Elder William, 448, 459, 460, 461, 470, 482, 483, 484, 502, 546, 600, 626, 643, 648
Oberlin, Allen A., 531
Old Folks' Home, 93
Old Order Brethren, 338, 348, 377, 485
Oley, 15, 28, 55, 75, 79, 272, 289, 475, 477
Orr, E. A., 126, 127, 156
Otterbein, William, 382

Palatinate, 5, 7, 9, 32, 38, 56
Park, Asa, 173
Parkerford Church, 213, 228, 233
  Mission, 219
  Beginnings, 250
  First pastor, 255
Partman, Anna D., 76
Patches, Henry M., 496, 497
Patrick, Thomas, 442, 443
Paxton Boys, 376
Peach Blossom Church, 533
  Early history, 530
  Division, 531
Penn, John, 293
Penn, Thomas, 293
Penn, William, 13
Pennypacker, Joseph, 231, 247, 248
Pennypacker, Nathan, 230
Pennypacker, S. W., 9, 299
Pequea, 29, 30
Persecution, 7-12, 13, 58
Pettikoffer, Anna Elizabeth, 70, 90
Pettikoffer, Johannes, 70, 89, 90, 91
Pettikoffer House, 92-94, 96
Pfautz, Elder David, 462
Pfautz, Jacob, 330, 331, 332, 341
Pfautz, Elder Jacob (Conestoga), 328, 335, 356, 365, 457, 458, 521, 545, 548, 643, 648
Pfautz, Elder Jacob (Little Swatara), 448, 449, 451, 471, 648

Pfautz, Joseph, 335
Pfautz, Moses, 458, 460
Pfoutz, Elder Abraham, 448, 449, 453, 458, 469, 648
  Biography, 527
Pfautz, Elder Michael, 78, 82, 83, 85, 86, 166, 327, 328, 335, 373, 374, 381, 386, 514, 547, 548, 644
Pherson, O. P., 534
Pilgrim, The, 216
Pittenger, Elder J. M., 408, 412, 413, 632
Philadelphia churches
  First Brethren, 107
    On Crown Street, 108
    Elders and ministers, 112
    Poor fund, 118
    Sunday School, 119
    On Marshall Street, 124
    On Dauphin Street, 128
    Recent history, 134
  North Philadelphia Church, 127
    Geiger Memorial, 128, 136, 244
    Pastors, 137
    Work of Mary S. Geiger, 141
  Bethany Mission Church, 142
Pietists, 2, 3, 9, 34, 35, 36, 42, 45, 57
Poor Fund
  At Philadelphia, 118
  At Coventry, 227
  At Harmonyville, 268
Poulson, Elder Israel, Sr., 168, 169, 170, 172, 173, 314, 648
  Biography, 198
  Visions, 199
Poulson, Elder Israel, Jr., 155, 159, 162, 170, 172, 179, 180, 181, 182, 183, 184, 189, 570, 581, 648
  Biography, 201
Preisz, Johannes (Jakob), 20, 27, 291, 294, 302, 306, 644
Presbyterians, 235
Pressel, Valentine, 381
Price, Caleb, 294, 313, 316
Price, Elder D. E., 293
Price, Daniel, 217, 292, 293
Price family, 291
Price, F. W., 105
Price, Elder George, 211, 217, 218, 219, 222, 223, 230, 231, 240, 241, 294, 323, 479, 545, 547, 648
Price, Elder Henry A., 294, 306, 320, 648
Price, Elder Isaac, 122, 219, 230,

INDEX.

231, 236, 238, 241, 246, 250, 251, 252, 274, 278, 294, 573, 581, 583, 588, 648
Price, Elder Jacob M., 295, 303, 306, 642, 648
Price, Elder John, Sr., 211, 220, 223, 224, 235, 240, 274, 294, 548, 550, 648
Price, Elder John R., 211, 215, 223, 294, 581, 589, 649
Price, John W., 153, 162, 294, 581, 588, 642
Price, John (Antietam), 293
Price, John (Indian Creek, poet), 291, 294
Price, Elder John (Indian Creek), 293, 294, 295, 302, 306, 314, 315, 457, 458, 462, 479, 521, 545, 546, 642, 644
Price, Johannas, 292
Price, Jonas, Sr., 317, 396, 469, 479, 499
Price, Jonas H., 157, 295, 600
Price, Samuel H., 309, 312
Price, William (Ephrata), 337, 338
Price, W. S., 128, 257, 258, 259, 260, 261, 262
Price, Elder William W., 238, 240, 294, 298, 304, 305, 306, 314, 315, 317, 346, 457, 521, 649
  Biography, 295
Pricetown meeting house, 476
Primitive Christian, 216
Progressive Church, 187, 204
Protestants, 8
Prussia, 1, 5, 291

Quaker Church, 492
Quakers, 45, 64
Quinter, Elder James, 56, 57, 60, 119, 120, 132, 140, 174, 181, 182, 185, 213, 220, 233, 234, 237, 238, 239, 241, 244, 248, 251, 252, 255, 275, 278, 305, 314, 315, 401, 545, 551, 572, 580, 649
  Conversion, 231
  Early Christian life, 232
  Elected to ministry, 238

Rairigh, Elder George S., 411, 534, 535, 538, 592, 643, 649
Raudenbush, Henry, 372, 544
Rayman, Richard, 154
Reading City Church
  Church house, 492
  Organization, 493
  Church activities, 494

Ream, James F., 322
Reber, Aaron C., 534
Reber, Daniel H., 481, 482, 483
Reber, Elder D. C., V, VIII, IX, 86, 404, 408, 409, 415, 418, 420, 421, 505, 508, 537, 538, 540, 632, 633, 634, 636, 637, 649
Reber, Elias G., 482, 483
Reber, Frank L., 470, 628
Reber, Jonathan G., 479, 482, 483
Redcay, Jacob, 350, 352
Reed, Elder Samuel, 442, 649
Reformation, 8
Reformed Church, 9, 11, 21, 51, 56, 63, 67, 74, 225, 257, 281, 285, 365, 382, 392, 465, 468, 478, 530
Reidenbach, Elder Rudy S., 330, 331, 350, 351, 649
Reiff, J. B., 214, 253, 256
Reiff, J. C., 186, 188, 194, 247, 248
Reiner, Elder Jacob, 111, 122, 153, 162, 173, 279, 304, 313, 315, 317, 553, 581, 588, 589, 642, 649
Reiner, Joel K., 111, 126, 127, 185
Reinhart, Abraham, 211
Reinhart, Martin, 211
Reinhart, Peter, 211
Reinhold, Jacob, 329, 334, 468, 499, 587
Reisman, Johannes, 70
Reutsh, Joseph, 372, 544
Rider, Elder Jacob, 388, 390, 391, 392, 396, 398, 407, 430, 458, 569, 589, 649
Rider, Joseph H., 407, 414, 628, 629, 630, 631, 635
Ridgely Church, 531
  Organization, 533
  Officials, 534
Righter, Elder John, 111, 112, 131, 238, 649
Righter, Sara, 112, 131, 230, 252
Rittenhouse, David, 218, 238
Rittenhouse, F. H., 532
Rittenhouse, Elder Joseph, 530
Rittenhouse, J. Roy, 531, 598
Ritter, Daniel, 20
River Brethren (Brethren in Christ), 308, 382, 383, 453, 542
Roeller, B. F., 263
Rosenberger, Artemus, 318
Rosenberger, Jacob, 318
Rosicrucian, 34, 36, 48, 49
Rothermel, Elder Jeremiah, 479, 481, 483, 484, 649
Rothrock Cemetery, 283, 284, 285
Rothrock, Jacob, 285, 288
Rothrock, Elder Joseph, 462
Rouser, Gideon, 163, 164, 372, 544

INDEX. 667

Royer, Abram H., 331, 352, 626, 627
Royer, Aaron H., 352, 531, 532
Royer, B. Mary, 413
Royer, Cyrus, 346, 347, 348
Royer, Daniel, 457, 458, 460, 464, 521, 524
Royer, David, 331, 337
Royer, Elder G. B., 411
Royer, Henry, 338, 352
Royer, Elder J. G., 359, 410, 540, 556, 557, 639
Royer, John, 353, 544, 565, 568
Royer, John L., 459, 460, 471
Royer, John R., 338, 339
Royer, Joseph, 336, 363, 544
Royer, Reuben, 459, 461
Royersford Church, 213
   Sunday School organized, 258
   Organization, 261
Ruhl, Allen B., 397, 398
Rupp, Elder Christian, 329, 330, 356, 587, 649
Rupp, Levi, 332

Sabbath, 41, 47
Sabbatarians, 41, 47, 48, 49
Sachse, Julius F., 9, 19, 23, 27
Sand Brook Church, 175, 190, 191, 193
Sacon Township, 284
Sanger, H. E., 531
Sanger, W. E., 532
Sanger, W. H., 408, 633
Sanger, Elder S. F., 538, 557, 558, 567
Saylor, Elder D. P., 178, 179, 180, 182, 276, 391, 545, 550, 572, 579, 580
Saylor, Jeriah, 307
Saur (Sower), Christopher First, 67, 77, 292, 297
Schilbert, Peter, 89, 90, 91
Schlatter, 72
Schlosser, Elder John W., 338, 350, 352, 353, 643, 649, 652
Schlosser, R. W., 408, 409, 413, 415, 636
School house, 313, 355, 462, 463, 465
Schreiber, 77
Schreiber, George, 92, 372, 544
Schreiber, John S., 154, 155, 159
Schreiner, George D., 335, 359
Schriesheim, 56, 57, 62
Schumacher, Daniel, 544
Schuylkill Church, 526
   Early history, 485
   Meeting places, 486

Schwarzenau, 2, 4, 5, 23, 35, 36, 39, 45, 49, 50, 57, 59, 91, 281
   Geography, 1
   Religious conditions, 3
   Church at, 7
Schwaninger, Francis, 531
Schweitzer, Mattes, 372, 544
Schwenkfelders, 9
Secrist, Caleb, 531, 532
Seidensticker, 9
Sell, Andrew, 29, 205
Sell, Elder James A., 558, 559, 560, 561, 562, 584
Select School, 97
Seldomridge, J. Albert, 343, 344, 399
Separatists, 36, 53, 272
Seventh Day Baptists
   Relation to Brethren, 49
Shafer, Joseph, 30
Shaffer, J. J., 214
Shallenberger, Elder David, 457, 521, 545, 570
Shamokin Church
   Early history, 490
Shearer, H. B., 397, 398
Shearer, Elder S. S., 406
Shelly, Jeremiah, 303, 600
Sherman, George H., 492, 494, 495
Sherman, Samuel, 449, 454
Shimer, William, 534
Shirk, Isaac, 332, 337, 356
Shisler, Elder James B., 150, 194, 301, 324, 642, 649
Shlipfer, John, 372, 544
Shoemaker, Peter, 90, 96
Shope, Elder Adam J., 442, 443, 649
Shrab, Lorenz, 372, 544
Shroyer, Elder Reuben, 410
Shuler, Elder Moses, 319, 320, 321, 642, 649
Sieber, Elder Solomon, 499
Sisters' work, 225
Skippack, 15, 27, 289, 290, 304, 307, 308, 309, 312
Slingloff, Henry, 92
Slingluff, Casper, 154
Slingluff, Henry, 154
Slingluff, John U., 153, 155, 173, 323, 588
Slingluff, William, 154
Sluyter, Peter, 41
Smith, Benjamin, 459, 461, 470
Smith, Elder David, 442, 649
Smith, Elder George, 469, 485, 486, 487, 643, 649
Smith, John H., 496
Smith, Peter A., 311, 312, 494, 502

INDEX.

Smouse, J. M., 183
Snader, David, 334, 357, 358
Snively, W. F., 532
Snowberger, Joseph D., 533, 534
Snyder, Elder G. A., 590
Snyder, Hiram, 338, 352
Sonon, Elder Henry S., 399, 649
Sonon, Jacob, 392, 394
Sontag, Elder Jacob, 82, 83, 85, 327, 330, 644
Sophia, Hedwig, 1, 2
Sower, Charles, 77, 103
Sower, Elder Christopher, 77, 78, 92, 96, 98, 306, 323, 372, 374, 377, 409, 445, 475, 511, 544, 546, 644
   Biography, 101-103
Spanogle, Elder Andrew, 172, 391
Spanogle, Harry, 488
Spanogle, Jacob, 115, 118, 132, 134, 588
Specht, A. J., 263
Sperry, Henry, 154
Spicher, Levi, 534
Spidle, Wm. F., 322
Spiker, Milan H., 534
Spring Creek Church, 504, 506, 520, 594
   Organization, 472
   Elections, 472
   Houses of worship, 473
Springfield Church, 240, 293, 303
   Organization, 319, 321
   Stone meeting house, 320
   Present officials, 322
Spring Grove Church, 331, 347, 617
   Organization, 350
Springville Church, 354
   Organization, 352
   Church houses, 353
Statistical Tables
   Of churches, 642
   Of elders before 1800, 644
   Of elders since 1800, 645
   Of local Sunday School meetings, 652
Stauffer, Benjamin G., 398
Stauffer, Cyrus, 348, 349
Stauffer, D. F., 260
Stayer, D. B., 534
Steel, Edward, 534
Steel, George, 534
Steely, Harrison, 335, 346, 348
Steely, Mathias, 322
Stehman, Henry, 392, 394
Stehman, Jacob, 392, 394, 400
Steinmetz meeting house, 354
Stevenson, Theodore, 173

Stewart, Benjamin, 534
Stiefel, George, 36, 41, 42, 65
Stiegel, Baron, 392
Stoll, Elder Jacob, 326, 327, 328, 335, 336, 369, 374, 545, 547, 644
   Biography, 362-364
Stoner, Joseph, 403
Stoner, Elder Solomon, 533
Stony Creek Church, 74, 79
Stoudt, Harrison, 481
Stouffer, Daniel M., 493
Stover, Mrs. Rudolph, 222
Stover, Elder W. B., 104, 411, 546, 563
Strasburg, 33, 34
Strayer, Ephraim, 538, 540
Struphaar, Daniel, 472
Struphaar, Isaac, 472
Struphaur, Joshua, 485
Struphaur, Michael, 486
Stump, Jacob, 76
Stuntz, 36, 40, 42, 65, 66
Stutzman, Jacob, 372, 544
Sunday School
   District secretaries, 651
   Table of meetings, 652
Swatara Church, Big, 75, 79, 328, 445, 489, 504, 507, 512, 513, 514, 515, 517, 520, 524, 594
   Early history, 436
   Division, 441
   Elections, 442
   Meeting houses, 443
Swatara Church, Little, 75, 79, 166, 457, 462, 469, 481, 504, 514, 518, 521, 523, 525, 527, 577, 594
   Early history, 445
   Elections, 446-448
   Houses of worship, 449
   Union cemetery, 451
   Obituaries, 449, 455
Swigart, Elder M. C., 105, 147, 158, 162, 211, 563, 621, 642, 649
Swigart, Elder W. J., 126, 185, 240, 260, 559, 563

Täufer (Tunkers), 4, 9, 12, 50, 74, 79, 168, 291, 383, 480
Taylor, A. Z., 339, 350
Taylor, Elder I. W., 330, 331, 332, 339, 340, 343, 344, 345, 348, 350, 351, 354, 357, 359, 560, 561, 562, 563, 590, 592, 600, 612, 613, 614, 615, 617, 621, 628, 643, 649, 652
Taylor, Leonard, 324
Taylor, Elder S. W., 350, 351, 649
Texiere, Martin, 538, 540

INDEX.

Thomas, John S., 121
Tobias, George, 490
Towamincin, 304
Tower City Mission, 490
Traut, Balser, 20
Traut Bros., 17
Traut, Jeremias, 20
Traut, John H., 6, 17, 20, 65, 67
Traut, Magdalena, 20
Trout, Henry T., 177
Trumbauer, Harrison, 319, 321
Trumbauer, Henry, 322
Trutt, Daniel I., 494, 495
Tulpehocken Church, 346, 393, 482, 496, 501, 502, 521, 524, 594
    Organization, 457
    Elections, 458-459
    Obituaries, 460
    Division, 461
    Houses of worship, 462
    Sunday Schools, 470

Ulery, J. Edson, 536, 537, 538, 539, 562
Ulrich, Samuel, 543
Ulrich, Elder Stephen, 372, 381, 544
Umstad, Elder John, 131, 134, 153, 155, 172, 173, 216, 218, 219, 230, 233, 237, 238, 239, 240, 245, 247, 305, 315, 323, 346, 367, 545, 549, 550, 551, 579, 580, 581, 588, 642, 649
    Conversion, 231
    Election to ministry, 232
    Biography, 273-279
Union Church, 193
Union meeting house, 450
United Brethren, 346, 382, 410, 453, 485, 486
Universalists, 390
Upper Dublin Church, 183, 202, 293, 301, 313, 594
    Organization, 153
    Deacons, 154
    Oversight of, 155, 162
    Pastorate, 159
    Church auxiliaries, 160
Urner, Catherina Reist, 20, 22, 28, 205
Urner, Isaac N., 17, 209, 210, 215, 218, 220, 223, 226, 264, 267
Urner, Elder Jonas, 211, 221, 644
Urner, Elder Martin, 17, 18, 20, 21, 22, 28, 78, 205, 206, 209, 210, 223, 270, 271, 281, 282, 374, 642, 644
Urner, Elder Martin (Second), 211, 223, 377, 380, 381, 429, 445, 475, 511, 514, 544, 545, 547, 644

Utz, Daniel, 381, 545, 547

Van Bebberstown, 19, 20
Van Dolah, Cyrus, 173, 183
Van Dolah, Henry, 185
Virginia, 71, 209, 217, 276, 296, 523, 569, 579, 584
Visions, of Israel Poulson, 199
Von Bebern, Isaac, 40, 41, 42

Wadsworth, W. J., 263
Waggoner, Jacob, 170
Waggoner, William, 171, 173
Walking Purchase, 282
Waltz, B. Franklin, 345
Wanner, Andrew, 307, 309, 312
Wayland, J. W., 71, 73, 74
Weaver, Elder David W., 342, 343, 410, 494, 495, 503, 600, 601, 650
Weaver, Elam, 399
Weaver, George W., 339, 405
Weaver House, 96, 97
Weaver, John, 96, 112
Weaver, Philip, Jr., 96, 111
Weber, Jacob, 29, 36
Weidler, Michael, 331, 334, 356
Weiser, Conrad, 67
Weiss, Howard, 496, 497
Wells, David G., 253, 257, 259
Wenger, Christian, 331
Wenger, Elsworth, 357
Wenger, Elder Edward M., 448, 449, 453, 455, 459, 485, 487, 490, 503, 592, 600, 601, 632, 643, 650, 651
Wenger, Elder Israel, 337, 338, 350, 352, 353, 459, 494, 643, 650
Wenger, Jacob, 460, 470
Wenger, Elder Jacob, 304, 390, 446, 447, 448, 449, 455, 456, 526, 650
Wenger, Jacob F., 447, 448, 449
Wenger, S. G., 397, 398
Wenger, Samuel, 496, 497
Wenger, Samuel R., 332, 609, 612, 613
Werner, Peter, 388, 389, 390, 391
Westphalia, 1
Whisler, C. Alfred, 344
Whitefield, George, 72, 196
White Oak Church, 55, 75, 79, 81, 359, 360, 361, 399, 401, 402, 422, 423, 427, 430, 457, 458, 461, 516, 521, 541, 542, 587, 594, 609
    Hummer family, 369
    Zug family, 374
    Eby family, 378
    Longenecker family, 386

White Oak Church
  Divisions, 391, 394
  Later history, 393
Widder, D. H., 489
Wilhelm, Joseph, 459, 470, 496, 497
Wilson, Clinton B., 185
Wine, J., 172
Wine, Elder William M., 639
Winebrenarian Church, 569
Winebrenner, John, 382, 383
Wingard, Joseph D., 530
Winters, Cyrus, 504, 505
Wissahickon, 18, 19, 21, 24, 38, 45
Wise, Elder John, 122, 123, 125, 181, 182, 545, 552, 571, 572
Wise, Rachel Douglas, 94
Witmer, Elder J. H., 442, 443, 444, 474, 504, 592, 600, 643, 650
Witmer, Joseph, 472
Witmer, Elder S. Z., 377, 472, 506, 507, 592, 600, 619, 621, 643, 650
Wittgenstein, 1, 101, 291
Wohlfahrt, Michael, 42, 53, 63, 64, 206
Wolf, George B., 357
Wolf, Samuel N., 335, 355, 356, 357, 358
Wolgemuth, Harry W., 42, 53, 64, 206

Yocum, Howard, 248
Yoder, David, 320, 321
Yoder, Emanuel, 481, 483
Yoder, Elder Harry B., 342, 343, 344, 345, 415, 600, 601, 619, 620, 638, 642, 650, 652
Yoder, Henry, 322
Yoder, Jacob, 479, 480, 481, 483
Yoder, John, 475
Yoder, Nathaniel, 482
Yothers, David, 485

Zerbe, Samuel, 485
Ziegler, Amos, 310
Ziegler, Daniel P., 311, 312, 490
Ziegler, Elias P., 448, 456
Ziegler, Henry Z., 449
Ziegler, Elder Jesse, 105, 127, 158, 162, 260, 261, 309, 310, 311, 312, 324, 411, 494, 523, 562, 590, 592, 600, 601, 617, 618, 625, 626, 627, 628, 629, 631, 632, 642, 650, 652
Ziegler, John, 311, 312, 448
Ziegler, Katherine, 312, 343, 413
Ziegler, Levi, 310, 311, 312
Ziegler, Levi K., 534
Ziegler, Elder Philip (Chiques), 388, 389, 391, 392, 393, 396, 398, 430, 569, 587, 650
Ziegler, Elder Philip (Little Swatara), 456, 650
  Biography, 523
Ziegler, Samuel, 449
Ziegler, William, 456
Zigler, Elder D. H., VII, 71, 523, 562, 579, 583
Zinzendorf, Count, 72, 271, 272, 281, 477
Zion Children, 441, 447
Zobler, William N., 343, 399
Zook, Wallace, 334, 336
Zuck, Abraham, 315, 328
Zuck, David, 375
Zuck, John, 375
Zuck, Peter, 282, 283, 284
Zug, Elder Abraham, 377, 468, 520, 522, 650
  Biography, 365, 457
Zug, Benjamin (White Oak), 392, 396, 429, 572
Zug, Benjamin (Tulpehocken), 459, 460, 521
Zug, Benjamin R., 396, 397, 398
Zug, Elder Henry S., 397, 398, 431, 472, 643, 650
Zug, Elder John, 122, 123, 365, 367, 370, 441, 457, 458, 460, 469, 479, 480, 481, 529, 545, 552, 571, 581, 587, 588, 589, 643, 650
  Biography, 520–523
Zug, Elder Johannes, 328, 365, 374, 375, 376, 379, 380, 381, 384, 385, 387, 422, 426, 429, 471, 545, 644
Zug, Elder John C., 377, 397, 408, 409, 411, 434, 473, 495, 561, 592, 650, 652
Zug, Elder S. R., V, VIII, 134, 137, 158, 162, 185, 190, 191, 193, 320, 341, 342, 345, 364, 365, 367, 368, 377, 388, 392, 396, 397, 398, 406, 407, 408, 420, 421, 443, 448, 458, 469, 473, 488, 489, 506, 511, 516, 520, 523, 525, 533, 537, 554, 556, 557, 558, 559, 567, 572, 586, 587, 588, 589, 590, 592, 595, 600, 609, 612, 613, 616, 621, 624, 626, 627, 642, 643, 650
  Biography, 429–435
Zug, Ulrich, 374, 375, 376, 377, 378, 429